ABERDEEN
1800 – 2000
A NEW HISTORY

ABERDEEN
1800 – 2000
A New History

Edited by

W. HAMISH FRASER
AND CLIVE H. LEE

Introduction by James Naughtie

Foreword by Lord Provost Margaret E. Smith, JP

TUCKWELL PRESS

Published by Tuckwell Press Ltd
The Mill House
Phantassie
East Linton
East Lothian EH40 3DG
Scotland

First published 2000

ISBN 1 86232 175 2 *hardback*
1 86232 108 6 *paperback*

British Library Cataloguing-in-Publication data are available

Typeset and originated by Carnegie Publishing, Chatsworth Road, Lancaster
Printed and bound by Bath Colour Books, Blantyre

Contents

List of illustrations		vii
List of figures		xiii
List of maps		xiv
List of tables		xiv
List of contributors		xv
Acknowledgements		xvi
List of abbreviations		xviii
Foreword		xix
Introduction *by James Naughtie*		1
1.	The Growth of the City JOHN S. SMITH	22
2.	People in the City ANDREW BLAIKIE	47
3.	The Nineteenth-century Economy RICHARD PERREN	75
4.	Survival and Decline: The Economy 1918–1970 RICHARD PERREN	99
5.	The Oil Economy DAVID NEWLANDS	126
6.	Working Life in the City WILLIAM W. KNOX	153
7.	Politics Before 1918 W. HAMISH FRASER	176
8.	Twentieth-century Politics MICHAEL C. DYER	204
9.	Local Government CLIVE H. LEE	236

10. Social Welfare: Poverty and Health 265
CLIVE H. LEE

11. Housing 295
NICHOLAS J. WILLIAMS

12. Education 323
SYDNEY WOOD

13. Religion 348
PETER HILLIS

14. Elite Society 374
I. G. C. HUTCHISON

15. Leisure and Culture: The Nineteenth Century 398
IRENE MAVER

16. Leisure and Social Change: The Twentieth Century 422
IRENE MAVER

17. The Press 448
W. HAMISH FRASER

18. Villages and Suburbs 466
JOHN S. SMITH

Epilogue: The City and its People 490

Notes 494

Index of Names 510

Index of Subjects 516

Illustrations

Introduction   *page*

Aberdeen from the municipal tower, *c.* 1880s   6-7

The Castlegate, engraved by John Hay from the original drawing by
   J.W. Allan, 1840   8

'The Silver City with the Golden Sands' – Aberdeen's advertising slogan
   in the 1950s and 1960s   12

Celebrations in Union Street. Street party in July 1994   13

Cabs wait near the Joint Station   15

The market in the Green at the turn of the century   18-19

Chapter 1: The Growth of the City

Part of John Smith's 1810 plan of the city of Aberdeen   24

Archibald Simpson, architect   26

King Street, the new road north from the Castlegate   27

The harbour, vital to Aberdeen's development   28

John Morgan, 1883   29

Rubislaw Quarry, opened in 1740   29

Municipal housing development at Kincorth in the 1950s   37

The railway cutting through the valley of the Denburn, which opened
   the route to the west   39

Plan showing the proposed railway through the Links, successfully resisted
   in the 1850s   43

Chapter 2: People in the City

Cartoon of Matthew Hay, from *Bon-Accord*, 12 December 1891   54

Sir Dugald Baird   56

Dr Mary Esslemont   57

A few of the remaining cottages of old Footdee in the 1990s   66

Guestrow slum   68

Chapter 3: The Nineteenth-century Economy

Grandholm Mills, linen factory of Leys, Masson and Co. from the end of
   the eighteenth century until 1848, reopened as a woollen mill for Crombie
   Knowles and Co. in 1859   74

The harbour had to be expanded steadily to cope with increased shipping   77
Management and staff of Alexander Hall & Sons, 1862   85
Model of the *Thermopylae* built by Walter Hood and Co.   86
The fishing fleet heads to sea   88
William Pyper, poineering steam trawler owner   89
John Fyfe, quarry master   92
Pirie's Stoneywood paper works in the late nineteenth century   94

Chapter 4: Survival and Decline: The Economy 1918-1970
Women workers from J. M. Henderson and Co. on parade in Union Street
    during the Second World War   100
Coal being unloaded in the upper dock of the harbour   101
Funeral cortège takes air raid victims to Trinity Cemetery, 1943   102
Cod laid out for sale at Aberdeen fish market, 1969   103
The *Acklam Cross*, a Hall, Russell & Co. ship, *c.*1933   106
Workers leaving Hall, Russell & Co. shipyard in the 1950s   107
Sir Thomas Jaffrey, chief executive of Aberdeen Savings Bank, 1892-1929   113
Poster advertising the Northern Co-operative Society's shops in Aberdeen
    and district, 1932   115
Isaac Benzie's department store advertisement from the film *Out for Value*,
    1933   117
Edwardian beach scene: the bathing station, Aberdeen   117
Passengers board the bus at Aberdeen bathing station in the early 1900s   118
GNSR advertises for one of its hotels   119
James Hay, solicitor and town councillor   121
The beach in its heyday in the late 1950s   122
Hank winding at Richards Mills, 1978   123

Chapter 5: The Oil Economy
Harbour development in the 1970s   130-1
The Amerada Hess Building, Hareness Road   132
Oil workers disembark from a helicopter at Aberdeen heliport   137
Stewart Milne, builder   138
Sir Ian Wood, one of the few home-grown entrepreneurs who seized the
    opportunities presented by the oil industry   143
An oil rig in production   148
Calum A. Macleod, CBE   151

Chapter 6: Working Life in the City
Messrs A. Pirie & Sons, Woodside Works, *c.*1886   154
The crew of the Aberdeen trawler *Yorick*, *c.*1960   158

Sir James Taggart, granite merchant and lord provost, 1914-19   160
Granite cutting   161
Temperance Society card   165
A. S. Cook, clothier and shirtmaker, an indefatigable campaigner for the
    temperance movement   166
Prohibition notice about bonfires   167
Joseph Duncan, a leading figure in the Independent Labour Party from 1905   174

Chapter 7: Politics Before 1918
Sir Alexander Bannerman, MP from 1833 until 1847   179
Notice of polling places, 1835   180
W. S. Lindsay, radical activist, as portrayed in the *Northern Figaro*, June 1885   182
Col. W. H. Sykes, MP from 1857 until 1872   184
John Webster, lord provost 1856-59 and Liberal MP 1880-85   187
Trade union demonstration, August 1884   189
Rev. C. C. MacDonald, land reformer and campaigner   190
Professor James Bryce, Liberal MP for South Aberdeen from 1885 until 1908   190
Unitarian Rev. Alexander Webster addressing a meeting on the Broadhill
    in favour of socialism in the late 1880s   192
Duncan Vernon Pirie, MP for North Aberdeen from 1896 until 1918   194
Anti-suffragette cartoon, March 1909   198

Chapter 8: Twentieth-century Politics
Sir John Fleming, lord provost 1898-1902, Liberal MP 1917-18   209
Evening Express cartoon about the 1928 Aberdeen North election campaign   211
Hector Hughes, Labour MP for Aberdeen North, 1945-70   219
Election pamphlets from the 1966 General Election   220
Conflicting views in the posters for the 1979 referendum on Scottish
    devolution   224
The victors in the election of May 1997   228

Chapter 9: Local Government
James Hadden, lord provost 1801-2, 1809-10, 1813-14, 1830-31   239
Sir Alexander Anderson, lord provost 1859-65   244
The tower of the Town House   247
Peter Esslemont, lord provost 1880-82, Liberal MP for East Aberdeenshire
    1885-92, as seen in the *Northern Figaro*   248
The bustling heart of the city around 1900, looking east towards Castle
    Street   253
Corporation trams lined up awaiting the finish of a football match at
    Pittodrie   255
Lord Provost Sir Thomas Mitchell, civic leader during the Second World War   261

James Wyness, lord provost 1992–96   263

Chapter 10: Social Welfare: Poverty and Health
'Aid to the Unemployed' cartoon, November 1908   270
Campaign notice to prevent tuberculosis   277
Typhoid epidemic of 1964   278
Aberdeen Royal Infirmary, Woolmanhill, in the early twentieth century   279
Female medical ward, Woolmanhill, early in the twentieth century   281
Lord Provost Sir Andrew Lewis   283
John J. R. Macleod, a Nobel prizewinner as one of the discoverers of
    insulin   284
Aberdeen Royal Infirmary, Foresterhill, *c.*1937   285
Sir Alexander Ogston, the city's medical officer of health   290
Lady Matilda Baird, first chair of the North-East Regional Hospital Board   291

Chapter 11: Housing
James Matthews, architect, lord provost 1883–85   298
Floor plan, Urquhart Road tenements, 1897   306
Designs for bungalows in Back Hilton Road approved in 1928   315
An elderly woman salvages possessions from her home on Menzies Road,
    Torry, 1941   317
T. Scott Sutherland, architect, housing developer and endower of the School
    of Architecture   318
Kincorth Circle in the 1970s   319
High-rise flats, low blocks and terraces at Hazlehead in the 1960s   320
Post-war council housing surrounds 1930s private bungalows in Cairncry
    Road West, 1982   321

Chapter 12: Education
James Melvin, rector of Aberdeen Grammar School, 1826–53   324
Aberdeen Grammar School Return, 1833   326
Ashley Road School, opened in 1888   333
Robert Gordon's College, *c.*1900   336
Woodwork class in a late-nineteenth-century school   337
Charleston Primary School built by Stewart Milne Construction   338
Old Marischal College Quad   345
The Faculty of Management and Design library of Robert Gordon
    University, opened in 1998   346

Chapter 13: Religion
St Nicholas' Church, *c.*1850   349
The North Parish Church, opened in 1831   350

Dr James Kidd, evangelical minister of Gilcomston Church from 1796 until
    1834   352
Queen's Cross Free Church and Rubislaw Parish Church   354
Rev. George Adam Smith, minister of Queen's Cross Free Church, 1882–92   355
Carden Place Presbyterian Church, completed in 1882   356
Monsignor William Stopani, Dean of the Cathedral of St Mary of the
    Assumption in Huntly Street   357
Members of the Guild of St Agnes of St Margaret's Episcopal Church with
    Mother Annis Mary of St Margaret's Convent, Spital, 1883   358
Rev. James Cooper, controversial minister of the East Parish from 1881 to 1898 360

Chapter 14: Elite Society
Theatre Royal poster, 1837   377
Some of Aberdeen's elite, photographed by Washington Wilson, 1852–56   381
Rubislaw Terrace on the north side of Albyn Place, *c.* 1900   382
Sir David Stewart, combmaker, lord provost 1889–95   384
Mrs J. W. Crombie, wife of the leading textile manufacturer, J. E. Crombie   385
John Morgan's book label   386
County, university and town elites combine in 1931 to confer the freedom
    of the city on Sir George Adam Smith   392
Margaret Farquhar, Aberdeen's first woman lord provost, 1996–99   397

Chapter 15: Leisure and Culture: The Nineteenth Century
Jane Ronald's Lemon Tree Hotel off Castle Street   400
The Central Library, opened in 1892, and St Mark's Free South Church, built
    in the 1890s   404
Rev. A. M. Bannatyne, the Union Free Church's 'presbytery policeman', as
    shown in *Northern Figaro*, January 1885   407
John Henry Anderson, 'the Wizard of the North'   409
The Bool Road 'Penny Rattler' theatre in the early 1840s   410
Plan of Duthie Park as featured in a special supplement of the *Evening
    Gazette* in 1883   413
George Washington Wilson, Scotland's best-known photographer between
    the 1850s and 1880s   415
Office bearers of the Northern Bicycle meet, 1883   419
The Volunteer Movement   420

Chapter 16: Leisure and Social Change: The Twentieth Century
Pierrots at the Beach Pavilion around 1900   424
Beach Pavilion programme from the 1930s   425
Plans for Donald's 2,000-seater Astoria cinema in Clifton Road, built in 1934   429
Dr Walford Bodie, 'the Electric Wizard of the North'   430

James 'Jimmy' Spankie, presenter for Grampian Television in the 1960s   435
James Bryce MP, who campaigned for access to the mountains, as featured in
    Bon-Accord, November 1890   436
Lord Provost Lewis driving off the first ball at the municipal golf course at
    Hazlehead, July 1927   438
Aberdeen FC *v.* Third Lanark FC, as featured in *Bon-Accord*, February 1905   440
Richard 'Dick' Donald   441
Aberdeen FC's defeat of Real Madrid in the European Cup-Winners' Cup at
    Gothenburg, 1983   442
The beach in the 1960s, looking north to the Bridge of Don   444
Stephen Robertson, Buff Hardie and George Donald, of *Scotland the What?*   445

Chapter 17: The Press
William Carnie, journalist   454
William Alexander, editor of the *Evening Gazette* and author of *Johnny Gibb
    of Gushetneuk*   455
The masthead of *Bon-Accord*, designed by Pierre Delavault   459
Bon-Accord cartoon supporting local MPs Bryce and Pirie in their criticism
    of the South African War   460
Cartoon of Sir Henry Alexander, editor of *Aberdeen Free Press*, 1914–22, lord
    provost 1932–35   461
Broad Street, home of Aberdeen Journals, in the 1960s   462
James C. Grant, editor of the *Press and Journal* from 1959 until 1976   464

Chapter 18: Villages and Suburbs
Trams in the late 1800s   470
Looking north in the 1970s to the expanding suburbs beyond the Bridge
    of Don   471
Salmon fishers at the mouth of the River Don, *c.*1900   475
Culter paper mills   481
Looking east towards Seaton along St Machar Drive   484
The airport at Dyce   487
Aerial view of Westhill in the 1980s   489

Figures

2.1	Population of Aberdeen 1801-2001	48
2.2	Natural rate of population change: Aberdeen 1861-1996	49
2.3	Infant mortality in Aberdeen 1861-1996	53
2.4	Composition of population change: Aberdeen 1861-2001	58
3.1	Landings of white fish (cwts): Aberdeen harbour 1888-1998	89
3.2	Distribution of employment in Aberdeen 1851-1911	97
4.1	Distribution of employment in Aberdeen 1931-91	124
5.1	U.K. North Sea oil and gas production 1975-96	126
5.2	Aberdeen harbour: tonnage of vessels cleared 1973-97	128
5.3	Employment in the oil industry: Grampian Region 1973-96	134
5.4	Average earnings in Grampian Region 1971-96	136
7.1	Distribution of votes by party in general elections in Aberdeen 1874-1918	188
8.1	Distribution of votes by party in general elections in Aberdeen 1918-97	216
9.1	Water abstraction from the River Dee for Aberdeen City 1820-2000	241
9.2	Number of passengers carried by Aberdeen Municipal Transport 1898-1974	254
11.1	Aberdeen housing stock by date of construction	310
13.1	Scottish Episcopal Church membership in Aberdeen	364
13.2	Social composition of church membership	369
14.1	Value of estates left by elite and non-elite citizens of Aberdeen	379
18.1	Passengers arriving at Aberdeen Airport 1960-97	488

Maps

1. A Bird's Eye View of Aberdeen   17
2. The developing city *c.*1840   60
3. Aberdeen Parliamentary Constituencies 1997   206
4. Westward expansion *c.*1900   250-1
5. Aberdeen's parishes 1848   267
6. Rubislaw and its fashionable residential streets *c.*1900   294
7. Areas of some of the worst housing in the city centre *c.*1900   300
8. Mainly working-class residential areas in the north *c.*1900   309
9. Ruthrieston and Mannofield areas to the west *c.*1900   468-9

Tables

2.1 Occupations by district   62
2.2 Distribution of birthplaces   63
2.3 Household typologies   65
7.1 Aberdeen parliamentary representation and election results 1832-1918   201-3
8.1 Aberdeen parliamentary representation and election results 1922-97   230-5
8.2 Results of the Election to the Scottish Parliament 1999: Aberdeen constituencies   235

Contributors

Andrew Blaikie, Professor of Historical Sociology, University of Aberdeen

Michael C. Dyer, Lecturer in Politics, University of Aberdeen

W. Hamish Fraser, Professor of History, University of Strathclyde

Peter Hillis, Head of Social Studies, School of Education, University of
Strathclyde

Iain G. C. Hutchison, Senior Lecturer in History, University of Stirling

William W. Knox, Senior Lecturer in Modern History, University of St Andrews

Clive H. Lee, Professor of Historical Economics, University of Aberdeen

Irene Maver, Lecturer in Scottish History, University of Glasgow

James Naughtie, journalist and presenter of *Today* on BBC Radio 4

David Newlands, Senior Lecturer in Economics, University of Aberdeen

Richard Perren, Senior Lecturer in Economic History, University of Aberdeen

John S. Smith, Senior Lecturer in Geography, University of Aberdeen

Nicholas J. Williams, Senior Lecturer in Geography, University of Aberdeen

Sydney Wood, Teaching Fellow, University of Dundee

Acknowledgements

Works such as this necessarily accumulate a large number of debts for assistance. Some acknowledgements are included in the notes accompanying each chapter in respect of particular help. More generally, the editors are indebted to Diane Morgan and Judith Cripps, both of whom read the entire manuscript and provided much helpful advice and comment. The final version is both factually more accurate and generally improved as a result of their efforts. Furthermore, Diane Morgan provided considerable information and advice with regard to the biographical portraits, and we are particularly grateful for that help.

Particular thanks are also due to Siobhan Convery and Iain Gray of the Aberdeen City Archives, who undertook the formidable task of researching the material for the illustrations. They have been invariably helpful and enthusiastic, as were those who supplied the illustrations. More generally we are particularly grateful for the assistance given to those contributors who made use of the Aberdeen City Archives. Many of the contributors also made use of the Aberdeen Central Reference Library, and thanks are due to the staff who have always been pleasant and helpful. Librarians elsewhere, including the Mitchell Library in Glasgow and the National Library of Scotland as well as in the various universities and colleges from which the contributors come, also have our thanks. We are grateful to the National Archives of Scotland, as we must now learn to call the Scottish Record Office. We would also like to offer our thanks to Lynne Ballantyne, and colleagues in the Planning Department of Aberdeen City Council. We are indebted to many other organisations and individuals who answered specific queries or provided information. Iain Beavan and his colleagues in the Aberdeen University Library Special Collections have been an invaluable source of information and assistance. We appreciate also the willingness of the University of Aberdeen to reduce the reproduction fee normally charged on the use of material from the Washington Wilson collection and thereby to forgo any profit.

Others who have helped with illustrations and research are the Publicity and Promotions Unit, the Photographic Unit of the Arts and Recreation Department, the Property Services Department of Aberdeen Council; Aberdeen Environmental Education Centre; Aberdeen Maritime Museum; Robert Gordon University; Northern Health Service Archives; Marischal College Museum; Aberdeen Medico-

Chirurgical Society; Aberdeen Journals Ltd; and the Scottish National Portrait Gallery. To all of these the editors, who were responsible for the illustrations, figures, maps and biographical detail in the text, are most grateful.

Finally our thanks must go to ex-Lord Provost James Wyness and his colleagues on the original Working Party established by the Aberdeen District Council to commission the New History. At an early stage in those discussions, the Lord Provost indicated that he hoped that this study would stimulate interest in the history of the city, especially in schools, and that it would encourage others to carry forward the study of local history. We are certainly aware, despite the length and weight of this present volume, that numerous opportunities for further investigation exist. We share the hope of James Wyness that the publication of this study might mark the beginning of such labours for others, as well as the completion of our own.

WHF
CHL

ILLUSTRATION ACKNOWLEDGEMENTS

Aberdeen City Libraries 15, 29, 39, 54, 68, 101, 117, 160, 161, 165, 189, 220, 336, 349, 350, 356, 400, 409, 424, 425, 430, 445, 475

Aberdeen City Archives 8, 10, 24, 37, 43, 74, 94, 103, 106, 115, 121, 122, 137, 154, 167, 180, 198, 255, 270, 298, 306, 315, 320, 321, 326, 333, 345, 358, 377, 386, 392, 410, 413, 415, 419, 420, 429, 438, 461, 462, 470

Aberdeen City Publicity and Promotions Department 397

Aberdeen Environmental Education Centre 337

Aberdeen Journals Ltd 11, 13, 85, 102, 107, 118, 123, 211, 219, 224, 228, 278, 317, 435, 441, 442, 464, 481, 487, 488

Aberdeen Property and Technical Services 338

Aberdeen University Medico Chirurgical Society 56, 284, 290

Aberdeen University, Department of Medical Illustration

Aberdeen University, Department of Special Collections and Archives 119

Aberdeen University Library, George Washington Wilson Collection 6, 18, 77, 253, 354, 381, 382

Amerada Hess 132, 148

City of Aberdeen Art Gallery and Museums Collection 89, 92, 100, 113, 158, 179, 187, 209, 277, 384, 385, 453, 455

Dr John Smith 130, 319, 471, 484

Judith Cripps 358

Fiona Watson 285

Mrs G. Scott Sutherland 318

Northern Health Service Archives 279, 281, 285, 291

Professor Andrew Blaikie 66

Robert Gordon University 318, 346

Scottish Film Library 117

Scottish National Portrait Gallery 57, 184

University of Aberdeen Public Relations 151, 355

From Alexander Webster, *My Years in the Ministry* 192

From William Diack, *A History of the Trades Council and Trade Union Movement in Aberdeen* (Aberdeen, 1939) 174

From *Supplemental History of the Society of Advocates in Aberdeen* 121

Bon-Accord 436, 440, 459, 460

Abbreviations

AAICP	Aberdeen Association for Improving the Conditions of the Poor
ACA	Aberdeen City Archives
ACRL	Aberdeen Central Reference Library
AGMA	Aberdeen Granite Masters' Association
ALU	Aberdeen Ladies' Union
ARI	Aberdeen Royal Infirmary
AULSC	Aberdeen University Library Special Collections
BBC	British Broadcasting Corporation
BPP	British Parliamentary Papers
BP	British Petroleum
CALA	City of Aberdeen Land Association
GNSR	Great North of Scotland Railway
ILP	Independent Labour Party
MOH	Medical Officer of Health
NAS	National Archives of Scotland
NSA	New Statistical Account
NLS	National Library of Scotland
NHS	National Health Service
NUR	National Union of Railwaymen
OILC	Offshore Industry Liaison Committee
OMGCU	Operative Masons' and Granite Cutters' Union
OSA	Old Statistical Account
PAL	Poverty Action Liaison
RAHSC	Royal Aberdeen Hospital for Sick Children
RGIT	Robert Gordon's Institute of Technology
RGU	Robert Gordon University
SAR	Samples of Anonymised Records
SED	Scottish Education Department
SDF	Social Democratic Federation
SNP	Scottish National Party
SSHA	Scottish Special Housing Association
TSA	Third Statistical Account (Aberdeen)
TSAC	Third Statistical Account (Aberdeenshire)
UDC	Union for Democratic Control
UOMA	United Operative Masons' Association
WSPU	Women's Social and Political Union

04 October 2000

Now we have entered the new Millennium, the City of Aberdeen faces an exciting and challenging period ahead, but we must never forget the part that the past has played in the foundation and progress of Aberdeen. This city, the capital of the North-East of Scotland, is steeped in history and tradition, and in the Granite City we are fortunate in that we have one of the most complete sets of civic records in Scotland. For example, the earliest Charter to be found was granted by William the Lion in about 1179.

However, to come to more recent times, the last 200 years cover an immensely interesting period of change, transformation and fascinating progress; and this book focuses on that period.

In 1891 Oscar Wilde wrote: *"The one duty we owe to history is to rewrite it"*. I cannot agree with this assertion as no fictional account could ever be as spell-binding as the real thing!

I commend this book to you – take up the challenge – read and enjoy!

Yours sincerely

Lord Provost Margaret E Smith, JP

Introduction

JAMES NAUGHTIE

A city must have a sense of itself, or it hardly counts as a city. A cathedral was once the badge that mattered and now there are rules - or conventions - that are meant to update the old test. But whatever the mechanism by which it is decided that somewhere populous deserves to have the grand word attached, the feeling is the most important part of it. Aberdeen knows what it is.

The history of this place is more than the story of a community clustering around an obvious spot, between two rivers and facing the sea. That would simply be a question of geography and economic history, an explanation of why there was an Aberdeen here and not somewhere else. However fascinating the course of that story might be, by itself it can't catch the essence of what the place has become, what it has made of itself. That is a much more elusive question, and the answers are somewhere in the people and the way their lives have been shaped, in the landscape itself and in the buildings, in the chance twists of fate that have come Aberdeen's way. The truth may be that those answers have to be absorbing and have to have some hold on a community's imagination for a city to be able to prosper. It can't seem somewhere permanent without that instinctive understanding of why it has lasted. A profitable factory - even an oil well that doesn't run dry - or a chance settlement of people can't by itself give a city its confidence. Something more mysterious has to be at work too. People need to want to claim it as their own.

So it must feel distinct, first of all. Aberdeen has never found it difficult to manage that. Glasgow and Edinburgh have seemed to be great lumbering beasts baying at each other across a landscape lying between the Forth and the Clyde which sometimes appears to have been laid waste in a battle for supremacy. The one so big and dark, the other so conscious of its outward elegance - surely Aberdeen has benefited from wanting to have no part of it. They can fight for their territory and wage their various social struggles, but somehow the North-East can stay happily remote.

Inescapably, remoteness has shaped Aberdeen. Nowhere else tries to crowd it out. Of the bigger places near at hand, Dundee is hardly mentioned, of course. Perth seems a city that is not quite a city, more a town with ideas above itself. Inverness is so different - and so *small* - as hardly to count. And in the real business of establishing an identity, it has always suited Aberdeen to be clear that, even with the long-delayed arrival of roads that could get you safely and quickly south, this was always a place that wouldn't be sucked into a great wen where all its character would be subsumed into something much more metropolitan, or at least something too big for comfort.

Happily, the south has always acquiesced in this. Although the Grampians were never more than a symbolic barrier, they appeared high enough and impenetrable enough to everyone but the fabled drovers of old to act like a kind of rocky curtain beyond which were people who were different and went their own way. Like all such intangible feelings, there was a good deal of nonsense involved. It was not as if North-East folk wore strange clothes or didn't know how to catch the train to Glasgow ... but enough incomprehension persisted (real and manufactured) to allow Aberdeen to hold on to a certain distinctiveness that somehow survived and prospered.

Language, landscape and climate all have something to do with it, and the combination has been enough to create a special feeling that has survived social and economic upheavals and, even, the blundering efforts of some architects to undo the work of their more distinguished predecessors. Union Street is still Union Street, just. The beach still sweeps cleanly away north towards the Ythan and Buchan. The granite still sparkles after the rain. And the voices, which sound to outsiders as broad as those from the countryside but which are so different in the city, still speak of an Aberdeen that has managed to keep hold of itself.

Perhaps that is a surprise at the end of a century in which so much was washed away in the great tides of change that followed the Second World War and, especially, the coming of oil from the North Sea. Yet in the physical reshaping of the city and the huge social changes that came with a new kind of economy, something did remain that echoed the solidity of the past. It was as if the granite was heavy enough and the wind strong enough to resist the rush of the new. Of course this is a feeling as much as a fact. Like nostalgia that shapes history to expunge the awkward bits - and dwells on the grand rather than the workaday, the prosperous rather than the poor - all of us on whom Aberdeen exerts a grip try to spy the permanent and the familiar in the landscape, even when it changes beyond recognition. The good news is that the signs are still there.

The cities that live in our minds are the cities which have imprinted a personality on us. All of us who know Aberdeen's intimacies, some more attractive than others, pretend to ourselves that we understand them. To be honest, we also pretend that such is the particular character of this place - its *difference* - that no-one else can share that knowledge. Absurd, of course, but a telling symptom of the power of this place.

The poet Iain Crichton Smith was a student in Aberdeen in the 1950s, when the city would have looked familiar to a student of thirty years before. The big changes that were to mark the last quarter of the century were still some way off. Looking back to these days quite a few years later Crichton Smith caught something of the sharpness and pride in the way the city disported itself, and the tradition that underpinned that feeling.

ABERDEEN

Mica glittered from the white stone.
Town of the pure crystal,
I learn't Latin in your sparkling cage,
I loved your brilliant streets.

Places that have been good to us we love.
The rest we are resigned to.
The fishermen hung shining in their yellow
among university bells.

Green lawns and clinging ivy. Mediaeval
your comfortable lectures, your calm grammar.
The plate glass windows showed their necklaces
like writhing North Sea fish.

Nothing will die, even the lies we learn!
Union Street was an arrow
debouching on the crooked lanes, where women
sweated like leaking walls.

That poem is in tune with the city. Springing from its history is a continuity and warmth that many of us absorbed in the fold of those high alcoves that marched towards the great window in the old library at King's, now transformed into a quite different kind of place, which some may find congenial but which still reminds many others of what was lost. In Old Aberdeen a sense of permanence was and is inescapable, with Bishop Elphinstone there in his sarcophagus to remind anyone who forgets. And in the city itself, that 'sparkling cage' is still there, though some of its simple elegance has long since been despoiled. There are fewer fishermen now and some of those crooked lanes are gentrified corners rather than real byways, but there is still the Aberdeen that can be sensed by those who come home.

When they do, many of them no doubt feel twinges of the guilt that comes with nostalgia. Everyone understands the danger. You think of the high-mindedness of architects who knew what was in Rubislaw quarry and were willing to think on a suitably majestic scale, you think of the best preachers and teachers who perpetuated the belief in what George Davie called 'the democratic intellect', and you tend to see the city shining under an imaginary rainbow, as a special place. You forget, easily, the social battles and the poverty and the sheer churning hardships of the lives that were led far away from the granite palaces west of Queen's Cross. When they built the sleek span of the Victoria bridge in the 1880s to link the city with Torry across the Dee, which was one of the foundation stones of the modern city, they were creating a community in which comfort and hardship would have to acknowledge each other.

Affection for the place, and pride in its characteristic steadfastness, shouldn't produce a maudlin and misty-eyed Aberdeen. Much of its character, after all, has been hewn from rough terrain and a hard life.

Start with the countryside. No-one can begin to understand this city without taking account of the hinterland. Many cities seem to exist on their own, clutching satellite communities to their outer rims but hardly touching the rural spaces beyond. Aberdeen is quite different. For those of us who grew up in the villages and towns of the North-East it was the hub of a solar system, connected to all the life that went on around it. The railways ran through it; it was the place of business; the fish market and the parade of beasts at Kittybrewster spoke of its dependence on the life that went on outside the city; and it had all the power of a place that hadn't suddenly sprung up but had been doing this for generations.

Culturally, this is as important a fact about Aberdeen as any other. You can't separate the urban place from the rural life. Some of us may be able to identify instinctively the accents from Strichen or Keith or Torry and contrast them as easily as we would if they were from Charleston and New York, but these are the distinctions that come with intimacy. The North-East corner of Scotland has a city and a network of rural and fishing communities, but it has never seemed anything other than a place that grew as one. The city sprang from that terrain, and everyone looked to the city for something.

This means that the character of Aberdeen can be found well outside the city limits. Rural life, like life at sea, was hard. There are fine big farms that spread far across the landscape of Buchan, and many grand estates on Deeside, but there are many more places where a living had to be teased out of rather inhospitable soil whipped bare by an unforgiving wind. The riches of the place – whether in beef or grain or fish – came at a cost.

No-one should be surprised that these communities developed their own kind of defence. They were solid. To outsiders there was something mysterious about the taciturn acceptance of the way things were, and about the unflinching dependence on the trinity of the minister, the laird and the teacher (the dominie, of course) which was the social architecture in the old days. But there was confidence. Lifted by that persistent belief in education which cast a shaft of egalitarianism into many lives, the day-to-day business of survival in modern times seemed one that would not change. As with miners who thought that coming generations would go down the pit because that was the way things were, the thought that everything might change in a flash just didn't seem to make sense. Such confidence is almost always misplaced, but the North-East found that there was a good deal of truth in it. For better or worse, it was for many generations a place in which the same rules held sway. The villages and the market towns fed off the land, and round the coast they depended on the sea. Only in recent times has that way of things had to be seriously challenged. And even with those changes the place still feels the same.

What a legacy this is. Frustrating though a sense of continuity can be when it turns into an instinct to resist change, that solidity has been a benefit. As the city began to take on its shape in the second half of the eighteenth century, and those great pits of granite were first put to use, it seemed a most elegant adornment on what had always been a rugged coastline shorn of the more cosy domestic charms. When architects like John Smith and Archibald Simpson came along and the masons began to work the stone with such confidence and flair, towers began to parade up the streets from the sea. There were plenty of church spires, of course, and public buildings that encapsulated the sort of defiance you find in the huge town halls of northern England. They apologised to no-one; they displayed a municipal confidence that could be sensed by anyone who walked down the street.

This was luck. The stone was there and the talent emerged to work it well. Enlightened civic leadership helped things along. Yet it seems impossible to separate the Aberdeen of its greatest physical flowering from, say, 1770 to the end of the Victorian era in 1901, from the broader streams that flowed with the Dee and the Don in from the countryside to the town. Partly perhaps because the smokestack enterprises of the industrial revolution were not the ones on which Aberdeen ever had to depend, the city seemed to rise from a landscape that didn't have to be fashioned for manufacturing but could maintain its links with the past and the way life was still lived away from the city.

This may be thought over-generous. Aberdeen had many of the problems that every city had to face, and its powerful figures often turned away from the uncomfortable sights and smells of poverty. No-one in our time can feel comfortable in comprehending the depth of the social divides that marked the map. But the city's golden era was a time that can justly be celebrated for its boldness and style.

Style. The very word seems to collide with the Aberdeen of the popular imagination. Cold streets and windy spaces have often been thought more apt mental images, and outsiders have often seemed grudging about the elegance of

*Overleaf:
'Town of pure crystal'. Aberdeen from the Municipal Tower, c. 1880s, with its many churches, horse-drawn trams and the haze from coal fires.
(Photograph by Washington Wilson)*

the place. Remoteness has something to do with it - that distance from the centre of gravity of Scotland's population which has always placed it, absurdly, on the fringe. There is something else too. Aberdeen is a different kind of city. Nowhere has granite been used like this, with such abandon. The architects who built the city streets - the crescents and residential corners as well as the public places - were in their way as notable as those who laid out the New Town in Edinburgh and indulged themselves so magnificently until the money ran out somewhere in the middle of Saxe Coburg Place in the middle of the 1830s.

The Castlegate became something as elegant as anything that could be offered by most cities. Union Buildings, overlooking the 'timmer market' at the bottom of the sparkling new Union Street, and put up in the second decade of the nineteenth century, was a kind of statement about what sort of place this was going to be. You stood in the teeming crowds around the mercat cross where the whole city seemed to converge, and alongside you saw the calm façade of a building that led you into a main street that was really a boulevard, rising up to the bridge that took you across the gardens where the railway would run, flanked by buildings that had a character quite their own, all of them in the same granite. When the town house was finished about sixty years later and became the anchor at the eastern end of Union Street a unique cityscape seemed complete.

So style there was. This was a city that knew it had been built deliberately. The curve of Rosemount Viaduct would, naturally, have library and church and theatre side by side – who could imagine any other combination? The gardens would have the Triple Kirks towering above to point up the way the city plunged down from the streets to the leafy places below. You could see the boats from Union Bridge (and smell the fish, of course). If you travelled west you would see a grand avenue – fit for the Queen's processions to Balmoral – which could be said to be the match of anything elsewhere. All this was stamped with confidence.

You might say that the last high point of that confidence was the building of the front of Marischal College in the twentieth century, long after Simpson had built the main part of the building and was gone. He had once famously described the Scott Monument in Edinburgh as looking like a spiky whin bush. What would he have thought of Marischal? It certainly grew in conception from what had already been built, and it drew a certain spirit from many of the buildings that now framed Union Street, but there was also something extraordinary about it, a headiness that is still there, despite some of the adjoining buildings that have tried to drain it of its character in recent times.

Surely Marischal College has a strange Aberdonian swagger about it. Here is a city famed for a particular kind of steadiness with a wholly unjustified reputation for dourness sometimes attached – and here is a building that is heady and wild, a festival of spires. Anyone who wants to capture the true spirit of Victorian and Edwardian Aberdeen need only gaze at it to understand how strong those currents of optimism and determination really were. This was no city caught in indecision or pallid conservatism. It was bursting out everywhere.

Those who confuse the North-East's continuity with some kind of shyness or calm must also confront the ferment of nineteenth-century politics in Aberdeen. Whether among the Chartists, who in Aberdeen were models of constitutionalism in their determination to proceed by rigorous argument and the force of persuasion, or among the Free Churchmen who broke away on issues of principle, this was a city where civic passions ran high. The schism in the church is, of course, a fine example. The ministers and their congregations who split in the Disruption in the 1840s were acting with a sense of outrage against what they believed to be corruption. No less fiercely than the reformers three centuries before, they believed that they had no choice but to reject their church and leave because a politically and financially indefensible establishment made it impossible to take any other course.

When the break came it was quite natural that in Aberdeen and the North-East it should be sharper than almost anywhere else. In caricatures of the nineteenth century in Scotland that were obsessed by the narrowness of the Calvinist legacy (for example, in the spectacular struggles between the drinkers and their enemies in the temperance movements) this simple truth once tended to be forgotten. The act had been something remarkably bold, and worthy of admiration from many of us who would not want much to do with some of the attitudes which flowed from the Disruption and took several generations to calm down.

It was a very particular part of the city's history, which had consequences in families and in the social structure of the place that could easily be discerned a century later, and it is good to remember that the granite façade always was a façade. Just because this was a city with a thoroughly respectable and immovable outward appearance there was no reason to think that its people didn't fight some remarkable political struggles. Nor, of course, was it especially immune from the daftness of some of the bumptious entrepreneurs who loped over the horizon in the mid-nineteenth century, carrying their prospectuses like the snake-oil salesmen and medicine men who were simultaneously perched on the back of their carts on the frontiers of the New World. South Sea bubbles swelled and burst. The banks wobbled from time to time. In Aberdeen, Alexander Anderson was the figure who somehow established that part of the character of a city that always seemed able to surmount these squalls and storms. In the mid-nineteenth century he was the lawyer and developer who harnessed the excitement of the railways, made several fortunes, and – to no-one's surprise – became lord provost as well. The point about Aberdeen was that it always seemed to prosper in the end. For more than two centuries it has been a story of success. The progress was interrupted from time to time, certainly, but it was success all the same.

This combination, of urban prosperity and a feeling of kinship with its rural hinterland, gave twentieth-century Aberdeen an enviable legacy. It appeared to be a big city that wasn't enveloped in soot and it had a particular character, in its speech and its social ways, that spoke of a world that stretched beyond its own modest limits. The writer John R. Allan, who was a man of the countryside and a sceptic as well as a romantic about this own land, once wrote this about the city: 'It is the only big town I know where, instinctively and without surprise, a gentleman will step off the pavement to make way for a cow, as he would do for any lady.' I can hardly think of a better way of putting it. We don't these days have gentlemen or ladies or cows in the street, but we know what he means.

For generations, that has been the Aberdeen caught in the photographs of George Washington Wilson. Without him would the perpetuation of the old Aberdeen be such a conscious act? I doubt it. Like a painter who could draw back a curtain with a new canvas, he fixed on paper a picture of the city in one of its fine periods that simply will not fade. The dip of Schoolhill and Upperkirkgate leading up to the tower of Marischal, the shoals of trawlers crowding round the harbour entrance on the grey North Sea, the cascade of fish spilling on to the quayside - all of them are images that have helped to build a bridge with the past. The city around us is also the city that was.

George Washington Wilson was once silly enough to say that he thought all photographs, after serving their temporary purpose, deserved oblivion. That his own collection survived is one of the reasons why Aberdeen was able for so long to connect the natural civic pride of the moment with its history. Even those of us who were students in the sixties could understand that the shape of our city was one that previous generations would know. Look at a photograph of Union Street in the early fifties and it is not very different from a Washington Wilson print of the 1890s, save for the long dresses and the horses. The only congestion comes from the trams, the familiar buildings are there - with the 'monkeyhouse' and its columns still the centre of gravity - and of course the clean lines of the city are just as they once were.

I suspect this was an unconscious reassurance to those who knew the city in the first seventy years of the twentieth century, and who absorbed naturally the fact that it hadn't been badly bombed and it had managed to preserve a particular sense of age - not the obvious antiquity you get in medieval towns but the genteel confidence of the nineteenth century. How do you quantify or measure a feeling of this sort? You can't but you can describe it.

When I first knew Aberdeen as a young boy in the 1950s it seemed, more than anything else, solid. Its main streets were long and straight and they appeared to mark out the contours of a vast map. You didn't feel as if you were caught in the dark rough and tumble of a Dickensian city, all byways and alleys, and whereas the tenement closes of Edinburgh seemed to plunge away into mysterious depths, in Aberdeen there was no sense of wandering in a maze. It was simple, clean and straight. You could almost see the sea from the top of Union Street away beyond the Salvation Army citadel at the bottom, and above the streets you could enjoy a tapestry of turrets and towers. It shone, especially after the rain. You felt (mistakenly as it turned out) that these stones were permanent.

What do those of us of a certain age remember about outings around the city? Places like Isaac Benzies' department store, which had been one of the first of its kind, the old grocers' shops like the original Chivas' emporium with their smells of ham and simple cheeses, the steep steps down the back way to the station from Union Street, the seagulls and the fishy smells flying across from the harbour, the wind across the beach sending everyone under cover, the vastness of the horizon and the dunes away to the north. Kennaway's restaurant at Union Bridge with its black-clad waitresses who came of a friendly breed that seemed to populate half the city, and in the earliest days the rattling trams which were to come to their end when the last of them was set alight in a kind of Viking funeral service at the beach.

I confess that I always believed the 'Silver City with the Golden Sands' advertisements of my youth to be making far too much of a goodish thing. I know why it was that families would come north every year during the Glasgow Fair for an Aberdeen holiday, but I could never quite sympathise with the desire. It was always true that on more days than not Aberdeen would be cold. There is no gainsaying that wind, and no point in trying. Yet the evidence is there, from the crackly Harry Gordon records and the persistence of the cafes on the Beach Boulevard, that attests to that bracing life by the shore that once helped to define Aberdeen for the outside world, along with the well-known postcard featuring a picture of a deserted Union Street with the legend underneath 'Aberdeen on a Flag Day'.

You sensed a potent mixture of the opulent and the hair-shirted. Here were elegant buildings that looked like castles, their revolving doors seeming to give into marbled places that spoke of permanence and wealth, gleaming in mahogany and brass. At the same time you needed a strong constitution to brave the seafront in all but the best of summers, and a certain clean-scrubbed look reminded you that whatever this was it wasn't a city of steamy fleshpots made for lotus-eaters. The luxury was rationed.

Later, many of us saw Aberdeen through student eyes and of course it is one of the best ways. Crichton Smith's 'university bells', 'calm grammar' and Latin learnt 'in your sparkling cage' may seem to be images from an earlier age but even in the early seventies, as the University was about to be thrown into a traumatic period of change, enough was still there to maintain the feeling of an academic tradition that could transport you back easily. You might believe the stories of students traipsing in from country towns carrying bags of meal on their backs to see them through the next term, and you certainly felt the weight of generations who'd trod the same stone flags and wooden floors. There were things here worth preserving. We wanted to throw much else out, of course – Aberdeen was no St Andrews, staying aloof from the fray – but I don't believe that there was a moment when some of the history didn't sit on our shoulders.

'The Silver City with the Golden Sands'. Aberdeen's advertising slogan in the 1950s and 1960s.

Definitely not a flag day? Two hundred years of Union Street celebrated at the world's biggest street party in July 1994. The Music Hall is on the right with classical pillars and the Free Church College is at the top centre. (Photograph by Sandy McCook)

Then it all turned. In a period of a couple of years in the seventies the tone of the city changed. To come back in early 1975 from abroad was to encounter a city that seemed to be shaken to its foundations. Many people enjoyed that, because it offered prosperity, though for many it was to prove fools' gold. Unquestionably the discovery of oil was the opening of a new era in the history of the city, and one that had more profound implications than any since the heyday of Victorian expansion. No-one can deny that Aberdeen survived some of the nastier economic moments of the 1970s and 1980s by the discovery of that oil and by the extraordinary influx of the brash, the rich and the hopeful that came with it. This was a time when money seemed to flow through parts of the city like the very oil itself, fuelling all sorts of wild schemes and social excesses that might have seemed alien. But they were welcome. Who would deny that?

Fortunes were made and lost, and there were cruel penalties to be paid by some of those who found that the new wealth eluded them, but Aberdeen boomed. Everyone felt the spin of the property roulette wheel and visitors used to speak of a city that had somehow lost its sense of balance. It hadn't, but there were forces on the loose that seemed uncontrollable. People would speak of hotels in Peterhead turned by the traffic of the oil workers into virtual speakeasies of which Klondyke itself would have been proud, and in the city itself a bizarre headiness took hold.

Old ladies would discover that their modest terraced houses in Mannofield, with manicured gardens front and rear, had doubled in price in a couple of years. Accents from the southern American states were everywhere and it seemed that if you weren't tied up with some oil-related business you weren't alive. Except, of course, that most people were not – they were vicarious participants in the whole business, their lives perhaps rising or falling with the price of a barrel, but looking on nonetheless. What a strange period it was.

For those of us of the post-war generation the coming of oil was a moment that divided the past and the present in Aberdeen. The past was the couthiness of the 'Inversnecky Cafe' or Alec Finlay at the Tivoli before the bingo came, a shimmering world of folk memories that aged like sepia prints in the attic. It was disappearing fast. The present, which was a relief because it was fresh, was bringing hope in a period when the industrialised world was reeling in the oil shock and preparing for years of decline. Now Aberdeen had its own oil, or at least that's how it seemed. There were enormous difficulties of course, and as someone who studied for finals in Old Aberdeen in the winter of 1973 with the help of candlelight, I would be the last to say that the North-East was spared the economic and industrial crisis which characterised the time. But there seemed to be a future. There would be jobs, and the city would prosper.

Many cities across the country would happily exchange their experiences in that period for Aberdeen's, and it can generally be said that the worst attacks of

recession and unemployment in the 1970s and 1980s treated Aberdeen more lightly than most. So the junction between past and present was one that was met with promise rather than fear.

The city, however, was changing in other ways that seemed inexplicable. You do not have to be a rigid traditionalist to question the kind of development that began to creep into the city centre. Here was a place that was blessed with a natural shape giving it Union Terrace and the gardens at its very heart, with a fine Georgian and Victorian parade of buildings rising up dramatically around it. There were vistas even in such unpromising corners as the approaches to the station - always, in my youth, the 'Joint Station' in a genuflection to earlier days - and especially around the Castlegate where the old city gave way to the Beach Boulevard and the sea. Ruin was visited on nearly all of them.

I am conscious that any criticism of this sort can be seen either as a piece of reactionary sullenness or a failure to realise that development means business. I

Cabs wait for the expected arrivals near Joint Station in its heyday. Note the milk delivery on the left.

plead not guilty to both. It is certainly not true that economic development necessitated a shopping centre between St Nicholas Church and Upperkirkgate that would have the effect of flattening out the natural contours of the city and the surrounding buildings, nor that the original sweep of George Street, always a great trading thoroughfare in the city, should be blocked by a structure quite out of keeping with its surroundings.

The more serious complaint is that those who criticise that period of development are engaging in saloon bar conservatism, damning progress at every turn and lamenting the passing of the good old days. This is surely a much more serious question. Take the centre of the city, from the station along the line running north as far as the course of the old Denburn behind the theatre. Though some semblance of the shape has been saved – not without a struggle – this is but a shadow of the simple elegance that was once there. The shopping centre on Union Bridge has become a monument to its time and to the attendant design practices that have now been consigned by most cities (including Aberdeen) to the dustbin. Around the station there has been a glaring failure to think of buildings grouped together, as a part of a landscape. And above Union Terrace gardens? Of the Triple Kirks there is only the skeleton of a spire now, reminding people of a structure which John Betjeman thought one of the finest pieces of brickwork in Britain.

There is certainly nostalgia involved. The older city seemed more comfortable with itself. But it is more than that, and a reflection of the obvious truth that city planners by the end of the century were putting more store by that indefinable essence of place and less on the 'build at any cost' feeling which seemed to take hold in the seventies and produced some terrible scars. The civic leaders who are now thinking of development in sympathy with the natural lines of a city, and with proper acknowledgement to the past, are the ones who are going with the grain.

It is an observable fact that there are many Aberdonians, at home and far away, who believe that there was a period in which considerable damage was done not just to the façade of the city but to its self-confidence. Some would say that the erection of St Nicholas House opposite Marischal was the first step down that road; others would choose less prominent changes, like the ripping out of the fine old booking office at the station in the early seventies in favour of a rent-a-station look; many would say that Aberdeen's architectural legacy was simply taken for granted, and damaged as a result.

Much has gone but much remains. There is still the city that has grown up over two hundred years and many of its finest buildings have survived the neglect that destroyed some of their lesser imitations. But it is certain that if attention is not paid to them they will be swept away: they don't look after themselves. This has

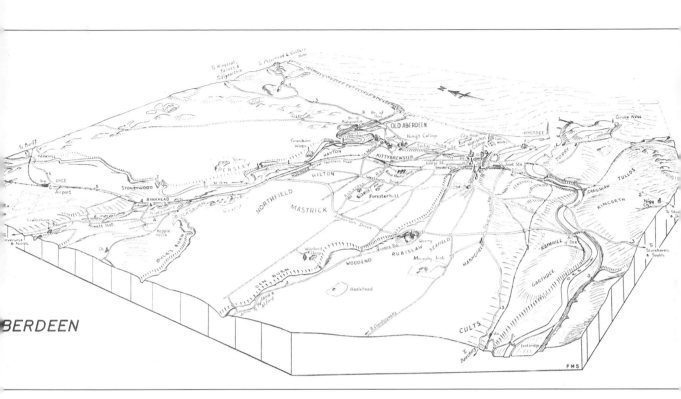

more to say about the city than the appearance of a single street or a building. It speaks of the history encapsulated for all the citizens in the feel of the place - the myriad vistas and buildings, details and special character marks that have made it what it is.

This history, in these many pages, is a story that deserves recognition for its weight and its significance for generations past. It can't be put aside lightly. New cities can be built and sometimes they are successful, but it is not easy. How much simpler it is to inherit a place that has established itself and made its way in the world. It is so obvious as to hardly need saying that people respond to their surroundings: they give to a place that seems to be home, and they recoil from somewhere that seems distant. Aberdeen's strength is that. It has that force of personality which has been able to survive economic troubles, war and the ebb and flow of people over the centuries. That is the strength that this history explains and celebrates and it needs to be renewed.

We must all speak personally when we feel about a place as so many of us feel about Aberdeen. For me, the evidence is plain: this is a city worth defending and supporting. We can't feel neutral about a place that has such a history in learning, in trade, in human discourse, in its connections with its rural and coastal hinterland. And we feel it is ours.

Map 1.
A Bird's Eye View
of Aberdeen.

Country comes to town for the market in the Green at the turn of the century.

19

On my wall I have a George Washington Wilson print which was taken from a spot on Union Street just opposite the Music Hall, looking east. Against the sky the spire of the town house is a misty pinnacle in the distance. Trams are proceeding up the street, a No 45 bound for Rubislaw to the fore. There are no cars, of course, but a flotilla of bicycles is making its way along the cobbles, many of them ridden by elegantly turned-out women with broad late-Victorian hats. The pavements are crowded, most of the men wearing strong flat caps, though the odd bowler and a spectacular straw boater can be seen. The shops are solid and welcoming. Down the streets the crowds flow across Union Bridge. Away down near the Castlegate the street seems black with people. This is an Aberdeen of a hundred years ago, but it is one that is still recognisable, despite everything.

The buildings, from the corner of Silver Street, where a rather finely dressed group is talking, to the buildings beyond the bridge, the corners and windows and chimney pots are as they are today. This is continuity – not simply a pleasurable memory, but evidence of the persistence of place. This is the street that I knew as a boy, wide-eyed in from Banffshire for the day, and that Aberdeen boys know today. I can imagine the conversations along the pavement. In that crowd there will be farmers and chandlers, lawyers and teachers, fishwives and traders of every kind, country folk and town folk – it's a marketplace of people.

Somehow the history of the place is captured in this picture. The granite shines, the sheer style of the early architects can be seen on every corner, the sense of commerce pervades everything. All of us will add personal memories and let our imaginations run a little wild. The point, though, in all the work of Washington Wilson is that a portrait emerges of somewhere alive: not a dormitory, nor a functional place of industry, but a place that breathes its fascination.

Each generation expresses this in a different way. For those of us who knew Aberdeen in the last part of the twentieth century, I suppose our folk memory will certainly include two of the most affecting cultural accoutrements of the city – *Scotland The What?* and the Dons. Within the hard covers of a book there is little to be said about Aberdeen Football Club except that any temporary lapse in performance will no doubt be rectified in time and that in the meantime we can all remember what it was like to be in Gothenburg in 1983 to watch Alex Ferguson's team beat Real Madrid – Real Madrid! – to win the European Cup Winners' Cup. I remember on that rainy night thinking it extraordinary that this most fabled of teams from one of Europe's great cities, a place of rich and extraordinary culture, was being taken to pieces by our own Dons. But then . . . why the surprise? It says something of our tendency to underrate ourselves that this seemed a little bizarre. And afterwards, as bemused but friendly Swedes gamely tried to master the *Northern Lights*, led as I recall by a moonlighting organist from an Aberdeen church who had done rather well by the *aquavit*, we felt confident that there would never be any need to feel downtrodden again. I am sure that future sociologists will track from that moment a stirring of the old spirit in Aberdeen.

And of *Scotland the What?* we can say that they have taught us how to laugh at ourselves. Buff Hardie, Stephen Robertson and George Donald were for more than twenty years much more than polished masters of the stage revue. They understood the nature of the North-Easter's phlegmatic and unblinking view of the world, whether from Rhynie or Mastrick, and they discerned the humanity underneath it.

Is it simply loyalty that makes that word humanity seem particularly appropriate? I think not. Aberdeen is a city built with an eye to its people. It feeds on the land around it and it has been a focus for lives lived far outside its borders. Those who built the modern city were enlightened and determined. It had, as all of us like to recall, two universities when the whole of England only had two, and it has always had education in its bloodstream - championing the cause of learning open to all and pioneering the entry of women into higher education, for example. In civic affairs its values in its best periods have always been generous rather than mean-spirited, and it has mostly been on the side of progress rather than reaction.

Against all the black patches in its history, these are the achievements that deserve to be celebrated. After all the toast of Bon Accord is '. . . happy to meet again'. At its best that happiness has always flourished behind the austere granite frontages and the place has held our affections because somehow it has managed to reflect the people who built and sustained it.

Those who direct it in the future can do no better than to look to this history and learn it.

1

The Growth of the City

JOHN S. SMITH

Aberdeen in 1800

At the conclusion of the eighteenth century, the outer limits of Aberdeen's built environment had scarcely changed for a century. The boundaries at that time were defined by the Denburn Valley to the west, the south end of the Spital (now St Peter Street) to the north, and the tidal estuary of the River Dee to the south. The industrial suburb of Gilcomston, north of the Denburn, lay in Oldmachar parish. The town was thus remarkably constricted in housing a population of some 27,000. Indeed there had been a considerable increase in population in the eighteenth century from a little over 5,000 in 1708 and 15,000 in 1755.[1] This growth had been accommodated primarily by the infill of open space thus greatly increasing the density of the urban population.

It is not surprising that the civic leaders were both fully aware of these restrictions and were actively planning the physical expansion of the town as the new century approached. Charles Abercrombie, an eminent surveyor, was engaged in 1794 to report on the best means of providing improved access to the town, bearing in mind the example of Edinburgh's New Town. Consideration was given to the possibility of creating a new street running eastwards along the banks of the Dee which would cross the largely unreclaimed estuary to meet the lower end of Marischal Street with its elegant Georgian houses. But the final decision favoured a street running westwards from Castle Street over a series of gravel hillocks interspersed by streams and running into the Denburn Valley which constituted the principal barrier to urban expansion. The new street had to bridge this natural obstacle but would then open up the possibility of future expansion over a vast greenfield site to the west. The new street was called Union Street, in recognition of the proposed union between Great Britain and Ireland which was eventually accomplished in 1801. The expansion scheme included provision for a second new street, with a projected north-south axis, which became King Street, thus providing a second new entry to the town. A number of turnpike roads further increased ease of access. This planned development was formally agreed in 1799, and the new street trustees advertised for designs combining the appropriate architectural and engineering requirements. The skeleton of the two new streets was in place by the end of the first decade of the new century, although the occupation of the building stances was slower than anticipated. In parts of lower Union Street high building costs, arising from the sharp fall of the ground from the new street level to the Green, discouraged purchase. Not until the second half of the nineteenth century did Union Street become the granite canyon which has been its enduring characteristic. It developed, initially, in typically Victorian style, surrounded by the cottage slums and smoky factories of Schoolhill and the lower Denburn area.

The Pattern of Urban Growth

The creation of Union Street and King Street allowed the town to overcome the principal obstacle to physical expansion, the Denburn. During the past two centuries the population has increased by more than tenfold, and this has necessitated a massive increase in the physical scale of Aberdeen. The initial development was confined primarily to the central area and the destruction of existing slum property, to allow the widening and refashioning of streets and their replacement by better buildings, was as important as the construction of new streets. The construction of the bridge to support the new Union Street, necessitated the destruction of a considerable amount of slum property built on the banks of the Denburn. The Police Act of 1795, secured as the culmination of two decades of local debate, opened with a statement which demonstrated the growing pressure of urban growth.

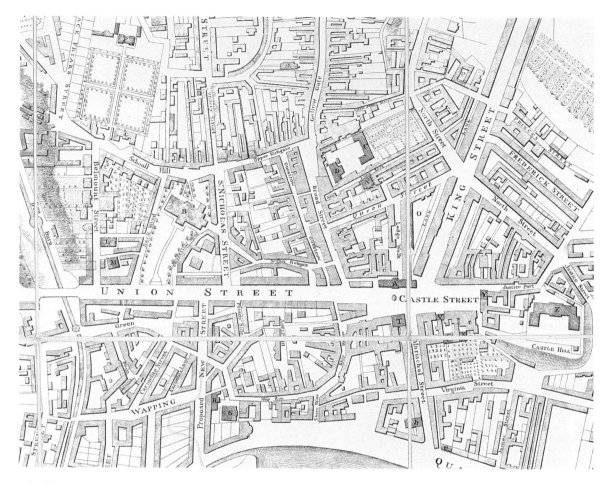

The developing city: part of John Smith's 1810 plan of the city of Aberdeen.

Whereas the city of Aberdeen has of late years greatly increased in buildings and inhabitants, and the roads, avenues, streets, lanes, and other public passages, within the said city and royalty thereof, are at present too narrow, indirect, and incommodious, and are not properly paved, lighted and cleaned, nor are the inhabitants sufficiently supplied with fresh water: And whereas it would be greatly for the safety and accommodation of the inhabitants of the said city, and of all persons resorting to the same, that the said roads, avenues, streets, lanes and other public passages were enlarged and altered, and that they were more sufficiently paved, lighted and cleaned, and the said city better supplied with fresh water; that all incroachments, annoyances and obstructions of every kind upon the said roads, streets, avenues, lanes and other passages were removed and prevented; and that all persons dealing in gunpowder within the said city were prevented from keeping at any one time in their houses, shops, or warehouses, more than a certain quantity of gunpowder: But these useful and statutory purposes, for want of proper powers and a sufficient fund to pay the expence thereof, cannot be accomplished without the authority of parliament.[2]

In the course of the nineteenth century, Aberdeen grew outwards from its historic centre around the Castlegate and the harbour and expanded along the channels marked out by the new streets and their hinterland. The first half of the nineteenth century saw the appearance of many of the public buildings which still characterised the central districts of the city in the year 2000. These included the Assembly Rooms, which subsequently became the Music Hall, the Royal Athenaeum, the Triple Kirks, the Medical Hall, St Andrew's Chapel, and the headquarters of the North of Scotland Bank, all of which were the work of Archibald Simpson. At the same time John Smith contributed the screen at St Nicholas Churchyard, the North Church (now the Arts Centre), Trinity Hall, the Old Town School, Crimonmogate House and the first Advocates Hall. Golden Square (1817) and Bon-Accord Crescent and Square (1823) were developed to offer more gracious housing beyond the town centre. Nor was the development unsupervised. The town council made its contribution by ensuring architectural quality. Thus, in the 1850s, a proposal on behalf of the Congregational Church, Frederick Street, for a feu on the south side of Union Street immediately west of Dee Street for a chapel failed to gain approval on the grounds that its elevation was inconsistent with the general plan of the street and that it would thus destroy the uniformity which was intended.

For much of the nineteenth century the expansion of the city was concerned with the redevelopment of the central area. In part this was a problem of dealing with the existing slums and with the health hazards they contained. The demolition of slum property was a persistent, albeit sporadic, process from the beginning of the nineteenth century onward. By the later decades of the century slum clearance had also become a matter of public health as properties were condemned by the medical officer of health in places like Shuttle Lane and the Cowgate. In the 1890s, for example, an 'unhealthy area' was identified in Exchequer Row which had a density of one person per 6.3 square yards compared with one to 27 in Greyfriars, one to 37 in St Nicholas and one to 250 in the city as a whole.[3] On other occasions demolition was an effect of the process of development. The construction of the Denburn Railway necessitated the clearance of existing buildings and dispossessed 'a great number of families of the poorer classes from their dwellings'. The town council offered temporary accommodation, erecting a long brick shed in Lower Don Street, and providing an alternative domicile in the west prison.[4]

Perhaps the most obvious indicator of perpetual redevelopment was the experience of the harbour. Over forty pieces of parliamentary legislation were passed in the two centuries after 1800 relating directly to the harbour, and several others which impinged upon it.[5] While the city was fortunate enough to have highly-skilled local architects who shaped the built environment, the harbour benefited from the work of some of the greatest engineers in the United Kingdom, John Smeaton advising on developments in the 1770s and 1780s and Thomas Telford providing designs for improvements in the 1800s. As seaborne trade increased, so the need to accommodate more and larger vessels meant that the harbour had to be made both wider and deeper. In addition new quays, locks, and cargo sheds were required. By 1900 the harbour had assumed its modern shape,

Archibald Simpson 1790–1847

Archibald Simpson, 'an architect of genius ... head and shoulders above the men of his time' according to Sir John Betjeman.

Son of a merchant, born in the Guestrow, Archibald Simpson was educated at the Grammar School and Marischal College. He had to curtail his education when his father died in 1804 and he was apprenticed to a mason in the Castlegate. He moved to London to work for an architect in 1810, subsequently visited Italy, and returned to Aberdeen in 1813 to start business on his own account. His first public commission was St Andrew's Chapel, now the Episcopal Cathedral, and his first major design was the Medical Hall on King Street, for the Medico-Chirurgical Society, followed by the Assembly Rooms, Royal Athenaeum, Bon-Accord Square and Bon-Accord Crescent. He later created designs for the new market, the Mechanics' Institute, Exchange Street, Market Street, Marischal College, the Royal Infirmary, Mrs Emslie's institution, later Harlaw Academy, the Triple Kirks and Marine Terrace. He contributed to the domestic architecture of Rubislaw Place, Waverley Place, Victoria Street and Albyn Place. But his most celebrated building was probably the headquarters of the North of Scotland Bank, which was refurbished in the 1990s as Archibald Simpson's Bar.

and was handling an annual tonnage of shipping almost ten times that of a century earlier. The twentieth century witnessed equally extensive redevelopment work in widening and rebuilding quays and sheds, together with the improvements in handling by the introduction of powerful new cranes. The most extensive redevelopment was necessitated by the radical restructuring of the work of the port as fishing declined and as oil-related demands appeared. The lease of land at Torry to Shell UK Exploration and Production in 1965 marked the beginning of the new development which transformed the harbour and greatly increased the tonnage of shipping handled. The continued demands of ferry services to the Northern Isles, but accommodating larger vessels with roll on/roll off facilities, required extensive restructuring of freight handling, and the entire crane capacity of the port was replaced in the second half of the twentieth century.

Beyond the city centre, the principal impetus towards the expansion of the city was manifest in the need for housing as the population grew. Towards the end of

King Street, the new road north from the Castlegate. Archibald Simpson's North of Scotland Bank is on the left. John Smith's North Church is in the centre.

The harbour coming right into the heart of the city was vital to Aberdeen's development.

the nineteenth century, developers such as John Morgan had taken the middle-class suburb as far as Argyll Place, Argyll Crescent, Westburn Drive, Hamilton Place, Fountainhall Road and Belvidere Street in the west end. Morgan's own house, at 50 Queen's Road, built in 1886 in Scottish baronial style, stands as a memorial to the quality of such work. As the more prosperous citizens moved west, their houses were colonised by less-affluent successors.

> The nobility and gentry who had estates in the country had a town residence in Aberdeen, where they usually passed the winter months ... Castle Street, Upperkirkgate, and Guestrow had several of these mansions, which are still to be seen. They usually had their entrance by a narrow court from the street, and though now let to numerous tenants, the oak panelling on the walls and the wide stone stairs are still there – the relics of their ancient grandeur.[6]

The physical expansion of the city was seldom a matter of consensus, principally because expansion involved expense and risk. The decision to develop Union Street was argued about for at least twenty years before work commenced, the costs of developing the harbour were a persistent source of animated debate, and the two major conflicts in local politics in the nineteenth century both concerned disputes about expansion. In each case the expansionists were successful and their victories were realised in the Aberdeen Municipality Extension Act of 1871 by which the city incorporated parts of Rosemount, Fountainhall, Mannofield, Broomhill, Ferryhill and the Dee estuary, and in the 1891 legislation by which the city incorporated Old Aberdeen, Woodside and Torry. Each of these three distant, and hitherto independent, areas were drawn into the city, initially through shared amenities. In 1882 residents of Mannofield applied to the town council to have the city gas supply extended to their area, and both Woodside and Old Aberdeen relied on the city gas supply before they were incorporated into its jurisdiction. The extension of the city boundary in 1891 more than doubled the area of the municipal burgh. But at the end of the First World War, there were still cultivated fields immediately to the west of Mannofield Reservoir, west of Rubislaw Quarry and around Summerhill and Woodhill.

The Anderson Drive ring road, which became a major landmark in the configuration of the modern city, was constructed, section by section, in the first half of the twentieth century. The first part, between Great Western Road and Carnegie Crescent was completed in 1902. The northern stretch of the road to Great Northern Road, and the southern extension to the Bridge of Dee were completed between the wars. Even so, in the early 1950s Anderson Drive effectively marked the boundary between the city and open countryside. Only Hazlehead, the suburban villages of Deeside like Cults and Bieldside, and their equivalents on other fringes of the city, such as Dyce and Cove,

John Morgan, leading property developer and city treasurer, 1889-92.

One of the main sources of Aberdeen's distinctive grey granite was Rubislaw Quarry, opened in 1740.

existed beyond the ring road. The second half of the twentieth century witnessed a marked expansion in the physical area of the city, characterised by housing development. This included council estates such as Northfield, Mastrick and Kincorth and private housing developments at Danestone/Bridge of Don, Portlethen, Bieldside, Milltimber and Peterculter as well as at Kingswells and Westhill. Considerable areas of land around the airport at Dyce, along the coastal fringes both north of the city at Denmore and south of the city at Altens and Tullos and, in the west, at Westhill, were developed as industrial estates.

LAND OWNERSHIP AND USE

The development of the city involved a variety of agencies working sometimes in collusion and occasionally in opposition to each other. The initiative for the new streets, which effectively started the process of expansion at the beginning of the nineteenth century, was taken by a small number of civic leaders who were the developers of their day and who also constituted the town council. Following the democratisation of local government in the 1830s, the town council became the principal agent responsible for initiating growth, and for supervising the form that the process took, and with an obligation to balance the competing requirements of expense and amenity. In the 1830s, for example, reports were commissioned from several prominent architects concerning the most suitable location for a public market, which should be 'most commodious and central' and at as moderate an expense as possible. The final report recommended the construction of a new street to link Union Street with the harbour, namely Market Street.

Perhaps the most basic responsibility for development which fell to the town council was the determination of land use. Throughout the nineteenth century the town council sought to buy land as it became available using the accumulated resources of the common good fund. This had been the traditional source of income for the town council since medieval times, and comprised rent on properties and land, and feu duties, held by the town council to provide charitable benefits for the citizens of the town. The purchase of land on which the town stood or onto which it might expand was a manifestly appropriate form of investment. Such investments had obvious economic benefits and, by the late twentieth century, the portfolio of the common good fund had increased to comprise property and land worth £24.5 million together with £8 million in reserves.

In the nineteenth century the town council had to buy land on the open market and was not always successful. An attempt to buy 66 acres of land at Angusfield in 1894 fell more than 10 per cent below the successful offer. When a civic bid was successful, as at Rosehill and Burnside in the 1890s, then land was frequently let on short-term leases for nursery gardens until required for residential construction. Some purchases were strategically important for future development. One offer, to buy from the town council the feu relating to a piece of land in Torry, was rejected because the proximity of the land to the harbour would be likely to increase its future value, and because the land might be required for future expansion of the harbour. Other strategic purchases were made possible by the foresight and philanthropy of civic dignitaries. In 1876 Lord Provost Jamieson and several colleagues together bought five acres of land at Leadside, and offered it to the town council at the same price. This purchase made possible the construction of the Rosemount Viaduct some years later. When estates came onto the market, in locations where future expansion might be needed, the town council became an increasingly important bidder. The 832 acres at Hazlehead were bought from the estate of Donaldson Rose, merchant and shipowner, most of which consisted of farms, nurseries and market gardens in 1920.[7] Other lands were acquired from institutions. The lands at Kincorth and Craigshaw were purchased from the Aberdeen Bakers' Incorporation, including the Hill of Kincorth, in 1928. In 1946 the land portfolio was increased by the purchase of Seaton House and its surrounding policies. The condition of this sale was that the owner of the house, Major Malcolm Hay should enjoy use of the house and lodge for his lifetime and that, in due course, the property should be transferred to the links and parks department for use as a public park.

The potential for the development of land within and adjacent to the city was not lost on private developers, so that the city authorities often had to deal with them, although the individuals concerned were seldom unknown to the town council. Private builders feued for development land owned by the incorporated trades in Golden Square and Diamond Street. There was also some opportunism. A petition from the inhabitants of properties near Trinity Quay, Market Street and Shiprow in 1853 complained about the nuisance arising from the 'great quantities of fish brought into and cleaned in the Fish Market situated at the Shiprow and Quay, and which was injurious to the health and comfort of those living in the neighbourhood', and requested that the fish market might be moved elsewehere. Shortly afterwards the town council received a letter from the lawyers Adam and Anderson, proposing that the north basement of the market buildings, of which they were part-owners, might be set aside as a fish market.[8]

The need for the city to acquire land was closely linked to housing problems. In the 1920s, some slum properties were bought, using the common good fund, in the Guestrow, Upperkirkgate, Barnett's Close and Broad Street from the trustees of the estate of John Lyall Grant to allow the clearance of what had been defined as the Guestrow insanitary area.[9] Some housing schemes were developed precisely for the purpose of housing those displaced from the slums. The Cattofield scheme of 373 new dwellings built in the 1920s was intended for those expelled (or saved) from the Guestrow, Shuttle Lane and Shoe Lane, although the town council, ever economical, did manage to persuade the Scottish Board of Health to relax the regulation governing the maximum number of dwellings per acre from 24 to 36.[10]

Sir Alexander Anderson 1802–1887

Born at Strichen, a son of the manse, Alexander Anderson was educated at the parish school at Strichen, and then in Aberdeen at the Grammar School and Marischal College. He became a lawyer, in partnership with William Adam, and was admitted to the Society of Advocates in 1827. He acted as treasurer for the dispensary, and administered the estate of an uncle, George Watt, who left bequests to establish a house of refuge for the poor (Oldmill) and a reformatory for youths (Oakbank). In 1837 he launched the North of Scotland Insurance Co and the North of Scotland Bank. He was involved in the establishment of the new market in the 1840s, the planning of Market Street, and started a gas company to break the monopoly power of the existing supplier which, after a few years, was obliged to merge with his company. He was deeply and extensively engaged in the promotion of railways, sponsoring the North British Railway from Friockheim to Aberdeen, the Great North of Scotland Railway and the Deeside Railway. In 1859 he was elected to represent the third ward on the town council and served as lord provost 1859–65. During his term of office he promoted the new waterworks at Cairnton, inaugurated the new site for the Grammar School and the new town house. In 1875 he promoted the City of Aberdeen Land Association (CALA) to exploit feuing land in Rubislaw and Torry which he had bought some years earlier.

Anderson was knighted in 1863, an occasion which created an important precedent. Later in the same year, a large body of civic dignitaries was assembled for the inauguration of the Albert Memorial in London, and precedence in the procession was a matter of some import. The provost of Dundee, as current convener of the Convention of Royal Burghs, claimed precedence over his counterparts in both Aberdeen and Glasgow on the grounds that, while they used the higher title of lord provost, they had no right to do so. However, some months earlier, Queen Victoria had attended the unveiling of the statue commemorating the Prince Consort in Aberdeen and marked the occasion by conferring a knighthood on Alexander Anderson. She had also accorded him the title of lord provost, which had hitherto been used, with increasing frequency, as a courtesy title.

Increasingly, in the twentieth century, land was needed for the expansion of the city. An estate at Foresterhill, comprising 45 acres, was purchased in 1906 'for the behoof of the Common Good of the city' as the town council minutes recorded. In the 1920s, the 198 acre Hilton estate was purchased and, in the 1930s, 390 acres at Tullos and 520 acres at Sheddocksley were bought for council house building.[11] An agreement between the town council, Aberdeen University and John George Burnett of Powis enabled the city to acquire Powis House and its grounds together with land between St Machar Drive and Bedford Road. The land was subsequently developed as a housing scheme, a new school and a sports field. Other purchases allowed the use of brownfield sites for redevelopment. The Froghall housing scheme occupied a site made available by the demolition of the jute works.

Long-established patterns of land ownership also caused problems, not least in the celebrated and highly controversial purchase of the Torry Farm estate for development. In the 1860s the acquisition of the estate was essential for the development of the harbour and the extension of the city onto the southern bank of the Dee estuary. The history of the ownership of the estate greatly complicated that project. The estate had been part of the barony of Torry, and virtually coterminous with Nigg parish. Half of the barony was bought by the town council in 1704. In 1785 the lands were divided. The ownership of the village of Torry, Balnagask and the land along the coast towards Loirston was allocated to the town, while the lands of Torry Farm and Kincorth became the property of Menzies of Pitfodels. The town council feued its land off in small estates, while the Torry Farm estate remained in the hands of Menzies and the trustees of his estates until it was sold at public roup in 1859 for £15,000. The purchasers were a consortium comprising Sir Alexander Anderson, Milne of Kinaldie and John Blaikie, the lawyer acting on behalf of the Menzies Trust.

Within the decade, it was recognised that land on the Torry Farm estate was essential for the improvement of the harbour. The harbour board planned to divert the Dee into an entirely new channel to produce a net gain of about 90 acres of land in addition to the existing available Inches, together with a strip of land running from the lowest bridging point to Torry village and to Craiglug at the site of the Wellington suspension bridge. The diversion of the channel of the river and the additional land were both regarded as essential for the development of the harbour.

There were thus several interested parties concerned about the ownership, sale and use of the land. In 1864 the consortium of owners offered the land to the harbour board for £28,000, but that body was unable to proceed since the cost exceeded the limits of its financial powers under the Harbour Act. In the following year the town council proposed to buy the Torry Farm estate for the asking price of £28,000 if it could not be secured for less. It agreed that the harbour board should be permitted to acquire such parts of the estate on both sides of the river as it might require, provided that the harbour board agreed to build a bridge across the new bed of the river in line with Market Street. An additional benefit of the project, according to its supporters, lay in the fact that the new bridge would be a recreational benefit 'answering as it would in many respects, the purposes of a public park, might enable the community to dispense with an outlay of money for that object'. In 1867 the town council made further preparations for this project by purchasing the salmon fishing rights.

By 1869 the matter had become a major source of controversy and wrangling. The majority view within the town council was willing to purchase the estate at a price which had risen to £32,000 and to promote a bill in Parliament to build a new bridge using £12,500 from the Bridge of Don Fund. In April 1869 the trades council presented a petition to the town council, in support of the scheme to purchase Torry Farm and to construct a bridge over the Dee, which contained 6,000 signatures. This enabled James Barclay, a leading supporter of the scheme, to place before the town council a resolution in favour of adopting the terms of the petition, with a request that a meeting of the citizens, a head court, be called to consider the matter. This meeting was held one week later on 27 April in the Music Hall which was 'nearly filled with an audience comprising all classes'.[12] This boisterous meeting rehearsed the arguments for and against the proposed development. While there was general agreement about the need for a bridge, there were sharp divisions about the purchase of the land.

The main proponent of the development was Barclay who spoke at length, arguing the need for expansion of the city, and seeking to provide reassurance that there would be no need to tax the citizens to pay for the venture since the Bridge of Don Fund could be used to finance it. An even more glorious prospect was painted by Mr Miller of the Sandilands Chemical Works. 'But give them access across the river to the south, and in twenty years they would see another town raised there. In twenty years they would have ship-building yards, iron ship-building yards, and factories and workshops all along the river, making Torry to Aberdeen what Gorbals is to Glasgow and Birkenhead to Liverpool.'[13] The president of the trades council also supported the project on the grounds that it would create employment.

Against the purchase of the land were Lord Provost Nicol and his associates. He phrased his objections in terms of a long-standing commitment to 'purchase for the harbour commissioners every foot of ground at the cheapest possible price'. The strongest case against the venture was articulated by an ex-lord provost, John Webster. He disputed Barclay's argument that the Bridge of Don Fund could be redirected to pay for the new project. He also argued vehemently that, while the construction of a bridge lay in the public interest the development of land across the river did not.

I say, at once, that I have throughout maintained the opinion that a Town Council, having itself to borrow every shilling that it has to employ for the purpose, has no business at all to speculate in land. (cheers and hisses) The purchases and management of agricultural property, or of building lands, is much better, depend upon it, in the hands of private individuals, who have direct interest to overlook it and make it pay. (applause)[14]

The meeting became even more noisy when Adam Mitchell, who presented himself 'merely as a citizen of Aberdeen', spoke. 'I say I have always been in favour of a bridge across the river. [A Voice] To get the contract. [Mr Mitchell] Yes to get the contract and to get work for the people of Aberdeen. [cheers, hisses, and uproar which continued for some time].' Eventually the meeting dissolved in chaos, the lord provost walked out, two opposing motions were put to the audience but the second was ignored amid the din. Six months later, in the town council elections, the 'Party of Progress' finally secured its mandate to build the bridge and buy the land.

THE BUILT ENVIRONMENT

The physical growth of the city has been primarily reflected in the erection of buildings for public, commercial and private use. The bulk of nineteenth-century building was undertaken by private developers. The architects and builders of the nineteenth century shaped the built environment of the city, although the town council did seek to maintain and enhance high architectural standards. A report from the superintendent of works, William Smith, paid particular attention to the required architectural characteristics of the residences which would overlook Victoria Park, along the difficult curved alignment of Argyll Place. Smith recommended that the appearance of the houses from the park would be best served if the ground 'were let off in portions for separate villas and not built in uniform style', although he was aware that the gradient would mean that each house would have to be at a different level. This option was recommended by the improvements committee.

While most of nineteenth-century building was conducted by private contractors for individual or institutional clients, a major change occurred towards the end of the century which profoundly influenced building thereafter. This was the Housing of the Working Classes Act of 1890 which was the first of a series of legislative measures which allowed local authorities, and later other agencies such as the Scottish Special Housing Association, to build public authority housing. This not only became a major task of local authorities in the twentieth century, but played a central part in giving shape to the growth of the built environment.

The acceptance of such extensive financial commitments by the town council took some time. In 1853, accepting a motion put forward by the lord provost, it was agreed to contribute £40 towards the cost of widening Hadden Street only with the proviso that 'this subscription to have no reference, and to form no precedent from bringing any expense whatever on the town council in regard to further or other improvement which may be proposed in connection with the said street or its neighbourhood'.[15] In the twentieth century, as public sector housing increased so its influence upon the spatial growth of the city became overwhelmingly important. Immediately after the First World War the first phase of the Torry housing scheme, comprising 100 dwellings, a mixture of three-roomed flats and four-roomed cottages, was built. Plans were prepared at Hilton for 'concrete dwelling houses of the flatted type, each dwelling a 3-apartment house with scullery, bathroom and coal-cellar, at a contract price per house of £400'.[16] In the 1930s the construction of council houses extended to Tullos and Sheddocksley. Many of these housing estates were constucted on greenfield sites, often on hills between major arterial roads, as at Hilton and Kincorth. While money and materials were in short supply, the land for construction was easily available and relatively cheap, and the housing schemes themselves did not constitute a contentious use of land. Such conflicts emerged later.

Pressure for housing was even greater after the Second World War. Some temporary houses were erected at Tillydrone and Hayton and over 750 aluminium

Municipal housing development at Kincorth in the 1950s.

houses were placed at Cornhill and Stockethill, while plans to build similar houses at Walker Road and Wood Street had to be abandoned because of drainage problems. In 1947 the town council commissioned a civic survey and advisory plan, which was published in 1952. The Chapman-Riley Report envisaged the development of housing estates at Northfield and Kincorth, and proposed one major area for private residential development at Seafield, which was to be bounded by Springfield Road, the Craigiebuckler estate and a proposed outer ring road. Additional land for private housing was identified at Woodend and Hazlehead, while industrial requirements were to be met by the construction of an industrial estate at Tullos.[17]

In the post-war era, the need for housing land began to threaten the requirement to maintain open-space amenities. An early sign of the erosion of such amenities had been the gradual disappearance of allotments in favour of construction. The development plan submitted by the town council to the Scottish Office in 1953 defined the inner green belt as 'an area where the normal occupations of agriculture, horticulture, or forestry predominate, and in which the townsman enjoys the pleasures of the countryside'.[18] It expressed an equivocal commitment to maintaining the green belt, indicating that 'there will be absolute prohibition of development except such as can be shown to be necessary, and any planning consents given will contain provisions for the safeguarding of amenity'.[19] Having accepted restrictions on the outward expansion of the city, the town council considered the alternative of upward expansion, and its representatives examined multi-storey tower blocks in London and Glasgow. In the 1960s such tower blocks appeared in Aberdeen, the result of pressure to relocate people from slum clearances in the central districts and of the inability to expand the city boundaries. Five-storey blocks were built at Cornhill-Stockethill and at Tillydrone. Later and higher tower blocks were constructed at many other locations throughout the city.

By the 1970s housing policy was changing under the influence of new policy preferences on the part of central government. The construction of council housing gave way to a programme which concentrated on the refurbishment of existing stock. But the pressure for new construction moved to the private sector fuelled by rising prosperity and by the oil boom. In the 1970s the town council, and its successor the district council, undertook a programme of land acquisition for private housing development, aiming initially at the provision of 500 houses per annum. Three areas were identified as providing the suitable location for most of this programme, the Bridge of Don and Dyce to the north, an area south of the Dee and east of the main Stonehaven road (Portlethen), and parts of the ribbon development along the valley of lower Deeside.[20] The district council was also keen to develop land in its ownership at Carnie for housing, but faced the difficulty that the land lay within the jurisdiction of another local authority, Gordon district.

The 1970s and 1980s witnessed a massive programme of new office building, mainly attributable to the oil industry. The oil companies tended to favour less central sites, BP being based at Dyce, Shell at Altens, Occidental at the Bridge of Don and several companies located on Anderson Drive close to Rubislaw Quarry. The British National Oil Corporation proved to be an exception choosing a central location in a tower block close to the railway station. In spite of the upsurge of office construction, vacancy rates fell and commercial rents rose sharply. There was also substantial investment in new warehouse and factory space.

TRANSPORT NETWORKS

The geographical spread of the city and its increase in population brought additional demands for transport links. The Inverurie canal, opened in 1807, represented an early attempt to link the agricultural and textile producers of the hinterland to wider markets by way of Aberdeen harbour. But the growth of the city required the development of an adequate road system, while the railway transformed external links from the middle of the nineteenth century onward.

The Aberdeen Railway, eventually part of the Caledonian Railway, first linked the city to the south in 1850. The original intention was that the railway would penetrate into the heart of the city crossing the partially reclaimed Dee estuary to

terminate on what subsequently became the site of the new market. But this ambitious scheme, with obvious advantages for the convenience of passengers, failed to meet the conditions imposed by the harbour board. Thus the line initially terminated at Ferryhill Station, but was eventually extended across the estuarine flats to reach Guild Street Station. The Great North of Scotland Railway (GNSR) was inaugurated in 1854, running initially from Kittybrewster to Huntly. Since Kittybrewster was deemed to be too far distant from the industrial quarter, in 1855 the line was extended along the old canal bed to a new terminus at Waterloo Quay. Although short, the gap between the stations at Waterloo Quay and Guild Street caused much inconvenience for connecting passengers. In the following decade a proposed line to link the two railway systems was projected to run from Guild Street along Albyn Place to Kittybrewster, then beyond the city boundary. Residents objected that this 'circumbendibus route' would result in the 'unnecessary marring of the most ornamental suburb of the city' and advocated the direct route through the Denburn valley. The problem was resolved in 1863 when the town council agreed to sell the land along the Denburn for the rail link. This involved the constuction of tunnels and the negotiation of steep gradients, but enabled the aptly-named Joint Station to be opened in 1867. It was subsequently rebuilt in largely its modern form in 1915. The feeder Deeside line to Ferryhill Junction opened in 1853.

Until the end of the nineteenth century, private transport relied heavily on the horse. Public transport, in the form of buses pulled by horses, appeared in the 1860s. By 1866 a horse bus service operated from the town to Bieldside and to Blairs as well as between Queen's Cross and Old Aberdeen.[21] The horse buses lasted until the

The railway cutting through the valley of the Denburn opened the route to the west. The building with Simpson's elegant spire housed the Triple Kirks, while the church on the right is Belmont Street Congregational.

1890s. From Market Street routes provided a service to Bieldside, Woodside, Bucksburn and Stoneywood, although both the passenger capacity and the frequency of services were very limited. The Aberdeen District Tramways Company opened in 1874, the first horse tramway service running from the North Church on King Street to Queen's Cross, and from St Nicholas Street to Causewayend. This service, operated with 24 horses, relied on four double decker trams, each drawn by two horses, and each having a carrying capacity of 40 passengers.[22] The service operated on a 15 minute frequency between 8 am and 10 pm on weekdays only. Private bus companies serviced the growing suburban villages. In the 1870s William Bain had three buses running to Cults, and McBeg had four running to Woodside. The first suburban train linked the city to Stoneywood in 1887, and the success of this line encouraged the opening of the Deeside line to Peterculter in 1894. These 'subbies' ran until 1937 when they were supplanted by bus and tram competition. They provided a highly efficient service, unrivalled for speed and frequency of service and density of stations, there being eight intermediate stations on the Dyce line and nine on the Peterculter line.

The Aberdeen District Tramways Company was taken over by the town council in 1898. Municipalisation brought progress in the form of electrification of the system, double track routes and formalised tramstops. The network also began to expand, reaching the sea beach and bathing station in 1901. The bathing station had already preceded the tramways into public ownership, having been bought by the town council in 1892 after councillors had satisfactorily completed site visits to Scarborough, Ramsgate and Boulogne. The boundaries of the tramway system at the turn of the century were Bayview Road, Mannofield, the Bridge of Dee, Woodside and the Bridge of Don. Both Ferryhill and Torry were linked to the tramway in 1903. In the following decade the network penetrated further into the west end, running along Fountainhall Road, Beechgrove Road and along Rosemount Viaduct to Woodside. More controversially, Sunday services started in 1902. Their absence earlier had marked a temporary success for the Rev. Thomas Gardiner, convener of the Sabbath observance committee of the Free Presbytery of Aberdeen, who wrote to the town council asking that a clause be inserted in the bill prohibiting all tramway traffic on Sundays. It proved to be a temporary respite against the encroachment of secularisation. The provision of transport links to the outer fringes of the civilised world was a task still left to private operators. The Aberdeen Suburban Transport Company started operating in 1904 with tram routes from Woodside to Dyce and Mannofield to Bieldside.

The tramway reached the limits of its network in the 1920s. Several factors conspired against it. At the end of the First World War, the tramways faced high costs in renewing and possibly extending track, and in replacing cars. Furthermore, the new estates built between the wars were not close to tram routes. Residents of

Hilton and Torry 'Garden City' faced a steep walk to the nearest tramstop. In 1931 the Torry route was closed as was, amidst public controversy, the Ferryhill route. The tram was replaced, of course, by the bus which offered a more flexible and economical alternative, and one less irritating to suburban motorists. The city's service started in 1921 running from the city centre to Ferryhill and Torry. The first double decker, with 52 seats, was introduced on the Hilton to Garden City route in 1930. The construction of new housing estates in the 1950s at Northfield, Mastrick and Kincorth finally ended the tramway era.

In the twentieth century, as the volume of motor transport grew, the road system and traffic management became major issues. As early as the 1920s the town council was seeking urgent support from the Ministry of Transport to finance the construction of the northern and southern portions of the ring road. Until the 1950s the centripetal structure, by which the Great Northern, Great Southern and Great Western roads provided access to a single hub of activity for employment, shopping and cultural activities in the city centre, sufficed. But in that decade the first problems of traffic congestion appeared, occasioned by the volume of public transport in Union Street which was traversed by six tram routes and five bus routes. At peak hours, the trams operated a three-minute service frequency so there were constant interruptions to the flow of traffic as passengers headed across the granite setts to board the trams. Traffic lights caused further delays so that it frequently took ten minutes or more to travel a quarter of a mile.

The bus and the private car, in due course, created other types of traffic problem. In 1959 the town council was asked to consider the practicability and probable cost of raising Union Terrace Gardens to street level so that four floors of underground parking could be built below.[23] New housing developments had now to take account of the need to provide parking. The Gallowgate housing redevelopment scheme, based on multi-storey flats, was designed to include covered car parking accommodation, while a more radical solution to access came in the form of a request from the Chamber of Commerce that land be allocated in the central area of the city to provide a heliport.[24]

In the later decades of the century the problem of congestion within the city centre became less contentious, or perhaps less severe, than the problem of access. There were two major problems. In the north of the city, there had been extensive housing construction at the Bridge of Don and beyond, together with commercial development in the creation of an industrial estate, a science park, an international conference centre and office blocks for oil-related companies. But access across the Don was still restricted to two bridges located at Persley and the Bridge of Don. This problem became very apparent in the 1980s and increasingly desperate in the following decade, but any progress towards the establishment of a third bridge was hampered by disputes between the two authorities concerned, Aberdeen district council and Grampian regional council. Similar, although less acute, traffic problems developed at the other end of the ring road, at the Bridge of Dee, where traffic entering the city from the south encountered traffic flowing from several superstores and, in the late 1990s, the development of the new Robert Gordon University campus, all located on Garthdee Road.

The essential traffic problem facing Aberdeen in the later years of the century centred upon the ring road. Virtually all traffic seeking to by-pass the city needed to travel along the ring road while, for a great many journeys from the suburbs to the city centre, the ring road was an unavoidable crossing point. This problem necessarily reactivated the discussions about a new ring road, now designated the western peripheral route, which had been mooted first in the early 1950s. Since such a road would necessarily pass through the fashionable suburbs of lower Deeside, at Pitfodels, Milltimber or west of Peterculter, according to the various routes proposed, it became an obvious focus for well-articulated opposition. As the century neared its end, there was little sign of immediate action to deal with any of these traffic problems.

SOCIAL AMENITIES

The quality of life in any urban centre relies upon the quality of its amenities for leisure and social life as much as upon the provision of buildings and transport systems. Aberdeen town council consistently sought to protect social amenities in the form of open space for recreation, and most notably the Links. The popularity of the Links placed them at risk from unregulated use, as a report from the ground officer in 1850 demonstrated.

> The Links although a great privilege to the inhabitants of Aberdeen, have in many cases been deteriorated by certain classes who have frequented them. The parties most blamable are idle and disorderly boys, some of them with dogs – cab drivers and others with vehicles and on horse back, going to and returning from the Bathing Machines, grooms exercising and breaking horses, also persons playing with quoits, cricket and other games. To these may be added that of making pits and driving stakes, also laying down and taking up water pipes at Cattle Shows.[25]

The race course also contributed to this wear and tear. The town council was so worried that it closed some entrances to the Links for carriages and drew up a list of regulations for future use. Far more threatening was the proposal of the Aberdeen, Peterhead and Fraserburgh Railway Co., formulated in a parliamentary bill in 1856, to build a railway line from Waterloo Quay to the north and thus running through the Links. The town council 'dissented from and objected to' this

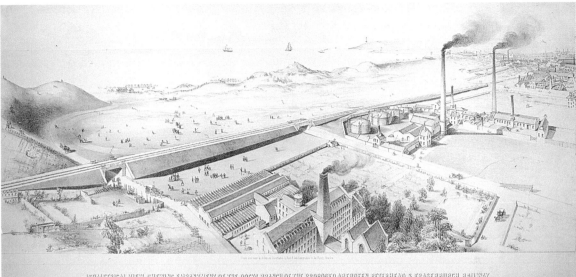

ISOMETRICAL VIEW SHEWING EMBANKMENT OF THE DOCKS BRANCH OF THE PROPOSED ABERDEEN PETERHEAD & FRASERBURGH RAILWAY, THROUGH THE PUBLIC LINKS OF ABERDEEN, 1866.

proposal, as did a public meeting, or head court, of the citizens held at the Lemon Tree Tavern. This meeting produced a petition, presented to the House of Lords by the Earl of Aberdeen, noting with righteous indignation civic opposition to a wanton and inexcusible abuse of popular rights and privileges. The evidence taken by the parliamentary enquiry reflected a variety of different perceptions about the Links. The supporters of the railway reckoned that few respectable people went there owing to the predilection of boys to re-enact the battles of the Crimean War, even on the Sabbath. But the opposition stressed the great benefit afforded by opportunities for robust and respectable activities such as cricket, quoiting and golf. Sir Thomas Blaikie, as lord provost, gave a sterling defence of the Links, and stressed the value to working-class people of the healthy environment provided there.[26] The Links, it was argued, provided a secure play area for children, space for sportsmen to compete, and a suitable review ground for the militia. The protesters won the day and the railway line was never authorised.

The amenity value of open space was increased and improved by the provision of parks, although a report commissioned by the town council in the 1870s prudently observed that the high marketable value of land in the vicinity of large towns, eagerly sought after for building purposes, would preclude the possibility of acquiring large areas for public parks. In 1873 Victoria Park was opened, subject to an exhaustive set of regulations for use. In the same decade the newly completed embankment on the north bank of the Dee, later Riverside Drive, was recognised as having considerable amenity value as a broad carriage drive with ornamental verges. James Matthews, an architect, produced detailed proposals suggesting that

Attempts to push a rail line through the Links were successfully resisted in the 1850s.

the town council should obtain the surrender of feuing rights from owners in Union Terrace and Belmont Street with a view to upgrading the open area north of the Union Bridge as a social amenity. This became Union Terrace Gardens. Some amenities were gifted to the city, such as the public park given in 1880 which still bears the name of Miss Duthie of Ruthrieston.

In the nineteenth century urban land was relatively cheap and more abundantly available than it became by the late twentieth century. The town council sought to maintain an informal green belt of land for amenity purposes. Council house building between the wars did not ignore such considerations, seeking to leave high ground as an amenity space, so that Brimmond Hill and the 'rough ground on Kincorth Hill' were reserved as open spaces. In later decades, as the pressure to build increased, especially from private builders, resistance to further development came from both the local authority and local community groups. Applications for residential development were frequently refused on the grounds of preserving good agricultural land, the maintenance of areas of high landscape quality and the possible threat to natural resources.

By the last decade of the twentieth century the defence of the green belt against the encroachment of builders had become a major political and planning issue. The Aberdeen district local plan, produced in 1989, espoused a strategy by which the greater part of future development in the Aberdeen area would be located in the suburbs and in settlements with easy access to the city. The green belt would be maintained with the objective of delimiting the built-up areas immediately adjacent to the city in order to maintain its 'landscape setting'.[27] The strategy for the city centre was to strengthen its role as the commercial, cultural and entertainment centre of the region, and to accommodate additional housing needs by building on brownfield sites and city-centre infill. The realisation of the last aspect of the policy became very visible in the 1990s in the form of developments of new flats in locations such as the Green, in the George Street and Gallowgate areas, and in Union Glen. But this did not fully satisfy demand for construction. Proposals such as that put forward by a consortium to build both a business park and 1,000 houses on Kincorth Hill, at the close of the 1990s, on land still designated as green belt, proved to be extremely contentious. It was vigorously opposed by residents with initial success, although some uncertainty as to the longer-term prospects remained. Similarly attempts by developers to erode the green belt between Bieldside and Peterculter and between Cults and Hazlehead met fierce local resistance, as did attempts to secure planning permission for new supermarkets adjacent to the ring road. Similar but unsuccessful outrage accompanied the decision of the town council to allow the construction of new Asda and Safeway supermarkets in Garthdee and a new campus for the Robert Gordon University (RGU) on land which had previously been an amenity area.

Control and Planning

In the early nineteenth century, the decision to pursue urban expansion by building Union Street was a local decision taken by the civic leadership. It was a matter of little or no interest to distant places such as Dundee, or even Stonehaven. As the city grew in the course of that century, and even more in the twentieth century, the desire and need to expand impinged upon neighbouring authorities. In the 1860s the cost of the new county and municipal buildings was shared by the city, the county, and a number of small burghs. The allocation of the relative shares of that financial burden was the subject of debate and close scrutiny between the different authorities.

Thereafter, there were frequent negotiations concerning the adjustment of boundaries as the city sought to expand. In the late 1920s discussions were held with the two neighbouring counties with regard to the appropriate jurisdiction for villages at the margins of the city such as Peterculter, Newhills, Dyce and the rural parts of Oldmachar. This led to the establishment of the Aberdeen and district joint town planning scheme, whose report took five years in preparation, but which provided the largest and most comprehensive analysis then available when it was approved by the Department of Health for Scotland in 1933. It provided an integrated planning scheme for an area of 96 square miles including the city and parts of its two adjacent counties. In the 1960s further discussions with the county authorities of Aberdeenshire and Kincardineshire considered both the city's ambitions to take over an area lying between the Skene Road and Bucksburn Farm, known as Sheddocksley, for housing, and land east of the Stonehaven Road and the coast at Altens where the city hoped to locate an industrial estate.[28] The latter site had been identified in the Gaskin Report, published in 1969, as a potential location for industrial development. An attempt made by Aberdeen district council to secure boundary changes which would bring the Westhills–Carnie area into its jurisdiction, hence obviating the need to obtain planning permission from rival neighbouring planning authorities to develop land it had bought, caused controversy. The attempt failed. The residents of Westhill, fearing the imposition of high rates, strenuously and successfully opposed the move to change their local jurisdiction.[29] It had been hoped and intended that the new two-tier local government structure introduced in 1974, whereby Aberdeen's local government was divided between the district council and Grampian Region, would have facilitated the co-ordination of policy. The reality was very different and the two-tier structure became a source of conflict largely because the majority of councillors elected in one tier never represented the same political interests as the majority elected in the other tier. The tensions were most apparent in the struggle over a new bridge across the Don, favoured by the regional council but implacably opposed by the district. In the 1990s, local government was radically restructured, but no new bridge crossed the Don.

The passage of time brought another interested party into the political and planning equation, namely central government. Even in the nineteenth century, the town council never enjoyed a completely free hand in development matters, and the supervisory control of central government increased over time. Parliamentary legislation was required for all developments, and this set the borrowing and tax limits for each project. Later changes in boundaries also required government legislation. In the twentieth century both local planning and central government intervention in that process became more formal and extensive, usually operating through the agency of the Scottish Office.

Modern planning procedures were introduced in the 1947 legislation in the form of the Town and Country Planning (Scotland) Act whereby each authority was obliged to submit to the Secretary of State for Scotland a survey report and development plan, indicating its programme for land use. Both the Scottish Office and the Scottish housing advisory committee kept a watching brief on town council policy and there emerged a set of working rules which were the antecedents of national planning guidelines. The agreed conventions stipulated that the area developed should be part of a planning scheme and, if required, zoned as a housing area. Location and accessibility were identified as the key factors, although danger to residents of proximity to major traffic routes was to be considered. Fertile land should be retained whenever possible for agriculture and market gardening, and appropriate sanitary and water supplies should be easily accessible. This allowed positive development objectives to be identified and pursued, and greatly enhanced the powers of local government. In the 1950s, plans for completing the Northfield and Cummings Park building programme, and the Seafield private housing programme, brought the built-up area of the city close to the boundary with Aberdeenshire. Any further expansion of those projects would cross the city boundary. To explore the possibility of this development, and to prepare for its possible eventuality the Department of Health for Scotland produced a range of population projections. It also conducted discussions with the city authorities and the representives of its two adjacent counties concerning the distribution of future population growth and the preservation of the green belt.[30]

While the city experienced little population growth in the final decades of the twentieth century, there was a substantial increase in surrounding rural areas and satellite districts. Aberdeen became the heart of an extensive city region within which the distinction between town and countryside became increasingly blurred. This was recognised by the structural plan devised prior to the reorganisation of local government in 1995-96.[31] Aberdeen's links with its hinterland were augmented and reinforced rather than severed by late twentieth-century development.

2

People in the City

ANDREW BLAIKIE

THE GROWTH OF POPULATION

One of the most obvious and important differences between the past two centuries and earlier historical periods lies in population growth. The medieval and early modern world experienced limited increases in population. Since then growth has been much more sustained.[1] In 1755 Dr Webster estimated the population of the two city parishes of Aberdeen, St Nicholas and Oldmachar, to be 15,433. Forty years later, the *Statistical Account* noted that 'owing chiefly to the rapid progress of manufactures' the city had 'greatly increased' in size to 24,493. A variety of economic and social stimuli created the basis for this expansion. The extensive cultivation of waste in the surrounding agricultural land had 'found occupation for many additional hands', while the 'great demand for paving the streets of London' with granite setts had 'brought a multitude of labourers from all parts of the country … and after that demand slackened, many of these remained with their families in Aberdeen, as a proper place for obtaining employment as day-labourers'. Less direct stimuli also contributed to urban growth. 'Many likewise, who have come up as patients to the infirmary, have, after being cured, settled with the same view', while 'many aged persons [from country parishes] particularly single women, retire to towns, and accommodate themselves in small rooms'.[2]

The pattern of growth is shown in Figure 2.1. In 1801 the city's population stood at 26,992, but with the growth of the textile industry the first three decades of the new century brought spectacular rates of growth of close to 30 per cent per decade. The rate slowed down during the following two decades but, in the first half of the nineteenth century, population increased by two and a half times to reach 71,973 by 1851. The 1840s crisis in textiles cut the rate of growth thereafter, although recovery in the final quarter of the century stimulated by the fishing boom ensured that the population doubled between 1851 and 1901. The first half of the twentieth century witnessed a modest population growth of 20 per cent followed by a decline in the two decades following the end of the Second World War, during which time there was a marked outward migration from the city. The oil boom generated a revival, boosting the population to 215,930 in 1997.[3] In the context of the late twentieth century, however, concentration on the city alone is highly misleading. In the last decade of the century the towns and villages of the surrounding commuter belt, bounded approximately by Stonehaven, Banchory, Inverurie and Ellon, greatly increased their populations. This 'greater' Aberdeen is expected to continue to enjoy population growth in the new century.[3]

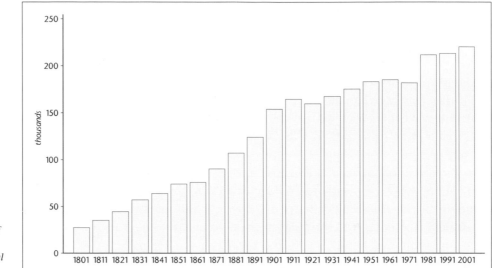

Figure 2.1
Population of
Aberdeen,
1801-2001.
(Source: Census of
Population for
Scotland, Decennial
Reports)

The growth of population is determined by a number of factors in combination with each other. The birth rate, measured as the number of live births per thousand population, is the principal means of increase. This may, in turn, depend on social factors such as the age of marriage and the acceptability of illegitimate births. The death rate, also expressed conventionally per thousand population, is the natural counterpart to the birth rate. It has tended to fall over time during the past two centuries as the population has become healthier and thus more resistant to disease. The difference between the two rates, in any given year, indicates the rate of natural increase. Population change overall is the rate of natural increase modified by the effects of migration, outward migration diminishing the overall growth and inward migration increasing it. The aggregate pattern of Aberdeen's population over the past two centuries was determined by this balance of variables.

Natural Increase

From 1861 onward, vital rates are calculable using the civil registration statistics which began in 1855. The birth rate fell by half between the early 1860s when it was 34.6 per thousand and 1950 when it was 17.2. However, the post-war baby boom saw the figure rise to 24.4 during the first half of the 1960s before declining again to just over 12 by the end of the century (see Figure 2.2). Changes in the birth rate may be caused by changing fertility levels both within and outside marriage. The age at which couples marry and the number of people who decide to marry affects the likelihood of children being born. However, knowledge and availability of birth control and social attitudes towards it clearly effect such decisions. Aberdeen's marriage rate rose slightly between the mid-nineteenth and mid-twentieth centuries, from around 8 per thousand to 12 per thousand. During that period, the age of first marriage did not alter appreciably. Although illegitimacy rates were considerably higher in Aberdeen than they were in other Scottish cities in the mid-nineteenth century, by the 1930s they had fallen by half, even though by that time 41 per cent of women in the city were unmarried. It thus appears probable that declining reproduction rates before the baby boom were, in some measure, attributable to Aberdeen's unusually high number of single women.[4]

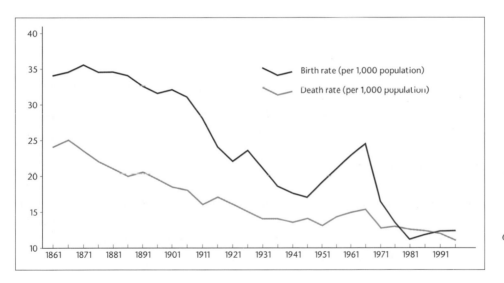

Figure 2.2 Natural rate of population change: Aberdeen, 1861-1996. (Source: Registrar General for Scotland, Detailed Annual Reports)

Although low compared with its hinterland, the level of illegitimacy in Aberdeen in the later 1850s stood at 15.2 per cent of births, compared with 10.4 per cent recorded by Dundee. This provoked an intriguing discourse on 'immorality'. Sheriff Watson's explanation pointed to the fact that factory closures in 1854 alone resulted in over 500 young women being made redundant. Being able-bodied they could not claim poor relief and were forced to live from soup rations, 'but this supply was insufficient ... and many of them were driven by dire necessity to prostitution and gave birth to illegitimate children ... and it was ascertained that of 272 illegitimates born in Aberdeen during 1855, the mothers of 101 of them were factory servants'.[5] Others were migrant mothers from surrounding rural parishes, although many were domestic servants who had been forced to leave their situations in fashionable areas when their pregnancies were discovered. A report found that the residences of mothers bearing illegitimate children between January and June 1859 were, 'very distinctly … in the districts where the lower class of houses are situated … No case is reported to have occurred in Union St, King St, Crown St, Dee St, Bon-Accord St, Bon-Accord Tce, Albyn Place, Victoria St, Union Tce, or Skene St'.[6]

After the 1850s illegitimacy maintained its relatively high level, falling below 10 per cent for the first time in 1883 and ranging between 8 and 12 per cent, with occasional exceptions, until the 1930s.[7] The pattern since then has been volatile. From 1933 to 1940, the ratio hovered between 6 and 8 per cent, rising to over 10 per cent during the Second World War. The post-war era saw a marked decline, dwindling to an all-time low of 3.7 per cent in 1962. However, the late 1960s brought the start of a protracted rise. By 1973, 9.7 per cent of births were to unmarried women. In 1983 the proportion had almost doubled to 17.3 per cent, doubling again to 34.1 per cent by 1993.

Before the mid-1970s most women bearing illegitimate babies in Aberdeen were young and primiparous, and there was no evidence of increased cohabitation. Moreover, Filinson's study of sample cohorts bearing children in 1954, 1964 and 1974 found that higher illegitimacy rates in the last sample were compensated neither by a higher rate of deferred marriage nor by quicker entry into marriage. Any rise in cohabitation would be indicated by a rise in the proportion of cases where both parents registered a birth. However, across the three cohorts, the proportion of joint registrations rose only marginally, from 42 per cent in 1954 to 45 per cent in 1974, while the probability of marriage to the registering father remained constant at 40 per cent.[8] These post-war changes are consistent with nationwide trends, and reflect the growing preference for living in stable relationships but without the sanction of marriage. While more sharply escalating illegitimacy in the last decades of the century might have a different explanation, it is likely that over the longer term both lone parenthood and cohabitation with the father were less common than the reliance of single mothers on their parents for support, an arrangement that has been an abiding facet of unmarried motherhood in the North-East for over two centuries.[9]

More generally, it seems that increased contraceptive knowledge, together with the desire to have fewer children, explains the fall in fertility. Although Aberdeen led the way in pursuing policies of providing both the contraceptive pill and sterilisation facilities, trends in reproductive behaviour have broadly mirrored the national pattern. A voluntary birth control clinic, founded by Mrs Fenella Paton, daughter of Liberal MP John Crombie and wife of John Paton of Grandholm, began in Aberdeen as early as 1926, with the town council providing annual grants after 1935 and assuming direct responsibility in 1948. Significantly, the clinic had been organised to deal with discretionary referrals, and its use appears to have been somewhat circumscribed by medical considerations. In 1934 Dr Marie Stopes, the pioneer of birth-control clinics, addressed a public meeting in the city on constructive birth control, and announced that the Aberdeen clinic would henceforth open daily. A minute of the meeting reported that:

> This meeting of Aberdeen citizens passed unanimously a resolution asking the Department of Health for Scotland to take into account the strong feeling in the country in favour of controlled and racially serious parenthood, which views with concern the bearing by diseased and out-worn women of children doomed to defective health, and to permit the Medical Officers in charge of state-aided clinics to give, at their discretion, advice on simple scientific contraceptive methods to all women requiring it.[10]

The contraceptive pill was introduced in 1964 and became universally free in 1966. The popularity of this more liberal provision was reflected in an increased number of clients, from 1,540 in 1965 to 4,244 by 1970, while birth control through sterilisation and abortion also increased. However, the use of contraception varied by social class. Askham's study of women who married in Aberdeen in 1960/61 and

---

Dr Agnes Thomson 1880–1952

Born in Brechin, Agnes Thomson attended Aberdeen University intending to become a teacher, but changed to medicine. She commenced general practice in Aberdeen in 1912, having a surgery on Union Street until 1929 when she moved to Albert Street. During the First World War she worked as an anaesthetist at the Children's Hospital. She was a founder member of the Medical Women's Federation, and served on its council and as local president. She also served as president of the Aberdeen Women Citizens' Association, and supported the Soroptimist Club, St Katherine's Community Centre, Aberdeen Old People's Welfare Council, and the National Council for Women. She played a major part in establishing the Mother and Baby Home. From 1914 onwards she acted as a medical officer to the Mother and Child Welfare Association at Holburn clinic. In the Second World War she served as a medical officer at the air raid post at Walker Road School, Torry, the stress of which caused a marked deterioration in her health. In 1945 she became president of the Scottish Council of Women Citizens' Association.

who were still living in the city in the early 1970s indicated that differences in family size were clearly linked to the effectiveness of birth control. Over half of those women with two children claimed they had the number they wished to have, but the same proportion of those with four or more children had more children than they would have wished. Less effective birth control or non-use and lack of knowledge about the more efficient methods were clearly significant, but relative deprivation also predisposed couples to have less positive attitudes. Because they had to adapt frequently to economic insecurities, poorer families were unlikely or unable to engage in long-term family planning, and consequently adopted fatalistic behaviour more readily than those perceiving material benefits from having fewer children. The type and level of stability of the husband's occupation was thus an important variable.[11]

Despite such variation, there has been a general trend towards delayed family-building. Between 1961 and 1979, the age at which married women in Aberdeen bore their first child rose. Whereas the 20–24 age range remained the most popular time throughout the period, after 1970 the relative proportion of women starting a family in the age group 25–34 years increased, while there was a pronounced decline among teenagers.[12] Such bunching reflected a considerable increase in the proportion of first births occurring after three years of marriage. A second factor was the growing divergence between first pregnancies and first births. After the 1967 Abortion Act the number of terminations increased, continuing a trend already well established in Aberdeen. Fewer married women bore a first child in their teens because of two factors, namely that an increasing number of teenage first pregnancies ended in abortion, and because more women bore their first child illegitimately.[13]

DEATH RATES AND INFANT MORTALITY

Like birth rates, death rates have undergone a secular decline, as shown in Figure 2.2. Between 1861 and 1950 the death rate fell from 24.9 to 12.2 per thousand, showing a minor rise to around 15 by the mid-1960s, but a steady decrease thereafter, so that by the 1990s it had reached a nadir of under 11 per thousand. In the long term the reduction was attributable to a fall in a limited number of infectious childhood and respiratory diseases, with the most significant decline occuring between 1870 and 1945 in the age ranges between 5 and 29. It also reflected a greatly reduced infant mortality rate after World War Two (Figure 2.3). Underpinning such successes lay improvements in health services, housing, sanitary conditions and the working environment. Of course, Aberdeen was not unique in its demographic transition, for the combined pattern of declining fertility and declining mortality occurred throughout Western Europe after the

1870s. What was distinctive, however, was the contribution of socio-medical research in the city to the better understanding of these matters.

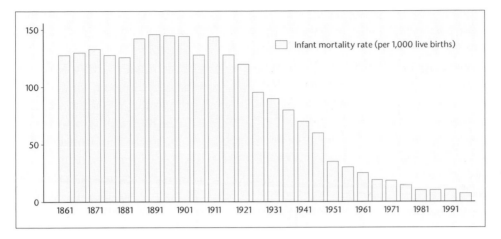

Figure 2.3 Infant mortality in Aberdeen, 1861-1996. (Source: Registrar General for Scotland, Detailed Annual Reports)

Individuals, groups and institutions within Aberdeen played a central role in British research on both fertility and mortality, and pioneered innovations in maternity care. The original stimulus for much of this work lay in the very high infant mortality rates recorded in the city in the later nineteenth century. In many areas of Britain infant mortality levels fell during the later Victorian period. However, the North-East was distinctive in that between 1861 and 1901 the infant mortality rate rose substantially, from 86 per thousand live births in 1861 to 116 in 1901, while in Aberdeen the rate rose from 128 to 144.[14] Among the major towns in Scotland, Aberdeen's infant mortality rate of 142.8 in the early years of the twentieth century was worse than that of Glasgow and ranked second only to Dundee. An inverse relationship clearly existed between income level and the likelihood of death from all groups of causes, with the highest infant mortality rates in one study being found among the offspring of seafarers (165.9) and metalworkers (183.7). In Aberdeen, overcrowding was notorious in that part of the city where fisherfolk were concentrated, and the connection between this and high numbers of infant deaths appears unassailable. Metalworkers were more scattered, and their link to high mortality is less apparent, especially since in Dundee the offspring of this occupational group fared much better.[15]

One of the pioneers tackling the problem was Matthew Hay who became medical office of health (MOH) for the city in 1888. By the age of 35, Hay was already both a university professor and medical practitioner, married with four children, and living at the smart end of Union Street. His household was typical of the elite part of town. The 1891 census recorded that he kept four servants, including a nurse and an undernurse.[16] However, as MOH for the city, his principal

THE PUBLIC HEALTH.

Matthew Hay, professor of medical logic and jurisprudence 1883-1926 and medical officer of health from 1888 until 1923, tackles the furies of typhoid, measles, influenza, whooping cough and scarlet fever, the great nineteenth-century killers. Bon Accord, 12 December 1891.

concerns lay less with the welfare of the children of his own class than with those living in poverty. In 1907, he deployed staff armed with 30-question schedules to visit the parents of all infants who had died under the age of two. The inquiry revealed the circumstances of some 659 deaths. Among the findings was the fact that 92.7 per cent of deaths in the sample occurred in houses of three rooms or fewer, 68.1 per cent occurred in houses of two rooms or fewer, and just 7.3 per cent in houses containing four or more rooms. Secondly, bearing in mind that crowding tended to be greater in small houses, Hay found that 'the mortality rate in houses with an average of more than three persons per room was twice as high as in houses with an average of one person or under'.[17] This conclusion was supported by later research suggesting that density per room was the crucial component in Glasgow during the same period.[18] Hay observed that: 'generally, for every disease the mortality decreases with increase in size of house … the death-rate from prematurity among breast-fed children distinctly lessens with increase in size of house, as it would appear to indicate that prematurity, as the single largest cause of death, might be considerably reduced if only the prematurely born child could be nurtured under better conditions'.[19]

Hay's pioneering work laid the foundations for other medical and scientific research in the city. Most notable was the work of Professor Sir Dugald Baird and Lord Boyd Orr, Director of the Rowett Research Institute. Like Hay, they were concerned to identify the link between social factors and early death, and thus showed a particular interest in the problems of infant mortality.[20] A World Health Organisation meeting in the 1950s hailed the city's antenatal care standards as 'the best in the world'.[21] Baird left the maternity hospital a uniquely catalogued set of case records. The value of this, coupled with Aberdeen's location as a disease

Professor Matthew Hay 1855–1932

Born at Slamannan, Stirlingshire, the son of a colliery owner, Matthew Hay was educated at Dollar Academy and at the universities of Glasgow and Edinburgh. He subsequently studied at Strasbourg, Munich and Berlin. He was appointed demonstrator in materia medica at Edinburgh 1878–83, and served as professor of medical logic and jurisprudence at Aberdeen University 1883–1926. He acted as an expert witness in forensic science in many court cases. He was medical officer of health for Aberdeen 1888–1923, promoting the introduction of health visitors and child welfare schemes, and founding the residential homes at Linn Moor and Scotstoun Moor. He demonstrated in 1905 that the typhus epidemic was transmitted by body vermin, but did not publicise the discovery and a French scientist was awarded the Nobel Prize in 1909 for the same work. Hay initiated the scheme to bring all the hospitals in Aberdeen together on a single site, and was rumoured to spend his weekends scouring the suburbs for a suitable location, eventually identifying Foresterhill.

Sir Dugald Baird 1899–1986

Born in Gourock, Dugald Baird was educated at Greenock Academy, and the Universities of Glasgow and Strasbourg. He practised medicine in several hospitals in Glasgow including Rottenrow Maternity Hospital where he was deeply affected by the effects of poverty on women. He served as regius professor of obstetrics and gynaecology at Aberdeen 1937–65, where he sought to rid women of the burden of unwanted fertility through contraception, sterilisation and abortion. He was obstetrician-in-chief at the Aberdeen Maternity Hospital, and honorary director of the Obstetrics Medical Research Unit established in 1955 by the Medical Research Council. He pioneered the termination of pregnancies on social grounds. He was awarded honorary degrees by several universities, was knighted in 1959 and was given the freedom of the city of Aberdeen in 1966. He is commemorated at Aberdeen University through the Dugald Baird Centre for Research on Women's Health.

Lady Matilda 'May' D. Baird 1901–1983

Educated at Glasgow High School for Girls and Glasgow University, Matilda Baird graduated in medicine in 1925. She moved to Aberdeen when her husband was appointed to the regius chair in 1937. She served on the town council, representing Gilcomston 1943–45 and Cairncry 1945–52, and was convener of the health committee. She was the first chairman of the North-East Regional Hospital Board 1947–66, served as a governor of the BBC in Scotland 1966–70 and was awarded a CBE in 1962. She received the freedom of the city jointly with her husband, Sir Dugald Baird.

Sir Dugald Baird, regius professor of obstetrics and gynaecology 1937-65 and strong advocate of birth-control and of abortion on social grounds.

regional centre made it ideal for epidemiological research. This was recognised by the Medical Research Council which supported a medical sociology unit to investigate a wide range of issues from reproductive behaviour to health inequalities and maternity services.

In 1943, prompted by the unacceptably slow decline in Scottish infant mortality, compared with England and other countries, the Boyd Orr Committee established by the Scottish Health Department and convened by Baird, produced a report on *Infant Mortality in Scotland*. It attributed the differential in infant mortality to poor housing conditions and poverty, and in particular to overcrowded tenements which encouraged the spread of droplet infections especially where sanitation was inadequate. With an infant mortality rate of 71 per thousand in 1938, Aberdeen fared better than the urban areas of west central Scotland (88) or Dundee (77), but markedly worse than Edinburgh (61), Greater London (50) or New York (38). Nutritional factors were significant, especially class variations in the incidence of breastfeeding, generally agreed to provide resistance to infection and promote good health. A local study of some 205 nursing-home mothers compared with the same number of women in a poor district indicated large variations in the ability to maintain lactation, with 80 per cent of the former still breastfeeding at six months, judged as 'outstandingly successful' compared to only 29 per cent of the latter, dismissed as 'outstandingly unsuccessful'. Inability to continue successful lactation was linked to the poor diet of the mothers living in poverty.[22] However, postwar improvements clearly had an impact, and by the 1960s Aberdeen's infant mortality rate of 18.6 was lower than that of the other Scottish cities. Furthermore, the use of child welfare services in terms of clinic attendance, immunisation rates and consumption of welfare foods was far higher in Aberdeen than anywhere else in the country, 23.9 bottles of orange juice being consumed per annum per liveborn child, compared with 10.5 in Glasgow. Stillbirth rates, associated with the same conditions as infant mortality, also demonstrated a pronounced decline from 36 per thousand in 1939-41 to 6.5 in 1992-94.[23]

Dr Mary Esslemont 1891–1984

Mary Esslemont was of a strongly liberal family; both her grandfather, Peter, and her father, George, represented the Liberal Party as MPs as well as being partners in the family business. She was educated at Aberdeen High School for Girls and Aberdeen University, where she became the first woman president of the Students' Representative Council. She was assistant in the botany department of Aberdeen University 1915–17, science lecturer at Stockwell Training College, London 1917–19, and assistant medical officer of health for Keighley, West Yorkshire 1924–29. She returned to Aberdeen in 1929 to enter general practice with surgeries in the west end and Torry. She was also appointed as a gynaecologist at the free dispensary in Guestrow. She was the first women president of the Medico-Chirurgical Society in 1957. She was also the first woman chairman of the British Medical Association, later becoming a life president, having been elected a fellow in 1959 and a vice president in 1970. She became a fellow of the Royal College of General Practitioners in 1969 and received a CBE in 1955. She was a JP and served on the University Court 1947–74. She was awarded the freedom of the city in 1981. She was president of the Soroptimist Federation, and on her death her home, Mile End House, passed to the society to provide housing for single women.

Dr Mary Esslemont, distinguished GP and indefatigable campaigner to improve the position of women in the poorest areas of the city.

THE IMPACT OF MIGRATION

The combined effect of the secular decline in both birth and death rates was a diminution of the impact of natural increase (the excess of births over deaths) on the overall population size such that between 1861 and 1951 the rate of natural increase fell from 9.7 to 5.0 per thousand.[24] By 1956-60 it rose slightly to 7.8 and, buoyed by the baby boom and declining death rates, reached 9.1 per thousand in 1966-70. Thereafter, however, it struggled to remain positive. Indeed, from 1976 to 1985 the death rate rose above the birth rate, albeit temporarily, with a net increase of just 0.8 achieved in the following decade.

Using census figures for total population, and then comparing intercensal increase with natural increase, it is possible to compute net migration flows. Aberdeen made gains through migration until 1901, then lost population at each census until 1971, as shown in Figure 2.4. Household domestic service was a major stimulus to young women who left the countryside in droves in the nineteenth century, a phenomenon sufficiently severe in its impact to provoke Lady Aberdeen into forming the Onward and Upward Association as an incentive to retain youngsters in rural employment.[25] Despite her efforts, girls continued to forsake the farms, a trend exacerbated in the early twentieth century by the growth of opportunities in typing and clerical work in the city. The effects of this were clearly evident in Aberdeen's skewed sex ratio in 1931 when, in the over-16 age groups, there were 125 females for every 100 males, a situation to which the loss of men killed in the Great War doubtlessly contributed. Among the unmarried, the disparity increased to 156 females for every 100 males, a statistic explained by the 'many opportunities for women to lead independent lives'. Such imbalances are likely to have had the effect of reducing the marriage rate, thereby depressing fertility levels. The greater part of the population of the city has always comprised native Aberdonians, leavened by migrants from the rest of the North-East. In 1871, 56.2 per cent were Aberdonians, while a further 31.4 per cent came from North-East Scotland. By 1931, the respective proportions were 62.9 per cent and 24.2 per cent. The continuing replenishment of cities by migrants from local rural areas has been a worldwide phenomenon as part of economic modernisation. For much of the twentieth century, however, Aberdeen lost population through outward migration. Immediately before the oil boom, migration from the Aberdeen area was the highest in the United Kingdom, with a net outflow in excess of 15,000 in the decade 1961–71. In the following decade this became a net inflow of over 30,000. At the same time natural increase, which had made a healthy contribution

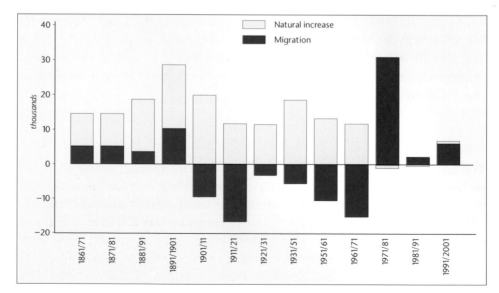

*Figure 2.4
Composition of
population change:
Aberdeen 1861–2001.*

ABERDEEN 1800–2000

to population growth in the 1950s and 1960s, fell to a state of virtual stagnation. The apparent stability of population growth, therefore, was the result of relatively buoyant natural increase combined with high outward migration until the late 1960s, followed by falling vital rates coupled with inward migration thereafter.

Population change was also influenced by the dispersal of population throughout the region's commuter belt. The population of Grampian Region increased by 5.3 per cent between 1988 and 1993 compared with a rise of 0.5 per cent in Scotland overall.[26] The last three decades of the century witnessed considerable growth in the number of people residing in satellite and dormitory towns such as Ellon and Inverurie and in new town developments like Portlethen, while Gordon district was the fastest growing commuter area in Scotland during the 1980s and 1990s especially in communities close to Aberdeen, like Westhill. Although projections forecast an overall decline in the Scottish population in the first decade of the new millennium, with losses incurred by Glasgow, Inverclyde and parts of the west Highlands, Aberdeenshire is expected to grow by 8 per cent. Allied to this was the development of both suburbia and exurbia. While Deeside continued to attract business and professional people and the northerly Donside suburbs engulfed former villages between Woodside and Dyce, the expansion of Bridge of Don was spectacular, its population rising from about 1,500 in the early 1950s to an estimated figure in excess of 25,000 by 2001.[27]

Aberdeen enjoyed sustained population increase through the nineteenth century as death rates fell more sharply than birth rates and as migrants were attracted from the surrounding rural areas. Population growth was more modest during the first seven decades of the twentieth century as birth rates continued to fall, rising only briefly during the post-war baby boom and as migrants moved away from the city rather than to it. The final three decades of the twentieth century witnessed very low and sometimes negative rates of natural increase. But these were offset by inward migration.

FAMILY AND HOUSEHOLD STRUCTURE

This analysis of demographic trends has thus far focused on aggregate patterns. To set births, marriages, deaths and mobility in context it is necessary to explore the processes of family formation, and this requires more detailed analysis at the level of the household. Fortunately, the existence of census data facilitates a degree of comparability between the nineteenth century and the present day. To assess the composition of households in different parts of Victorian Aberdeen three sample areas were analysed using the census enumerators' books for 1861 and 1891.[28] The

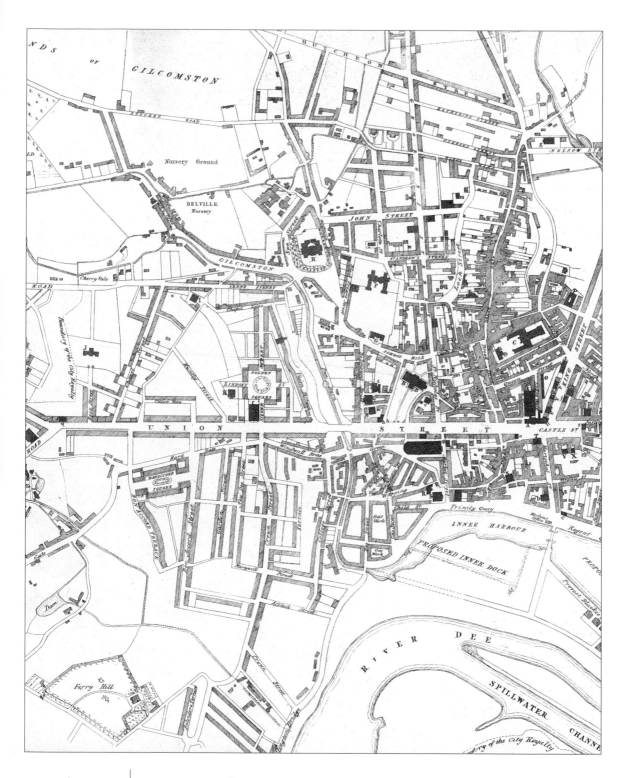

Footdee squares provide an example of an area in which one of the city's staple industries, fishing, predominated. The people working in the other key industries, textiles and granite, were more scattered throughout the city, as were many of the clerks, labourers and artisans that comprised the workforce of a regional capital. The other samples were thus chosen according to different criteria. The area around Netherkirkgate and the Guestrow was at the heart of the city and represented a densely urbanised milieu. Meanwhile, the exclusive zone around the Bon-Accord developments and the west end of Union Street affords a glimpse into the rarefied domestic sphere of the city's elite.

OCCUPATIONAL STRUCTURES

The homogeneity of Footdee is evident, in Table 2.1, from the fact that the proportion engaged in fishing and ancillary work was very high, 71.7 per cent in 1861 and 81.6 per cent thirty years later. By contrast, the central city pattern was much more variegated and reflected considerable change over time. In 1861 almost half the sample, 46.6 per cent, were involved in skilled crafts, but by 1891 this percentage had more than halved to 22.9 per cent. The number of tailors and shoemakers fell, to be offset in part by an increase in shopkeepers and small entrepreneurs, although most impressively by an increase in factory workers in textiles from 10 per cent to 21.5 per cent. A perceptible decline in the occupational standing of the area is also evident in the growth of general labourers and a decline in the number of households keeping servants. Changes in recording practice make it difficult to compare levels of unemployment but six paupers were recorded in 1861 while, in 1891, 20 were returned as unemployed and 11 as being 'at home'. Significantly, by 1891, the Victoria Lodging-House (omitted from the sample) took up a considerable part of the Guestrow, housing some 71 persons and heralding the general decline of the district in the following decades.

The elite quarter presents a different picture. The wealth of this neighbourhood is immediately apparent from the number of property owners, rentiers, and those recorded as 'living on private means'. Taken together this category represented about 13 per cent at each benchmark date. As might be expected, the proportion of servants was very high, comprising 53.9 per cent of all persons returned as occupied in 1861, the great majority working as female domestics, as cooks, tablemaids, lady's maids, nurses or undertaking general duties. Thirty years later, their number and proportion had decreased, but they still comprised 44.3 per cent of the total. This decline did not correspond to any reduction in number or status among their household employers, since those enumerated in the upper professional bracket almost doubled, from 4.9 per cent to 8.4 per cent. All other groups, except shopkeepers and traders, who increased from 2.3 per cent to 11.4 per

Opposite:
Map 2.
The developing city
c. 1840.

Table 2.1 *Occupations by district*

A. Footdee Squares

	1861 Male	1861 Female	1891 Male	1891 Female
Fishermen/women	82	0	116	68
Fish dealers/sellers	0	40	1	5
Fish curers	0	4	0	19
Pilots	29	0	17	0
Seamen	3	0	4	0
Boatbuilders/joiners/ropemakers	11	1	22	1
Servants	0	36	0	3
Other	12	20	36	18
Total	**137**	**101**	**196**	**114**

B. City Centre

	1861 Male	1861 Female	1891 Male	1891 Female
Textiles	7	16	10	51
Tailors/dressmakers	17	8	7	8
Shoemakers	15	3	5	0
Other skilled crafts	62	5	49	1
Shopkeepers/traders	13	6	27	12
Labourers	9	0	50	0
Servants/charwomen	1	25	1	21
Others	17	28	17	25
Total	**141**	**91**	**166**	**118**

C. Elite Quarter

	1861 Male	1861 Female	1891 Male	1891 Female
Rentiers/annuitants/private means	8	44	6	41
Professions	39	5	55	9
Manufacturers/merchants	21	0	5	0
Shopkeepers	10	0	36	13
Artisans	13	0	15	0
Lodging house keepers	0	5	0	12
Students	18	0	12	0
Servants	2	228	0	191
Others	13	21	20	16
Total	**124**	**303**	**149**	**282**

Sources: General Register Office, Census of Population Enumerators' Books, 1861, 1891.

cent, remained relatively static. The reason for the decline in the number of servants lies in the reduction in those employed by each individual household. In 1861, the majority of the 76.9 per cent of households which maintained servants had two or more while, by 1891, only 60.3 per cent of households kept servants and just over half employed more than one.

BIRTHPLACES

The three sample areas show considerable variation in birthplace, as indicated in Table 2.2. While in 1891, 56.5 per cent of Aberdeen residents were born in the city, 95.2 per cent of the residents of the Footdee squares were native Aberdonians, as were 68.4 per cent of the people in the central area sample. But in the elite quarter just 41.6 per cent were native to Aberdeen. In 1839, the Rev. William Henderson wrote that the fisherfolk of Aberdeen 'seldom marry with persons not of their own community'.[29] Their endogamous character certainly is apparent from the very high concentration of inhabitants born locally. Indeed, all bar one of the Kincardineshire natives in Footdee had moved no further than across the mouth of the Dee from Nigg parish. The remainder hailed from the fishing towns and villages of Buchan and the East Neuk of Fife, with just four other individuals from Ardersier, Inverness, Glasgow and Greenock. Eight surnames encompassed over two-thirds of the population, and one-third were named either Baxter, Morrice or Guyan. This connection between occupational concentration, birthplace proximity and surname frequency is typical of fishing communities so that it was necessary to distinguish individuals, some sharing the same first names as well as surnames, by means of tee-names. For example, 'Bowfer', 'Pokie's Dod' and 'Foveran's Ondy' were all Baxters, as were Annie Baxter One and Annie Baxter Two.[30]

Occupational considerations also influenced birthplace in the elite quarter, reflecting the two extremes of the social spectrum. The relatively high proportion of migrants from Aberdeenshire and the rest of the North-East, 41.3 per cent of the

Table 2.2 *Distribution of birthplaces (per cent)*

Birthplace	Footdee Squares		City Centre		Elite Quarter	
	1861	1891	1861	1891	1861	1891
Aberdeen	91.8	95.2	63.3	68.4	47.6	41.6
North-East Scotland	7.7	3.9	23.3	20.9	34.6	41.3
Rest of Scotland	0.5	1	10.3	7.3	8.6	7.4
Outside Scotland	0	0	3.1	3.4	9.3	9.7

Sources: General Register Office, Census of Population Enumerators' Books, 1861, 1891.

1891 total, can be explained largely by the influx of domestic servants born in the rural hinterland. This partially offset the markedly low proportion of indigenous inhabitants. Furthermore, a much greater share of the population was drawn from outside Scotland than was evident elsewhere. While just 3.4 per cent were non-Scots in the central sample, and none at all in Footdee, in the elite quarter 9.7 per cent of residents came from England or overseas. Analysis shows that, of these 67 individuals, 12 were classed as 'living on private means', 12 were professors or members of their families, nine were surgeons, dentists and their families, three were governesses, and the remainder were professionals and merchants. Only two were servants. In 1861, half of all non-Scots in the elite quarter had been born outside the British Isles. The fashion for ex-colonials to settle to the west of Aberdeen, particularly on Deeside, was mirrored in the popularity of Bon-Accord Square and its environs, where nine persons had been born in the Indian sub-continent, six in South Africa, three in Australia, and one in each of the Indies and Nova Scotia. In both this and the later census, the link to colonial administration, military careers and commercial expansion was quite clear. In 1891, eight persons born in the colonies were related to colonels while a further 17 were children of indigo planters, shipowners, landed proprietors and merchants. Tea planters and consular officials also appeared, while overseas medical connections were represented by a surgeon's widow from Bengal, medical men from Ceylon and even an ophthalmic surgeon born in South America.[31] Although no further than two miles distant, the cohesive localism of the Footdee squares appears a world apart from such grand cosmopolitanism. Nevertheless, these two ways of life were bound together by the common factor of Aberdeen's status as a port. As well as tea and wine merchants, the 1861 elite sample included shipowners and shipbuilders, among them John Duthie, William Thompson and the Williamson family.

Household Structures

Given the fundamentally different character of the three sample populations as regards origin and occupation, it seems likely that family and household patterns would differ. Size variations reveal relatively little, since a domestic group could be smaller or larger either for reasons of poverty or reasons of affluence, and both the Footdee squares and the elite quarter had a mean household size of about five persons. However, the density of individuals per dwelling varied greatly with between four and five persons per windowed room in overcrowded Footdee, but closer to two windowed rooms per person in the spacious west end (that is half a person per windowed room). The city centre fell between these two extremes averaging about two persons per windowed room.

Table 2.3 *Household typology (per cent)*

Type	Footdee Squares		City Centre		Elite Quarter	
	1861	1891	1861	1891	1861	1891
People living alone	4.5	5	17.2	15.4	18.5	23.1
People living in non-family unit	0.9	7.5	5.7	3.5	11.6	19.9
Married couples without children	5.4	5.7	7.9	9.8	7.7	5.1
Married couples with children	58.9	57.2	41.8	41.3	34.5	24.9
Widows/widowers with children	11.6	10.7	10.1	11.2	10.8	13.5
Parent alone with children	1.8	2.5	5.1	4.2	5.4	4.5
Extended family households	16.9	11.4	12.2	14.6	11.5	9

Sources: General Register Office, Census of Population Enumerators' Books, 1861, 1891.

As shown in Table 2.3, most people lived in nuclear family units, but only in Footdee did the proportion of such units account for a majority of all households. In assessing the overall predominance of simple family households, married couples living alone can be added to this group on the presumption that most would intend to have children. Similarly, widows and widowers with children can also be included. Taken together, these simple family households consistently comprised just above three-quarters of the total in Footdee. The high incidence of nuclear family units in Footdee may be explained by several possible factors. The contemporary saying among the Moray Firth coastal villages, that 'no man can be a fisher and want a wife' was equally relevant here, where the womenfolk were pivotally involved in all aspects of the domestic order of free enterprise, from mending nets and baiting lines to selling the fish.[32] In the later nineteenth century, fishing still relied on the combined labours of the family unit. Secondly, however, the fact that many of the residents of the squares lived in one-room cottages, in which nets and other equipment had also to be stored, militated against the inclusion of additional family. A mean family size of five is not unduly large, yet the overcrowding of North and South Squares was the main reason why the town council resolved to develop Pilot's Square in the 1870s. At that time, tenants were given the opportunity to buy their homes, and new storeys were added by owner-occupiers, facilitating multiple occupancy, but in separate households.[33] Thirdly, most residents were closely related to one another as well as being native to the district. As they came of age, young men and women in the village married one another and moved into houses a matter of yards away, rather than residing with either spouse's parents. This conforms to a broader British pattern, as it does to other close-knit fishing communities in the North-East. In Findochty in 1881, for example, where 72.9 per cent of households were simple, 84.4 per cent of married women between the ages of 16 and 49 had been born in the parish.[34] In Footdee, a few widows lived alone, but most non-nuclear households consisted of interdependent relatives in

A few of the remaining cottages of old Footdee in the 1990s.

extended families. In mid-Victorian Footdee, 22 per cent of households each employed a single living-in servant. By 1891, only 2 per cent of families kept a servant. By this time the fishing community was overwhelmingly characterised by close-knit family units, with very little extra-familial support.

In the central urban district, households were similarly structured, but a smaller proportion of nuclear and extended households was offset by a greater number of solitary occupiers, especially widows and widowers. Their self-sufficiency, enforced or otherwise, is evident in that, among the 26 widowed individuals, only five had obtained live-in support. One had a sick nurse, one a servant, one a boarder, and one a lodger, while another, an innkeeper, had both a lodger (her coach guard) and domestic servants. Few households in this area kept servants, just 7.9 per cent in 1861 and 5.6 per cent in 1891. Only three of the 19 families maintained more than one servant. Eight families took in boarders and lodgers in 1861, but only three did so in 1891.

The picture in the elite quarter was markedly different. In 1861, 76.9 per cent of households contained servants, the majority of them depending upon two or more. By 1891, the proportion was 60.3 per cent with the majority still reliant on two or more servants. These were relatively high proportions compared with other parts of the country.[35] As in the other two areas, most servant-keeping households were simple family households, 65.0 per cent in 1861 and 59.6 per cent in 1891. But a high number of solitary individuals and non-family households were also sufficiently wealthy to keep servants, 51.9 per cent doing so compared with only 6 per cent for the other samples taken together.

The enumeration of boarders and lodgers as separate households reflects the spare dwelling space available to accommodate them in such a manner. The number of boarders and lodgers recorded as living with families in the same dwelling was not great. However, no fewer than 32 households consisted purely of lodgers, living alone or with other lodgers, while four single boarders and four pairs of servants were also given as occupying separate premises. Two such groups, both being sets of lodgers, resided in the central area in 1891; otherwise, the arrangement was non-existent. Not only did servant-keeping denote affluence, but considerably more boarders and lodgers resided in the elite quarter. While their existence has conventionally been regarded as an indicator of financial support for impoverished families, there is little evidence of this among these samples. Their very separateness from the household suggests that, in many instances, the occupation of otherwise unused available space contributed to the rentier capital of already wealthy citizens.

CHANGES IN FAMILY BEHAVIOUR: HOUSEHOLDS IN THE 1990s

The level of disaggregation provided by the census schedules allows comparisons between the composition of households to be made for the Victorian period. But, since access is restricted to material over one hundred years old, it is difficult to make comparisons with more modern data. However, it is possible to obtain some information from Samples of Anonymised Records (SAR) drawn from the 1991 Census of Population. Although the 1 per cent sample of households cannot be disaggregated beyond the regional level, it is possible to analyse families within city households from a 2 per cent sample consisting of 4,275 individuals in Aberdeen.[36] The data indicate that the married family remained the conventional and majority social structure, with cohabiting households and single parent households being much fewer in number. Similarly the most common family unit contained dependent children, although a significant minority, of 15.5 per cent of families, included non-dependent children. Individuals were further subdivided to indicate the proportion above legal marriageable age included in each group.[37] About 20 per cent of these were married with no children in the household, while another 21.8 per cent did have dependent children. Fewer in the sample were married with no dependent children, about 14 per cent, while 13 per cent cohabited or were single parents.

It might be assumed that the combined effect of slum clearance, municipal

Until it was cleared in the 1920s Guestrow was one of the city's worst slums, as new tenements cut off light from older property. This close, photographed probably in the 1890s, looks remarkably clean. (Photograph by Washington Wilson)

housing construction and the flight to the suburbs, coupled with changes in occupational structure and methods of working, would have been to weaken links between generations. However, the age structure of households indicates the continuing significance of co-residence between generations. As parents age, most children grow up and leave home so that 71 per cent of all individuals in households containing married couples but no children were over the age of 50. Nevertheless, when relationships between household members are examined, it becomes evident that a considerable number of adult offspring lived with their parents and in-laws. In households characterised as 'married with no dependent children', 39 per cent of the total occupants were the adult offspring of the head of the household. The overwhelming majority of them were under the age of 30, and almost half of them were in their early twenties. Skilled white-collar and skilled manual workers together accounted for the highest proportions of persons both in families with dependent-age children and those containing adult offspring who were no longer dependants. Their offspring were themselves likely to be included in households of the same category. This might reflect the straitened circumstances of many young adults, unable to afford to live in independent accommodation because of factors such as unemployment, low incomes and the high price of rented property and housing for purchase in a local economy affected by inflation due to the impact of oil. A small number of students also lived at home.

Whereas 48.9 per cent of married persons in households with no children were of pensionable age, less than 2 per cent of households with dependent children also contained pensioners. Almost one-fifth of the 'married with no dependent children' households included at least one person of pensionable age, but all of these were the married partners themselves. Thus, as in 1861 and 1891, most people in the sample lived in nuclear families, consisting of couples either living alone or with their children. While scant evidence of extended family co-residence exists, nevertheless a sizeable proportion of adults, particularly those in early adulthood, lived with their parents while a smaller quota of pensioners stayed with their offspring. It might plausibly be assumed that such patterns of adult co-residence reflected a degree of economic interdependence between kin. More generally, successive generations have moved within and beyond Aberdeen, while increased numbers have arrived from farther afield. However, although the kind of localism seen in nineteenth-century Footdee has vanished, it is less easy to establish whether or not social and economic changes have resulted in a diminished sense of neighbourhood identity.

Given the post-war reorganisation of housing stock in Aberdeen and attendant improvements, a reduction in the density of persons per room is to be expected. Moreover, earlier reductions in completed family size and in servant-keeping, boarding and lodging inevitably contributed to the contraction of the mean household size. By 1991, over 80 per cent of all people in the sample inhabited households of between two and five individuals. A useful, and comparable, measure of changed density is the number of persons per room. The aggregated set of samples taken in 1861 gave a mean figure of 1.1 persons per windowed room, and those for 1891 gave a mean figure of 1.2. Since the samples were deliberately drawn to indicate contrasts these figures ought not to be interpreted as indicating a representative average of the entire city. However, taking into consideration the consistently higher mean values for the constituent samples in both the Footdee squares and the city centre, they do suggest that densities were much higher than today. The 1991 sample clearly shows that the vast majority of inhabitants occupied properties where the ratio of persons to rooms was less than one. Only 8 per cent of individuals lived in accommodation where there was more than one person per room while almost 30 per cent of them lived in accommodation where there were at least two rooms per person.

Migration and Counter-Urbanisation

The 1991 census did not ask respondents to give their birthplaces, so direct comparisons with Victorian data are not possible. But a more exact measure of migration is afforded in that the place of last residence is recorded and its distance from Aberdeen can be calculated. The vast majority of those included in the sample, 86.4 per cent, were non-migrants. The 13.3 per cent proportion of people who had moved into the city within the year before the census date was slightly higher than the average for the United Kingdom as a whole and, indeed, was higher than the proportion for Edinburgh, Glasgow and Dundee which ranged from 11.3 to 12.5 per cent. In keeping with both historical and contemporary trends, the majority of migrants fell into the 20-44 age range (63.9 per cent), with people in their twenties particularly predominant (38.8 per cent). Over half the incomers were single, although a significant minority of 43.8 per cent of them were both under twenty and dependent children.

Although most inward migrants came from the North-East hinterland, following the advent of the oil industry greater numbers arrived from farther afield. Once the prevalence of North-East origins among its populace was cited as the reason for Aberdeen having a more provincial character than most cities of comparable size. Indeed, before the Second World War no more than 5 or 6 per cent of the population came from outwith Scotland. Since then, however, and particularly since the 1970s, the city has become increasingly cosmopolitan. During the period 1974-79, an estimated 64 per cent of migrants into the North-East came from England, Wales and overseas compared with 36 per cent from elsewhere in Scotland.[38] Nevertheless, of those moving to Aberdeen during 1990–91 from within the United Kingdom, three-quarters had moved less than 30 km, and half less than 5 km, compared with a fifth moving more than 100 km. The clear implication is that migrants came either very short or relatively long distances, but not from within the commuter belt itself because it too had become a receiving area for inward migration.

The impact of counter-urbanisation was reflected in distance-to-work patterns which clearly indicate the existence of a late-twentieth-century trend towards commuting dependent upon modern transport facilities, especially the widespread use of the motor car. While over 90 per cent of Aberdeen residents in the sample travelled less than 10 km from home to work, almost half of the inhabitants of Gordon district and Kincardine and Deeside travelled farther than this distance. The dichotomy is perhaps all the more remarkable considering the much higher proportion of residents in the commuter belt who claimed to be working at home. Presumably, a sizeable number of these were farmers and other rural workers who, in terms of their work patterns, fall into a distinctively different category from commuters.

The cohort of migrants to Aberdeen during 1990–91 exhibited a greater share originating in England and Wales than had been the historical norm. The Aberdeen ratio of 9.5 per cent was just below that of Edinburgh but almost double that of Glasgow or Dundee. Aberdeen's commuter belt grew at a greater rate than the city itself and the city's profile at the end of the twentieth century has to be depicted within a regional perspective. Both Gordon district and Kincardine and Deeside enjoyed considerable inward migration during the final quarter of the century, with a substantial minority coming from England and Wales and from overseas.

Balancing the Population Equation

During the nineteenth century, steady rises in population were checked by relatively high infant mortality rates, which depressed overall life expectancy, and by endemic infectious disease. One of the penalties of concentrating an expanding population within a relatively small area, without providing adequate public health infrastructures to accommodate it, was a high rate of turnover, that is of births and deaths. However, the inflow of migrants from the rural hinterland ensured a steady replacement. Like cities elsewhere, Aberdeen experienced the profound effects of the demographic transition. With better public sanitation, diet, and especially improved prospects for infant survival, death rates fell. Birth control practices diffused from the middle classes to the working classes so that fertility rates also dropped. As Flinn concluded in his survey of Scottish demographic change, 'a principal feature of the general decline of mortality in the late nineteenth and early twentieth centuries is the reduction in mortality from infectious diseases, including tuberculosis'.[39] Aberdeen was no exception. The typhoid epidemic of 1964 has been the only significant outbreak of a major infectious disease in the past half century.

The years following the Second World War saw continued improvements in health and maternity and child welfare, stimulated considerably by scientific and social advances made in the city itself. In the earlier twentieth century, Hay, Baird and Boyd Orr each contributed substantially, not only to the diagnosis of the social causes of death and disease, but also to improvements in public health practice. Slum clearance led to reductions in damp and overcrowding. Meanwhile, innovations in the provision of birth control eventually aided women in regulating their fertility, although enduring cultural differences, such as relatively high levels of teenage pregnancy, remained as testimony to the distinctive demography and culture of the North-East.

The samples taken from 1861 and 1891 enumerators' books indicate considerable differentiation in household structures within different neighbourhoods. The occupational and social expectations of the fishing community clearly differed from those of the urban elite, and in such matters as the employment of servants and the density of persons per room, the east and west ends of the city were clearly worlds apart. Similarly, the close, almost in-bred cohesion of the fisher squares contrasted markedly with both the infusion of migrants to the city centre and the attractions of the Bon Accord quarter for relatives returning from the far corners of the Empire. Although each of the sample communities demonstrates interdependencies between household and family members, in Footdee extended family households were considerably exceeded by simple family units, whereas in the elite quarter, where the nuclear family might be expected to prevail, simple family units were least in evidence. It would be unwise to infer too much from such evidence since the differing degrees of dependency *between* households cannot be known. But there is anecdotal evidence in the case of fishing communities, and some historical research into support networks amongst the bourgeoisie. These patterns point to the inadequacy of a simple analytical dichotomy between a 'traditional' world inhabited by extended families and 'modern' societies characterised by the nuclear family.

Evidence from the 1991 Sample of Anonymised Records was examined for comparative purposes. The age structure of households indicates some degree of dependency between generations although there was very limited evidence of extended family residence within the same accommodation and a much decreased density of persons per household. To an extent this must be taken as indicative of a growing measure of generational self-sufficiency, particularly by older persons.

Anderson pointed out that 'while an average woman in the 1970s could expect to live 25 years after the birth of her last grandchild, a woman of the mid-eighteenth century could expect to die 12 years before her last grandchild was born'.[40] The demographic realities of Aberdeen at the end of the millennium were very different from those of 1800. Fertility was lower, births tended to be clustered in the early years of marriage, and life expectancy had greatly increased. Taken together, these changes mean that older people were more likely to live alone.

In the final three decades of the twentieth century, the impact of the oil industry had a profound effect on the local economy and labour force. This was also manifest in demographic change as the long-established pattern of outward migration was reversed to become a substantial inflow. There were also signs of growing cultural diversity. The first Chinese restaurant opened in 1961 and was followed in the oil boom by hotels, restaurants, cafe bars and gambling casinos. Scottish-born residents fell from 91.6 per cent of the population in 1971 to 88.5 per cent in 1981. The largest non-Scottish group were the English whose numbers doubled in the 1980s to reach almost 7 per cent of the total. They were followed, in numerical importance, by American and Spanish incomers. The population remained predominantly white, and less than 1 per cent of the ethnic population of Grampian region was non-white in 1995.[41]

Some of these incomers settled in the city. But many established themselves in the booming satellite towns around the city, such as Ellon and Inverurie. At the same time native Aberdonians moved outwards to new housing developments at Portlethen, Westhill, and north of the Bridge of Don, so that the newly emergent economic and social reality reinforced the links between the city and its hinterland.

Grandholm Mills,
linen factory of
Leys, Masson & Co.
from the end of the
eighteenth century
until 1848, reopened
as a woollen mill
for Crombie,
Knowles & Co. in
1859.

3

The Nineteenth-century Economy

RICHARD PERREN

In the period of modern economic growth, Aberdeen has been heavily influenced by its location distant from the main centres of population. The city did not have the natural resources of coal and iron which underpinned the first phase of British industrialisation. But Aberdeen has had the advantage of being a seaport, and the natural distribution and processing centre for a hinterland rich in natural resources. It is not surprising, therefore, that industrialisation should have depended very heavily on the exploitation of those natural resources in agriculture, fishing, granite and in processing activity which used those natural resources to produce commodities such as textiles, paper, soap and candles, leather, food and drink.[1]

As late as 1800, the predominant form of industrial production was domestic or cottage industry. At that time the chief industry was textile manufacture, wool, linen and cotton, in that order of importance. There were at least eight important textile factories, of which three were engaged in cotton production, three in wool manufacture and two making linen goods. There are only imprecise estimates of the number employed but an estimate of 8,000 to 10,000 in the 1830s has been quoted by one source, and the 1841 Census of Population returns offer some support for this sort of figure.[2] If the burgh's still sizeable number of handicraft textile workers are included, it seems that the industry employed a total of about 14,000 in the 1840s in a workforce of some 30,000.[3] The huge Woodside cotton works of Gordon, Barron & Co. was started in 1785 and employed 3,000 by 1820. In 1800 Forbes, Low & Co. established a cotton mill at Poynernook, and in the 1820s the family firm of Thomas Bannerman & Co. built the Bannermill. The woollen industry was represented by Charles Baird's mill at Stoneywood, established in 1789, and Alexander Hadden's mill in the Green established about 1798. Crombie, Knowles & Co. had a small wool mill on the Don some 10 miles from Aberdeen at Cothal from 1805 onward. The linen industry's first representative was Leys, Still & Co. established as early as 1749, but by the end of the century it had become Leys, Masson & Co., based in a huge mill on the Don at Grandholm. Some time between 1808 and 1811 the linen firm of John Maberly & Co. acquired land and a flax spinning mill at Broadford.[4]

Shipbuilding was firmly established with seven shipyards building small fast short-haul wooden sailing vessels, mainly less than 100 tons. In 1800 the port had 281 registered vessels with a total tonnage of 23,235, trading mainly with London and the Continent. The largest yards were Alexander Hall & Co., founded in 1790, William Duthie Sons & Co., which became John Duthie & Co. in 1815, and John Vernon & Sons. The others were all smaller concerns, of which the best known was John Duffus & Co. A later, but prominent, yard that opened in 1839 was Walter Hood & Co.[5] One firm that was to leave Aberdeen in 1830 was that of Alexander Stephen who first moved to Dundee and then later established a substantial firm on the Clyde at Linthouse. As a Scottish shipbuilding port, Aberdeen held an important place in the early nineteenth century.

Aberdeen yards were not leaders in the earliest technical developments of steam power and iron hulls, and only after some lapse in time did they eventually enter these fields of construction. The first steam-powered ship, the *Comet* was launched on the Clyde in 1812, but Aberdeen's first steamship was not built by Duffus & Co. until 1829.[6] This was a wooden-hulled coastal paddle steamer, the *Queen of Scotland*, built for the Aberdeen Steam Navigation Co. Aberdeen's first iron-hulled ship was the *John Garrow*, built in 1837 in the Vernon yard. With the introduction of iron hulls the size of Aberdeen's vessels rose, although the increase in the size of ships had already begun with wooden vessels independently of the introduction of iron. In 1818 construction of the *Asia*, which had, at the time, the exceptionally large displacement of 528 tons by Alexander Hall & Co. had earned this firm a place in the front rank of British shipbuilders. These larger 'packet' boats were first used in the coasting trade but were soon competing on longer routes. The demand from shipowners for fast bulk-carrying ships in the late 1830s and early 1840s led to further changes in design. Speed was needed for long-distance trade, and Aberdeen was able to take advantage of the growth of British trans-oceanic trade with the introduction of the clippers that were specially designed as fast long-distance carriers.[7]

The paper industry, with three mills, also began before the nineteenth century. The first successful paper mill was established in the mid-eighteenth century when Bartholomew Smith, a paper-maker from England, set up the Culter paper mill by the burn of Culter with a labour force of six men to make fine and coarse paper. He visited Aberdeen each Friday to purchase raw materials of rags, flax and hemp. In 1803 another mill was started at Ferryhill. In 1807 Lewis Smith, grandson of Bartholomew Smith, bought it and transferred the plant to Culter. The Stoneywood paper mill on the Don had been in operation since 1770 and, after some early changes in ownership, in 1778 Patrick Pirie, an Aberdeen merchant, entered into partnership to manage the business. This was the start of an association which lasted through five generations of the Pirie family. Mugiemoss mill, also on the Don, was established in 1796 by Charles Davidson who, in the 1770s, had been a partner in the Stoneywood mill. From its outset this mill concentrated on the manufacture of wrapping papers and continued this line of production into the twentieth century.[8] An inventory of the Stoneywood mill made in 1796 showed it had a labour force of 16 employees.

From the 1760s onward Aberdeen granite had been used for London pavements.[9] In the eighteenth century the use of this material was restricted because contemporary blasting technology placed limits on the size of the blocks of stone that could be quarried. The expansion of Georgian London, with its ready market for building stone, paid for some of the investment made by North-East landowners in the improvement of local farming. The developments in quarrying technology, as well as in agriculture, provided an opportunity for local farmers to supplement their incomes by carting stones. The city also benefited directly from the industry as civil engineering work carried out on improvements to Aberdeen harbour at various times in the late eighteenth and early nineteenth centuries made ready use of local granite from the quarries at Greyhope and Nigg, the latter being renowned for its stones and pebbles. As granite was in demand as a building material in other places besides Aberdeen and London, it made an excellent ballast

The harbour had to be steadily expanded to cope with increased shipping.

for ships sailing south and reduced the overall cost of ocean freight.[10] Aberdeen granite was used in building the Roker Pier in Sunderland, and this allowed the town to purchase coal from the north-east of England in the 1830s at a price 5 per cent cheaper than would otherwise have been possible. Local transport development in the early nineteenth century allowed the granite industry to advance the frontier of quarrying increasingly farther from the coast and the city. The construction of the 19 miles of the Aberdeenshire Canal from Aberdeen harbour to Inverurie, opened for the passage of vessels in June 1805, allowed the exploitation of granite deposits as far as Kintore, as long as they were within easy reach of this waterway.[11]

THE ECONOMIC INFRASTRUCTURE: TRANSPORT, TRADE AND FINANCE

The principal impediment to the city's growth throughout the nineteenth century was its distance from readily available supplies of raw materials and more populous markets, and there was no really substantial change to the dependence on sea transport before the coming of the railway in the 1850s, in spite of the development of turnpike roads. In the 1820s there were only ten stage coach services out of Aberdeen with just three travelling to the south. By the 1840s this had increased to about 20 stage coaches, including eight to the south and two postal services each day to Edinburgh. Some improvement in coastal shipping was effected by the introduction of regular steamship services from Aberdeen to London in 1827. These ships were capable of carrying heavy loads unlike the steam yachts which had hitherto travelled no further south than Leith. After 1829 the new service allowed the transport of cattle to by pass the long road journeys south, and thus removed one of the major transport problems previously facing Aberdeenshire livestock farmers.[12]

At the end of the eighteenth century Aberdeenshire produced a surplus of fat cattle after the requirements of Aberdeen and other local towns had been met. At the end of each summer a large part of this surplus was bought by English drovers who then sent the cattle south.[13] Early in the nineteenth century further progress in agricultural improvement, resulting in the increased supplies of roots and other fodder crops, added to the production of finished cattle in excess of local requirements. From the 1830s Aberdeenshire farmers could obtain the full value of fattened cattle, less the cost of the ocean freight, by sending their own cattle south by sea. This was more profitable than selling surplus animals at a cheap price to drovers who would then sell them on to farmers in England for fattening. The rise in the livestock trade acted like the increase in the granite trade in fostering the growth of the shipping firms operating out of the port of Aberdeen, as well as the prosperity of the port itself.[14]

The early nineteenth-century development of industry and transport required a more highly developed financial infrastructure for marketing, banking and insurance services than hitherto. Although Aberdeen acted as an agricultural marketing centre, it had always shared this position with other markets and fairs held in the country towns. In the early years of the nineteenth century it was estimated that 180 of these took place annually in various parts of Aberdeenshire. In 1800 the city's market sites were dispersed, although over time there was a tendency towards concentration at one location at Kittybrewster. In 1806 the Corporation of Fleshers built a market in the east end of the town with fifteen slaughterhouses and 86 meat stalls. In opposition, butchers who were not members of this corporation and thereby excluded from it, built themselves a smaller new flesh market in George Street in 1816. At both of these markets meat was sold only on Friday and Saturday, but in 1821 additional small retail markets where meat was sold daily were opened in the Gallowgate and Chapel Street. Wholesale livestock markets came to Aberdeen relatively late, and there is evidence that livestock and dead meat were shipped from the city before formal marketing arrangements had evolved. The same problem of widely dispersed markets applied to retailing as well. In 1839 the formation of the Aberdeen Market Company and the start of work on a new market hall in the Green, marked the beginning of the concentration of retail services in the central part of the town around the junction of Union Street and St Nicholas Street, realising one of the express aims of the new street trustees.[15]

In 1800 there were two city banks, the Aberdeen Banking Company, established in 1766, and the Commercial Banking Company of Aberdeen, established in 1788. In the late eighteenth and early nineteenth centuries there were banking wars between the Aberdeen banks and their Edinburgh and Glasgow competitors over geographical spheres of influence. Naturally, the Aberdeen banks believed they should have control over the city and its region. By 1800 broad agreement had been reached between the two sides to refrain from inconveniencing each other by demanding payment in specie at their branches on presentation of their respective notes. In return the Aberdeen banks were allowed to establish agencies or branches in the north relatively free of competition. But within the city itself, where the largest amount of business was to be had, competition with other banks continued.[16] This was intensified in 1818 when John Maberly, owner of the Broadford linen works, opened the Exchange and Deposit Bank. Although this institution only lasted for fourteen years until Maberly's bankruptcy in 1832 it was important, both locally and nationally, because Maberly reduced the time of remitting drafts from Scotland from 60 days to 20. This increased customer convenience and effectively reduced banking charges. It is also likely that resentment and opposition from the Edinburgh banks helped to undermine

Maberly's operations and possibly contributed towards his business failure.[17] In 1826 a third local bank, the Aberdeen Town and County Bank was established. By 1836 its paid-up capital was £112,000, and in that year the North of Scotland Bank was formed with a capital of £200,000 and 1,563 shareholders. In 1833 the Commercial Bank of Aberdeen was absorbed by the National Bank of Scotland and in 1849 the Aberdeen Banking Company was taken over by the Union Bank. In spite of these changes local banking initiative remained strong. By the end of 1837 the remaining three independent Aberdeen banks had a total of 60 branches in the region; the Town and County with 13, the North of Scotland with 32 and the Aberdeen Banking Company with 15.[18]

Beside the banks, there were also 24 insurance agencies and offices in the city in 1822, dealing in both fire and life policies. Early local initiatives in the insurance market were by no means as successful as those in banking, and all of these agents represented businesses with head offices elsewhere, mainly in Edinburgh and London. In 1817 an unsuccessful local attempt at marine insurance was tried but was abandoned a few years later with the loss of most of the subscribers' capital. In 1826 another attempt was made when the Aberdeen Fire and Life Assurance Company was established with a capital of £750,000. This company was a success and this prompted the formation of a rival in 1836, the North of Scotland Fire and Life Assurance Company. Both concerns survived, and part of the reason for this was that they were each closely allied to one of the two major local banks, the Aberdeen Fire and Life with the Town and County Bank and the North of Scotland Fire and Life with the North of Scotland Bank. By the 1840s the local economy had grown sufficiently to support a wider range of financial institutions than in the very early years of the century. Development of industry and commerce provided a wide range of premises requiring fire insurance, and the expanding number of professional people raised the demand for life assurance.

THE ECONOMIC COLLAPSE OF 1848

The growth and prosperity based on textiles came to an end in the late 1840s, with the failure of a number of the businesses and closure of their mills. In Scotland as a whole the immediate crisis was linked to speculation in railway shares, and in no place was that connection stronger than in Aberdeen, where a number of proposals competed for public support.[19] One of these was the North of Scotland Railway scheme, floated in March 1845 to link Aberdeen with the south. It was wholly subscribed and managed by Aberdeen businessmen, and involved a share and loan capital of £1,100,000. Its list of subscribers included all the leading city magnates, and according to the *Aberdeen Herald*, which also gave its unstinting support, it had the backing of

... the Bannermans, the Lumsdens, the Haddens, the Blaikies, the Burnetts, the Forbeses, the Piries, the Hogarths, the Kilgours, the Jopps, the McCombies, the Davidsons, and, in short, of every name of any note in our good city ... the most enterprising of our moneyed and mercantile men ... have been equally forward in promoting the undertaking.[20]

This scheme eventually became part of the Aberdeen Railway, but the Great North of Scotland Railway (GNSR) also had plans to link Aberdeen with Inverness and projected branch lines to Deeside, Alford, Buchan, Turiff and Banff. Local speculation in railway projects was so widespread that 44 individuals from Aberdeen were responsible for over £350,000 worth of railway stock. One of those, who had committed himself to the tune of £10,000, was James Adam, editor of the *Aberdeen Herald* who had so earnestly puffed the whole railway project in his own editorials.[21]

Some of these investors no doubt hoped to resell at a profit, and others certainly needed to. In the late 1830s, as a response to slack local trade, Aberdeen investors subscribed to colonial investment companies and American companies based on an urban property boom. One of these, the Illinois Investment Company, was promoted locally by the Aberdeen law and business partnership of Alexander Anderson and William Adam and managed in the United States by Anderson's cousin George Smith, later known as 'Chicago' Smith. The Illinois Investment Company was intended to bring fortunes into the pockets of Aberdonians who were persuaded to become shareholders, but instead they lost around £100,000 when it failed. Smith, however, augmented his fortune, and it is likely that Adam and Anderson managed to do the same. Anderson was also a prominent figure influencing the switch to railway investment at home in the 1840s when this and most of the other overseas projects of the 1830s had proved unsuccessful. Anderson promoted a number of bills for the construction of lines in the North-East after 1845, but when the national market in railway securities collapsed in 1847 there was insufficient ready cash to meet the outstanding calls on railway stock, and in the ensuing crisis many of the city's middle class lost heavily. Railway construction ground to a halt and had to be restarted later on a firmer financial base.[22]

No group of enterprises was hit more seriously than the textile factories because their owners had been leading speculators, and had lost heavily on overseas investments in the 1830s as well as on domestic railways in the 1840s. The linen firm of Leys, Masson & Co. stopped business in May 1848, and with it the allied woollen business of Alexander Hadden & Sons, both of which were controlled by the Hadden family. Although the Hadden mill in the Green resumed work two years later, Leys, Masson & Co. remained closed until its premises were taken over by Crombie Knowles & Co. in 1859. In 1850 the cotton factory of Gordon, Barron

& Co. closed and the Bannermill passed into new hands. Forbes, Low & Co., also in the cotton trade, finally closed and the linen works of Milne, Cruden & Co., at Spring Garden, and Gordon's mills ceased operation in 1854.[23] These failures cannot simply be ascribed to the financial crisis. Aberdeen textile firms had for some time neglected to undertake new investment and their plant and machinery had become obsolete. Furthermore, the distance from coalfields and major markets put Aberdeen textile mills at a long-term disadvantage relative to producers in the south, as well as depriving them of the short-term resilience to cope with economic fluctuations. Only four larger mills, the Broadford linen works, the Grandholm mills (converted to woollens in 1859), the Hadden mill in the Green, and the Bannermill (under new management), survived the depression of 1848-54.[24]

Besides its consequences for the textile industry, the crisis following the collapse of the railway investment bubble had a general effect upon the whole economy of the city, and helped to slow down the rate of growth at mid-century. The disappearance of the Aberdeen Banking Company in 1849 was linked to speculation and the railway crisis.[25] The closure of the mills threw several thousands out of work for a year or more, forcing them to subsist on the charity of soup kitchens, church collections and subscription funds until the shattered local economy started to revive. The mid-century years were characterised by slow growth in all the Scottish cities, but Aberdeen was the worst affected. The growth of population between 1851 and 1861 was only 2.6 per cent, the lowest recorded for any decade in the nineteenth century, whereas the average increase was 19.2 per cent. For over a decade the textile districts, especially Woodside, remained in a state of depression. The 1850s were also difficult years for other sectors of the economy. The Aberdeen Steam Navigation Company entered into collaborative price agreements with the railway, but its profits fell sharply after 1850 and its authorised capital fell from £150,000 in 1851 to £50,000 in 1871.[26] Even railway building experienced a hiatus as construction on the GNSR came to a halt. No lines extended north of the city before 1850. The Aberdeen to Huntly line opened in 1854, the Huntly to Keith extension in 1856, and a connection through to Inverness in 1858. The Aberdeen to Banchory line opened in 1853, and was extended to Aboyne in 1859 and to Ballater in 1866. The Buchan line was opened in 1862 and the Speyside line in 1866.[27]

THE GROWTH OF TRADE

The difficulties of the 1850s engendered a defensive spirit among the business community. One symptom of this pessimism was the formation in November 1853 of the Aberdeen and North of Scotland Trade Protection Society which acted largely as a local debt collection agency for members, as well as lobbying Parliament on national matters of local concern. In the 1860s it was engaged in opposing railway amalgamation bills on the grounds that reduced competition might cut services and raise transport costs.[28] Investment in railways had been undertaken in the hope that it would bring wealth and prosperity, and the railway certainly did benefit the cattle trade by offering a quicker and easier route to southern markets. By 1850 a weekly cattle train left from Ferryhill, and accommodation was provided at Torry Farm for animals awaiting shipment.[29] Livestock traffic reached its peak in 1859 and thereafter declined as more cattle were slaughtered in the city and sent south by rail as fresh dead meat. But the transport of meat did not entirely replace that of livestock. The great Donside cattle breeder, William McCombie, estimated that in 1865 the equivalent of 33,800 cattle left Aberdeen as dead meat, 9,000 by rail as live animals, and a further 4,450 by sea.[30] The livestock trade was never entirely abandoned, and a few animals were still sent south from Aberdeen as late as 1935. One factor that kept the trade alive was the practice of awarding prizes at livestock shows in London and the provinces in the week or so before Christmas. On these occasions, animals sent by Aberdeen traders and local farmers were frequent winners. Although the most important firms in the meat and livestock trade were based in Aberdeen, a large volume of meat was also sent from Inverurie and other parts of the county and, for thirty years after 1850, the quantity of dead meat sent from Aberdeen regulated the London meat market at Newgate. Not necessarily all the meat sent from Aberdeen was locally fed. The city's reputation for quality even encouraged some salesmen to buy animals in Glasgow, bring them to Aberdeen for slaughter, and send them to London to supplement local supplies. With the increasing number of livestock passing through the city, better marketing arrangements were required. Aberdeen's first formal cattle auction mart was John Duncan's in King Street, which started in 1867. Duncan was a dealer who imported cattle from Orkney, and he started his auction business on a piece of open ground where he sold by private bargain. Soon the site was divided by portable wooden fences, then a rostrum was added and, later, permanent buildings.[31]

The meat trade stimulated industries processing the inferior parts of the carcass meat, and making use of animal by-products. In the 1860s there were five firms which together employed about 500 people and produced 2.5 million lb of tinned and salted meat for the export market and the armed services. The city was at the forefront in the processing of other preserved foodstuffs. The firm of John Moir & Son started in 1825 canning lobster, trout, crab and salmon. It moved from fish to meat, poultry and vegetables and by the 1870s had built up a considerable export trade in tinned fruits and vegetables.[32] This feature of the local economy was further stimulated when increasing quantities of herring and white fish became available to food manufacturers. In the processing of animal by-products the most important example was the manufacture of horn combs. By the 1840s more combs were produced in Aberdeen than anywhere else in Scotland. The Aberdeen Hide Skin & Tallow Market Co., at the city's main slaughterhouse in Hutcheon Street was also geared up for by-processing. In 1868 it was estimated that a total of 17,500 tons of hides were handled by dealers in Aberdeen and that 15,000 tons of these were sent south.[33] In the 1860s there were tan works in Jack's Brae, Rodger's Walk and the Hardgate, the last of which, owned by William Sim, was the largest.

The railways supplemented the continuous improvements being made to the harbour, which because of its superiority to local competitors was able to engross most of the coastal traffic of the region, while its link between regional and national rail networks made the city the prime distribution point for the region. But, while there were beneficiaries from transport improvements, there were also losers. The Aberdeenshire Canal had never been a directly paying proposition. But it had been a considerable benefit to its investors, most of whom owned the land through which it passed, in the improvements it allowed them to make to their properties. By 1850 the canal had outlived its usefulness and was bought by the GNSR which closed it in 1853 and then, after draining it, used about a third of its route as a permanent way for the Aberdeen to Inverurie railway line.[34]

THE CLIPPER SHIPS

Changes in technology at this time posed problems for shipbuilding. Aberdeen, unlike Glasgow, had been poorly placed to experiment extensively with coal and iron in the early days, hence attempts to improve the sailing ship to compete with the early Glasgow-built paddle steamers. With the switch from wood to iron and then to steel, Aberdeen was again hampered by its distance from coal and iron, as well as by a shortage of land for extending its shipyards to accommodate the increased size of vessels. As early as 1846 John Duffus & Co., one of the major shipbuilding firms, was forced to merge with the ironfounders Blaikie Brothers and to close down its shipbuilding operations as a consequence of these difficulties. Others were only able to survive by improving their performance in the later stages of sail technology.[35] Alexander Hall & Co. built the *Scottish Maid* in 1839, designed specifically for speed to compete with the new steamboat service between Aberdeen and London. Thereafter, this yard built all its large sailing ships with a raked stem. The origins of this feature of design are disputed among maritime historians. However, the raked stem, carrying the extreme forepart of the ship clear of the water, and over the roughest seas with relative buoyancy and smoothness, was exploited by city shipbuilders with such success that it became

known as the 'Aberdeen bow', and was regarded as the hallmark of the long-distance fast sailing vessel.[36] In 1845 the yard built the *Torrington*, the first clipper to compete with American opium clippers in the trade from Bengal to south China. From 1850 onward these vessels competed with American clippers in the China 'tea races' with ships that were built specially for this trade. Alexander Hall & Co. remained the major firm in Aberdeen during the final stages of the age of sail and built 290 of this type of vessel before the end of the clipper era in the 1870s. Walter Hood, from its inception in 1839, until it merged with Alexander Hall & Co. in 1881, built about another 40 such vessels. The success of the clippers was relatively short-lived and ended with the construction of the Suez Canal in 1869 and the establishment of convenient coaling stations abroad. But it was this class of vessel that maintained Aberdeen as a shipbuilding port with an international reputation throughout the 1860s.[37]

In 1864 James and William Hall, the family members currently responsible for Alexander Hall & Co., established with Thomas Russell, a Glasgow engineer, the

Management and workers of Alexander Hall & Sons in 1862, when the firm specialised in building fast clippers for the 'tea races' from China.

George Thompson Jr 1804–1895

Born at Woolwich, George Thompson Jnr moved to Aberdeen at the age of two to be brought up by his grandparents. He was educated at the Grammar School, and started work in the office of the London Shipping Company. He set up as a ship and insurance broker about 1825 and later became a shipowner and timber importer. He established the Aberdeen White Star Line, engaging in the clipper ship trade with South Africa and Australia. He was the main partner in Walter Hood & Co., shipbuilders, which built the famous *Thermopylae*, the fastest sailing ship ever built. In 1850 he was joined in partnership by William Henderson, later his son-in-law, who acted as London agent. He was dean of guild, 1840–41, represented the first ward on the town council, 1842–44, and the third ward, 1847–51, serving as lord provost 1847–50. He was MP for the city 1852–57. He was a Liberal radical who campaigned for the repeal of the Corn Laws and was sympathetic to the demands of the chartists. He was a director of the North of Scotland Bank, and of the Great North of Scotland Railway. A member of Trinity Free Church, he supported church disestablishment. He was a substantial benefactor to good causes, especially to the Royal Infirmary and the University Medical School.

Model of the Thermopylae, *built by Walter Hood & Co. to carry wool from Australia, the fastest sailing ship ever built.*

marine engineering firm of Hall, Russell & Co. The premises of the Aberdeen Iron Works were acquired and equipped to modern standards. The original intention was to supply the latest designs of engines, shipbuilding equipment and other marine machinery to the parent company, but in 1867 the firm started to build iron-hulled vessels. In the 1860s Alexander Hall & Co. had other problems. In 1863 the rope-making firm of Catto & Thompson, in which Hall had a 50 per cent shareholding, collapsed leaving the firm responsible for £40,000 worth of debts. In 1866, £4,000 was lost on one clipper when its intended purchasers could not reach the contract price, and a further £500 was lost when James Hall underestimated the cost of a vessel for the Japanese navy. Although the business was put into receivership, the reserve price was not reached and the company began trading successfully again late in 1867. The firm maintained its links with Japan, and by the end of 1869 had built three modern gunboats for the Japanese navy, two built by Hall & Co. and the other by Hall Russell & Co., before it became necessary for that country to turn to the Clyde for larger warships than Aberdeen could produce. By the mid-1870s the transition from wood to iron was almost complete, and the era of the clippers was almost over.

THE TRAWLING INDUSTRY

The fishing industry was long established in Aberdeen, but on a relatively small scale compared with neighbouring ports like Findhorn, Buckie, Fraserburgh, Peterhead and Montrose. In the eighteenth century, Aberdeen was most noted for the salmon in its rivers, which were dispatched throughout Europe. Aberdeen was also the first Scottish port to send ships to whaling from about 1750 and, in 1834, six of the 40 Scottish whalers sailed from Aberdeen to the Arctic. But the whaling fleet never matched the scale of Peterhead or Dundee. By the middle of the nineteenth century, therefore, Aberdeen was a much smaller fishing port than either Fraserburgh or Peterhead. But the building of the railways provided the fishing industry with options other than salted herring and cod. Rising prices not only stimulated catches of traditionally acceptable fish but also encouraged consumers to switch to other species that the North Sea could provide. However, unlike the meat trade, fishing could not take immediate advantage of the improved transport for its highly perishable products and, in any case, the largest sales of herring continued to be for salted fish even in 1914.

In fishing, reliance on small sailing vessels, which restricted the time and distance that could be covered in voyages and the quantity that could be landed, still acted as a constraint on output. The advent of the steam trawler changed this situation dramatically. Its origins in Aberdeen may be traced to 1882 when a wooden Tyne-built tugboat, the *Toiler*, was converted in one of the Aberdeen yards

The fishing fleet heads to sea in the 1870s before the coming of the steam trawler.

to carry fishing gear and successfully operated in Aberdeen bay for a season before showing signs of wear. The *Toiler* was soon followed by more efficient iron-built screw vessels, which were used both for trawling and drifting.[38] Steam power meant revolutionary change for both white fishing and herring fishing. White fishing became highly organised and used both steam trawlers and liners, while the steam drifters engaged in herring fishing. This meant the industry was divided into two parts, each with its own type of vessel. White fishing concentrated on Aberdeen, as steam trawlers were too large for the small harbours of the fishing villages along the coast. In addition, Aberdeen had the advantage of the excellent railway facilities that had been developed for the meat trade and which were now vital for the expanding fresh-fish trade. The change from sail to steam necessitated much larger capital investment in a modern fishing vessel and this led to a greater concentration of capital. In the days of sail, boats and gear had been cheap enough for fishermen to finance themselves from their earnings, savings and loans, or sometimes with assistance from a landowner. As the financing of steam vessels was largely beyond the capacity of the ordinary fisherman, this provided an opportunity for the multi-vessel-owning fishing firm to appear, although some vessels were still owned by individuals or small companies. By 1912, 61 per cent of

William Pyper 1833–1909

Born at Newhills, William Pyper was educated at Ellon by his uncle who was a schoolmaster. At the age of 14 he was apprenticed to Robert Stevens, a grocer, in George Street. He became manager of the shop, and later opened his own grocery business in Queen Street. He engaged in many business activities and belonged to the syndicate which purchased the first steam trawler in Aberdeen. He became managing director of the company, called the North Line, and built up the fleet. He was a pioneer and director of the North Eastern Ice Company. He also had business interests in the China trade and the North of Scotland Equitable Loan Company. He represented the second ward on the town council 1874–77, the first ward/St Clement's 1880–88, and served on the harbour board throughout these terms. He served as chairman of the St Nicholas parochial board and the Aberdeen parish council. He was a governor of Robert Gordon's College. Politically he was a staunch Conservative and a member of the council of the Primrose League. He was a member of Craigiebuckler Parish Church.

William Pyper, pioneering steam trawler owner. The portrait is by R. Brough.

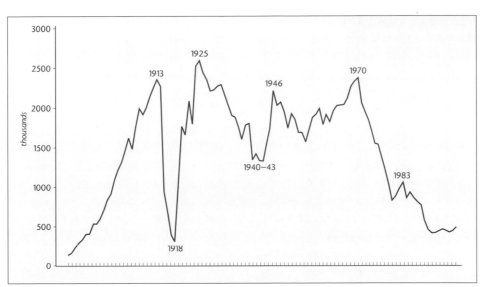

Figure 3.1 Landings of white fish (cwts): Aberdeen harbour, 1888-1998. (Sources: Aberdeen Harbour Board. Data: Annual series for years ending on 30 September)

the 161 steam trawlers belonging to the port of Aberdeen were owned by 10 companies each with more than five vessels, 37 per cent were owned by 19 companies with two to five vessels, and only three trawlers were operated by single-vessel owners or companies. The smaller and cheaper line-fishing vessels and drifters allowed more single-vessel ownership, but even here there was some concentration.

As the new industry offered handsome profits, capital was readily forthcoming. Investors in trawlers also took an interest in the supply of coal, ice or stores which gave rise to a structure of interlocking directorates between trawling firms and the subsidiary industries. The marketing of fish remained the preserve of merchants and there was little connection, or common interest, between them and the trawl owners. The herring industry, unlike the white fishery, did not become concentrated in Aberdeen. Although the herring drifter abandoned sail for steam, it was smaller and cheaper than the trawler and could be accommodated in the smaller harbours of the local outports.

Trawling brought about a series of profound changes to the port itself, and to the entire Aberdeen economy.[39] Before 1850 the harbour was a tidal basin but in that year the first lock gate was added to convert it to a wet dock where vessels could ride in water at low tide. The final stage of this process, authorised in 1868, gave the harbour a deeper wet dock when the Albert Basin was opened. Nearby land, reclaimed from the river as a result of this work, was put to commercial use. As the white fishery expanded, the town council opened the first stage of its new fish market at the north end of Albert Quay in May 1889. By 1904, after two extensions, this establishment covered an area of more than 85,000 square feet and was the largest in Scotland.[40] Aberdeen not only became the headquarters for most Scottish and a large number of English trawlers, it also attracted Danish and German vessels. Buyers and fish salesmen for both British and international businesses made Aberdeen their headquarters. In 1888 the tonnage of white fish landed at Aberdeen was 133,180, by 1914 this had risen to 2,268,860.[41]

The harbour improvements and better access to the south side of the river meant that Torry began to grow and became heavily dependent on the modern fishing industry after 1890. The whole district around Point Law, and on the south side of the Dee between St Fittick's Road and Wellington Road, became a processing centre for both white fish and herring, acquiring in the process a collection of curing yards, smoking kilns, fish houses, provision works, coopers' shops, box factories, ice manufacturers and net makers. In the early twentieth century the city had four ice-making plants with a combined cold storage capacity of over 60,000 cubic feet, and another one was under construction.[42] At the same time 200 steam trawlers, 40 steam liners and about 30 sail boats operated from Aberdeen, and employed some 3,000 to 4,000 fishermen, but more than double that number were required to carry on the fishing industry ashore. In addition, there were other businesses like sawmills, shipyards, carriers, and railways that owed a portion of their trade to the demands generated by the fishing industry. In 1905 the *Aberdeen Journal* estimated there were 70 businesses employed in the preparation of white fish, 31 in herring curing, while the canning industry employed nine firms in the city. It went on to say that the 'number of women employed in preparation and curing of white fish alone is estimated at 2,600, and altogether it is calculated that the number of fishermen, curers, and workers engaged in Aberdeen in connection with the industry amounts to the huge total of 9,200'.[43]

THE GROWTH OF THE SHIPYARDS

Although after 1870 the local yards still built ocean-going vessels, the distance from supplies of raw materials, absence of deep water, and restricted space to expand the yards, prevented the industry from entering the market to supply vessels over 4,000 tons. In these circumstances it was natural that, by 1914, Aberdeen shipyards specialised heavily in fishing and coasting vessels, including colliers. The transition to trawling was reflected in the tonnages launched in the three decades before the Great War. Aberdeen yards did, however, continue to build some long distance cargo and passenger vessels, but now in iron, and later steel, and powered by steam instead of sail. For example, Messrs John T. Rennie, Sons & Co. ordered fourteen steamers between 1882 and 1910 for their South African trade. The Aberdeen Line took delivery of the steamer *Thermopylae* in 1891, named after the firm's famous sailing ship, and of the *Salamis* in 1899. Both of these were fully-equipped luxury passenger steamers for the Australian trade. But not all the yards in Aberdeen survived the transition to iron and steel and steam. The larger yards were better placed to invest in the more expensive capital equipment and to recruit workers possessing the wider range of technical skills now required, such as boilermakers and fitters. In 1870 only three yards remained in Aberdeen: Alexander Hall & Co., John Duthie Sons & Co., and Hall, Russell & Co.

Shipbuilding came to rely very heavily on fishing, both for new orders and repair work. Between 1882 and 1903 the three surviving yards produced between them 267 steam trawlers.[44] The Aberdeen yards probably reached their peak output in 1907 when a total of 67 vessels were built, although in some other years before the First World War an output of more than 40 trawlers was recorded. In the 1890s some steam-powered line fishing boats were built, but after 1895 these were designed for easy conversion to trawling if required. From 1903 the Aberdeen yards also built steam drifters, and John Duthie's yard in Torry specialised in this kind of vessel. But it was still possible at this time for new entrants to begin shipbuilding and a new firm was set up at Cove by John Lewis who moved to Aberdeen in 1876 when he established a small yard at Point Law. He filled the gap left by the larger yards by confining himself to wooden vessels for local use, fishing cobbles for the royalty at Balmoral, as well as in-shore fishing boats up to 55 feet long, and ferry boats for Aberdeen harbour.

THE CITY OF GRANITE

The other great industry of the late nineteenth century was granite. Output of Aberdeenshire granite more than doubled between 1850 and 1870. The expansion of stone finishing in the city's granite yards developed after the first polished granite funereal monument was exported from Aberdeen to London by Alexander MacDonald in 1832. At first growth was slow and there were only ten stonecutters' yards in the city in 1846-47,

Mr. JOHN FYFE.

John Fyfe 1830–1906

Born at Newhills, John Fyfe took over the family quarrying business at Tyrebagger at the age of 16 on the death of his father. He moved to Kemnay in 1857 to take advantage of richer granite deposits and improved transport provided by the Alford Valley Railway which opened in 1859. He established the largest granite quarrying firm in the north, and invented the Blondin transporter. He provided the granite for the Forth and Tay Bridges, for the Thames embankment and Holburn viaduct. As a contribution to the city, he built the Victoria Bridge in Aberdeen for a price well below the cheapest commercial estimate. He served on the Aberdeen Quarrymasters Association and the Aberdeen Granite Manufacturers Association. He was a director of the Aberdeen Lime Company, the Town and County Bank, and the local branch of the London and Lancashire Insurance Company. He served as a JP and on the Aberdeen University Building Committee, contributing £1,000 towards the construction of the new frontage of Marischal College, which was built in Kemnay granite. He was a member of Rubislaw Church and, in politics, supported the Unionists.

but after the emergence of the American market the number grew to 32 by 1875-76.[45]

Output from local quarries grew rapidly when many of the original technical problems had been overcome by the 1870s. The demand from the building industry had the effect of promoting the granite finishing yards within the city which numbered 46 in 1879-80 and had risen to 100 by 1913-14.[46] Since top quality polishing stone never constituted more than 10 per cent of total granite output, local supplies of the flawless stone required by the stonecutters and granite polishers were soon exhausted and replacements were hard to find. By 1910 more than 50 per cent of the granite cut in the manufacturing yards was imported from northern Europe, mainly from Norway, Sweden and Russia. Economy dictated that the preparation of granite street setts, kerbs, and crushed granite for building hardcore were quarry-based operations. Only a small amount of the granite quarried went into finished products and, as the output of a quarry was far too large for a single yard, there was a natural division between the two branches of the industry. Few of the largest finishing yards had quarrying interests and only one or two of the largest quarry owners were involved in cutting and polishing. Output from the Aberdeenshire quarries reached its peak in 1898 with 332,140 tons, but output had dipped to 137,000 tons by 1911 because of the national downturn in building work. The activities within city stone yards were shared between the manufacture and finishing of small-scale pieces and monuments and the production of constructional blocks and polished slabs for various kinds of building work. Monumental work required a good deal of equipment like saws and polishing machines, as well as a substantial input of the most essential factor, skilled labour, which was concentrated in Aberdeen. Before 1914 Aberdeen enjoyed both national and international domination of the finishing trade, and polished granite was one of the city's main exports, rising from 2,000 tons in 1880 to over 9,000 in the decade before 1913. In the 1880s the American market for tombstones was of particular importance but, by 1900, in response to American tariffs and a national building boom, the domestic market had become the main outlet.[47]

Like the fishing industry, granite supported a number of subsidiary activities. Chief among these were the engineering trades. Improved blasting meant that shallow workings gave way to deep quarries that required steam-powered cranes with fixed jibs, derricks with moveable jibs, and the 'Blondin' suspension cableway, to raise the stone to the surface. Steam-powered rock drills, and electric detonating devices were brought in to increase output and meet the rising demand for stone. Although there were no major technical advances between 1880 and 1914, other than the introduction of the pneumatic drill, the further application of these techniques to existing quarries was sufficient to ensure the industry's steady demand for new machinery. To meet this need Aberdeen's small but already thriving engineering industry diversified after 1870. It was to local firms like those of Wilson, Henderson, Blaikie, and Abernethy that the quarry-masters went for their cranes, steam-borers, Blondins and other equipment. Local blacksmiths also made a valuable contribution to the trade by maintaining the drills, hatchets, chisels and hammers used in stone-working.[48]

PAPER AND PROCESSING

Pirie's Stoneywood paper works in the late nineteenth century. Note that it is the men who control the machines.

In 1848, when textile mills were shutting down, the Stoneywood paper mill was greatly extended and more machines installed. In 1856 the firm bought the neighbouring print mills at Woodside which were turned over to the preparation of the rags used in paper manufacture. Against a background of slow growth in the local economy, Alexander Pirie managed to transform a relatively modest business into a large prosperous firm with a national reputation for high-quality stationery and envelopes. The introduction of the penny post in 1840 had given

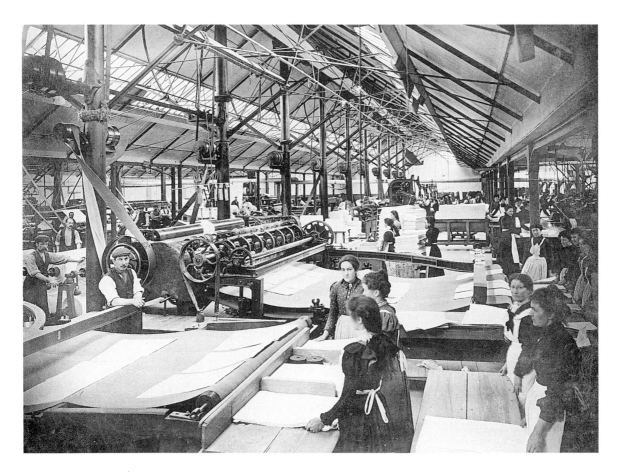

a great boost to the production of envelopes, as before that date an additional
charge was levied on letters that had an outer wrapping. Originally Pirie's made
envelopes by hand at premises in the Adelphi in Aberdeen. Demand was so great,
and hand production so slow, that the firm's engineers designed special machines
for envelope manufacture and, by the second half of the nineteenth century, Pirie's
was among the world's leading envelope manufacturers. At the Stoneywood site
there was a steady expansion of premises and capacity, and almost every decade
saw the installation of some new machine. The discovery of the potentialities of
esparto grass and, later, the introduction of wood-pulp gave a new impetus to
output, although rags continued to be the main raw material. The expansion of
Pirie's firm was not at the expense of the other paper firms who maintained their
position. There was also a new entrant to the industry. Further up the Don, outside
Aberdeen but certainly within the industrial orbit of the city at Inverurie, Thomas
Tait & Sons began making paper in 1860. This family had previously been
important farmers in the area, and leading investors in the Aberdeenshire Canal.
The money obtained when the canal was sold to the railway was used to finance
the paper mill.[49]

While the industry had a rising market, there was strong foreign competition
in the last quarter of the nineteenth century. Before the 1880s imports of paper
represented about 10 per cent of home consumption but by the 1900s they were
about 30 per cent of United Kingdom output, and between 1870 and 1900
approximately one-quarter of the firms in the British paper industry disappeared

each decade.[50] Not only did the three original local firms survive but, by 1900, were joined by two others. The policy for survival was aggressive expansion and heavy investment. In 1892 Davidson & Sons of Mugiemoss were compelled to add to their buildings, install further machinery, and open two new agencies in England to reach a wider range of customers. In 1888 Gordon's mills on the banks of the Don between Old Aberdeen and Woodside, which had been used for various purposes and latterly as a meal mill, were converted by Patrick Shand for the manufacture of brown paper wrappings. In 1893 the business was taken over by John Laing & Co. of Dundee. The name of the business was changed to the Donside Paper Company, under the chairmanship of Sir John Laing, and the premises renamed as the Donside mills. The Aberdeen paper industry was able to take advantage of the increase in demand, initiated by the growth of population and real incomes, and expressed in the spread of mass literacy, an increased volume of business correspondence, an expansion in the activities of local and central government, and a mounting consumption of wrapping paper and other packaging materials stimulated by new retailing methods. It was able to achieve this growth by constantly enlarging the scale of its operations and adopting new technology to reduce costs.

The Uncertainty of Economic Growth

For some industries the late nineteenth century was a period of decline. Improved transport technology may have been a crucial factor for the development of the fresh food industry, as both meat and fish required speedy access to distant markets, but for other local products these changes brought exposure to competition from more efficient producers elsewhere. Competition from larger units in the ports of London, Liverpool and Glasgow led to the extinction of trades like flour milling and leather tanning. In the early nineteenth century Aberdeen had five flour mills processing local wheat as well as imports from the Baltic and, in 1873, Joseph Rank, founder of the Rank milling empire, was sent from Hull by his father to work as a journeyman at the city flour mill in Aberdeen.[51] By 1914 many of the local mills had closed, and most of the flour and meal used in Aberdeen was brought in by rail. Leather tanning, which had been important in the city and the region, was almost eliminated by competition from large works in the south of Scotland and England that drained away the supply of hides from local butchers. Transport changes may have led to the reduction of some of the city's agricultural processing trades, but for its meat processors these were years of positive growth. Although falling corn prices meant this period was regarded as one of agricultural depression, local farmers readjusted successfully by specialising heavily in livestock products, particularly high quality beef, whose price was more buoyant.[52] One sign of this success was an increased purchase of agricultural inputs, often using traders based in Aberdeen and its locality. From being mainly an importer, carrier and seller of manures and feedstuffs, after 1870 the Aberdeen Lime Company gradually acquired a range of mills, presses and blending machines enabling it to produce a wide range of compound fertilisers and oilcakes for animal feed and by 1912 had £25,000 worth of plant and machinery for this purpose.[53] Before the First World War there were about a dozen firms in Aberdeen serving farmers in the North-East with a range of agricultural implements, machinery, feed stuffs, fertilisers, and other products.

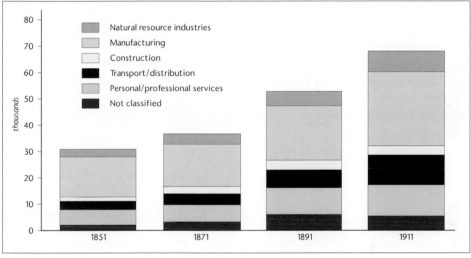

Figure 3.2
Distribution of
employment in
Aberdeen.
(Sources: Census of
Population for
Scotland, Decennial
Reports)

But the textile manufacture continued to struggle. In 1904 both the Hadden mill and the Bannermill were forced to close, and this finally brought to an end Aberdeen's participation in the cotton industry. The woollen firm of J. & J. Crombie at Grandholm experienced some lean years in the 1880s but managed to survive, and in 1898 the linen manufacturer, Richards & Co. was forced to suspend business, although it resumed business after a public flotation, as Richards Ltd.[54] Both these firms survived by serving very specialised sectors of the market, and purchasing raw materials directly from abroad to eliminate the middleman, while ensuring a control of all stages of production. But in addition to these two textile giants there were a number of smaller woollen firms producing items like hosiery and gloves. In 1873 James Kilgour and Thomas Walker took over a small woollen mill in Bucksburn and in 1875 moved to premises within the city at Berryden and specialised in carding, spinning and dyeing, together with the weaving of wincey.

Other parts of the local economy faced not closure but loss of independence. The history of Aberdeen banking from the 1830s onward was characterised by the steady erosion of control as local banks amalgamated with larger concerns which had come to dominate them. As these companies had head offices elsewhere, decisions on bank policy were increasingly taken outside the city. However, this tendency was resisted for longer than in most other areas, and in 1900 the North-East remained the only Scottish region outside Edinburgh and Glasgow to have its own bank. The North of Scotland Bank remained free of either Edinburgh or Glasgow control throughout the nineteenth century and when it did amalgamate, in 1907, it was with the Town and County Bank, the other successful independent Aberdeen bank, to form the North of Scotland and Town and County Bank. In the nineteenth and twentieth centuries the 'North Bank', as it was usually known, built up strong connections with all local industries, although it was most prominent as a financier of farming and fishing. Its link with fishing was crucial before 1900 when it provided skippers with much of the finance for building the Aberdeen fleet.[55]

4

Survival and Decline: The Economy 1918-1970

RICHARD PERREN

ECONOMIC DECLINE AND REGENERATION

Economic growth throughout the nineteenth century proceeded at a steady rate. The effects of national and international market forces on the Aberdeen economy were mainly beneficial, offering opportunities to exploit natural resources rather than creating problems. The twentieth-century experience marked a sharp departure from this relatively benign environment. The disruption of two world wars, the intensification of international competition, and the juxtaposition of phases of high growth against periods of deep depression were the salient characteristics of economic life in the twentieth century. Like many other cities and their regions, for Aberdeen and the North-East the twentieth century brought the manifold problems of structural transformation in changing work patterns, unemployment and instability although it also brought some new opportunities.

THE IMPACT OF WAR

War disrupts economic life. Normal activities are abandoned or reduced in order to support the war effort. At the most obvious level, some workers leave their jobs to enlist in the forces. In the First World War, half the granite workers in the North-East joined the forces and the North of Scotland Bank lost about 40 per cent of its staff through enlistment or conscription. Some of these jobs were filled by women. The Bank appointed its first women clerks in 1915 and employed 160 by 1918. Employers in the granite industry faced strong resistance to the employment of women from their male workers, so that women were eventually allowed to work in the polishing branch of the trade but not in the cutting branch.[1] Some industries lost raw material supplies as trade was disrupted. Granite was affected by the prohibition on foreign imports and the loss of export orders as government restrictions were placed on shipping space. But the distortion of war brought opportunities for some firms. Richards supplied military orders for heavy linen,

Women workers from J. M. Henderson & Co., engineers, on parade in Union Street, to encourage other women to take up work during the Second World War.

and paid dividends of 10 per cent plus substantial bonuses every year between 1915 and 1919.[2] Food-preserving businesses also secured military contracts for rations. Boot and shoe factories adjusted to military demands, producing ankle boots, field service mounted boots, and sea boots for the British forces. Since Aberdeen offered the only direct sea route to Russia, the local industry was able to secure large orders for Cossack boots for the Russian army.[3] The city's shipyards found employment in converting trawlers and drifters into minesweepers and patrol boats. Fishermen, like their boats, were commandeered to the service of King and Country.

The Second World War caused further distortions, some temporary in nature and others of a more permanent character. In common with other British cities, Aberdeen was attacked by the Luftwaffe and although its main targets were the harbour and industrial sites in the central and northern parts of the city, bombs also fell on houses and tenements. A raid by a single aircraft in July 1940 damaged the Hall, Russell shipyard and killed 32 workmen during their lunch break.[4] In April 1942 the heavy engineering firm John M. Henderson's, King Street works was

Coal being unloaded in the upper dock of the harbour.

hit, while Crombie's Grandholm works suffered the loss of over 9,000 square feet of glass broken in an air raid during April 1943.

In the Second World War, as in 1914, local industries lost workers to the forces. By the end of 1941 there were only 547 skilled workers and 13 apprentices left in the granite yards, although output of hard-core from the quarries was increased because it was needed for military building works.[5] The problem of the loss of labour was compounded by restrictions on raw materials. Rationing had a severe effect on paper manufacture, and some productive capacity was converted to manufacture military supplies. At Wiggins Teape this took the form of producing containers, not only for explosives and lubricating oils, but also for 90 and 45 gallon drop fuel and napalm tanks carried by Mosquito bomber aircraft for the Royal Air Force and by Mustang fighter and ground attack aircraft for the United States Air Force.[6] Much of Aberdeen's trade with the south was diverted from coastal shipping to the railways, partly for reasons of safety. In 1938–39 most of the coal used in the North-East still came into Aberdeen harbour, the colliers carrying 65 per cent of the total while the balance was handled by the railways. By 1944–45 the colliers' tonnage had dropped to 38 per cent and had fallen in volume by almost half, while that carried by rail had increased substantially.[7] Colliers, like fishing vessels, were

*Residents line
Seaforth Road as a
funeral cortège takes
air raid victims
from Bedford Road
and Cattofield
district to Trinity
Cemetery on
21 April 1943.*

diverted to other work and trawlers were again converted to minesweepers. The war also saw an increase in the volume of fish carried from Aberdeen by rail.[8]

As in the earlier war, some industries found their skills in great demand. Henderson's wartime production list was typical of that of most city engineering firms, and included gun carriages, ammunition hoists, Churchill tanks, aircraft and Bailey bridge parts.[9] Before the war William McKinnon & Co., Spring Garden, had specialised in plantation machinery for hulling and crushing crops like coffee, cocoa, sugar and rice. Between 1939 and 1945 production was switched to mortar bombs, howitzer and naval shrapnel shells, baffle plates, chemical containers, and aero-engine parts.[10] Throughout the war Crombie & Co. found a ready market for high-quality cloth, sustained by British and United States government orders for soldiers' uniforms and material for officers' greatcoats. Most of what was produced for civilian use was exported to the United States to earn dollars.[11] In the main, war constituted a temporary disruption to the Aberdeen economy. But the end of war never leads to the resumption of normal pre-war routines. After both world wars, the economic environment was fundamentally altered and, on each occasion, the impact on the Aberdeen economy was to intensify the economic pressures of adjustment to a declining resource base, a relatively isolated location and increasingly competitive markets.

THE FISHING INDUSTRY

The fishing industry was adversely affected by wartime conditions in both world wars, as vessels and crews were requisitioned and allocated to minesweeping and coastal defence duties while other fishermen were redirected to serve in the navy and coastal shipping. But for those who remained in the industry, the higher prices offered for their catches provided some compensation for inconveniences

Cod laid out for sale at Aberdeen fish market in 1969 before the decline in the industry set in.

such as restricted access to fisheries, and shortages of spare parts and servicing as local shipyards fulfilled military contracts. On the return of peace, and the release of crews and vessels from Admiralty service, the industry hoped for government support to rebuild the fleet after years of run-down and capital decline. After the First World War the Aberdeen trawling fleet, which numbered 218 in 1913, continued to grow and reached 255 in 1938. However, the number of the city's workforce engaged in the industry had shrunk from 12,000 in 1920 to 9,000 by 1939.[17] At the same time dominance in herring fishing was increasingly challenged by boats from Germany, the Netherlands and Norway which raised their catches between 1920 and 1938 while Britain's catch fell.[13] Although Aberdeen continued to account for about 70 per cent of Scottish white fish landings between the wars, the industry suffered from the higher cost of coal and its distance from the main markets. These factors, together with low prices, meant that Aberdeen owners experienced the highest financial losses among the five major fishing ports in Britain between the wars. Increased use of road transport helped to offset the extra rail costs imposed on fish landed at Aberdeen, but by 1935 there was a real anxiety that Aberdeen would be unable to keep its place in the British fish trade.[14]

By 1950, after years of inter-war neglect, the fishing industry was handicapped by a run-down and out-of-date fleet of vessels, a large proportion of which were still coal-burning. Out of 197 ships operating from Aberdeen, 172 had been built before 1929 and of these 154 had been built before 1919. Between 1945 and 1950 Aberdeen yards built 30 trawlers but only five of them were for local owners. When owners were able to expand their businesses they followed pre-war practice and bought second-hand vessels from other ports. Some owners had decided to sell during the war to take advantage of the increase in capital value, so there were fewer trawlers operating out of Aberdeen in 1950 than there had been in 1939. The slender financial base of many firms did not allow them ready access to capital or encourage new investment, especially given the overcapacity in the industry. In 1950 there were 105 fishing firms, 67 of which owned just a single ship. In addition to the fragmented nature of the fishing fleet, the subsidiary services of salesmen, merchants and curers were in a similar atomistic disorganised state.[15] Accordingly, the industry proved incapable of any really concerted action in response to competition from other ports, or increased landings from foreign vessels, although some companies were still very successful. In the 1960s and 1970s the fleet size remained fairly stable at just over 100 vessels, and there was some renewal of vessels, aided by government grants. But, in the early 1970s, catastrophic decline set in.

The immediate causes of recession were low quayside prices, high fuel costs following the Arab–Israeli war of 1973, restricted access to fishing grounds, and the imposition of quotas on landings. In a final burst of frustration at what was seen as government inactivity and betrayal, Aberdeen fishermen took part in the national blockade of ports, including Aberdeen, in April 1975.[16] However, this demonstration could do nothing to avert the long term reduction of the Aberdeen

David Craig b.1916

David Craig left Robert Gordon's College at 15 to join the family trawling company George Craig & Co., and secured his skipper's ticket at the age of 21. During the Second World War he served in the Navy on minesweeping and anti-submarine patrols. He remained at sea until 1960 when he opted for an administrative role on shore. By that time the company owned ten trawlers. He served as chairman of the Aberdeen Fishing Vessel Owners' Association, and as vice president of the British Fishing Federation. He was closely involved with the Royal National Mission to Deep Sea Fishermen as chairman of the local advisory committee and as a member of the national council. In 1978 he was awarded an OBE.

trawler fleet from 161 in 1958 to 25 by 1980, while between the same dates the tonnage of fish landed fell from 98,100 to 15,600 and its value fell by 79 per cent. Although the depletion of fish stocks and quota restrictions on catches played a part, at the root of the problem lay competitive failure rooted in a lack of investment. While the industry in Aberdeen shrank to a fraction of its former size, sections of the industry in other ports of the region held on to their market position. The decline at Aberdeen was in the larger 'deep sea' vessels of over 80 ft, whereas the other ports of the North-East retained their fleets of smaller coastal vessels.[17]

The Shipyards: A Struggle for Survival

Before 1914 the Aberdeen shipyards had come to depend on fishing industry orders. In the Great War the yards were fully employed, both in converting existing vessels and fulfilling orders to design and build minesweepers. A few special types were selected by the Admiralty, and Hall, Russell & Co. was parent of the 'strath' type of ship and Alexander Hall & Co. of the drifter type of minesweeper. Their construction was not limited to Aberdeen and vessels of these designs were copied by shipbuilders in other parts of Britain. Immediately after the return to peace, local yards were kept busy as Admiralty orders gave way to civilian orders to replace wartime losses, augmented by those orders that had been deferred because of war. Although the demand for fishing vessels never approached pre-war levels, for a few years the yards enjoyed full employment building cargo boats. One of the largest of these was the *Maryland*, built in 1921 for the Det Forende Company of Copenhagen. At 360 ft in length this was one of the largest and heaviest cargo boats built in Aberdeen and it operated on the transatlantic route. However, post-war depression cut orders and for Aberdeen, like all shipbuilding centres, the 1920s and 1930s were lean years, the last remaining part of the Duthie shipbuilding interest at Torry was forced to close in 1925. The expansionary phase of the Aberdeen fishing industry was almost over and, by the mid-1930s, 38 per cent of the stock of the port's fishing vessels was more than 25 years old.[18] However, Aberdeen yards still retained the ability to produce modern fishing vessels, as several large and powerful trawlers 200 ft long were built, for owners in France and Spain, to operate in the Newfoundland cod fishery. But foreign orders were never enough to make up for the decline in domestic demand. In the 1920s employment of all kinds in shipbuilding and marine engineering in Aberdeen fell by one-third.

The collapse of the demand for fishing vessels led Aberdeen yards to seek new customers. The strategy for survival adopted by the shipbuilders took the form of a moderately successful search for alternative markets, although this still left about half the productive capacity unused.[19] Alexander Hall & Co. specialised in orders

The Acklam Cross,
a Hall, Russell &
Co. ship, c. 1933.

for dredgers and hopper barges, and also built many tugs, both steam and diesel
engined. Two suction dredgers built for the James Dredging Towage and Transport
Co., the *Foremost Chief* and the *Foremost Scot* were used in the reclamation work
required to extend Southampton docks. Hall, Russell & Co. tended to build more
passenger vessels including the passenger and cargo steamers required for the
North of Scotland and Orkney & Shetland Steam Navigation Co., a business
connection that went back to 1883. The last vessel built for this purpose before
the war was the *St Clair*, completed in 1937, which had all the characteristics of a
modern medium-sized passenger steamer. But the firm also built other vessels. The
Acklam Cross completed in 1933 was the first diesel electric tug built in Britain, and
the sailing yacht *Trenchemer*, built in 1934 for the leisure market, came second in
the Fastnet Race that year. Four boom defence vessels were built for the Admiralty,
but Aberdeen shipbuilders found it harder to secure military orders than yards
elsewhere.[20]

Some shipyards prospered by combining fishing with shipbuilding. The John
Lewis yard opened at Torry in 1907 as a base for trawling. In 1927 the yard built its
first steam trawler, and soon extended production to include coasters and colliers.
Between the wars 15 steamers were built for John Kelly of Belfast. By the late 1930s
the yard had secured Admiralty contracts for corvettes, and later produced tank
landing craft. After 1945 the firm returned to building trawlers, including the
world's first fish factory steam trawler launched in 1954. The 1950s represented its
best decade and, in 1959, the Montrose Shipyard Co. was taken over. Shortage of
space in this yard also limited production to smaller ships with a maximum length

of 300 feet and about 3,500 tons dead-weight. In the 20 years after 1945 orders were completed for about 140 vessels for customers in Iceland, the Faroes, Norway, Canada, France, Panama, Pakistan and Australia, as well as for British owners.[21] But in 1972 the trawling and fish distribution divisions of the company were sold to British United Trawlers and the Torry shipyard passed into the ownership of the John Wood Group.

In the 1950s the main demand was for bulk carriers. In that decade Hall, Russell & Co. built ships up to about 9,000 tons dead-weight and about 450 ft in length. The firm sought to compensate for restrictions on the size of ship it could build, imposed by the absence of space to extend the yard, by building a wide variety of specialised vessels, such as bulk sugar carriers supplied to Silvertown Services Shipping to carry raw sugar from the West Indies to the Tate & Lyle refineries at Plaistow in Essex. Another bulk sugar carrier was built for the Adelaide Steamship Co., and a vessel able to carry liquid molasses in side tanks was built for the Colonial Sugar Refining Company of Australia. The *Esso Preston* was built as a

Workers leaving Hall, Russell & Co. in the 1950s as shipbuilding experienced its final phase of decline.

specially designed steam tanker to carry liquid bitumen. In 1953, Hall, Russell purchased the share capital of Alexander Hall and Co., bringing the two companies, once again, into close co-operation.[22] Shipbuilding in the city suffered its final demise in the 1990s. Hall, Russell & Co., after some expansion of its premises in the 1960s, was nationalised by the Labour Government in 1977 and then offered for sale in 1984 under the Conservative Government's privatisation plans. In 1986 it was acquired by a local consortium, Aberdeen Shipbuilders. But the viability of the yard, which had come to depend heavily on defence orders, was undermined by a government announcement in 1985 that no further naval work would be placed there. After two years struggling for orders the yard closed in 1988 and, after passing through the hands of two further shipbuilding concerns, both from outside the North-East, the yard and its equipment was auctioned off in May 1993.[23]

The Decline of Granite

In 1918 the granite industry had high hopes of a revival in the domestic market based on war memorials, and anticipated a building boom that would further help recovery. But there was no substantial revival of the building industry in the 1920s, and the granite industry entered a period of protracted decline. In part, it was caused by a fall in demand for major constructional projects like harbours and bridges, although in the 1930s there was some revival of the demand for Aberdeen polished slabs for the frontages of banks, insurance offices and shops. But the home market faced other more serious problems. Before 1921 no manufactured monumental or architectural granite was imported, but in that year there were substantial imports of granite, heralding competition from German, Czechoslovakian and Finnish manufacturers of gravestones and memorials. The industry reacted to this competition by experimenting to improve product finishes, such as the introduction of the mirror polish, and by attempts to increase productivity.[24] What really determined the fate of the industry was the fact that labour costs in the Aberdeen yards were often considerably higher, and the hours worked often fewer, than in competing continental countries. Even the introduction of tariffs on imports after 1932 could do little to counteract huge differences in productivity. By 1939 import duties on raw granite were 10 per cent, which actually added to the costs in those yards using imported granites, but even duties of 30 per cent on finished work did not prevent continental imports undercutting the prices of Aberdeen yards. In 1920 the industry expected it would eventually be able to restore some of its position in export markets, but throughout the inter-war years it was unable to compete with generally lower wages abroad, import tariffs in practically all export markets, and government subsidies in some countries. By 1939 Aberdeen's granite export trade was all but dead.[25] There was a sharp drop in the number of granite manufacturing businesses in the 1920s, and the number of firms in the city was reduced from 85 in 1919 to 49 by 1939.[26] Those firms which moved into the heavy construction sector of the industry fared better. In the later years of the nineteenth century William Tawse & Co. had engaged in extensive construction work in the Aberdeen area, renovating the harbour, building roads and constructing the Girdleness sewage scheme. Between the wars the company concentrated on road and bridge construction, building roads through the Great Glen and Glencoe.

The years of attrition continued after 1945. By 1958 the number of firms belonging to the Aberdeen Granite Association had shrunk to 34. A new reason for decline was the change in architectural fashions. In the inter-war years there was still a strong market for slabs of polished granite up to 2 inches thick for public buildings, but demand for this style of commercial embellishment receded in the immediate post-war years of austerity, although in the 1950s there was a revival of demand for thin granite slabs as a facing material for the head offices of banks and similar buildings. But the resumption of imports of finished granite and competition from yards in Devon and south-west Scotland made further inroads into the business of the Aberdeen firms.[27] In the 1960s a few companies, such as the Pittodrie Granite Turning Co., survived by catering for niche markets. This firm had originally been established in 1912 to produce columns for buildings and with the decline of this fashion in the inter-war years had concentrated on the production of granite rollers for the paper industry. By the 1960s it was turning out rollers over 30 tons in weight and 27 feet in length. In addition to plain rollers for the paper industry in Scotland, Europe and North America, the firm manufactured a variety of other industrial rollers for the paint and foodstuffs industry, including chocolate, as well as some grooved rollers used in the production of galvanised wire for the main cables of the Forth Road Bridge which was under construction in the 1960s. Granite was an ideal material for this purpose as the galvanising process required the wire to pass through tanks of acid.[28] In the post-war years the quarries at Kemnay and Rubislaw concentrated on the manufacture of bricks and composite building blocks known as fyfestone, as they no longer produced granite suitable for monumental or ornamental architectural work. At Rubislaw production costs rose to unacceptable levels and the quarry that had produced the foundation materials for the Forth and Tay rail bridges and a large proportion of nineteenth-century Aberdeen, finally closed in 1970. In 1975 the link with locally produced granite was broken when 500 tons of French granite were imported to Aberdeen to be used partly to face the new Town House extension, and partly for the gravestone and monument trade. It was estimated that this would provide enough stock for two years work in the remaining half-dozen city granite yards.[29] The Aberdeen Granite Association folded at the end of 1983. By 1987 there were only two firms left in the city processing granite, employing together only about 120 workers, A. & J. Robertson (Granite) Ltd and John Fyfe (Concrete and Quarry Products) Ltd.[30]

PAPER MANUFACTURE

The paper mills initially were able to maintain their market position in spite of the increased competition from imported papers. In the 1930s local mills had a capital of around £2,000,000, and employed 3,500 workers of whom 60 per cent were males.[31] In comparison with mills farther south that were closer to coal mining areas the Aberdeen firms were worse off as about £40,000 in transport costs was added to their combined fuel bill. The Donside paper mills developed their manufacture of newsprint by selling overseas, and by the early 1920s were exporting a large tonnage to Commonwealth countries, with regular consignments of 1,500 tons going direct from Aberdeen to Australia.[32] Wiggins Teape continued to extend its range of commercial stationery production for overseas and domestic markets, with the Union Works in Aberdeen concentrating on envelopes while the manufacture of other items was transferred out of the city in the early 1930s to the firm's factory in London.[33]

One successful local firm which expanded its operations by taking over sites outside the region in the process of becoming part of a large conglomerate was the Davidson paper mill. By 1978 it had become part of the Davidson Radcliffe group, a wholly owned subsidiary of BPB Industries, comprising nine companies with twelve manufacturing sites throughout the United Kingdom. At the Mugiemoss site over 1,200 people were employed making paper sacks, refuse bags, paper liner for plasterboard, and packaging cartons.[34] But not all establishments survived the process of take-over. The Culter Paper Mills Company became part of a group which included the Guardbridge paper mill in Fife and was called Culter-Guardbridge Holdings. However, when the decision was taken by the Guardbridge group to reduce the number of its sites it was the Deeside plant that was closed in 1981. The mill was demolished and the site of Aberdeen's longest serving paper mill was turned into a private housing development.[35]

COMPETITION AND SURVIVAL

The experiences of some of the major sectors of the local economy in the twentieth century demonstrate the multifaceted pressures faced by the modern company. Some businesses survived by introducing new technologies. In the inter-war years the Aberdeen Combworks suffered from depressed trade, partly due to slack exports and reduced domestic demand, accentuated by changes in women's fashions in the 1920s, and severe competition from cheap Japanese celluloid combs. The firm responded by diversification of production into combs made from a cheaper composite material, marketed under the trade name 'keronyx', which it also used to manufacture a variety of shallow moulded goods like shoe-horns, spatulas, drinking cups, letter openers, toothpicks and nail cleaners. In addition, as keronyx was fireproof, unlike celluloid which was highly inflammable, it was sold to other firms for the manufacture of fancy goods, buttons, pocket knife handles and electrical insulators. Under further competitive pressure the company commenced injection moulding of plastics in 1937, with a complete range of combs and other domestic items such as egg cups, egg spoons, containers, bathroom tiles, and cutlery trays.[36] The remaining representatives of the textile industry, Richards and Crombie, both managed to survive the inter-war depression. Richards experienced another crisis in 1934, mainly as a result of mismanagement but provoked by a decade of slack trade. This necessitated refinancing the firm and imposing a new board of directors and fresh managers.[37] In the depth of the depression Crombie & Co. modernised the machinery and layout of most of the works, scrapping over 300 older looms and investing in 200 new Hattersley looms, demolishing rambling and inefficient buildings that dated back to the eighteenth century, and installing a modern weaving shed with a steel roof. This resulted in a smaller, but more efficient firm, and still one of the largest woollen manu-facturers in Scotland.[38] Other companies survived through their traditional links with the natural resource base of the region. The Caledonian Milling Co. and Scottish Agricultural Industries both included among their products animal feed manufactured from waste material provided by fish processors, while food processors Robert Lawson & Sons, Dyce, established in 1934, was capable by the 1960s of killing and processing 6,000 pigs a week, providing employment for 200 people.[39]

Some manufacturers were able to take advantage of new developments to compensate for the loss of traditional markets. Furniture making was a nineteenth-century workshop industry that was adversely affected by an influx of cheap mass-produced articles from factories in the south. But one local firm of cabinet makers, J. & A. Ogilvie, successfully moved into the production of seating and all types of furniture for public places of entertainment like theatres and the growing number of cinemas. In 1914 this firm had begun by furnishing the city's first purpose-built cinema, La Scala. When it gained the seating contracts for the Capitol (1931) and His Majesty's (1932) theatres respectively, it became the North-East's largest supplier of theatre seats and fittings. Other companies survived by an increasing reliance on contracts for office furnishings and public contracts such as those for the new Royal Infirmary in 1936.[40]

Another strategy for survival was to merge in order to take advantage of economies of scale and to secure an enhanced competitive position. The construction firm of Alexander Hall & Son, which had started in 1880, sought and received co-operation from William Tawse & Co. in the 1960s. These two companies, which were already large, worked together successfully on a number of greenfield sites before examining the possibility of a more formal pooling of resources. Each company had already acquired substantial financial holdings in three other public companies working on the fringes of the building and civil engineering industries: John Fyfe & Co., initially granite quarriers but now with wide interests in the supply of building materials, G. W. Bruce & Co., a precast concrete manufacturer, and Lewis Middleton & Co., a civil engineering contractor. In 1967 these firms came together to form the Aberdeen Construction Group. The rationale of the strategy was to achieve a sufficiently large-scale operation to enable successful competition against the national giants of the building industry in bidding for large public works contracts and development schemes.[41] Some companies, like the timber firm of John Fleming & Co., sought to secure survival by buying out competitors in the same trade. The Morayshire sawmills at Elgin were taken over in 1958, followed by the firm's oldest Aberdeen rival, George Gordon & Co., in 1959, and James Walker & Co. of Inverness in 1962. These purchases were followed by further expansion in the take-over of J. Watt Torrance & Co. of Glasgow and Grangemouth in 1968 and Hay & Co. of Lerwick in 1975.[42] One of the most successful amalgamations of local companies began in 1955 when John Wood bought out the other shareholders in the Aberdeen ship repair company of Wood & Davidson. By a process of acquisition and fresh investment the firm developed three main divisions in the 1960s and early 1970s, respectively in fishing, engineering, and general industries. By 1974 the John Wood Group had become one of the largest private industrial companies in Scotland operating over 50 trading companies with a turnover of £18 million and 1,750 employees. With 15 years' experience of rapid expansion, much of it linked to harbour-based enterprises, this conglomerate had become one of the few Aberdeen companies to have established the necessary economic base to take full advantage of the opportunities offered to providers of locally based services by the advent of North Sea oil after 1970.[43]

As the scale of businesses grew, the pressure to create ever larger and more fully integrated firms, controlled through a national headquarters, in Edinburgh or London, increased. Financial institutions were particularly vulnerable to such amalgamation, and in 1950 the North of Scotland Bank disappeared in name when it was taken over by the Clydesdale Bank. This change was more illusion than reality, as the North Bank had been owned by the Midland Bank since 1924, so that the disappearance of the name of the last Aberdeen bank was only a symbolic

Sir Thomas Jaffrey, chief executive of Aberdeen Savings Bank, 1892-1929 and leading philanthropist, in a portrait by W. Orpen.

break with the past. Before it finally disappeared the North Bank had some 160 branches, seventeen in Aberdeen itself, two in London, and the rest scattered throughout Scotland, particularly in the more important farming and fishing villages of the North-East.[44]

Some local firms were absorbed into national concerns, like Scottish Agricultural Industries, which became a subsidiary of Imperial Chemical Industries. The local soap firm of Ogston & Tennant, which had been formed from the merger of two hitherto major Scottish companies in 1898, was eventually taken over by Unilever, the detergent giant.[45] After almost 70 years of independent operation, the Great North of Scotland Railway lost its identity in 1923, when it became the Northern Scottish area of the London and North Eastern Railway. The GNSR had offered more than just trains and provided a comprehensive service for the city and its region. It had been one of the earliest railways to develop feeder bus routes as well as a comprehensive carrier business using steam lorries. Its non-rail services had included the ownership of three large hotels, two in Aberdeen and one at Cruden Bay which had its own adjoining golf course.[46]

The Economics of Structural Change

The transformational difficulties of the Aberdeen economy were partly caused and then exacerbated by the erosion of the resource base of the region, the severe restrictions upon the realisation of economies of scale, and the relative isolation of the city from major population centres. The city produced none of the new consumer goods that were to become items of high mass consumption in the immediate post-war years, such as automobiles or household electrical goods like televisions, radios, vacuum cleaners and kitchen equipment. These industries required a far larger market base than the North-East of Scotland had ever been able to provide, and a far more diversified industrial structure than Aberdeen's to sustain them. A national survey of manufacturing industry in Scotland, undertaken in the early 1950s showed that, out of a total of 565 large firms, only 17 were located in Aberdeen itself, although there were a further five elsewhere in the North-East. Of those in Aberdeen, six were connected with the paper industry, five with shipbuilding or engineering, three were in textiles, two served agriculture and the remaining one manufactured boxes, chiefly for the fishing industry.[47] The region suffered from external control more effectively through financial constraints than from take-over at board room level. One agency set up after the War by the principal banks in England and Scotland to provide capital for small to medium-sized businesses was the Industrial and Commercial Finance Corporation. It did not even have an office in Aberdeen until September 1974 but, operating from Edinburgh, it already had a sizeable number of Aberdeen and North-East firms among its customers before it moved into premises in the city.[48]

Against a general background of higher levels of unemployment than the national average and doubts about the future growth of some of Aberdeen's industries, several studies were conducted into aspects of the local economy in the 1950s and 1960s. There was considerable anxiety that the area was so dependent on primary production that the annual fall in the employed labour force in agriculture and fishing would constitute the main problem in the future, and that there existed a need to attract new industries to counteract this.[49] As 17.5 per cent of Grampian's labour force was employed in agriculture, forestry and fishing in 1961, whereas the figure for Great Britain as a whole was less than 4 per cent, there was some substance to this fear.[50] In 1969 the *Chamber of Commerce Journal* observed that since 1859 there had been at least eight reports written about the state of the city and its hinterland, excluding the annual state of industry and trade surveys printed in the *Chamber of Commerce Journal*, and the local press.[51] The report on the investigation carried out by a group headed by Professor Maxwell Gaskin in the mid-1960s provided a detailed snapshot of Aberdeen and the North-East on the eve of the discovery of North Sea oil.[52] It confirmed the picture of a highly diversified pattern of activities within the Aberdeen employment exchange area but with a higher than average level of unemployment and a persistently slow decline in the population of the city's employment area since the 1930s, although that of the city itself was rising slowly. Shifts within the manufacturing sector had occurred so that the most important industry had become food processing, principally of bacon, meat and fish, followed by paper, textiles and lastly shipbuilding. In other areas of employment fast growth had taken place in the provision of professional and scientific services and also in construction. The size of many industries in Aberdeen remained small by national standards. Although there still remained a mixed textile industry with heavy linen, hosiery and woollens, in 1971 it only employed 2,600 people.

THE GROWTH OF THE SERVICE ECONOMY

The structure of the urban economy, especially as reflected in the distribution of employment, changed dramatically in the twentieth century. As those industries which had provided substantial employment before 1914 struggled against decline, new sectors emerged and offered alternative forms of employment. The service sectors were prominent in this structural change. The growth of services in the modern economy had many different causes. In part, they reflected the growth of social services and welfare provision through local government, the health service, education and housing, each of which is considered separately in later chapters. Other services reflected the increasing complexity and affluence of society, as in the growth and diversification of the distributive trades and in the expansion of the professions.

Changes in the pattern of distribution and retailing between the wars were a continuation of the retreat from the smaller nineteenth-century type of shop with its highly localised customer base. The Northern Co-operative Society had long played an important part in the lives of many citizens. In 1861 the amalgamation of two existing co-operative societies created the Northern Co-operative Society which opened a small corner shop in the Gallowgate. Like all retail co-operative societies it traded with the aim of supplying its customers with good-quality goods at moderate prices on a cash-only basis. The original capital was £1,000 in £1 shares, which shareholders

Poster advertising the Northern Co-operative Society's shops in Aberdeen and district, 1932. The Northern was for long one of the most successful of co-operative societies.

DO YOU KNOW?
THAT IN ABERDEEN AND DISTRICT THERE ARE

Co·op **32** GROCERY SHOPS
AND IN EACH YOU WILL FIND THE SAME HIGH-QUALITY GOODS.

★ SPECIALLY BLENDED TEAS ★
AT PRICES TO SUIT ALL POCKETS

FRAGRANT & REFRESHING	YOU'LL ENJOY THIS
PER 1/8 LB.	PER 2/- LB.
HOUSEHOLD FAVOURITE	FINEST BLEND
PER 2/4 LB.	PER 2/8 LB.

SERVICE BUILDS GOODWILL — AND GOODWILL PAYS A BIG DIVIDEND!

SHOP AT THE **CO-OP**

could buy in instalments. Profits were divided between shareholders in proportion to their purchases with the company. It was soon able to expand from its Gallowgate premises, opening up a chain of shops throughout other districts of the city. The Northern Co-operative Society, which became a limited company in 1918, followed a similar path to the other multiple stores. It was immediately successful, paying good 'divis' and, by 1918, the Society had 87,000 members, which meant that one in every two Aberdonians was a shareholder. After the Second World War there developed a marked trend towards larger units, and an increasing concentration of trade in the main thoroughfares of Union Street and George Street, where a wider choice of goods was available in large modern shops, and away from the small local shops of the residential districts. As a result the small shop-keeper lost ground to the Northern Co-operative Society, the multiple shop and department store. These highly capitalised businesses also had a network of delivery vans to take goods to people's homes, enabling them to keep contact with their customers as the suburbs expanded and population shifted from the more congested inner areas of the city. It was still possible, however, for the individual business to prosper.

Similar tendencies towards enlargement and amalgamation were experienced in the retail and distributive trades after 1945. The immediate post-war years were probably the high point of the phase in which the city-based retailer operated from premises in the city centre. Some of these organisations also had large networks of branches that stretched well beyond the suburbs into the regional hinterland. In the grocery trade two city firms together had 45 branches, in the meat trade three firms had 41 branches, and in the bakery trade five firms had 95 branches. In the early 1950s there were thirteen departmental stores in the city, eight in or near Union Street and the remainder in the vicinity of George Street and St Nicholas Street. The wide choice of goods at low prices available from these

---

Thomas 'Cocky' Hunter 1867–1925

Born in Water Lane, off Virginia Street, Thomas Hunter left school at the age of 13 and was employed by a fish dealer operating in the small coastal villages between Aberdeen and Collieston. He later worked as a boiler maker in the shipyards in Aberdeen and West Hartlepool. He returned to Aberdeen in 1903 and opened a second-hand furniture store on East North Street. In 1908 the business had prospered sufficiently to warrant a move to larger premises on Commerce Street. Several of his 16 children also engaged in a variety of retailing trades. At his funeral, the coffin was carried by fellow boiler makers, and a large crowd lined the streets to pay their respects.

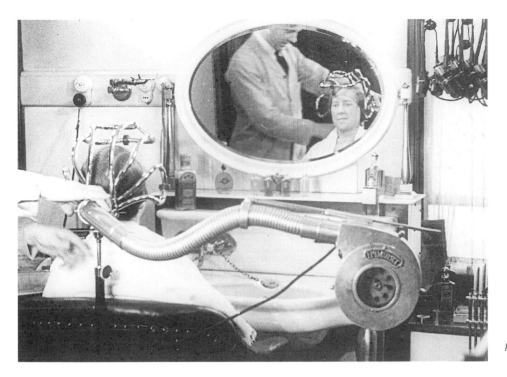

Isaac Benzie's department store advertised one of the many services which it offered women in this still from the film Out for Value, *1931.*

Edwardian beach scene: the bathing station, Aberdeen. The clothes worn proclaim the bracing air.

THE BATHING STATION, ABERDEEN

establishments made the centre of Aberdeen the principal shopping centre not only for the city itself but for the region. These larger stores such as Isaac Benzie's, Falconer's, Watt & Grant, and Esslemont & Macintosh, served customers as far away as, Peterhead, Fraserburgh, Banff, Speyside, and Orkney and Shetland. They offered a postal delivery service for those at a distance from the city, and a day's entertainment for those who lived near enough to the city for a personal bus, rail or car trip to be convenient.[53] Many of these stores were still locally owned but various national store groups became visible in Aberdeen after 1960. But it was still possible for small businesses with a strong local base to survive in the very long term. Jamieson & Carry, continuously trading since 1733, provides an obvious example. This business was started in Broad Street by a silversmith and passed into the ownership of the Jamieson family in the middle of the eighteenth century. William Carry joined the partnership in 1881, extending its range of activities as he was a jeweller. In 1907 the Carry family became sole owners.[54] Esslemont & Macintosh remains the one department store to remain in local, and family, ownership.

LEISURE AND TOURISM

Insofar as the North-East developed an early specialised service industry, tourism must take pride of place. In the Victorian period the city was a gateway to the

Women in the early 1900s board the omnibus to Market Street, having enjoyed the delights of the bathing station.

The GNSR advertises its hotels.

'Royal Highlands' for royalty and aristocracy mainly intent on enjoying the field sports. A few of these people might stay in Aberdeen for a short time and the Palace Hotel in Union Street had a private suite of rooms for Queen Victoria. With improvements in public health the incidence of epidemics was reduced, and from the 1880s it became possible to persuade local residents to remain within the town for more of the summer without endangering their health, as well as to tempt some outsiders to stay there for purposes other than business. Sea bathing from the beach dated from the 1830s, but the beach bathing station there did not open until 1895. The existing swimming baths in Constitution Street thus became redundant and the building was converted to become a tram depot. For those who preferred the sea, a 'qualified rescue' service was provided. In the 1890s the foundations of Aberdeen's popular tourist industry were laid. During bank holidays the beach was particularly busy and on spring bank holidays around the turn of the century, held on the first Monday in May, extra tramcars to Torry and the beach bathing station were always needed. In addition to those who thronged the improved facilities within the city, there was also an increased demand for access to places beyond, and during the holidays passengers left Aberdeen station for destinations which included Deeside, Buchan, Arbroath, Edinburgh, Glasgow and Loch Lomond. By 1908, between 1 July and 30 September, the Great North of Scotland Railway was advertising its 'Three Rivers Tours'; a series of day trips by train from Aberdeen combined with motor and charabanc tours of sites and places around the upper reaches of Deeside, Donside and Speyside, returning to Aberdeen by rail in the evening.

By the early 1920s, during the shooting season as many as 70 sleeping car passengers might reach Aberdeen in a morning. Some would choose to have a bath and breakfast at the station before proceeding straight to estates, mansions and hotels on Deeside and beyond. Others, if they wished to remain in Aberdeen for a day or two, could stay either at the Palace Hotel, which had 81 bedrooms and was frequently used for balls and public dinners, or in the more restrained Station Hotel in Guild Street which catered more for families and commercial visitors. At that time both hotels were owned by the GNSR.[55] There were further developments between the wars with the appearance of a network of cheaper boarding houses designed to cater for a growing number of working-class holiday makers. Throughout the inter-war period Aberdeen was particularly popular with Glaswegians, who arrived at the station in large numbers for the Glasgow Fair holiday.

However, there were limits to this expansion. The cool climate and the consequently shorter holiday season, as well as distance from other large population centres, made it difficult for Aberdeen to compete on an equal basis with towns in the warmer south. Nevertheless, in spite of its geographical disadvantages, the number of insured persons employed in hotels and boarding houses rose between 1923 and 1937 from 1,080 to 1,850.[56] As an encouragement to visitors, both the London Midland Scottish Railway and the London and North Eastern Railway issued tickets in the summer months at special holiday and excursion fares from a number of towns to Aberdeen.[57] The working-class holiday makers, arriving by train and without access to personal transport, needed to make Aberdeen the base from which part of their stay would be spent in short trips further afield. In the 1920s the city transport department began short bus tours of

an hour or two in and around the town to give visitors an impression of the Granite City's special sites and activities. In addition, and in competition with the railways, there were at least three private coach hire firms who offered cheap Deeside day trips to Balmoral and Braemar, as well as to popular beauty spots in Aberdeenshire and Kincardineshire.[58] One of the arguments put forward in 1927 in support of a direct road link between upper Deeside and Speyside from Braemar through Glenfeshie to Kingussie, was that it would bring more day excursion routes within the reach of tourists from Aberdeen.[59]

The beach in its heyday in the late 1950s.

By the 1920s, for those who decided to stay in the city, the parks were described as 'numerous and finely laid out' and the construction of the beach esplanade made both the Links and bathing station more accessible to visitors, and neither money nor effort was spared to popularise the whole of the beach area.[60] In the 1930s boating and fishing were added to the attractions of Aberdeen bay, and a total of four 18-hole golf courses at Balgownie, Murcar, Balnagask and the Links provided opportunities for a further recreation that could be enjoyed on dry land but within sight of the sea. In addition, there were tennis courts, bowling greens and 'every form of indoor amusement'.[61] This development of a general environment to attract tourists was linked to the further progress of municipalisation, which catered both for the needs of permanent residents as well as the summer visitor. By 1938 the city's public parks and sports grounds covered 656 acres, children's playgrounds 58 acres, and golf courses, football pitches, school playing fields and other open spaces, including the Links, extended to 1,019 acres.

In the inter-war years a total of £61,000 was spent on the beach's entertainment buildings which included the ballroom, the bathing station with a swimming pond and private baths, and £108,000 on improving and extending the esplanade.[62] Municipal improvements also acted as a stimulus to private investment, which on the eve of the war also numbered among its attractions Mark Cordona's carnival pleasure park with its 'scenic railway', built in 1929, 'chair-o-planes', and 'automatic speedway'. At this establishment it was optimistically claimed that, 'the holiday maker could spend many a carefree afternoon and evening at ... infinitesimal cost.'[63]

In the immediate post-war years the majority of visitors still had no access to personal transport and the array of rail and coach trips to the surrounding countryside was still needed.[64] In 1948 the town council established a publicity department to advertise the general amenities, advantages and attractions of Aberdeen. Although not solely concerned with tourist advertising, the department issued copies of the accommodation register, holiday guides, and publicity leaflets in response to postal enquiries, as well as advertising in newspapers and on display posters. By the mid-1950s the local register of hotels, boarding houses and guest houses contained more than 700 addresses and the growth of Aberdeen as a holiday resort led to the opening of a number of new private hotels and boarding houses, as well as a number of private caravan parks on the outskirts of the city,

For women the textile industry remained an important source of employment. These women are hank winding at Richards Mill, 1978.

and a municipal one at Hazlehead. A survey by the Scottish Tourist Board showed Aberdeen to be the most popular resort in Scotland and the publicity department dealt with approximately 20,000 personal enquiries per annum.[65]

As part of the campaign to attract visitors in the 1950s, the city continued to place strong emphasis on the beach, a feature which had always figured prominently in inter-war publicity drives. But by now more use was made of slogans, with Aberdeen described as 'the silver city with the golden sands' with a climate that was 'bracing, dry and healthy'.[66] Even stronger emphasis was placed on the bus tours provided by local authority transport which, at the peak of this activity, advertised no less than eleven separate routes lasting from one to two-and-a-half hours. They now covered every possible permutation of city, suburb and immediate hinterland, and even included one excursion exclusively devoted to the city's inter-war and post-war municipal housing schemes. But by the early 1960s the range of attractions offered by the city had begun to look unexciting and traditional. More holiday makers had their own transport, and, like all British resorts, Aberdeen began to notice the first effects of the boom in foreign holidays. In 1964 a typhoid outbreak severely reduced the number of summer visitors, and it was realised that there was a need to improve and modernise the image of the city. As a result more emphasis was placed on organised events held in the city's open spaces and a properly managed holiday calendar was introduced. This series of events, which began as the Aberdeen Festival Fortnight and evolved into the Bon-Accord Festival, involved the recognition that the average tourist of the late 1960s demanded higher standards of entertainment and was no longer content simply to brave the rigours of the beach. Instead, more emphasis was placed on

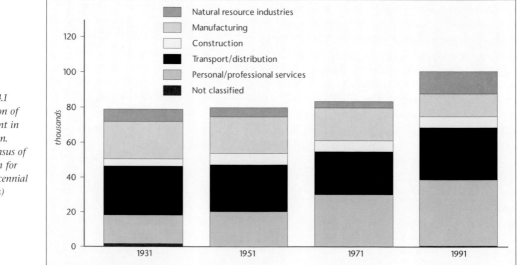

*Figure 4.1
Distribution of
employment in
Aberdeen.
(Sources: Census of
Population for
Scotland, Decennial
Reports)*

ABERDEEN 1800–2000

indoor attractions like the reconstructed Winter Gardens and Hazlehead Zoo, and on light cultural events like pipe band competitions, folk-song and popular orchestral concerts. Some of the more remarkable features of the local economy like the fish market and Rubislaw quarry continued to act as attractions.[67]

THE ECONOMY ON THE EVE OF OIL EXPLORATION

Against this background of declining traditional industries the city economy remained surprisingly buoyant. Before the advent of North Sea oil, the explanation was to be found in Aberdeen's broad industrial base which spared both the city and region from some of the high levels of unemployment that were experienced by other regions suffering from de-industrialisation. As late as 1973 one commentator, rather implausibly, listed the increased prosperity of fishing, higher prices partly compensating for the decline in landings, as one reason for the general prosperity of the region. Further advantages included the substantial expansion of employment in food processing and the continued rapid growth of employment in the service sector. Thus the manufacturing sector was squeezed by competitive pressure, especially after the Second World War, and was replaced as the mainstay of local employment by personal, professional and distributive service industries.

5

The Oil Economy

DAVID NEWLANDS

THE GROWTH OF THE OIL INDUSTRY

Many of Aberdeen's traditional industries have been based on the exploitation of natural resources. The same is true of its newest major industry, oil. Although only significant in the last thirty years of the twentieth century, the oil industry came to dominate the Aberdeen economy and will probably continue to do so well into the twenty-first century. There were three distinct periods in the growth of the industry, its establishment in the late 1960s and early 1970s, the period of uninterrupted growth from the early 1970s to the mid-1980s, followed by recession in the mid-1980s and renewed growth in the mature phase of the industry's development.

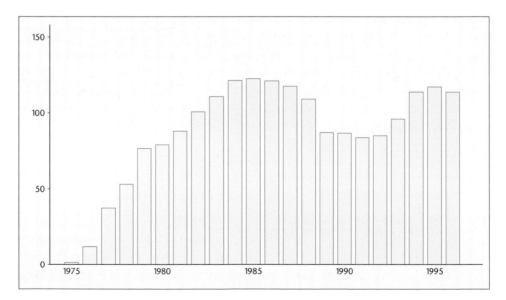

Figure 5.1
UK North Sea oil and gas production (million tonnes), 1975-96.
(Source: Scottish Office, Scottish Economic Bulletin)

The first discovery of oil or gas in the North Sea was the British Petroleum (BP) West Sole gas field in 1965. This was discovered in the relatively shallow waters of the southern North Sea and was serviced from English ports, notably Great

Yarmouth. Thereafter, as improvements in technology permitted work in deeper waters, the focus of the oil companies' attention shifted to the northern North Sea. The first discoveries of commercial quantities of oil in the British sector of the North Sea were in the Montrose field in 1969 and the enormous Forties field in 1970. Most of the large oil fields were discovered in the first half of the 1970s including Auk and Argyll in 1971, Piper in 1973, Claymore in 1974 and Brae in 1975.

Oil production consists of several distinct processes: exploration, drilling, extraction and transportation of petroleum products for processing on shore. A complex structure of companies was involved in oil production. There were the oil companies themselves, such as BP and Shell, often termed the oil majors. Then there were the multitude of firms which supplied various products and services to the oil majors and which were collectively known as the oil supply industry. They can be classified according to the phase of oil production in which they are involved. The exploration phase involves surveying, exploration and appraisal drilling. The oil majors did some of this work themselves but most was contracted out to the large drilling companies, a number of which were based in Aberdeen. The development phase involves the construction, installation and equipping of offshore production platforms, the laying of pipelines and the building of onshore terminals. Very little of this work was done by firms based in the Aberdeen area. Most of the construction companies which were involved in this phase were based in the Highlands, at Ardersier or Nigg, on Clydeside or Tyneside, or abroad. The operating phase involves the running and maintenance of the platforms once production has begun. The firms which received work from the oil companies in this phase included suppliers of drilling equipment, supply boat and helicopter operators, diving companies, employment agencies, catering firms and suppliers of a wide range of other goods and services. Many of these firms were based in Aberdeen with a smaller number based in Shetland. While there were suppliers of a large variety of products used in oil production in Aberdeen, very few of these products were manufactured locally.

THE OIL INDUSTRY IN ABERDEEN

The oil industry did not transform Aberdeen overnight. Indeed, the beginnings of the industry which was soon to dominate Aberdeen almost went unnoticed. In the year that oil was discovered, 1969, the *Press and Journal* devoted just 33 words of a sixteen page *Review of the City of Aberdeen* to exploration for oil and gas.[1] The Gaskin Report, a major government-sponsored study of the North-East published in the same year, did not even mention the oil industry.[2] Aberdeen did, however, have very considerable advantages over other potential locations during the exploration phase.

When oil prospecting started in Scottish waters in the mid 1960s only four ports could provide the 24-hour all-year-round availability needed by survey and supply vessels – Grangemouth, Leith, Dundee and Aberdeen. Of these, only Leith and Aberdeen had air services adequate to the needs of the industry and, of all four, Aberdeen had the best accessibility to the sea areas being searched and was very seldom closed by bad weather.[3]

Pressure on Aberdeen harbour for quay and storage space escalated after BP's discovery of the Forties field in 1970, and prompted serious consideration of alternative sites. BP transferred its marine operations to Dundee in 1971 and a service base was created at Peterhead harbour. Somewhat later, in 1975, the peak year for exploration activity, capacity problems in Aberdeen led the oil companies and drilling contractors to use other ports including Lerwick, Montrose and Peterhead. However, these transfers were temporary and, as capacity pressures eased, companies returned to Aberdeen.

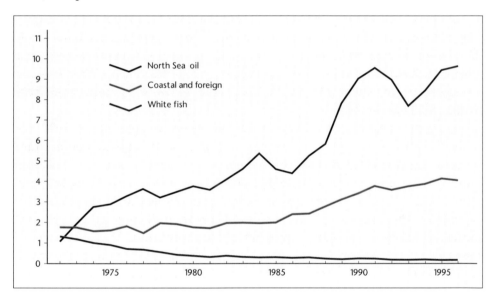

Figure 5.2
Aberdeen harbour:
tonnage of vessels
cleared (000 gross
tonnes), 1973-97.
(Source: Aberdeen
Harbour Board,
Annual Reports)

The oil industry had to be accommodated in a harbour which at the time was still a major fishing port, an active commercial port, and the site of two shipbuilding yards. At first, the burden of handling the oil service vessels fell mainly on Pocra Quay and Maitland's Quay East. Then, in October 1971, Aberdeen harbour board decided upon a major investment programme involving the reconstruction of the quays in the Victoria and Upper docks and the removal of their dock gates to make the entire harbour tidal. Harbour board investment was supplemented by private development. In the early 1970s, five new quays were constructed by private interests. Four were marine bases for individual companies and the other was a multi-user facility. Oil developments did not just put additional pressure on quay space. Warehousing and office accommodation close to the harbour was also in short supply. However, the harbour board encouraged firms for which a facility close to the harbour was not essential, to move elsewhere while other firms moved away of their own accord. Initially, many of the service bases were simply adaptations of existing warehouses and factories. Then, in the early 1970s, once it was recognised that the oil industry's presence in Aberdeen was not to be a fleeting phenomenon, newer premises better suited to the particular demands of the industry were built. While some were close to the harbour, many others had to be accommodated on industrial estates elsewhere in the city. Moreover, the rate of expansion was such that the oil companies and other large businesses often had to find several premises. The new industrial estates were crucial to the establishment of the oil industry. It was fortunate for the industry that the town council in the 1960s had secured substantial areas for these estates, only a short distance to the south of the harbour. More recently, an extension of the city boundary south eastward made possible a rezoning for industry of further land at Altens. The Farburn estate at Dyce was almost fully allocated at a single meeting of the Aberdeenshire planning committee in 1972.[4] At the same time, a shortage of land within the city encouraged developers to look further afield, to the south, north and north-west. The new industrial estates were filled very quickly.

Industrial developments to the north of the city were notable for the establishment of an oil-related manufacturing capacity. Subsidiaries of three American oil tool manufacturing companies, Vetco Offshore, Baker Oil Tools, and Smith International, set up at the Bridge of Don. The airport provided a twin and complementary focus to the harbour in the establishment and development of the oil industry at Aberdeen. There was rapid growth in the number of scheduled and charter flights. Helicopter traffic grew particularly quickly. The number of passengers increased from 135,000 in 1970 to 450,000 in 1974. On the other hand, limited handling facilities constrained the growth of freight traffic other than for fairly small items. Access to the airport was an important factor for firms at the neighbouring industrial estate, operated by Aberdeenshire county council. These included firms involved in oilwell testing, directional drilling, underwater engineering and other highly specialised activities. Subsequently, a number of private property companies sought to develop sites near the airport. In a very important development, BP established its United Kingdom exploration and production headquarters at Dyce.

During the exploration phase in the late 1960s and early 1970s, a comparatively small number of companies were involved and on a relatively modest scale. Shell's first office in Aberdeen consisted of a few rented rooms above the Church of

The harbour was gradually developed in the 1970s to cope with supply vessels.

The oil boom brought many new offices to the city. The Amerada Hess building, Hareness Road.

Scotland Bookshop in Union Street, while BP had a similar base in Bridge Street. Gradually, more of the oil companies established a permanent presence in the city to supervise exploration. From 1970 onward, this included a significant number of American companies. Once Aberdeen had become established as the principal exploration base and the oil majors had opened offices in the city, firms in the oil supply industry saw an advantage in being located nearby. Oil companies expected their suppliers to be close at hand so that the quality of production could be easily monitored and any problems with materials and services which arose could be sorted out quickly. In addition, oil supply firms in Aberdeen were in the best position to learn of new orders, to identify the precise specifications of the product or service sought by the oil companies, and to bid successfully for those orders. The economies generated by the concentration of a large number of oil supply firms in the same location contributed to the rapid consolidation of

Sir Maitland Mackie 1912–1996

Educated at Aberdeen Grammar School and Aberdeen University, Maitland Mackie started farming at Westertown in the Garioch, Aberdeenshire, in 1932. He served on Aberdeenshire county council 1951–75, and was convener 1967–75. He was chairman of the North East Development Authority 1969–75, the Aberdeen Milk Marketing Board 1965–82, Peterhead Bay Management Co 1975–86, and Hanover (Scotland) Housing Association 1981–86. His directorships included Scottish Telecommunications 1969–85, and Aberdeen Petroleum 1980–96, and Aberdeen Cable Services 1983–87. He was a governor of the North of Scotland School of Agriculture 1968–82, and of the Rowett Institute 1973–82. He served on the agriculture subcommittee of the UGC 1965–75, the Scottish Council for Development and Industry, chairing the oil policy committee and playing a distinctive role in the early development of the oil industry in the region. He was awarded the CBE in 1965, KStJ 1977, and knighted in 1982. He was a JP, and served as lord lieutenant of Aberdeenshire 1975–87.

Aberdeen's dominant position as the principal onshore centre for the North Sea oil industry. The rate of growth was astonishing. In October 1971, there were an estimated 56 firms in Aberdeen and district for which oil-related business was the principal activity. By October 1972, this had risen to 109 and by October 1973 to 217. At this time, two oil supply firms each week were arriving in Aberdeen or being founded or transferred from some other line of business.

There has been some debate about the inevitability of Aberdeen's establishment as the main centre for the oil industry. Some commentators have emphasised the crucial role of the local authorities in the area which

> have been willing and able to provide the necessary infrastructure and support to attract oil-related companies to the area and to keep them there. This has been particularly important in relation to landfall industrial development and offices, the ease and speed in obtaining planning permission and the improvement of transport facilities at the harbour and the airport.[5]

The response of local government certainly did Aberdeen's case no harm. However, with hindsight, it is probably fair to conclude that only monumental failure to respond to the opportunities offered by the public authorities and private developers would have led the oil companies and oil supply industry to have gone elsewhere. Such were the inherent advantages of the location of the city and the facilities it offered.

EMPLOYMENT AND EARNINGS

There is a paucity of good statistics relevant to the economic impact of oil on the Aberdeen area. There are no statistics relating to output, investment or profits. There is information on the number of firms and on wages but it is very limited. The main statistics on the impact of oil relate to employment and unemployment. However, there seems little reason to believe that the trends revealed by the employment figures would be contradicted by other indicators. Oil-related employment in the North-East constituted a large proportion of the Scottish total, over 60 per cent in most years. Moreover, about 90 per cent of oil-related jobs in the North-East were located in Aberdeen itself. Peterhead was the only other location within the region where there was a significant number of oil-related jobs. The increased number of such jobs in Aberdeen reflected trends in both offshore and onshore employment. Those who worked offshore might live in the Aberdeen area but would be more likely to live in northern England, central Scotland, or elsewhere. The pattern of working two weeks offshore, followed by two weeks onshore leave, was established at an early stage and meant that offshore workers could continue to live two or three hundred miles from Aberdeen.

During the 1970s and early 1980s, more and more offshore workers moved to make their permanent home in the North-East. In some cases, these were workers who might be called upon to go offshore at short notice. However, most were employees who simply believed that the medium term future of the North Sea industry was secure and recognised that Aberdeen would remain the dominant onshore base. Nevertheless, it has been estimated that, even in 1985, only 37 per cent of offshore workers were permanently resident in the region. In the recession in the oil industry following the collapse in world oil prices in the mid-1980s, that proportion fell to 32 per cent in 1987. The number of onshore oil workers increased steadily until the mid-1980s as Aberdeen became the centre for the North Sea oil supply industry. The growth of onshore employment was particularly marked as the offshore platforms entered the operating phase of production, from 1975 onward.

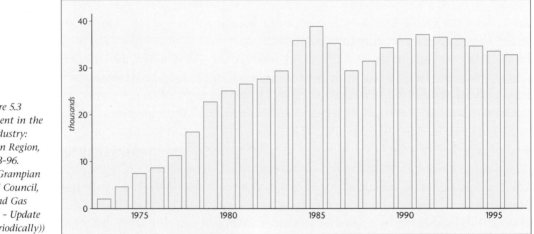

Figure 5.3
Employment in the
oil industry:
Grampian Region,
1973-96.
(Source: Grampian
Regional Council,
Oil and Gas
Prospects – Update
(issued periodically))

The arrival of the oil industry in Aberdeen created thousands of jobs directly but also had a significant indirect stimulative effect upon the local economy. The increase in the number of people in employment, and earning high incomes, gave a boost to the local economy. Some of the increase in income was spent on the purchase of locally produced goods and services. This, in turn, led to greater employment in the provision of those goods and services, generating a further round of employment and income creation. Increased spending provided a big boost to retailing and to the hotel and restaurant sector. At the end of the 1960s, there were a number of empty shop premises in Union Street and on the southern part of George Street, but from 1973 onward these shops were rapidly occupied. Eight new hotels opened in Aberdeen in the 1970s and most of the others expanded. The number of hotel rooms increased by 27 per cent between 1970 and

1975 and by 58 per cent between 1975 and 1980. The number of city centre restaurants, excluding those in hotels, also increased rapidly in the 1970s from 17 to 36. In addition, the growth in the population of the area provided an indirect boost to employment and income. The provision of public services such as education and the health service is related more to population than to income. Therefore, as the population of the Aberdeen area grew as a result of oil developments, so too did the demand for publicly provided services.

In the 1980s an attempt was made to calculate the size of the so-called multiplier effect by which jobs created in the oil industry had an additional impact upon total employment.[6] The estimated figure, for 1981, was 1.78. This means that, for every 100 jobs in the oil sector, a further 78 jobs were created in local shops, pubs, restaurants, hotels, transport, schools and hospitals. With the inclusion of these jobs in non-oil industries, the total employment generated by the oil industry in 1981 was 40,560. The number of oil-dependent jobs represented a very high proportion of total employment in the North-East. In 1981, there were 196,800 employees in Grampian Region and 144,905 employees in the Aberdeen employment office area. More than one-fifth of the jobs in Grampian Region were attributable, directly or indirectly, to oil and more than a quarter of total employment in the city itself was dependent on oil. The oil industry continued to grow very rapidly until the slump in world oil prices in 1985 and 1986. The estimate reported above would suggest that the number of oil-dependent jobs was 68,890 in 1985. In that year, more than 40 per cent of the workforce in Aberdeen relied upon oil. The effect of the enormous boost to the Aberdeen economy, both directly and indirectly, from the oil industry was that unemployment in the city fell. More particularly, unemployment in Aberdeen was low compared with the Scottish average, especially in the early years at the beginning of the 1970s.

Many of the jobs created by oil in Aberdeen were well paid. Earnings in the oil sector, both offshore and onshore, were much higher than in non-oil industries, with average earnings in the oil industry being about 1.67 times those in non-oil industries.[7] Of course, working conditions were very different. Oil workers were often highly skilled, worked long hours, and spent long periods away from home, particularly in the case of people working offshore. The work could be physically demanding and even dangerous. This was especially true for offshore workers. Nevertheless, even making allowances for these differences, earnings in the oil industry in Aberdeen were clearly above the average for the area and for Scotland as a whole. The result of the establishment of the oil sector in Aberdeen was that average earnings in the city increased considerably by comparison with the rest of the country, at least for men.

The earnings of men in Aberdeen were well below the national average in the early 1970s. As the level of oil related employment grew, and as the higher earnings of oil workers began to have a greater impact, so the earnings of men in Aberdeen rose to 15 per cent or more above the national average. The comparison of the earnings of women in Aberdeen with female earnings elsewhere is more complicated. Account has to be taken of the fact that many more women than men were employed only on a part-time basis. Nevertheless, it is clear that the oil industry did not provide women with many well paid job opportunities. The jobs which women obtained were not in the core occupations which offered the best rates of pay but in peripheral service areas which had traditional low wage levels.

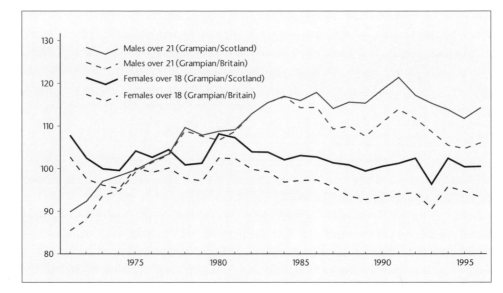

Figure 5.4
Average weekly earnings in Grampian Region, 1971-96. (Source: New Earnings Survey)

THE EFFECT ON THE INFRASTRUCTURE

Oil developments were associated with some marked changes in the infrastructure of the Aberdeen economy. The harbour board invested in improved facilities, notably in the form of better-serviced quays and the provision of two 'roll off/roll on' terminals. The use of the harbour by oil supply vessels increased markedly in the 1970s at a time when other demands upon the harbour were declining. The airport was completely transformed. The number of aircraft movements increased fivefold in the 1970s and the number of passengers increased tenfold. By the late 1970s, the Aberdeen-Sumburgh route was the busiest in Europe. In April 1979, there were 1,050 aircraft movements between Aberdeen and Sumburgh compared with 900 betweeen London Heathrow and Paris. Aberdeen became one of the busiest heliports in the world. The number of helicopter passengers grew from 15,000 in 1972 to 226,000 just five years later. There was substantial investment in the airport itself. A new £3.5 million terminal was completed in 1977. This, and a greater

One of the busiest heliports in the world. Oil workers disembark from a helicopter.

frequency and range of destinations of scheduled flights, conferred an additional benefit to non-oil business passengers and to domestic passengers. On the other hand, the quality of road and rail links deteriorated in the 1970s. Government funding was not provided to upgrade the main road south of Aberdeen despite large increases in the volume of traffic. Similarly, British Rail did not invest in the east-coast line and lost freight traffic to the roads as a result.

THE HOUSING MARKET

The 1970s and early 1980s witnessed a rapid increase in the demand for housing in Aberdeen. The arrival in the city of thousands of new people together with the rise in average incomes put pressure on all available housing. There was an increase in the number of people looking for rented accommodation, including council housing, but the sharpest rise in demand was for houses to buy. Much new housing was then built, primarily by private firms. To some extent, this was simply a reflection of the pattern of increased demand, but the concentration upon building for sale rather than for rent was also due to government restrictions on funding which limited the building programmes of the Scottish Special Housing Association (SSHA), Aberdeen district council and the other district councils in the North-East.

Although there was an expansion of private housebuilding in Aberdeen, it always lagged behind the increase in demand for housing. House building in the Aberdeen area happened to be at a low level in the early 1970s. In addition,

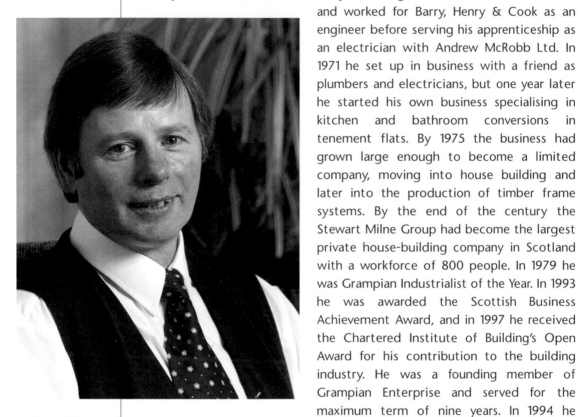

Stewart Milne b. 1950

Born at Torphins, Stewart Milne was brought up at Tough, attending Tough Primary School and Alford Secondary. At the age of 15 he moved to Aberdeen and worked for Barry, Henry & Cook as an engineer before serving his apprenticeship as an electrician with Andrew McRobb Ltd. In 1971 he set up in business with a friend as plumbers and electricians, but one year later he started his own business specialising in kitchen and bathroom conversions in tenement flats. By 1975 the business had grown large enough to become a limited company, moving into house building and later into the production of timber frame systems. By the end of the century the Stewart Milne Group had become the largest private house-building company in Scotland with a workforce of 800 people. In 1979 he was Grampian Industrialist of the Year. In 1993 he was awarded the Scottish Business Achievement Award, and in 1997 he received the Chartered Institute of Building's Open Award for his contribution to the building industry. He was a founding member of Grampian Enterprise and served for the maximum term of nine years. In 1994 he became a director of Aberdeen FC, and was appointed executive chairman in 1998.[8]

Stewart Milne, builder, created the largest private house-building company in Scotland in the quarter of a century from 1975.

at the very time the local house building firms needed more people to build more houses, they lost large numbers of workers to oil-related construction ... It was not until large outside firms – such as Barratt and Wimpey – moved in with their own itinerant labour that the level of new building improved significantly.[9]

Moreover, the shortage of land in the city meant that most new building was in the suburbs, such as Bridge of Don, Cults and Cove, or in surrounding towns and villages, such as Ellon, Inverurie, Kemnay, Banchory, Westhill and Stonehaven, the populations of which grew substantially during the 1970s and 1980s. The result was that available housing in Aberdeen did not increase sufficiently to match the growth of demand. For over ten years, house prices in the city rose much faster than elsewhere and, not surprisingly, the gap between house price inflation in Aberdeen and elsewhere was greatest in the early 1970s when the arrival of people in the city to take up jobs in the oil industry was at its peak.

The effect of above average increases in house prices was that, while houses were rather more expensive in Aberdeen than in many other parts of Scotland before oil developments, by the early 1980s they were very much more expensive. In 1983, the price of a three-bedroomed semi-detached house in Aberdeen was 64 per cent above the British average.[10] The rapid increase of house prices in Aberdeen was probably due almost entirely to oil development, with the implication that oil provided house owners in the city with a windfall gain as they saw the value of their property rise. It has been estimated that the average windfall gain between 1971 and 1983 was over £15,000 per house.[11] This increase in personal wealth affected a large number of people since the number of owner occupiers in Aberdeen in 1971 was nearly 23,000. Approximately 5,000 new owner occupiers bought houses in Aberdeen between 1971 and 1983. They too made a windfall gain although obviously it was smaller the later the date that the person concerned entered the market. The sharp increase in house prices represented a gain to established owner occupiers in Aberdeen but, simultaneously, they became the source of major housing problems for others. Shortage of housing, high house prices, long waiting lists for council houses, and high private sector rents combined to make it very difficult for young couples and others wishing to enter the housing market to find an affordable place to rent or buy.

DISPLACEMENT AND DETERRENCE

The output and employment of certain non-oil firms were less than they would have been were it not for the growth of the oil industry. Those sectors already in difficulty experienced an acceleration in their decline. Some firms seeking to maintain or expand output were unable to do so. The establishment and expansion of the oil industry created a considerable demand for labour in Aberdeen. Some of the new jobs were filled by migrants to the city and some by people who were previously unemployed, but the availability of well-paid jobs in the oil sector also proved attractive to people employed in other industries. Firms in the non-oil sector experienced a number of difficulties as a result. According to one report,

We have established that a significant number of companies in the indigenous manufacturing industries in the study areas faced higher labour turnover, recruitment problems, labour shortages, and increasing labour costs (sometimes accompanied by declining quality of labour), during the 1970s. These problems were created by the labour market disruption caused by oil related activity.[12]

It might be expected that firms experiencing difficulty in recruiting or retaining labour would respond by increasing the wages they offered. There is evidence that this happened. An annual survey of non-oil earnings in Grampian Region in the 1970s showed wages increasing faster than the national average. Non-oil earnings rose from 78 per cent of the Scottish average in 1974 to 84 per cent in 1978. McDowall and Begg suggested three reasons why some firms might not have chosen to increase wages. Firstly, some firms in Aberdeen were subsidiaries of larger companies and wages were negotiated nationally for the whole group. Secondly, the management of some firms made a deliberate decision not to compete directly with oil-related companies in a wages 'rat race', adapting to consequent shortages of labour by reducing the skill content of the work or by substituting female for male labour. Thirdly, the Government's incomes policy which operated from 1972 to 1974 created a number of problems for firms in Aberdeen. The policy did not provide for exceptional wage increases to reflect labour scarcity. In theory, the incomes policy should have constrained incoming firms as much as established ones but, in practice, new firms found it relatively easy to evade the incomes policy. They were required to pay the 'going rate' but this could seldom be defined. Those firms which could not, or would not, increase wages to counter the attraction of jobs in the oil sector naturally faced the most severe labour shortages but this was a widely experienced problem. There was a diversity of experience. Printers and skilled workers in the paper industry tended to remain in their existing jobs while fitters, welders and instrument mechanics, whose skills were more readily transferable from one industry to another, tended to be more attracted by opportunities in the oil sector. The growth of the oil industry also increased the demand for commercial property. Office rents rose faster in Aberdeen in the ten years after 1973 than in any other place in Britain and by the early 1980s Aberdeen was the fifth most expensive location outside London for commercial property.[13]

Two other factors contributed to the displacement effect. There were a few years in the early 1970s when non-oil firms found it very difficult to obtain certain services locally. Frequently quoted examples were delays in getting equipment repaired and problems in finding electricians, builders and painters. In addition, firms in the area ceased to be eligible for assistance under the terms of regional policy. In 1978, Aberdeen was downgraded from having full development area status to become an intermediate area, and even this status was lost in 1982. Firms in industries such as paper making, textiles and food processing found that grants and loans, which were available to their competitors in other parts of the country, were now denied to them. There was an attempt to measure the displacement effect by making a comparison between the two periods, 1971–1976 and 1976–1981. This found that a number of industries in Aberdeen had rates of growth lower than the national average for those industries. In particular, fishing, food and drink, clothing, building materials, and timber and furniture experienced a faster decline in employment in both periods than might have been expected given national trends. In addition, the chemical, shipbuilding and leather industries, as well as professional and scientific services, had a faster decline, or slower growth, in employment between 1971 and 1976 than the national average for those industries, and the same was true of papermaking for the second period, 1976–81. Two main points emerged from these results. Firstly, it was mainly manufacturing industries which experienced faster than expected decline. This was consistent with the view that competition from the oil industry for labour and property most severely affected manufacturing firms. Secondly, there was a strong displacement effect in the earlier of the two five-year periods. The national economic recession of the late 1970s and early 1980s led to an easing of labour and property shortages, and thus of the displacement effect of oil developments.

It may be, of course, that the relatively poor performance of these various industries was due to factors other than the pressure of oil developments. The fishing industry was very seriously affected by the exclusion, in 1977, of its trawler fleet from traditional Arctic fishing grounds after Iceland, Norway and the Faroes extended their fishing limits to 200 miles. In addition, until its abolition in the mid-1980s, Aberdeen was the only Scottish port covered by the national dock labour scheme which laid down staffing levels covering the employment of fish porters, and it was claimed that the scheme increased the landing costs of boats in Aberdeen.[14] It has been estimated that, for every 100 jobs created by the oil industry in Aberdeen in the 1970s, eight jobs were lost in traditional industries. By 1981, displaced employment amounted to more than 3,000 jobs. Only about 25 per cent of these were absorbed by the oil sector. This implies that some 2,500 of the 6,207 people who were added to the unemployment register in Aberdeen in the 1970s lost their jobs as the direct result of oil developments.

The displacement effect related to the adverse impact of oil developments on established firms in Aberdeen but there was a further related phenomenon, the deterrence effect. High labour and property costs and the absence of regional aid may have deterred new firms which might otherwise have come to Aberdeen. This deterrence effect is not easy to measure. Nevertheless, there are indications of its operating especially in new industries. The best example was provided by electronics, which in Aberdeen and the North-East was very much under-represented. In 1976, the main locations of the electronics industry in Scotland were in Strathclyde, which had 50 per cent of total Scottish electronics employment, in Lothian which had 24 per cent, and in Fife which had 17 per cent. The situation did not change greatly after 1976.[15] These employment figures do not prove that electronics firms were deterred from setting up in the North-East but they are certainly consistent with that argument. Were it not for oil developments, the Aberdeen area might, particularly given the number of graduates in electronics and computing from Aberdeen University and the Robert Gordon Institute of Technology (RGIT), have been an attractive location for electronics firms.

Ownership and Control

In the 1960s, most businesses in Aberdeen were locally owned and controlled with only a few examples of external ownership. Among the latter were a number of the paper mills controlled by larger British concerns such as Wiggins Teape, and the meat products company Lawson of Dyce, taken over by Unilever in 1966. The pattern of ownership of industry in Aberdeen changed radically as a result of the arrival of the oil industry. From the beginning, most of the firms involved in the oil supply industry were incomers to the area. The proportion of local firms was 29 per cent in 1970 but fell to 22 per cent in 1979.[16] A survey conducted in 1984 suggested that the figure had fallen to as low as 11 per cent.[17] Indeed, only 20 per cent of firms were Scottish. Not only were there comparatively few local firms, they tended to be involved in the more peripheral, less specialised areas such as retailing and transport. American-owned companies dominated such specialised activities as oil exploration, drilling, well stimulation, and electrical and electronic engineering.

Despite this evidence, some commentators felt that the development of the oil industry showed Aberdeen entrepreneurs in a good light, and that 'Aberdeen has taken initiatives which would not have occurred elsewhere in Scotland'.[18] Certainly, there are a few examples of Aberdeen companies grabbing the opportunities afforded by the development of the oil industry. The best example is the Wood Group which expanded as an offshore supplier and rapidly moved into other areas, although the very frequency with which it is cited as evidence of the entrepreneurial prowess of Aberdeen business suggests that it is one of the exceptions that prove the rule.

The *Sunday Times* list of the 100 richest Scots, published in 1999, showed 12 entries from Aberdeen and its hinterland, the majority of which reflected fortunes made in the oil industry. Sir Ian Wood took pride of place with assets which placed him in the top 150 wealth holders in the United Kingdom. Others who prospered in the oil industry included Alasdair Locke, chief executive of Kelt Energy and later

Sir Ian Wood b. 1942

Educated at Robert Gordon's College and Aberdeen University, he joined the family engineering firm, John Wood & Sons, in 1964. In 1967 he became chairman and managing director of the John Wood Group PLC, and chairman of JW Holdings in 1981. He won the Scottish Free Enterprise Award in 1985 and the Scottish Business Achievement Award Trust Award in 1992. He was awarded a CBE in 1982, and a knighthood in 1994. He accumulated an extensive record of public service having served on the harbour board, the offshore industry advisory board, and the offshore industry export advisory group. He also served on the Scottish Development Agency, the Scottish Economic Council, the Scottish Enterprise Board, the Scottish Higher Education Funding Council, and the Sea Fish Industry Authority. He chaired Aberdeen Beyond 2000 and Grampian Enterprise, and served as a director of the Royal Bank of Scotland.

Sir Ian Wood, one of the few home-grown entrepreneurs who seized the opportunities presented by the oil industry.

of the Abbot Group. James Milne, owner of the Balmoral Group, manufacturers of marine equipment, Klass Zwart, owner of Petroline Wellsystems, toolmakers for the industry, and Ian Suttie, owner of the Orwell Group which provided oil services, were also included. The established firm of George Craig & Sons moved successfully from trawling to the provision of standby vessels, while Stephen Bond transformed a family crop-spraying business into a helicopter service to take advantage of the oil boom. Less directly, the Stewart Milne Group benefited from the impact of the oil industry upon the construction industry.[19]

GAINS AND LOSSES FROM ECONOMIC CHANGE

Additional employment was the major benefit of the growth of the oil industry. However, the oil sector was a highly specific occupational structure and this was reflected in the pattern of job opportunities in Aberdeen. Whereas the unemployment rate is accepted as a measure of the job opportunities open to men, this is less true of the female unemployment rate. Women are influenced by a wider range of considerations in deciding whether or not to seek work, and more women than men are in a position to withdraw from the labour market completely if few jobs are available. The female unemployment rate is still relevant but a better indicator of the employment opportunities for women is the participation rate. The female participation rate is the proportion of women of working age who are economically active, that is in a job or seeking work. During the period 1971–1981 there was a rapid increase in female participation in Aberdeen, rising from 64 per cent in 1971 to 73 per cent in 1981. This represented a higher rate of increase compared with Scotland as a whole. These figures suggest that there were more employment opportunities for women in Aberdeen than in the rest of Scotland.

The unemployment rates confirm this. In Aberdeen, the female unemployment rate increased from 4.3 per cent to 4.7 per cent in the 1970s while the Scottish average increased from 5.9 per cent to 9.6 per cent. Furthermore, the number of women in full-time employment increased in Aberdeen but fell in the rest of Scotland. In addition, there was a greater than average increase in part-time female employment in Aberdeen than elsewhere. While the effect of oil developments in Aberdeen was to provide many new job opportunities for women in the city, the oil industry itself did not employ many women. Most of the new job opportunities were in those sectors which were stimulated by oil activity, including retailing, catering and entertainment. Moreover, jobs created in these sectors outweighed the loss of women's jobs in traditional industries, such as food processing and textiles, which were subject to the displacement effect.

After the oil industry became established in Aberdeen, there was a considerable increase in average earnings in the city. In 1971, earnings for men were less than 90 per cent of both the Scottish and British averages. During the next 15 years, however, male earnings rose almost without interruption by comparison with the rest of the country. The available statistics strongly suggest that women did not experience the same steady and pronounced rise in relative earnings as men. Adjustment of the average earnings figures to take account of the disparity between the oil and non-oil sectors transforms the picture. In 1979 male earnings in Grampian region were 107.6 per cent of the British average. However, if oil workers are excluded, the corresponding figure was 94.4 per cent. In other words, after nearly ten years of oil development, male workers in Aberdeen who were not actually employed in the oil industry still received average incomes well below the British average. There had been some improvement in their relative position but only a modest one. In 1979, female earnings for Grampian region were 97.1 per cent of the British average. If oil workers are excluded, the figure becomes 92.5 per cent. Thus, the relative earnings of women in the non-oil sector were lower in 1979 than before oil developments began. The creation of jobs in Aberdeen as a result of oil developments favoured men rather than women, and middle-class rather than working-class people. Moreover, the evidence on employment and earnings taken together suggests that the Aberdeen economy, from the beginning of the 1970s until the fall in world oil prices, consisted of an expanding oil sector with a high level of average earnings existing alongside, and largely separate from, a stagnant or declining non-oil sector in which average earnings remained well below the national average.

The impact of oil on the housing market was also very uneven. Established owner occupiers in Aberdeen enjoyed a windfall gain as house prices rose sharply. Many owners did not realise their windfall gain which can only be obtained when the house is sold. Nevertheless, these windfall gains represent a very significant redistribution of wealth from the high income earners associated with the oil industry, whose entry into the housing market caused the rapid increase in house prices, to established owner occupiers. Moreover, many oil workers were migrants to the area while the majority of established owner occupiers were native Aberdonians. The housing market may be seen, therefore, as compensating for the failure of the labour market to diffuse higher oil-related incomes more widely. Many Aberdonians not employed in the oil sector received some of the additional wealth which the oil industry brought to Aberdeen, through the windfall gain they enjoyed as owner occupiers.

This evidence on the differential impact of oil-related developments is complemented by survey evidence of the perceptions people held about the effects of oil. A survey of 800 people drawn from the electoral register in Aberdeen in 1985 asked questions about their views on the effects of the oil industry on them personally and on the city generally.[20] Over 80 per cent of respondents thought that 'oil has been a good thing for Aberdeen generally' and that 'oil has increased job opportunities for Aberdeen people'. However, 50 per cent thought that 'oil has been of little benefit to Aberdeen people' while 42 per cent thought that 'oil has changed the character of Aberdeen for the worse'. Asked about the effects of oil on their own life, 25 per cent of respondents thought it had been 'good' while 21 per cent answered 'bad', 22 per cent 'mixed' and 32 per cent 'no difference'. Mirroring the objective differences according to gender, social class and housing tenure, men were more likely than women, middle-class people more likely than working-class people, and owner occupiers more likely than council tenants to view the effects of oil on themselves as 'good'.

The Contribution of Local Government

Successive British governments have chosen mainly not to intervene in oil production. Their greater concern has been with the balance of payments and tax revenue benefits of oil. The result was that the multinational oil companies had considerable freedom to determine the pace and manner in which North Sea oil was developed. Local authorities in the North-East were not prepared for oil, which is not surprising. Not only did the industry develop extremely quickly in the early 1970s, it occurred at the same time as the introduction of the new structure of local government. The local authorities were also unwilling to delay changes while they prepared a local government strategy. Given the region's experience of long-term population and economic decline, local government did not want to frighten off any new investment.

Could local government in the North-East have behaved differently? The experience of Orkney and, in particular, of Shetland suggests that there was an alternative.[21] When Shetland was first proposed as a base for some oil-related developments, many Shetlanders expressed reservations about the effects of oil on traditional industries such as fishing and knitting, their way of life, and the environment. Shetland county council sponsored a private act of Parliament, passed in 1974, which gave powers not normally available to a local authority. These powers included the right to levy various charges on oil-related facilities which were paid into a reserve fund which was then used to protect, and ensure, a future for traditional industries. Shetland's experience was not identical to that of the North-East. In particular, while central government was prepared to permit a private act of Parliament for an island authority like Shetland, the chance of similar legislation being passed for an area of the mainland like the North-East was much slimmer. Nevertheless, in Orkney and Shetland local government was active in trying to control oil development to limit potentially damaging effects upon the islands. Local authorities in the North-East do not seem to have tried actively to do this.

The new Grampian regional council, which was set up in 1975, followed a policy of trying to disperse oil developments around the region. This was a sensible strategy. Most oil-related activity was based in and around Aberdeen, as were most jobs and higher incomes. Dispersal of the oil industry more widely within Grampian Region could have spread the benefits of jobs and higher incomes more widely while simultaneously reducing the adverse effects of oil arising from over concentration in Aberdeen. The problem with this strategy was that Grampian regional council always flinched from adopting the measures that were required to implement it. In particular, a dispersal strategy could have been built upon a policy of selective planning permission in which a proposed development in

Aberdeen could be refused planning permission to redirect it to another part of Grampian Region where permission would be available. Such a discriminatory planning permission policy was legal in the 1970s and much of the 1980s. If it had been used then, the impact of oil developments on the North-East might have been different, with more benefits and fewer costs.

Aberdeen district council showed more awareness than Grampian regional council of the disadvantages of oil development induced by a high cost of living in the city and a shortage of affordable housing. Throughout the 1970s and most of the 1980s, council house rents in Aberdeen were kept below the Scottish average. Council house rents were subsidised everywhere, but Aberdeen district council provided a greater subsidy than other councils. This low rents policy was useful in cushioning council house tenants from the rise in the cost of living which resulted from oil developments. However, government legislation forced Aberdeen district council to abandon the policy. From the mid-1980s onward, the Government first restricted, and then prevented, local authorities from subsidising rents from the rates. Local authorities were forced to put up council house rents to the levels necessary to cover costs. While rents rose everywhere, they increased in Aberdeen by greater amounts than elsewhere precisely because they had begun from a lower level.

THE RECESSION OF THE 1980s

Through its own growth, and by displacing and deterring other industries, the oil industry came to dominate the economy of Aberdeen. There are risks from such dependence upon a single industry, as were illustrated by the recession in the oil industry in the 1980s which followed the collapse in world oil prices. The activities which were most affected by the fall in oil prices were exploration drilling and the development of new fields. Exploration activity was reduced dramatically when oil prices fell below the cost of developing new fields in deeper or more inaccessible waters. By March 1987, only 22 rigs were operating in the British sector of the North Sea, the lowest level of activity since 1979. Only about 40 per cent of available rigs were in use. The cut in exploration activity provided the most visible evidence of the downturn in business. On several occasions, the string of redundant exploration rigs moored just off the North Sea coast extended from the Firth of Forth to the Moray Firth. However, with the partial recovery of oil prices, the level of exploration activity recovered fairly quickly. By August 1987, the proportion of rigs in use had risen to about 70 per cent. Another response to lower oil prices was the delayed development of new fields. This most seriously affected the engineering and construction companies which built and equipped production platforms. The Scottish Highlands, Clydeside and Tyneside, where the

An oil rig in production.

principal yards were situated, were the hardest hit. The Loch Kishorn yard provided the most prominent casualty.

The recovery of both exploration activity and expectations of future field development between 1986 and 1987 were due to both rising oil prices and enormous reductions in costs. The project cost of the South-East Forties field, which began production in 1987, had originally been $675 million but the final cost was $450 million, a 33 per cent saving. On the Clyde field, the budgeted cost had been $1,370 million whereas the eventual cost was only $825 million, a reduction of 40 per cent. These cost reductions partly reflected continuing technical progress although the identification of new savings became an urgent consideration with the fall in oil prices. However, the reduction in costs also reflected the oil companies' success in passing a large share of the burden of the recession to others. There were job losses within the oil companies, facilitated by the widespread use of short-term contracts and agency labour. Offshore workers were affected, but so too were office staff. For example, Britoil reduced its staff by 35 per cent between June and September 1986. Nevertheless, the vast majority of the job losses in the oil industry itself were in oil supply firms. 'This constitutes an exploitation of the subcontract to enable the multinational corporations to respond to the fall in the world oil price and manage the rationalisation and concentration of its distributional impact upon the offshore suppliers'.[22] Grampian regional council estimated that oil-related employment in the region fell by only 4,100, from 38,700 to 34,600, between 1985 and 1986. However, these figures do not appear to match the estimates of total Scottish job losses or the view of most commentators that 'the direct job loss effect is bound to fall most heavily in the Grampian Region'.[23]

These different impressions are difficult to reconcile, but two considerations are relevant. The first is that job losses did not affect offshore oil workers who lived in the region to the same extent as workers who lived outside it. Many of the 13,000 oil workers who lived outside Grampian Region in 1985 were employed as roughnecks, roustabouts and drilling technicians and these were precisely the occupations where cutbacks were greatest. In other words, many of the job losses were 'exported' to other parts of the United Kingdom and to other countries. The second is that, while oil companies and oil supply firms were concerned to reduce labour costs, such cuts did not necessarily translate into reductions in employment. The oil industry was characterised by the extensive use of agency labour, the employment of many people on short-term contracts, and an extreme hostility to trade unions. All of these combined to make it much easier for firms in the oil industry to react to a downturn in business by cutting wages than was possible in other areas of British industry. Reductions in wage bills may have taken the form of cuts in wage and salary rates rather than job losses to a greater extent than elsewhere.

To the job losses which took place in the oil industry must be added the multiplier effect. For every four jobs lost in the oil sector, three more jobs were lost in the rest of the local economy. In this case, it does not matter whether cutbacks in the oil industry took the form of job losses or reductions in wages. Both had the effect of reducing spending in shops, restaurants or hotels. Total job losses in Grampian Region may have been of the order of 7,000 even if the conservative estimates of Grampian regional council are the most accurate. These job losses created the sharp rise in unemployment during 1986. The unemployment total in Grampian region increased by nearly 6,000 between the beginning of 1986 and the beginning of 1987, an increase of 31 per cent. Most of the job losses occurred in Aberdeen where unemployment total rose by over 4,600, by 42 per cent. In contrast, the Scottish total increased by only 1.4 per cent over the same period.

The fall in oil prices had a significant effect upon the Aberdeen housing market. In the 1970s and early 1980s, the rise in house prices caused by oil development brought substantial windfall gains for existing owner occupiers. The recession in the 1980s put this process into reverse. People experienced cuts in wages, lost their jobs or left the area altogether, at a time when the building of a substantial number of new houses was reaching completion. More houses came on to the market, took longer to sell, and sold at lower prices. House prices fell by 1.4 per cent between June 1985 and June 1986 and by a further 3.3 per cent between June 1986 and June 1987, compared with a rise of 9.3 per cent for Scotland as a whole. Thus, just as the rise in house prices in the 1970s and early 1980s represented a substantial increase in the wealth of people in Aberdeen, so the reversal of the trend of house prices devalued what, for most people, was their most valuable personal asset.[24]

As oil prices rose from the low point in 1986, the Aberdeen economy began to recover from the recession in the oil industry. New jobs were created and incomes began to rise again. In some respects, therefore, the effects of the fall in oil prices can be seen as a hiccup in what was otherwise a continuous period of buoyant oil-related activity. However, the importance of the fall in oil prices provided an illustration of the risks of excessive dependence on the oil industry, which was dominated by large foreign companies with few roots in the local economy. Hence, in any downturn in business, it is not a primary concern of the company to ensure a minimisation of the economic damage imposed upon the local area.

THE OIL INDUSTRY IN THE 1990S

The cost cutting which began almost as a panic response to the collapse in world oil prices in the 1980s subsequently became a central objective of the oil industry. It became known as 'cost reduction in the new era' which allowed the maintenance of high levels of oil production for much longer than most commentators had previously predicted, but also generated fears that cost cutting had been at the expense of safety. The Piper Alpha explosion in 1988 which cost 167 lives was by far the worst accident experienced in the North Sea. The subsequent Cullen Report was supposed to ensure that safety considerations were paramount. Nevertheless, there is evidence that the rate of fatalities and serious injuries were higher in the 1990s than at any other time in the history of the industry in the North Sea.[25]

Apart from these persistent concerns about safety, after the recession the oil industry entered a mature phase. New fields continued to be developed. Indeed, in terms of the number of new fields, the peak year, with eight new fields in development, was 1989.[26] However, cost reduction programmes and a variety of technological innovations meant that new oil developments did not generate the same employment opportunities or rates of pay that they had earlier. From the perspective of the late twentieth century, it seemed likely that growing employment opportunities offshore in future would be related to the decommissioning and abandonment of installations as an increasing number of fields reached the limit of their economic use and ceased production. In the mature phase of production, the North Sea increasingly faced competition from new areas of oil exploration around the world. The North Sea came increasingly to be seen as a 'high cost, modest reward (in new reserve terms) province'.[27] Competition with new oil provinces would be likely to intensify if the low oil prices of the late 1990s persisted into the twenty-first century.

Counteracting these tendencies, the scale of the exporting business of Aberdeen based firms increased steadily. Skills acquired in the deep waters of the North Sea could be applied in new offshore oil provinces, in Canada, China, the former Soviet Union, and elsewhere.[28] Aberdeen also continued to be the beneficiary of office relocations. In 1992 and 1993 alone, BP Exploration was transferred to Aberdeen from Glasgow, Chevron and Texaco transferred functions and personnel to Aberdeen from London, and the Department of Trade and Industry relocated its oil and gas division to Aberdeen from London.

The oil industry continued to dominate the Aberdeen economy in the 1990s and promised to retain that pre-eminence well into the new millennium. Nevertheless, in the late 1990s, there was evidence of the emergence of new major growth centres within the Aberdeen economy. These were all within the service sector. Aberdeen had two universities. Foresterhill was one of the largest hospital complexes in Scotland. Aberdeen was the financial base and the main media centre in the north of Scotland. Transport and tourism also held promise for future employment. The fortunes of some of these service industries were themselves closely linked to those of the oil industry. This was true of the financial sector and parts of the transport sector, the airport being the best example. However, other

Calum A. Macleod, CBE, continued the tradition of linking the legal profession and the business world.

services in Aberdeen, such as health care and education, existed largely autonomously of the oil industry and made increasingly important contributions to the Aberdeen economy. A recent study of the economic impact of Aberdeen University on the North-East found that staff numbers had risen by 30 per cent in the first half of the 1990s.[29] The student population had increased by over 50 per cent during the same period. Direct expenditures associated with Aberdeen University injected £129 million into the North-East economy in 1995–96 but the total financial impact, including indirect knock-on effects, was £187 million, implying a multiplier effect of 1.46. A survey of participation in higher education, undertaken by the Scottish Higher Education Funding Council in 1998, measured variations in a standardised participation ratio, the number of students living in an area in relation to the number who might be expected to be there given national age and participation rates. The

Scottish average was set at 100 and Aberdeen, scoring 137, was the highest in Scotland. In some areas of the city the expected rate was 160 but the actual rate was 526.[30]

THE IMPACT OF OIL

The oil industry brought many benefits to Aberdeen. In the 1960s, there were few well paid job opportunities in the city and people responded by moving elsewhere. Oil development reversed this pattern of outward migration and brought jobs, higher incomes and greater wealth to the city. However, the oil industry in Aberdeen was not the unqualified success story that the image of a 'boom town' suggests. Oil developments involved certain costs, notably the displacement of Aberdeen's traditional industries, a variety of housing problems and the risks of dependence on a single dominant industry. Moreover, the benefits of oil were very unequally distributed. After the recovery from the recession of the mid-1980s, the oil industry entered a mature phase. It no longer offered the same employment opportunities or rates of pay as it did in the period of rapid expansion from the early 1970s to the mid-1980s. Moreover, other growth industries, principally in the service sector, began to emerge. Nevertheless, the oil industry was still the dominant force in the Aberdeen economy at the end of the twentieth century with every prospect of continuing to be so for some years into the new millennium.

6

Working Life in the City

WILLIAM W. KNOX

INDUSTRIALISATION AND SOCIETY

The social effects of industrialisation on Aberdeen were less dramatic than those on Glasgow or Dundee. There was not the mass immigration which altered their social balance in the mid-nineteenth century. The vast majority of migrants to Aberdeen were drawn from the agricultural counties of the North-East, and only a tiny number of Irish immigrants made their way to the city. Less than one in fifty were Irish born in 1851 compared with one in five in Dundee. This allowed the city to escape most of the ethnic and religious tensions which characterised some other parts of Scotland. On the other hand, the slower pace of industrialisation meant that Aberdonians experienced a standard of living below that of the industrial west for most of the nineteenth and twentieth centuries. Aberdeen's different pattern of development has led historians on various occasions to refer to it as a flexible city or a diversified city. Each description has its origins in the economy of Aberdeen rather than the social structure of the city. Looked at from the vantage point of the social structure a better characterisation might refer to Aberdeen as a stable or an unspectacular city. But in terms of its economy and employment structure, the city's diversified economic base would have been welcomed by many other cities.

MASS EMPLOYMENT IN THE TEXTILE MILLS

During the course of the last two centuries, like the rest of the industrial world, Aberdeen has experienced massive and continuous change in its economic and social structure, as has been demonstrated by the frequent restructuring of the city's employment. Information for the first half of the nineteenth century is less abundant or reliable than that compiled later, but there is no doubt about the most outstanding characteristic of the early Aberdeen economy, namely its reliance on textiles.

The growth of the textile factories was itself a manifestation of massive economic and social change. Aberdeen and its rural hinterland had a long

*Messrs A. Pirie &
Sons' Woodside
Works, c. 1886, was
established first as a
cotton mill by
Gordon, Barron
& Co. in 1785.*

association with the linen and woollen trades. Traditionally merchant-manufacturers, like James Hadden, supplied raw material to cottar women knitting stockings in their homes in rural Aberdeenshire and Banffshire and bought back the finished articles at an agreed price.[1] The same system operated in linen manufacture and, in that sector, the practice continued as late as the 1840s. Woollen factories began to appear towards the end of the eighteenth century in places like the banks of the Don at Woodside and Persley, where they could take advantage of the water power of the river. By the first decade of the nineteenth century over 1,500 handloom weavers were employed at the Woodside works and the number doubled over the next two decades. Furthermore the emergence of cotton manufacture brought spinning into factories. The significance of these changes was social as well as economic. No longer could crofting families supplement their incomes with spinning and weaving. Many were pushed into the city to find work, while those who remained found their earnings plummeting. On the other hand, factory labour offered the prospect of increased earnings for women and children as well as men. In the 1790s women in linen mills could earn five to six shillings (25-30p) a week, considerably more than they could have earned at home. The advent of steam power in the 1820s freed the mills from river locations, so that Hadden could build a new woollen mill in the Green, and Bannerman built a cotton mill on the Links. Steam power also gradually allowed the displacement of handlooms by powerlooms. The number of handloom weavers in the city fell sharply from a peak of 3,000 in 1820 to fewer than 1,400 by the early 1830s, with earnings shrinking to well below starvation level. The poet, William Thom, who worked at Gordon, Barron & Co.'s handloom weaving mill in Schoolhill, ' a prime nursery of vice and sorrow' as he recalled, saw his earnings fall so low that he was unable to afford a copy of the *Aberdeen Journal* in which his first poem was published in 1828.[2]

The new mills brought new job opportunities but also new disciplines. The majority of textile workers were single, young women, but men occupied the skilled jobs and supervisory posts such as flax dressers and tenters in the linen industry, and mule spinners in the cotton mills. There was also child labour. From 1819, children under the age of ten were not allowed to work but this restriction was often ignored, ostensibly on charitable grounds and under pressure from parents. The manager of Grandholm mill, Alexander Cooper, testified in 1833 that

… from ten to twelve years is the best time to teach a child to spin, and it takes from three to four years to make a good spinner. It is much more expensive to teach them at a later age, because they take as long to learn and during that time require larger wages.[3]

Some factories dismissed women when they married, others allowed them to remain as tutors to young operatives. But the percentage of married women employed in Aberdeen was the lowest recorded in any Scottish city. Discipline was harsh in the early textile mills and fines were imposed for lateness, singing and talking. Girls spoke of being 'frequently knocked about and kicked' by overseers. However, in spite of these common complaints, working conditions seemed to be relatively better in the cotton factories than in the linen industry. In Bannerman's cotton mill, dressing rooms, lavatories, drinking water, well-fenced machinery, a canteen, a sick fund and a library managed by the workforce were all provided under the paternalistic regime. Few matched the high standards of Bannerman's, although by the 1830s some factories offered canteen facilities. The worst conditions of work seem to have been in the linen mills at Broadford and Spring Garden. Girls attending wet frames were constantly sprayed with hot or cold water, and in the hot, wet spinning department the temperature rose to 100°F. Workers in the textile mills faced long hours tending their machines with the pace of work dictated by the speed of the machinery. The standard working day started at 6 am and ended between 7 pm and 8 pm depending on the number and length of breaks allowed. In effect, work lasted for twelve and a half hours each day, and for six days each week. The mills also worked night shifts, riverside mills needing to take advantage of a high water level to compensate for times when the river was low and power curtailed. The harshness of the regime led to a strike in 1834 when the girls at the Broadford mill walked out in protest against a series of wage reductions.[4]

Combmaking, like cotton, also faced problems connected with the management of labour, by the difficult transition from the domestic system to the factory. Combmakers had previously worked from home suiting themselves as to the effort and hours they worked. Their relocation in a new division of labour within a highly supervised factory regime, combined with rigid working hours, led to incessant conflict in the workplace. As one employer said, 'they resisted, rebelled and left their work on more than one occasion'. Only by persistently cajoling and lecturing the workforce was management able to convince the workers of the 'necessity of consistent labour for ten-hours a-day, six days a week'.[5]

For many young women workers, particularly those coming from the rural areas, domestic service remained a major source of employment well into the twentieth century. Aberdeen, by Scottish standards, had a substantial middle class comprising just under 9 per cent of the total occupied workforce in 1841, a figure that was lower than Edinburgh but much higher than Dundee or Glasgow. In 1861 there were 80 doctors, 170 male teachers and professors, 200 female teachers and 500 commercial clerks working in the city. The sizeable proportion of middle-class professionals in the city called for labourers and servants of all kinds. Over 40 per cent of the occupied female workforce in Aberdeen were so employed in 1841, a proportion which rose to nearly 54 per cent twenty years later. By 1861 there were almost 4,000 female domestic servants, of whom more than one-fifth were under 20.

SMALL-SCALE EMPLOYMENT: FISHING AND GRANITE

As a result of the changing nature of working practices, industrial conflict was endemic in factory-based industries, but the collapse of textiles, and the emergence of fishing and granite as important providers of employment, brought a change in favour of small production units and this reduced industrial conflict. In fishing, before the introduction of the steam trawler, the boats and tackle belonged to the men. However, this arrangement was to prove short-lived. From the 1870s onward the application of steam power transformed the social relations of the fishing industry as it put the cost of ownership beyond the reach of the small fishermen. Larger trawlers were needed to encroach into the rich fishing grounds of the northern waters. This added to the time at sea and the cost of fuel so that fishing became a huge commercial operation requiring substantial investment with the effect that large numbers of previously independent fishermen became employees.

In the first phase of expansion, ownership of the fleet was in the hands of fish salesmen, but as the industry grew the wider business community became involved and the market forces which determined the price of herring became more obviously apparent. Hitherto, the price of a cran had been agreed by the herring fishermen and the merchants, but by the 1880s the price was determined at public auction.[6] By 1900 the great majority of shareholders in the new fishing companies had no previous interest in the industry.

There existed a clearly defined hierarchical structure governing and controlling social relationships within the industry. Below the owner came the skipper who, in the early days of steam trawling, was rewarded with a share in the boat's takings. He also had his own cabin at sea which separated him from the men, and the structure of the trade encouraged him to drive the men hard. On shore, the skipper usually adopted a lifestyle distinct from that of the deckhands by living in the more salubrious parts of Aberdeen, in Rublislaw Den or Ferryhill rather than Torry. Occupying the intermediate position between crew and skipper were the first mate, usually a skilled and experienced fisherman, and the ship's engineer. At the bottom of the hierarchy were the deckhands, a rather disparate group, some with little or no knowledge of fishing, but employed because of labour shortages. The hierarchical structure of fishing was reflected in the wage structure. In 1913, a deckhand received 25p a day when at sea and a bonus of 1 per cent of the ship's net earnings, while the skipper and first mate received a 10 and 8 per cent bonus respectively after the ship's overheads and wages had been deducted. For the deckhand the wages received in a good year could put him on par with a skilled worker, for the skipper the returns could be a great deal higher. Stories of skippers bringing furs, diamonds and pianos for their wives in the prosperous years of the First World War were an established part of the folklore of the industry.

The prosperity of the trawlermen began to diminish after the end of the Great War as white fishing felt the effects of intense competition. The depression in white fishing affected social relationships in the industry as skippers came under increasing pressure to cut costs and maintain catches. Increasingly caught between loyalty to crew and to management, many skippers cultivated an authoritarian ruthlessness. As one put it: 'if you'd been a skipper you have to be like Joe Stalin, that was my idea, trust nobody but yourself'. If a skipper stood up against management he ran the risk of being blacklisted. Tensions also increased as risky practices and low levels of maintenance saw death rates remain high, and chronic sickness and accidents increase, a problem made worse by the long hours of work and high consumption of drink. On deep-water boats duty-free drink, the bond, was a perk added to wages. One ship's engineer recalled in 1918 that a fishing trip would 'start with a sing-song ... everybody ... had a good bucket in ... the men just sit down and get drunk and the skipper can't do anything with them ... it's

The toils of the deep. The crew of the Aberdeen trawler Yorick, *c. 1960.*

their money, it's their drink.' The drunkenness and danger of trawling made it unrespectable as far as many Aberdonians were concerned, an occupation 'nae fit for a dog' and its employees 'a heap of rubbish' with the result that many of the crews were recruited from cities other than Aberdeen.[7] Indeed, even as late as the 1970s, when the trawling fleet was a mere shadow of its former self, most of the places on training schemes for the industry were filled by boys from industrial cities rather than locals.

The initial success of white fishing had repercussions for shipbuilding in Aberdeen. The transition from sail to steam and wood to iron was the most dramatic transformation in the shipbuilding industry in the nineteenth century. The collapse of wooden shipbuilding made redundant not only established firms, but also traditional skills. The failure of the firm of Alexander Hall & Sons at the end of 1869 had a devastating effect on Footdee. Established in the 1780s, under the founder's son, James Hall, it had pursued a paternalistic policy, paying the best wages in the port, being first in the 1850s to concede the Saturday half-holiday, providing an evening school for apprentices, and housing for key workers. Others struggled to survive. The days of sea-going drifters were passing and shipbuilders in the North-East began to concentrate on steam-powered trawlers, with over half of the tonnage built in the period 1886–1914 earmarked for the fishing industry. The construction of steam trawlers called for a wider division of labour and a new range of skills. Carpenters and joiners saw their status fall as metalworkers became the new aristocrats of labour in the yards. As a consequence, demarcation disputes began to emerge as workers competed with each other for certain classes of work. The most serious dispute occurred in 1899 between carpenters and joiners and led to a six-week strike before a compromise was reached.[8]

Steam technology also led to a concentration of shipbuilding capital, with only three yards still operational by 1900, the largest being Hall, Russell & Co., which employed 1,400 men, over half of the total shipbuilding workforce of Aberdeen. In spite of its growth, Aberdeen remained a very small centre of shipbuilding activity compared with the Clyde. During the period 1870–1914 total output of the shipyards of Aberdeen was 337,790 tons, only 2 per cent of the output of the Clyde during the same period. The higher wages on the Clyde also attracted a steady stream of Aberdeen men, particularly after a lost strike for parity of payment in 1910. This began a trend which continued into the inter-war years. In the later period the heavy dependency on the fishing trade led to shipbuilding's demise. Although the yards did their best to diversify into building a variety of ships, employment in shipbuilding fell by about one-third between 1921 and 1931. Lewis Grassic Gibbon poetically remarked that 'Footdee sleeps with silent yards'.[9] White fishing also underwent a crisis in spite of a short-term boom after 1945. The old problem of the need to modernise the trawling fleet remained, with nearly half the trawlers more than 40 years old. It was only in the later 1950s that new and more modern boats were added to the fleet. The new additions, however, did little to halt the decline of fishing. But the processing branch of the industry remained active with 2,000 workers still employed in Aberdeen in the 1990s.

The granite industry was split into two distinct sectors, quarrying and stone polishing, with the latter concentrated within the city boundaries. It also witnessed a transition towards more capital-intensive forms of production, but unlike the other trades this did not involve a greater concentration of ownership. As the preserve of the small capitalist, the granite industry in 1900 had over 90 firms employing 2,500 men and boys, with the largest firm employing fewer than 100 men. The petty capitalist nature of the industry meant that it suffered from few disputes over pay and conditions. Indeed, between 1860 and 1913 there were only four recorded strikes. The industrial harmony which existed could be attributed to three factors, namely the face-to-face relationships in the workshops between worker and employer, the ability of journeymen to achieve master status,

Sir James Taggart, granite merchant and lord provost 1914-19. Portrait by Ambrose McEvoy, 1917.

Sir James Taggart 1849–1929

Born at Coldwells near Inverurie and brought up at Port Elphinstone, James Taggart came to Aberdeen at the age of 16 to be apprenticed as a stonecutter and studied at the Mechanics' Institute. He spent some time in the United States before returning to establish his own business as a granite merchant in 1879 in Great Western Road, initially in partnership but from 1883 on his own account. He represented Ruthrieston on the town council 1894–1919, and served two terms as lord provost between 1914 and 1919. He became celebrated in the First World War for recruiting for the forces and the local artillery brigade was nicknamed 'Taggart's Own'. He served on the University Court, was an active fund raiser for the Sick Children's Hospital and supported societies as diverse as the Scottish Cyclists' Union and the home for widowers' children. He was knighted in 1918.

and the high turnover rate of firms, which saw masters reduced to journeyman status during periods of recession. However, it is possible that high rates of temporary emigration to the United States also reduced tensions particularly at times of economic depression, when wages fell and work was in short supply. An annual 'exodus' of monumental stonemasons left Aberdeen for Vermont each summer between 1865 and 1914, encouraged during trade depressions by their trade union which subsidised the emigrants by as much as £2 a head.[10]

Aberdeen's granite industry suffered considerably during the inter-war years. Capital became more concentrated as the number of firms declined, a trend which undermined the ability of the working mason to achieve employer status. Costs were also rising rapidly. The capital outlay for a medium-sized yard in 1939 was about £38,000, and a small yard required at least half that sum. Yet despite the increase in fixed capital, productivity gains in large yards were minimal. Added to

Granite cutting was one of the two sectors of the granite industry.

this was the fact that recruitment to the industry was becoming more difficult. Sons no longer followed their fathers into yard management and on the death of the owner a yard was typically either sold or dismantled. However, the lack of new capital entering the industry was also partly the result of the desire of existing yards to minimise competition. All employers were members of the Aberdeen Granite Masters' Association (AGMA) and it was the practice of the organisation to charge high entry fees to discourage new members. An employer who refused to pay these entry fees found himself unable to recruit labour. The AGMA signed an agreement with the trade unions by which it agreed not to employ non-union labour provided the unions agreed that their members would only work for firms belonging to the AGMA. By adopting a policy of short-term security, the employers have been accused of unwittingly hastening the demise of the granite industry by discouraging the entry of new capital and ideas.[11]

After the Second World War the granite industry was even more badly hit. The number of firms steadily declined. Most of the quarries ran out and the few which were still in business produced crushed stone or dust for cement manufacture rather than blocks for cutting and polishing. As demand declined, employers attempted to reduce costs by introducing new cutting machinery which simplified the process and made it accessible to unskilled labour. The attempt to destroy craft-based production led to a strike lasting 14 weeks in 1955 concerning who had the right to operate stone saws: labourers or time-served men. The result was a victory for the skilled men, but the success was hollow and short-lived. The fact that very few boys on leaving school thought of an apprenticeship in the granite industry, preferring cleaner occupations, brought a crisis in the supply of labour. In these circumstances a more flexible approach to working practices was accepted by the trade unions and, as a result, masons were allowed to polish and polishers allowed to operate cutting machinery.[12] But the granite industry continued its spiral of decline and eventually collapsed in the 1980s.

THE STANDARD OF LIVING

The early textile industry was subject to violent swings in the trade cycle and thus large-scale unemployment became a phenomenon of modern society in Aberdeen as elsewhere. Indeed, the cotton industry experienced a major downturn in 1836, and another followed in 1842, although the telling blow to the fortunes of the industry was delivered in the recession of 1847-48. The massive fall in domestic and international demand for cotton products saw 3,000 workers made redundant and the domestic handloom weaving sector collapse. The two largest mills, Leys, Masson & Co. and Hadden & Sons closed. Few textile firms survived. One writer referring to the 1840s spoke of the scenes of 'squalor, vice and misery that were to be seen in broad daylight', particularly at the east end of Castle Street, and of the 'great many beggars with sore arms and legs … forming a disgusting sight'. The level of prostitution was also said to be alarmingly high in the Justice Port area of the city and there were food riots in both 1843 and 1848.[13]

The transition to a more diversified economy after the collapse of cotton saw the standard of living improve for many Aberdonians. Wages rose faster in Aberdeen than in many urban areas of Britain. Data for building wages shows that in 1800 Aberdonians earned only 43 per cent of what construction workers earned in London, but by 1901 the gap had been closed to 76 per cent and, although many of the trades in Aberdeen paid low wages in comparison to Clydeside metal trades, they were generally substantially above those paid in Dundee.[14] In the poorer areas of Aberdeen the people still struggled to make ends meet, and even second-hand clothes were a luxury. Older women remembered that 'lots of clothes were made out of flour bags'. One even remembered sewing flour bags together to make bed sheets.[15]

By the early twentieth century, however, Aberdeen had become a relatively prosperous and diversified economy. According to the *Glasgow Herald* 'the capable and energetic community that peoples Aberdeen … is making itself more and more independent of incidental depressions'.[16] The years of the First World War brought price rises and shortages, and the trades council was quick to call for government control of supplies and prices. But there was not the sharp rise in rents which triggered rent strikes in Glasgow, although hardly any houses were built in the city during the war years. The greatest anxiety seemed to be occasioned by the government regulation requiring potato or beanflower to be used for baking. This threatened the beloved 'buttery' and the trades council expressed its concern at 'the hardship resulting if the rolls are discontinued'.[17] In spite of the problems faced by its main industries between the wars, Aberdeen did not experience the high levels of unemployment which affected other parts of Scotland. In the mid-1930s Aberdeen had 12.8 per cent of its total insured population out of work compared with an unemployment rate of 22.1 per cent in Dundee and of 21.3 per cent in Glasgow. Some local industries like papermaking and combmaking actually prospered during the depression. There was also a marked increase in employment in the service industries. For those on the dole, however, life was harsh. One woman recalled that, rather than see her husband and daughters go without, she lived 'practically on bread and potatoes'.[18]

The Aberdeen economy stagnated in the decades after 1945. One survey concluded in 1963 that 'it is remarkable that no new industries have been founded … within the city itself'. The economic consequence of this was that wages were again substantially lower in Aberdeen than in other parts of Scotland. Men's wages in Aberdeen in the early 1960s were only 90 per cent of those of Edinburgh and Glasgow, and significantly below those in Dundee.[19] According to the 1951 census of population, Aberdeen had a larger proportion of adult males in the poorest social class than had Edinburgh, Dundee, or Scotland as a whole. If the next poorest social class, the semi-skilled, was added to the lowest then Aberdeen was in a less fortunate position than even Glasgow. The combined total of social classes IV and V for Aberdeen was 33.4 per cent, while for Glasgow it was 32.4.[20] The absence of well-paid employment opportunities in Aberdeen saw outward migration reach levels far higher in the North-East than in any other area of Britain.

The growth of the oil industry in the 1970s and 1980s dramatically changed the situation in respect to work and wages. Male unemployment in Aberdeen in 1981 at 7.2 per cent was the lowest of any large British city. Dundee had an employment rate of nearly double that figure and the disparity between the two cities was also reflected in the figures for unemployment among young males of 16 to 19 years, with Aberdeen at 11.8 per cent, and Dundee at 27.0 per cent.[21] As the travel writer, Paul Theroux, put it, 'most British cities were plagued with unemployed people. Aberdeen was plagued by workers'.[22] Twelve years later the situation was just as favourable with the Grampian Region recording a rate of unemployment of 4.6 per cent compared with 9.9 per cent for Scotland as a whole.

Wage levels were also transformed within a decade as the region moved from a low wage area in 1971, when adult male earnings were only 85.4 per cent of the United Kingdom level, to a high wage area. In Grampian Region in 1979 wages were

7.6 per cent higher than the United Kingdom average, and 7.8 per cent higher than the Scottish average. However, gross average earnings were pushed upwards by the high earnings in the oil industry. A survey of 81 Aberdeen firms covering 20,000 workers found that the gross earnings of non-oil workers were still 'well below the Scottish average' for 1978.[23] By employing more female labour, and substituting unskilled for skilled workers, employers were able to keep down wage costs.

Not all Aberdonians benefited from the oil boom, and, even those who did, faced a continuing struggle to maintain wage levels. But there were enough people on high earnings to sustain a sharp increase in the average standard of living in the city and the surrounding hinterland. As a result of oil expansion the increase in per capita income in the first half of the 1990s made Grampian one of the richest regions of the United Kingdom. In 1991, Scotland as a whole averaged 95.8 per cent of United Kingdom per capita income, while Grampian was an astonishing 134.8 per cent.[24] The increase in per capita income was reflected in car ownership. By 1981, 53.0 per cent of Aberdeen households owned a car, whereas in Dundee the respective figure was only 43.5 per cent.[25] Although after 1850 Aberdeen never experienced the social devastation of mass unemployment, it is possible that employment was sustained at the expense of wages. Oil changed this situation and from an area of low wages Grampian, with Aberdeen at its centre, became one of the most prosperous regions in the United Kingdom.

SELF-HELP AND TRADE UNIONISM

Aberdeen, like most of urban Scotland, in the nineteenth century provided little in the way of amenities or relief from exploitation and poverty. In the absence of a welfare state, life for many could prove to be a brutalising experience. The response to these conditions was self-help and self-improvement. As a consequence, various institutions, some initiated by workers and some by the philanthropic middle classes, were established to provide help and to preach the values of thrift and sobriety. Among the most important were the temperance societies. The first to be established was the Aberdeen Temperance Society in 1839, and by 1841 it had 10,829 members. The Rechabites also established themselves in the city with their brand of temperance and friendly society benefits and, in 1843, could claim to have 22 tents, as the lodges were called, and 1,000 members. In 1870 the Independent Order of Good Templars, a temperance friendly society with Masonic underpinnings which had spread from the United States, arrived in Aberdeen. The effect was electric, and had a major impact on local politics. Within a year of starting its operation, the Order could claim 4,000 members and 23 lodges. However, despite the efforts of leading activists like A. S. Cook and William Lindsay, such initiatives did little to stem the tide of the drink trade, and by 1898 the Order's

The temperance movement influence religion and politics as well as social life in the nineteenth century. Note the images of education, the 'improving' entertainment at the Music Hall, the savings bank and the tranquil domestic scene.

William Lindsay 1822–1900

Born in Newhills parish, the son of a shoemaker, William Lindsay subsequently followed his father's trade for some years. He then established himself as a newsagent, stationer and bookseller in the Gallowgate in the 1840s. In 1837 he became a member of the Owenite socialist society, and later joined the Aberdeen Chartist Association. He wrote articles for the *Commonwealth* newspaper after 1854 and distributed the Aberdeen edition of the *People's Journal* between 1861 and 1877. He was a founder member of the Aberdeen Liberal Association, having attended meetings of the Scottish Advanced Liberal Party as early as 1852. He was secretary of the forty shilling freehold committee in 1857 and a member of the Aberdeen Workmen's Peace Association from 1875. Besides his commitment to radical politics he was a staunch supporter of teetotalism. He joined the Aberdeen Total Abstinence Society in 1843, serving as vice president 1848–50, and belonged to the Scottish Temperance League. He also served as a director of the Music Hall Co., the New Market Co., the Aberdeen Cafe Co., and the Bon-Accord Investment Co.

membership had fallen to 1,339. However, trade unions continued to campaign for temperance and to call for municipal control of the drink trade.

The most obvious manifestation of self-help for the working classes was through the collective action of trade unionism which, in Aberdeen, had its roots in the eighteenth century. As early as 1732 there were complaints among employers that journeymen were associating to shorten their hours of work.[26] In the 1750s and 1760s a Woolcombers' Society established links with similar societies in England and tried to maintain a regular system of apprenticeship and, in 1768, the tailors formed a union to push up their wages from eightpence to tenpence per day.[27] In 1792 there was considerable panic among the magistrates when seamen went on strike and, in 1797, twelve tailors were given eight days in gaol by the burgh court for leaving their work without due notice.[28] As textiles were at the forefront of industrial development, it is of little surprise that unionisation took hold there at a fairly early date. In the first decade of the new century there were signs of organisation among handloom weavers and calico printers, but it was in the 1820s and 1830s that such organisation began to grow. Despite the paternalism of some of the early textile employers, recurring economic difficulties saw them seek to curb costs by holding down wages. At the same time there was growing industrial unrest among craft workers like weavers, shoemakers and tailors. In 1834, after the managers of the Broadford mill had reduced the wages of reelers and spinners, 156 women workers resolved to form an Aberdeen Female Operatives Union and some 1,000 women from 11 mills turned up to hear one Mary Brodie, who had refused

A. S. Cook, clothier and shirtmaker, an indefatigable campaigner for the temperance movement and one of the founders of the Liberal Association.

to take over work normally done by the striking men, denounce the petty tyrants who employed them. There were complaints that workers were fined sixpence for singing, or for stopping to remove a splinter, or for being 15 minutes late, and were fined one penny for speaking to a neighbouring worker.[29] They received support from the United Trades of Aberdeen and some held out for five weeks despite denunciation by the clergy. In the end the company conceded most of the strikers' demands, but the strike leaders, and others identified as militants, were dismissed. The final act of the union was to pay the travelling expenses of those victimised workers to enable them to seek work in Dundee.

Tailors and shoemakers tried to establish a branch of Robert Owen's Grand

National Consolidated Trades Union in Aberdeen in February 1834. The move encompassed the idea of 'one big union' for all the trades in Aberdeen, but the collapse of Owen's organisation later that year killed off any hopes of a concerted challenge by the workers to the power of capital. As the stonemasons' experience in 1842 showed, the idea of a general national union was rather impractical. The Aberdeen masons went on strike, unsuccessfully, against a reduction in wages, and, at the same time, as members of the United Operative Masons' Association (UOMA), they were being 'taxed' in support of strikes in Glasgow and London. Supporting two actions simultaneously was beyond the resources of the Aberdeen men and they withdrew from the UOMA 'partly on the ground that the strikes were, in nearly every case, in support of wage claims substantially in excess of the earnings of local craftsmen' and not until 1870 did they again join a national union.[30]

While industrial protest was becoming increasingly formalised, older patterns of popular protest persisted. An attempt to ban the traditional bonfire in Castle Street in celebration of the King's birthday in 1836 led to a riot and the smashing of the town house windows, and during the shortages of 1843 and 1848 there were meal riots in the Castlegate. But, by the end of the nineteenth century trade unionism had become an established part of workplace culture. The growing capitalistic nature of the fishing industry brought the first fishermen's union in 1904, the Aberdeen Steam Fishing Vessels' Enginemen's and Firemen's Union with 200 members. Strikes broke out in the period of industrial unrest before the outbreak of the First World War. Female fishworkers struck in April 1913 for an increase in wages. Their success encouraged the deckhands, and, in the autumn, they too won an increase in wages. However, permanent organisation was difficult given the highly personal nature of relationships at sea and, as a result, it was estimated that only five per cent of deckhands were members of a trade union in 1913, a situation further compounded by inter-union rivalries.[31]

BY AUTHORITY
OF THE HONOURABLE THE
MAGISTRATES OF ABERDEEN.

WHEREAS a serious Riot and Breach of the Public Peace took place in this City, on the *Anniversary of his MAJESTY's BIRTH-DAY*, last year, and considerable damage was done to Private Property by those engaged in the Riot---

The MAGISTRATES, while they re-commend to their Fellow-Citizens to use all due means in securing their Property, *do strictly prohibit* the kindling or making of BONFIRES upon any of the Streets of this City, on the approaching Anniversary of his *Majesty's Birth-day*; and warn and admonish every Person to conduct himself with becoming propriety on that occasion; to avoid all riotous and disorderly proceed-ings, and all unwarrantable interference with Public and Private Property, of every description.

CERTIFYING those who may in any respect offend in the Premises, or disturb the Public Peace in any way, that effectual measures will be adopted for securing and bringing them to condign punishment.

Council Chamber, Aberdeen, 16th April, 1829.

D. Chalmers & Co. Aberdeen.

The authorities increasingly tried to control and regulate popular celebrations, such as those on the King's birthday, which might lead to political protest.

Workers in the granite industry were faced with similar problems. Before 1888 union membership was 'small, being chiefly confined to enthusiasts ... with little influence on trade conditions'. Such was the premium placed on skill that bargaining was conducted through the individual workplaces. However, the establishment of the AGMA saw the stoneworkers join with the building masons to form the Operative Masons' and Granite Cutters' Union (OMGCU) in 1888. According to Donnelly, almost all the stoneworkers joined, a phenomenon assisted by the close proximity of the workshops to each other and the kinship network within the granite polishing trade. Only a few 'Doubting Peters', claimed the new union's journal, 'looked with suspicion on the favour shown by the employers and designated it a "bosses union"'. The decision to accept compulsory arbitration of disputes only served to reinforce that perception.[32] Such differences may also have reflected historic divisions within the workforce. The elite of the labour force were the stonemasons, followed by the polishers and sett-makers, who split and cut the different granites. At the bottom of the hierarchy were the yard labourers, or scabbers, who assisted the masons and performed general labouring tasks. The masons were historically paid at a higher rate than the polishers, although each were highly skilled, and this was a source of friction between the two crafts. This differential was not removed until 1969.[33]

At times divisions could be set aside when faced with a common challenge. An attempt in 1919, due to labour shortages, to introduce female workers in polishing work at Stewart's on Fraser Road led to the threat of an all-out strike. This was enough to see the women dismissed. Such was the power of the stoneworkers in the industry that they had established a 44-hour week by 1913, while most other craft workers were working 51-54 hours a week. Relations between the men and their employers were usually amicable and according to a 1905 report of the OMGCU:

> ... the peaceful policy which we have always pursued, and ardently wish to pursue in the future, largely accounts for this state of affairs. We have neither the desire nor the intention to do anything which will unfairly hamper or harass the employers.[34]

Women had been among the pioneers of trade unionism in the textile industry in the city, but remained poorly organised and the subject of much concern about their moral welfare. In 1883, a middle-class inspired Aberdeen Ladies' Union (ALU) had as its object the 'bringing together of all workers for the welfare of women and girls in Aberdeen'. Much of the work was aimed at the 11-15 year old female half-timers in the mills. The object was to create an 'atmosphere of Christian refinement' and to 'raise the moral standard in all ways possible'. This was to be done through the establishment of 'lily bands', whose main activities included reading circles, needlework and family worship. Within two years the 'lily bands' membership numbered 300. For older girls 'lily band' evening classes were established along the same lines and they had around 250 members in the late 1880s. The need of the expanding middle class of Aberdeen for domestic servants was also addressed by the ALU. It provided homes for 10–12 'country' girls in which they would be 'trained for service', since 'much difficulty has been found in inducing girls to go into service'. This reluctance was put down to the 'daily growing tendency for girls to go in for anything that will leave them with what they style "liberty"'. The report complained that the girls will 'labour in shops, in warehouses, in mills, in offices, in places of business of every imaginable kind, rather than go into service, where they would at least be ... prepared for keeping a house of their own.'[35] Those in the mills continued to show occasional signs of militancy with major strikes at the Broadford works in 1901 and again in 1910 and 1911. Messrs Richards, on more than one occasion, dismissed girls for joining the Textile Workers' Union.[36]

As elsewhere, the years just before the First World War were a time of intense industrial unrest. The trades council embarked on an intensive recruitment campaign among poorly organised groups of workers around the port, and members were particularly active in trying to press for improvements in the intolerable conditions of the fish girls. In 1913 the *Daily Journal* talked of a strike epidemic among granite workers, fishworkers, masons, coachbuilders, upholsterers and combmakers.[37] A strike at the combworks of Stewart & Co. lasted from June until October. According to the trades council the firm was 'the most unscrupulous employer around the district'.[38]

The inter-war period had an inhibiting effect on trade unionism in all sectors of the economy. Apart from a brief period of militancy in the immediate post-war years, trade-union organisation seems to have collapsed. In the fishing industry employers took advantage of the depression to break the unions. The only reported strike of deckhands in the inter-war years took place in 1919 and it was not until 1940 that another unofficial strike occurred. If the men complained about wages or conditions in this period they were told to 'roll 'em up ... and that was that ... you was finished.'[39]

According to a survey of membership carried out by the Scottish Trades Union Congress in 1924, only 20,000 workers, or 27 per cent, out of a total workforce of 74,000 belonged to a trade union in Aberdeen, much lower than in neighbouring Dundee where the figure was nearly 38 per cent, in spite of the large female presence in the working population of the city.[40] The aftermath of the General Strike of 1926 meant further decimation of membership with considerable victimisation and a requirement imposed on many workers to sign a declaration that they would never again join a trade union. In spite of this a few advances were made thanks largely to the work of the local trade-union organising committee set up by the trades council. In 1931, a permanent Aberdeen trade union women's group was set up with representatives from seven trades, including shop workers, bakers, tailors, textile workers, general and municipal workers, and female clerks. In 1935 the woodcutting machinists and boxmakers, who were making the new lighter boxes now used for transporting fish, were organised for the first time. In the following year a major breakthrough was achieved among the poorly paid women workers at the city's 17 cinemas. A strike at Pool's Palace Cinema in Guild Street during the Glasgow Fair week, when appropriately Chaplin's satire on capitalism, *Modern Times*, was showing, eventually resulted in the recognition of the union and acceptance of a minimum wage of £2 per week. Some success was also achieved by Donside papermakers, Broadford textile workers and mental hospital workers, despite a declaration by one matron that her nurses were 'God's own gentlewomen and not the riff-raff that joined trade unions'.[41] Nevertheless, trade unionism remained relatively weak and it would appear that defending what might be called the social wage, particularly housing and rent, was more likely to engender militancy than workplace issues. The inadequacy and shortage of housing was dramatised in 1946 when a squatters' movement, supported by the local Communist Party, took over some of the hotels in Aberdeen.[42]

Trade unionism began to flourish during the war years and after in conditions of full employment. The most spectacular gains were enjoyed in the public sector and, from the 1960s, women were increasingly likely to become union members. The peak period of union growth in Britain came in the decade 1968–78. However,

---

Robert S. Lennox b. 1909

Educated at St Clement's School, Robert Lennox left at the age of 14 to become apprenticed as a painter. He became one of the youngest members of the national executive committee of the Scottish Painters' Society and was active in the Labour Party, speaking against fascism in the Castlegate and being heckled. In 1939 he became a full-time official of the Painters' Society, serving simultaneously on the trades council. He represented Woodside on the town council 1945–52, Cairncry 1952–61, Mastrick 1961–75 and Cornhill 1975–80. In 1949 he left the Labour Group after a dispute about policy and sat as an independent socialist for three years. He served as treasurer for a total of 13 years, and held the convenerships of lighting and watching and of housing. He served as a JP and as lord provost 1967–70 and 1975–77. He played a major role in securing the status of Old Aberdeen as a conservation area. He was awarded the CBE in 1978.

the election of the Conservative Government in 1979, committed to rolling back the frontiers of the state and reducing the power of the trade unions, saw membership fall sharply. The situation in Aberdeen was compounded by the presence of oil companies hostile to trade unionism. Before the 1970s, 68 per cent of firms in Aberdeen were locally owned and, as in the case of the granite industry, were prepared to come to a *modus vivendi* with the unions over many issues of mutual concern. However, the discovery of oil led to the appearance of firms which were either opposed to trade unions or were lukewarm in their dealings with them.[43]

American management styles led to increasing tensions in the oil industry, particularly over wages, health and safety. There were complaints about contracts which were terminated automatically in the event of sickness or injury. One American foreman graphically expressed the situation as 'fall off that derrick, buster, and you're fired before you hit the deck'.[44] In the early days, conditions on the rigs were poor with overcrowded sleeping conditions, and unsatisfactory medical supplies. Complaints were not welcome and trade unions were regarded as manifestations of communist agitation. Casual attitudes to health and safety and the employment of a large number of inexperienced workers laid the conditions for many accidents and several fatal accidents. A major disaster occurred on 1 July 1988 when the Piper Alpha platform went up in flames. This was the catalyst which forced the offshore workforce to reappraise every aspect of its conditions of employment. Above all it underscored the consequences of the workers' lack of voice and powerlessness. The feeling that the official trade-union movement was failing adequately to address these issues with management led to a grassroots revolt in the wake of the 1988 disaster in the offshore sector, culminating in the establishment of the unofficial Offshore Industry Liaison Committee (OILC).

Even then trade unionism was slow to spread among the unskilled workers in the drilling sector, and it was among the catering and engineering workers that organisation developed. Four years after its founding as a pressure group, OILC constituted itself as a trade union in February 1992, setting a target of recruiting 3,000 members in a year. By August 1993 it had reached 2,774, but of these only 1,723 were fully paid-up members. Divisions and personality clashes hampered progress, and less than a dozen ordinary members were present at a special conference held in Aberdeen in February 1994.[45]

In spite of these divisions within the leadership, OILC remained active, but its short history is instructive when examining the problems of trade-union organisation within the oil industry. Firstly, there were immense logistical problems in trying to organise workers in over a hundred installations in three separate sectors, where 80 per cent of the workforce were employed by 300 different contractors and agencies. Secondly, there was an hierarchical division of labour in the drilling crews in which the leading hands were the pump and rig men, and the lowest were the roustabouts. The last constituted an amorphous pool of labour, and the former a regular and better paid core of the workforce. Opposition from established trade unions made recruitment difficult for OILC, although it was accepted as an affiliate of the trades council. Perhaps for these reasons, 25 years after the first development of oil exploration, some 35,000 workers were still without effective trade-union representation.[46]

THE TRADES COUNCIL

The transition to small master production which followed the collapse of the textile industry and the growth of the service sector inhibited the development of trade unionism in Aberdeen. But it encouraged collaboration between trades. During a strike in 1846 the joiners proposed to bring together all the organised trades so that they could support each other in the event of a strike. A 'delegated committee of sympathy' was formed which survived until 1849.[47] However, at the end of 1868 during a ten-week masons' strike in the city, 13 societies and branches came together under the chairmanship of John Jessiman of the associated carpenters, to form a trades council.[48] It was keen to get a court of conciliation established to mediate in labour disputes, but this received little support from employers. Such a body was established by the town council and the Chamber of Commerce in 1890, but neither side was prepared to be bound by its decisions. By 1873 the trades council had 50 delegates from over 20 trades, mainly from the construction industry and from granite and shipbuilding, but also including delegates from a Labourers' Society led by the republican John Nicol.

In the 1880s the trades council co-ordinated support for trade unions on strike and organised campaigns for shorter working hours, but it also played an active political role in campaigning for municipalisation of the gas works and, later, the tramways, free libraries, provision of free meals for needy children and the abolition of fee-paying in elementary schools. It collaborated with the powerful temperance movement in backing candidates for the town council. Because of the general weakness of individual unions in the city, the trades council had an influence disproportionate to its membership. But, as influential as it might have been, little could be done to disguise the fact that as late as the 1880s there were few trade unionists in Aberdeen, with only 2,000 workers represented by the trades council.

A new era dawned in the 1880s with the expansion of unskilled unions, a development which predated the explosion of 'new unionism' elsewhere in Britain. The trades council supported the formation of a union of women workers in 1882. In 1883, a shore labourers' strike in the docks ended successfully for the men and as a result the labourers sent delegates to the trades council. In the following year the seamen organised a branch of the South Shields-based Seamen's Union and J. W. Annand, of the Stonemasons' Union, spoke at the first meeting. A Workmen's Protection and Benefit Society sent two delegates to the trades council in October 1883 and a deputation from the gas stokers asked for assistance in forming a trade union, as a result of which a Gas Stokers' Society was formed in 1886.[49] Much of the success was due to the president of the trades council, J. C. Thompson. Thanks largely to his efforts, the Scottish Farm Servants' Union was established in 1884 and he became its secretary. In January 1889, the trades council established an organising committee which drew up a list of unorganised groups of workers in the city. From its efforts a branch of the Amalgamated Union of Seamen and Firemen was formed in February 1889.[50] Probably because of the large number of unskilled workers affiliated to the trades council, Aberdeen in 1888 took the lead in supporting the campaign for an eight-hour day to be fixed by legislation.[51] The Trades Union Congress held its annual meeting in Aberdeen in 1884, presided over by the president of the trades council, and it was on the initiative of the Aberdeen trades council that a Scottish conference was called in 1895 which led to the formation of the Scottish Trades Union Congress two years later.[52] The prodigious efforts of the trades council led to a growth in the number of affiliated societies from 12 to 40 between 1882 and 1895, representing 6,957 workers. But, in spite of these efforts, union membership represented less than 11 per cent of the total occupied workforce of Aberdeen. Moreover, some of the new unions, such as the Gas Stokers' Society, failed to survive the employers' and the judiciary's backlash in the later 1890s.[53]

The central role of the trades council in representing the interests of a wide

James C. Thompson 1848–1904

A native of Peterhead and the son of a harpooner in the whaling fishery, James Thompson moved to Aberdeen as a child and was subsequently apprenticed as an ironmoulder. He worked in Dundee and Glasgow before returning to Aberdeen in 1875. In 1880 he represented his trade on the trades council and two years later became president. In 1884 he was president of the Trades Union Congress when the annual conference was held in Aberdeen. He became secretary of the Scottish Farm Servants' Union in 1884, and served on the school board 1885–91. He was active in the temperance movement and served on the council of the Aberdeen Temperance Society. He was superintendent of the Sabbath school of the Band of Hope, and a member of John Street Congregational Church. In later years he started a window cleaning business and took little part in public life.

section of the organised workers in the city necessarily drew it increasingly towards political involvement. It was committed to securing working-class representation on public bodies, and regularly identified candidates for support in local elections. In 1884, the trades council was engaged in discussions to find a Labour candidate for the forthcoming parliamentary election. There were also signs of wider stirrings when, in October 1886, a motion by the blacksmith, George Bissett, who was president of the trades council, called for co-operation with working men outside the trade unions to consider 'the organisation of a strictly working class Political Association to secure more direct representation in Parliament and Public Boards'.[54] A few years later, the members of the trades council unanimously agreed to 'pledge themselves to make the interests of labour the first and determining question in all their political action imperial and local'.[55] By the beginning of 1891 a committee had been appointed 'to draw up a programme of labour questions of pressing importance' and to call a national conference. This conference, held in Edinburgh in August 1891, gave a fillip to the movement for Labour representation with demands for the payment of MPs and of election expenses, a statutory eight-hour day and the return of a body of Labour MPs for Scotland. There were still those within the trades council who believed that co-operation with the Liberal Association was possible in local elections, but as the election approached, the Liberal ward committees made no effort to hide their hostility both to the programme and to Labour candidates. The trades council broke with the Liberal Association and recommended five men as 'Labour candidates' and the Liberal Association noted that a large number of those returned in November 1891 were 'favourable to social reform'.[56]

Joseph Duncan, trade-union organiser of both fishermen and farm workers and a leading figure in the Independent Labour Party from 1905.

Indeed, an Aberdeen edition of the *Labour Elector* was able to claim that the town council was the only one in Britain in which the labour interest predominated, with five Independent Labour Party (ILP) members, nine other councillors who could generally be relied upon to vote in the Labour interest and eleven 'doubtful and squeezables'.[57] At the same time, the socialist society began to infiltrate the trades council and, by the beginning of 1893, as many as thirteen members of the socialist society, 'all of them speakers and writers of more than average ability' had been appointed as delegates.[58] In the early twentieth century the trades council was frequently the focus of the often acrimonious debates between the different sections of the labour movement. Affiliated membership grew only slightly to 16,684 at the peak in 1920. However, it continued to maintain a high profile in the local community and was able to settle many inter-union disputes concerning the demarcation of work.

After the excitement of the 1926 General Strike when it acted as the local co-ordinating committee, the trades council's task was to hold the much-weakened movement together. But, as trade improved in the late 1930s it, once again, embarked on recruiting campaigns among the poorly organised. The years of the Second World War and after gave a boost to trade unionism in Aberdeen and, under the vigorous guidance of James Milne, secretary from 1948-69, the trades council grew. By 1980, with Ron Webster as secretary, the number of affiliations to the trades council had reached 70 societies and branches with over 26,000 members. It was a sign of changing times that it was public service unions, such as the National Union of Public Employees, which predominated together with white-collar unions, such as the National Association of Local Government Officers and the Association of University Teachers. But the 1980s and 1990s were difficult decades for trade unionism and, although there was no collapse of membership, the trades council's affiliations and influence were much reduced.

The Diversification of Employment

Until recent decades Aberdeen's economy did not generate the same levels of wealth as Glasgow's or Edinburgh's, but its economic development created a more stable society and a less uncertain pattern of life than in many other cities. There was apparently less extreme inequality in the distribution of wealth. A greater sense of civic solidarity emerged and was reflected in the many progressive and philanthropic overtures by the middle class towards the working class, and in the latter's commitment to the values of self-help and self-improvement. Even the rise of trade unionism and the growth of radical politics did little to disrupt these social relationships. Progressive action on issues of health, particularly that of women and children, and housing, seemed to compensate for lower wages even in the 1950s and 1960s. In the last four decades of the century the deskilling of some working-class employment, and the decline in manufacturing, transformed family and social relationships. Aberdeen, by becoming more oil-dependent, moved some way from the diversified economy of the nineteenth and twentieth century. This process did, however, create more employment, particularly for women, and increased prosperity.

7

Politics Before 1918

W. HAMISH FRASER

THE OLD ORDER

The fears inspired in the ruling order of Britain by the events of the French Revolution had effectively ensured that there was little political life in Aberdeen at the end of the eighteenth century. Dissatisfaction among the growing merchant and business community at the lack of adequate representation of their interests had, in 1783, resulted in the formation of a committee of burgesses to press for burgh reform. Revolution in France and the writings of Thomas Paine had stirred wider popular enthusiasm for parliamentary reform, but such views were subdued in the repressive atmosphere which prevailed after 1793. In national politics Aberdeen was part of the Montrose district of burghs consisting of Brechin, Montrose, Arbroath, Inverbervie and Aberdeen. The selection of parliamentary candidates was made by delegates from each of the five town councils which usually meant that Angus interests prevailed. Between 1792 and 1802 the Member was Alexander Allardyce, a loyal cog in the Dundas machine which ran Scottish politics. He was succeeded by his brother-in-law James Farquhar of Inverbervie, a brother-in-law of James and Gavin Hadden and whose father was a partner in one of the Hadden enterprises.

Despite the sterility of political life, the city was growing and changing rapidly and challenges to the existing political order were eventually to appear. Worker discontent in the previous century had usually resulted in the propertied classes standing together. The fatal shooting of four young boys by troops during a minor fracas on the King's birthday in 1802, however, resulted in a united community challenge to the decision of the Lord Advocate not to prosecute, and deep indignation when the hand-picked Edinburgh jury acquitted the two officers and two sergeants brought to trial.[1] There was also widespread public criticism of the proposals to extend the Corn Laws.[2] But there were also divisions among the dominant groups about local issues. A growing population, coupled with post-war unemployment, led to a petty crime wave and demands for a 24-hour watch service and a new jail and court house, but also to appeals for relief work for the labouring poor. By the end of 1816 there was clearly mounting disquiet about the town's affairs, and the announcement by the city treasurer in February 1817 that he could no longer meet the interest payments on the city's debts confirmed the worst fears. There followed two years of bitter acrimony between the old ruling group and their critics, a struggle which probably did more than anything to create political awareness in Aberdeen. At a time when other parts of Scotland were being shaken by demands for political reform, many in Aberdeen saw the crisis as an opportunity to reopen the campaign of thirty years earlier for burgh reform in order to secure an elected town council. It was a measure of the bitterness of feeling that even the stoning of the members of the town council as they processed to the West Church for the kirkin', although condemned at a public meeting, was accompanied by a resolution expressing regret 'that any set of Magistrates should have persisted in pursuing measures contrary to their own recorded opinion, and to the opinion of the great body of the inhabitants'.[3]

A further sign of changing times was the decision of the Angus burghs, where there had also been a considerable agitation for reform, to rebel against Tory domination in parliamentary elections and to back a radical son of Montrose, Joseph Hume. James Farquhar had held the seat since 1802, apart from being ousted briefly for a few months in 1807 by a Whig, John Ramsay. By 1818 Montrose politics had been radicalised by a successful battle over reform of the local council. Aberdeen was conveniently disenfranchised at the time by legal battles over the civic debt, and Hume carried three of the remaining four burghs. A small man, with a great barrel chest, Hume, describing himself as 'the independent, unshackled representative of the only free and independent burgh in Scotland', quickly established himself as a campaigner for political and economic reform. He was an inveterate attender of the House of Commons, an irrepressible participator in debates, a dogged scourge of government expenditure and such an excruciatingly dull speaker that he was guaranteed to empty the chamber as he rose to his feet. The Tory-dominated town council was never reconciled to him, but its critics among the burgesses, such as George Still, Alexander Bannerman and Andrew Jopp, sang his praises, and in 1823, 1824 and 1825 he was elected rector of Marischal College. He quickly clashed with powerful forces in the University by taking up student grievances, investigating the use of bursaries and, for the first time for nearly a hundred years, calling meetings of the rectorial court. He saw it as his duty 'to ascertain the rights of students, and see justice done to them', not an attitude which endeared him to the professors.[4] However, Angus unity broke in the late 1820s, when Joseph Hume failed to support Brechin's case in respect of the Montrose road bill. Brechin switched its allegiance and went with Aberdeen and Inverbervie in supporting the Tory, Sir James Carnegie of South Esk, whose father had represented the burghs in the previous century, and who had a rent roll of £15,000 per annum in Brechin.[5]

In local government the Hadden dynasty dominated Aberdeen for the first three decades of the century. But by the 1820s they faced persistent opposition from Whig reformers. Alexander Bannerman, who emerged as head of the reform party, maintained a steady stream of political squibs against the ruling group and their associates, focusing particularly on the plans for harbour improvement.[6] The campaign succeeded in having control of the harbour transferred to a separate elected trust and out of the exclusive hands of the town council. There were mounting complaints at extravagance, corruption and exclusiveness on the part of the town council, kept up by a stream of short-lived newspapers and pamphlets, while more radical journals from south of the border also circulated. In July 1830, Hume, able to read the signs and unwilling to face the cost of buying off the challenge of Carnegie, announced his intention to give up the seat and to stand instead for the more democratic electorate of Middlesex. He urged his former constituents to support Horatio Ross of Rossie, a retired army captain and noted sportsman, but Carnegie was returned. His tenure was, however, short-lived. Wellington's ministry, after struggling to survive, at last resigned in November 1830. While the *Aberdeen Journal* was reassuring that 'no violent change' in the composition of the House of Commons was contemplated by the incoming Whig Government 'but merely such alteration … as will accord with the spirit of the times, and the wishes of the middle-classes of society', the departure of Wellington triggered universal demands for reform.[7] Carnegie found himself in a hopeless situation, opposed to political reform but knowing that it would be impossible for him to stand out against the proposal to give Aberdeen its own member of parliament. A Whig reform meeting, excluding the working classes by imposing a fivepence entry fee, and chaired by Alexander Bannerman, called for burgh reform and the end to self-elected councils.[8] These moderate reformers were manufacturers and merchants whose primary interest lay in burgh reform. But there was also a more radical, largely working-class demand calling for universal suffrage, annual parliaments, and votes by ballot. The more cautious voices, which argued that to press for these demands would threaten reform altogether, were shouted down.[9]

When the Whig government was forced to resign in April 1831, the Incorporated Trades instructed their councillors to support only a reformer. Carnegie, who had voted for the amendment which had brought down the Government, announced that he would not stand in the election since his views were 'out of tune' with most of the burgh's inhabitants. The Whigs struggled to keep control of the situation. It was a measure of the state of excitement that some 3,000 people attended a meeting in the Crown Street amphitheatre on 23 May 1831 while, it was claimed, another 8,000–10,000 could not secure admittance. The self-appointed working-class leaders - John Warden, a schoolteacher, John Cant, a

Sir Alexander Bannerman 1788–1865

Son of a wine merchant, Alexander Bannerman was educated at Marischal College. He became a partner in the family firm, the Bannermill, and in Milne, Cruden & Co., also a textile firm, as well as in Duffus & Co., shipbuilders. He joined the town council in 1811 initially as a supporter of James Hadden but eventually became a strong critic. Bannerman made his reputation as a reformer during the events of 1817–19, when he chaired many of the meetings condemning the town council. Bannerman was an easy-going, genuinely popular figure, with a clever and powerful wife. He was no radical, thought that vote by ballot was 'unnecessary' and saw 'no need' for a broader, household suffrage franchise. The rivalry with Hadden came to a head in the 1832 election to the first parliament following the Reform Act. Bannerman stood for the radical Whig cause as a Liberal and made a variety of allegations against Hadden's record in local government. Bannerman represented the city until 1847 when he was knighted and became successively Lieutenant-Governor of Prince Edward Island, Governor of the Bahamas and, finally, Governor of Newfoundland.

Portrait of Sir Alexander Bannerman, MP from 1833 until 1847, by George Hayter

tanner, and John Davidson, a printer, temperance reformer and self-publicist – all urged support for the Whig measure even if it did fall short of popular demand, and they won over the meeting. A petition in September 1831 secured 5,000 signatures in support of reform and there was considerable local anger when the Duke of Gordon asserted that the petition was unrepresentative, 'got up in the Old Town' and 'signed by very few respectable persons'.[10] The rejection of the bill by the House of Lords unleashed mass demonstrations across the country and raised the political temperature. Whigs and working-class radicals united in a meeting on the Links on 22 October, when, despite wind and rain which blew down the hustings, it was claimed that 10,000–15,000 turned out.[11] With the prospect of constitutional reform now becoming inevitable, a group of leading Whigs pressed Alexander Bannerman to stand.

When it eventually came in the autumn of 1832, the Scottish Reform Act gave Aberdeen 2,024 new electors and its own Member of Parliament. In the first post-reform election in December, Bannerman was elected unopposed. The Tory interest had supported James Hadden and there were accusations that Hadden was using his considerable economic influence to intimidate tradesmen. But in the end he withdrew and, indeed, failed to get elected to the reformed town council in November 1833 as a new 'dynasty' emerged in the shape of the influential Blaikie family.[12] Furthermore, at this time, James Adam came to Aberdeen as editor of the *Aberdeen Herald* and he set about creating a new Liberal movement from the Whig and Radical reformers, with a vigour and abrasiveness which belied his portly appearance. The emergence of the campaign against the Corn Laws at the end of the 1830s helped further strengthen middle-class commitment to Liberal politics. The *Herald* suggested that the Tories in 1835 had in fact harmed themselves by forcing an election in which they had no chance, though it did wish that Bannerman would be seen rather more often to align himself with Liberal Radicals in Parliament. Bannerman was securely returned against the Conservative, Admiral Sir Arthur Farquhar, despite the fact that he had had antagonised many by trying to push through a bill to unite Marischal College and King's College into a single university.[13]

In the election following Victoria's accession, Bannerman was again returned unopposed. There was some opposition from Alexander Hadden and others on the ground that he was no supporter of the Established Church. There was also growing criticism from radicals because he voted in favour of Irish coercion, for the maintenance of the Corn Laws and for amendments to the Factory Act which undermined its effectiveness. Generally, however, the politics of the city were moderately Whig, although there were signs of a Tory revival in local politics. This

ELECTION OF A
Member of Parliament,
FOR THE
CITY OF ABERDEEN.

NOTICE to ELECTORS or PERSONS entitled to *Vote* in the Election of a *Member* of *Parliament* for the *City of Aberdeen.*

The TOWN-CLERK hereby gives Notice, that, in terms of the Act of Parliament, 2d and 3d WILLIAM IV. Cap. 65, entitled "An Act to amend the Representation of the People in Scotland," the City of Aberdeen has been divided into Districts for Polling at the Election of a Member to serve in Parliament, and that POLLING-PLACES, in each of these Districts, have been fixed as follows :—

FIRST DISTRICT.
Comprehending East and St. Clement's Parishes.
POLLING PLACE,
At or near Weigh-house Square.

SECOND DISTRICT.
Comprehending North and Greyfriars Parishes.
POLLING PLACE,
At or near the North Side of Castle Street.

THIRD DISTRICT.
Comprehending West and South Parishes.
POLLING-PLACE,
At or near the North Gate of Robert Gordon's Hospital.

FOURTH DISTRICT.
Comprehending those parts of the Parish of OLD MACHAR, which are situated to the South of the Denburn, and that part of the Parish of BANCHORY-DEVENICK, near the Bridge of Dee, comprehended within the Boundary of the Burgh, as fixed by the said Act of Parliament.
POLLING PLACE,
At or near the crossing of Rose Street and Thistle Street, Northward from Union St.

FIFTH DISTRICT.
Comprehending those parts of the Parish of OLD MACHAR, which are situated between the Denburn on the South, and the River Don on the North.
POLLING PLACE,
At or near the Town-house of Old Aberdeen.

Town-Clerk's Chambers, Aberdeen, January 9, 1835,
D. CHALMERS AND CO. PRINTERS.

Notice of polling places, 1835.

cautious approach was evident in the Anti-Corn Law Association which, as late as 1841, was prepared to accept something less than total repeal of the laws, although 10,000 signed a petition in favour of repeal.[14]

The Whig talk of 'finality' as regards parliamentary reform left much dissatisfaction since the £10 burgh franchise was high by Aberdeen housing standards and excluded many middle-class people as well as the mass of the working class. Since 1830 there had been demands from the non-electors for the ballot, universal suffrage and shorter parliaments, as well as for abolition of the Corn Laws and reform of the House of Lords. These demands were brought together by the emerging Chartist movement. John Mitchell, a bookseller, attended the meeting of Scottish Chartist delegates on Edinburgh's Calton Hill in December 1838 and some 8,600 signatures were gathered in Aberdeen for the first Chartist petition. The city's Chartists were not represented at the Chartist Convention of May 1839, but sent a letter suggesting that, as soon as the fate of the petition was known, they should declare their loyalty, while warning that 'the conduct of the government in withholding their just demands, is calculated to endanger the peace of the country and the stability of the throne'.[15] Resolutions from the convention, asking local associations to consider the principle of arming for self-defence against tyranny, caused a split, with the moderate Mitchell breaking away and forming an Artisans' Association. But, despite the tensions, some 20,000 attended a great Chartist rally on the Broadhills and the movement was given a boost during the summer of 1839, when the powerful Chartist propagandist, George Julian Harney, visited the city. In September, when a number of Chartist leaders were arrested in England, there were protests from the Aberdeen Working Men's Association. This was followed soon afterwards by the imposition of severe sentences on the leaders of an attempted armed uprising in Wales and these reunited the movement, with Mitchell chairing a mass public meeting of protest. There were talks between the different wings of the movement and a new organisation, the Aberdeen Charter Union, was formed, with John Legge, a stonemason, as chairman. It received trade-union backing at a large demonstration in October 1840 held to coincide with the Highland Show and the opening of the new market.[16]

It was a time of considerable working-class agitation since unemployment was at a high level, and the wages of those still in work were falling. A full-scale meal riot against hoarders was narrowly averted in 1843. Ratepayers' meetings to protest against increased assessment for the poor rates were interrupted by Chartists, pushing for resolutions in support of the Charter, and Anti-Corn Law meetings were also disrupted.[17] It is true that, as a recent historian of Aberdeen Chartism has written, there was in Aberdeen 'no insurrectionism; no arming; no confrontations between the military, police and protesters; no rioting'. Even so social tensions could be real enough at times.[18]

These political debates were overshadowed, however, by the growing controversy over church government. Bannerman supported the evangelical, non-intrusionists and thus lost the support of James Adam's clergy-baiting *Herald*, which, while no admirer of the Established Church, was scathing in its treatment of the evangelicals.[19] In the July 1841 election, Bannerman was opposed by a Kincardineshire landowner, William Innes of Raemoir. The Chartists put up the lecturer, Robert Lowery, who was living in Aberdeen and presided over a popular Chartist Church. The show of hands by the non-electors at the hustings in the Castlegate was overwhelmingly in favour of Lowery although in the actual poll he gained only 30 votes. The issue of church and state relationships dominated this election coming, as it did, in the immediate aftermath of the suspension of the ministers of Strathbogie Presbytery by the General Assembly for their refusal to accept the Assembly's ruling on patronage. Church issues overcame social ones at a time when Chartist tactics were being re-evaluated. The strategy, emanating from the London leadership, of working towards political collaboration with middle-class radicalism, appealed to some Aberdeen Chartists. The increasingly popular and well-organised temperance movement also helped span social classes. Significantly, during the 1841 election, Bannerman was given a banquet in the new Temperance Hall although 'the idea of a banquet without wine or intoxicating liquors was something beyond the experience of the time'.[20] But other Chartists retained a deep suspicion of the motives of the middle classes. In October 1841 proposals to organise a trade-union demonstration in favour of the North of England Chartist leader, Feargus O'Connor, who was resisting collaboration, produced fear of riots, and the magistrates called on the mill owners not to allow their workmen to attend the demonstration. The lord provost and

W. S. Lindsay, radical activist, as portrayed in the Northern Figaro, *June 1885.*

magistrates panicked. Five hundred special constables were sworn in and the military were given 16 rounds of ball cartridges. A debate on strategy between the collaborationist Patrick Brewster and the more confrontational O'Connor polarised local divisions.[21]

The Charter Union, now chaired by John MacPherson, a combmaker, continued to admire O'Connor who reciprocated at the end of 1841 by claiming that

Chartism had never been so healthy in Aberdeen, with over 800 members of the Charter Union and a dozen new ones joining each week. There was also support among the local Chartists for female suffrage and Mrs Legge presided over a female association of some eighteen young women. They presented O'Connor with a tartan plaid when he visited the city in October.[22] Middle-class radicals, like James Adam and the bookseller William Lindsay, increasingly tried to defuse social discontent, and, during 1842, a branch of the Complete Suffrage Union, which sought to unite working-class and middle-class reformers, gained ground and attracted sympathetic support from Liberal businessmen such as the shipowner George Thompson, and the shipbuilder James Hall. Such radical businessmen were politically isolated in an area where support for the protection of farming was still very powerful and the Anti-Corn Law Association was struggling to survive. Mitchell and John McPherson both offered themselves for election to the town council in 1842, polling 88 and 82 votes respectively. But groups of Chartists continued to remain active, using the publicity of a meeting in the aftermath of the Disruption to push through a motion in favour of the Charter.[23] In July 1848 some 4,000–5,000 attended a meeting to protest at the harsh sentence passed on the English Chartist, Ernest Jones.

LOCAL CONFLICTS

Although the divisions generated by the Disruption of the Kirk were deep and long-lasting, as so often in Aberdeen, it was local issues rather than national ones which dominated the politics of the 1840s. The key debates concerned proposals for city improvements. A group of 'improvers' centred on the lord provost, Thomas Blaikie, and included the Conservative, James Hadden, and the most powerful lawyer and financial speculator in the city, also a Conservative, Alexander Anderson. Railway speculations and economic crises were also to prove, temporarily, the financial undoing of the group in 1847.[24] Perhaps, the same financial blizzard explains Bannerman's unexpected decision to resign his seat although he had been experiencing ever greater difficulty in picking his way through the hazards of church issues.[25] The search ensued for a successor. Blaikie was originally proposed, but there was too much opposition to his improvement schemes, and the Whig/ Conservative improvers put up a director of the East India Company, Colonel William Sykes, 'after hawking it through half the banking Houses in London, and ferreting every inn of court in search of a candidate', according to their opponents. The critics successfully nominated the 'rich and amiable' Captain Dingwall Fordyce of Brucklay, who had the Free Church and dissenting vote and even some Chartist support. The Conservatives, unable to field a candidate of their own, were split. The traditional elite had given way to a new Liberal middle class.[26]

Fordyce declined to stand again in the 1852 general election and George Thompson Jr, a successful ship and insurance broker, came forward. Thompson, a Free Churchman, had a reputation as a radical, 'one of the most zealous and liberal contributors to the Anti-Corn Law League'. He had the backing of the remnants of the Working Men's Association and gained the support of the *Herald* despite his church association. His opponent, a Palmerstonian Whig, Sir Andrew Leith Hay of Rannes, who had served with Wellington in the Peninsular War, tried to portray Thompson as an extremist bent on carrying out Chartist principles, although Thompson believed that any franchise lower than £5 was not politically practical. In effect, both candidates presented themselves as free traders and moderate reformers and, in a poll in which fewer than half the electors voted, Thompson was returned.

By the election of 1857, the highly controversial issue of the fusion of Marischal College with King's College was beginning to resurface. Thompson, who had voted with the Radicals against Palmerston's China policies, declined to stand again, retiring to the delights of his new estate at Pitmedden. Sykes, an opponent of University fusion, who had kept his contacts with the city by being made rector of Marischal College in 1854, was brought forward as a Liberal, backed by both Thompson and Fordyce and by a group of well-connected, bright young lawyers whom Adam of the *Herald* dubbed 'the wee clique'. A London barrister with links in the north and who had made his fortune in India, John Farley Leith, also stood, as a Palmerstonian Liberal, causing some offence by coming forward even before Thompson had declared his intentions. Attempts to find a Conservative candidate again fell through. There was not a great deal to separate the two candidates. Both supported the return of Palmerston's government, both favoured a limited extension of the franchise, both favoured an expansion of secular education and the abolition of church rates. Sykes leaned slightly further towards church disestablishment and Leith picked up both Established and Free Church votes. Old political and religious alignments crumbled. A rather rugged, unorthodox individual, Sykes was the more strongly opposed to college fusion and was returned with a majority of 186. His continued defence of the independence of Marischal College ensured his unopposed return

THE LATE COL. W. H. SYKES, M.P.

Col. W. H. Sykes, MP from 1857 until 1872.

in the 1859 election and again in 1865. A tall, upright ex-military man, with a 'rather seedy … swarthy cadaverous look', Sykes had advanced ideas on social reform, took a particular interest in licensing reform and was able to attract broad support. In Parliament he pursued a relatively independent line.[27]

The death of Palmerston in the autumn of 1865 unleashed a renewed demand for reform and a branch of the Scottish Reform League, led by John Sharar, had secured a local membership of 350 by early 1867. The League went out of its way to emphasise constitutionality and the renunciation of physical force, and, in the 1868 election, came out in support of Sykes, approving of his support for Irish Church disestablishment and for female suffrage. The new franchise gave the vote to householders in burghs and more than trebled the size of the electorate. Women were still excluded, although the city assessor, John Duguid Milne, initially agreed to include on the register 1,088 widows and single women who were householders. The sheriff overturned his ruling, but it did unleash a debate on women's rights in the press.[28] There was considerable disappointment that Disraeli's parliamentary manoeuvres dashed the hopes of an additional member for the city and Sykes was returned unopposed in what was described by the *Journal* as the quietest election ever.

John Duguid Milne 1822–1889

The son of a lawyer, John Milne was educated at the Grammar School and also became a lawyer. He was a friend of Alexander Bain and a correspondent of J. S. Mill. Throughout his life he campaigned for women's rights. In 1857 he published, anonymously, *The Industrial and Social Position of Women* in which he argued that middle-class women needed to be able to work and should involve themselves in public life. In 1870 a revised version of the book, *The Industrial Employment of Women*, was published under his own name. He served as city assessor, as secretary of the Aberdeen Philosophical Society and as a member of the University Council, advocating the claims of women to university education. He helped found the Aberdeen Ladies' Educational Association and was a strong supporter of free public libraries.

THE LIBERAL YEARS

Sykes' death in 1872, gave Farley Leith the opportunity to present himself as a moderate Liberal, who would be acceptable to many Conservatives. James Barclay stood against him as an 'advanced' Liberal, as did a South-Wales ironmaster, James Shaw, in the Conservative interest. Leith was comfortably returned. Gladstone's decision to call a snap election in January 1874 was fortuitous for Farley Leith, since Shaw was out of the country and was unable to return in time. None the less, it was a measure of the disenchantment with Gladstone's government that Shaw increased his by-election vote nearly fourfold and came within 1,200 votes of Leith. Leith took his cue from Gladstone with promises to abolish the income tax and to reduce taxes on consumer goods while Shaw focused on social issues affecting the working classes.

During the 1870s both the main parties improved their organisation. It is hard to assess the strength of Conservatism in the city, and, significantly, the Conservative Association, until 1880, called itself the Liberal Conservative Association. The leading figure in the Association was wine merchant and antiquarian, Alexander Walker, son-in-law of the prolific publisher Lewis Smith, and president of the Licenced Trades' Defence Association. It attracted some of the merchant and shipping interests who were beginning to have doubts about free trade, and had the partisan support of the *Aberdeen Journal*. It was a sign of the times that a major businessman, F. Logie Pirie, a paper manufacturer, openly identified himself with the Conservative cause. In 1882 the Conservatives also made a bid for wider support with the establishment of a Working Men's Conservative Association and a club house offering dining and billiards.[29]

A formal Liberal organisation, the Liberal Association, was set up in February 1877 largely due to the activities of William Alexander, the editor of the *Free Press*, William Lindsay, a long-time radical, A. S. Cook, a leading temperance campaigner, James Butchart, a lawyer, and Alexander Taylor, the manager of the Co-operative Coal Society. It claimed to be the first Liberal Association in Scotland 'formed upon a thoroughly representative and democratic basis' and was the first Scottish body to affiliate to Joseph Chamberlain's National Liberal Federation.[30] The new association began actively to organise for local politics, under the leadership of Peter Esslemont, and in November 1877 succeeded in securing the return of seven Liberals to a town council which, they claimed, had recently been pursuing Tory policies. It sought to attract the working class by inviting the trades council, which had been formed in 1868, to send representatives, and Thomas Gill, the president of the trades council, helped draft the constitution.[31]

The new association was intended to unite all shades of Liberal opinion, but from the start it was dominated by the radical wing of the party, particularly by Lindsay and Alexander, and these two succeeded in edging out Farley Leith as the candidate in 1880, and put up instead John Webster of Edgehill. The tall, lanky Webster proudly sported his honorary LL.D., recently awarded for long service on the University Court, but was still attacked for having betrayed Marischal College in the fusion of 1860. He was a compromise choice from thirteen prospective candidates who offered themselves for election. He stood firmly alongside

John Webster 1810–1891

Son of Alexander Webster, a lawyer, John Webster followed his father into the profession. He was elected to represent the first ward in 1853 and served as lord provost 1856–59. He strongly supported the fusion of Marischal and King's Colleges, and opposed a plan to route the Peterhead and Fraserburgh railway through the Links. He was responsible for setting up the Music Hall Company in 1859 to provide a meeting place for the British Association for the Advancement of Science. Initially rather conservative, he opposed the expansionist policies of the 'party of progress', but became more radical in the 1870s favouring church disestablishment and opposing Disraeli's foreign policy. He served as vice president of the Disestablishment Association and later of the Liberation Society from 1875 onwards. He was a member of the University Court 1861–80. He was the first chairman of the Aberdeen Liberal Association 1877 and MP for the city 1880–85, but joined the Liberal Unionists after 1886. He married a daughter of David Chalmers, publisher of the *Aberdeen Journal*.

John Webster, lord provost 1856-59 and Liberal MP 1880-85. Portrait by William Carter, 1887.

Gladstone in his condemnation of Disraeli's foreign policy and had organised a great Liberal demonstration in the city in 1878 in protest against the threat of war against Russia. However, in 1880, his main opposition came from his support for the disestablishment of the Church. Extraordinarily, there were moves by the Conservatives to persuade Alexander Anderson, now 78 years of age but still wheeling and dealing, to stand but he declined. Anderson instead gave his backing to James Shaw, but Shaw split the Conservatives since he was critical of Disraeli's foreign policy and, therefore, the influential Patrick Chalmers of the *Aberdeen Journal* family recommended a search for an alternative. But the Conservative Association in the city was largely defunct and, in a high poll, Webster was returned with a substantial majority.

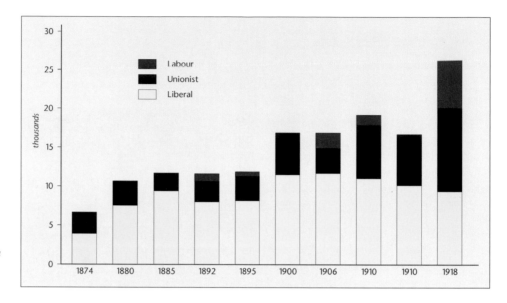

*Figure 7.1
Distribution of
votes by party in
general elections in
Aberdeen,
1874-1918.*

NEW VOICES

The hopes of radicals who swept Gladstone back into power in 1880 were quickly dashed by his disastrous government of 1880-85. Initially there was enthusiasm, particularly for the Irish land reforms and the Government's apparent readiness to challenge the House of Lords. There were hopes of land reform at home, with vigorous support for the Farmers' Alliance through which local farmers were pressing for greater rights for tenants. Disenchantment set in quickly, however, and support for the Liberal Association fell away. The tensions so apparent among the politicians quickly made themselves felt in the constituencies, and Aberdeen was no exception. A younger, more radical element tried to make its voice heard against the old guard by forming first the Junior Liberal Association in 1882 and then the Radical Association in 1884, which became the forum for discussion of the new intellectual ideas that were stirring younger radicals.[32] The Radical Association wanted to be free to criticise the Liberal leadership and to press for land nationalisation, abolition of the House of Lords, payment of MPs, women's suffrage, and triennial parliaments. The emergence of the Radical Association was probably also influenced by tensions over local issues. The town council, under the leadership of Peter Esslemont, was pushing forward a new City Improvement Act, involving the building of Rosemount Viaduct and the extension of the city boundaries. It aroused considerable resistance. The Act doubled the number of wards to be contested in local elections and required a local 'general election' when all council seats had to be contested. A big demonstration in August 1884, the largest in the city since 1832, gave support to the campaign for equalisation of the

ABERDEEN 1800–2000

THE MASONS WILL DO ALL THEY CAN FOR THE FRANCHISE AND THE GRAND OLD MAN.

county and burgh franchise, with the Keith-born surgeon Dr Maitland Moir as the main organiser. The great procession was led by nineteen carriages carrying survivors of the 1832 agitation, followed by 30 former Chartists. With unrest spreading among Highland crofters and the continuing agitation of tenant farmers, the issue of land reform came to the forefront of politics. The Rev. C. C. MacDonald of St Clement's Parish Church, a Gaelic speaker, was very active in the Land Law Reform Association and the local solicitor D. C. MacDonald, another Gaelic speaker and secretary of the Association, campaigned alongside the American reformer, Henry George. The Rev. MacDonald, a man whom a critic described as having 'his finger in every pie in Aberdeen', also had close links with the trades council. In his powerful sermon to the delegates gathered in Aberdeen for the 1884 meeting of the Trades Union Congress, he told them that 'it is not enough for you to exercise the franchise, and to give your votes to the best and largest-hearted men of the classes who have hitherto controlled legislation. You must represent yourselves. You must do your own work in Parliament and in the other councils and governing bodies of the nation'.[33]

A trade union demonstration, August 1884, in support of reform of the country franchise, passes the Criterion Bar on the top left and Joint Station on the right.

There was encouragement for the radicals in the redistribution of 1885 which divided Aberdeen into two constituencies, North and South, much against the desires of the Liberal Association which wanted an extra member but not a divided city. The radicals quickly identified William Alexander Hunter as a candidate for the more working-class northern division. The more middle-class Aberdeen South constituency selected the Oxford-based James Bryce, who had sat for Tower Hamlets since 1880, but was looking for a more secure seat and one which would be less distracting from his writing and travel commitments. An enthusiastic mountaineer and future president of the Cairngorm Club, Bryce had attracted notice in the North-East by his 'Access to the Mountains' (Scotland) Bill which he first introduced in 1884. He received numerous letters from Deeside artists and walkers who had experienced being peppered with lead shot from zealous gamekeepers, and had the backing of the Aberdeen Land Law Reform Association. Over the next few years he and other North-East MPs tried in vain to place freedom to roam legislation onto the statute book.[34]

Gladstone's conversion to home rule for Ireland provided an opportunity for those who disliked and feared the loud radical voices in the local Liberal Association to find a new home. By the spring of 1886 there were growing signs of disquiet within the Liberal ranks. It was not confined to people on the right of the party. It also split the Radical Association, whose chairman, ex-Baillie Alexander Duffus, disapproved of Irish home rule. A Liberal Unionist group, under the leadership of John F. White, tried to persuade the former MP John Webster to stand against Bryce. He declined, and both Hunter and Bryce were returned unopposed in the election of July 1886. Both the local daily newspapers now espoused the Liberal Unionist cause, and, although Bryce was not a particularly enthusiastic home ruler,

William Alexander Hunter 1844–1898

Son of James Hunter, granite merchant and president of the Northern Co-operative Society, William Hunter was educated at the Grammar School and Aberdeen University. He entered the Middle Temple and was called to the bar in 1867. He was professor of Roman law (1869–79), and professor of jurisprudence (1879–82) at University College, London. He came to local prominence in 1870 when he helped defend a right of way between the Bridge of Dee and Morrison's Bridge, Cults in a local *cause célèbre* which ended up in the Court of Session, and in 1879 when he had acted as counsel for the town council in a dispute with the harbour commissioners. He was also a prominent speaker on behalf of tenant farmers and in support of land reform. In 1884 he founded the People's League for the Abolition of the House of Lords and it was the Radical Association and the trades council which supported him in 1885. He served as MP for Aberdeen North 1885–96. He was a suppporter of the Farmers' Alliance and the Land Reform Movement. He favoured home rule for Ireland and Scotland, and introduced a Scottish Home Rule Bill in 1892. He supported the nationalisation of Highland estates. He was largely responsible for securing the use of probate duty to abolish school fees. He received the freedom of the city in 1890 for his services to securing free education.

he lost 'many of his oldest and best supporters'.[35] These included John Webster and John Crombie who successively chaired the Liberal Unionist Association. The key figure in the organisation was the lawyer William R. Reid, who organised visits from leading political figures and who prepared the way for the merger of Conservative and Liberal Unionist supporters in the 1890s.

THE EMERGENCE OF SOCIALISM

There were many who believed that only a drastic measure of land reform, not excluding nationalisation of land, could begin to solve some of the economic problems facing the country. The Unitarian Rev. Alexander Webster who, while based in Glasgow, had chaired the Scottish Land Restoration League, arrived in the city in 1884 and for the next seven years helped spread socialist ideas.[36] There was also strong support for Scottish home rule and the trades council agreed to collaborate with the Junior Liberal Association and the Radical Association in a home rule demonstration at the end of 1886.[37] Hunter remained a persistent campaigner for Scottish home rule as did Peter Esslemont who, in 1885, became MP for East

Opposite (top): Rev. C. C. MacDonald, land reformer and campaigner.

Opposite (foot): James Bryce, Liberal MP for South Aberdeen from 1885 until 1906.

Aberdeenshire. There were also signs of wider stirrings when George Bissett, president of the trades council, called for the organisation of a strictly working-class political association, in October 1886, to secure more direct representation in Parliament and on public boards. A more controversial declaration took place in the following autumn when the young propagandist for the socialist Scottish Land and Labour League, John Lincoln Mahon, addressed an open-air Saturday afternoon meeting in the Castlegate, chaired by James Leatham, a compositor. He knew his audience and immediately tapped into land issues: 'You sing of your bonnie Scotland and your heather hills. It's not your bonnie Scotland. It's not your heather hills. It's the landlord's bonnie Scotland. It's the landlord's heather hills. And if you want enough earth to set a geranium in you've got to pinch it.'[38] On the following Sunday, a meeting ended in the arrest of Leatham and Mahon for lecturing on politics on the sabbath. The two days before the pair were due to appear in front of the magistrates gave time for the radicals to rally to a defence of free speech, and Mahon and Leatham were triumphantly acquitted. Mahon was able to leave Aberdeen with a branch of the Land and Labour League launched under Leatham's leadership. The League encouraged trade unionists to focus on the issue of an eight-hour working day to be enforced by legislation. This became a test issue for socialists, and it is a measure of the influence of Leatham and his friends in Aberdeen that after months of debate, Aberdeen was, in August 1889, the first trades council in the country to declare in favour of a legislative eight-hour day.[39]

This focus on the eight-hour day issue was also influenced by Henry Hyde Champion, a former army officer who had resigned his commission in the midst of the Egyptian campaign and who had returned to England to become a founder member of the Social Democratic Federation (SDF) in 1884. Champion came to socialism from a Conservative rather than a Liberal background. His links with the North-East came through his mother's family, the Urquharts of Udny. He visited the city in 1887 and 1888 under the auspices of the Land and Labour League and the Scottish Socialist Federation. He returned for the first May Day rally in 1890 which was the largest in the country outside London. The loyalty to Champion displayed by the supporters of the Independent Labour Party (ILP) in Aberdeen was one of the more surprising features of a most unusual career. Like the Irish leader, Parnell, whom he wished to emulate by forming a party based on a single issue, the eight-hour day, Champion's force of personality was such that it was difficult for anyone to be indifferent to him. Aberdeen trades council took the initiative in forming the Scottish Trades Councils' Labour Party in rivalry with Hardie's Scottish Labour Party in 1892. They brought forward Champion to oppose Bryce in the 1892 election. Bryce had shown an arrogant insensitivity towards the trade unions, as, indeed, he often did to his entire constituency. Bryce had also been less than enthusiastic about Scottish home rule, thus losing the support of some of his traditional supporters.[40] Champion's platform consisted of one issue, an eight-hour day, but he was also able to tap into some latent support among Aberdeen trade unionists for a move away from free trade. As early as 1888 he had made the point that an eight-hour day could not be achieved 'without conceding the principle of Free Trade' and he later came to anticipate Joseph Chamberlain's calls for an imperial customs union. Otherwise his address consisted of no more than an assertion of his independent stance observing that 'my attitude towards these parties is one of impartial criticism. Any proposition which will effectively secure the social freedom of the people or advance their political liberty, will have my warm support, no matter what side of the House it comes from.'[41]

Not all socialists in the city supported him; the Liberals believed that, as a protectionist who was unsound on temperance, 'his whole programme smells of Tory subsidy', and the normally sympathetic *People's Journal* refused to back him. Despite that, he polled 991 votes, the highest for an Independent Labour candidate in Scotland, but considerably less than Bryce or the Conservative, McCullugh. In spite of some disappointment, the trades council did not go back on its independent stance and the delegate to the TUC was instructed to vote for 'entirely independent action by the working classes'. The local Liberal leadership was slow to recognise the changes which were taking place in politics: 'fossilized survivors of your younger days', a sympathiser told Bryce.[42]

A meeting of the trades council, the ILP and the SDF in May 1894 agreed to seek Labour candidates for both divisions of the city. Bryce had bitterly attacked the ILP with its emphasis on class representation as 'violating the true traditions of

English public life' and declared that he would rather that working men joined the Tory Party than the Labour Party. He also showed no sympathy for the demand for a legal eight-hour day. A motion from the Aberdeen ILP that, in the event of there not being a Labour candidate, support should be given to the Conservative, although never put to the vote, anticipated the appearance of the maverick Tory-Radical, Maltman Barrie, on the scene as a possible Conservative candidate. In the end the Conservative Association adopted the more orthodox Liberal Unionist, the wealthy combmaker and lord provost, David Stewart, as their candidate in Aberdeen South, and a number of Aberdeen ILP activists spoke on his behalf because he showed some sympathy for the eight-hours agitation. In Aberdeen North, John Lincoln Mahon was proposed as a Labour candidate, amid a great deal of controversy as the intrigues deeply divided both the Aberdeen ILP and the trades council. There was still a considerable residue of support for Hunter among trade unionists. Hunter had been largely responsible for bringing about free education and had introduced a private member's bill for Scottish home rule, but he was not keen on the demands for an eight-hour day. The trades council finally did not give official support to Mahon's candidacy and he polled only 608 votes.

The rumour in the following year that Hunter was to resign his seat allowed some of the old intrigue to reappear. Hostility by Champion's friends towards Keir Hardie, who had lost his seat at West Ham in 1895, was still a factor and the local movement backed the general secretary of the ILP, Tom Mann, as their candidate.

Duncan Vernon Pirie, MP for North Aberdeen from 1896 until 1918.

Hardie took the snub very personally and even considered resigning from the party, but his strong identification with the miners in west Scotland created no resonance in the North-East, while Mann's activities among dockers and seamen did. The outcome was a spectacularly close run contest in which Mann polled 2,476 to the Liberal Duncan Vernon Pirie's 2,909. The Liberals had toyed with the idea of finding someone who would be acceptable to Labour and approached the radical journalist A. E. Fletcher, but in the end chose Pirie.[43] He followed a well-established Aberdeen political tradition. Not only did he come from a local family, but he was still in military service as a captain of hussars, with a distinguished record in the Egyptian campaign. At the same time, his selection was in many ways a direct defiance of the local labour movement since the family firm was not noted for its good relations with trade unions.

Despite Mann's remarkable performance there was

no follow-up. The Aberdeen ILP, badly divided by the intrigues of 1895, struggled to survive and eventually merged with the national party. Three middle-class ILP candidates, Beveridge, Gray and Glass, continued to serve on the town council, as did Johnston, the secretary of the trades council, and William Cooper, a joiner and member of the SDF. It was the SDF which increasingly made the running in Aberdeen Labour politics after 1895, regularly holding propaganda meetings. The branch confidently proposed in 1899 to nominate H. M. Hyndman as a candidate at the next general election, but narrowly failed to win support from the trades council. Proposals from ILP supporters to run R. B. Cunninghame-Graham in Aberdeen South also fell through and in the khaki election of 1900 no Labour candidates were brought forward.

The trades council had, at an early stage, protested against the 'unjust and iniquitous' war in South Africa as being pursued in the interests of 'Jewish and British speculators'.[44] A 'stop the war' meeting organised by local socialists and pro-Boers such as the Rev. Webster actually took place on the day after the news came through about the relief of the siege of Mafeking. It ended in a riot and there were unpleasant assaults by 'patriots' against Webster, the ILP councillor Dr Beveridge, and one of the German lecturers at Marischal College. Bryce, although critical, was seen as someone who had 'wobbled a good deal' in his stance on the Boer War and there were considerable doubts among some trade unionists about supporting him. On the other hand, from the Conservative and Unionist side, Bryce and Pirie, both came under attack as 'pro-Boers' although the latter had actually returned to the colours in South Africa by the time of the election. Despite the jingoism which surrounded the election, Bryce in the end had a much increased majority against a Conservative, as did Pirie, who faced a strong challenge from a Liberal Unionist, Robert Williams, a former colleague of Cecil Rhodes, who tried to appeal to the working class with a combination of imperialism and social reform.

THE NEW CENTURY

The early months of 1900 saw the formation first of the Scottish Workers' Parliamentary Elections Committee in Edinburgh and then of the Labour Representation Committee in London. Aberdeen was not represented at either of these but, by the following year, Aberdeen SDF members were playing a vocal role in the Scottish committee. Alexander Ritchie moved a resolution, which was carried, 'that the nationalisation of land, railways and mines be made a plank in the Committee's programme' and Thomas Kennedy moved for 'free maintenance of children in all board schools', only to have the SDF withdraw its affiliation a few months later, against the wishes of the Aberdeen branch.[45] Kennedy was to continue to regard this as a fatally missed opportunity to influence the Labour movement from the inside. In September 1900, an Aberdeen Workers' Election Committee was formed to bring together socialists and trade unionists. Elrick, the president of the trades council chaired it, but its initial record was not impressive. Elrick, himself, failed ignominiously to win the Greyfriars ward in the town council election of 1901, a seat formerly held by an ILP councillor. In 1902, all three of the committee's candidates went down to defeat, including Johnston, who had represented the St Andrew's ward for 11 years. They made some progress on other bodies, and two candidates with trades council backing were elected to the parochial council in 1901. Further defeats in municipal elections in 1903 and recriminations between the SDF and the trades council led to the collapse of the Workers' Election Committee although Thomas Kennedy was elected to the school board in 1903.

An active and influential trades council, very conscious of its dignity and determined to be seen as the voice of the organised working class, found it hard to tolerate the sharper, more confrontational tones of the Social Democratic Federation (SDF). The Aberdeen branch of the SDF showed marked insensitivity to the trade unionists. The key figure in the branch was the Kennethmont-born former railway clerk, Thomas Kennedy, a highly experienced Clarion lecturer who in 1903 became Scottish organiser for the SDF. Kennedy, one of the ablest Marxists in the Federation and a prolific contributor to its paper, *Justice*, had little time for compromises of any kind with liberalism. He had denounced those socialists who were prepared to go along with pro-Boers by depicting the South African War as 'Chamberlain's war'. This to him was 'impractical sentimentalism'. War, he argued was the 'inevitable accompaniment' of capitalism.[46] Ramsay MacDonald's argument, when he spoke in Aberdeen in December 1904, that even the institutions of a capitalist state could be used to 'contribute to the building of the health, wealth and happiness of all the industrial classes' received equally short-shrift from Kennedy.[47] It was the young who were attracted to socialism and one of them, John Paton, later recalled how he and the members of the Clarion Club saw themselves 'in a perpetual state of simmering revolt' against Aberdeen bourgeois society. As he said, 'they were zealots in possession of a new revelation' and they revelled in their social ostracism. 'We conceived we were the stuff of the martyrs'.[48]

In 1905 a new, more moderate voice emerged when Joseph Duncan, secretary of the Scottish Steam Fishing Vessels', Enginemen's and Firemen's Union re-established a branch of the ILP. Duncan believed that only those who could rally 'the combined labour forces behind them' would succeed. He regarded the SDF tactics as counter-productive posturing, 'a cry in the wilderness', dividing the Labour movement. A deep rivalry developed between the two bodies, and the two leading figures in them, emerging when Duncan refused to support Kennedy in

Aberdeen North in the 1906 election, although the ILP branch did. Kennedy's relatively poor showing was not helped by Maltman Barrie's intervention for the Conservatives. Champion and Mann, both in Australia, were reputed to have written in support of Barrie, and the Conservative *Aberdeen Journal* reprinted Barrie's 1890 pamphlet in support of an eight-hour day, *The Labour Day*. But Duncan had no doubt that the fault lay with Kennedy himself and the lack of proper organisation. Pirie, who supported old age pensions financed by a tax on land, was duly returned with 63 per cent of the vote. R. B. Cunninghame Graham had once more declined a request from the local ILP to stand in Aberdeen South and Bryce was again returned with his largest ever majority, despite the attraction of Chamberlain's tariff reform to some local trade unionists.

Mrs Kennedy was more successful than her husband in that she was returned in the school board election of April 1906 to join her husband who was already a member. There was soon a renewed effort at unity when the trades council, the ILP, the Women's Political Association and the SDF agreed to establish an Aberdeen Labour Representation Council. Bryce's decision in December 1906 to accept the post of British ambassador in Washington occasioned a by-election and, a mere ten days before polling, the Labour Representation Council agreed to put forward the SDF nominee, Fred Bramley, a former Bradford cabinetmaker, who had been a well-known Clarion propagandist in Scotland, and had supported Kennedy in 1906. His platform was unequivocally socialist, demanding the nationalisation of land and the public ownership of railways, coal mines, canals 'and all other forms of Social Service that could be managed and controlled collectively in the interest of all'. There were no resources, poor organisation, a principled resistance to canvassing on the part of the SDF and many other tensions, including personal ones, although both Kennedy and Duncan took turns in chairing the public meetings held by the candidate. A small number of trade-union tariff reformers supported the Unionist, Ronald McNeill, a journalist.[49]

But the Liberal Party was also divided. Since the beginning of the century groups of young Liberals had sought to radicalise the party and secure a commitment to a programme of social reform, while the moderate old guard had resisted. A long list of possible candidates was considered and it was eventually narrowed down to two, the ex-lord provost and wood merchant, John Fleming, and the son of Peter Esslemont, the former MP. George Birnie Esslemont was chairman of the Liberal Association, and his selection over Fleming left a residue of bitterness among local party members. There was also the complication of women's suffrage. An Aberdeen Women's Suffrage Association had been working for some time to get women into public bodies. Although Esslemont, unlike Bryce who had always been strongly opposed, was a supporter of women's suffrage, Mrs Pankhurst's Women's Social and Political Union (WSPU) was campaigning against all government candidates, and

THE WANTS OF MODERN WOMEN.

Prominent Public Man—"Dear me, dear me! What will they want next? They demand votes, seats on the School Board, representation on the Technical College Committee, and—and—well, what would you like, my dear?"

Young Lady—"Oh, I am old-fashioned enough to be content if I get a good husband."

Public Man—"Well, I am glad there is one sensible woman left, and I have no doubt you will very soon get a good husband."

Anti-suffragette cartoon, March 1909.

leading suffragists like Teresa Billington, Annie Kenney, Helen Fraser and Emmeline Pankhurst herself all appeared in the city during the by-election. Bramley, standing under a socialist label, polled a respectable 1,740 votes in unfavourable territory for a Labour candidate, and Esslemont ended up with a majority of only 367.

In the aftermath of the campaign a branch of the WSPU was formed in the city with Lady Ramsay as president and Caroline Phillips, a journalist, as secretary. A visit by Asquith for his rectorial installation some months later provided another opportunity for publicity. But the violent tactics used by the stewards against Mrs Pankhurst, the elderly Rev. Alexander Webster and others, to prevent a motion on women's suffrage being proposed led the far from sympathetic *Evening Express* to denounce the 'methods of barbarism' that had been deployed.[50] A number of young women, many of them students, risked ridicule and violence to campaign for the cause. It was not helped by Emily Davison, soon to die under the King's horse at Epsom, thrashing a poor Baptist clergyman as he emerged from a train at the Joint Station in the mistaken belief that he was Asquith. Militant tactics were employed. In November 1912, four women were charged with trying to disrupt a Lloyd George meeting in the Music Hall, and in 1914 there was an attempt to burn down Ashley Road School.

The winding up of the Scottish Labour Party in January 1909 and the affiliation of the Aberdeen branch to the British Labour Party shattered the precarious unity of the left. The SDF branch could not be affiliated to the Labour Party, and since Kennedy, already identified as prospective candidate for Aberdeen North, would not adhere to the Labour Party constitution, the Aberdeen Labour Party would not commit itself to support him. The bitterness between Duncan and Kennedy reappeared, with accusations that Duncan had secretly undermined Kennedy's candidacy in 1906. The left was hopelessly divided. Only the trades council and the ILP were affiliated to the Aberdeen Labour Party. But outside it stood the Social Democratic Party (as the SDF had now become), the Aberdeen Socialist Club, the Marxian Socialist Club, the Socialist Labour Party, the Industrial Workers of the World, the Industrial League and the Clarion Club, almost all offshoots of the Social Democrats. The socialists focused their campaign on demands for the medical officer of health to take action to force owners to improve the notorious slums of the Guestrow and Shuttle Lane. Not surprisingly when the general election came in January 1910, Kennedy did even less well than he had in 1906. Pirie was returned with a clear, although reduced, majority against Kennedy and a Liberal Unionist. In the December election of that same year Kennedy's name was again proposed as candidate by the SDP but withdrawn just before nomination day, deliberately leaving no time for any other body to find a candidate. Pirie was again comfortably returned against the Liberal Unionist candidate. In Aberdeen South, Esslemont faced a Conservative in January 1910 and a Liberal Unionist in December and on both occasions won more than half the votes. In Labour politics the squabbles continued.

THE FIRST WORLD WAR

The war changed much. Labour organisation continued to improve and trade unionism expanded. The new constitution of the Labour Party united trade-union and political interests. The Liberal Party, in contrast, began to disintegrate as Liberals saw the great principles which had sustained them in the nineteenth century sacrificed to the needs of total war. The local Liberal Party split over the introduction of conscription and a number of key figures resigned. Esslemont made it clear that he was deeply unhappy about it although he could not bring himself actually to vote against the government. At the end of 1916, increasingly committed to the idea of a negotiated peace, he announced his resignation. In the ensuing by-election, held at one of the most critical junctures of the war just as news of the February revolution in Russia began to filter through, Liberal acrimony could not be suppressed. Lloyd George had nominated Sir James Murray, but Asquith's supporters were determined on their own man and proposed first Asquith's private secretary, Vivian Phillips, and then the former lord provost, Sir John Fleming. Murray withdrew, but some Lloyd George supporters put up J. Robertson Watson, professor of chemistry at the Royal College of Science and Technology in Glasgow. Watson had stood as a Labour candidate in Glasgow Bridgeton in 1895, but now he presented himself as a 'democratic patriot', bent on combating pacifist propaganda, and a supporter of tariff reform. The Labour Party had decided against participating since it was deeply divided by the war and also because so many of its potential supporters were away from Aberdeen. But the Union for Democratic Control (UDC), pressing for peace by negotiation, was determined to seize the propaganda opportunity of the by-election and brought forward the well-known London pacifist and campaigner for women's rights, F. W. Pethick-Lawrence. There was no UDC branch in Aberdeen and little to build on, and Pethick-Lawrence and his supporters had a rough time. Gordon Highlanders broke up his meetings and Ramsay MacDonald, who came to speak in his support, seemed to rouse a special ire.[51] The trades council and the local Labour Party declined to back him. That apart, the election stirred little enthusiasm. On a snowy day, only 37 per cent of the electorate turned out. The Unionists gave no backing to Watson and most rallied to Fleming who was returned, with Pethick-Lawrence gaining a surprising 333 votes.

The expanded electorate of 1918 tripled the city's electorate and enfranchised more than 12,000 women. The Liberal Party was divided and the national mood was swinging to the right. Aberdeen South went overwhelmingly to a Conservative Coalitionist, F. C. Thomson, who ousted Sir John Fleming, who had been refused the coalition 'ticket' and again had to face opposition from Professor Watson standing as an independent. Meanwhile, in Aberdeen North, Pirie, a Lloyd George Liberal, was defeated by the journalist, Frank Rose, standing for Labour. Pirie had opposed votes for women and had refused to commit himself to a minimum wage for farm workers, neither of which helped him with the new electorate. Rose, a staunchly pro-war Labour man, who had first been considered as a possible candidate in the 1907 by-election, ran an unashamedly 'Hang the Kaiser' campaign, demanding that conscientious objectors be deprived of the vote for five years. There was little of socialism in his speeches and with no Conservative opposition he duly reaped his reward, with a majority of 210.

Since the reform of 1832, Aberdeen had developed a strong tradition of Liberal radicalism. It was always Liberals who were chosen as representatives of the city, but concern about particular local issues was vital for the success of any candidate. Conservatism was unable to make much impact after the decades of Tory dominance by the Haddens had been brought to an end. From 1885 onward, in Hunter and Bryce, the city returned two leading Liberals, with the more radical Hunter frequently pressing the demand for Scottish home rule. When, from the 1880s, the Liberal Party nationally failed to respond quickly enough to the new demands coming from the working class, Aberdeen trade unionists were among the first to support independent Labour representation. But this also manifested a distinctively Aberdeen approach which was not always in tune with those in the west of Scotland who dominated the Labour movement.[52]

Table 7.1 *Aberdeen parliamentary representation and election results, 1832–1918*

Pre-reform Members

1792-1802	Alexander Allardyce
1802-1806	James Farquhar
1806-1807	John Ramsay
1807-1818	James Farquhar
1818-1830	Joseph Hume
1830-1831	Sir James Carnegie
1831-1832	Horatio Ross

Election results

1832	Alexander Bannerman (Lib)	unopposed
1835	Alexander Bannerman (Lib)	938
	Sir Arthur Farquhar (Con)	372
	Majority	566
1837	Alexander Bannerman (Lib)	unopposed
1841	Alexander Bannerman (Lib)	780
	William Innes (Con)	513
	Robert Lowery (Chartist)	30
	Majority	267
1847	Alexander Dingwall Fordyce (Lib)	918
	William Henry Sykes (Lib)	422
	Majority	496
1852	George Thompson (Lib)	682
	Sir Andrew Leith Hay (Lib)	478
	Majority	204
1857	William Henry Sykes (Lib)	1,085
	John Farley Leith (Lib)	840
	Majority	245
1859	William Henry Sykes (Lib)	unopposed
1865	William Henry Sykes (Lib)	unopposed
1868	William Henry Sykes (Lib)	unopposed
1872 [by-election]	John Farley Leith (Lib)	4,392
	James William Barclay (Lib)	2,615
	James Shaw (Con)	704
	Majority	1,777
1874	John Farley Leith (Lib)	3,910

	James Shaw (Con)	2,724
	Majority	1,186
1880	John Webster (Lib)	7,505
	James Shaw (Con)	3,139
	Majority	4,366
1885 North	William Alexander Hunter (Lib)	4,794
	C. B. Scott Foster MacGeogh (Con)	894
	James Wallace Thom (Indep)	177
	Majority	3,900
1885 South	James Bryce (Lib)	4,548
	Colin Mackenzie (Con)	1,455
	Majority	3,093
1886 North	William Alexander Hunter (Lib)	unopposed
1886 South	James Bryce (Lib)	unopposed
1892 North	William Alexander Hunter (Lib)	4,462
	Bremner Patrick Lee (Unionist)	870
	Majority	3,592
1892 South	James Bryce (Lib)	3,513
	James Gordon McCullugh (Unionist)	1,768
	Henry Hyde Champion (Lab)	991
	Majority	1,745
1895 North	William Alexander Hunter (Lib)	4,156
	John Lincon Mahon (Indep Lab)	608
	Majority	3,548
1895 South	James Bryce (Lib)	3,985
	D. Stewart (Lib Unionist)	3,121
	Majority	864
1896 North [by-election]	Duncan Vernon Pirie (Lib)	2,909
	Tom Mann (Lab)	2,479
	Majority	430
1900 North	Duncan Vernon Pirie (Lib)	4,238
	R. Williams (Con)	2,251
	Majority	1,987
1900 South	James Bryce (Lib)	4,238
	W. C. Smith (Unionist)	3,121
	Majority	1,117

1906 North	Duncan Vernon Pirie (Lib)	4,852
	T. Kennedy (SDF)	1,935
	Maltman M. Barrie (Con)	931
	Majority	2,917
1906 South	James Bryce (Lib)	6,780
	W. G. Black (Unionist)	2,332
	Majority	4,448
1907 South [by-election]	George Birnie Esslemont (Lib)	3,779
	Ronald J. McNeill (Unionist)	3,421
	Frederick Bramley (Lab)	1,740
	Majority	358
1910 (Jan.) North	Duncan Vernon Pirie (Lib)	4,297
	R. Scott Brown (Lib Unionist)	2,314
	T. Kennedy (SDF)	1,344
	Majority	1,983
1910 (Jan.) South	George Birnie Esslemont (Lib)	6,749
	Ronald J. McNeill (Con)	4,433
	Majority	2,316
1910 (Dec.) North	Duncan Vernon Pirie (Lib)	4,282
	R. Scott Brown (Con)	2,546
	Majority	1,736
1910 (Dec.) South	George Birnie Esslemont (Lib)	5,862
	W. C. Smith (Lib Unionist)	3,997
	Majority	1,865
1917 South [by-election]	Sir John Fleming (Lib)	3,283
	J. R. Watson (Indep)	1,507
	F. W. Pethick-Lawrence (Indep)	333
	Majority	1,776
1918 North	Frank Herbert Rose (Lab)	6,128
	Duncan Vernon Pirie (Coalition Lib)	5,918
	Majority	210
1918 South	Frederick C. Thomson (Coalition Con)	10,625
	Sir John Fleming (Lib)	3,535
	J. R. Watson (Indep)	2,868
	Majority	7,090

8

Twentieth-century Politics

MICHAEL C. DYER

THE ELECTORAL SYSTEM

The Representation of the People Act, 1918, had a greater impact on British politics than any other single piece of legislation since the Reform Act of 1832. The introduction of universal male suffrage and the extension of the franchise to women aged 30 years and over greatly increased the parliamentary electorate, while a redistribution of constituencies increased the importance of the large cities and industrial counties. Subsequently, there were few major changes. The extension of the franchise to women on the same basis as men, following the Equal Franchise Act of 1928, resulted in females, having been excluded from the parliamentary register before 1918, outnumbering males in all the general elections since 1929.

It is indicative of the scale of the 1918 reforms that only about one in four of the electorate in 1922 would have had the opportunity to cast a ballot in 1910. Furthermore, between the general election of December 1910 and the census of 1921, while the number of enfranchised males more than doubled in Aberdeen North, they increased by little more than 50 per cent in Aberdeen South, and while females constituted a somewhat modest 39.8 per cent of the roll in the North they comprised 43.0 per cent of the register in the South. Following the equalisation of the franchise, women accounted for fully 58.5 per cent of all electors in the South, making it one of the most female-dominated constituencies in Scotland. Amendments to the electoral system after 1928, such as the abolition of the business vote before the 1950 general election, were of much less significance. The most important development after 1945 was the reduction of the voting age to 18, following the Representation of the People Act, 1968, but its political consequences were unimportant.

A critical factor influencing the politics of parliamentary representation has been the configuration of the constituencies. In social terms, the two seats which emerged in 1918 were sharply contrasting. Aberdeen North, in which almost half the inhabitants lived in dwellings of two rooms or less, was an overwhelmingly working-class seat heavily concentrated around the harbour. It might have been better described as Aberdeen East, for it had newly gained the fishing suburb of

Torry from Kincardineshire, while its northern extremities, which encompassed the former police burgh of Woodside and burgh of barony of Old Aberdeen, were sparsely populated. The massive municipal housing estates, filled by refugees decanted from inner city wards, that were to be Aberdeen North's dominant features from the late 1950s onward, had yet to appear. Aberdeen South, by contrast, remained a south-west wedge including all the middle-class wards, with almost 70 per cent of its constituents living in dwellings of three rooms or more.

Before 1983, the boundaries of Scottish parliamentary constituencies were based on the historic division between burgh and county, but in that year they were brought into conformity with the regions and districts of the post-1974 local government system. In Grampian, however, the quest for parity of size made it necessary for some of the new constituencies to infringe the lower tier district boundaries. Aberdeen District, consequently, while wholly incorporating the former city divisions, also included parts of parliamentary constituencies of both Kincardine and Deeside and of Gordon. Furthermore, the council estates of Kincorth and Garthdee, together with the middle-class electors of Mannofield, were moved out of Aberdeen South into the Kincardine and Deeside parliamentary seat, though the acquisition of St Clement's from Aberdeen North provided an element of compensation. As a result, Aberdeen South came to include the whole of the harbour area of Torry and St Clement's, which had contained a large proportion of the Aberdeen North electors between 1918 and 1950. The changes did not greatly upset the socio-political balance in the South, though they were held to favour Labour marginally.

The representation of Aberdeen was rationalised in 1997, when the commissioners found it possible to establish three seats coterminous with the local authority. Inevitably, there were major consequences for the former burgh divisions that had maintained a recognisable degree of continuity since 1885. Although Aberdeen South regained the areas it had ceded to Kincardine and Deeside in 1983, it lost its traditional Unionist heartland, Union Street and parts of the west end including Beaconsfield Place, Carlton Place, Devonshire Road, Hamilton Place and Stanley Street, to the new Aberdeen Central division. Although solid, prosperous middle-class suburbs along Deeside were added, they had proved vulnerable to the Liberal Democrats in local elections. Aberdeen North was also much changed, for not only did it include post-war housing estates, but it was also associated for the first time with parts of suburbia in the former Gordon constituency in the lower middle-class owner occupier estates extending from the mouth of the Don to Woodside, and incorporated developments around the airport at Dyce. Only Aberdeen Central, predominantly working class and confined to the pre-1974 municipality, retained a traditional social profile. Thus, whatever the contemporary circumstances, institutional factors alone promised to

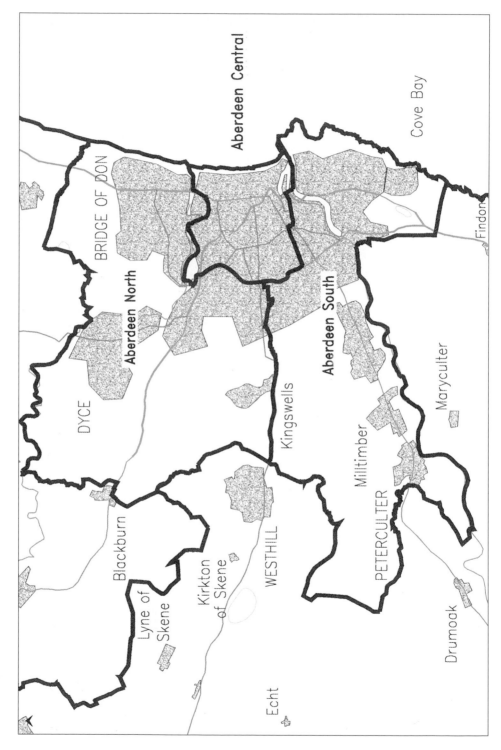

Map 3.
Parliamentary
constituencies 1997.

ensure that 1997 would mark a new phase in the politics of the city's parliamentary representation.

THE ECLIPSE OF THE LIBERALS

Before 1918, Aberdeen politics had been dominated by the Liberals, but subsequently the fortunes of the Labour movement dictated the pace of change. Even before 1914, the trades council and socialist parties had begun to challenge the bourgeois hegemony of both local politics and parliamentary representation, but the restricted franchise had hindered their progress. The Act of 1918, however, enabled Labour to redefine the parameters of partisanship. The main instrument for the political advancement of the left in Aberdeen during the inter-war period was the trades council, which acted as a focus not only for the socialist fight against capitalism, but also for the struggle between Labour and the Communists for power over the working-class movement. As with other Scottish trades councils, its strength represented a local centre of political power which challenged the centralising pressures emanating from national leaderships, both political and industrial. In 1920 the trades council established a council of action to resist British intervention in the Russo-Polish war.[1] During the 1926 General Strike, which its members fully supported, the trades council organised the distribution of food in association with the Northern Co-operative Society.[2] Face-to-face relationships made it easy for left-leaning Labour supporters to co-operate with Communists in organisations such as the Minority Movement, against the wishes of their national leaders and, in 1937, the trades council disaffiliated from the burgh Labour Party in order to participate in the activities of the Communist-dominated Unemployed Workers' Committee and the United Front against Fascism.[3]

The pressure exerted by the left inevitably forced changes on the centre-right. Socialist successes in municipal elections after the Great War threatened and gradually undermined the non-partisan ethos of municipal politics, as electoral pressures forced independent councillors, mostly Unionists and Liberals, to act more and more like a political party in opposition. Similarly, Labour's capture of Aberdeen North in 1918 and its emergence as the second party in Aberdeen South in 1923, persuaded most Liberal voters that their historic dispute with the Unionists was an unaffordable luxury. This process was fiercely encouraged by the traditionally Conservative, *Aberdeen Journal*, and its sister paper the *Evening Express*. The development of a defensive anti-socialist alliance proved successful in carrying both parliamentary constituencies in 1931, and denied Labour a majority on the town council until 1945. Thus, while the left was forcing political developments, more traditional attitudes, deference to local elites and doubts about the competence of Labour politicians, both local and national, still prevailed.

By temperament the centre-right was less active than the left, but its possession of power across a range of social, economic and political institutions was sufficient to support its interests without recourse to overt political activity. Nevertheless, when confronted with the challenge of the General Strike the authorities liberally employed the Emergency Powers Act, 1920, and the lord provost threatened the tramwaymen individually with dismissal and loss of superannuation.[4] Throughout Britain the leading political question in 1918 was not whether Labour could replace the Liberals, but whether the Liberals or the Unionists were best equipped to meet the socialist threat. In the event, burgh Liberalism in Scotland was to survive only where Labour was weak as in Edinburgh, or divided as in Greenock, or had understandings with the Unionists as in Dundee, the Montrose Burghs, and Paisley. Only in Leith, a constituency not unlike Aberdeen North, did Liberalism retain sufficient strength to survive unaided against strong Labour and Unionist opposition during the 1920s. What was most to distinguish political change in Aberdeen was less its character than the speed with which it took place.

In 1918, the Aberdeen Liberals, defending both constituencies, faced not only the consequences of electoral reform, but also the debilitating influence of the split between Lloyd George and Asquith. The outcome of the 1918 election, when they lost both seats, proved to be a disaster for them. In Aberdeen South, Thomson crushed Fleming while, in Aberdeen North, Pirie was the only Coalition Liberal to be defeated in Scotland, although the margin of Rose's victory was slight. His success was quite remarkable, because in Scotland as a whole Labour had carried only a handful of seats.[5] Undoubtedly, his position on the War had been crucial, for not only had the ILP's stance been a major problem for Labour nationally, but in a constituency where two-fifths of adult males were in the armed services anything less than a patriotic platform would have been censured by those left at home. Rose's continuing success was to be characterised by a willingness to articulate the aspirations of his working-class constituents, even at the expense of antagonising a majority on the trades council and losing the party whip from time to time in the House of Commons.[6]

In 1922, following the formation of the National Liberal Party, Liberal divisions at Westminster could no longer be obscured at the local level, particularly so in Scotland where the electoral pact between supporters of Lloyd George and the Unionists was sustained. Consequently, the Asquithian Liberals fought both seats, led by Sir Charles Mallet (South) and James Johnstone (North), with the Unionists (South) and National Liberals (North) forming an electoral pact or understanding. Even so, Mallet, facing a straight fight with the Unionists, indicated to the electors that 'he would support Mr. Bonar Law's government under certain conditions.'[7] It was little wonder that Sir Charles, commenting on the campaign, observed that 'the Liberal Party was suffering from political apathy, and a certain lack of enthusiasm'. Not so Labour supporters who, reflecting an election in which the issue of rent control had been of central concern for working-class voters, shouted to electors as they arrived at the polling stations, 'Vote for Rose and you'll get your rent money back!' In a year when Labour achieved a major breakthrough in Scotland, the outcome proved particularly satisfactory for Thomson, for not only did he increase his vote, but comfortably carried the South for Unionism against a single opponent. Most Unionist voters, however, probably gained more solace from the *Journal's* observation on the overall result: 'Fortunate it is, therefore, for Scotland that it has not today a Parliament in Edinburgh, and that it can still depend on a predominant partner that is able to hold the extremists within reasonable check.'[8]

Sir John Fleming, lord provost 1898-1902, Liberal MP 1917-18. Portrait by R. Brough.

Shortly before the 1923 general election, the Liberals were united for the first time since 1916, and the composition of the platform parties was once again rearranged. Sir John Irvin, president of the Aberdeen Liberal Association described the accord as a miracle, and James Ogilvie, president of the Aberdeen District Council of National Liberals, at a joint meeting, observed, 'who would have thought that three weeks ago they would all be there smiling at each other, but there it was'.[9] More problematical for the Liberals, however, was the fact that their new-found accord opened the way for the Unionists to contest Aberdeen North. The Liberals also found themselves opposed for the first time by Labour in Aberdeen South, where, despite the lack of trade-union support, the ILP, unhappy with Rose, ran a pacifist, John Paton, a former Schoolhill barber who had become a leading national official of the ILP.[10]

On one level the election was about tariff reform. With no small feeling did Sir James Taggart, recounting difficulties in exporting granite to New York, emphasise to an audience at Holburn Street School that 'with Protection they could be able to say to countries "If you dinna let in our gravestones we won't let your stuff in here",' while Lumsden, the Unionist candidate, favoured a levy on German-caught fish.[11] On a more fundamental level, however, the election was about straight-forward social prejudice and fear of Labour. The *Journal* reminded its readers that 'the Socialists are committed to obey the behests of a Russo-German-Jewish combination of incipient Bolshevists in Europe … [and] are eager to bring Britain to the level of Russia by nonsensical Capital Levies and ruinous nationalisation.'[12] Labour supporters, who spent much of their time heckling opposing candidates, enlivened the votes of thanks at an overflowing combined Liberal rally at the YMCA with a rendition of 'The Red Flag' and 'Yes, We Have No Bananas'.

Although 1923 produced a revival in Liberal fortunes generally, the performance of the party in Aberdeen was humiliating as it was outpolled by the Unionists in the North and by Labour in the South. Consequently, at a meeting of the Liberal Party executive in 1924, a proposal to contest both seats received only four votes, and although it was decided to fight one of them, no candidate was adopted. No Liberal was to stand in Aberdeen South again until 1945. The problem for the Liberals was that the rise of Labour deprived them of their radical constituency, and the electoral system left the centre exposed to attack on two fronts. In 1924, Liberal support for the first Labour government had provided ammunition for the Unionists, while its role in bringing down that administration had undermined its credibility with the left. The polarisation of the party system was well illustrated in Aberdeen North, where both the Unionist and Labour parties were to run ex-Liberals as candidates. In 1924, the Unionists adopted the first female to stand in the city, Laura Sandeman, a local doctor and admirer of John Bright, who had associated with the National Liberals on her return from France at the end of the War, and had spoken for Cameron, the Liberal candidate, in 1922. At the 1928 by-election, the new dispensation was to be underlined by the adoption of Wedgwood Benn, the former Liberal member for Leith and severe critic of Lloyd George, as the Labour nominee. Thus, the candidates of both the major parties had been Liberals earlier in the decade.

Labour made no attempt to placate the Liberals. Rose insisted that he had 'always been, and was still, an opponent of political Liberalism … there was nothing to choose, as far as bedrock principle was concerned, between Liberal and Tory'.[13] Archibald, the 1924 Labour candidate in Aberdeen South, was particularly uncompromising, virtually forcing the centre into the Unionist camp: 'I come here at the invitation of the Aberdeen Trades and Labour Council, representing the organised workers of Aberdeen, and it [is] mainly to the organised workers of Aberdeen that [I will] look for support.'[14] The Liberal voters of 1923, however, seemingly split evenly in both constituencies, afforded both Rose and Thomson comfortable majorities. Following the 1924 general election, relations between Rose and the trades council, which he publicly characterised as Communist dominated, deteriorated to such a degree that it unanimously adopted Paton as his replacement in October 1925. By 1928, Rose had also lost the parliamentary whip, although the withdrawal of Paton's candidacy and the threat of a general election had produced national pressure for a resolution to the local conflict. The crisis was only resolved by the member's death but, even then, the trades council having expressed sympathy to his widow, lacked the magnanimity to recognise Rose's contribution to the cause.[15]

The 1928 Aberdeen North by-election was notable for the intervention of the Communist Party. The Communists had hitherto sought to influence Labour through its party members on the trades council, but a change in Comintern policy ended the tactic of entryism, thereby formalising the conflict between the democratic and revolutionary strands of socialism. Aitken Ferguson, a boilermaker on the Glasgow trades council and the Communist candidate, led the attack.

> You find Mr Maxton protesting … against this influx of Liberals, of captains, colonels, and managers and bankers, and reverend gentlemen … carrying the flag of the Labour Party as opposed to the workers … he pointed out that most

A by-election for North Aberdeen in August 1928 involved Wedgwood Benn (Labour), Sandeman (Unionist), Rutherford (Liberal) and Ferguson (Communist). Benn was the clear winner. Cartoon from Evening Express.

of the houses built ostensibly for the working class were being occupied by clerks, doctors and other professional men ... The Communist solution was to get bigger State grants for housing on which no interest would be charged ... homes of wealthy people with ten, twelve, and fourteen rooms would have to be relinquished to the local authorities.[16]

He advocated higher unemployment relief, the forfeiture of every fortune over £1,000 at death, and a minimum wage of £4 a week. At an open-air meeting on the Links, Harry Pollitt declared, 'We are a class party, our slogan is Class against Class,' and Bob Stewart, another speaker, recalled a prison minister asking a Communist incarcerated in Perth jail, 'What is it you fellows want?', receiving the reply, 'We want the lot for the lot.'[17] It was stronger stuff than Sandeman's 'belief in whole-hearted democracy ... Imperial preference and all measures of health reform', and Benn's stand 'against private interest and the mastering of trusts by the state.'[18] Significantly, the Communist saved his deposit, and the Liberal, despite introducing the new technology of loud-speakers to address lunch-hour meetings at factory gates, was ignominiously pushed to the bottom of the poll.

In 1929, following the death of Dr Sandeman, the Unionists in Aberdeen North, whose organisation was chronically weak, failed to stand, while the Liberals did not contest Aberdeen South. Labour, predictably, chose to present this denouement as a pact between their opponents. Although there is no evidence of such an agreement, the character of the contest almost inevitably became defined in those terms. Bob Boothby, a Unionist beneficiary of Liberal support in East Aberdeenshire, called upon the Unionists in Aberdeen North to support the Liberal candidate, and the chairman of the Aberdeen North Unionist Association made an appeal for party supporters to vote for Captain Berkeley, 'the anti-socialist'.[19] In the South, the theme was picked up by the minister of Mannofield Parish Church, the Rev. James Kellas, who, at a public meeting addressed by Thomson, asked whether in the light of Boothby's request for Unionists in the North to vote Liberal that 'something should be done in some way to influence the Liberals of this constituency to vote for Sir Frederick'.[20] Similarly, Henry Hutcheon of the Aberdeen Granite Works wrote to the press, 'I feel great credit is due to the Rev. J. Kellas ... [that] Liberals should vote for Sir F. C. Thomson in South Aberdeen, and I would add, be proud of the opportunity to do so ... This is a fight between constitutional government and ultimate chaos and ruin to our industries if Labour win.'[21] On the same day, Sir John Irvin, president of the Aberdeen Liberal Association and fishing magnate, stated that 'I counsel any fisherman in East Aberdeenshire ... to cast his vote for Mr Boothby ... I do not consider the return of Socialists pledged to nationalisation, would lead to the prosperity of the fishing industry.'[22] The implicit signal to Liberals in Aberdeen South could hardly have been more clear. Although Sir Frederick indicated that he 'hoped to get the support of Liberals in this constituency', he was under no pressure to make concessions to them, and made none. The result in the South was virtually the same as in 1924, while Benn, despite the intervention of the Communist, performed as well as Rose in his last contest.

Thus it appeared that Aberdeen had two safe seats shared between Labour and the Unionists, but the 1931 general election, dominated by the financial crisis that had induced MacDonald to form the National Government, produced a result remarkable even by the circumstances of the time. Compared with 1929, Labour's share of support throughout the city fell from 49.0 per cent to 20.2 per cent, while the Unionist share rose from 33.3 per cent to a massive 74.6 per cent. Consequently, Aberdeen displaced Glasgow as the most pro-Unionist area of Scotland. In the North, Councillor Burnett of Powis, a lawyer, and chairman of the reorganised Unionist Association, carried the seat with more votes and a higher share of the poll than any candidate of any party before 1945, while Thomson's performance in the South has never been surpassed. A significant feature of the result was the exceptionally high turnout, 73.4 per cent in the North and 75.8 per cent in the South, whereas the average participation in other general elections between the wars was only 58.0 per cent and 62.3 per cent respectively.

Benn's explanation for his defeat was that 'they felt very much handicapped by the Press ... the wireless had been used with great effect against them, particularly the comments of Mr Snowden. Another thing that killed them was fear. People were scared that the Socialists wanted to take their savings and give them to the unemployed, and not pay them back again.'[23] The tone of the contest, however, was sober rather than strident. At a meeting for Sir Frederick at Ashley Road School, two classrooms were filled to overflowing thirty minutes before the opening of the meeting, and it was necessary to hold two overflow meetings in other classrooms. 'During his three speeches, while he uttered grave words of warning ... Sir Frederick was not once interrupted ... [despite] the presence of many Socialists in the audiences.'[24] In the North, Burnett addressed overflow meetings at Woodside and Frederick Street schools, where he criticised the Labour government for having taken duties off paper imports and for not imposing them on monuments, 'which was supported not only by the association of employers, but also by the operative unions'.[25] Labour did not always help its own cause, as when George Catto, a leading member of the trades council, standing in the South, stated at a public meeting that, 'if the [Liberal] voter belonged to the "nice" people he should join the Conservative Party.' Benn, by turning up late to a meeting, provided an opportunity for Mrs George Collie, a leading Unionist, to address the audience in his absence.[26] Benn was also given a rough time by the Communist candidate, Helen Crawfurd, a Glasgow-based party organiser, particularly over his support for 'cuts at the expense of the working class'.[27] Crawfurd was almost to double her party's vote of 1929.

Given that the circumstances in Aberdeen were similar to those applicable elsewhere, the scale of the National Unionist victory in the city cannot simply be ascribed to media bias or the popularity of tariffs in certain industries. A more likely explanation is that the financial crisis had a strong resonance in a region noted for its belief in financial rectitude, fear of debt, the virtue of balancing the books, and the value of personal savings. It would seem that the electors blamed a feckless Labour Government living beyond its means rather than the bankers for the impasse, and agreed with Sir Frederick that 'to promise glibly to restore all benefits, to repeal the Economy Act, and indulge in further expenditure was a pleasant thing to do, but they were not really helping people in the end'.[28]

Sir Frederick C. Thomson Bt 1875–1935

Born at Balerno, Midlothian, the son of an Edinburgh shipowner, Frederick Thomson was educated at Edinburgh Academy, Edinburgh University and University College, Oxford. A lawyer, he was called to the Scottish bar in 1901, became a member of the Inner Temple in 1904 and King's Counsel in 1923. He distinguished himself in the First World War, serving in Egypt and Greece, and was badly wounded. He served as Unionist MP for Aberdeen South 1918–35. He was Scottish Unionist Whip and was Parliamentary Private Secretary 1919–22, Solicitor General for Scotland 1923–24, and Junior Lord of the Treasury in 1923 and 1924–28. He served as vice chamberlain of HM Household 1928–29 and 1931, and Treasurer 1931–35. He was created a baronet in 1929.

A by-election, occasioned by the death of Sir Frederick, was held in Aberdeen South some few months before the 1935 general election. It was a measure of the popularity of the 'tall and courtly' appearance and 'kindly and courteous disposition' of the deceased MP that his son, Sir Douglas Thomson, was invited to represent the Unionist interest.[29] At the time of his adoption, Sir Douglas, an alumnus of Eton and Oxford, where he had won a rowing blue, was an active partner in the family shipping firm. His Labour opponent, Joseph Duncan, had been active in the city's labour movement since early in the century and, in 1904, had become general secretary of the Scottish Steam Vessels and Firemen's Union, and was president of the trades council, 1911-12. It was, however, as the leader of the Scottish Farm Servant's Union after 1915 for which he was best known, and in that capacity had been appointed to the highly influential Royal Commission on

Housing.[30] Since 1919, however, he had been based in Stirling, and it was a measure of his commitment to the by-election, that he was frequently absent during the campaign, serving on various government commissions. The result was never in doubt, and the broad base of Thomson's coalition was underlined by letters of support from Liberal leaders, Sir John Simon and Sir Godfrey Collins, Secretary of State for Scotland, expressing the opinion that 'neither for international nor for domestic purposes has the time come when we can safely return to party politics'.[31]

The 1935 general election found the political equilibrium restored, when Labour recaptured Aberdeen North. The Labour candidate in Aberdeen South changed yet again. This time it was a local joiner, George R. McIntosh, or 'GR', as the popular veteran socialist was known. He had been both secretary and treasurer of the trades council, and, aided by his wife, had been Wedgwood Benn's election agent. Fighting a hopeless seat, he was more than relieved to save his deposit because it had been subscribed by his Unionist father-in-law. In the North, the contest was far less straightforward, because a well-liked local trade unionist and town councillor, Fraser Macintosh, had decided to contest the seat on behalf of the ILP, which was now distinct from the Labour Party. It was considered by some Labour supporters that their prospective candidate since 1932, Henry Hetherington, chairman of the Aberdeen branch of the National Union of Railwaymen (NUR) and president of the political section of the trades council, would be vulnerable to Macintosh's appeal, thereby assisting the Unionists.[32] Sniping at Hetherington caused the Aberdeen NUR to take umbrage and disaffiliate from the trades council. This enabled his critics to secure the intervention of the Labour Party national executive, in the summer of 1935, as the first step towards removing the prospective candidate. Although separate constituency parties were not established until 1936, it was arranged through the Scottish Labour executive for trades council representatives connected exclusively with the North division to discuss the matter, and in late September they voted to reject Hetherington. They did not, however, have a replacement, so that when the election was sprung they looked to the national party to find a candidate. It obliged by producing Garro-Jones, a lawyer and sometime editor of *The Daily Dispatch*, who had stood as a National Liberal in Bethnal Green in 1922, and had been the Liberal MP for South Hackney between 1924 and 1929. As Fraser Macintosh was to remark at a public meeting, 'With regard to Mr Garro-Jones, that gentleman had never seen Aberdeen until the election came on, and he would not have been in Aberdeen if the local Labour Party had been able to face an election – they had neither the money nor courage to face an election … the local Labour Party had made a gift of North Aberdeen to the so-called National Government.'[33] Despite the split on the left, Garro-Jones defeated the incumbent, Burnett, having strongly criticised 'the National Government's record and policy in health and housing services, unemployment and armaments manufacture', and the local member for supporting the household means test.[34] He was also assisted by open backing from the Communists who were unsympathetic to Fraser Macintosh's pacifism. Labour, however, rebuffed Communist attempts to negotiate a formal alliance. Perhaps even more crucial than Communist support in producing the Labour majority was the 7.5 per cent drop in turnout, the equivalent of almost 4,000 electors.

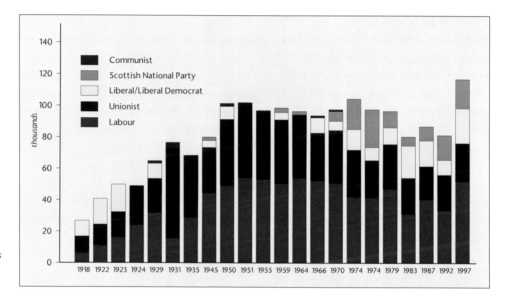

Figure 8.1 Distribution of votes by party in the general elections in Aberdeen, 1918-97.

TWO-PARTY POLITICS

Although the general election of 1945 was an important landmark in British politics, the main effect in Aberdeen was to underline the two-party dominance which had been imperfectly evident since 1918. Most local attention centred on the replacement of Garro-Jones, whose reasons for his decision to step down were not clear. He was, however, ennobled as Baron Trefgarne in 1947, and subsequently joined the Liberals in 1958. The six hopefuls wishing to replace him included Dr C. E. M. Joad of BBC Brains Trust fame, nominated by the Fabians, and the ubiquitous G. R. MacIntosh, but the former fell on the first ballot and GR withdrew. The eventual winner was Hector Hughes, an Irish and English King's Counsel, nominated by the Electricians' Union, with a single vote majority over J. E. Harper, an engineer-come-barrister, who had contested the Montrose Burghs in 1935, and was backed by the Amalgamated Engineering Union. Hughes' Unionist opponent was Lady Grant of Monymusk. The novel feature of the election was a Scottish National Party (SNP) intervention, in the person of Austin Walker, a Motherwell chartered accountant. Although the Unionists retained Aberdeen South, a Liberal

ABERDEEN 1800–2000

candidature helped reduce the majority to only 1,816. The highlight of the election was an eve-of-poll stramash in the Music Hall, when the Unionists booked the main auditorium and Labour the other three main rooms. More than 2,000 members of the public crammed into the building, and the doors were closed well before the advertised commencement times.

A by-election in Aberdeen South in November 1946, following the resignation of Thomson for business reasons, restored one of Unionism's more comfortable majorities, and saw the return of Lady Grant as Aberdeen's first female MP. A lawyer and former secretary to the Lord Chief Justice of England, Arthur Irvine, was the Labour candidate. He was an Aberdonian, and a graduate of Edinburgh and Oxford, where he had been president of the Union. In 1935 and 1939 he had stood as a Liberal in Kincardine and West Aberdeenshire. His major contribution to the campaign was an attack on the *Press and Journal* as 'a paper controlled from London, capitalist controlled, designed by every subterfuge and every kind of stratagem to achieve certain political ends'.[35]

Lady Tweedsmuir 1915–78

Born Priscilla Thomson, the daughter of a brigadier, Lady Tweedsmuir was educated privately in England, Germany and France. Her first husband, Major Sir Arthur Lindsay Grant, was killed in action in 1944 during the battle for Normandy while serving with the Grenadier Guards. She married Baron Tweedsmuir of Belhelvie in 1948. In 1945 she unsuccessfully contested Aberdeen North for the Unionists, but was subsequently elected to represent Aberdeen South 1946–66. She was a delegate to the Council of Europe 1950–53 and to the United Nations General Assembly 1960–61. In government, she was Joint Parliamentary Under Secretary for State at the Scottish Office 1962–64, Minister of State at the Scottish Office 1970–72, and at the Foreign and Commonwealth Office 1972–74 and was appointed a Privy Councillor in 1974. She was principal deputy chairman of committees 1974–77 and chairman of the Select Committee on European Communities 1974–77. She held directorships in Factoryguard and Cunard Lines.

The transfer of Torry to Aberdeen South before the 1950 general election lit a slow fuse that had an important impact on the city's electoral politics. But equally important was Labour's capture of municipal power in 1945 because it was followed by a massive programme of council house building with subsidised rents. Although most municipal housing construction was in the North constituency, estates were developed south of the Dee, creating new Labour-voting suburbs to challenge Lady Tweedsmuir (as Lady Grant had become). Nevertheless, it was not until 1964 that the vulnerability of the South became clear, so that the overwhelming characteristic of the early post-war period was that of representational stability, exemplified by the regular return of Hughes and Lady Tweedsmuir. Consequently, only the most ardent activists on either side believed the post-war settlement could change, even when the evidence was to the contrary.

Hector Hughes 1887–1970

Born in Dublin, Hector Hughes was educated at the Diocesan School, St Andrew's College, Dublin and Dublin University where he studied law. He was called to the Irish bar in 1915 and the English bar in 1923, taking silk in 1927 and 1932 in the respective jurisdictions. He became a member of the Middle Temple. He was a founder member of the Socialist Party of Ireland in 1918 and the Irish Co-operative Labour Press Ltd. He wrote extensively on legal matters. He represented Aberdeen North 1945–70. His wide array of memberships included the Ghana bar, the Board of the Church Army, the National Union of Seamen, and the National Union of General and Municipal Workers. An enthusiastic swimmer, he served as president of the National Council for the Promotion of Education in Swimming.

In Aberdeen North, elections were enlivened by the episodic intervention of minor parties. For the Communists, Bob Cooney, a popular Spanish Civil War veteran, fought the general election of 1950, though with less success than his predecessor in 1931. His comrade, fortuitously bearing the same name as the Queen's sister, Margaret Rose, who ran a guest house in Maberly Street, appeared in 1966. In 1950 and 1966, Liberals stood to the disadvantage of the Unionists, and the SNP made a token foray in 1959. The inclination of Liberals towards the centre-right was underlined in 1951 when 'some members of the [Liberal] Association … including one Progressive on the Town Council, assisted the Unionist candidate'.[36] One of the more innovatory features of the period was the election address format adopted by Frank Magee, the 'battling baillie', the Unionist candidate in 1951. It eschewed the lengthy prose characteristic of traditional appeals for a series of bullet-style points, and was coloured black and claret, red with a tinge of blue, out of deference, no doubt, to the political prejudices of his electorate.[37] It was also indicative of contemporary political discourse that the text unselfconsciously made a specific reference to 'the working class', whose interests the Unionist claimed he had promoted as housing convener. Magee certainly had a better feel for the electorate than the fresh-faced laird of Dinnet, Marcus Humphrey, the

Hector Hughes, Labour Member of Parliament for Aberdeen North 1945-70. Like Mao, he liked to demonstrate his fitness by a swim in the sea.

Conservative candidate in 1966, who admitted to finding running up and down tenement stairs somewhat exhausting. Hector Hughes proved an adept constituency MP, moving periodic parliamentary questions on local matters, as when he asked the Minister of Food whether there would be enough 'currants, raisins and other ingredients required for Christmas puddings in the City of Aberdeen'. He generated most publicity by arranging for the *Press and Journal* to photograph him swimming in the North Sea whenever there were unhelpful rumours concerning his retirement.

THE DECLINE OF THE TWO-PARTY SYSTEM

Despite the apparent stability of post-war representation, important changes were taking place in the culture of local politics. After 1945, the increasing nationalisation of politics reduced the importance of local institutions, accelerating the process whereby local political activism increasingly constituted a sub-culture of private politics divorced from the concerns of the wider public. In particular, the trades council became little more than a 'talking-shop', providing an opportunity for leftists to pass resolutions critical of the Labour leadership, and a platform for non-Labour forces within the working-class movement including members of the ILP, Communists, Scottish Labour Party supporters, and the occasional Scottish Nationalist. Nevertheless, a respected Communist, James Milne, graduated through the trades council, having served as secretary in Aberdeen 1948-69, to become general secretary of the Scottish Trades Union Congress.

Nowhere was political change more marked than in the collapse of the local campaign as a means of political communication. From the early 1950s, radio and television undermined attendances at public meetings, which rapidly assumed a purely ritualistic significance. The local press ceased to cover such events, relying, instead, on party press releases for news of what the candidates had said. The *Press and Journal* adopted a policy of restricting such 'coverage' to two meetings per party and none in the last week of the campaign. Similarly, Grampian Television devoted few resources to campaigns in its area. It was a measure of the reduced impact of the local campaign that a survey undertaken in Aberdeen North a week before the election of February 1974 indicated that only 42 per cent of the electorate could name the Labour candidate, 23 per cent the SNP candidate, 9 per cent the Liberal candidate, and 8 per cent the Conservative candidate.[38] More remarkably, a study of Aberdeen South in 1979 indicated that only a small proportion of the electorate appreciated the highly marginal character of the constituency.[39]

In other respects, the culture of politics established in the 1920s was changing. Before the 1966 general election, the Scottish Unionists reverted to designating

Election pamphlets from the 1966 general election.

themselves as Conservatives for the first time since 1912. Following the 1970 general election, a revolt by a new generation of Tories in Aberdeen South, led by Sandy Mutch, forced the intervention of Conservatism into local government. Consequently, the consensual style of Unionism that had come to incorporate traditional Liberalism was replaced by a more abrasive partisanship, symbolised by Iain Sproat, whose 1970 recapture of Aberdeen South was technically the first Conservative victory in the city since before the 1832 Reform Act. Ignoring his Wykehamist background, his campaigning focus on law and order and welfare scroungers heralded the new dawn. These local developments mirrored wider changes in a party whose leadership was rapidly shifting down the social scale from the Old Etonians to Heath, Thatcher and Major.

On the left, Labour's dominance in Aberdeen North, accompanied by a virtual collapse of the Conservative Association after 1966, was characterised by increasing complacency and a decline in political participation. Labour's relationship with the working-class electorate also became somewhat ambivalent, for while the party retained the language of protest it had become entrenched as the local political establishment and landlord to most of its target voters.[40] Party organisation, such as it was, centred on working-class councillors who had little interest in encouraging a wide membership, which by the early 1970s was well under 200, the lowest ratio of members to voters in Scotland. It was appropriate, therefore, that when Hector Hughes was finally persuaded to retire, the nomination was contested by two local councillors, James Lamond and Robert Hughes, the latter being successful. In Aberdeen South, a similar decline in working-class participation was offset by an increasing middle-class membership. The capture of the parliamentary seat by Donald Dewar, a Glasgow lawyer, in 1966 typified the change. Consequently, there was a marked cultural distinction between the two Labour parties. Whereas social events in the North centred on the trades council bar at the Adelphi, with catering by the Co-operative Society, in the South claret and canapés in the spacious private residences of individual members was more characteristic. A feature of the social distinctions in the South was that working-class members felt disadvantaged by a growing tendency for ward meetings to be held in private homes rather than in the more neutral fora of public premises.

A challenge to the complacency of two-party politics was slow to develop. The Liberals, whose survival had depended heavily on Dr Mary Esslemont, were racked by 'petty jealousies which had grown up within the General Executive Committee'. Consequently, despite the post-1959 Liberal 'revival', they failed to contest either seat in 1964, because Major Adam, the former party organiser for the city, was rejected as a candidate in North Aberdeen following 'opposition to him at the Scottish Liberal Party as well as from one or two members in South

Aberdeen'.[41] Instead, local activists were directed to a more promising contest in West Aberdeenshire. In 1966, however, Liberals intervened in both seats, and they may have been instrumental in securing the defeat of Lady Tweedsmuir. But, following the intervention of the SNP and a swing to the right, the Liberal performance in 1970 compared unfavourably even with those of candidates twenty years before. The SNP promised more when, following devaluation in 1966, they severely damaged Labour in municipal elections, which enabled the Progressives to seize power on the town council for the first time in two decades. Nevertheless, by 1970 the Nationalist tide had passed, and both SNP candidates lost their deposits, coming a poor third in the North and fourth in the South.

The first credible threat to the post–1918 settlement came in 1974, when the SNP put Labour under severe pressure in Aberdeen North, and may well have been a factor in preventing Labour recapturing the South. The miners' strike, which had precipitated the election, had reflected poorly on both major parties, and the capture of Glasgow Govan in late 1973 from Labour, coupled with the 'It's Scotland's Oil' campaign, found the SNP well-placed to capitalise on general unease with the operation of the political system. In addition, the SNP in Aberdeen seemed to have found a seam of political enthusiasm on the part of the public that had not been evident since the inter-war years. Whereas the established parties seemed atrophied, as demonstrated by their persistence with poorly attended public meetings, as a modern movement the SNP seemed more attuned to a campaign style which reflected the age of advertising. Hundreds of small posters featuring the party's slogans appeared all over the city on walls, deserted shops, derelict buildings and workmen's huts, and St Andrew's flags bearing the appropriate candidate's name sprouted in windows across the municipal housing estates. Children proudly boasted SNP stickers on their clothing, as did younger bus conductors on their ticket machines. Appreciating the importance of publicity, the SNP was successful in engineering stunts that secured coverage in the newspapers as when Sandy Stronach, the candidate in Aberdeen South, was photographed by the press canvassing on a bus. A huge saltire flag draped from the balcony of a high rise flat in Mastrick not only appeared in the local newspapers but a heavy-handed response from council officials brought even more publicity. In the North, where the SNP had a better chance of success, such activities were supplemented by leaflets designed by Ian Hughes, a university psychology lecturer, which, with the purpose of boosting confidence in the capacity of Scotland to go it alone, included material contrasting Scotland's success in qualifying for the World Cup finals in West Germany with England's failure so to do. Neither Labour nor the Conservatives found themselves able to compete with such vibrancy. Not that Labour felt vulnerable in the North, where its minimalist February 1974 campaign was typified by Bob Hughes, the incumbent member, who sat alone in the North's headquarters on the Saturday before polling dealing with constituency correspondence. In the South, however, the marginal nature of the seat meant that both Labour and Conservatives, who had a full-time agent, were able to counter the SNP's highland charge with superior organisation and detailed canvassing.

Lord Hughes b. 1932

Born at Pittenweem, Fife, Robert Hughes was educated at Robert Gordon's College. He emigrated to South Africa 1947–54 and completed his education at Pietermaritzburg Technical College. He returned to Aberdeen and was employed as chief draughtsman by C. F. Wilson & Co 1954–70. He was a member of the Amalgamated Engineering Union. He represented Ferryhill on the town council 1962–70 serving as convener of the health and welfare and the social work committees, and was chairman of the Aberdeen Labour Party 1961–69. He stood unsuccessfully as Labour candidate in South Angus and Mearns in 1959, and subsequently represented Aberdeen North 1970–97. He served as Parliamentary Under Secretary of State at the Scottish Office 1974–75. He was vice chairman of the Tribune Group in 1984–85, and a member of the shadow cabinet 1985–88, during which time he was the principal opposition spokesman on agriculture and transport. He was strongly associated with the anti-apartheid movement and the campaign for nuclear disarmament, and served as chairman 1976–94. He became a life peer in 1997.

The result of the February election worried Labour in Aberdeen North, for although its majority was almost 12,000 it had won fewer than half the votes and, with the SNP in second place, the prospect of losing the seat had become a distinct reality. Consequently, Hughes, who was an opponent of devolution, included in his election address of October 1974 a section entitled 'Powerhouse Scotland', endorsing support for the Scottish Assembly proposals which Harold Wilson, the Prime Minister, had imposed on a reluctant Scottish Labour Party. Furthermore, on the Saturday afternoon before polling, in contrast to the previous February, not only was the North's headquarters a hive of activity, but the MP himself was in the city centre distributing leaflets. Even so, half an hour before the close of polling on the following Thursday Labour had no idea how well it had performed, and Hughes, fearing defeat, was still campaigning hard. The problem lay in the fact that with such a moribund organisation Labour had no systematic canvass returns. In the event, although another 2,000 was removed from the Labour majority, Hughes' share of the poll increased to just over 50 per cent. The main loser was

Conflicting views in the posters for the 1979 referendum on Scottish devolution.

Peter Fraser, the Conservative candidate, whose campaign was noted for a meeting at Hilton Academy attended almost exclusively by Tory activists, to whom he had to defend his liberal views on crime and punishment. Similar developments in the South, however, proved insufficient for Robert Middleton, a trade unionist and prominent Labour councillor, to displace Iain Sproat. The Conservatives, nevertheless, had suffered such a severe mauling throughout the city as a whole that they were outpolled by the SNP.

By 1979, the traumas of the mid-seventies appeared past, and a more traditional politics returned. Hughes re-emerged as an opponent of devolution, and felt sufficiently secure to advocate a 'No' vote in the referendum, which carried the day in the Grampian region.[42] His Nationalist opponent, Maureen Watt, who was the daughter of the SNP member for Banffshire, addressed several exceptionally sparsely attended meetings during the referendum campaign.[43] She was easily pushed into third place by Gordon Adams, leader of the Conservative group on the district council. In Aberdeen South, Stronach collapsed into fourth position behind the Liberals, while Sproat doubled his Conservative majority. Aberdeen had reverted to a two-party system.

The failure of the SNP to consolidate progress in the late 1960s and early 1970s reflected the lack of a distinctive social or organisational base. In February 1974, a survey in Aberdeen North indicated that support mirrored the social composition of the electorate as a whole. The SNP candidate, an Angus seed potato merchant, made references to the closure of a sugar beet factory, but neglected the problems of the inshore fishing industry and rising house prices, thereby demonstrating little understanding of the constituency. Similarly, Watt, although working in Aberdeen, had no obvious affinity, apart from nationality, with the people she sought to represent. She came from a rural background, the daughter of an MP who had started his political career as a Unionist before transferring his support to the SNP. Aberdeen South, with its high concentration of professional middle-class electors, was even less fertile ground for the nationalists. The lack of SNP strength in depth, even in 1974, was emphasised by its inability to achieve more than a token breakthrough in local government. It is possible, too, that prosperity brought by the oil industry weakened discontent with the status quo on which the SNP had fed.

The redistribution before the 1983 general election persuaded Sproat that his interests would be best served by decamping to a safer seat in the Borders, and his place as the Conservative candidate in Aberdeen South was taken by Gerald Malone, a Glasgow lawyer. The Conservatives were in office and unpopular in Scotland, while the SNP was pre-occupied with internal divisions and still suffering opprobrium for having helped Mrs Thatcher bring down the previous Labour government. Thus Labour was less exposed to the Nationalist threat than in the 1970s. Although the shift of Labour to the left had precipitated the formation of the Social Democratic Party (SDP) and its electoral alliance with the Liberals, the new party posed a less credible threat to Labour than had the SNP in working-class seats like Aberdeen North. On the other hand, the Liberal/SDP Alliance, with its capacity to appeal to middle-class electors, who in no circumstances would vote Labour or SNP, was in a strong position to mount a challenge in Aberdeen South, with the assistance of disaffected Labour voters. Such hopes were reinforced by the displacement of the Tories by the Alliance as the second largest party on the district council, though its local government strength lay principally in areas incorporated within the city in 1974, but which were outwith the parliamentary burgh. Responsibility for fighting the Alliance campaign fell to the SDP in both constituencies. The main effort was concentrated on the South where a small group of middle-class activists, mostly new to politics, worked with much gusto for the cause. Their problem was that both the Labour and Conservative parties were well-organised.

Although the SDP had organisationally failed to attract more than the occasional Labour activist, its candidates had seemingly won a substantial proportion of Labour voters keen to send a message to the leadership. Middleton, in a third vain attempt to capture the South, suffered from a drop of more than

40 per cent in the Labour vote, and Hughes' vote was 28 per cent lower than in 1979. The Conservatives, however, increased their share of the poll in the North, and Malone comfortably won Aberdeen South, although with 5,000 fewer votes than Sproat's previous tally. The disappointment for the SDP was that it failed to come second in the South, though pressing Labour hard, and prospects of improving in the North seemed slender. Both SNP candidates, and a lone Ecologist, lost their deposits.

In 1987 Labour was in a stronger position than in 1983 because the oil industry was in a recession, and in Scotland generally the party had recovered its losses from the Alliance. Consequently, Labour hoped to capture the South with a new candidate, Frank Doran, a Dundee lawyer. The SNP remained in the doldrums. Ian Philip once again ran for the SDP in the South, but the party presented a new aspirant in the North, Sir Robert Smith, grandson of a former Unionist member for Aberdeenshire Central, and a relative of Buchanan-Smith, the Conservative MP for Kincardine and Deeside. Although Malone's vote fell by less than 700, Labour increased its vote by more than one-third to give Doran a narrow majority over a surprised incumbent. The SDP retained second place in the North, but Hughes' majority grew by more than 7,000. Again, the SNP performed miserably in both constituencies. The general election of 1987 had reduced the Scottish Conservatives to a mere 11 seats. Consequently, in 1992, they concentrated their efforts on retaining the seats they held together with a few marginals they hoped to recover. Aberdeen South was clearly one of their targets, and the prospective candidate, Raymond Robertson, a former history teacher, was not only *in situ* well before the contest, but his appointment to a central office position in Aberdeen virtually made him a professional candidate. The nature of the seat, which could be secured with the support of barely one-quarter of the registered electorate, put a high premium on locating and mobilising supporters rather than agitating the electorate as a whole. Consequently, the Conservatives mounted an extensive telephone compaign directed towards electors in the middle-class parts of the constituency in the pre-election period, while the candidate retained a generally low profile even in the three weeks before polling. Telephone campaigning also formed part of the Labour strategy, and both the major parties were supported by professional agents and modern technology. The contrast with Aberdeen North, continuing to exhibit all the moribund features of a safe seat, was stark.[44]

The Conservatives were assisted in their efforts by revival in the oil industry, and the concerns of a relatively prosperous electorate about the implications of Labour's taxation proposals for income tax rates and mortgages. The Conservatives also pointed out to a local electorate, which had been at best lukewarm about devolution, the implications of a tax-raising Scottish Assembly. Although such matters appealed particularly to the traditional middle classes in the South, first-generation working-class home owners and oil-rig workers were voicing similar concerns. The Conservative strategy seemed to work, for while there was strong evidence to indicate that turnout in middle-class areas increased markedly, it fell away in places of Labour strength. As a result, Robertson recaptured Aberdeen South for his party. A secondary feature of the contest was an SNP revival, largely at the expense of the Liberal Democrats, so that the Nationalists resumed their status as the second party in the North and third party in the South.

REDISTRIBUTION

The division of Aberdeen into three constituencies produced what in normal times would be regarded as a safe Labour seat, Aberdeen Central, and two marginal constituencies, Aberdeen North and Aberdeen South. In Central, the main conflict centred on the struggle for the Labour nomination between Bob Hughes, the sitting MP for the North, and Frank Doran, who had held the South between 1987 and 1992. Under the new Labour Party selection rules, one member one vote, the traditional union block vote no longer applied. This was to the disadvantage of Hughes so that Doran, who heavily canvassed the party membership, narrowly won the nomination over the veteran socialist. In the South, a second innovatory rule change had produced a mandatory all-female Labour short leet, which resulted in the selection of Anne Begg, a schoolteacher from Brechin. The Labour candidate in the North was Malcolm Savidge, an English-born maths teacher and local councillor, who had fought the Kincardine and Deeside by-election in November 1991.

Predictably, Labour easily carried Aberdeen Central. The Conservative candidate, a flamboyant local councillor, Jill Wisely, 'the lady who makes things happen', took second place.[45] She relied on a strong upper-middle-class vote in those parts of the west end which had been formerly in Aberdeen South. Labour also won very comfortably in the less predictable North, reflecting the temporary preferences of a politically volatile electorate found in the new private housing estates along the northern bank of the Don, allied to a more traditional council-house vote in the working-class schemes hitherto in the North. In addition, the level of Labour local campaigning was unprecedented, well-resourced, highly professional, and completely unmatched by their opponents, whose efforts were concentrated elsewhere. The SNP candidate, Brian Adam, a highly respected councillor who represented one of the most disadvantaged council wards in the constituency, held second place. The Liberal Democrats were pushed into fourth place behind the Conservatives in a seat they might have hoped to win in circumstances less favourable to Labour.

By far the most hotly disputed constituency in 1997 was Aberdeen South, a seat targeted as winnable by the Conservatives, Labour and the Liberal Democrats. In social terms, the new constituency was more favourably delineated for the Conservatives than hitherto, but redistribution had removed crucial areas of traditional Tory strength to Aberdeen Central. Furthermore, in local elections in the new constituency the Liberal Democrats had been the leading party in 1992 and only marginally behind Labour in 1995. The Liberal Democrats ran Nicol Stephen, a local lawyer, who had been MP for Kincardine and Deeside from November 1991 to the general election of 1992, as their candidate. It was hoped, thereby, that many of those Labour voters who had tactically voted for Stephen in his former constituency and now transferred to Aberdeen South, would either be unaware of the new dispensation or would stick with him, while at the same time retaining and expanding middle-class support in places like his former local government ward, Mannofield. Liberal Democrat literature, assuring the electors that Labour could not win the seat, was designed to encourage tactical voting on the left and to reassure the right that to desert the Conservatives would not let Labour in.[46] Liberal Democrat literature also personalised the contest by printing photographs of a hang-dog looking Robertson, the incumbent Tory, seemingly glancing sideways at a charismatically smiling Stephen marching confidently to victory.

Inevitably, the Labour campaign attacked the Liberal Democrats in an attempt to establish the credibility of its own challenge, while the Conservatives doggedly sought to shore up their own vote in an attempt to minimise middle-class

The happy victors in the election of May 1997. From left to right: Frank Doran (Aberdeen Central), Anne Begg (Aberdeen South) and Malcolm Savidge (Aberdeen North).

desertion to Stephen.[47] Both parties used telephone canvassing extensively, with not a few of the calls coming, in Labour's case, from Clydeside. Even the local campaign had become national in organisation. Despite being swamped in an ocean of paper noted more for its mendacity than enlightenment, the electors of Aberdeen South placed the parties in the order established at the local elections of 1995, though Labour's margin of victory was more decisive. In conformity with the recent past in Aberdeen South, the winner attracted barely a quarter of the registered electorate. More novel was the success of the Liberal Democrats in taking second place, raising the possibility that the party might replace the Conservatives as the focus of an anti-Labour coalition.

RETROSPECT

Although the history of parliamentary representation in Aberdeen can only be understood within the context of national developments, the city continued, in sharp contrast to its rural hinterland, to be at the forefront of the wider evolutionary process. At the same time, a combination of social, geographical and institutional factors produced a political culture sufficiently distinctive to merit attention beyond the merely idiosyncratic. The collapse of Scottish Liberalism, which was not generally completed until 1931, was effected as early as 1918 in Aberdeen, and the Labour movement made its parliamentary breakthrough in the burgh four years before the party established its position in Glasgow and Clydeside. Perhaps more remarkable, given the powerful Liberal tradition of Aberdeen, the Unionists replaced the Liberals at the end of the Great War, which contrasted with a lingering urban Liberal survival elsewhere in Scotland.

An important institutional factor hastening the twentieth-century developments was the configuration of the constituencies which created an essentially homogeneous working-class seat in the North and concentrated middle-class voters in the South, thereby embedding class-based politics following the realisation of universal adult suffrage. To that extent Aberdeen was a microcosm of the British polity as a whole. The major beneficiaries were the Unionists/ Conservatives, particularly after 1945, because the constituency boundaries limited the consequences of their declining support, although Labour certainly enjoyed the cushion afforded by its usually redundant majorities in Aberdeen North in the crises of 1974 and 1983. The popular politics of Aberdeen, as elsewhere, were shaped by the consequences of franchise extension. Between 1832 and 1918, the emancipation of the middle class was the central theme, and since then the rise to power of the organised working class has been the dominant motif. It is, therefore, unclear what factors, in the absence of franchise extension, will shape future political developments. Although the challenges to class-based politics posed by the SNP and Liberal

Democrats from the 1970s onwards failed to destroy the firmament, they shook the foundations sufficiently to indicate that the certainties of the previous fifty years were under threat as the century moved to its close.

These forces were reflected in the last major election of the twentieth century which took place in May 1999 to select members for the new Scottish Parliament. The Aberdeen electorate repeated some of the responses found elsewhere in Scotland, as in the low turnout, so that the votes cast in the three city constituencies were just 75 per cent of the vote recorded in the general election of 1997. As elsewhere the Labour vote suffered most heavily, and the Conservatives continued to lose support. Only the SNP showed a modest increase in its vote. But other features of the election reflected the importance of local matters. Labour barely managed to hold Aberdeen North, scraping home by 398 votes over the SNP candidate, Brian Adam, a long-serving and well-liked local councillor, whose vote was almost certainly augmented by personal support. In Aberdeen South, another candidate with a strong local presence, Nicol Stephen, won the seat for the Liberal Democrats, thus providing a reminder of the city's long tradition of radical Liberalism.

Table 8.1 *Aberdeen parliamentary representation and election results 1922-97*

1922 North	F. H. Rose (Lab)	10,958
	W. M. Cameron (National Lib)	6,615
	J. Johnston (Lib)	2,113
	Majority	4,343
1922 South	F. C. Thomson (Unionist)	13,208
	Sir C. E. Mallet (Lib)	9,573
	Majority	3,635
1923 North	F. H. Rose (Lab)	9,138
	W. F. Lumsden (Unionist)	4,820
	W. M. Cameron (Lib)	4,099
	Majority	4,318
1923 South	F. C. Thomson (Unionist)	11,258
	J. Paton (Lab)	6,911
	Sir C. E. Mallet (Lib)	5,641
	Majority	4,347
1924 North	F. H. Rose (Lab)	13,249
	Dr L. Sandeman (Unionist)	8,545
	Majority	4,704
1924 South	F. C. Thomson (Unionist)	16,092
	G. Archibald (Lab)	10,699
	Majority	5,393

1928 North [by-election]	W. W. Benn (Lab)	10,646
	Dr L. Sandeman (Unionist)	4,696
	A. Ferguson (Communist)	2,618
	J. R. Rutherford (Lib)	2,337
	Majority	5,950
1929 North	W. W. Benn (Lab)	17,826
	R. C. Berkeley (Lib)	9,799
	A. Ferguson (Communist)	1,686
	Majority	8,027
1929 South	Sir F. C. Thomson Bt (Unionist)	21,548
	W. H. P. Martin (Lab)	13,868
	Majority	7,680
1931 North	J. G. Burnett (Unionist)	22,931
	W. W. Benn (Lab)	8,753
	Mrs H. Crawfurd (Communist)	3,980
	Majority	14,178
1931 South	Sir F. C. Thomson Bt (Unionist)	33,988
	G. Catto (Lab)	6,627
	Majority	27,361
1935 South [by-election]	Sir J. D. W. Thomson Bt (Unionist)	20,925
	J. F. Duncan (Lab)	10,760
	Majority	10,165
1935 North	G. M. Garro-Jones (Lab)	16,952
	J. G. Burnett (Unionist)	13,990
	A. F. Macintosh (ILP)	3,871
	Majority	2,962
1935 South	Sir J. D. W. Thomson (Unionist)	25,270
	G. R. McIntosh (Lab)	11,817
	Majority	13,453
1945 North	H. S. J. Hughes (Lab)	26,753
	Lady Grant (Unionist)	9,623
	A. W. Walker (SNP)	2,021
	Majority	17,130
1945 South	Sir J. W. D. Thomson Bt (Unionist)	19,214
	W. Mclaine (Lab)	17,398
	J. L. Milne (Lib)	4,501
	Majority	1,816
1946 South [by-election]	Lady Grant (Unionist)	21,750
	A. J. Irvine (Lab)	17,911
	Majority	3,839

1950 North	H. S. J. Hughes (Lab)	31,594
	A. Tennant (Unionist)	15,705
	J. G. Wilson (Lib)	3,574
	R. H. Cooney (Communist)	1,391
	Majority	15,889
1950 South	Lady Tweedsmuir (Unionist)	26,128
	Mrs O. R. Chruchley (Lab)	17,302
	R. T. Pirie (Lib)	5,248
	Majority	8,826
1951 North	H. S. J. Hughes (Lab)	33,711
	F. Magee (Unionist)	18,365
	Majority	15,346
1951 South	Lady Tweedsmuir (Unionist)	28,947
	S. Shaw (Lab)	20,325
	Majority	8,622
1955 North	H. S. J. Hughes (Lab)	33,153
	C. A. B. Malden (Unionist)	16,357
	Majority	16,796
1955 South	Lady Tweedsmuir (Unionist)	26,817
	Mrs J. C. M. Hart (Lab)	19,627
	Majority	7,190
1959 North	H. S. J. Hughes (Lab)	32,793
	J. Stewart-Clark (Unionist)	15,137
	W. A. Milne (SNP)	2,964
	Majority	17,656
1959 South	Lady Tweedsmuir (Unionist)	25,471
	P. M. Doig (Lab)	17,349
	Mrs E. T. Dangerfield (Lib)	4,558
	Majority	8,122
1964 North	H. S. J. Hughes (Lab)	31,844
	J. C. McInnes (Unionist)	14,366
	Majority	17,478
1964 South	Lady Tweedsmuir (Unionist)	25,824
	D. C. Dewar (Lab)	21,926
	J. B. Reid (SNP)	2,197
	Majority	3,898
1966 North	H. S. J. Hughes (Lab)	28,799
	J. M. M. Humphrey (Con)	8,768
	Mrs D. W. MacPherson (Lib)	4,350
	Mrs M. Rose (Communist)	719
	Majority	20,031

1966 South	D. C. Dewar (Lab)	23,291
	Lady Tweedsmuir (Con)	21,492
	N. W. King (Lib)	5,797
	Majority	1,799
1970 North	R. Hughes (Lab)	27,707
	D. J. Williams (Con)	9,807
	J. McKenna (SNP)	3,756
	F. McCallum (Lib)	2,835
	A. J. Ingram (Communist)	521
	Majority	17,900
1970 South	I. M. Sproat (Con)	23,843
	D. C. Dewar (Lab)	22,754
	K. J. B. S. MacLeod (Lib)	3,135
	B. M. Cockie (SNP)	2,777
	Majority	1,089
1974 (Feb.) North	R. Hughes (Lab)	23,193
	J. A. McGugan (SNP)	11,337
	N. G. M. Dunnett (Con)	8,115
	F. McCallum (Lib)	6,001
	Majority	11,856
1974 (Feb.) South	I. M. Sproat (Con)	21,938
	R. Middleton (Lab)	18,380
	A. Stronach (SNP)	7,599
	A. A. Robbie (Lib)	7,447
	Majority	3,558
1974 (Oct.) North	R. Hughes (Lab)	23,130
	J. A. McGugan (SNP)	13,509
	P. L. Fraser (Con)	5,125
	F. McCallum (Lib)	3,700
	Majority	9,621
1974 (Oct.) South	I. M. Sproat (Con)	18,475
	R. Middleton (Lab)	18,110
	A. Stronach (SNP)	10,481
	A. A. Robbie (Lib)	5,018
	Majority	365
1979 North	R. Hughes (Lab)	26,771
	G. C. Adams (Con)	7,657
	Miss E. M. Watt (SNP)	5,796
	Miss L. J. MacMillan (Lib)	4,887
	Majority	19,114

1979 South	I. M. Sproat (Con)	20,820
	N. A. Godman (Lab)	20,048
	Mrs H. M. Pitt-Watson (Lib)	5,901
	A. Stronach (SNP)	4,361
	Majority	772
1983 North	R. Hughes (Lab)	19,262
	C. S. Deans (SDP/Alliance)	10,118
	Miss G. E. C. Scanlan (Con)	7,426
	J. A. McGugan (SNP)	3,790
	Miss E. M. Harty (Ecology)	367
	Majority	9,144
1983 South	P. G. Malone (Con)	15,393
	R. Middleton (Lab)	11,812
	I. G. Philip (SDP/Alliance)	10,372
	S. Coull (SNP)	1,974
	Majority	3,581
1987 North	R. Hughes (Lab)	24,145
	Sir R. Smith Bt (SDP/Alliance)	7,867
	Miss G. E. C. Scanlan (Con)	6,330
	P. B. Greenhorn (SNP)	5,827
	Majority	16,278
1987 South	F. Doran (Lab)	15,917
	P. G. Malone (Con)	14,719
	I. G. Philip (SDP/Alliance)	8,844
	M. F. Weir (SNP)	2,776
	Majority	1,198
1992 North	R. Hughes (Lab)	18,845
	J. A. McGugan (SNP)	9,608
	P. Cook (Con)	6,836
	M. Ford (Lib Dem)	4,772
	Majority	9,237
1992 South	R. Robertson (Con)	15,808
	F. Doran (Lab)	14,291
	J. Davidson (SNP)	6,223
	Miss I. Keith (Lib Dem)	4,767
	Majority	1,517
1997 Central	F. Doran (Lab)	17,745
	Mrs J. Wisely (Con)	6,944
	B. Topping (SNP)	5,767
	J. Brown (Lib Dem)	4,714
	J. Farquharson (Referendum)	446
	Majority	10,801

1997 North	M. Savidge (Lab)	18,389
	B. Adam (SNP)	8,379
	J. Gifford (Con)	5,763
	M. Rumbles (Lib Dem)	5,421
	A. Mackenzie (Referendum)	463
	Majority	10,010
1997 South	Miss A. Begg (Lab)	15,541
	N. Stephen (Lib Dem)	12,176
	R. Robertson (Con)	11,621
	J. Towers (SNP)	4,299
	R. Warton (Referendum)	425
	Majority	3,365

Table 8.2 *Results of the Election to the Scottish Parliament, 1999:*
Aberdeen constituencies

Central	L. MacDonald (Lab)	10,305
	R. Lochhead (SNP)	7,609
	Dr E. Anderson (LD)	4,403
	T. Mason (Con)	3,655
	A. Cumbers (SSP)	523
	Majority	2,696
North	Ms E. Thomson (Lab)	10,340
	B. Adam (SNP)	9.942
	J. Donaldson (LD)	4,767
	I. Haughie (Con)	2,772
	Majority	398
South	N. Stephen (LD)	11,300
	M. Elrick (Lab)	9.540
	Mrs N. Milne (Con)	6,993
	Ms I. McGugan (SNP)	6,651
	S. Sutherland (SWP)	206
	Majority	1,760

Parties:

Con	Scottish Conservative and Unionist Party
Lab	Scottish Labour Party
LD	Scottish Liberal Democrats
SNP	Scottish National Party
SSP	Scottish Socialist Party
SWP	Scottish Workers' Party

9

Local Government

CLIVE H. LEE

THE UNREFORMED TOWN COUNCIL

Two hundred years ago local government did not comprise a clearly identified element within a coherent and comprehensive system of administration as it does today. Indeed, very few of the services associated with local government at the end of the twentieth century were provided at the close of the eighteenth century, and those that were available were primarily provided by charity. The structure of local government at the beginning of the nineteenth century was the creation of a rural and slow-changing society, and of largely self-sufficient communities. The growth of urban population, however, created demands to which these traditional structures could not respond effectively and, consequently, generated a radical transformation in the scale and range of activities undertaken by local government.

The structure of local government which existed in 1800 was very restricted, as were the tasks it undertook. Aberdeen town council had evolved from the medieval merchant guild. An Act of Parliament, passed in 1469 in the reign of James III, made the town council self-elected since the outgoing administration was charged with the responsibility for appointing its successor.[1] Each year the outgoing town council selected a new town council, and then the two groups together chose the officers to serve as provost and baillies. Its functions were largely prescribed by the common good, a fund comprising land, property and feu duties accumulated over many centuries and held by the town council on behalf of the citizens. To this money was added traditional bell and petty customs whereby local authorities obtained income by imposing a tax on markets, harbours and other commercial activities. The right to collect these taxes was auctioned off, and in the 1820s this generated an income of some £800–900 for the common good. Property was also taxed according to a sliding scale. Houses with an annual rental between £2 and £7 were assessed at an equivalent of 10p in the pound, while shops and warehouses in the same valuation range were charged at 8p in the pound. Private houses with a water supply attracted an additional levy bringing them to 10.5p in the pound.[2] But the town council had no right to tax the burgesses further without securing the express authority of Parliament through legislation.

This type of local government could function effectively only in the context of a static society requiring a low level of public taxation and expenditure. Urban growth disturbed and then rapidly destroyed this archaic regime. The need for financial powers was recognised, and the town council and the merchant guild together sought the parliamentary legislation which would establish a police commission with a legal right to raise funds through taxation. The police commission was empowered to borrow up to a limit of £5,000 and to levy an assessment of one shilling (5p) in the pound to fulfil its remit to improve the paving, lighting and cleaning of streets, provide a better water supply, and develop new streets. The first police commission was established in 1795, but when it reached the limits of its financial resources the town council refused to help by drawing on the common good. Thus the police commission had become effectively defunct before the close of the century.

The need for finance for development remained. A major physical obstacle hampering the development of the town lay in the fact that the valley of the Denburn effectively prevented westward expansion. The town council obtained an Act of Parliament in 1800 to develop two new streets at an estimated cost of £37,000. These were to form the crucial axis for expansion, Union Street running west from the town and crossing the Denburn by bridge, and King Street running north from the Castlegate. This imaginative and bold strategy reflected the confidence and adventurousness of the city fathers, although it eventually exposed their financial misjudgement of the scale of the undertaking. The expenditure required soon exceeded the sum authorised. The town council raised additional money by securing another Act of Parliament in 1810 to improve the harbour, with authority to borrow £140,000 and to impose shore dues at almost double the previous rate. This money was raised but the docks were not built. Other financial expedients were adopted as the crisis deepened, including the sale of charitable assets.

> Previous to the insolvency of the burgh, several of the office-bearers of the corporation were possessed, as trustees of lands destined for charitable purposes, almost all of which appear to have been sold by order of the magistrates and council, not from any want of money on the part of these charities, but that the price might be lent to the treasurer, to supply the expensive speculations of the magistrates.[3]

One such transaction concerned a loan of £3,000–4,000 made to the town council by Baillie McCombie. To repay this debt, the town council sold McCombie a plot of land at Skene which belonged to the common good for £12,000 and allowed him to deduct the amount of his loan from this sum. By 1817 the town council was receiving less income than the cost of servicing its accumulated debts, and the treasurer was obliged to declare it insolvent in February of that year.

This state of affairs meant that control of the finances of the town council had to be relinquished to a committee of 21 trustees. In part the problem was recognised as one that time would alleviate, having occurred as the result of a rapid and over optimistic expansion.

> At first, the Projectors of these Improvements entertained sanguine expectations that the Ground Rents to be drawn for the Stances in the lines of New Streets, would be adequate to the Interest of the monies which had been borrowed for those purposes; but they seem at no time to have adopted, or even had in contemplation, any plan for extinguishing the principal sums. Owing to the state of the Town at the commencement of these Improvements, and for several years afterwards, the great extent of valuable Property thrown into the market, and other unfavourable circumstances, the feuing of Stances in the lines of those Streets made very slow progress. The consequence was, that the expectations of the Projectors were not realised; and the Debt contracted increased every year, by the accumulation of Interest, to a very great amount.[4]

Time, it was hoped, would improve the market for commercial property so that the sale of ground rents could eradicate the debt. In 1820 a sinking fund was established to pay the creditors, of whom there were 570 individuals. They were owed sums of between £10 and in excess of £2,000, making a total of £165,000, while the office-bearers of the town, as trustees for various charities, were owed a further £70,000. In the event, the debt was discharged by 1825 as the market recovered rather more quickly than had been hoped or anticipated, as a result of the large income generated from feuing the ground along the new streets. The trustees were thus able to hand back to the town council the property they had been managing on its behalf.

The declaration of civic insolvency, the subsequent embarrassment of a parliamentary enquiry, and the need to reassure creditors, focused critical attention on the undemocratic nature of the town council which was controlled by a small group of people. Especially significant in the development of Aberdeen in the first three decades of the nineteenth century were the Hadden family, prominent textile manufacturers. James Hadden, and his brother Gavin Hadden, held the office of lord provost between them for almost half the period 1801–32, and their terms of office coincided with crucial initiatives in urban development. James Hadden served as lord provost at the time of the early improvement scheme to build the Union Bridge over the Denburn, and earned the sobriquet of 'father of the city'.[5] His business partner, Thomas Leys, preceded Hadden as lord provost in 1797-98, and chaired the committee of ratepayers which finally decided to undertake the extension scheme. He served a further term as lord provost in 1803-04. When the development scheme fell into financial difficulties, the closed nature of the town council enabled the true state of affairs to be concealed from all but a very small group of individuals.[6]

In September 1817 the beleaguered magistrates and councillors unanimously supported a motion criticising the oligopolistic nature of self-appointment 'tending to give any individual or party who may be so inclined, an excessive and unnatural preponderance, and to foster and encourage a system of secrecy and concealment … and to the absence of such checks in the constitution of this burgh [to which] the subscribing members of the town council ascribe the heavy calamity which has befallen it'.[7] A similar view had been expressed twenty years earlier. The burgesses of guild passed a resolution stating that 'they attributed the present disaster to the bad system under which the burgh had been governed, by the town council being self-elected, and to its administration having become, as it were, the inheritance of a few individuals, who forming a secret junto considered themselves irresponsible for their management to their fellow citizen's'[8]

James Hadden, lord provost of Aberdeen, 1801-02, 1809-10, 1813-14, 1830-31.

Aberdeen was not unique in encountering such difficulties and local government in general, before 1833, was 'characterised by want of co-ordination, purpose or policy'.[9] Eventual reform, and with it the beginnings of modern local government, was introduced by the Royal Burghs (Scotland) Act 1833 which turned municipal councils into elected bodies, although they were still denied the power to tax. The detail of the evolution of the modern system of local government is complex and idiosyncratic. But it did have three outstanding characteristics. Firstly, new activities were usually introduced and operated by ad hoc bodies. Secondly, they were subsequently absorbed by local government or fell under its control. Thirdly, as the town council increased in authority and obligations, it too fell increasingly under the power of central government. Local government grew in both scale and range of activities under pressure from two forces, namely the emergence of new and urgent problems consequent upon urban expansion and the attempts of central government to deliver public services through the agency of local administration.

DIVIDED AUTHORITY: TOWN COUNCIL AND POLICE COMMISSION

For much of the nineteenth century, local government was based on a dual system of administration as the police commission operated in conjunction with the town council. The Police Act of 1795 established the first police commission, membership of which was restricted to the most affluent citizens, being residents of property worth an annual rent of £15 per annum, elected on a franchise which was only a little more extensive, being restricted to the inhabitants of property worth £5 in annual rent. The police commission was given the power both to raise an assessment and to borrow up to a specified limit, an authority not available to the town council.[10] After quickly running out of funds, the police commission remained dormant for almost two decades, but it was revived in 1818 and, thereafter, maintained an uneasy duplication of function with the town council.

The rapid expansion of nineteenth-century towns created an immediate and obvious demand for improvements in infrastructure, with the lighting and paving of streets, the provision of sanitation services with drainage systems to remove sewage, and a supply of water to meet increasing demand. The Police Act of 1818 gave enlarged powers over drainage, paving and lighting to the police commissioners. The 1829 Police Act effectively provided the commission with responsibility for public health, particularly for the provision of a water supply as a public utility financed by capital raised locally. Water provision became a major priority as the town grew. At the beginning of the century Aberdeen relied on a series of wells and a piped supply from the Hazlehead spring. As this became increasingly inadequate, by the 1820s, the police commissioners sought new supplies of water. Possible sources included the Loch of Skene, the Burn of Culter, the Aberdeen to Inverurie canal and the River Dee. The last was finally chosen and, in the 1830s, water was pumped from a point close to the Bridge of Dee by steam engines and through an infiltration tunnel to the waterhouse in Union Place (now the western end of Union Street). Local reaction to this improved provision was mixed. For some, the existence of piped water constituted a selling point for property, for other consumers the possession of property outside the jurisdiction of the police commission, with well water but no water rate, offered a greater attraction.

In the 1830s the pumping system only needed to operate for six hours per day to satisfy demand, but by the 1850s it was in operation for 22 hours each day.

Several other sources were again considered, including the Don and the Denburn as well as further exploitation of the Dee. The last was again the preferred source and parliamentary legislation passed in 1862 made provision for the city water supply to be taken from the Dee at Cairnton almost 20 miles from the main storage depot at Mannofield. The scheme was officially opened by Queen Victoria in 1866. This was helped, a few years later, by the construction of a steam pumping station at Cults and additional reservoirs at Mannofield and Slopefield. In response to continued growth in demand, the system was periodically renewed, a new electrically driven pump being installed at Cairnton in 1960 and a dam at Tillyfumerie, on the Water of Dye, was built in the 1970s to discharge a regulated flow of water into the Dee to compensate for the increased abstraction of water by the city. Despite the rising demand, the River Dee was still able to meet the needs of the city at the close of the twentieth century.[11]

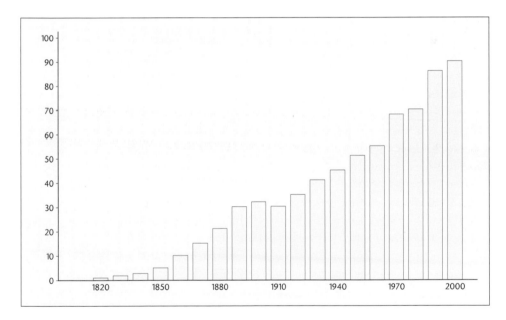

Figure 9.1
Water abstraction from the River Dee for Aberdeen City, 1820-2000.
(Source: North of Scotland Water Authority, Rate of Abstraction Ml d)

The Police Act of 1818 also gave the police commissioners authority to provide a night watch. The day watch remained the responsibility of the town sergeants under the authority of the magistrates and town council. Relations between the two forces were not always harmonious and one town sergeant was suspended for assaulting the superintendent of the watchmen. The legislation of 1829 enabled the police commissioners also to provide a day watch. Gradually the policing responsibilities of the police commission increased. By agreement with the harbour commissioners in 1854, the police commissioners undertook to maintain law and order in the harbour area by merging the respective watches of the two bodies. But, when the city police force was inspected by Colonel Kinloch, first HM Inspector of Constabulary in Scotland, under the terms of the 1857 Police (Scotland) Act, the colonel complained that his efforts to inspect the Aberdeen force had been persistently obstructed. When he eventually succeeded in making an inspection in 1859 his report was damning.

> The Constables are divided in the old fashioned way into 'Day Constables' and 'Night-Watchmen'; the latter being so far considered of an inferior class that they have less pay and are not thought worthy of putting into uniform like the day Constables, being provided only with a great-coat, a broad flat bonnet and a big stick ... the cells are very cold, the windows being unglazed; inferior to any Prisons of the present day, and in my opinion not fit for the confinement of prisoners who are only taken up by the Police on suspicion, or for drunkenness, and who are not yet convicted of any crime ... Altogether, I consider this force to be behind the age, inefficient in organisation and discipline and to require a thorough reform.[12]

The police commissioners furiously repudiated this verdict, noting that Aberdeen was a cheap and healthy place in which to live, and observing that the town enjoyed 'comparative good order and quietness'. A review of the required reforms in the following year indicated that an increase in spending of £1,061 would be needed to implement them, but the government grant which was available to help was worth £1,152 representing a net gain of £91. In these felicitous circumstances, the reforms were adopted.

While the town council and police commission co-existed from 1818 onward, they were never entirely separate bodies. Indeed the Police Act of 1818 established a police board of 13 elected members plus the lord provost, city treasurer and dean of guild as ex-officio members. The 1829 Police Act increased the elected membership to 18 and added a fourth ex-officio member, namely the convener of the Incorporated Trades. By 1871, five of the 18 elected members of the police commission were also town councillors. Furthermore, the lord provost chaired the police board and several other leading councillors played important roles by virtue of their office. Alexander Duffus, a member of the police board, stated that 'some of these parties, by virtue of their office, claim several convenerships of committees at the police board. The dean of guild, in virtue of his office, claims the convenership of the street committee; and the city treasurer, who is also an ex-officio member, claims in virtue of his office the convenership of the watching and lighting committee.'[13] The police commissioners maintained generally cordial links with the town council and, in 1838, the lord provost was presented with two elegant lamps bearing the town's arms, which were placed at the entrance to his house by the police commissioners in recognition of his position as chief magistrate, thus commencing a tradition which still continues.[14]

During this period, the responsibilities of local government were shared with a variety of other institutions. Historically the town council had acted as the harbour board, and the Harbour Act of 1810 established a harbour commission under its control. In 1829, after years of debate, another Harbour Act added six members to the existing 19 members of the town council to constitute the harbour trustees. This organisation was reformed as the harbour board in 1843, comprising the members of the town council plus 12 burgesses. The constitution was again modified in 1868 to increase the level of representation. The 19 councillors remained and were joined by 12 elected commissioners drawn from individuals who paid at least £10 per annum in harbour rates, partners nominated by ratepaying companies, owners of shipping of 50 tons belonging to the port, and the burgesses of guild and trade.[15] In fact, the representation of the town council on the harbour board lasted until 1960 when its power was transferred to the port authority. Other institutions also enjoyed overlapping representation. The St Nicholas parochial board which, after 1845, bore responsibility for poor relief, comprised four delegates appointed by the magistrates and town council plus four from the kirk session and 15 elected by ratepayers. The Oldmachar parochial board comprised heritors (possessing property worth at least £20) plus 20 members elected by ratepayers, six elected by the kirk session, plus the provost and baillies of all royal burghs in the parish.[16]

All these bodies were, in effect, run by the same small network of the most prosperous citizens. When the town council became at last subject to the whims of an electorate it was, initially, based upon a highly restricted franchise. The first election took place in November 1833. Each of the three wards returned six out of 12 candidates. The franchise extended only to burgesses, so that the electorate numbered only 1,627. This electorate comprised almost certainly less than 5 per cent of the adult population and was exclusively male. The first elected town council comprised 19 members, six elected for each of the three wards, plus the dean of guild elected by the guildry alone.

THE BATTLE FOR POWER

Mid-Victorian local government was fragmented into a diversity of institutions, each holding responsibility for the delivery of some specific service. This had an important effect on political activity with regard to the main issue which divided opinion within the Victorian establishment of most cities, including Aberdeen. This reflected the conflict between expansion, implying increased expenditure the cost of which would fall upon the local elite, and fiscal prudence which would limit the burden of that taxation. Those who wished to follow an expansionist policy were hampered by the fragmentation of power while those who wished to restrict expenditure found it a useful political tool. In Aberdeen the spectre of the civic bankruptcy of 1817 also provided a focal point for opposition to any perceived financial extravagance.

Attempts to follow an expansive policy had to be pursued by way of the reorganisation and concentration of civic power. One early and imaginative scheme, which fell foul of conservative caution, comprised an attempt to reorganise and integrate a number of administrative bodies. This was proposed by Lord Provost Thomas Blaikie in 1846. He led a group of aspiring improvers which included conservatives such as Alexander Anderson and James Hadden, and was reputed to have financial, business and masonic links. Their political opponents attacked the clique of 'improvement jobbers' as self-seekers who wanted to exploit their shareholdings in the market and the gas company. Blaikie's scheme proposed the establishment of a new administrative body comprising three members of the town council, two from the Incorporated Trades, two from the police commission, and six members elected by the ratepayers. The programme proposed included the abolition of the bell and petty customs, the acquisition of the new market, with power to build a cattle market and slaughter house, the purchase of the United Gas Company's works and the formation of several new streets. The town council was willing to adopt most parts of the scheme, but omitted the proposals to buy the gasworks and markets. A joint committee of councillors and ratepayers, appointed by a public meeting, examined the details of the scheme. It included the provision for a tax equivalent to 1.7p in the

Sir Alexander Anderson, lord provost 1859-65, the most dynamic of the mid-century civic leaders and promoter of many schemes.

pound to be levied on owners of property and 0.9p on occupiers of property, but the scheme was rejected by a public meeting held in the quadrangle of Marischal College in January 1847.[17] Blaikie withdrew his bill and retired from the town council at the subsequent election, although he did return to serve another term as lord provost in the 1850s.

The next serious attempt at reconstruction produced a major power struggle in the late 1860s and early 1870s in one of the principal local political conflicts of the century. This time the reformers were successful. The extension of the franchise in 1868 provided a powerful new base of support as the electorate was increased from 2,926 to 9,347. This enabled the 'party of progress' to attract sufficient support to gain a majority on the town council in order to implement its radical programme which involved both the extension of the city boundaries and, more fundamentally, a major redistribution of power within local government. The second and critical effect of the 1868 extension of the franchise was to undermine the democratic credibility of the police commission. Hitherto the police commission had been elected on a wider franchise than the town council. Indeed the lower property qualification required for the police commission had proved attractive to some radical politicians. But the change in the franchise in 1868 meant that the town council was subsequently elected on a franchise 60 per cent larger than that which selected the police commission.

The 'party of progress' was a loose political grouping of people which had formed partly as the result of a wrangle between interest groups in the 1860s about plans to improve the harbour and to link the city to Torry by means of a bridge. The proposed purchase of Torry Farm for development by the town council proved to be a major basis for dispute.[18] Lord Provost Nicol, who opposed the venture, lost his seat in the critical town council election of 1869, as did many of his supporters. Following victory in the town council elections, the 'party of progress' brought forward the Aberdeen Municipality Extension Bill of 1871 which proposed a major reform of local government, and was by far the most substantial change since the establishment of the police commission and the introduction of an elected town council. The central proposal was the abolition of the police commission and the assumption of its responsibilities by the town council, as well as the municipalisation of the gas company. These changes threatened a number of interests and generated a fierce parliamentary battle which ended substantially in favour of the town council. Its promoters, who appeared before the parliamentary committee in support of the bill, included Lord Provost Leslie, and eminent local politicians such as Sir Alexander Anderson, Peter Esslemont and James Barclay.

Petitions in opposition to the proposed legislation were presented by a number of vested interests. The police commission was split, the minority being roughly the size of town council representation on the police commission. The majority, arguing in favour of pluralism in representation, made an assertion that the citizens were quite satisfied with the management of the police commission, and that the town council already had sufficient power and responsibility. John Webster, appearing as chairman of the gas company, claimed to represent many small investors, argued that the citizens were satisfied with the supply and price of gas, and rejected the threats of competition issued by the town council. Further support for this petition came from prominent industrialists in the city who enjoyed price discounts as large customers, from wealthy citizens wishing to protect the dividend on their shares, and from the ratepayers who feared an additional tax levy if the company fell into the hands of the town council. The elected representatives on the harbour board objected because they feared that an increase in the size of the town council would reduce their own influence on the harbour board. As Duffus observed in his evidence, 'All I know about the harbour is that when the harbour commissioners want anything from the town, they are very anxious to let us know that the interests are identical - and sometimes they can make it appear that they are not so'.[19] The guildry objected to the proposal to remove the dean of guild from the town council, fearing that its funds would be sequestered by the town councillors. The guild was in some difficulty. Since the loss of commercial privileges, under the 1845 legislation, membership had dwindled from 700 early in the century to reach 300 by 1871. Finally the Incorporated Trades objected to the proposals which would rob it of representation on the police commission. In the event, the town council prevailed over both the police commission, which was abolished and its functions and responsibilities transferred to the town council, and the gas company, which was taken into municipal ownership. The guildry was allowed to maintain control of its assets which provided for the needs of retired members and the widows of deceased members. The dean of guild was allowed to remain on the town council as an interim measure (which lasted for 104 years), but the Incorporated Trades failed to retain its representation.

The victory of the town council over the police commission marked the way ahead. Legislation empowered the transfer of waterworks to town authorities, allowed them unlimited rating powers and made them responsible for paving, lighting and street maintainance, and for connecting domestic drainage to the sewer system. They were also empowered to acquire land for parks, establish a gas supply and build their own hospitals. Dual administration throughout Scotland was ended by the 1892 Burgh Police (Scotland) Act and confirmed by the Town Councils (Scotland) Act of 1900, which insisted on uniform constitutions vested in the offices of provost, baillie and councillor. Eventually local authorities absorbed the powers and functions of all the ad hoc bodies. School boards, for example, established in 1872, lasted until 1918 when their functions were absorbed by the local education authorities.

THE GROWTH OF THE CITY AND LOCAL GOVERNMENT

The second great conflict of the century in local government occurred in the final decades, and was occasioned by another surge of expansion. It was also accompanied by a further extension of the franchise to a wider range of property owners including, from 1882, single women who were ratepayers. This increased the electorate to 15,168 men and 4,345 women by 1888-89 but, even so, it included only about 35 per cent of the adult population.[20] In 1894 married women became eligible to vote in local elections and were allowed to stand for office if they were qualified to vote. Not only was the local franchise restricted to ratepayers, and to those who had paid their dues in full before the election, occupiers of the cheapest properties where rates were compounded with rents were automatically excluded. Even at the end of the century, the local electorate was

The tower of the Town House built 1867-74, symbolising the new confidence and power of local government.

Peter Esslemont, founder of Esslemont & Macintosh, drapers, lord provost 1880-82, Liberal MP for East Aberdeen-shire 1885-92, as seen in the Northern Figaro.

limited to middle-class and skilled working-class citizens. The greatest extension of the franchise, eventually reaching universal adult suffrage, was delayed until after the First World War.

The size of the town council itself grew as both its functions and the city expanded. As a result of this, in 1871 the number of wards was increased from the original three to four, and the number of town councillors increased from 19 to 25. In 1883 the Aberdeen Extension and Improvement Act created eight new wards to replace the existing structure. The new wards were now named as St Clement's, St Andrew's, Greyfriars, St Nicholas, Ferryhill, Rosemount, Rubislaw and St Machar. Each ward had three elected representatives, one of whom stood down or sought re-election each year.

Another important ingredient in the new expansionary phase lay in the foundation of the Liberal Association in 1877. The group of young and radical Liberals being led by Peter Esslemont, and supported by the trades council and temperance interests, managed to secure seven seats in the town council election of 1877. This reforming group held sway through the following decade, and the temperance councillors managed to use their strategic power to make a clean sweep of the magisterial bench in 1887. This followed a renewed campaign by the temperance organisations in the city to obtain a local veto on public houses or at the very least to reduce the number of licences. Subsequently, in 1893, they managed to secure a sub committee report recommending the municipalisation of the drink trade although it was eventually rejected, albeit narrowly, by the full town council.

The expansionists vigorously pursued their policies through the 1880s and Esslemont Avenue, laid out in 1882, provided a memorial to Esslemont's term as lord provost. He was responsible for the Extension and Improvement Act of 1883 which allowed substantial developments later in the decade. A new road, projected from Union Terrace and crossing a viaduct of arches over the Denburn to reach the higher ground at South Mount Street, gave much improved access to Rosemount. In the other direction, the extension of the road towards Schoolhill necessitated the demolition of Denburn Terrace and Mutton Brae and the construction of a bridge, Denburn Viaduct, over the railway. Elsewhere in the city,

---

Alexander Macdonald Munro 1860–1911

Born in Aberdeen and educated at Robert Gordon's Hospital, Alexander Munro joined the staff of the town house in 1877. He spent his entire career in the department of the city chamberlain, and was appointed to the office of chamberlain in 1905. According to his obituary, he was kind and considerate, and especially generous to the poor who, when rates were due and money was scarce, were almost invariably granted an extension of the period of payment. He was a noted antiquarian and was a fellow of the Society of Antiquiries of Scotland, and of the Aberdeen Philosophical Society. He wrote extensively about the history of the city, including *Records of Old Aberdeen, 1157–1891* (2 vols, 1899, 1909), *A History of the Common Good of Aberdeen* (1888), *Memorials of the Aldermen, Provosts and Lord Provosts of Aberdeen 1272–1895* (1897), and *MPs for Aberdeen 1357–1886* (1887). He also produced a 'Register of Burgesses of Guild and Trade in Aberdeen 1399–1700' in the *New Spalding Club Miscellany, Vols 1 and 2* (1890, 1908). He was an office bearer of Gilcomston United Free Church.

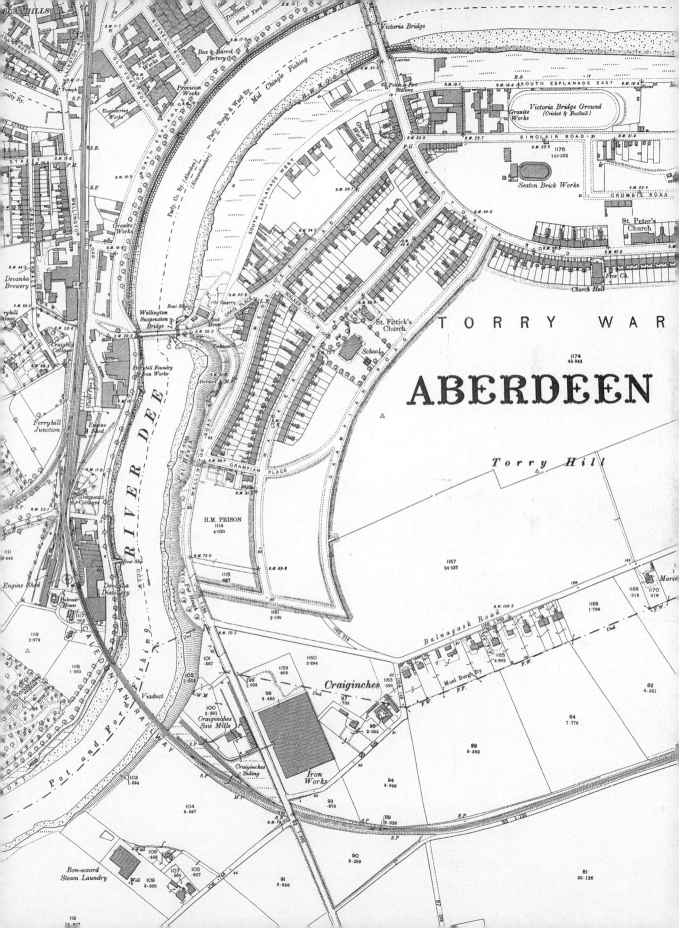

the Ferryhill area was developed by extending the road from Springbank Terrace, at the foot of Bon-Accord Street, to run through the grounds of Ferryhill House, which had been purchased by the town council from the common good fund, to Fonthill Road. This new road, also Bon-Accord Street, provided improved access to the Duthie Park.

The stimulus for expansion was given further impetus by the County Councils Act of 1889 which threatened to hamper future growth by establishing the boundaries between the city and its two adjacent counties. The continued success of the expansionists in the town council election of 1889 came to fruition in the Corporation Act 1891 which increased the boundary of the city to encompass the barony of Old Aberdeen, the old village of Torry and the Woodside police burgh. These additions together increased the area of the city from 2,681 acres to 6,748 acres. In 1891 parts of Mannofield and Rubislaw were also added to the city, and the wards of Ruthrieston, Torry and Woodside were created, raising the total number to 11 and the number of councillors to 31. Torry was restricted to a single representative until 1899, an additional offence to those Torry ratepayers who had voted against incorporation in 1890 by 289 votes to 58. The ratepayers of Woodside had agreed to incorporation in return for a park, duly delivered by Lord Provost Stewart, and opened in 1904.

MUNICIPAL TRADING

One of the major factors determining the growth of the town council's responsibilities during the Victorian period was the growth of public utilities. Aberdeen town council, like many other local authorities, acquired control over a range of services which had originally been provided by commercial organisations. Gas was first supplied to the town by a private firm, the Aberdeen Gas Light Company, established in 1824 in Guild Street. The New Gas Light Company was established in Cotton Street in 1844. The two companies subsequently merged in 1846, and the town council took over control of the undertaking in 1871 as municipalisation achieved growing popularity. Increasing demand was reflected in the massive new gas holder built at the Gallowhills in 1892-94. The Electric Lighting Act of 1882 allowed local authorities to take over electricity provision from private companies and to set maximum charges. In that year Guild Street, Bridge Street, Market Street, Union Street and Castle Street were illuminated by electricity for a four month trial period, although the electricity supply for the city did not come into operation until 1894 when an electricity generating station was set up on the Cotton Street site of the gas works. The electrification of the tramways further expanded demand and warranted the construction of the Dee Village generating station which opened in 1903 adjacent to the new tramway depot.[21]

NION STREET, ABERDEEN.

The bustling heart of the city around 1900, looking east towards Castle Street.

Local transport needs grew with population and a variety of private local transport services existed before the advent of municipal control. The Aberdeen District Tramways Act 1872 contained provision for the town council to purchase, at a fair valuation and at a later date, the lines constructed. The first proposal for purchase was placed before the town council in 1895 and was received favourably by the District Tramways Company. But negotiations broke down in dispute about the purchase price. The situation was further complicated when the Great North of Scotland Railway Company (GNSR) expressed an interest in buying the tramways. Its plan was to bring the line from Echt into the city along Queen's Road, across the bleachfields and down Albyn Place. Not surprisingly, an offer from the railway company to buy the district tramways was blocked by the town council on the grounds that it wished to provide a municipal service to benefit ratepayers rather than shareholders. A further dispute arose over the proposal, embodied in the parliamentary legislation, to allow the town council to impose a supplementary rate to cover any deficit in the tramways operating budget. Councillor Alexander Wilkie strenuously opposed this, arguing that it was unfair to tax the entire community for benefits which were enjoyed by a limited number of them. He also argued that a subsidised tramway would offer unfair competition to the Woodside train service of the GNSR, especially as the latter was a major ratepayer. The rating issue roused more controversy than the proposal to take the tramways into municipal ownership. The Aberdeen House Proprietors' Association joined the GNSR and the Caledonian Railway in objecting to the proposed powers to levy an additional rate. Underlying this was a fear, articulated by the *Free Press*, that the tramways might be deliberately run at a loss on social grounds with the costs being borne by the ratepayers. The legislation was amended to require the town council to fix fares annually at a rate that would cover all expenses. Wilkie was hailed as a hero in the local press, and this may have helped his subsequent appointment as convener of the tramways committee. The town council assumed control of the tramways in August 1898 for a purchase price of just over £100,000, enabling the city to assume ownership of 38 cars and 244 horses.[22]

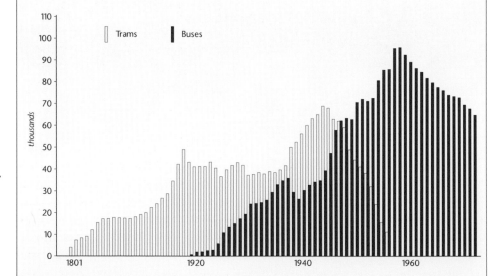

*Figure 9.2
Number of
passengers carried by
Aberdeen Municipal
Transport,
1898-1974.
(Sources: Aberdeen
Town Council,
Public Transport
Accounts)*

The Aberdeen District Tramways Act had authorised five lines. But owing to shortage of subscriptions only two were opened in 1874 and this left a gap in the market for private companies to provide transport to the suburbs. Alexander Wilkie, the convener of the tramways committee, was deeply involved in the

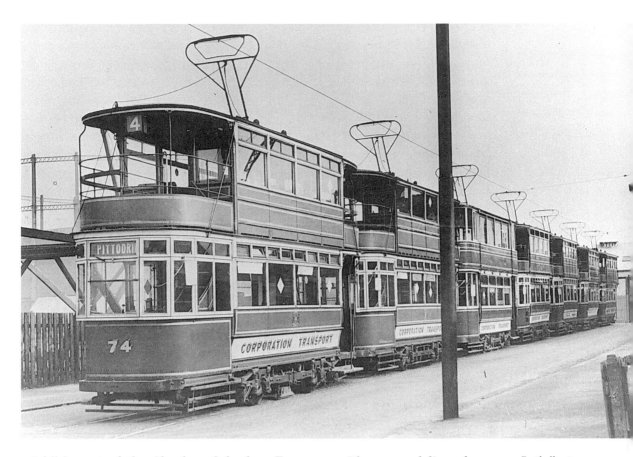

Football extras:
Corporation trams
lined up awaiting
the finish of a
football match at
Pittodrie.

establishment of the Aberdeen Suburban Tramways with proposed lines from Woodside to Dyce and Mannofield to Bieldside. Originally a photographer and apprenticed to Washington Wilson, he became a police commissioner for Woodside and subsequently represented the Woodside ward on the town council between 1891 and 1911. He served as managing director of the Aberdeen Suburban Tramways throughout its existence 1902–27. Agreement was reached with the town council about through-running (Wilkie was both convener of the transport committee and city treasurer), including free use of the track but offering compensatory payments for the mileage covered plus 5 per cent commission on tickets.[23] The company provided the track outside the city and its own cars. The official opening took place in June 1904. The town council tried to take over the company in 1914 without success. But by the 1920s both track and cars were in a poor state of repair and derailments became frequent. In 1925 the town council terminated the through-running agreement with effect from June 1926. This blow, together with bus competition, effectively killed the company which ceased operation in July 1927.

The power of the magistrates was also demonstrated by the resolution of the bus war of the 1920s manifest in the appearance of private operators normally offering their services at the bus stand in the Castlegate at the top of Shiprow. Some of these offered tours, or travelled beyond the city limits, and some operated very small vehicles with less than ten seats. By 1927 there were 28 independent buses operating in the city, 11 of them owned by the Town and County Company. The bus war ended, and the independent operators had their activities curtailed abruptly, when the magistrates refused to renew operating licenses in October 1927.

Control over competition did not save the trams. At the end of the First World War the tramways faced high costs in renewal and extensions of track, and replacement of cars. Buses offered a more economical and flexible alternative, and new housing developments built between the wars were not close to tram routes. The tramway system enjoyed little capital investment after the 1920s. Route closures took place steadily through the 1950s as the buses, travelling to increasingly distant estates, duplicated the tram routes. The final tram disappeared in 1958. The city's control of public transport ended in 1975 when the bus service was placed under the control of the new Grampian regional council. In 1989 Grampian Regional Transport bought itself out of public ownership, and became GRT Holdings PLC. In the 1990s the company played a prominent role in the series of mergers and take-overs which characterised the privatised bus market, becoming part of the First Bus Group.

THE GROWTH OF CENTRAL CONTROL

In the course of the Victorian era, local government became a coherent system for the delivery of important services and, in this process, it assumed the activities and responsibilities hitherto carried out by other official bodies and by the voluntary sector. The Local Government Act of 1929 completed this process and marked the high point of local government power. After 1945 central government transferred to its direct control several of the most important responsibilities previously undertaken by local government. This accelerated the process by which local government became ever more closely controlled by the state as an agency for the implementation of redistributive policies. Furthermore, the functions of local government changed and some of the main duties it had undertaken in the nineteenth century were lost in the twentieth century. Gas, water and electricity were all removed from local control by 1950 and, later, privatisation removed control of local bus services. Central government also assumed control of health provision and care of the poor through the social security system. Public sector housing and education became the main services local authorities were required to deliver.

Financial issues lay at the heart of the relationship between local and central government as the former became increasingly dependent on transfer payments from the state to fulfil its obligations. This did not become a serious problem until after 1914. The greatest expenditures by far, before the First World War, involved the delivery of water, gas, electricity and local transport. Municipal trading activities were legally required to generate income to cover expenditure and thus did not impose a burden on ratepayers. But the scale of capital investment required could not possibly have been met through local taxation and had to be borrowed. As a result of such capital spending the total debt outstanding against Aberdeen town council in 1901 stood at £1.3 million. The main items were debts on capital investment on gas provision £253,000, on the tramway system £183,000, on the waterworks £178,000, on the city improvement scheme £114,000, on electricity supply £107,000 and on the sewerage system £88,000. Other components of the debt included the City Hospital, parks and roads, the cost of the burgh court house and police building, the corporation lodging-house, and workmen's dwellings.[24] In fact local government was fiscally prudent and a firm control was maintained over expenditure. Aberdeen town council balanced its books in almost every year before the First World War. Exceptional expenditures, such as the purchase of properties to clear land for the construction of the new Greyfriars Kirk in 1901, represented one of the few exceptions.

Placing the main thrust of expenditure on self-financing utilities postponed serious conflict about public spending. Even so, the principle was clearly established at an early date that local taxation was to remain firmly based on property. The allocation of the burden between owners and occupiers varied. The Police Act of 1833 and the Prisons Act of 1839 both imposed the costs of the respective services upon burghs and stipulated that they should be derived from assessments on property. But the former legislation imposed the burden upon the occupiers of property while the latter divided the cost equally between occupiers and owners. In Aberdeen by the last quarter of the nineteenth century assessment fell primarily on occupiers rather than owners in a ratio in excess of three to one.[25] The growth of public policy in Victorian Britain was driven by the imposition of obligations and standards by central government upon services which were to be delivered by local government. The result was that, as the century progressed and the burden of local provision increased, transfer payments from central government became increasingly necessary to bridge the gap between local authority income and expenditure.[26]

In the twentieth century political conflict became concentrated on the dispute between those who wished for additional or better services from local government, partly as a means of income redistribution, and those who opposed the expenditure involved, possibly because it fell disproportionately upon themselves. Central government became responsible for an increasing proportion of local government spending paid through transfer payments. The provision of financial support enabled central government to increase its grip on local government. 'The history of local government finance then is one of piecemeal development and change to accommodate service expansion and growth, followed by consolidation of rates and grants to facilitate expenditure control.'[27] The inflation of the 1960s and 1970s seriously eroded the weak tax base of local authorities since it was linked to property which was not revalued sufficiently frequently to keep pace with inflation. But the complaints of Scottish business about the revaluation of commercial property in the 1980s led to the expedient introduction of the community charge, known more commonly as the poll tax. By 1999-2000 central government grants accounted for 47.4 per cent of the revenue required for the expenditure of Aberdeen city council, having grown from a very modest contribution in the 1950s.

The growth of control was confirmed and strengthened by central government through the allocation of duties to local government. After the reorganisation of 1929, local authorities were given responsibility for social welfare spending until the introduction of the welfare state legislation after 1945. Education was a major part of the spending of Aberdeen town council comprising 32-42 per cent of the total from the 1930s onwards, except between 1975 and 1996 when responsibility for education was delegated to Grampian regional council. In the 1930s public health and public assistance were important, while in the post-war years public sector housing represented a major source of expenditure accounting for 11 per cent of the total in 1947-48, rising to 24 per cent in 1973-74 and 38 per cent in 1983-84 by which date, in the absence of education, it constituted the major single item of expenditure. By the close of the century housing had fallen to just over one per cent of expenditure and the main items, other than education, were social work and the police and fire services.[28]

THE EMERGENCE OF PARTY POLITICS

For much of the nineteenth century local political conflict was based on personality and faction. But the beginnings of a different type of local politics, based on organised party interest, and stimulated by the extension of the franchise, appeared through the agency of the trades council, which brought together the interests and representatives of many trade unions. Its concerns were far from revolutionary. Its views were sympathetic to ratepayers' anxieties and, until the 1890s, represented liberal as well as more radical perspectives. One early success was achieved when the trades council played a leading part in the establishment of a free public library in 1884 helping to secure a successful vote at the critical public meeting, an earlier attempt having failed in 1872. Its first attempt to influence local representation came in 1877 when it made clear its opposition to the re-election of Lord Provost Jamieson. The trades council determined in future to find suitable candidates to support and thenceforward it regularly named those candidates which it favoured.[29] In 1879 it identified acceptable candidates for the school board whose membership had hitherto been determined by private agreements between the various churches. In 1882 the trades council tried to force an election but the churches withdrew two of their candidates to avoid a poll. In 1885 the trades council supported two Labour candidates in the town council election.[30] Both candidates were successful. A poem, circulated in pamphlet form, regretted the success of the 'slumocrats'.[31] It concluded with the verse:

> The crowd have now had length of rope,
> The scum has risen to the top,
> And given the death-blow to all hope
> Of civic fair repute;
> The bloom prefigures a poor crop
> If this be Franchise fruit.

The two successful candidates were James Forbes, a boot and shoe rivetter, and George Maconnachie, a compositor, who won respectively the St Machar and St Andrew's wards. The latter was able to combine his duties with his job which involved night work. Forbes was partly compensated by the trades council for loss of wages, as were some elected representatives on the management boards of the public library and Aberdeen Royal Infirmary. A major part of the radical platform focused on the quest to change the time of meetings of the town council from the afternoon to the evening to enable working men to serve as councillors. The platform for the town council election of 1891, adopted from that of the Glasgow trades council, included the taxation of land values, fair wages to be paid on municipal contracts, a commitment to build artisan dwellings, evening town council meetings, and public control of the liquor trade.[32] Briefly, in 1895, town council meetings were held in the evening but reverted back to the traditional afternoon sessions a few months later on the grounds that there had been frivolity at the evening meetings, that serious business could not be conducted at the end of the day, and that the new regime was inconvenient for those members living outside the city.

Before 1914 local political activity was shaped by bargaining between groups, representing the middle classes, the skilled working classes, the Church of Scotland and the free churches. The Liberal influence on the trades council was declining by the 1890s as membership swung in favour of emerging Labour groups and anti-socialist conservatives and unionists standing under independent and later progressive labels. In 1893 there were four Independent Labour Party (ILP) men on the town council, a small representation of the labour interest which grew slowly before the First World War. The Aberdeen Workers' Election Committee was set up before the municipal elections of 1900. It represented the first attempt by trade unionists and socialists in Aberdeen to create a unified organisation with representatives from the trades council, the Social Democratic Federation (SDF) and the ILP. One of their few successes was William Chalmers, a postman, who represented St Andrew's between 1909 and 1912. Labour and socialist candidates found it easier to secure places on the school board and parochial council, perhaps because they were less important bodies which were perceived as posing less of a threat of socialist extravagance in expenditure.[33] School boards were also elected on a wider franchise, including everyone on the valuation role as owner or occupier of land or property worth £4 per annum, although lodgers remained excluded.[34]

By 1919 the trades council had merged with the Labour Party to form the Trades Council and Burgh Labour Party. In the 1919 municipal election five of the six Labour candidates were elected. Four more seats were gained in 1925, the first election in which the independents offered a combined front against Labour. The *Press and Journal* carried an advert urging readers to vote against the socialist menace, warning of higher rates and arguing that party should be kept out of local politics. Progress remained slow for Labour, hampered in part by the fact that the support for radical candidates had to be shared with competing groups such as the communists. There was little variation in the issues given priority by Labour candidates between the wars, housing and unemployment representing the principal areas of concern, together with pressure for the provision of employment by the town council and support for fair wages for its employees. In 1933 Labour secured electoral victories over an independent Marxist in St Clement's, over the Unemployed Workers Committee Movement in St Machar, and against a Communist Party candidate in a by-election in St Clement's. In 1936 Labour candidates stood against ILP candidates so that a split radical vote prevented possible victories in Woodside and St Machar.[35] Party organisation developed rapidly from the informal grouping of 1919. The Labour group had formulated rules and procedures by the mid-1920s, restricting membership to official Labour Party members who accepted policies consistent with those of the national party. In 1936 the hitherto crucial link between the burgh Labour Party and the trades council was severed as a further support to party discipline.

The redistribution and growth of the urban population was reflected in ward changes. In 1928 the Holburn ward was created increasing the total number to 12 and the membership of the town council to 36 plus the dean of guild as an ex officio member, a structure of representation which lasted until 1975.[36] In 1929 the St Andrew's ward disappeared, squeezed out by three adjacent wards, while Gilcomston was created and those wards on the western and southern boundaries of the city were extended both in that year and again in 1934. In 1952 there was further restructuring of wards as Gilcomston and Greyfriars disappeared, St Andrew's reappeared, and the western half of Woodside became Cairncry. In 1961 St Andrew's again disappeared and Cairncry was divided to form Northfield and Mastrick. These adjustments reflected two developments, the expansion of the population of the city and its geographical spread away from the east coast with the redistribution of population from wards close to the city centre to new locations on the periphery, Torry at the turn of the century, Northfield and Mastrick after 1945, and Bridge of Don in the last three decades of the century. By 1938 Labour representation had risen to 17, concentrated in central wards with a high proportion of manual workers, such as St Clement's, Greyfriars and St Nicholas, as well as in the developing housing estates at St Machar and Torry. By the end of the decade, the determination of ward elections was set firmly by their relative prosperity. In 1938 Labour won all the wards in Aberdeen in which housing averaged an occupancy level over 1.6 persons per room, and lost all the others.[37]

There is little doubt that the ratepayer's traditional fear of high spending socialism held together the coalition of opposition to Labour or that it was eroded as the franchise was extended to those who had high hopes of being beneficiaries of such spending. Local elections were suspended for the duration of the Second World War. After 1945 Labour enjoyed an almost unbroken majority on the town council. Only in 1951 did the Progressives secure a majority, although there was no overall majority in the elections of 1949, 1950, 1959 and 1968. Majorities in the 1950s were small but, apart from a revival late in the 1960s,

Lord Provost Sir Thomas Mitchell, civic leader during the years of the Second World War.

Alexander C. Collie 1913–99

Born in St Nicholas Lane, Alexander Collie later lived in a flat above Ma Cameron's public house before moving to Dee Street. He was educated at Ferryhill School and Ruthrieston School. He was apprenticed to Adam Gordon as a baker, and later worked for the Northern Co-operative Society. He became secretary of the Aberdeen Bakers' Union, and a member of the national executive of the Scottish Bakers' Union. He served as secretary to the Torry branch of the Labour Party. He represented St Clement's ward on the town council 1947–75 and Castlehill ward on the district council 1975–95. He served on the harbour board 1947–74, and as a JP. He served as convener of the links and parks committee, and was lord provost 1980–84. He also was a member of the North of Scotland Hydro Electric consultative committee, and the Scottish Sports Council. He was awarded the OStJ in 1981, and the MBE in 1979. He received the freedom of the city in 1995.

the Progressives, and the Conservatives who succeeded them, fared increasingly poorly.[38] After 1945 the town council's principal responsibility lay in education and housing as determined by central government, and the delivery of such services became the basis of Labour policy and electoral success.

In Aberdeen local elections, the Conservative Party did not appear until the 1970s. There was increasing tension within the political right, as some favoured the traditional practice of keeping party politics out of local government while others believed that Labour's success meant this was no longer possible. Supporters of the latter view argued that effective opposition required the demonstration of explicit party allegiance on the part of candidates who had hitherto passed under a variety of non-party names, usually as independents. In Aberdeen, the Progressives renamed themselves in the 1971 local election as Conservatives, forcing Conservative Party candidates to stand as Official Conservatives. This split the local activists. The South Aberdeen Conservative Association supported the Progressives renamed as Conservatives while the North Aberdeen Conservative Association supported the Official Conservatives. The two variants of conservatism contested four wards against each other and the Conservatives beat the Official Conservatives in three of the four.[39] The national Conservative Party then accepted the new regime. Prominent in this conflict was Alexander 'Sandy' Mutch, a self-made businessman who had represented Holburn ward since 1961 and became leader of the Conservatives in 1974. He led the process of transition from Progressive to Conservative identity, and became first convener of the Grampian regional council 1974-90, still representing Holburn.

James Wyness, lord provost 1992–96. Portrait by A. Fraser.

LOCAL GOVERNMENT AT THE MILLENNIUM

The seemingly perpetual reorganisation of local government continued throughout the final quarter of the twentieth century. Aberdeen town council was replaced by the district council under the local government reorganisation of 1975 which introduced a two-tier system of administration by which duties were shared with Grampian regional council. The new district council had 50 members, each representing a single ward. The long-established membership of the dean of guild on the town council ended. By the time that the city council replaced the district council in 1996, a reversion to unitary authorities, it had 50 wards each with a single representative, extending in the west to Culter, in the north to Dyce and in the south to Loirston. As the result of a more modest restructuring of boundaries, the number of wards was reduced to 43 in 1999.

The increasing dependence of local government upon subsidies from central government to carry out its programmes, and underpinned by legal obligations, continued to erode the capacity for independent action. It also broke the link between local benefits and payments. By the time that the Labour Government lost office in 1979 local spending had been brought under control. But further substantial reductions in central government support under the new Conservative Government in the early 1980s generated further substantial increases in rates. The Local Government (Miscellaneous Provisions) (Scotland) Act 1981 was a watershed in that it allowed central government to intervene selectively in the expenditure decisions of individual councils. The Scottish Office thus determined when local expenditure became 'excessive and unreasonable'.[40] By the end of the century local government was firmly controlled by central government. Consquently major policy decisions required the consent of the Scottish Office. The major local government policy issues at the close of the twentieth century, as in the past, related to development and modernisation. Two stood out: the new ring road, the western peripheral route, intended to ease the pressure of traffic on Anderson Drive, and the third bridge over the Don, also needed to ease traffic congestion. Both ventures required financial assistance and planning approval from central government as well as political commitment on the part of the city council.

10

Social Welfare: Poverty and Health

CLIVE H. LEE

SOCIAL DEPRIVATION AND ITS CAUSES

All societies, however prosperous, contain relatively disadvantaged individuals and groups unable to provide for themselves satisfactorily when faced with a loss of income through unemployment, disability, sickness or old age. In virtually all societies the same groups are most at risk and for the same reasons. Poverty is most likely to strike at three times in the life cycle, in childhood, young parenthood and in old age. The inspector of poor for Aberdeen testified, in 1909, to the effect that

> the chief classes of persons applying for relief are widows with families, deserted wives with families, wives whose husbands are in prison, wives whose husbands are in an infirmary or lunatic asylum, women with illegitimate children, sick, aged and infirm persons, weak minded persons, orphan children, deserted children, separated children, insane persons whose relatives are unable to maintain them in a private asylum or institution, men and women suffering from venereal disease, and those who are sometimes certified able-bodied although suffering from that disease.[1]

In societies with little or no welfare state provision, it was the inability to work which exposed individuals and families to poverty. The young, the old, and those who relied on unskilled or casual work were thus most at risk. In Aberdeen men were employed periodically by local relief committees to repair streets, as in 1817, in 1832 and again in 1842 to alleviate unemployment, and received wages paid from public subscriptions. Lawrence Don, in evidence to the Select Committee on Handloom Weavers, stated in 1834 that wages for handloom weavers had fallen by half in the last 20 years even though weavers now undertook a longer working day.[2] Life was so precarious that the sale of oatmeal for export occasioned public riots. 'Multitudes of disorderly persons nightly assembled in the streets, setting at defiance the civil power and committing every species of mischief.'[3] Estimates made in the late nineteenth century by English social reformers suggested that approximately 30 per cent of the population lived in poverty and did not consume enough of the necessities of life to maintain physical efficiency.[4] It is highly improbable that the proportion in Aberdeen would have been different or lower at any earlier date. At the beginning of the century those in need had to rely on family and charity for any assistance. Only when these failed could they turn to a church-run poor law. Estimates of the number of people poor enough to require public relief in Aberdeen indicated that 3.1 per cent of the citizens qualified at the beginning of the century.[5] In the 1840s the proportion was estimated at 2.4 per cent.[6] These data are consistent with estimates for Scotland as a whole.[7]

Such estimates of the proportion of people living in deep poverty must be highly restrictive, since the definition of those eligible for relief from public funds was very narrow and confined to the totally destitute. A census taken in Aberdeen on 31 March 1906 showed that 748 paupers were lodged in the poor house, including 110 children. In the two parishes of Aberdeen and Oldmachar 2,100 paupers and 1,426 of their dependents were receiving relief. For most of them this meant outdoor relief, and only 13 per cent of the total receiving help were given indoor relief, mainly in the Poor's House.[8] Despite many changes and the general and substantial increase in prosperity in the twentieth century, society has failed to eradicate poverty. In part, as societies become more prosperous, the definition of an acceptable minimum standard of living becomes periodically and imperceptibly redefined. As a result, the threshold for assistance rises through time. Even so, there still exists a minority who live at standards which are regarded as low enough to qualify for aid in the form of supplementary income. Both public assistance and private charity have been both active and necessary throughout the past two centuries.

THE ALLEVIATION OF POVERTY: CHARITY

Throughout the nineteenth century, the majority of the population was vulnerable to poverty induced by unemployment or ill health. Only the most wealthy could be certain of being able to pay their way through such crises. The state played a minimal role in providing safeguards against such events or in offering support when they occurred. Individuals were thus obliged to try to provide for themselves through savings or insurance or, if they were unable or unwilling to do this, they had to rely on charity.

In Aberdeen, the magistrates and town council had instituted the beginnings of welfare provision by establishing the Poor's Hospital in the early 1740s. This marked a response both to the inconvenience of begging and a recognition that there did exist a body of elderly and infirm individuals who would be deserving recipients of public assistance. A major landmark in poor relief followed in the establishment of the United Fund in 1768. This brought together the support of

Opposite:
Map 5. Aberdeen
Parishes 1848.

PLAN OF THE PARISHES OF ABERDEEN

1848

three public bodies: the kirk session of St Nicholas, which agreed to contribute £241 annually; the managers of the Poor's Hospital who agreed to contribute £100, their estimated surplus of revenue over expenditure; and the managers of St Paul's Church who agreed to pay £30 annually and to continue their quarterly collections. The United Fund was jointly managed by the town council which nominated 30 representatives, the kirk session which provided 14 representatives, and the managers of St Paul's Church who contributed six representatives.[9] Its funds were supplemented by donations and bequests from a wide variety of sources, including the Lemon Tree Club (patrons of the tavern), the Northern Shooting Club, the Aberdeen Society of Shipmasters, the seven Incorporated Trades, and the stewards of the race meeting. Entertainments also contributed to the charity, the theatre occasionally devoting one night's takings to help the poor. Other charities also benefited in this way. The public soup kitchen enjoyed the proceeds of a ball held in 1800, from charges levied on spectators witnessing the launch of a hot air balloon from the grounds of Gordon's Hospital in 1812, which came down in the sea at the mouth of the Don, and in the following year from a concert.[10]

The United Fund relied on charitable contributions. If deemed insufficient they could be supplemented by a legal tax assessment on the citizens. Sentiment appears to have been strongly against such a development, and the case for an entirely voluntary system was articulated by Robert Hamilton, professor of mathematics at Marischal College in an address published in 1822, and based on his experience as a manager of the United Fund. Various groups, he argued should be excluded from charity, including the able-bodied unemployed, anyone in employment, and mothers of illegitimate children although they could be given private charity. He identified four means of giving charity. Almsgiving to beggars was the worst since it was degrading and should not be allowed. This was consistent with the aims of the Society for the Suppression of Begging, founded in Aberdeen in 1815, and which countered the traditional practice by which the poor were supposed to supplement charitable help by begging. When this society merged with the United Fund in 1818, recipients of largess from the latter were prohibited from begging. Hamilton was almost as strongly critical of the English poor law, which did give to the able-bodied and which, in some areas, supplemented low wages. Having excluded begging, Hamilton reviewed the three alternatives. Private charity was, he thought, by far the best. It was personal and direct and combined voluntary giving with grateful receipt. Support from public funds, supplemented by voluntary giving was an acceptable alternative. But he strongly opposed the fourth option, compulsory taxation, which lost the spirit of charity, combining reluctant giving and thankless receiving. This, he feared, would encourage the idle not to work, the managers of funds to be less careful of their responsibilities, and attract country people to the towns in the hope of greater relief.[11] Hamilton also presented a series of accounts for the United Fund, covering the period 1813-21, which indicated that almost half the income came from church collections and the kirk session, that close to one-quarter came from subscriptions and almost one-fifth from feu duties. The principal expenditures were upon food and clothing, together with payments to the Poor's Hospital, to the soup kitchen and to support orphans and deserted children.[12]

The views expressed by Hamilton were widely held. In 1818 a survey was undertaken on behalf of the General Assembly of the Church of Scotland which reiterated the traditional strong emphasis on voluntary help, and suggested that any marked increase in legal assessments would both reduce church collections and increase the number of claimants. A further report in 1839 repeated these conclusions although, by then, the medical profession was expressing a contrary view that the increase in fever epidemics, closely linked to levels of poverty, constituted a more potent threat to public order than any increased demand on public funds.

In fact the United Fund managed to fulfil its obligations from its usual sources of income until 1818. Unemployment, following the discharge of men after the conclusion of the Napoleonic Wars together with the impact of the introduction of machinery on manual textile employment, necessitated the raising of the first voluntary assessment in that year. Thereafter it became an annual event, but the contributions fell in value as some citizens chose not to pay. By the second half of the 1830s, the average expenditure incurred by the United Fund was 37 per cent higher than it had been in 1813-21 but, none the less, in 1838 it had become necessary for the magistrates to impose the first legal assessment on the proprietors and occupants of houses, lands and fishing rights. This brought further problems. The ratepayers claimed control over the money raised from them, but the kirk session demanded its traditional voice and, from 1840, withheld its contribution to the United Fund. As the income from the legal assessment increased from £570 in 1836 to £4,800 in 1841 so church collections fell. Consequently the revenue from the compulsory assessment increased from 21.6 per cent to 75.8 per cent of the total.[13] Furthermore, the migration of the most affluent citizens to the west of the Denburn took them out of St Nicholas parish into Oldmachar where the assessment was much lower. Thus the burden in the urbanised St Nicholas parish fell upon its less affluent citizens.

Despite local concern and bickering, the situation was resolved by the establishment of a new system of poor relief in Scotland under the provisions of the Poor Law Amendment Act 1845 which made the mitigation of poverty a statutory public responsibility. This legislation was prompted by the collapse of the old poor law system as one effect of the Disruption which seriously undermined the capability of the established church to fulfil its traditional welfare responsibilities. The legislation created parochial boards under the control of a central board of supervision based in Edinburgh. Local parish boards were offered three alternative ways of funding poor relief. The most popular method took the form of a tax on all lands and heritages, half of which fell on the owner and half on the tenant or occupier.[14] This did little more than regularise the existing

AID TO THE UNEMPLOYED.

Art to the Rescue.

The Aberdeen Art Gallery Committee has resolved to give the use of the Art Gallery for a Sunday concert in aid of the funds of the Distress Committee; and Mr Robert Arthur has granted the use of His Majesty's Theatre for a Sunday concert, admission to be free, but a collection to be taken on behalf of the unemployed.

With common aim, two different forms of Art
  Seek to give succour to poor, needy mortals;
And each, well fit to play the noble part
  In this great cause, now opens wide her
      portals.

Art's constant mission is to elevate the mind,
  A path from which her footsteps never stray;
Save when, with a benevolent spirit kind,
  She seeks to help the needy on the way.

Unemployment was widespread in 1908. Before unemployment insurance, workers had to depend on their own efforts or on charity.

situation in Aberdeen although, as elsewhere, the stated aim of the legislation, to cut the cost of poor relief, was not realised. In fact the burden on ratepayers continued to rise.

The general provision of welfare support offered by the United Fund was supplemented by a host of smaller charitable undertakings, each with a more specific focus. The public soup kitchen started in 1800, operating originally from St Mary's Chapel until 1834 when it moved to the Vennel which later became St Paul Street. A grain fund was also started in the harsh winter of 1800 to maintain a basic minimum supply of food, and raised £3,000 for that purpose. As the century progressed many other charities were founded, including the boys' hospital, the girls' hospital, the Aberdeen female orphan asylum, the industrial feeding school more popularly known as the ragged school, and three schools of female industry all providing for orphaned or deserted children. The Aberdeen Female Society for the Relief of Aged and Indigent Women and the Sick Man's Friend gave a titular statement of their aims, as did the House of Refuge, the Coal Fund, the Rent Aid Association, the Association for Teaching the Blind at their Homes, and the Clothing Society. The Aberdeen Ladies' Working Society supplied sewing and knitting to unemployed women, while the Repository for Female Industry sold the clothing made by such women. The Ladies' Fund sought to help women during 'confinement in child-bed'. The majority of the associations

---

Alexander Walker 1825–1903

Born in Old Aberdeen, Alexander Walker was educated at Strath's Academy and the Grammar School, under Dr Melvin, before joining the family firm, William Walker & Sons, merchants. He served as dean of guild 1872–80, and as a governor of Robert Gordon's College during the same period. He served as chairman of the Licence Holders' Association for 15 years and was vice president of the Traders' Defence Association. He belonged to the educational trust which managed schools such as Mrs Emslie's and the boys' and girls' hospitals. He served on the school board, and on the St Nicholas parochial council for six years, and was president of the Mechanics' Institute, playing a major role in arranging the donation of the library of the institute to the public library. He was a visiting manager of the Aberdeen Savings Bank, and supported a wide variety of charities such as the Sick Man's Friend, the Soup Kitchen, the United Coal Fund, the Paupers' Lunatic Fund and the Association for Improving the Condition of the Poor. He wrote *A History of the Workhouse or Poor's Hospital of Aberdeen* (1885) and *Robert Gordon: His Hospital and His College* (1886), and many other booklets and pamphlets which were either anonymous or simply signed 'AW'. He was president of Whitehall Bowling Club and of the Conservative Association. He was an elder of the West Parish Church, and a fellow of the Society of Antiquiries of Scotland. His portrait was painted by Sir George Reid.

directed towards helping women were organised primarily, and often totally, by well-meaning ladies from the more prosperous sections of society.

Church organisations continued to contribute to the care of the poor. In 1862, the Roman Catholic Nazareth House opened a branch in Chapel Court where the sisters devoted themselves to the care of the elderly and sick, irrespective of creed. A new building was erected in 1877 as a result of the efforts of Monsigneur Stopani. It also included an industrial schools for girls. The House of Bethany, situated in the Hardgate, was founded in 1870 by the widow of a clergyman and provided a home for orphan girls. It was run by the Scottish Society of Reparation, a society of sisters devoted to the care of orphans.

THE ALLEVIATION OF POVERTY: MUTUALITY AND INDIVIDUALISM

The alternative to charity is self-help, provided either independently or through a mutual benefit society. Several of these existed in Aberdeen before the nineteenth century. The Narrow Wynd Society had been favoured by genteel society in the eighteenth century, offering assistance to elderly members, widows and orphans. The seven Incorporated Trades had joint and separate funds to support 'decayed' members and widows. Other friendly societies which were active in the early nineteenth century included the Dyers' Society, the Society of Porters, the Barber and Wig-makers' Society, the Merchants' Society of Old Aberdeen, and six masonic lodges. Mutual benefit societies relied on their members' willingness to maintain contributions, and failure to do so occasioned difficulties. The Shipmaster Society had been founded in 1598 to support aged and infirm seamen. All seamen belonging to the port of Aberdeen were obliged to contribute to the 'box' from their wages, irrespective of rank. The society was granted a Royal Charter of Incorporation in 1801. There was, however, a growing problem of non-payment and, in 1808, it was decided that all non-contributors should be struck off the membership list. The scale of this was indicated by the fact that in the following year, the society had 110 master members plus 87 ordinary members in good standing, and 60 master members and 330 ordinary members who had been struck off.[15]

Friendly societies were established, some by working people, to cover sickness, life assurance and funeral costs. By the end of the nineteenth century the city had over 50 societies providing insurance for sickness and funeral expenses. From the 1830s co-operative societies also existed as 'associations, the members of which enter into an agreement to purchase, by wholesale, every article which their families may require in the provision way, and appoint a committee and salesman to superintend their purchasing and disposal'.[16] The societies later became a vehicle for saving through the payment of a dividend, the trading surplus of the society being divided amongst its members relative to the amount each had purchased.

In Aberdeen the first co-operative started at the Broadford works in 1833 when 150 members subscribed. This early venture collapsed fairly quickly, although a few trading clubs survived into the 1850s when William Lindsay, with the support of the local Chartists, convened a meeting to consider unification. The outcome was the formation of the Northern Co-operative Company, modelled on the celebrated Rochdale Co-operative Society, which issued 1,000 shares valued at £1 each. The first shop opened on the Gallowgate in July 1861, supported by 223 subscribers. By 1903, membership had increased to 17,317 with annual sales of almost half a million pounds and a dividend payment of £79,000.[17]

For those who sought self-reliance, even on the basis of low wages, the savings banks provided an important avenue for modest saving. The Aberdeen Savings Bank was established in 1815, the outcome of a public meeting called by the lord provost to consider measures for the suppression of begging together with proposals for a savings bank. Its purpose was to hold small sums saved from the earnings of tradesmen, mechanics and labourers which might otherwise 'be squandered away, unsafely deposited, or lost altogether'.[18] A survey of depositors in the early 1820s showed an almost equal division between domestic servants and skilled tradesmen. The list of members in 1822 showed 1,354 depositors, a figure which rose to 5,420 by 1838, 27,000 by 1896 and 57,000 by 1914, equivalent, at the last date, to one-third of the population of the city. Initially deposits had to be at least two shillings and no more than five pounds, and no account was allowed to carry a balance above £25. A room in the Poor's Hospital was set aside for an hour each Saturday morning for the Savings Bank to receive deposits. As it prospered it moved into rented premises in the Guestrow in 1832, to an office in Exchange Street in 1857 and finally into its imposing new headquarters in Union Terrace in 1896. The Savings Bank did not hold a monopoly despite its popularity. By the 1870s the city had over 30 penny banks together with a number which were not linked to the national security savings bank, which guaranteed the deposits of such institutions.

THE ORIGINS OF THE WELFARE SYSTEM

The enduring prominence of belief in voluntary provision, was reflected in the endorsement of the virtues of thrift to counter the problems of those brought down by 'bodily weakness or loss of character', and also by the fact that nationally the annual receipts of registered charities in 1911 exceeded total state expenditure on the poor law. In spite of the impressive range and accumulated value of welfare provision through private provision (self-supportive and charitable), central and local government played an increasingly important role in controlling and delivering such help.

The establishment of the Board of Supervision for the Relief of the Poor in Scotland under the 1845 legislation marked the first step towards central control. The board had the power to examine and control each local parochial board which, in turn, was empowered to levy a legal assessment and carried an obligation to provide for the poor in its jurisdiction. There was substantial pressure on local resources for welfare expenditure. The inspector of poor for Aberdeen, C. B. Williams, reported that efforts to control relief expenditure had met with little success. An investigation into the Poor's House in 1903, to see if any inmates might be lodged elsewhere, had found that only nine inmates over the age of 65 out of a total of 299 could be moved. The rest either had no relatives (78), had families who could not accommodate them (39), could not be taken into their families 'on account of their habits' (49), or it had proved impossible to trace their relatives (124). Williams estimated that the parochial board spent £56,000 per year directly on the poor and a further £16,000 indirectly through support given to the District Lunacy Board.[19]

Alexander Duffus 1832–1906

Educated at Ledingham's Academy, Alexander Duffus followed his father into business as a confectioner, with shops in Castle Street and Market Street. Later he moved into the wholesale part of the trade. In public service he was a police commissioner, and sought election to the town council on several occasions before representing the third ward 1878–83. He was an outspoken opponent of Peter Esslemont and opposed the Improvement Act of 1883. He lost his seat while seeking election to the new St Nicholas ward. He was a member of both the St Nicholas and Oldmachar parochial boards, and served as chairman for each of them. He was regarded as a great authority on the poor law and played a major part in the discussions which led to the creation of the Poor Law (Amendment) Act 1894. He was a strong opponent of both the Oldmill poor house and Kingseat asylum, believing that a combined institution should be provided in the city. He was a Liberal and president of the Aberdeen Radical Association but opposed Irish home rule.

A major local initiative was the formation of the Aberdeen Association for Improving the Condition of the Poor (AAICP) in 1870 with the intention of co-ordinating the charitable activities within the city. Inspired by the philosophy of the Charity Organisation Society, it became the major agent for poor relief in the late nineteenth century. As its secretary and superintendent, Peter Diack, affirmed, 'It was sought to inculcate the virtues of thrift and self-reliance, to promote temperance, to discourage mendacity, and to secure co-operation amongst other charitable organisations. The chief method to be adopted in carrying out these objects was to be personal visitation of the poor.' In 1906 the expenditure of the AAICP amounted to £800 in response to some 2,000 applications, all being cases of temporary need, although Diack estimated that the total charitable outlay in the city might reach about £5,000 per year.[20] At this time, the Association had 65 district vistors, who were volunteers and primarily business or professional men. On the basis of their recommendations, the AAICP disbursed help from the funds it received from legacies and subscriptions. Relief took a variety of forms including grants to buy food, admission to the Association's workshops to collect firewood, furnishing to start work as a pedlar, fares to seek employment, temporary work, old clothing and cash. In the late nineteenth century, the Association was primarily concerned to find work for the poor, to improve sanitation and hygiene, and to provide a day nursery. Laudable as its aims were, the AAICP faced difficulties. Those societies which existed to provide for distressed gentlewomen were anxious to maintain the privacy of their clientele and resisted absorption into a larger organisation. The AAICP's co-ordinating role grew slowly, often through the absorption of smaller bodies. During the inter-war years, it added adult homelessness to its range of concerns and started a children's shelter in 1925.

The role of local government in delivering welfare changed in the late nineteenth century under direction from central government. The Local Government (Scotland) Act 1894 transferred the powers of the board of supervision to the local government board. The introduction of pensions in 1908 for the elderly poor, and the introduction of compulsory national insurance to provide cover against sickness and unemployment in 1911, began the erosion of local responsibility for the alleviation of poverty. A new Local Government (Scotland) Act 1929 transferred the functions of the parochial council to town councils. But local responsibility for unemployment lasted only until the introduction of welfare reforms after the Second World War.

In the late 1940s both the town council and the local charities were obliged to reconsider their roles and relationships. The AAICP became the Aberdeen Association of Social Services, and its work became closely co-ordinated with that of the town council's statutory obligations. The Association necessarily adopted a regulated and subsidiary role, but contributed services in regard to discharged prisoners, children's homes, unmarried mothers and care of the elderly. One of its most successful activities related to the Aberdeen Old People's Welfare Council in establishing residential homes and providing voluntary support staff.[21]

Despite the greater prosperity of the most recent past, and the additional benefit of oil-related employment, the enduring need for charitable help is evidenced by the foundation of a new local charity, Instant Neighbour, in the middle of the oil era in 1986. A report produced by the Church of Scotland poverty committee in 1999 identified numerous pockets of deprivation in the city, the worst areas including Seaton, Tillydrone, Powis, Middlefield and Rosemount Square. These statistics demonstrated the enduring link between poverty and poor health. People living in the Printfield, Ferrier/Sandilands, and Rosemount Square areas were found to be twice as likely to suffer from coronary disease as the city average, while those in Hayton were three times as likely to have a stroke. Those living in areas of deprivation were also more likely to suffer from mental health problems. The Instant Neighbour charity estimated that it provided food for 30-40 people per week, and that some families were reduced to sleeping on the floor and living without furniture.[22]

Instant Neighbour started as the result of an initiative by the Rev. Michael Mair, minister of Holburn West Church, to help unemployed young people aged 16-18. He was assisted by Dennis Nicol, who subsequently became the director of the project, which was supported by a £30,000 grant from the community programme. Initially Instant Neighbour offered unemployed teenagers a guaranteed income for one year in return for a commitment to undertake work in the community doing jobs such as house painting for the elderly. Eventually the organisation moved from its base at Holburn West Church to the Gallowgate. This move, together with rising government restrictions on benefit payments, increased requests for help primarily from young people and young families facing destitution. As it grew Instant Neighbour extended its range of activities, providing emergency food and clothing, furniture and free removal services. Recognising that children from impoverished homes were most vulnerable to accidents, the 'safe and sound' project was initiated specifically to provide for children's needs in the form of clothing and equipment such as cots, high chairs, fire guards and stair gates. The poverty action liaison (PAL) project sought to match individual clients and volunteer helpers to provide personal support.

The growth in the volume of activity in less than two decades was considerable, at a rate of 5-10 per cent annually, and the early informality of the organisation had to be replaced by formal structures. Instant Neighbour became a charitable company with a board of management, sustaining a full-time professional staff of 16, supplemented by voluntary workers. Growing responsibilities necessitated increased income. The church congregations of the city remained the principal supporters of Instant Neighbour providing both finance and gifts such as food.

Support was obtained from a diversity of other sources including the common good fund, the national lottery, the BBC 'Children in Need' fund, and from personal donations often given under a cloak of confidentiality. The business community also offered support directly, as in the sponsorship of the PAL project by Halliburton, and indirectly, as in the free refurbishment of the Gallowgate premises by the Stewart Milne Group. In addition the charity received gifts of furniture, clothing and food from throughout the city for distribution to its clients.

While Instant Neighbour was a product of the later decades of the twentieth century, its antecendents may be found in the more distant past since many of its characteristics were similar to charitable undertakings in the city in the nineteenth century. The ecclesiastical origins of the charity, the enduring support it received from the churches, its reliance principally on local support, and its association with other charities and with the city council replicated earlier experience. Its board of management had a composition similar to its Victorian predecessors combining church interests with business expertise. In the nineteenth century the industrial school movement started in Aberdeen and was subsequently copied throughout the country. Similarly Instant Neighbour was emulated in many other parts of the United Kingdom from Inverness and Glasgow to Canterbury.[23]

MEDICAL PROVISION: PRIVATE AND VOLUNTARY

Medical services evolved substantially during the nineteenth and twentieth centuries. In the early nineteenth century medical problems and their treatment were closely linked to poverty. The growth of the population of the city at a rate well in excess of the growth of new accommodation created an environment which was perfect for spreading infectious disease. Nineteenth- century medicine was thus much exercised by the problems of infection. Not surprisingly there were periodic epidemics including measles in 1807-08, typhus in 1817-19, 1831-32, 1835-39, frequently throughout the 1860s, and in 1904-05. There were cholera outbreaks in 1832 and 1854 which caused, respectively, 100 and 200 deaths. In 1866 there was yet another outbreak of cholera which caused 64 deaths. In

Tuberculosis was a major cause of death and chronic ill-health against which there were many campaigns before it was eventually brought under control in the 1950s.

The typhoid epidemic of 1964 brought Aberdeen an unwelcome notoriety and much anxiety. A boy patient in the City Hospital.

1863 an outbreak of typhus started in the Gallowgate and Causewayend areas, lasted for three years and claimed 1,731 victims including 225 fatalities, while a smallpox epidemic in 1871-72 lasted for fifteen months and claimed 163 deaths. The latter event prompted, somewhat belatedly compared with elsewhere, the opening of the city fever hospital in 1877.

The risk of infection came from many sources. In 1881 an unknown epidemic affected 322 people and caused three deaths. Subsequent investigation found that a dairy run by the Oldmill reformatory had used water from a local ditch when the supply pipe froze during the winter, and this was blamed for the incident. Other causes of illness were more avoidable. In his annual report in 1902, the medical officer of health (MOH), drew attention to the use of methylated spirit as an intoxicant. It was available at four pence per pint and, served with an equal volume of water, it was only 25 per cent of the cost of whisky. Perhaps the most celebrated epidemic recorded in the city was the typhoid outbreak of May 1964. In total 469 cases were identified although there were no deaths from the typhoid itself.[24] The cause of the outbreak was eventually traced to a consignment of corned beef supplied to a local supermarket. The MOH, the lively but reassuring Dr Ian MacQueen, appeared frequently on television to reassure the public as part of a skilful use of the media. His high-profile approach was not approved by those who would have preferred the affair to be kept as quiet as possible. An impromptu visit by the Queen helped restore morale. While the publicity far exceeded the seriousness of the outbreak, the impact on the local tourist industry was very severe for several years.

It was not coincidental that the Poor's Hospital was founded at the same time as the Infirmary which was an essential adjunct to it. The Infirmary was opened in 1742 with accommodation for 40 beds, additional wings being added in 1754 and 1760, and new wards for fever patients in 1802. Hospitals, like poor relief, were funded by church collections, and the Infirmary drew on the charitable resources of the city and its adjacent counties, Aberdeenshire, Kincardineshire and Banffshire; its services were available to the people of those areas. The first board of managers, appointed by the town council, included past and present provosts, two medical practitioners, the principal of Marischal College and representatives of industry. In 1772 a petition was prepared to seek a royal charter. It indicated that the hospital was currently treating 800 people per annum and that it had accumulated assets worth £5,000 while discharging its duties. In 1773 Aberdeen

Aberdeen Royal Infirmary, Woolmanhill, designed by Archibald Simpson, 1832-38. This photograph by G. & W. Morgan dates from the first decade of the twentieth century.

Royal Infirmary (ARI) obtained a royal charter and a formal management structure which included the present and previous provost, the dean of guild, four baillies, the convener of the Incorporated Trades, the professor of medicine, the moderator of the synod, plus contributors of £50 and subscribers of £5, or their representatives.[25] Additions were made to the ARI in 1818 and construction of a new wing with 230 beds, designed by Archibald Simpson, was started in 1833. Further expansion took place periodically throughout the rest of the century: the Queen's Jubilee in 1887, for example, provided an opportunity to raise funds (in this case, £30,000), for development.

As with welfare provision, a variety of charitable institutions were established to offer medical assistance. A lunatic asylum for the mentally ill was founded in 1799, enabling the Infirmary to be released from this task, although the common treatment of pushing the heads of patients under the spill-water of the wheel of Gilcomston mill continued. An institution for the deaf and dumb opened in 1817, and an asylum for the blind in 1843. All these institutions relied on charity in some form. The asylum for the blind, in Huntly Street, was funded by a bequest of £7,000 from Miss Christine Cruickshank and offered training and work for 100 people making mattresses, upholstery and baskets. The legacy of a piece of land allowed the establishment of the lunatic asylum while a donation from the Honourable County Club in 1829 helped found the ophthalmic institution. The Morningfield Hospital for incurable diseases was established in 1857 by the trustees of John Gordon of Murtle. A house of refuge for the elderly at Oakbank and a reformatory at Oldmill were founded in the 1830s from the proceeds of a bequest left by Dr George Watt of Old Deer who left an estate of £40,000 following a career in general practice. His will was executed by his nephew, Alexander Anderson. In 1877 the Royal Aberdeen Hospital for Sick Children (RAHSC) was founded and housed at Castle Terrace. It was extended in 1885 to create a fever ward, adding cottage homes and, in 1898, a nurses' home. The management was exercised by all those who subscribed at least one guinea (£1.05). The maternity home, founded in 1896 in a house in Barnard's Close, also moved to Castle Terrace in 1900.

In spite of the impressive range and volume of financial support, voluntary medical establishments were nearly always under financial pressure. In 1883, as a sign of increasing anxiety, the ARI launched an appeal directed at the working classes intended to broaden the base of its income. A succession of civic leaders played an important role in fund raising. Lord Provost Henderson played the leading part in raising funds for the extension to the ARI designed to coincide with the Queen's Jubilee in 1887, while Lord Provost Taggart launched an important appeal on behalf of the RAHSC in 1919. Beyond these civic efforts, voluntary medicine often needed substantial, if occasional, benefactions, such as that given by George Stephen, the first Lord Mount-Stephen, a native of Dufftown who served

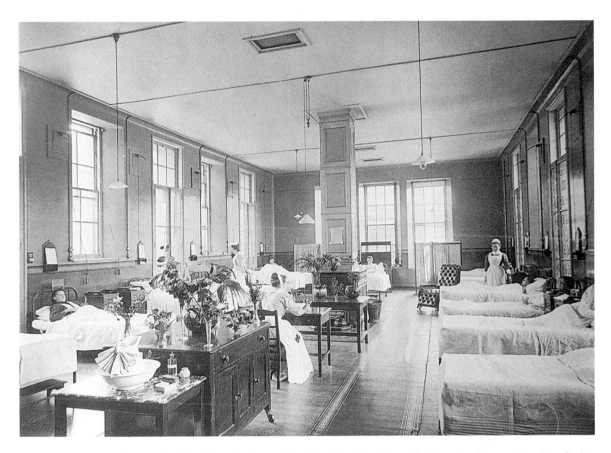

as an apprentice draper in Aberdeen before migrating to Canada and rising to be chairman of the Canadian Pacific Railway Company. Among other donations, he provided £25,000 in 1900 to clear the outstanding debt of the Jubilee Extension Scheme. Local industrialists and philanthopists, such as Thomas Jaffrey, were also important supporters on a lavish financial scale. James Crombie, the woollen manufacturer, was a substantial benefactor of the RAHSC, and an original trustee of the Newhills convalescent home. He also gave generously to the ARI which, during the second half of the twentieth century, benefited from the MacRobert Trust, as did Aberdeen University and so many other institutions in the North-East.

Those at the bottom of the social scale relied on dispensing druggists for cheap or free medical treatment. The dispensary was opened in 1781, and was originally funded by the Royal Infirmary. It became a separate charity in 1786 and remained open until 1948. A new dispensary was opened by the town council in 1803 to vaccinate children against the smallpox. By 1822 there were five separate dispensaries, and they were subsequently brought together in 1834 as the General

Female medical ward, Woolmanhill, early in the twentieth century.

Dispensary, Vaccine and Lying-in Institution. The dispensary used free student labour to curtail costs, in return providing them with practical experience. Everything at the dispensary was initially supplied free of charge and no recommendation had to be provided by applicants, although patients could be turned away if the medical staff believed they were able to afford payment. The dispensary, however, experienced much more difficulty than the ARI in attracting donations, as indicated by the frequent refrain in the annual report. As early as 1831 the matter was an issue of public debate, and the *Aberdeen Magazine* was highly critical of the large 'hoard of wealth' accumulated by the Royal Infirmary, suggesting that some be allocated to the dispensary.[26] By the beginning of the twentieth century the dispensary, located in the Guestrow since the 1870s, had a staff of six medical officers, each in charge of a different district within the city. In 1908 the dispensary reached the high point of its activity treating 13,877 cases while its staff made 10,010 home visits.[27]

THE REORGANISATION AND INTEGRATION OF MEDICAL SERVICES

Government legislation brought local government into the arena of health. The Public Health (Scotland) Act 1867 allowed local authorities to provide isolation hospitals for fever cases. In 1877 Aberdeen town council built a fever hospital, and it subsequently became the City Hospital. In 1879 the town council established a health department. One of the major advantages which contributed to medical provision in the city was the long and close relationship between the town council, the medical school and the hospitals. The lord provost had served as president of the corporation of the Royal Infirmary since the granting of the royal charter in 1773. This close relationship provided the base for one of the great triumphs of health provision, and a pioneering development, in the unification of the wide variety of private and local authority health services into an integrated unit on a single site. It was also self-financed at a time when funds were especially scarce. The idea of a joint hospital scheme was first proposed by Matthew Hay, the MOH, at a meeting of the Medico-Chirurgical Society in 1920. He proposed that hospital provision should be concentrated on a single site, to increase the number of available beds, and to improve the quality of service. A site at Foresterhill was soon approved by a working party in 1923 and the town council agreed to sell the land for £35,000, although it was valued at £46,776, to a consortium which included the ARI, the public health department, the RAHSC and the medical school.[28]

The transition from Hay's original idea to the completion of the first phase of the project, marked by the opening of the new Royal Infirmary, did not proceed without obstacles. Indeed the project became the subject of bitter controversy in the 1920s when Hay was succeeded as MOH by J. Parlane Kinloch in 1923. The new incumbent wished to expand the health services of the local authority, and was unwilling to support the reorganisation scheme in which the voluntary hospitals played a central role, especially if it threatened to draw resources away from the City Hospital. In 1924 Kinloch proposed that the venereal diseases department, which had been jointly run by the local authority and the private hospital since 1920, should be transferred from the ARI's site at Woolmanhill to the City Hospital. He also proposed that the City Hospital should assume responsibility for the treatment of tuberculosis, pneumonia and poliomyelitis, in anticipation of legislation which would place these diseases under the control of public health authorities. In 1926, the town council took over Oldmill Hospital, which had been vacant since 1919, from the parish council as a dedicated centre for the treatment of patients suffering from pneumonia and tuberculosis.

Lord Provost Sir Andrew Lewis, a moving force behind the establishment of a new infirmary at Foresterhill. Portrait by W. Orpen.

These initiatives caused considerable anxiety in the voluntary hospitals and the medical school since they threatened to sabotage the joint hospital project and to diminish their own practices. The ambivalence of the town council, caught between the warring factions, did not help the situation. Other pressures helped reinstate the scheme. The Scottish Board of Health, whose permission was needed to sanction the transfer of Oldmill Hospital, agreed to the scheme on the condition that the town council agreed to co-operate with the voluntary sector and with the medical school, and to allow full access to the newly opened Woodend Hospital for teaching purposes. In 1927 the Scottish Board of Health pressed the town council to co-operate with the ARI in the treatment of venereal diseases, and advised that treatment should remain at Woolmanhill. At the same time the managers of the ARI invited Lord Provost Andrew Lewis to convene a meeting of all the bodies interested in the question of hospital accommodation. Lewis was a director of the ARI and thus sympathetic to

John J. R. Macleod, regius professor of physiology at Aberdeen 1928-35, a Nobel prizewinner as one of the discoverers of insulin.

Professor John J. R. Macleod 1876–1935

Born at Cluny, near Dunkeld, the son of a free church minister who moved to take charge of the John Knox Gerrard Street Church, John Macleod was educated at the Grammar School and Aberdeen University. He studied for two years in Leipzig before being appointed assistant in physiology at the London Hospital Medical School. In 1903 he was appointed professor of physiology at Western Reserve University, Cleveland, and subsequently moved to the University of Toronto in 1918. In 1923 he was awarded the Nobel Prize in Medicine and Physiology, jointly with a colleague Frederick Banting, for the discovery of insulin. In 1928 he returned to Aberdeen to the Regius Chair of Physiology. He served as a consultant to the Rowett Research Institute and the Torry Fishery Research Station. The gold medal, awarded as part of the Nobel Prize, was bequeathed to Aberdeen University. He also left a legacy to fund a chair in biochemistry. The first appointment to the Macleod-Smith Chair was made in 1947.

the development scheme. He was also able to ensure that the town council now adopted a less equivocal stance, empowered by the support of the Scottish Office. In 1927 he established a consultative committee to review medical services in the city, comprising representatives of city and voluntary hospitals, the Medico-Chirurgical Society, the medical school, the health insurance societies, and the town council. This became the vehicle for moving the plans forward. In 1929 Aberdeen University clinical professors were given honorary status at the ARI, and the University gave honorary status to the hospital staff who contributed to teaching the medical degree programme. The medical officer of health received honorary status at the maternity hospital. This series of acts of mutual professional recognition enabled the project to move towards the creation of an integrated medical service in the city.

The new RAHSC opened in January 1929 on the designated site with 134 beds. Its managers had formulated plans for rebuilding in a new location in 1914, and would have built a new hospital in Ashley Road had not war intervened. In 1925, unwilling to tolerate further delays and the increase in building costs that would have entailed, the management board authorised the start of construction. The finance was raised by public subscription, as was the cost of the new ARI, following

Aberdeen Royal Infirmary, Foresterhill, c. 1937.

the tradition of the previous two centuries. The Royal Infirmary and the University decided to purchase their sites jointly and to make free provision of land for the maternity hospital. The town council withdrew its own interest in the site in favour of extending the City and Oldmill Hospitals. There were still some further difficulties. The town council was indecisive about the specialised use of Woodend Hospital, as Oldmill was renamed, there remained disputes about the allocation of specialisms between hospitals, and there was a row about the appearance of the buildings when it became known that steel and brick were to be used instead of granite which was much more expensive. A compromise on the last issue involved the adoption of a mixture of granite and concrete.[29] Construction work on the new Royal Infirmary started in 1930, and the building was opened in September 1936 by the Duke of York, the King having called off at the last minute to go to meet Mrs Simpson. The creation of the Foresterhill complex was the last of the voluntary hospital schemes. It was also the first such joint scheme in Britain. It was the last flowering of the voluntary system about to be swamped by a rising tide of medical knowledge that needed facilities beyond the financial capacity of local charity. But it was a remarkable achievement.

THE NATIONALISATION AND PRIVATISATION OF HEALTH CARE

During the Second World War an embryonic national organisation for health care emerged on an ad hoc basis as local health boards were drawn into close co-operation with central government. In return for their co-operation, the emergency medical service provided the finance for new beds and operating theatres to deal with the increased demand caused by wartime casualties. The National Health Service (NHS), which came into being in July 1948, was based on regional hospital boards. There were five such boards in Scotland, including one for the North-East region. This structure remained in effect until 1974 when a new round of reforms created a hierarchy of regional health authorities, regional areas and districts.

The development of the Foresterhill complex in the 1930s had a profound effect on later developments. The Royal Infirmary and the University jointly funded several developments between the wars, including the cardiovascular department and biochemical/clinical laboratory service, and a pathological laboratory. This provided an important precursor to later developments, encouraged by two main causes. The medical impulse came from the fact that technological and pharmaceutical advances had the effect of concentrating treatment into hospitals, while the organisational structure of the NHS after 1948 confirmed this trend. The result of these influences was to create, at Foresterhill, an unusually strong concentration of specialist acute services for the entire North-East region, much higher than in any other region in Scotland. While the city accounted for about half the population of its region, it had about 80 per cent of specialist medical services. The economies of scale which this allowed meant both efficient expansion and a wider range of services than would otherwise have been possible.[30] The growth of health expenditure nationally grew substantially under the NHS stimulated by technological advance and an ever-rising demand for better treatment. The Royal Infirmary responded with an extensive building programme, starting with the east wing in the early 1950s. Planning for further expansion was approved by the Scottish Office in 1959, and construction work on Phase I began in 1963 and was completed in 1966. Phase II was planned between 1964 and 1970, and completed between 1971 and 1976.

Most recently, the National Health Service and Community Care Act 1990, implemented in April 1991, created an internal market in health by splitting purchasers from providers. District health authorities became purchasers of services, and some medical practices with over 7,000 patients became fundholders with a share of the regional budget allocation, while the hospitals became suppliers competing for their patients. Hospitals were offered the opportunity to become independent trusts, and the ARI was among the first in Britain, and the first in Scotland, to take advantage of this opportunity. The Aberdeen Royal Hospital Trust was established in April 1992. The application for trust status stressed the benefits to be obtained from maintaining a centre of medical excellence at the Royal Infirmary, promised an increase in diagnostic facilities, as well as support to locally provided facilities. The Grampian Healthcare NHS Trust covering most of the rest of the North-East was established in 1993.[31] In April 1999 these two trusts joined with the Moray Health Trust to form two new trusts from the three existing operations, covering a huge area bounded by Portsoy, Braemar, Laurencekirk and the North Sea. Under the new scheme, the Grampian Acute Hospital Trust, based at Foresterhill, was to provide all the acute services for the Grampian Health Board region with a projected budget at the turn of the century of £140 million per year. The Grampian Primary Care Trust, based in Elgin, was to be responsible for other medical services in the region including general practitioners, dentists, pharmacists, mental health and services for the elderly.

THE MEDICAL SCHOOL

While King's College and Marischal College had long-established chairs of medicine, dating from 1505 and 1700 respectively, medical instruction in the late eighteenth century comprised essentially of practical work provided at the Royal Infirmary. The foundation of the Medical Society in 1789, which subsequently became the Medico-Chirurgical Society in 1811, represented a student initiative seeking to establish a programme of systematic teaching to overcome the inadequacies of the current diet of instruction. The courses which this produced were gradually adopted by Marischal College despite opposition both within the college itself, particularly from the influential professor of chemistry, George French, as well as from King's College. A joint medical school was established by the two colleges in 1818, prompted primarily by Marischal College. But the phase of co-operation foundered in 1838 as the King's Mediciner maintained his traditional right and refused to teach. King's College subsequently opened a medical school in St Paul Street, and both sets of medical students attended the nearby ARI to receive clinical instruction from the staff.

The early development of medical education faced other problems. The legacy of Burke and Hare's exploits in robbing graves in Edinburgh brought the study of anatomy into widespread public disfavour, and this intruded on the pioneering work of Andrew Moir in Aberdeen in advancing teaching in this medical discipline. Rooms in Flourmill Brae and in the Guestrow, in which he conducted his classes, were attacked and the windows smashed. In 1831 he obtained a specially built lecture theatre in St Andrew's Street with three false windows at the front. This deception was ineffective since the dreadful smell which emanated from the 'burkin hoose' indicated its purpose. The failure to bury remains satisfactorily, and the excavationary efforts of a local dog which revealed the remains of part of a body, caused a riot in December 1831. A large crowd forced its way into the building, attacking and chasing Moir and his students. The building was then burned to the ground, an event observed by the lord provost and magistrates, and a large number of special constables. Eventually a detachment of the 79th Regiment had to be brought to ensure the maintenance of public order. Moir later secured £235 in compensation from the town council and three alleged ringleaders were sentenced to twelve months in prison. But he had to endure public notoriety for several years before resuming his work and serving as lecturer in anatomy at King's College for five years before his early death in 1844.[32]

Medical instruction remained primarily but not exclusively based at Marischal College until the union of the colleges, an event to which medical issues made a significant contribution. Reform of the Scottish universities, including a proposed merger between King's and Marischal, had been a live issue since the 1820s, and had been recommended by a royal commission which reported in 1831. But there was considerable suspicion between the two colleges, spiced with animosity and rivalry. Furthermore each represented a different constituency. King's College was ultra-conservative, strongly connected to county landed interests, and to the church. Marischal College stood in the centre of the town and shared its liberal traditions and urban concerns. Each college feared that its power and independence might be reduced by amalgamation or that, at least, it would be severely diminished. Relations were not helped by the active involvement of Alexander Bannerman, the new Liberal MP, in the 1830s. He prevailed upon the Treasury to release a large grant which had been frozen pending discussions about reform, and ensured that the entire sum of £18,000 was spent on the rebuilding of Marischal College which, under the proposals of the royal commission, was to be closed to allow expansion of the new University on the abundant lands available at Old Aberdeen. Bannerman followed this coup by introducing a parliamentary bill proposing that the new University be located in the town on the Marischal College site, that the land at Old Aberdeen be sold and, for good measure, included a ferocious attack on the 'corrupt Tory corporation of the Senatus of King's College'.[33] This intervention generated a furious reaction, and the bill was withdrawn. There followed in the later 1830s a number of commissions designed to advance the proposed merger, but they made little progress and were ignored or opposed by the professoriat in Old Aberdeen. The only tangible outcome was the decision by King's College to withdraw from its only co-operative venture with Marischal College, namely the medical school.

It was this event, however, which created the eventual need for union. In 1848-49 a medical bill came before Parliament seeking to improve training. In conjunction with this, in August 1849, both colleges were informed by the University of Edinburgh that, in future, class tickets showing attendance at lectures in other universities would be accepted as valid towards graduation at Edinburgh only if those classes had been taught by members of the senatus, that is by full professors. This represented a massive threat to both colleges in Aberdeen since many of their students customarily proceeded to Edinburgh. But much of the teaching in Aberdeen was provided by non-professors and on an extra-mural basis, like Moir's anatomy classes. Indeed King's College still had only one medical professor. Medical teaching in both colleges was thus seriously threatened. While both colleges lobbied the Treasury for additional professorial appointments, the urgency for a merger became increasing apparent. Negotiation and posturing continued for almost a further decade before the decisive intervention of the new Lord Advocate, John Inglis, ensured the enactment of the Scottish Universities Act in 1858. As a result of the fusion, teaching in medicine and law was concentrated at Marischal College, and arts and divinity, except for natural history, were concentrated at King's College.

The close collaboration of the medical school with the ARI continued under the NHS. As a result they became almost indistinguishable and the influence of medical school staff and their laboratory support became integral parts of the NHS provision. In effect the University subsidised local health services. In the 1960s the University rapidly expanded its senior staff in the medical school, and the integration with clinical services drew them into the work of the Royal Infirmary.

Sir Alexander Ogston 1844–1929

Born into a medical family at Ogston's Court, Broad Street, Alexander Ogston was educated at the Grammar School and Marischal College. In 1863 he undertook a tour of the major medical centres in Europe including Prague, Vienna, Berlin and Paris. In 1865, when he qualified as a

doctor, he was appointed assistant to the professor of medical jurisprudence, his father Francis Ogston, a position he held until 1873. He ran the eye dispensary in Castle Street. He was appointed ophthalmic surgeon at Aberdeen Royal Infirmary in 1868, and lecturer in practical ophthalmology in 1869. In 1868 he was appointed joint medical officer of health, sharing the post with his father. He became a full surgeon in 1874, senior surgeon in 1880, and held the Regius Chair of Surgery 1882–1909. He served in the Egyptian campaign 1884–85, the Boer War and in the First World War, and considerably influenced the establishment of the Royal Army Medical Corps in 1898. His major contribution to medical research lay in the identification of the importance of bacteria in wounds and their treatment, and his discovery of the staphylococcus aureus. He served as surgeon to the Royal Household in Scotland, and was president of the Medico-Chirurgical Society in 1905.

Sir Alexander Ogston, the city's medical officer of health, in 1868 (with his father); regius professor of surgery, 1882-1909.

Furthermore, since this was a phase of general expansion in the university sector the increase in staff exceeded the growth of student numbers, because it was driven by the agreement made in the 1920s to share the costs of developments. In the 1970s when university funding became more closely scrutinised and then curtailed, the medical school was no longer able to maintain its unusually large share of the cost of the rapidly expanding service.

This exceptional pattern of development of medical services had effects which were both beneficial and adverse. On the credit side, the close integration of the Royal Infirmary and medical school helped both patient care and the training of doctors, and many important clinical advances occurred within the combined departments. It also led to an improved distribution of resources, and the creation of health information systems which were considerably in advance of those in other parts of the country.[34] The weakness in this development eventually had a substantial impact on the University. Involvement in clinical duties precluded the staff appointed by the University from maintaining a sufficient volume and quality of academic research because the focus of their efforts had been on the improvement of care rather than upon fundamental research. When the university funding mechanisms changed in the 1980s to take account of research performance, the medical school, and thence the University, faced stringent economies from loss of resources. The adverse results of the research review conducted in 1981 cost the medical school a reduction of almost 25 per cent in clinical and support staff. In the final two decades of the century the University was obliged to review its strategy on research and teaching, particularly with regard to the medical school which was a relatively costly component of the system. From this emerged a strong commitment to recover lost ground in developing a strong research base. The Institute of Medical Sciences, opened in 1996 with an academic staff of 200 plus 100 support staff, was intended to generate world class medical research, and thereby to keep Foresterhill at the forefront of medical advance.

Lady Matilda Baird, a leading campaigner for improvements in health provision; first chair of the North-East Regional Hospital Board 1947-66.

MEDICAL SERVICES BEYOND FORESTERHILL

While the growth of the Royal Infirmary continued to commandeer public attention, the provision of other medical services continued to expand, especially after 1948. At that time, the town council undertook duties such as the provision of health foods like orange juice and cod liver oil, and home visits with the introduction of a mobile health clinic in 1952. In some areas, the city remained in the forefront of national developments. A family planning clinic was established in 1926, the gynaecological service became operational in 1948 and, from 1966, offered free contraceptives. The authority also pioneered the integration of the work of doctors and health visitors in Scotland, assigning health visitors to specific general practices from 1959 onward.

Together with the hospitals and the dispensary, medical services were provided by the general practitioner. In the nineteenth century, the position was often combined with the dispensation of drugs. Dr Alexander Kilgour rose from poverty to become a well-liked and greatly respected Aberdeen GP. He started in practice at the age of 23, in the late 1820s, living above his drug-shop in the Gallowgate. Together with Dr Galen he acted as secretary to the committee of the town council set up in 1840 to enquire into the sanitary conditions of the poor. Kilgour's view was that cholera was closely related to the existence of open sewers. As well as maintaining his practice, Kilgour served for many years as senior physician to the ARI.[35] He was reputed to have built up the best consulting practice in the north of Scotland before retiring to the distant rural quietude of Cove.

General practice offered one of the earliest opportunities of a professional career for women. One Aberdeen practice, which was started by Dr Elizabeth Ewan in 1896, was run by a succession of distinguished women doctors. Dr Annie Watts took over from Dr Ewan in 1900 and, three years later, was joined by Dr Laura Sandeman. They had consulting rooms in Waverly Place and in Torry. Both were supporters of the mother and child welfare movement which was founded in 1909, and they were elected as the first two women members of the Medico-Chirurgical Society.[36] Dr Mary Esslemont joined the practice in 1929, filling the vacancy caused by the death of Dr Sandeman. The practice was maintained entirely by women doctors until the early 1950s.

The services offered by general practitioners changed radically in the course of the twentieth century. In the mid-1970s over half the practices in the city were still run by a single doctor. But the trend to larger practices had started in the 1950s and came to full fruition in the final decades of the century with multiple-doctor practices located in large consulting clinics such as the Denburn Centre or Foresterhill. Other services became extended and co-ordinated. In 1996 G-Docs began as a co-operative venture between practices, enabling a more effective use of manpower and providing an efficient but less stressful system of night visits. This meant that a doctor could always be contacted in emergency although not necessarily one from the practice with which the patient was registered.

A Distinguished Tradition

Throughout these two centuries the treatment of health and those aspects of social deprivation which compound medical problems were treated together as part of the same problem. In so doing, there emerged some of the strongest and most unique traditions in the history of the city, in dealing with slum clearance, in providing welfare and medical aid, and in advancing research in medicine and related disciplines. This was the forum for the activity of some of the city's most distinguished citizens and some of its most distinctive achievements, of which the creation of the Foresterhill medical complex, and the distinctive growth which emerged from that structure, must be accorded great prominence.

11

Housing

NICHOLAS J. WILLIAMS

NINETEENTH-CENTURY HOUSING

Aberdeen in 1800 was a town in which rich and poor lived cheek by jowl. Although the rich enjoyed housing which was both more spacious and less insanitary, they shared with the poor a generally squalid urban environment.[1] The more affluent lived for the main part in large dwellings on the main streets, notably Upperkirkgate, the Gallowgate, Guestrow, Castle Street and Marischal Street. The poor lived in the backlands behind these dwellings reached by vennels, tunnel-like passageways, giving access to courts of poorer housing, and in separate but proximate areas such as the Shorelands, east of Marischal Street, and around the Green. Sanitation was primitive, with open sewers, a reliance on ash-pits and cess pools and no piped water. Water was obtained from wells, which became increasingly inadequate as population grew. The most affluent lived in mansions, of which only two survive today, Provost Skene's and Provost Ross' houses. By 1800 some of these mansions may already have been subdivided, a process which accelerated in the course of the nineteenth century as the better-off left the more unhealthy areas. The characteristics of the poorest dwellings are not certain, but were in the main stone tenements and smaller but equally squalid buildings. Robbie's description gives a graphic picture of living conditions.

> The few streets of which the town consisted about the year 1800 were, as a rule, narrow, ill-paved, and by no means cleanly kept. But such as they were, the main streets were spacious compared with the numerous closes which, in the poorer parts of the town, entered from the more open thoroughfares. These closes were frequently but a few feet wide, with houses on either side into which the free air of heaven could scarcely penetrate. The windows were small, and the apartments low-roofed, dark and unhealthy; an open ash-pit was to be seen in every close, and apparently was an indispensable adjunct to every property. Water was a scarce commodity, and as a natural consequence everything of the nature of sanitary arrangements was entirely wanting.[2]

Opposite:
Map 6. Rubislaw and its fashionable residential streets c. 1900.

These conditions persisted throughout the nineteenth century and, in some areas, into the twentieth century. As the economy began to grow, inward migration from the surrounding rural areas to work in the new industries increased, and the population of the town grew rapidly. Low wages, the need to live close to work, total reliance on private agencies for housing provision, and the rate of population growth combined to increase population densities, overcrowding and squalor. Such physical expansion of the town that did occur was predominantly for the growing middle classes, and the working classes were in the main accommodated in already existing quarters at increasing densities. Backlands were further developed and existing tenements were 'made down' or subdivided to increase their capacity. The construction of Union Street, George Street and Market Street entailed the destruction of much slum property which further increased the pressure on the remaining areas. Although the town as a whole experienced growing prosperity, this was not reflected in the housing conditions of the working classes or the general urban environment. The central parts of the town remained socially mixed, insanitary and overcrowded.

The Flight to the Suburbs

The major beneficiaries of Aberdeen's economic growth were the middle classes, industrialists, shopkeepers and professionals. Their wealth gave them the means to escape from what was becoming an increasingly unpleasant, insanitary and dangerous urban environment. The poverty and lifestyle of the poor were obvious and offensive to the bourgeoisie, and the unseen but more dangerous factor of disease was an increasing hazard for rich and poor alike. The obvious mechanism of escape for the middle classes was to relocate to the suburbs. Here they could invest their wealth in property and create residential environments at lower densities with an improved sanitary infrastructure, with sewers, internal piped water, baths and, later in the century, water closets. This entailed a different lifestyle, more private than communal, with semi-detached and detached villas set in their own gardens rather than tenements, and which created physically separate neighbourhoods. It has been argued that middle-class economic power created and maintained the differentials between slum and suburb. The middle classes derived a rentier income through their ownership of slum property and used their local political control to redirect business profits away from environmental improvements and into housing investment in the suburbs.[3]

The growing middle class generated the necessary effective demand which was exploited as capital sought new investment outlets and profits. The professional classes were effective in securing access to capital for speculative investment in suburban property, the single most significant agency being the Land Association, later the City of Aberdeen Land Association (CALA). The prospectus of the company stated in 1874 that 'the rapidly increasing value of land in and around cities and large towns has been well known for many years, and has enabled many persons to realise handsome profits out of limited adventures'.[4] Its Memorandum and Articles of Association stated the objectives

> … to purchase, lease, or acquire land in Aberdeen and its vicinity; to hold, let, feu or re-sell the same; to build, or make advances on buildings, and to construct or contribute to the construction of roads and bridges; to borrow money on mortgage, as well as on Debentures and on Deposit, as the same may be deemed advisable and beneficial to the company; to afford facilities for persons becoming proprietors of their own dwelling houses, shops, or other heritable property, by assisting them with advances, which they may repay gradually by monthly or other instalments.[5]

The considerable initial investment, in land and infrastructure, would be offset by income from feuing, capital gains from the sale and resale of land and buildings, and the capital appreciation of the stock. It was hoped that the initial prospectus would stimulate the purchase of 12,000 shares at £10 per share, the capital raised to be supplemented by borrowing. In the event, the paid-up capital amounted to only £52,900 by 1876.[6] Immediate investments were made in the purchase of land on the outskirts of the city. The Rubislaw, Fountainhall and Morningfield estates were purchased for £105,000 and the Torry and Craiginches estates for £29,000. The Torry estate was to be socially mixed, with lower Torry catering for herring fishermen, whereas upper Torry was to have 'villas and first class housing'.[7] The most attractive investment, however, was at Rubislaw, and it was here that activities were concentrated. The Rubislaw and Torry estates were purchased from Alexander Anderson himself, the establishment of the land association thus yielding him an immediate increase in personal wealth as well as a stake in a potentially profitable enterprise, since he had also played a leading part in the establishment of the Association. Roads and sewers were constructed at the Land Association's expense,

James Matthews, architect, trained by Archibald Simpson and Sir Giles Gilbert Scott; lord provost 1883-85.

James Matthews 1820–98

Son of a clerk at the Commercial Bank, James Matthews was educated at Robert Gordon's Hospital and apprenticed to Archibald Simpson in 1834. He subsequently spent five years in London working for Sir Gilbert Scott. He established his own business in Aberdeen in 1844 in partnership with Thomas Mackenzie and later with his son, Marshall Mackenzie. He designed the St Nicholas Poor's House, in Nelson Street, which was adopted by the Board of Supervision as the model to be adopted throughout Scotland. His architectural designs included the Grammar School, the Town and County Bank, the Concert Hall in the Music Hall, Rubislaw Terrace, the Northern Assurance headquarters, the Art Gallery and Gray's School of Art, the harbour office, the Palace Hotel, the Free West Church and Ardoe House. He represented the third ward on the town council 1863–71. He returned in 1883, representing Rubislaw, and served as lord provost 1883–85. He also served on the school board 1879–82. He served as a harbour commissioner, as a governor of Robert Gordon's Hospital, and as chairman of the Scottish Equitable Liabilities Company. His directorships included the North of Scotland Bank, the Northern Assurance Company and the Mechanics' Institute. He was a deacon of Belmont Street Congregational Church.

including Stanley Street, Gladstone Place, Queen's Gardens and Forest Road, and the building plots so created were feued and sold off. In Torry, a considerable investment was made in infrastructure in collaboration with the town council. The sum of £5,750 was contributed towards the cost of the Victoria Bridge and £10,000 for the construction of the associated roads, sums which were expected to be easily recouped as the land was subsequently feued. In the event, most of the land was sold to the town council for municipal housing in 1919.

MacLaren noted that at the Disruption of the Church of Scotland in mid-century, many of those who seceded from the Church in Aberdeen had already moved out of the city centre to Union Place, Bon-Accord Square, Crown Street and Dee Street.[8] These were largely the new petit bourgeois business people and professionals who rejected the patronage of the old order. The established merchant class, with links to the gentry in the country, tended to remain in the older parts of the city. There was thus a spatial schism as well as a religious divide among the middle classes for a time. Even the old order moved out eventually, their formerly desirable dwellings being sold off and subdivided to provide cheaper accommodation for lower-income tenants. This completed the exodus from central Aberdeen by the middle classes.

HOUSING AND POVERTY

The experience of the working classes in nineteenth-century Aberdeen was considerably different from that enjoyed by the middle classes. Rapid urbanisation and population growth, and a decline in housing standards, meant that new demand was met by subdividing existing tenements and infilling backlands. This permitted a rapid increase in the housing stock close to the workplace. Later in the century, real wages rose and stimulated increased supply and the development of new working-class areas. The housing in these areas was poor compared with the middle-class suburbs, but a considerable improvement on the accommodation previously available to such people. A few areas, such as Ferryhill, George Street and Mounthooly, had a social mix of housing. For those not in regular employment, housing remained miserable throughout the century.

As the population density increased, conditions deteriorated, and the need for an improved water supply became urgent. Robert Anderson, water works engineer for the city, reported in 1865 that two thirds of the city had no sewers and that foul drainage found its way down open channels in the streets to the nearest stream or sewer grating. In the Shorelands, at high tide sewage could flood up into the streets and floors of the dwelling houses.[9] Dr Henry Jackson, lately a police commissioner, giving evidence to the House of Commons Select Committee with reference to the Aberdeen Police and Waterworks Bill of 1862, observed that in the

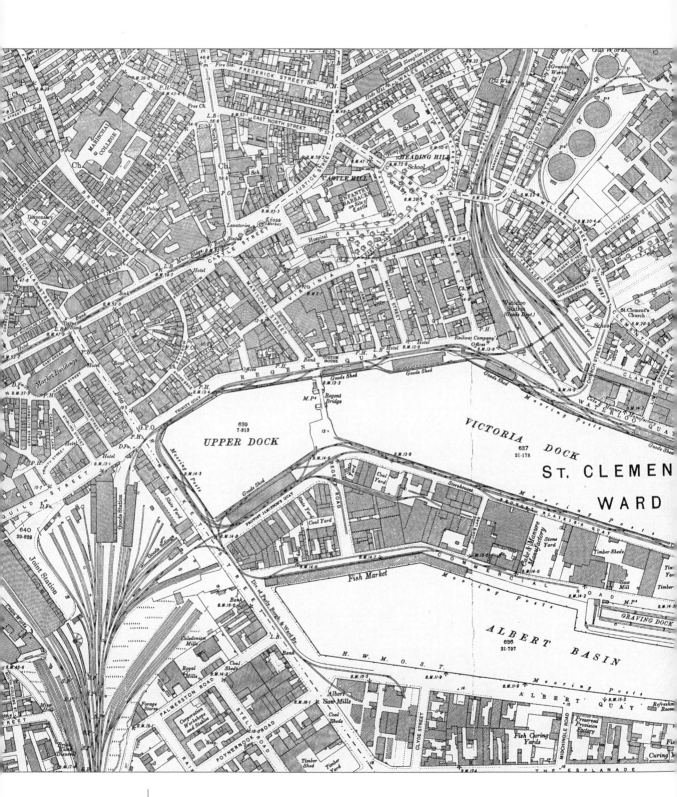

poorer parts of the city in mid-century, each well supplied about 400 families and often dried up early in the day.[10] The cess-pools and ash-pits in these areas were uncovered and offensive, and the liquid from them passed into the street channels or infiltrated into the soil. Solid matter was carted away periodically by scavengers. Refuse from slaughter houses, skinners, soap manufacturers and other industrial enterprises also found its way into these open channels, industry and working-class housing being intermixed in the areas around the city centre. Back courts were often unpaved and soon became muddy and a health hazard.

At the bottom of the housing hierarchy were cellars and underground dwellings. These were basement dwellings, often of one room only, with no water supply or solid floor and no chimney. They were damp, dark and cold in winter. Sanitation took the form of communal privies and cess-pools and the water supply was obtained from wells. Lodging-houses for communal living were also widespread, and these persisted into the twentieth century. Originally used as temporary accommodation for migrants to the city, in the face of housing shortage they became long-term hostel accommodation, often for families. They were grossly overcrowded and sources of disease, vice and criminality. Some of the larger dwellings abandoned by the middle classes became lodging-houses, especially in the area south of Castle Street and east of Shiprow. Tenement housing was the least objectionable. The oldest was to be found in the backlands behind the main streets, and from mid-century onwards new tenements of three and four storeys were built on the outskirts of the city. Although the best of the working-class housing, these tenements were by no means comfortable. There was no piped water, families often lived in one room, and the privies were communal. The newer areas, largely on the northern outskirts of the town along King Street and George Street, and later in Rosemount and Torry, did have underground sewers and the general environment was less crowded and offensive. Access to the different standards of housing was obviously determined by income. The best, and newest, housing was occupied by the skilled artisans with regular employment. Those with no skills whose employment was irregular, and those who suffered from misfortune such as illness which prevented them from working, were condemned to basement dwellings, the lodging-houses or the older tenements.

Despite Aberdeen's growing prosperity, therefore, a considerable number of Aberdonians were living in unhealthy and squalid conditions. Moreover, this poverty was situated close to the centre of the town and could not be hidden. Prostitution and drunkenness were regularly observed in the Castlegate and the proliferation of bars throughout the poorer quarters offered an immediate, albeit temporary, relief from poverty. The first significant philanthropic response to housing problems in Aberdeen occurred in 1850, following the precedent set in Edinburgh in 1844, in the establishment of a model lodging-house. This was

Opposite:
Map 7. Areas of some of the worst housing in the city centre c. 1900.

intended to meet the needs of travellers, migrants from the country in search of employment, and others in need of temporary lodging. It was run on a non-profit basis, any surplus accruing from rental income being used to improve or extend the accommodation.[11] Funds were raised by subscription and, in 1864, the Aberdeen Lodging-House Association leased the former residence of Provost Skene in the Guestrow from Miss Duthie (who later gave the city the park which bears her name). It became the Victoria Lodging-House with space for 75 lodgers. The Guestrow had become, by this time, a dingy and confined lane, belying its former status as a street for the rich and powerful. There was a strong moralistic element in the aims of the Association. Religious services were held in the lodging-house every Sunday, and efforts were made to protect the lodgers from immorality as well as to provide them with hygienic and comfortable accommodation. In this latter respect, it was very successful. In 1856 not a single case of infectious disease was encountered, such disease being common in other lodging-houses. The Association, although it had discussed establishing other model lodging-houses throughout the town, appears to have disbanded in 1885. The lodging-house itself continued on a private profit-oriented basis, into the twentieth century. The third annual report in 1852 observed that accommodation had been provided for 'working people, and those even below that rank'. In its first year the majority of the lodgers were railway labourers, and in the second year tradesmen in search of employment.[12] The vast majority of the indigent continued to live in the other privately owned lodging-houses, basement dwellings and the worst of the tenement and other slum accommodation.

The second philanthropic contribution to housing was the Aberdeen Association for the Improvement of the Dwellings of the Labouring Classes, founded in 1863. The objectives of this association were to provide high-quality dwellings for the working classes, either for rent or purchase, while at the same time yielding a modest return on capital. Subscribed capital amounted to £2,000, consisting of 80 shares at £25 each, shareholders including Lord Aberdeen and the Lord Provost.[13] Tenement property was purchased in Hutcheon Street for £286 and in Loch Street for £536, providing accommodation for 32 families, all tenants. These properties, although they yielded a dividend of 5 per cent, were not considered ideal, presumably because they were not of sufficiently good quality, and it was decided to build new dwellings at Gilcomston. Three three-storied tenements and ten cottages were to be constructed, the tenements costing £800 each and the cottages £150 each. The dwellings were equipped with water closets, facilities at the time restricted to the middle classes, and rents were paid half-yearly. The tenants were drawn from the artisan classes and included weavers, combmakers, cobblers and confectioners. The properties at Hutcheon Street and Loch Street were sold in 1870 for £317 and £416 respectively. The Association maintained its properties to a high standard, and insured them against fire. Dividends of between 4 and 6 per cent were declared in its early years, but despite this the Association found it difficult to raise capital and hence its stock of dwellings was not augmented. Furthermore, the rents charged and the half-yearly terms ensured that only the more affluent of the working classes could afford to be tenants. The Association continued in operation until 1930.

SLUM CLEARANCE AND PUBLIC PROVISION

Private philanthropy thus made little contribution to improving the housing of the working classes in Aberdeen. The number assisted was small, and those that were helped came largely from the artisan class. Philanthropy scarcely touched the housing needs of the poorest. As in most, if not all, British towns, however, there was considerable resistance to the extension of the activities of the state. This stemmed from an unwillingness to incur public expenditure, and a belief, strongly asserted by the churches, that much of the misery of the poor stemmed from fecklessness and immorality, rather than because wage levels were too low so that the necessities of life were unavailable. Cholera epidemics, for example, were often ascribed to a punishment from God for immorality as much as a result of insanitary living conditions.[14] Slum conditions were seen as a consequence of choice, the poor opting to spend their incomes on drink and licentiousness rather than better housing. Thus an improvement in the living conditions of the poor was to be achieved by moralising rather than through institutional reform and public action.

The Aberdeen Corporation Act of 1881 gave the town council widespread powers to close uninhabitable dwellings and this provided the mechanism for an attack on the city's slums. Much of the stimulus for civic action came from the medical officers of health (MOH). They repeatedly drew attention to the slums and their influence in spreading infectious disease. Although cholera had been absent since 1854 it was still much feared. Typhus, scarlet fever, measles, typhoid and tuberculosis were common in the poorest parts of the town, but by no means restricted to them, and smallpox made periodic appearances. With respect to the outbreak of typhus in 1882, the MOH, W. J. Simpson, described conditions in one court in the Gallowgate area where the illness had struck:

> … there were three families in four rooms. The height of the highest room was 5 feet 11 inches and the lowest 5 feet 4 inches; besides being in a confined court, they were slightly underground … In the same court, a room under statutory size for occupation by one person was inhabited by eight inmates … Others were found much the same.[15]

The source of the outbreak was eventually traced to a house in Sugarhouse Lane in the Shorelands area, a dwelling which had also been the source of typhus outbreaks on three other occasions in the previous 20 years.

The 1881 Act gave the town council powers to close uninhabitable buildings and they were used extensively for most of the following 30 years resulting in the closure of many slum properties. Some areas were so bad that it was easier to deal with them on a comprehensive basis in which properties could be closed on the grounds of high density as well as unfitness, even though some of them might be sound. National legislation gave town councils the powers to define such areas and compulsorily purchase all the property within them. Clearance and redevelopment could then proceed. The most significant legislation consisted of the Artisans' and Labourers' Dwelling Improvement Act 1875, and the Housing of the Working Classes Act 1890. Aberdeen town council took advantage of both to proceed with clearance schemes in the Shorelands and Exchequer Row areas. In July 1883 Simpson reported that Pork Lane, Water Lane, Sugarhouse Lane and Watt's Court, and Virginia Street in the Shorelands area constituted an unhealthy area in terms of the 1875 Act and should be the subject of an improvement scheme. He referred to the 'general insanitary conditions, defective sewer arrangement, the closeness and narrowness of the streets, and the want of light, air and ventilation.'[16] The Aberdeen Improvement Confirmation Act was passed by Parliament in 1884 permitting the town council to proceed with the Shorelands improvement scheme, and marking the first large-scale slum clearance in the city. The area contained 788 persons, and the improvement involved closure of most of the dwellings and the construction of a new road, Mearns Street, to replace Pork Lane. In the event, some of the dwellings were improved rather than demolished. The net cost was £13,962.[17]

In 1888 the town council appointed Matthew Hay as medical officer of health. Hay was convinced that the most effective means of improving public health was to improve the housing conditions of the working classes. In his reports he repeatedly drew attention to the insanitary conditions and disease in the poorest areas. Hay went further, however, in persistently urging the town council to take direct action to improve housing conditions. He instigated surveys of the poorer housing in collaboration with the sanitary inspector and, although hampered by a shortage of staff, was able to build up a comprehensive picture of the scale and location of the worst areas. In 1889 Hay recommended that the Exchequer Row and Shuttle Lane areas should be the subject of improvement schemes under the 1875 Act, but the town council failed to respond.[18] In 1894 Hay repeated his suggestion that the Exchequer Row area should be the subject of such a scheme, stating that a considerable time had elapsed since his last report on the area, and that the 1890 Act conferred greater powers on local authorities which the town council should consider.[19] Conditions in the area had not improved, and Hay referred to great overcrowding, insufficient space for the erection of sanitary conveniences, the dilapidated nature of most of the dwellings, and the high death rate among the inhabitants, one-third of whom lived in common lodging-houses. There was opposition from some councillors on the grounds of cost, but in August 1894 the public health committee was authorised to formulate a scheme for submission to Parliament.[20] The Aberdeen Improvement Scheme Provisional Order Confirmation Act was passed in 1896, defining an area containing 736 persons.[21] The net cost was estimated at £14,286, the gross cost for purchase of the properties of £25,776 being defrayed by subsequent sale of the cleared land. Most of the property lying within the area behind the buildings on the periphery was cleared over the next few years, leaving open space near the heart of the city. In addition to the closure and demolition of dwellings under the improvement schemes, the town council, on Hay's recommendations, continued to close uninhabitable dwellings on an individual basis in other areas under the terms of the 1881 Aberdeen Corporation Act. Legislation for a further improvement scheme dealing with the area east of the Gallowgate was confirmed in 1904 although some property along the Gallowgate had been demolished earlier to allow street widening, notably Mar's Castle in 1897. By 1905 Hay felt able to declare that, with the closure of sixteen dwellings in Scott's Court, Regent Quay, one of the last of the genuinely slum courts of the city had been dealt with.[22]

Closure orders for slum dwellings provided only part of the solution to Aberdeen's housing problems. Without replacements for the condemned housing, and indeed an increased supply of dwellings to cope with population growth, the housing problem, and in particular overcrowding, would have intensified. There had been a building boom in the last quarter of the century supplying both middle-class and working-class demand. Most of the working-class tenements in Torry, Rosemount and King Street were built during this period, but they were let at rents affordable only by the artisan class. For the poorest households, closure of slum property in the absence of replacements led only to greater overcrowding in the property that remained. In 1902, Hay gave evidence with respect to the contemporary housing situation.

I have had experience in my own city of proceeding too rapidly with the closure of slum properties without some provision for the accommodation of the displaced occupants. In some instances we have had to reopen closed properties for want of proper accommodation, and have had to delay for several years closing other houses that were clearly unfit for human habitation. Private builders are, in my experience, not eager to erect houses for the accommodation of such occupants. They fear the introduction of tenants with such experience and habits into their properties, and the deteriorating effect which the tenants and their families will have on the property. They also dislike the trouble of collecting the rents of such tenants. They naturally prefer to cater for the artisan and the higher-placed of the labouring classes … The sole motive guiding the private builder may not unfairly, and without aspersion, be said to be profit, and as much profit as possible. He will not build merely to provide accommodation for the displaced occupants of slums. There is no legal or moral obligation resting upon him. He will move only if he has hope of sufficient gain … For these and other reasons I am clearly of opinion that the Corporation should obtain power to provide themselves the accommodation required for the displaced population.[23]

While the town council was willing to follow Hay's advice to clear slums, it was

The town council's first venture into municipal house building in Urquhart Road, 1897. The communal WC on the landing was typical.

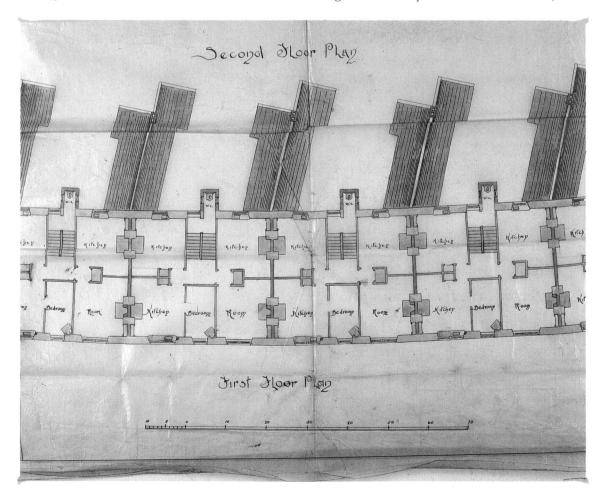

less responsive to the proposal that it should build and manage housing. The Housing Acts of 1875 and 1890 gave local authorities the powers to construct dwellings for the working classes, the former for persons displaced by improvement schemes and the latter more generally. No use was made by Aberdeen of the 1875 Act in this way, although a site was considered where dwellings could be built. In 1890 the town council considered building a lodging-house given the unsatisfactory nature of those in private ownership, and the decision to proceed was taken in 1896.[24] The Corporation Lodging-House in East North Street was completed in 1899 and continued to provide emergency accommodation until 1988.[25] It is significant that it consistently operated at a loss, whereas the Victoria Lodging-House returned an annual surplus. The former was built, furnished and managed to a higher standard and thus necessitated a subsidy. A more significant step was taken in June 1893 when the town council requested the finance committee to 'consider as to the propriety of the Council erecting dwelling-houses, consisting of one, two and three-roomed tenements, for the accommodation of persons belonging to the labouring classes, and as to the probable cost and the most suitable site for the purpose.'[26] No action was taken, however, and in May 1896 a committee was set up to investigate the erection of cottage dwellings. It reported in February 1897 and recommended that tenements rather than cottages be built on the grounds of cost since the 1890 Act provided no subsidy from central government so that local authorities had to bear the entire cost.[27] The construction of cottages would have required rents, if they were to cover costs, beyond the means of those for whom the houses were intended. The site chosen for the tenements was the south side of Urquhart Road between Park Road and Roslin Street, an area of private working-class tenements between the (St Nicholas) Poor's House and the fever hospital. Eight tenements of six houses each were proposed, four being two-roomed and two three-roomed. Each house was to have its own water supply, and there would be one water closet for every two houses. Further land was available in the area to be kept for later development. The original plan for self-contained cottages was abandoned in favour of tenements, for four, six or eight tenants, in plain but substantial granite blocks. The original specification included one water closet for every two tenancies, a wash house with fixed tubs for every three tenancies, each tenement to be fitted with grates and gas fittings ready for occupation, and at a total cost of £750 per tenement. The decision to proceed with the development was taken by 17 votes to 13, but was subsequently suspended so that the design of the dwellings could be changed 'to be more suitable for the class for whom it was intended that such dwellings be provided.'[28] The amended design increased the number of houses per tenement from six to nine, consisting of three two-roomed houses and six one-roomed houses. Individual rents were reduced, but the total rental per tenement was increased, thereby making the development more financially acceptable.

The reduction in quality, however, made the flats little better than those that were being constructed by the private sector. Even so, the development was approved by only 16 votes to 13, indicating that a significant minority of councillors thought that municipal involvement with housing construction was misguided. The dwellings were completed in 1899 and remain Aberdeen's oldest council-owned dwellings, other than the houses built in Footdee in 1808. They were still in use a century later although considerably modified internally. A further six tenements were subsequently built along Park Road, amounting to 131 dwellings in all, but progress was slow and in 1913 parts of the site originally acquired in 1897 still remained vacant.

Conditions in some of the older tenements built in the 1870s still left much to be desired. They could not accommodate individual water closets and had communal lavatories in the back courts. In the MOH's annual report of 1908, Hay referred to their filthy conditions.[29] Building more or less ceased completely during the First World War and hence by 1918 there was both an acute housing shortage and a backlog of unfit dwellings. The housing situation of Aberdeen's working classes in the period before 1919, notwithstanding the improvement schemes, was thus less than desirable. Only in comparison with the period before 1900 could the situation be considered in any way favourable, the removal of the worst of the slums and the improvement in the quality of the water supply having reduced death rates.

Even in 1921, however, 37 per cent of Aberdonians lived in dwellings of two rooms or fewer, and 11 per cent were living at a density of three or more persons per room, statistics that had barely changed since 1901. Most working-class Aberdonians were still sharing water closets and had no baths. Gaffron collected accounts of housing conditions at the time.

> We lived in Littlejohn Street where there were only two toilets for the fourteen families. We each had just the one room with no gas or electricity, only the open fire to cook on so you had to get the fire going in the morning before you could get a cup of tea even and coal was 1/- for a half bag. For lighting we used paraffin and that was another tuppence.
>
> You didn't have a bathroom. You filled a zinc tub in front of the fire or you might sometimes go to public baths. Hanover Street School had showers - I think it was sixpence they charged.[30]

Opposite:
Map 8. Mainly
working-class
residential areas in
the north of the city
c. 1900.

MUNICIPAL HOUSING

From 1919 onward, housing provision in Aberdeen was transformed with profound consequences for the urban landscape of the city. The major elements of the

change were the growth of owner occupation as the major form of tenure for the middle classes and the transfer of responsibility for working-class housing from the private sector to the town council. This resulted in improved housing quality for all, and in particular a reduction of the inequalities which were such a feature of the nineteenth century. Social segregation persisted, albeit in a different and more complex form. The working classes became increasingly concentrated in the council schemes as these increased in number, and a growing proportion of the middle classes became owner occupiers.

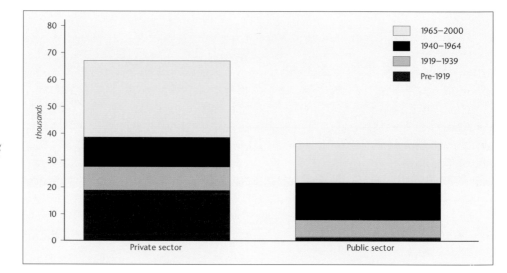

Figure 11.1 Aberdeen housing stock by date of construction. (Source: The Planning Department, Aberdeen City Council)

In 1917 the Local Government Board issued a circular to local authorities requesting information on their post-war housing requirements. The assumption made by the Government was that, given the cessation of building during wartime and the anticipated economic difficulties thereafter, private enterprise would be unable to meet the need for working-class housing. In these circumstances, a subsidy would be available from central government for those local authorities willing to embark on municipal schemes. It was assumed that this would provide a short-term solution to the housing problem, and that once normal market conditions were restored private enterprise would take over from the local authorities as the major provider of working-class housing. Aberdeen town council responded by assessing its immediate post-war need at 1,500 houses.[31] It stated that since the private sector would be incapable of meeting this need in the short term, it would be willing to embark on municipal provision of dwellings provided that adequate financial assistance was forthcoming from the Treasury.[32] The last condition was crucial, since the town council had not used its powers to build any dwellings other than the tenements in Urquhart Road and Park Road. In July 1918, a subcommittee was set up to prepare schemes in response to the circular, this subsequently becoming the housing committee. This committee was to become the most powerful force in local government and its activities were to transform the city.

The housing situation in the city after 1918 was acute. There existed both a shortage of housing, leading to overcrowding, and a considerable number of slum properties outwith the improvement scheme areas. In addition, there were rising expectations of what was acceptable as a minimum standard of housing, and this included exclusive access to a bath and water closet for all households. Such a standard would render unacceptable much of the working-class tenement stock even though, in other respects, it was acceptable and far superior to the remaining slum properties. The town council was thus faced with the need to increase the general stock of housing, eradicate the slums, and satisfy rising expectations. The nature of its response was largely governed by the policies of central government in terms of housing legislation, and hence Aberdeen's housing history in the inter-war period was similar to that of other Scottish cities. Broadly speaking, the legislation from 1919 to 1924 was aimed at increasing the general stock of housing, whereas the later legislation was designed to deal specifically with overcrowding and slum clearance. The dwellings built under the Housing Acts under the two regimes differed in quality and design, and the tenants who were allocated the properties differed in income. The result was an hierarchy of estates from the most popular with the most affluent tenants to the least popular with the poorest tenants.

Faced with acute shortage, the first action taken by the town council in June 1919 was to convert part of the King Street barracks into 18 one-roomed, 26 two-roomed and two three-roomed temporary dwellings. The 1919 Housing Act was generous to local authorities, requiring them to meet any financial deficit only up to the product of four fifths of a penny rate, the remainder being borne by the Exchequer. Under this legislation, the town council proposed to build a mixture of over 600 cottages and tenements in Torry on land owned by the Land Association. They would have a minimum of three rooms and all the dwellings were to have their own bathrooms and water closets. Compared with general housing conditions for working-class families at the time, these were houses of high quality, and without a generous subsidy the rents would have been beyond the means of most working men. In fact, rents were fixed at between £22 and £32 10s. per year. Almost all the tenants were from the ranks of the better-off and white-collar workers. The hope was that the properties vacated by the new municipal tenants would filter down to poorer households in slum or overcrowded conditions. In the event, government alarm at the open-ended nature of spending by the Exchequer caused the subsidy to be suspended and only 242 dwellings were built in Aberdeen. The cottages built under the 1919 legislation remain some of the most desirable of council dwellings.

The 1923 housing legislation transferred the responsibility for housing provision back to the private sector, although councils could receive a subsidy to build if it could be shown that private enterprise could not build sufficient dwellings. Councils could also build specifically for slum clearance for which they would receive 50 per cent of the capital cost. Private builders were eligible for capital subsidies from the Exchequer, administered by local authorities which could also supplement this grant from their own resources. Aberdeen adopted a scheme whereby builders could obtain a capital grant of £100 for each dwelling that had a minimum of three rooms plus scullery, bathroom and toilet. There was no maximum price or restriction on who could buy or rent the properties. Most were sold to individual buyers. Capital subsidies were given to provide housing not for the poor, but for the middle classes and the affluent working classes. In the event, over 1,600 dwellings were built by private enterprise with a capital subsidy between 1919 and 1934, when the scheme terminated.[33] Most were built in the expanding suburbs in the west and south of the city, notably Deemount (Ferryhill), Mannofield, Broomhill, and Midstocket, although some were also built in the Hilton area. Companies which took particular advantage of the subsidy included Northern Garden Suburbs, John Bisset & Son, Joseph Shirras & Son, the North of Scotland Housing Company, and Tesswell Construction. Scott Sutherland established Modern Homes (Aberdeen) Ltd to build and market houses, and employed himself as the architect.[34]

The election of a Labour Government in 1924 heralded a more sympathetic approach to council housing, and legislation shifted the responsibility for housing provision for the poor back to the local authorities with a more generous subsidy from central government. This enabled local authorities to increase significantly their production of housing, and in Aberdeen over 2,600 dwellings were completed between 1925 and 1935, almost all being four-flatted properties of two or three apartments.[35] They were located in the Hilton, Pittodrie, School Road, Ruthrieston and Torry areas. Population growth, the need to eradicate slums, and rising expectations, especially with regard to overcrowding, meant that the rate of construction of new dwellings could not keep pace with rising demands. Although the subsidies for houses built under the legislation of 1919 and 1924 were generous, they were still let at rents beyond the reach of most working-class households and continued to be occupied by those with skilled occupations and in regular employment. Even the schemes built specifically for slum clearance purposes had rents at levels which caused about half of the tenants decanted from the cleared areas to refuse offers of rehousing in those schemes. Private rents in the clearance areas ranged from £4 to £11 per annum for one to three apartment dwellings, whereas the rents for the municipal flats were £12 for two apartment and £15 for three apartment flats. Many families rehoused in the two apartment council flats soon became overcrowded. By 1925, the need for new dwellings had risen to over 5,300 compared to 2,600 in 1921.

By the end of 1929 over 1,900 new council dwellings had been built, but only about 100 of these were for slum clearance purposes. Municipal building had little effect on the poorest households. The housing legislation of the 1930s was designed to achieve a reorientation of local authority effort. Subsidies were restricted to slum clearance or relief of overcrowding, and were paid according to the number of persons rehoused. The effect of these legislative changes was that local authorities built bigger and cheaper dwellings. Most of those built in the 1930s were three-storey walk-up tenements of three, four and five apartment flats. The 1935 legislation enabled local authorities to grant rent rebates to poor families. It also amalgamated council dwellings into one housing revenue account. Previously there had been separate accounts for the properties built under each Housing Act, which imposed constraints on the rents that could be charged for particular schemes. The response of the town council in Aberdeen to this legislation, as in most towns in Scotland, created a hierarchy of council estates and produced chronic management problems in those schemes at the base of the hierarchy. The problem estates were those built in the 1930s and 1940s at Powis, Middlefield, Seaton, and Sandilands.

The problem had its origins in the physical form of the dwellings and the social and economic characteristics of the new tenants. Three-storey walk-up tenement flats, although consistent with Scottish architectural tradition and the experience of working-class families, were less popular than other council properties. Indeed, some councillors were unhappy about the policy of building tenements and registered strong dissent when it was suggested that the town council build four-storey tenements on the grounds of economy.

> It is a retrograde step in the rehousing of the working classes, one which will be welcomed by private speculative builders, whose desire has all along been to rehouse the working classes in huge tenement or balconied blocks. True, we have supported the building of tenement blocks, with not more than three storeys, and, provided the density rate for the areas was not being exceeded, our sole reason for doing so being the urgent demand for more houses. We realise full well that even a modern tenement house falls far short of the type of house we desire, and to which the working classes have as much right as any other section of the community.[36]

Most of the tenants moving into the new tenements were either from slum clearance schemes or from overcrowded conditions, and were largely at the lower end of the income scale. The town council introduced a rent rebate scheme in 1937 taking advantage of the provisions in the 1935 Housing Act. To limit the loss of revenue that the granting of rebates entailed, they were made available only in certain schemes. These were primarily those built under the slum clearance provisions, and almost all the dwellings were tenement flats. Rebates were not available in the rest of the stock, which consisted mainly of the popular cottage and four-flatted types commanding high rents. The effect of this rebate structure was to channel the poorer tenants into the schemes where rebates were available, and ultimately to create management problems in the post-war period. Only the better-off tenants with secure and reasonably well-paid employment could afford to pay the higher non-rebated rents charged for the rest of the stock.[37] At the time, however, tenants moving into the new tenement flats were delighted with the improvement in their housing conditions. Many were still living without baths or water closets, and many more were living in overcrowded conditions. The memories of those who were rehoused at the time provide vivid testimony to their pleasure.

> When we got a shift to Froghall we thought we were in a mansion. We were feert to go to sleep in the other rooms all by ourselves for we were used to everything going on around us.
>
> We brought up four children in two attics. Then we got one of the first houses in Garthdee. I walked in. I looked around upstairs and I looked around downstairs and I stood in the middle of it and said, 'This is aa mines'.[38]

These were the lucky families, since the housing shortage was so acute that many were reduced to living in tents and shacks. Seaton Place and Canal Road were the sites, among others, of such temporary accommodation. Attention was drawn in 1936 to a particularly unpleasant site at Haudagain, two fields off Great Northern Road, owned by the Land Association but leased to a local businessman. He had sublet the land to various tenants living in tents and temporary shacks. There was no water supply on site, and the ground was muddy and rat-infested.[39] In the face of such urgent need, the town council provided a variety of temporary accommodation at the King Street barracks, the Aberdeen jute works, Castlehill barracks, and the Torry Point battery.[40]

The construction of private houses in the city became increasingly significant in the inter-war period, and actually rose after 1934 despite the withdrawal of the capital subsidy. This was due to falling construction costs and the ready availability of finance from the growing building societies. Just under 5,000 houses were built by private enterprise between 1919 and 1939, almost entirely for owner occupation. They were generally smaller than the older private houses, being mainly bungalows, terraced houses and flats, and house prices were stable or falling. The

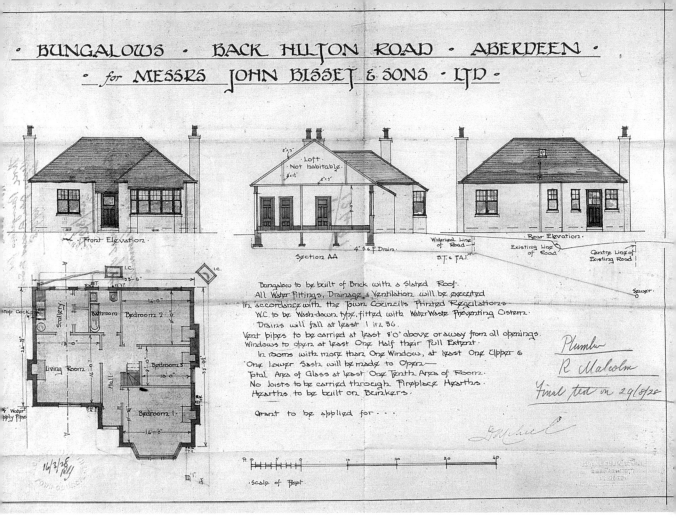

cheapest new houses were priced at £500 and required a minimum £50 deposit. The middle classes were increasingly drawn into these new owner-occupier suburbs.

The serious housing shortages and quality deficiencies existing in 1939 were exacerbated by the Second World War. The town council built fewer than 1,000 dwellings during wartime, and the private sector none. Aberdeen escaped relatively lightly from the *Luftwaffe* and there were only 35 raids in total. In sum, 78 houses were destroyed by bombing, 117 were irreparably damaged, 828 badly damaged and 12,175 were slightly damaged.[41] The marriage rate increased as demobilised servicemen returned home, further raising the need for new dwellings. The general standard of housing was still low despite the efforts of the town council and slum clearance programmes. In 1946, over half of all dwellings in Aberdeen were still without separate water closets, and 10 per cent were without internal piped water. These statistics compared very unfavourably with other Scottish towns, and are explained by the durable nature of the town's nineteenth-century granite tenements. These were difficult and expensive to modernise and landlords were reluctant to commit themselves to the required expenditure. Since the lack of a

The bungalow was very popular in private housing between the wars. These designs are for bungalows in Back Hilton Road, approved in 1928.

bathroom was not sufficient reason to close dwellings, landlords could not be forced to take action. Those living in substandard dwellings did at least have a home. More urgent was the problem of homelessness which afflicted returning servicemen in particular. The town council estimated the city's need for new dwellings, taking into account overcrowding, amenity deficiency, and sub-letting at 15,000. This was 50 per cent greater than the need estimated in 1939 and there was a consensus view that the most urgent problem facing Aberdeen in 1945 was the housing shortage. Rising expectations of what was acceptable, the Victorian legacy, the aftermath of war and social change combined in the post-1945 period to generate an acute housing problem.

THE PEAK OF MUNICIPAL HOUSING

An immediate response to this crisis was squatting, especially by demobbed servicemen. Targeted buildings included those requisitioned by the services during wartime, for example the Balmoral and Willowbank Hotels, and the redundant military quarters at Balnagask, Hayton, Girdleness and Torry, which had no light or running water, but did have stoves.[42] The official response to the general housing situation, both central and local, was determined by the profound political change that had occurred in 1945 with the election of a Labour Government which identified housing as a priority issue. This was paralleled by the election of Aberdeen's first Labour town council, and the policy decided at Westminster was enthusiastically implemented in Aberdeen. This policy relied on the town council to provide the bulk of the required housing and restricted the access of the private sector to materials and labour. The lessons from the inter-war period, when the town council had to compete with the private builders for resources, had been well learned, and a direct labour department was established in the face of fierce opposition from the non-Labour members on the town council. The demand for housing was so acute, however, that to meet immediate needs the Government supplied local authorities with temporary houses in the form of pre-fabricated bungalows. Aberdeen was allocated 1,500 of these dwellings, all of which were erected by 1948, some using German prisoners of war. They lasted longer than was

An elderly woman salvages possessions from her bombed home after a raid on Menzies Road, Torry, in August 1941.

Thomas Scott Sutherland 1899–1963

Born in Walker Road, Torry, Thomas Scott Sutherland was brought up in Ferryhill and later in Burns Road, attending Ferryhill and Ashley Road Schools. At the age of five he lost a leg as the result of a fall on holiday. He studied at Robert Gordon's College 1913–16 and won a bursary to the new School of Architecture, qualifying in 1922. He entered into partnership to build houses in Broomhill and Mannofield, and later in Fraserburgh. In 1931 he opened a midget golf course in Forbesfield Road, building four houses on the site when the craze passed. In 1932 he formed the company Modern Homes (Aberdeen) to sell his houses in the west end. He also designed and built cinemas, including the Majestic, the Regent (later the Odeon), the City and the Astoria. He built the new Scottish Amicable building on Union Street, and renovated the Tivoli theatre. In 1934 he was elected to represent Ruthrieston on the town council, a position he held until his death. As housing convener he pursued an active slum clearance and building programme at Hilton, Powis, Woodside and Kaimhill, and planned the Kincorth estate. His fortune, made through part ownership in the Fettercairn distillery and Moore's medicinals, distributing proprietary medicines, was used to establish the Scott Sutherland School of Architecture. Garthdee House and estate were gifted to house the school which was opened in 1957.

expected, the first being removed in 1960 from Tullos and Rosehill, those at Wellington Road lasting into the 1970s. The acuteness of the situation persuaded the town council to legalise much of the squatting. Lighting, water and communal toilets were provided at Balnagask and a rent of eight shillings a week charged.[43] Other emergency measures included the requisitioning of large unused properties for housing the homeless.

Other features of the immediate post-war period were the greater integration of housing development with town planning following the 1947 Town Planning Act,

the beginning of activity by the Scottish Special Housing Association (SSHA) in the city, and the increased use of non-traditional building techniques. The first major municipal scheme to benefit from the marriage of housing and town planning was Kincorth. The design of the estate had been the subject of a competition in 1937, the specification requiring entrants to include schools and other social facilities, industry and an element of private housing. When work began in 1947, the private houses had been deleted and the first dwellings to be constructed were granite council houses. Most of the dwellings built in the early post-war period were semi-detached cottages and terraced houses. Construction continued into the 1960s and Kincorth was to become one of Aberdeen's most popular housing schemes. The SSHA began building rented dwellings, the first developments being at Cummings Park and Garthdee. Both the town council and the SSHA made use of non-traditional building techniques at this time in order to accelerate the building programme, including steel, concrete and timber houses.[44] Non-traditional techniques had been used before 1939, notably for the concrete flats with flat roofs built at Pittodrie in 1928, but the range of techniques and dwellings involved increased significantly after 1945. Concrete houses, such as the Orlit houses at Garthdee, were not a long-term success and many later required extensive modernisation or were declared defective and demolished.

Kincorth Circle in the 1970s, with Kincorth Academy on the left.

The large council estates at Northfield and Mastrick were started and completed in the 1950s and 1960s, and the last major municipal developments were built at Altens, South Sheddocksley and Denmore in the 1970s. Although restrictions on the private sector were lifted in the early 1950s and the pace of private house construction increased, by 1979 half of all the dwellings in Aberdeen were owned by the town council. These included a variety of dwelling types, the proportion of flats increasing with time. By 1980 approximately 60 per cent of the municipal housing stock was flatted, including 11 per cent as multi-storeys and 28 per cent as tenements. The first multi-storey flats were built for the council by Alexander Hall Ltd in Ashgrove in 1960 and this form of construction dominated until the mid-1970s. By the end of the century there were over 50 multi-storey blocks in the city. The social segregation within the public sector stock which had been apparent before the war persisted and increased as the stock grew.

THE REVIVAL OF THE PRIVATE SECTOR

Two factors had a profound influence on housing policy in Aberdeen in the final two decades of the century. A policy change was brought about by the advent of a radical right-wing government in 1979 bent on injecting market forces into housing provision and allocation. The effect of this was to introduce a policy of selling council houses, primarily to sitting tenants. In the last two decades of the twentieth century almost 10,000 of Aberdeen's council houses were sold.[45] The town council was also forced by government to cut back sharply on construction and from 1982 onward more dwellings were being bought by tenants than were being built by the local authority. By the 1990s more than half of the dwellings in Aberdeen were privately owned. The second factor was the impact of the rapid growth of the North Sea oil industry. The latter attracted highly paid inward migrants whose incomes had an immediate effect on house prices and boosted the building of executive dwellings at the top end of the market. Less well-paid

The public and the private. Post-war council housing surrounds 1930s private bungalows in Cairncry Road West, 1982.

incomers faced difficulties in that rented accommodation was in short supply, both in the private and public sectors, and hence they were forced into the owner-occupied sector with its inflated prices. The rise in house prices was particularly strong at both the top and bottom of the market, with one-bedroomed tenement flats fetching prices of £20,000. This also created difficulties for local households attempting to enter the owner-occupied sector for the first time. Demand for housing resulted in rapid suburban expansion, particularly in the Bridge of Don, Altens, Cove and Portlethen areas, and for a time Aberdeen was the most rapidly growing urban area in Britain. Supply was unable to keep pace with demand and real house prices rose rapidly. By the late 1970s Aberdeen had the most expensive house prices in Britain outside London.[46] The new private sector housing was varied in both type and price and catered for a wide range of incomes. This created a variety of neighbourhood types in the expanding suburbs and increased the complexity of social segregation in the city.

The housebuilders responded to these market pressures within the constraints of the planning system and land availability to create a further differentiation within Aberdeen, based on price and market segmentation, which added to the social segregation which could already be observed in the public sector. New executive dwellings, for example, were built by preference in the more fashionable western parts of the city, such as Cults, Bieldside and Peterculter, but available sites were in short supply. The shortage of sites and the scale of inward migration, however, forced housebuilders to look further afield, and a feature of the 1980s and 1990s was the construction of dwellings outside Aberdeen but within the wider commuting area. This affected neighbouring settlements such as Banchory, Ellon and Stonehaven which, although physically separate from Aberdeen, were functionally a part of the city.

12

Education

SYDNEY WOOD

SCHOOLS IN THE NINETEENTH CENTURY

Pre-eminent among Aberdeen's educational provision in 1800 was the town's Grammar School. It stood in Schoolhill where its single-storey 1757 structure, fronted by a tiny playground, contained four classrooms crammed with around 200 pupils.[1] From their raised desks the masters directed their pupils' endless labours on Latin, for the Grammar School focused on entry to Marischal College. The abilities in mathematics and English of the 9 to 12 year olds who entered the school had to be developed by private tuition or voluntary attendance at the English School and the Mathematics School. Revenues from charitable donations as well as fees of around 50p per quarter sustained the school. Boys spent five hours a day on their studies, remaining for three years with an assistant master before moving on to face the formidable gowned figure of the rector.

Melvin himself summarised teaching at the Grammar School as 'construing, parsing, exercises and composition with full examinations and explanations' and

James Melvin 1794–1853

Born in Aberdeen to poor parents, James Melvin studied at the Grammar School and Marischal College. He started teaching at a private academy at Udny before moving to Old Aberdeen Grammar School. He became assistant master at the Grammar School in 1822 and rector in 1826. He was an outstanding Latin scholar, known to his pupils as 'Grim Pluto', and also held an appointment as lecturer in humanity at Marischal College. He was a licensiate of the Church of Scotland and did not support the Disruption. He was a bachelor who lived with his mother and sisters in Belmont Street close to the school. He was awarded an LL.D by Marischal College but was passed over for the chair of classics. The disappointment was reputed to have hastened his early death. He is commemorated by Melvin House at the Grammar School.

James Melvin, rector of Aberdeen Grammar School 1826-53 : 'Grim Pluto' to his charges

his system of control as 'reproof, disgrace, extra employment and corporal punishment'.[2] By the 1830s the school was being criticised for the narrowness of its curriculum and its tedious teaching methods. A town council committee wondered whether 'repeating by rote ... the rudiments and Grammar of a dead language be not establishing one of the worst habits of the human mind – that of reading without comprehension'.[3] Change crept into the curriculum slowly, with geography, French, Greek, English, mathematics and history being offered by the 1850s. But the school was still primarily driven by the requirements of the university bursary examination and had changed less than other burgh schools in Scotland. By 1866 the roll had grown to 308 of whom over one-third were the sons of merchants, traders, farmers and shopkeepers and nearly one-third came from professional families. Of the remainder, nine were from the landowning class, 47 from families with small businesses, farms or shops, and 51 were identified as from the labouring class.[4] An official inquiry in 1868 compared the work of the highest class with that required of Edinburgh High School pupils and found that Aberdeen pupils were far less widely read in classical works and that 'non classical subjects ... are sacrificed to the classical'.[5] Teachers of English, mathematics and modern languages all grumbled to the commissioners of the impossibility of expecting pupils to work hard at subjects that were optional, and suggested that the application of strict discipline and high expectations resulted in pupils abandoning their subjects. The commissioners found the boys' behaviour, especially to strangers and foreigners, to be ruder and more boorish than at other similar schools. Masters struggled to manage classes of around 60 pupils. The huge range of ability in classes posed especial problems notably 'a number of ignorant boys who are a drag upon the class ... and keep down the general standard of the attainment in the school'.[6] Prominent among this group were pupils who were there as a result of privately-funded bursaries. The Grammar School provided a curriculum that was narrow at a price that most Aberdonians could not afford. But in 1863 it did move to much superior premises, which form the core of its modern site, and which were able to accommodate a far greater number of pupils.

The two schools that filled the gaps in the Grammar School's curriculum both occupied accommodation that was far too cramped to properly house the pupils wishing to attend, but which had the merit of being maintained by the city. The

English School, in Drum's Lane until 1841 thereafter in Little Belmont Street in much improved premises, offered teaching in reading, spelling, grammar, recitation and composition whilst 'two pitiful apartments' in Correction Wynd housed the Commercial, Mathematics and Writing School.[7] By the 1850s well over 200 pupils attended the latter and over 170 the former. Nearly half of them were pupils from the Grammar School, which hampered the capacity of the teachers to plan systematic work; this, together with the inadequate accommodation, was a regular source of complaint. Visitors to the schools were usually impressed by the teachers' efforts, and by their competence in teaching, by firstly providing an exposition then requiring pupils to use their slates to show their understanding.[8]

Whereas the Grammar School's curriculum was shaped by the bursary requirements, Robert Gordon's Hospital provided its 130 to 150 pupils with an education aimed at employment. George Melvin, brother of James, who was head of the Hospital from 1832 to 1841 summarised it as including 'English, reading, grammar and composition; writing, arithmetic, book-keeping, geography, mathematics, natural philosophy, music, drawing, French, Latin'.[9] The main intention of this education was to fulfil the founder's wishes to see the grandsons and sons of decayed merchants and brethren of guild apprenticed to local merchants or tradesmen.[10] Boys who obtained apprenticeships received grants of £10 or £5 according to whether it was a merchant or a tradesman who took responsibility for their five years of training. Former pupils became employed in almost every trade and profession. By 1867, a growing number 'become apprenticed as clerks in respectable offices, large mercantile houses, railways, etc; some become shopkeepers, not a few, though not as many as formerly, become seamen'.[11]

The early-nineteenth-century Hospital housed both staff and pupils. Only in 1842 were the strict rules relaxed that required the staff to be both resident and celibate. The confined circumstances seem to have encouraged tensions. In 1841 quarrels between staff were so serious that the governors dismissed the head, one other master, and the matron. The matron, under attack for her cooking, responded with complaints about staff drinking and swearing.[12] Penned into their buildings, the boys lived a bleak life that began at 6.00 am. Worship began and ended a working day that, did not finish till 8.30 pm, broken only by half an hour of play after breakfast and by meals that consisted of variations on porridge, milk and broth, with occasional bread and butter, potatoes and other vegetables, and beef, washed down with 'small beer'.[13]

CHURCH SCHOOLS

The Grammar School and Gordon's Hospital had nothing to offer to the majority of local children. Yet a survey of schooling carried out by the town council in 1833

ABERDEEN SCHOOL RETURN.

Name of the School or Seminary, *Grammar School.* when begun,

where it is, *in Schoolhill* and in what Parish, *West.*

If superintended by a Clergyman, his name, and designation,

If superintended by a Corporation or Society, its name, *Magistrates, and Clergy, & Professors.*

and the names and designations of the Acting Office-Bearers,

Days of Teaching, *Six days a week*

Hours of Teaching, *from 8 to 9 morning — 10 to 12 forenoon — 3 to 5 afternoon (in winter from 1/2 past 2 to 1/2 past 4 afternoon No afternoon meeting on Wednesday & Saturday; on Saturday we dismiss as soon after 11 as business is completed.)* Certified by *James Melvin, Rector. 5th Decr. 1833.*

TEACHERS' NAMES.	His or her Age.	WHOLE NUMBER OF SCHOLARS AT PRESENT.		Ages of Scholars.	English.	Writing.	Arithmetic.	French, Italian, &c.	Latin.	Greek.	Mathematics.	Drawing.	Music.	Geography.	Elocution.	Sewing.	Dancing.
		Male.	Female.														
1st Class, Robert Forbes*	72	37		From 7¾ to 14					37								
2d Class, James Watt	61	30		9¾ to 13½					30								
3d Class, John Dun	36	63		9½ to 14½					63								
4 Class,		33		11 to 16					33	33							
5 Class, James Melvin	39	26		12 to 19					26	26							
6.		189		to													

State the Fees in this line, if agreeable, *10/6 per quarter.*

. Be pleased to send with this Return, filled up, the last Report on the School, and any other information connected with it ; such as the State of Funds, Mode of Teaching, Description of the Class of Persons Taught, &c. &c.

* *Assisted by Robert Forbes Junr aged 21 years*

Aberdeen Grammar School Return, 1833. Note the age of one of the masters and the size of the 3rd Class.

showed that 4,605 pupils were receiving education, one-quarter of them girls, in 56 different schools.[14] A significant part of this provision came from the efforts of the churches. In 1838 there were 11 schools supported by the Church of Scotland accommodating around 1,300 children. Only three of these schools were, however, of long standing; the rest were less than five years old and marked the response of the ministers and kirk sessions of the six parishes to a sense of an urban educational crisis. This was further stimulated by legislation. From 1833 the various churches in Aberdeen were able to draw upon government funds made available to support school building, especially in working-class areas. From the 1840s there were wider opportunities to tap this source of funding managed by the Privy Council's education committee but dependent on satisfying the newly-established schools inspectorate, which required that pupils were organised into standards, achieved satisfactory levels and were taught by suitable staff. Furthermore, the 1833 Factory Act required children under 13, who were employed in textile mills, to attend school for at least two hours each day. In 1844 this was increased to two and a half hours in winter and three in summer, and a number of factories provided schools. At Stoneywood one of the proprietors undertook the teaching himself.[15] Gordon's mill employed a woman to teach the 3Rs (reading, writing and arithmetic) to around seventy boys and girls under the general supervision of the mill manager.[16] A match-factory owner, John Marshall, suggested that only a shift system with two sets of children would allow his young workers adequate education and recreation but that 'would diminish their earnings very much and increase the trouble of accounts and management'.[17] Otherwise parents had to turn to private, profit-making 'adventure' schools or perhaps to one of 50 dame's schools (wifie's squeels) of variable quality which proliferated. Often the needs of poorer families for income ran counter to attempts to educate working children. As a committee of well-meaning Aberdonians noted 'there are many parents in the parish who have no desire for having their children educated'.[18]

It was no accident that the expansion of school provision came after the 1833 Factory Act placed limitations on the employment of children in textile mills. The early-nineteenth-century textile mills in the Aberdeen area employed well over 1,000 children under eighteen years of age, two-thirds of whom were girls, and of whom one in ten could not read.[19] A census taken at the Grandholm linen mills in 1833 found that only 28 per cent could read and write, that 45 per cent could read only and that 27 per cent were illiterate.[20] In evidence to the Sadler Committee, an indefatigable campaigner for better education provision, the Rev. Abercromby Gordon, voiced the belief that no worthwhile educational provision for children would be possible until their hours of work were much reduced from the 14 per day that even children under ten years old were currently working. The arguments offered by Gordon focused especially on moral issues, on the language and behaviour of young people, especially young women. Evidence gathered from teachers, however, supported the views that factory children attending school after a day's work were 'stupified with bodily exhaustion and the noise ... the children sometimes fall asleep, even the grown-up girls are wearied ... too tired to pay attention'.[21]

The newly-established church-supported sessional schools in the 1830s benefited from the recently introduced state grants for new school building, yet suffered the consequences of the poverty of the people they served. The curriculum they offered focused on religious instruction and the 3Rs, a narrower diet than that offered at older-established parish schools in Footdee, Oldmachar and St Nicholas. Session school teachers were not provided with houses and struggled to survive on school fees from parents who could ill afford them; only three were guaranteed an annual salary of £10 whereas the St Nicholas teacher received £22. The work undertaken in Bon-Accord parish illustrates what this effort by the churches to reach poorer families involved. The aim of the churches was to help destitute parents in the crowded area of Lower Denburn, College Street and Windmill Brae where many well-intentioned parents could not find schooling they could afford. With a government grant of £250, a further £50 from a charitable fund and subscriptions from well-to-do parishioners a school was built on the south side of Marywell Street that left the committee, chosen by a meeting of parishioners and church members, with a £70 debt to clear and, consequently, with a need to fix fees at two pence a week, a figure beyond many parents.

Other churches supported schools too. In 1825 a school in Flourmill Lane to serve episcopal congregations was made possible by funding from a benefactor. By 1837 it served 50 day pupils and over 140 Sunday pupils. By 1872, 340 day pupils studied in episcopal schools.[22] Roman Catholic parents were offered places for their children in separate schools for boys and girls that opened in 1832. By 1837 they were offering teaching for both 70 boys and girls as day pupils but over 300 children on Sundays. The Roman Catholic schools did not charge regular fees, while the episcopal school found it necessary to exact them on a quarterly basis. It was, however, the Disruption that produced the biggest ecclesiastical effort at educational provision beyond the Church of Scotland's influence. Newly-established Free Churches moved rapidly to set up schools of their own so that just three years after the church split, over half of the fifteen Free Churches in Aberdeen had opened schools for day pupils and were busy establishing Sunday schools and making efforts to reach the poorer sectors of society.

CHARITY SCHOOLS

Most schools that catered for poorer pupils charged a weekly fee and needed further financial support to make them viable. The Aberdeen Infant School asked for two pence a week, often had to make do with a penny, and relied on gifts and subscriptions from the charitable. Similar establishments included a charity school in the Shiprow funded by a merchant, James Thain, and a school in Footdee funded by a £1,000 endowment left by John Davidson, a goldsmith saved from drowning by two Footdee fishermen, to provide schooling for the children of fisherfolk too poor to afford fees. In 1864 Ross's School in Holburn Street opened funded by £7,000 left by James Ross, a successful upholsterer who practised in Upperkirkgate and who was moved by the mean and laborious lives of workers in the Holburn Street area.

Those keen to see large numbers of children being educated at very low cost looked to the ideas of two reformers of the time who argued that by training a small core of pupil monitors able to transmit their knowledge to small groups of other pupils, teachers could handle huge classes of slate-using pupils. Dr Andrew Bell, an Anglican clergyman of Scottish origin who spent much of his life in India, not only developed a highly disciplined form of the monitorial system, whereby older pupils transmitted learning to younger pupils, but also endowed schools in Scotland, including establishments set up in the mid-1830s and overseen by the town council in Oldmachar and Frederick Street. Although Bell's schools used the monitorial method, it was the rival scheme developed by Joseph Lancaster that tended to be preferred by English nonconformists and Scottish Presbyterians. A lecture that Lancaster gave in 1815 in Aberdeen inspired the setting up of the Aberdeen Educational Society to advance his ideas. A boys' school was opened in Harriet Street, moving in 1821 to the newly laid-out Blackfriars Street. In order to reach working-class children the society needed to raise money that would allow the fees paid by pupils to be kept at a very low level. Money came from a large number of half-guinea subscribers and from bigger donations given by businessmen like John Maberly. In 1824 a collection taken in city churches raised a further £145. In 1828 a girls' school opened in Charlotte Street. By 1839 the society's work was focused on its Charlotte Street building within which there were divisions for boys and girls. In 1845 control of the school passed to the South Free Church.

Industrial Schools

All these efforts still failed to provide education for a section of the city's children. Numbers of them wandered the streets begging, stealing and occasionally being arrested and placed in the house of refuge. In 1839 there were 120 boys and 93 girls under 14 years of age in this institution. Neither the bridewell nor the female penitentiary provided a sufficient deterrent to young vagrants and delinquents. In 1841, it was estimated that there were about 280 of them living from begging and theft, over a quarter of whom had been in prison in the previous year.[23]

Charitable funding underpinned an effort in 1840 based on offering children of the poorest families tickets entitling them to free education for three months, to be renewed provided their attendance and progress were satisfactory. Sheriff William Watson led the search for a way to tackle poor children's education and training by providing 'what they stood most in need of, three wholesome meals during the day'.[24] Voluntary subscriptions enabled Watson to hire a room and pay for three meals, of porridge, broth, bread and potatoes, a day from the house of refuge kitchens. These meals were given to children who accepted the discipline of four hours of lessons and five hours of work in a day, the products of their labours being sold to help defray costs. An initial small group of boys was assembled by the police and the number edged up to about fifty. Data for 1844 showed that 8 to 11 year olds attended most regularly, but by the age of 13 years the attendance rate had fallen sharply. Of the 69 boys and 64 girls in the 1844 sample most were children cared for only by mothers or were orphans. In 1845 the revival of an old Police Act enabled the police to arrest juvenile beggars and to force them to attend school if they wanted to get food from the soup kitchen.

Sheriff William Watson 1796–1878

Son of a Lanarkshire sheep farmer, William Watson was educated in Edinburgh at the High School and University. After graduation he was apprenticed to Andrew Storie, Clerk to the Signet for four years and subsequently secured a commission as Writer to the Signet. He remained in Storie's office as principal clerk until 1829 when he was appointed Sheriff-Substitute for Aberdeenshire. He was responsible for the first industrial school, established in Chronicle Lane in 1841, and encouraged the foundation of an equivalent school for girls which opened in 1843 in Long Acre. He opened a school in Skene Street in 1845 funded by subscriptions worth £700. His efforts pre-dated those of the Rev. Thomas Guthrie in Edinburgh. Watson sought to encourage the foundation of industrial schools elsewhere and addressed public meetings throughout the United Kingdom on the subject. He was an enthusiastic supporter of the Volunteers and convened the meeting in 1859 which revived the movement in Aberdeen.

Attendance at Watson's schools had risen to 474 by 1875 with a child's asylum committee overseeing operations and a general sense of pride in falling crime levels and the success in securing employment which many former pupils enjoyed. The voluntary funding that sustained the industrial schools included money raised by a meeting of working-class people pleased that their own children were no longer being led astray.[25] For children still unwilling to conform the reformatory school movement emerged, and, in 1857, opened a school at Oldmill. Charitable effort established two 'schools of industry' for girls in the early nineteenth century and a boys' hospital that in 1829 moved from the Gallowgate to Upperkirkgate. In 1828 a girls' hospital too was set up and, by 1871, the two institutions had moved to a single building in King Street. All these enterprises sought to provide not only basic teaching, instruction in morals and religious education, but also some practical skills useful for working-class employment. Girls learned sewing, knitting, clothes repair, washing and ironing, food preparation, cooking and cleaning. The aim was to train them to be capable domestic servants though in fact many girls were, a schools inspector noted, 'tempted to go to mills and manufactories'.[26]

Church and charitable efforts were aimed at poorer children. For the better off a range of 'adventure' schools existed. They were run for profit and many offered an education thought appropriate to the needs of young women. The Rev. Abercromby Gordon dismissed adventure schools as 'established by individuals on whatever plan and in whatever place they choose' and as being quite unaffordable to many families.[27] The origins of both St Margaret's and Albyn School are to be found in such projects. In 1867 Harriet Warrack began offering girls pianoforte and singing, modern languages, English and Latin at the school which eventually became Albyn.[28] St Margaret's grew out of the classes begun in her father's drawing room at 13 Union Row given by Miss Stephen. Young women were provided with teaching in music, French and German and singing as well as the 3Rs. In 1887 the formidable Duncan sisters, Jean and Isabella, took over and developed the school moving it first to Union Grove House and then, in 1900, to Albyn Place.[29] Most adventure schools were run by just one teacher, though Ledingham's Academy had two. Some stressed particular subjects. Clark's writing school in Rhind Court, for example, drew attention to its instruction in plain and ornamental writing, while Miss Clark's Gallowgate school emphasised the teaching of needlework. All encouraged the use of what J. M. Bulloch called 'Albyn Place English'.

THE SCHOOL BOARD

The Education (Scotland) Act of 1872 created local school boards, each responsible for ensuring that all five to thirteen year olds received an education in reading, writing and arithmetic. The boards operated under the supervision of the Scotch Education Department (SED), re-named 'Scottish' in 1918, whose initial concern was to see Scotland provided with a sufficient number of school places so that attendance at school could be required of pupils, and that within these buildings its approved curriculum would be delivered by appropriately trained teachers. Aberdeen schools, like those elsewhere, had to follow SED requirements if they wished to satisfy its inspectors and thus receive grants. Schooling in Aberdeen was, henceforward, increasingly determined by national policy.

Throughout Scotland school boards were elected in 1873 by adult voters owning or occupying property to an annual value of £4. Women who met the criteria were entitled to vote and candidates too could be male or female. When elections were held in March to choose the thirteen members of the Aberdeen school board, no woman stood and two-thirds of qualified women did not exercise their right to vote. Male candidates were labelled according to their religious affiliation. The successful included six from the Free Churches, five from the Church of Scotland, and representative Episcopalian and Roman Catholic Ministers. A total of five clergy were elected, as were two professors. Board members chose the Rev. Dr Pirie, soon to become University Principal, as chairman and appointed two officials. A former policeman became attendance officer and a former GNSR employee served as clerk and treasurer. The board occupied offices in King Street, moving to Union Terrace in 1898.[30] A survey undertaken by Professor Black established that the city contained 31 schools receiving government inspection, 27 private schools aimed at the more prosperous families, and 52 elementary schools not subject to inspection. Of the 13,904 children in Aberdeen the school board excluded from its area of responsibility Roman Catholic and Episcopalian children who were accommodated in their own church schools. It decided that it was directly responsible for 10,306 children, and was 2,500 places short of being able to provide for all of them.[31] Five new schools were urgently needed in the heavily populated areas of the Upper Denburn, Causewayend, Upperkirkgate, Dee Village and Virginia Street.

The Grammar School also became the responsibility of the school board. It was not permitted, however, in the early years to draw on the income from the parliamentary grant which was intended only for elementary education. Instead, a local rate, initially set at two pence and collected by the parochial board, was levied to sustain teaching at the Grammar School. The school board also took control of a number of existing church schools, initially those in poorer areas like Marywell Street and St Clement's, and began a building programme that, by 1877, had led to the construction of Commerce Street, Skene Street, Causewayend, Ferryhill and Gallowgate (Middle) Schools. Five years later it had also taken over sessional schools in Albion Street and St Paul Street, plus four Free Church and three endowed schools. None of these buildings offered a satisfactory level of accommodation. They lacked teachers' rooms, cloakrooms and playgrounds while their classrooms were vast areas housing four or five classes. Between 1887 and 1891 an additional 3,415 school places were created, often through expanding provision in hard-pressed areas like Skene Square but also through building new schools such as Rosemount (1887) and Ashley Road (1888). From 1891 yet more extensions were required as well as new schools like Victoria Road, Walker Road, and Sunnybank (1906), which was the most advanced school of its era and even generated its own electricity. Dr Bell's school in Frederick Street had to be completely replaced with

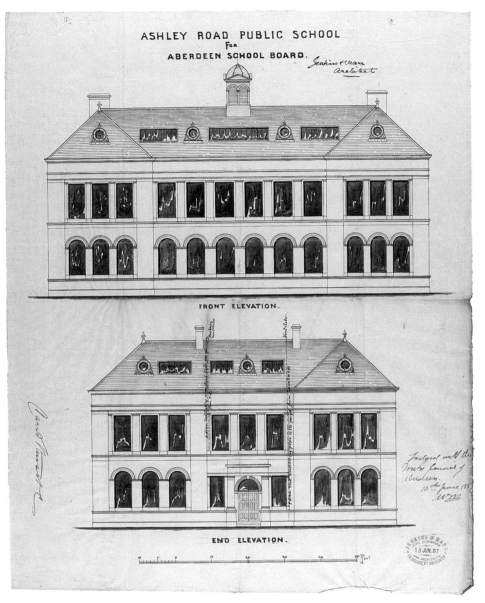

ASHLEY ROAD PUBLIC SCHOOL
For
ABERDEEN SCHOOL BOARD.

FRONT ELEVATION.

END ELEVATION.

The school board embarked on an extensive expansion of school provision in the late 1880s. Ashley Road school was opened in 1888.

a new building (1905) where the desire to offer play space in a crowded built-up working-class area led to the creation of a rooftop playground. By the 1900s it was expected that schools should have specialised provision for physical exercise, science and practical work.

By 1913 the school board not only controlled 23 elementary schools, it also managed three schools with claims to be offering a higher level of education. As well as the Grammar School, the board turned the English School in Little Belmont

Street into a higher-class school for girls in 1881. In 1891 Mrs Emslie's Orphan Asylum in Albyn Place was purchased and in 1893 a new High School for Girls, which soon had 600 pupils, opened on the site. The third higher-class school, the Central, was also constructed complete with a rooftop playground. It opened in 1894 and, unusually for the time, had no elementary pupils. It was not a full secondary school but took in 12 to 15 year olds and offered education above elementary level including practical work in science, art, cookery, shorthand and typing, and book-keeping as well as the usual academic subjects. This expansion of higher-grade schooling came in response to local pressure and, especially after 1885, from the increased readiness of the SED to fund secondary schooling as part of its policy of developing a system with two distinct and separate strands, namely elementary and secondary schooling.

The 1872 legislation also gave school boards the power to decide if adventure schools were efficient and to prosecute parents using unacceptable schools. The number of pupils in dame's schools and adventure schools fell from 1,805 in 1873 to 550 in 1883. The abolition of school fees for elementary schooling (1890), thanks largely to the efforts of William Hunter MP, was a further blow to some, while the building of a school like Ashley Road damaged the fortunes of those offering places in more prosperous areas. By 1898 only six private schools survived providing schooling for a mere 163 children.[32] Even when fees were ended, Ashley Road retained them as, for a brief period, did Rosemount and Ferryhill, using the regulation that permitted the imposition of fees if free places were available elsewhere and thereby reinforcing the school's middle-class character. This expansion of state-supported and rate-supported schooling inevitably required increasingly heavy borrowing and pushed up the charge on the local community. Aberdeen's school rate of two shillings, in 1913, was the highest among the Scottish cities and was attributed to its providing schooling for 94 per cent of its children. By 1913 the school board's 810 teachers were predominantly women although it was men who occupied school headships and served as second and third masters.

As school places increased, so the school board was able to begin to enforce school attendance more vigorously. In 1875 absenteeism amounted to one-quarter of the total potential attendances; by 1913 the figure had fallen to 8 per cent. Poverty accounted for many of the absentees. In 1886 a fall in attendance of about 1,000 pupils was attributed to serious unemployment caused by an exceptionally severe winter.[33] Destitution affecting school attendance could also be the consequence of irregular employment, the presence of only one parent, and the excessive consumption of alcohol.[34] The poverty of many families meant that children's earnings were important. It was possible for pupils of 10 to 13 to work in local factories and workshops for half the day and attend school for the rest of the day. Initially the school board sought to ensure that only those engaged in appropriate work were half-timers. In the late 1870s there were well over 500 half-timers, principally at Porthill (293) and Albion Street (141). Broadford, Bannermill, two rope works and two comb works all continued to employ children, but by 1899 the total had dropped below 100.[35] By 1900 the school board was waging war on the very concept, seeking to persuade employers that they should not employ children until they were over 13 years old. Support for poor children came from the Aberdeen Educational Trust which was formed from ten different charitable trusts in 1882. Its funds supplied meals for the destitute and provided clothes, books and stationery. It helped to pay fees including bursaries at the Grammar School and for evening classes.[36] The Trust ran the former boys' and girls' poor hospital on King Street where, by 1892, it provided three meals a day for over 400 children and basic education, including cooking and housework for girls, who were orphans or the offspring of very poor working mothers.

The Extension of Secondary Education

In the 1880s educational change focused on the reform of endowed establishments like Robert Gordon's Hospital. The Balfour Commission laid out a national framework that was taken up by endowed schools throughout the country. In 1881 Robert Gordon's changed its title from hospital to college, boarded out its formerly resident pupils, and transformed itself into a higher-grade day school sustaining a full range of academic subjects and offering very effective competition to the Grammar School.[37] Enrolment regulations were changed to let in boys from families living outside the city while open competitive bursaries allowed boys from poorer backgrounds to join the fee-paying pupils.[38] Whereas the number in the school before 1881 never exceeded 200, by 1886 there were 800 pupils, 120 of whom were foundationers whose fees came from bursaries. The school board viewed this development of a rival to the Grammar School with mixed feelings and managed to force a reduction in fees to make it very clear that the College was intended to serve a lower social class than the Grammar School.

The administration of education was reshaped by national legislation in 1918 that swept away the school boards, replacing them with directly elected education authorities chosen by a system of proportional representation. From April 1919 until its final meeting in May 1930, city schools were overseen by the triennially-elected Aberdeen Education Authority. The 1918 Act asserted the principle of free secondary education but failed to turn it into a reality for all. However, this phase of increasing education witnessed improvements in the provision of secondary education. In Aberdeen the Grammar School, the High School and, from 1921, the Central School in Belmont Street, where secondary provision was based, offered five-year courses. The education authority developed certain schools as centres for

Robert Gordon's College, c. 1900 with old school in the background and a statue of Gordon of Khartoum in the foreground.

intermediate studies providing three-year courses that were more demanding than those offered in the 'advanced divisions' of elementary schools that now replaced the old supplementary courses. The city was divided into districts, each with its own intermediate centre. In 1922 Ruthrieston shed its elementary pupils to become the first of these, to be followed in 1923 by Rosemount and Frederick Street and then by Middle, Torry, Woodside, Sunnybank, St Margaret's (Episcopal) and St Mary's (Roman Catholic). Housing development in Hilton led in 1931 to the opening of a further intermediate centre. Pupils were selected for intermediate centres through tests and the personal evaluation of headteachers. The director of education in the new authority began his term of office by having to quell a panic among pupils and their parents that the new authority was so obsessed with health matters it was going to shear off the hair of all girl pupils. Angry protests even took the form of smashed school windows.

The authority's responsibilities soon included Roman Catholic and Episcopal elementary schools, for the 1918 Act allowed local authority responsibility for the funding of denominational schools while allowing denominational bodies to insist that staff satisfy their requirements in terms of religious belief and character. Ambitious plans to raise the leaving age to 15 were hit firstly by the inter-war depression and then by the advent of the Second World War. Reform of local government in 1929 transferred educational control from directly elected bodies to local authorities. Aberdeen's educational administration began to assume the shape it was to retain until regionalisation provided a much broader context in the 1970s.

Although the war disrupted schooling it stimulated hope of social reform. The Education (Scotland) Act of 1945 at last brought secondary schooling for all in the form of separate junior (three year) and senior (five year) secondary schools together with the raising of the leaving age to 15, a reform deferred until April 1947 to allow for suitable classroom provision and teacher recruitment. In 1972 the leaving age was raised, once more, to 16. Aberdeen's intermediate schools were the

Practical skills in woodwork in a late-nineteenth-century class.

basis from which the junior secondary schools emerged that were attended by the majority of post-primary pupils. The educational experience of pupils in these schools probably did not greatly differ from that of their predecessors in the intermediate centres. The introduction of 'O' grade certification in 1962, however, offered a challenge to which first Ruthrieston, then other junior secondaries responded. The result was a developing connection between junior and senior secondaries as both offered Scottish Examination Board courses and pupils who did well enough could transfer, at 16, to a senior secondary school in order to study for highers. In 1965, for example, 44 Ruthrieston pupils sat 'O' grade examinations, taking 15 different subjects and achieving 162 passes. Thirteen of these pupils went on to join fifth-year senior secondary classes.[39]

Such opportunities were, inevitably, somewhat restricted while the selection procedures that distinguished junior from senior secondary pupils were increasingly seen as badly flawed. A move to comprehensive provision in the 1960s brought a transformation in the character of the Grammar School, the High School and Aberdeen Academy (the re-named Central School). Not only did all become area comprehensives, but the Academy left its Belmont Street premises for new buildings at Hazlehead and the High and the Grammar became co-educational. The High School became Harlaw Academy, absorbed Ruthrieston into its structure in 1972 and, in 1973, admitted 150 boys. The Grammar changed name briefly, soon abandoning its new title of Rubislaw Academy, to revert to its original name. The school's historic reputation continued to attract parents to send pupils there creating serious problems of overcrowding. The policy of neighbourhood schools meant that new buildings were needed elsewhere, leading to the opening of academies at Kincorth, Linksfield and the Bridge of Don to meet the needs of expansion. This left selective education to the private schools, namely the all-girl establishments of Albyn and St Margaret's, together with Robert Gordon's, which decided to change to a co-educational intake. The one Roman Catholic secondary school, the Convent of the Sacred Heart, closed in 1971. Changes after the 1960s created a network of schools whose differing characters were strongly shaped by the areas which they primarily served. While new schools developed in the expanding sprawl of suburban private housing and council housing, an older school at Hilton suffered a falling role that led to its closure and the transfer of its pupils to join those at Powis Academy to form the new St Machar Academy.

The character of education offered was shaped by national policy guidelines and the requirements of the Scottish Examination Board. One Aberdeen school in particular was the focus of an attempt to develop a less authoritarian approach, an attempt that split the school concerned. In 1968 Robert F. Mackenzie was

Exciting new design at Charleston Primary School, built by Stewart Milne Construction, 1998-99. (Photograph by Daniel Stewart)

appointed to the headship of Summerhill Academy, built a few years earlier to serve a new housing scheme. Mackenzie's work at Braehead School in Fife, his writings and speeches, identified him as highly critical of traditional forms of discipline, especially corporal punishment, of the effect of SED courses on learning and teaching, and of the authoritarian ethos commonly found in Scottish schools. The impact of his policies stirred sufficient concern among some of his staff to lead over half of them to draw up a petition defining pupil behaviour they saw as unacceptable and asking for the imposition of firmer discipline. After meetings involving staff, some parents and the education committee, Mackenzie was suspended in 1974 and remained in this situation until retiral age. He vigorously defended his policies, supported by some of the staff. The school roll began to fall, and in 1990 Summerhill Academy was closed. By then one of Mackenzie's key beliefs, that corporal punishment should be abolished, had become a general policy throughout Scotland.

TEACHER TRAINING

The development of the educational system necessarily required more and better trained teachers. In the early nineteenth century, parochial schoolmasters began to teach without any prior training. Although the setting up of an Aberdeen 'normal school' to train teachers was actively considered in the later 1830s, nothing was done at that time. Aberdeen teachers seeking training had to go to Edinburgh or Glasgow to normal schools overseen by the Church of Scotland's education committee. In 1846 the pupil-teacher system introduced in England was applied to Scotland too. By 1864, for example, Dr John Brown's school on Skene Square, was run by a master, a female assistant, and four pupil teachers (pupils who did some teaching as part of training for later entry into the profession).

In 1874 the Church of Scotland opened a new normal school for teacher training in Aberdeen. Initially just 30 young women enrolled under the tutelage of the first principal, James Ogilvie, who provided all their lectures in the various subjects of the school curriculum other than music, drawing, sewing and French.[40] In the following year the free churches followed suit, opening a normal school of their own. Students observed lessons by teachers and were themselves watched as they too attempted to teach. They worked in local primary schools, moving from one class to another after a month, as part of their two-year course. Neither school impressed visiting inspectors who found them poorly organised, ill-lit and unimpressively furnished. Reform turned these establishments into a single 'demonstration school' in 1909 led by Alexander Bremner, who adopted a more adventurous approach with fieldwork trips to Hazlehead and the Bridge of Don.

Teacher training in Aberdeen greatly benefited from the construction of hostels at Hilton in 1927-28, and from the concentration of study in a new building on St Andrew's Street, where the college remained until it moved to Hilton in the 1960s. From 1920 to 1958 the development of the teacher training college was overseen by a committee representing the interests of educational authorities in the north of Scotland. Thereafter a governing body, responsible to the SED took charge. The last two decades of the century saw the college facing considerable difficulties. An enforced merger with Dundee College of Education created the Northern College with all the problems and costs consequent on operating from two sites 70 miles apart. The college was required to enter the world of the research assessment exercise, fighting for funds in competition with much larger organisations, and trying to retain independence while other teacher training centres in Scotland merged with nearby universities. By 1998 the college was struggling to remain viable and entered into negotiations with universities in Aberdeen and Dundee with a view to each merging with its local component of the Northern College.

FURTHER EDUCATION

Improved education and technical training constitute a necessary response to the increasingly complex and specialised character of industrial society. In January 1824 Aberdeen emulated Glasgow by opening a mechanics' institute 'to afford to tradesmen, at a cheap rate, out of their own subscriptions, opportunities of instruction by means of books, lectures and models in the various sciences connected with the exercise of their calling'.[41] With over £100 donated by local businessmen and a further £247 in fees and subscriptions, the Mechanics' Institute was able to establish a library of 500 books and a lecture theatre where, beginning with chemistry and natural philosophy, it aimed to achieve 'the diffusion of useful scientific knowledge among the working-classes'.[42] By 1830, although the library stock had more than doubled and continued to be used by subscribers, the lectures had lapsed. In 1835 the reorganised Mechanics' Institute began to offer inexpensive classes in a wide range of subjects including French, geography, drawing, mathematics and English as well as science. It also began what proved to be highly popular 'mutual instruction' classes where members read and discussed papers on topics other than controversial theological and political issues. By 1856 courses began to offer training for jobs in the shipbuilding and engineering industries. Shipowners, who were suspicious of the Mechanics' Institute, backed the separate establishment of a school of navigation in 1859 under the control of the local marine board.[43] Helped by the growing number of skilled and clerical workers, the Mechanics' Institute flourished and its library grew to hold nearly 10,000 books with over 300 subscribers ready to find its annual five shilling fee. About a quarter of the membership in the 1860s were under 20 years old and one in six were women. Alexander Bain, later a professor at Aberdeen University, attended classes, used the library, spoke at mutual instruction classes and paid tribute to the Mechanics' Institute's value to his career. The library proved an excellent basis on which the city's free public library could build. In 1885 the Mechanics' Institute handed over its stock of books to the new public library and its Market Street premises to the town council.

The Act of 1872 handed the task of providing further education for those who had left school at the earliest opportunity to school boards. Within a year of beginning its work the school board had established evening classes offering reading, writing, grammar, arithmetic, history, geography and sewing, and attracting over 700 students. Further subjects were added as these 'continuation classes' developed a role ranging from remedial education for those who had achieved little at school, to trade and technical education and even to classes with a recreational purpose. By the end of the century well over 3,000 students were studying at one of the 13 centres that were open in the evening.[44] The SED took a growing interest in this activity, and legislation enacted in 1908 allowed local authorities to make attendance at continuation classes compulsory up to the age of 17 should they deem it appropriate for certain categories of pupil. Aberdeen required attendance at evening classes up to the age of 16 for children exempted from attending school until they were 14, making such exemption conditional on employers giving their young workers reduced working hours, a policy that sharply diminished the desire of employers to give any work to those under 14. In total, the number of Aberdonians attending evening classes reached 6,000 by 1913.[45]

Further education also benefited from philanthropy. John Gray was the son a Buchan millwright who became head of McKinnon & Co., ironfounders in Spring Garden. He was convinced of the importance of practical and technical education, became a director of the Mechanics' Institute in 1859 and, in 1883, was the benefactor who funded the establishment of the School of Art and Science. Thus, in 1885, art teaching transferred from the former Mechanics' Institute to John Gray's new buildings next to the recently constructed Art Gallery. A third component of the developing Robert Gordon's complex grew from the support of the Aberdeen Endowment Trust for a school of domestic economy in King Street. In 1910, Robert Gordon's Technical College took form as a central institution funded by a block grant, administered by independent governors and organised into three schools providing respectively engineering and chemistry, arts and crafts, and domestic science; 380 daytime and 456 evening students attended its courses.

The First World War inevitably affected attendance at continuation classes. At the end of the war, therefore, a big effort was made to attract students through the distribution of leaflets at Pittodrie football stadium, in schools, to employers and through showing advertising slides at the city's 13 cinemas. Attendance rose in the post-war years with 14 to 15 year olds especially in evidence. The Rosemount centre was particularly crowded while the least busy, Ferryhill, was seen as suffering merely because so many children in that area remained at school. Domestic courses, like needlework, cookery and dressmaking, were especially popular at the High School. Working-class women in Torry proved least inclined to attend such courses: only 89 students registered there, less than one-fifth of the number at the High School. However, the education committee's pleasure at the popularity of continuation classes soon soured as attendances slumped, provoking the gloomy observation that 'the general unrest is blamed and the attractions of the street and the picture house seem to make greater appeal than the classes … an attendance of three evenings a week is required of the pupils and the youth of today seem to find this demand rather irksome'.[46] Attendances gradually recovered, helped by the readiness of some employers to pay their employees' fees. By 1931–32 there were 8,439 students attending continuation classes, but the economic depression affected their popularity since 'it is only natural that a suspended apprentice who is beginning to doubt the possibility of ever returning to his trade should begin to lose interest in the technical classes … It is equally reasonable to expect the student of a Domestic Class whose material is exhausted and who if financially unable to obtain further supplies should cease to have the same interest.'[47] Changing social and economic conditions can be seen in the appearance of classes in motor engineering, in the termination of classes for the boot and shoe trade, and in the disappearance of apprentices from tailoring classes. In the mid-1930s purely recreational classes expanded, including gymnastics, dancing, community singing and whist drives, a development felt to be a 'useful social service particularly in the poorer districts of the city where recreational facilities are more limited'.[48] From these developments emerged the modern mixture with academic, practical and leisure pursuits on offer in a wide range of centres and the organised development of post-school education leading to a whole range of qualifications focused on Aberdeen College, and building on post-war developments like the establishment of Aberdeen Technical College in 1964 with its practical courses in subjects like hairdressing, meat processing, radio and television repairs.

Robert Gordon's Technical College had a range of academic and practical courses which grew during the century, and included the establishment of one of the earliest school's of architecture to be recognised by the Royal Institute of British Architects. The expansion of the college placed pressure on accommodation and led to the construction of new buildings that were opened in 1932. The effect of the depression was to bring about a fall in the number of students from 2,094 in 1930 to about 1,700 in the course of the decade, while the Second World War further aggravated problems of recruitment. Educational legislation in the latter stages of the war, however, required local authorities to provide adequate further education facilities. A post-war programme for day-release students was adopted and a students' union was established. The growth in numbers created further accommodation problems that were partly addressed by Scott Sutherland's decision to convey Garthdee House and estate to Robert Gordon's College and to carry out all the planning, redesign and supervision at cost. In May 1957 the Scott Sutherland School of Architecture was officially opened, to be joined, ten years later, by a new Gray's School of Art. When Scott Sutherland died in 1963 he left generous donations to the school which bears his name.

Many of the changes in the post-war period were overseen by the principal, Dr Alexander West, including the transfer of domestic science training in 1963 to new buildings on Queen's Road on the site of Kepplestone Farm. Expansion continued under West's successors, including a school of social studies to train social workers in 1968, and a school of librarianship in 1967. The endless search for accommodation led to the acquisition of the College of Education premises in St Andrew's Street in 1968 when the college moved to Hilton although, before long, Robert Gordon's occupied parts of the Hilton site too. Growth and diversification helped the college to secure degree-awarding status in the mid-1960s together with a new name, Robert Gordon's Institute of Technology (RGIT). Robert Gordon's elevation, in 1997, to become Robert Gordon University (RGU) meant that, by the 1990s, Aberdeen once more had two universities. By 1998 RGU was able to expand on the site at Garthdee, and work towards developing it as a single location for all its activities.

HIGHER EDUCATION

Aberdeen's two universities at King's College and Marischal College had existed in an uneasy relationship since the founding of the latter in 1593. Marischal College was regarded as the more modern, town college, while King's still had not entirely thrown off its Jacobite past. Attempts to unite the colleges in the 1830s had been met with bitter resistance from both institutions, and the eventual merger in 1860 was forced by external circumstances. In the 1830s Marischal College's old buildings had been demolished and replaced by a new building designed by Archibald Simpson which eventually opened in 1844. The re-building at King's had to wait for the unification of the colleges. New lecture rooms and a new library at King's soon followed. University courses changed too, moving away from their narrowly limited character, allowing students to choose from a range of courses for the three-year ordinary degree or from specialist studies like classics, history, English or modern languages for the separately taught honours degree.

One other change brought about by the fusion between Marischal and King's was less predictable. The legislation which brought about the fusion made explicit that it would be neither expedient nor financially feasible to maintain two professors in each discipline under the new regime. There was thus a surplus of professors. In the majority of cases, the senior man retired, but there was one notable exception. David Thomson, the professor of natural philosophy at King's, retained his post, rather ironically since he was known to be the author of an anonymous and scurrilous attack on the fitness of Marischal College to university status some years earlier. This meant that the professor of natural philosophy at Marischal College, James Clerk Maxwell who was still under 30, was pensioned off, even though he had married the daughter of the principal of Marischal College. He did not, however, sink into complete obscurity being subsequently appointed as professor of experimental physics at Cambridge University and achieving recognition, in due course, as a pioneer of the study of electricity and one of the greatest of British scientists.

By the 1890s the re-building programme had shifted back to Marischal College, where the new science faculty, created in 1892, was located. Applied science courses in agriculture and forestry became available by 1895 and, in 1904, the Aberdeen and North of Scotland College of Agriculture was founded.[49] The casual approach to studies that had characterised student behaviour for much of the nineteenth century began to decline. In the 1860s and 1870s no less than 53 per cent of students failed to graduate, but by the 1890s a course of at least three years before graduation was taken by most students. Degree examinations had become serious exercises in the assessment of knowledge and understanding, in contrast to examinations at the beginning of the century which had consisted of no more than oral tests of information dictated a week earlier.

During the half century after 1918 the University of Aberdeen remained a small institution of about 1,000 students. Until the 1960s, and the opening of the first mixed hall of residence in the country, Crombie Hall, all students lived at home or in lodgings. In the 1960s a period of rapid growth began that had increased the student population by almost tenfold by the late 1990s and necessitated a vigorous construction programme of halls of residence and flats to provide sufficient accommodation. The balance between male and female students changed too, with an approximate equality being achieved by the 1990s. In terms of appointing women to the University's staff, however, Aberdeen tended to lag behind other institutions with, in 1939, only one female lecturer in post in her own right and no female professor until 1964. Although Aberdeen's student population remained strongly rooted in the North-East, increasingly after 1950 students were attracted from more distant parts of the United Kingdom and from overseas. By the end of the century this trend had brought substantial numbers of European and North

*Old Marischal
College Quad.*

American students to join the increasing number from other parts of Scotland and the rest of the United Kingdom.

The movement of departments away from the constricted space of Marischal College had already begun in the inter-war years with the opening of a medical school in 1938 on the Foresterhill site so that it could be close to the Royal

The Faculty of Management and Design library of Robert Gordon University, Garthdee, design by Sir Norman Foster & Partners, 1998.

Infirmary. The trend to relocation continued after 1945, as the sciences moved to new buildings at King's College in Old Aberdeen. The financial cuts that were imposed on the University after 1981 accentuated and accelerated this policy so that, by 1996, the Marischal College site had been almost abandoned and other uses were being sought for its splendid granite buildings. The impact of cuts showed how dependent the University had become on massive state funding that had been the major source of its post-war growth. The cuts caused the closure of courses, the merging of departments, and the loss of a considerable number of staff through early retirement or transfer to other universities. The new regime brought an increasing emphasis on research since success in this activity had become a key element in determining funding and status. In 1945 a mere 27 postgraduate students had engaged in further study and research. By 1994 there were 1,625 postgraduates in residence. The University converted its old library at King's College into a visitor centre in 1991, sought to attract conferences, and joined the heritage industry with a shop selling memorabilia to tourists.

The increasing importance of research excellence in securing funding which became clear in the 1980s was an apt reminder to the University that it had a history of scholastic distinction. Professor Frederick Soddy for chemistry and Sir George Paget Thomson for physics, both Nobel laureates, spent part of their careers at Aberdeen, as did J. J. R. Macleod who was awarded the Nobel Prize for his work in medicine. Research activity was not confined to Aberdeen University. The Marine Research Institute at Torry, the Rowett Research Institute established at Bucksburn in 1922 to study nutrition, and the Macaulay Institute established in 1930 at Craigiebuckler to work on soil research all achieved substantial international recognition.

Lord Boyd Orr 1880–1971

Born at Kilmaurs, Ayrshire, John Boyd Orr was educated at Kilmarnock Academy and Glasgow University. He trained as a teacher and taught for four years before returning to the University to study medicine, qualifying in 1914. He was appointed first director of the Institute of Nutrition established by Aberdeen University and the North of Scotland School of Agriculture. In the Great War he served in the Royal Army Medical Corps and the Sherwood Foresters. He was awarded the Military Cross (with bar) for his service at the Battle of the Somme, and later was awarded the Distinguished Service Order. After the War he persuaded John Quiller Rowett to provide the funds to establish the Rowett Institute to study nutrition and diet. The institute opened in 1923 under his directorship. He was elected fellow of the Royal Society in 1932 and was knighted in 1935. He served as professor of agriculture at Aberdeen University 1942–45, as independent MP for the Scottish Universities 1945–46, and as first director of the United Nations Food and Agriculture Organisation 1945–48. He became rector and then chancellor of Glasgow University. In 1949 he became a baronet, was awarded the Nobel Peace Prize, and became a companion of the Legion of Honour. He received twelve honorary degrees, and was an honorary member of the New York Academy of Sciences and of the American Public Health Association. In 1968 he was made a Companion of Honour for services to human and animal nutrition.

The substantial expansion of higher education powerfully affected the local economy, providing employment, creating needs for accommodation, and supplying a flow of highly educated graduates to the local economy and beyond. By the late 1990s, the higher education institutions in the city, Aberdeen University, RGU and Northern College, were together catering for some 20,000 students. By 1995-96 Aberdeen University was responsible for a direct financial injection into the local economy of £129 million plus a further £41 million through the cumulative effect of these activities within the local economy.[50] Apart from its more obvious and primary role, education had become one of the major components of the Aberdeen economy.

13

Religion

PETER HILLIS

MEMBERSHIP AND ATTENDANCE

To the casual observer Aberdeen presents an image of a city in which the church plays a prominent part. Together with the tower blocks of the 1960s, church spires and towers dominate the skyline. A tour of the city further confirms the impression with imposing church buildings on many streets. The statistics of religion are also impressive at first sight.[1] In 1797 Aberdeen had 27 churches.[2] In 1851 the Census of Religious Worship recorded 43 churches with a total attendance of 41,622 at morning, afternoon and evening services.[3] Another census of church attendance, half a century later on Sunday 14 April 1901, recorded that 27,293 people were present at morning services in 94 places of worship.[4] In 1990 the 48 congregations comprising the Church of Scotland Presbytery of Aberdeen had 34,892 communicant members of whom 20,590 communicated at least once in the year.[5] In the same year the Roman Catholic Churches in the city recorded 128 baptisms, 115 confirmations and 56 marriages.[6] Outwith the Christian denominations the Jewish Synagogue was opened in 1893 and a Mosque in 1978.

Nonetheless, a closer examination of some church buildings reveals a different situation. In September 1995 the following notice was displayed outside St Nicholas' Congregational Chapel in Belmont Street:

> The final service in this building will be held on Sunday 17 September 1995 at 11.00 am. From Sunday 24 September 1995 the congregation will continue to worship within the kirk of St. Nicholas with the Rev. J. Ross MacLaren as minister.

With the exception of a very small congregation, served by a divinity student in Mastrick, St Nicholas was the last Congregational Chapel in Aberdeen and represented a dramatic decline in the denomination's presence. In 1851 Independents, or Congregationalists, had six churches with an attendance of 4,530 at all three Sunday services, while in October 1865 the deacons' court of George Street Congregational Chapel 'agreed to apply for two policemen to be in attendance on Sabbath evenings at the door to prevent crowding and confusion'.[7]

By 1901 the Congregationalists had expanded to eight chapels with 1,951 people attending the Sunday morning service.[8]

Elsewhere churches survive in different guise, including the Triple Kirks part of which was temporarily converted into a restaurant, the North Parish Church of St Nicholas which became the Arts Centre, and the Union Grove Church which was turned into residential accommodation. But the statistics suggesting greater devotional zeal in the nineteenth century can be misleading. The 1851 Census of Religious Worship counted everyone who attended all three Sunday services which led to double counting of those who attended more than one service. A recent analysis of the census data for Aberdeen suggested that 75 per cent of those attending were present at more than one service which gave an amended total attendance of 28,412, or 38.6 per cent of the city's population.[9] The 1901 Census of Church Attendance recorded an impressive total figure but it only represented 18 per cent of the population. A Census of the Churches in Scotland in 1984, however, revealed that Aberdeen had the lowest percentage of its population attending church compared to all other areas of Scotland.[10]

THE PHYSICAL PRESENCE OF THE CHURCH

By the beginning of the nineteenth century the parish of St Nicholas was spread over three congregations, the East and West Churches of St Nicholas and the old

St Nicholas' Church c. 1850 housed two separate congregations. On the left, the West Church designed by James Gibb was completed in 1755 and, to the right, the East Church was rebuilt by Simpson in 1837.

*The North Parish
Church at the top of
King Street was
opened in 1831.*

Greyfriars Church. In the old town there was the former cathedral of St Machar. As the city expanded, some 'chapels of ease' were created to deal with the pressures of population increase. Gilcomston, under the control of Oldmachar parish, was erected in 1788 to meet the needs of the growing working population on what was then the fringe of the town. Trinity Church dated from 1794 and a Gaelic Church was established in 1795. Yet another chapel, the Union Church, was established in 1822. In 1828 the St Nicholas churches were divided into three separate parish churches and three other parishes were created. A North Church at the top of the new King Street, which many regarded as Aberdeen's most beautiful nineteenth-century building, was opened in 1831. St Clement's Church at Footdee was built in 1828, and a South Church was completely rebuilt in 1830. These were the six parish churches, the funding of which the city was responsible for. In addition, Trinity, Union and Gilcomston were allowed their own kirk sessions. Bon-Accord was formed in 1828 as an overflow from Gilcomston, and Holburn hived off from Gilcomston in 1836 after disputes over the appointment of ministers. John Knox's Church, which opened for worship in 1835, was an extension to Greyfriars, and Melville was a former Secession Church, dating from 1772, which rejoined the Church of Scotland. In addition there were, by the 1830s, three Secession churches, three Baptist chapels, three Episcopal churches (St Paul's following the English style while St Andrew's and St John's followed the Scottish tradition), one Roman Catholic congregation (St Peter's), one Relief Church in Shiprow and a breakaway body from it known as the United Christian Church. There were also three Congregational churches, and the city claimed to be the home of the first Congregational church in Scotland, based on nonsectarian principles, which opened in 1797. There were also tiny groups of Wesleyan Methodists, the Society of Friends, Glasites, Irvingites, Southcottians and the Unitarians. The *New Statistical Account* suggested that, in the 1840s, 20,000 citizens were attached to the established church, nearly 9,000 to dissenting churches and just over 2,000 had no affiliation.

THE DISRUPTION

The most significant event to influence the modern religious history of the city was undoubtedly the Disruption of the established church in 1843. The split came at the end of decades of wrangling over the issue of lay patronage, and how far congregations had the right to veto the selection of a minister. However, the disagreement between evangelicals and moderates ran deeper than the right of patrons to appoint ministers. There were disagreements over theology, philosophies of life, and about relations with the state which had become entangled in the politics of the city. Challenges to the dominant theological moderatism of most of the parish clergy, usually accompanied by deeply conservative political views, had come from the secession churches. But at the beginning of the nineteenth century there were signs of change within the established church. Dr James Kidd of Gilcomston launched an evangelical tradition in Gilcomston which continued throughout the next two centuries.[11] After Kidd's death, the Rev. Gavin Parker at Bon-Accord and Dr Daniel Dewar of Greyfriars who, after 1830, was Principal of Marischal College, among others, took up the evangelical cause.

Dr James Kidd 1761–1834

Born at Loughbrickland, County Down, James Kidd studied and then taught for four years in Belfast. In 1784 he emigrated to the United States and worked as a tutor to a family in New Jersey and then as an usher at the College of Pennsylvania, where he also studied. In 1792 he returned across the Atlantic to study with the celebrated scholar, John Brown of Haddington, and at Edinburgh University. In 1793 he was appointed professor of oriental languages at Marischal College, and also served as lecturer at Trinity Chapel. He was appointed to the Gilcomston Chapel of Ease in the late 1790s and remained there until his death. He was a highly regarded and enthusiastic preacher in the evangelical tradition, offered three services a day, opened Sunday schools, took up the temperance cause, generally flouted the authority of the Oldmachar clergy, and was continually at loggerheads with someone or other.

The irascible and campaigning evangelical minister of Gilcomston Church from 1796 until 1834, Dr James Kidd, who was also professor of oriential languages at Marischal College.

But, as MacLaren's seminal analysis of religion and social class in Aberdeen demonstrated, social and economic factors also contributed to the Disruption.[12] The Free Church kirk sessions were dominated by the newer, more upwardly mobile section of the middle class. By way of contrast many Church of Scotland elders were drawn from the established merchant and landed élite. A feature common to all kirk sessions was the lack of working-class representation resulting from the social and economic obligations attached to an eldership. MacLaren argued that many church practices, including kirk session discipline and the financial obligations of church membership, discouraged working-class attendance. Only the Rev. James Stirling of the Secession Church and the Unitarians showed much sympathy with Chartist demands and many workers turned to their own Chartist Church, presided over by Robert Lowery, in the early 1840s.

The Disruption had a particularly devastating effect on the city because all fifteen of the established clergy came out taking with them a large part of their congregations. In Greyfriars, for example, only one elder was left although in the prosperous West Church, the 'high church', the majority stayed. For a time the new churches had to make do with temporary buildings, wooden huts or even were obliged to share buildings with earlier seceders. But, there was a powerful determination to challenge the Auld Kirk and to more than match its churches, and by the census of 1851 there were 15 free churches in the city compared with only seven established churches. Among the new churches was the Triple Kirk at the junction of Belmont Street and Schoolhill, deliberately located with the intention of challenging the established St Nicholas parish churches. It incorporated the East, West and South Free Church congregations and was ready for occupation by the beginning of 1844. The construction of the Denburn Railway in the 1860s damaged the West Church and the decision was made to move to Union Street. Not all the congregation agreed and some broke away and stayed in the old building, renaming it the Free High Church, which remained in existence until 1930. In the 1890s, the South Free Church, which had always attracted some of the leading figures in the city, moved across the Denburn to a large new building topped by a replica of the dome of St Paul's, and financed largely by John Gray who had also endowed the nearby Art School.

There was some temptation to build churches in areas that were most convenient for the more prosperous members of the congregations on whose voluntary contributions the new church depended. The dissident members of Greyfriars Church proposed to build in Crown Street rather than in Broad Street, where the old Greyfriars had been, and were accused of moving west to get 'close to the gentry'. In the end they were prevented from doing so and the church was instead built in George Street. This tendency for congregations erecting new churches to move to the west end of the city was frequently commented upon. Gray, in giving his money to build the new South Free Church, insisted that it must remain close to its original site. Gammie, the historian of Aberdeen's churches, commented that it was one of the very few churches where 'the successful city man and the toiling artisan rub shoulders week by week'.[13]

The scale of the impact of the Disruption was demonstrated by the figures collected for the Census in 1851. By denomination the allegiance of those church attendances was as follows: 16.2 per cent attended at the Free Church, 7.3 per cent at the Church of Scotland, 5.2 per cent at the Episcopalians, 4.3 per cent at the Congregationalists, 1.2 per cent at the Roman Catholic Churches. The rest attended at a variety of dissenting churches such as the Methodists and the United Presbyterians formed in 1847 from the merger of the Relief Church and the United Secession Church. While the Free Churches accounted for 41 per cent of total church attendance, none of the other denominations were able to reach half of this total.

Rivalry between the Free Church and the Church of Scotland continued throughout the century. Both were affected by the religious revival which swept

A fine example of denominational rivalry, with Queen's Cross Free Church in granite in the foreground and Rubislaw Parish Church in sandstone behind. Both aimed to attract the middle class of the West End. Photograph by George Washington Wilson.

the North-East and elsewhere in 1858–60, and became involved in home missionary activities. Both embarked on an extensive building programme in the 1870s. The Free Church erected buildings at Ruthrieston, Ferryhill, Torry, Causewayend and Queen's Cross. The last, opened in 1881, attracted the Rev. George Adam Smith as its minister, one of the great nineteenth-century preachers, a 'glowing young Evangel' who packed his church 'with congregations more eager than anyone had ever seen, before or since' according to one writer.

By the 1870s the Free Church was beginning to lose ground and the Church of Scotland formed the Aberdeen Church Extension and Territorial Home Mission Association, inspired by the Rev. Henry Cowan of the West Church and Lord Provost Nicol, and sought to match Free Church building with Rubislaw Church at Queen's Cross and other churches in Rosemount and Ferryhill. Trinity Church was rebuilt and another church, St George's, was provided in the west parish to meet the needs of the crowded, poorer areas off George Street. In 1882 the long-established Gaelic Church moved to Dee Street as St Columba's Free Church, occupying premises which, by the late 1990s, had become 'The Ministry of Sin' nightclub.

Sir George Adam Smith 1857–1942

Born in India of Scottish parents, returning home at the age of two, Adam Smith later studied at Edinburgh University and trained for the ministry at New College, Edinburgh. He became assistant minister at Brechin. He moved to Aberdeen and became the first minister of Queen's Cross Free Church in 1882, replacing William Robertson Smith who had been suspended from his church for heresy. Adam Smith taught at the Free Church College in Aberdeen and, in 1892, was appointed to the chair of Hebrew and Old Testament at the Free Church College in Glasgow. In 1910 he was appointed principal of Aberdeen University. He served as moderator of the General Assembly, and was knighted in 1916. Author of *A Historical Geography of the Holy Land* and many other works, he was awarded 13 honorary degrees. From 1924 to 1936 he was patron of the seven Incorporated Trades. He was given the freedom of the city in 1931, and was appointed chaplain to the King in Scotland in 1933. He retired in 1936 to Balerno.

Rev. George Adam Smith, one of the city's great preachers as minister of Queen's Cross Free Church from 1882 until 1892. From 1910 until 1935 he was principal of Aberdeen University.

The United Presbyterians, in particular, saw their mission as being focused upon the middle classes and they built their very grand 'cathedral church' in Carden Place in 1882 to replace the former very modest edifice in George Street. In the next decade, they also quit the small church in St Nicholas Lane, which had once belonged to the seceders, in favour of a huge new edifice in Union Grove. The Methodists, after years of difficulties struggling with the debts of earlier phases of chapel building, built a new church in Crown Terrace. It opened in 1873 and replaced the previous church building in Long Acre. The Roman Catholics outgrew their chapel, St Peter's in Justice Street, and in 1860 erected the Church of St Mary of the Assumption in Huntly Street. Built in the gothic style by the architect,

Carden Place United Presbyterian Church was completed in 1882 at a cost of £5,000. It replaced the precentor with an organ and with its lofty spire it was tagged the UP 'cathedral'.

Alexander Ellis, it was grand enough, when the Roman Catholic hierarchy was restored in 1878, to become the cathedral of the Aberdeen diocese. Its appearance was further enhanced and a spire added under the guidance of the vigorous Dean Stopani in the 1880s.

Some of the most extensive mission work was carried out in the 1860s and 1870s in the notorious Gallowgate area of the city by the Rev. John Comper of St John's

Episcopal Church. He and his Sisters of Mercy ran a day school, evening classes and guilds for young men and women. He resigned the incumbency of St John's in 1870 to work full-time at the Gallowgate mission which, in 1879, became St Margaret's Episcopal Church.

DEBATES AND CONFLICTS

No church was permanently free of theological and personal debate. Militant protestantism and fear of the advance of Roman Catholicism continued to stir sections of the population and the tendency to schism which had been such a feature of the eighteenth century persisted into the nineteenth century. Catholic emancipation in 1829, giving Roman Catholics the right to be appointed to public office, stirred vitriolic attacks against the spread of liberal ideas, with petitions against it. The success of a visiting Jesuit in attracting protestants to his lectures led to the formation in 1830 of the Aberdeen Society for Promoting the Religious Principles of the Reformation, chaired by the lawyer Patrick Bannerman. It continued to torment the small local Roman Catholic community with pamphlets and sermons.[14] The Rev. Shanks at the new North Church preached fiery sermons suggesting that Popery and infidelity were connected. Fr Charles Gordon

was prevented from taking his seat as one of the managers of the house of refuge, and money collected at the Roman Catholic chapel in 1836 to help the unemployed was refused.[15] Similarly, the conversion of a young divinity student to Unitarianism and the establishment of a Unitarian Church in George Street in 1838 was perceived as a threat and led to a campaign against unitarian views.[16]

The Disruption, of course, left a generation of bitterness which was often personal. Principal Daniel Dewar of Marischal College, who had been the main spokesman for the evangelicals but who failed to 'come out' in 1843, found himself ostracised as someone who had sacrificed principle for money. The Disruption also created rivalry not just between between the Free Church, which still saw itself as the new establishment, and the established church but also between the Free Churches and the dissenting churches who wanted a complete separation between church and state. Proposals in the later 1860s for a possible merger of the Free Church with the United Presbyterians led to schisms at Gilcomston where the Rev. Walter MacGillvray strongly opposed the proposals. But union was eventually achieved with establishment of the United Free Church in 1901. The debates over disestablishment rumbled on in both the Established and the Free Churches through the 1880s and 1890s, with the Rev. James Cooper of the East Parish, leading the campaign against with dire warnings that it would lead to other acts of confiscation and let loose 'all the elements that disintegrate society'.[17]

Nor did the new structures prevent further schism. Disputation about the validity of the Calvinist doctrine that salvation would only be for the elect raged in the 1840s, and led to the formation of the Evangelical Union and the spread of independent churches. The first of these was set up in 1846 after the Rev. John Kennedy purged his revisionist Sunday school officials. In time it became associated with the Congregational Union.[18] Dr J. H. Wilson, who abandoned his editorship of the *North of Scotland Gazette* in favour of home mission work, opened a Congregational Chapel in 1848 in the notorious Bool Road in what had been a wild theatre known as the 'Bool Road Penny Rattler'. A new church was erected in 1854 in Albion Street, as the Bool Road had now been renamed, the so-called 'ragged kirk', kept going largely by the financial support of David Macallan and George Maitland. It offered a school for poor children, a penny bank, as well as the usual temperance and tract activity. The success of this church by the 1870s, thanks to the preaching of John Duncan, led to the creation of an overflow church, Trinity Congregational which, by the 1990s, had been converted into a maritime museum.

Divisions and tensions were not confined to presbyterian churches. An attempt to unite the 'English' church of St Paul's with the Scottish Episcopal Church ended in a rancorous battle in the 1840s between the priest, Sir William Dunbar, and Bishop Skinner, which led to the former eventually being declared to be in a state of schism. Soon afterwards the Scottish Episcopal Church in the city, which consisted of two churches, St Andrew's and St John the Evangelist, was rent by a bitter battle, over the extent to which the catholicism of the Episcopal Church should be emphasised. It was a time when a number of leading figures in the Church of England, under the influence of Pusey, Newman and the Oxford Movement, were moving their theological allegiance to the Church of Rome. The Rev. Patrick Cheyne, who had been minister at St John's for nearly 40 years and had been largely responsible for ensuring that a new church was built in 1851, caused controversy as early as 1844 with sermons that leaned, according to his critics, 'to the peculiar doctrines and observances of the Church of Rome'.[19] His former colleague at St Andrew's Chapel, the Rev. Thomas George Suther, who succeeded Skinner as Bishop of Aberdeen in 1856, was determined to halt the advance of tractarian influence in Scotland and suspended Cheyne from his office. But Cheyne's successor, the Rev. F. G. Lee, was soon in conflict with the authorities, also after introducing rituals, eucharist vestments and candles on the altar. He survived only 15 months before resigning with some of his congregation and establishing a new church, St Mary's in Carden Place which bankrupted him.[20]

The Church of Scotland did not escape such battles about doctrine and religious practice. In 1857, Marshall Lang, minister of the East Church, proposed that the congregation should stand for singing, rather than following the traditional practice of sitting for singing and standing for prayers, and was duly censured by the Presbytery.[21] Demands for change were coming from various directions, and one group tried to raise money for a new church under a liberal-minded minister with the services conducted 'on improved principles including the use of an organ'. Dr Pirie, backed by other Aberdeen ministers, led the attack against service innovation at the General Assembly. He denounced what he saw as a 'tendency to sentimentalism and sensuality' which would lead to the loss of 'spiritual mindedness' and he pushed through the 1865 General Assemby what became known as Pirie's Act. This deprived ministers and kirk sessions of independent jurisdiction on the form of service and decreed that form had to be regulated by the Presbytery.[22] A quarter of a century later the question was still a live issue for debate at Gilcomston Free Church. Hymns were not introduced there until 1887 with instrumental accompaniment not being accepted until a decade later. A successor of Lang at the East Parish, in the early 1880s, Dr James Cooper, faced a rebellion when nearly half his kirk session protested about his 'High Church doctrine and practices'. Dr Cooper, too, had been influenced by the ideas of the Oxford Movement and he sought to promote union between the Church of Scotland and the Church of

Rev. James Cooper, controversial minister of the East Parish from 1881 to 1898, who hoped for union with the Church of England. He became professor of ecclesiastical history at the University of Glasgow.

The Rev. Professor James Cooper 1846–1922

A native of Elgin and the son of a farmer, James Cooper was educated at Elgin Academy and Aberdeen University. He subsequently travelled on the Continent and studied at Heidelberg. He was licensed by the Presbytery of Elgin in 1870 and acted as assistant at Banchory-Ternan, the East Church in Aberdeen, Stirling and Elgin Parish Churches before serving as minister of St Stephen's, Broughty Ferry 1873–81 and of the East Parish Church, Aberdeen, 1881–98. During the last period he served on the school board. In 1898 he was appointed as professor of church history at Glasgow University. He was president of the Scottish Ecclesiological Society and edited its transactions for many years. He was moderator of the General Assembly of the Church of Scotland in 1917. He wrote extensively on church history.

England. He believed that the Church of Scotland was the 'National Branch of Christ's Holy Catholic Church'. Before coming to Aberdeen he had been the first Church of Scotland minister to hold Christmas and Holy Week services, but he found at St Nicholas a church with no organ, no lectern, and with the communion table used by the choir to keep their hats on. Among his misdemeanours, in the eyes of his dissenting elders, were seeking to assimilate 'the worship of the Church to the practices of Anglicanism', of wanting to develop a priest's role for himself, of holding prayer meetings at which he knelt, giving communion to the sick in private and intoning a litany at the children's service. The Presbytery court rejected the accusations, but warned him to take care to act in accordance with the doctrine of the Church of Scotland.[23] His style seems to have had some appeal since church membership rose from 1,535 to 2,280 within a decade.

Most notorious of all was the case of Professor William Robertson Smith, who held the chair of Old Testament at the Free Church College which had been set up in 1860. Influenced by German biblical criticism, Smith published an article on the Bible in the 1875 edition of the *Encyclopaedia Britannica* which, among other 'heresies' in the eyes of his critics, claimed that the books of the Pentateuch were not all written by the hand of Moses but involved various authors. He was charged with propagating opinions 'which contradict, or are opposed, to the doctrines set forth in the scriptures and Confession of Faith' and were 'of a dangerous and unsettling tendency' and 'tend to disparage the Divine authority and inspired character of these books'. Smith, only 25 years of age and 'a fiery little man' according to the wife of his successor, defended himself vigorously and with an arrogance which riled his critics. Others, including the *Free Press*, rallied to his support, calling for tolerance, and an extensive pamphlet war resulted. It seemed at one point that the church might actually split over the issue. After years of wrangling, Smith was dismissed from his chair in 1881.[24]

Relations between church and state remained an issue of continuing contention. But in the twentieth century debates were generally focused on the role of the church in society and its contribution in providing social welfare. Different congregational traditions offered a variety of responses to events such as the evangelical campaigns imported from the United States periodically since the 1950s. The churches also had to learn to cope with an increasingly secular society. However, the response of the Aberdeen press and churches to broadcasts on scientific humanism given by Margaret Knight, wife of the professor of psychology at Aberdeen University, in 1955 was much less hysterical than that of the metropolitan press who denounced her as 'A Dangerous Woman' and 'The Unholy Mrs Knight'.[25] Perhaps the most acrimonious debates, however, concerned congregational mergers as the Christian churches sought to cope with dramatically falling numbers.

CHURCH ATTENDANCE AND MEMBERSHIP

Although the Disruption was a significant event at the time, viewed in the context of the past two centuries the long-term decline in church attendance was even more significant. Surveys which attempt to measure levels of church attendance and/or membership must be treated with some caution. The 1851 census recorded the number of attendances, while later surveys taken in 1901, 1984 and 1994 recorded the number of people who attended. Not all religious denominations agreed on a common criterion for church membership. For example, the Roman Catholic Church counted baptised Roman Catholics as members, while Presbyterian churches counted those in full communion with their church. Statistics of church attendance and membership exclude attendance at other types of religious gathering such as the annual New Year's Day revival meeting of the Brethren churches which commenced in 1874. Information about church membership can only provide part of the picture regarding levels of religious belief since church attendance does not always equate with a devout faith, and non-attendance does not necessarily imply atheism. Despite these qualifications the statistics show general trends in church attendance and membership, together with the strengths of a particular denomination or church.

The evidence for the nineteenth century is contradictory. Church attendance rates as a percentage of Aberdeen's population showed a decline from 38.6 per cent in 1851, to 26.1 per cent in 1878 and 18.0 per cent in 1901.[26] The last figure highlights one of the difficulties in any census of church going since it was based on the number of people attending morning service on a day when 'the rain became heavier just about the time many people were ready to leave their homes for church, and it is to be feared that numbers of the intending worshippers, especially amongst the fair sex, elected to stay at home'.[27] Church attendance, in terms of the percentage of the total population, showed a decline although in many denominations the number of members actually increased. In 1888 the Aberdeen Presbytery of the Church of Scotland recorded 30,177 communicant members, a total which had risen to 38,691 by 1903.[28] In 1865 there were 86 confirmations in the Roman Catholic Church whereas the average annual number of confirmations between 1891 and 1894 rose to 133.[29] The Roman Catholic Church benefited from Highland and, to a lesser extent, Irish migration into Aberdeen while, in a similar manner, migration from eastern Europe in the 1890s led to an expansion of the Jewish community. The growth of the city's population during Victoria's reign demonstrates contradictory evidence on church attendance as the rate of population increase outstripped the growth in church membership. Evidence for declining attendances in the twentieth century is unequivocal, and even less reassuring, for most Christian churches.

The major Presbyterian denominations experienced a declining rate of growth in the early decades of the twentieth century, a decline which became a sharp drop in attendance and membership from the 1960s onward. Despite reunification with the United Free Church, in 1929, membership of the Church of Scotland fell between 1921 and 1941. The decline in membership levels of city centre churches was partly offset by expansion in the suburbs with, for example, Beechgrove Church growing from 720 communicants in 1933 to 953 members in 1988. Notwithstanding these exceptions, the overall downward trend accelerated in the 1960s and continued in subsequent decades with a 27 per cent drop in the membership of the Church of Scotland between 1980 and 1994.[30] Moreover, communicant membership did not always equate with regular church attendance. Average adult Sunday attendance in March 1984 at Church of Scotland services in Aberdeen was 9,770 compared with a membership total of 42,520.[31] National figures for the Church of Scotland from the late nineteenth century onward show a denomination whose members attended church at increasingly infrequent intervals. Equivalent figures for Aberdeen were not recorded until the 1930s but from this date they mirror the national trend with 61,048 adults communicating at least once in 1934, compared with 81,309 church members. The equivalent figures for 1989 were 20,590 communicants from 34,892 members.[32] The unified Church of Scotland has been the dominant denomination in the city since 1929 but its attendance and membership statistics show a reduced rate of growth turning into an accelerating decline from the 1960s. Until the 1950s the Church of Scotland recruited progressively fewer new members, thereafter it lost increasing numbers from its existing membership. This failure in recruitment is most vividly illustrated by the decline in membership of Sunday schools and Bible classes once regarded 'as the most important agency for recruiting church members'.[33] This fell from 24,000 in 1930 to fewer than 3,000 in 1990.

The 1851 Census of Religious Worship recorded one Roman Catholic Church but by 1901 there were three.[34] Despite continued growth until the 1930s the evidence, with the exception of the period 1957-66, suggests a long-term trend of declining church membership. Indications of decline come from estimates of the Roman Catholic population taken from several parishes. In 1950 St Mary's Cathedral had an estimated Roman Catholic population of 2,665, a total which had fallen to 1,469 in 1994.[35] The equivalent figures for other parishes during the same period showed a fall from 1,000 to 547 in St Joseph's, and from 2,000 to 286 in St Peter's. Although the 1994 Census of Religious Worship recorded an overall growth in the membership of the Roman Catholic Church this was probably due to the inclusion of some churches outwith the limits of the city. The level of attendance did not fall so rapidly in the Roman Catholic Church as in the Church of Scotland largely because it had a higher membership/attendance ratio, 35 per cent compared with 29 per cent in the Church of Scotland.[36] Consequently, 1,380 people attended Easter mass in St Mary's Cathedral in 1994 out of an estimated Catholic population for the parish of 1,469.[37] Nevertheless, the Roman Catholic Church experienced a similar decline as the Church of Scotland in attendance by young people, registering a fall of 39 per cent in the number of children attending between 1980 and 1994.[38]

The Scottish Episcopal Church also expanded in the nineteenth and early twentieth century, but between 1960 and 1990 many of its congregations too recorded declining levels of church adherence. Membership figures for 1994, however, suggest that the Episcopal Church had countered the downward trend with some congregations registering increased levels of membership. Between 1985 and 1994 membership at St Andrew's increased from 453 to 537, and at St Margaret's from 153 to 500, although St James' continued to decline and St John's remained stable. The recovery was partly the result of English migration, so that the substance and permanence of this revival remained uncertain.

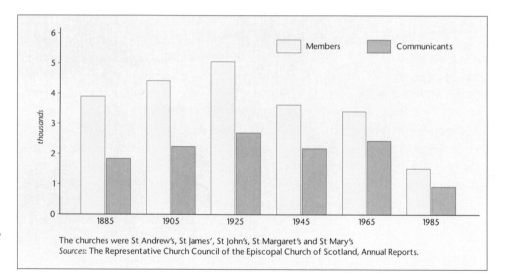

Figure 13.1
Scottish Episcopal
Church membership
in Aberdeen,
1885-1985.

It is more difficult to discover accurate data for many of the smaller Christian denominations in the city. The first Baptist church opened in 1821 in Crown Terrace. In 1901 there were four Baptist churches, a total which had been reduced to three by 1990. In 1980 these three churches, Crown Terrace, Gilcomston Park and Union Grove, had a combined membership of 451.[39] According to the 1901 census, 440 people attended Sunday morning service at the same three churches which suggests that the Baptist Church was relatively successful in retaining its levels of membership and attendance. Moreover, the 1994 Census of Religion recorded an increase in both membership and attendance since 1980, a growth partly explained by the inclusion of churches at the Bridge of Don and Cults. The same survey also recorded an increase in those attending independent meetings of bodies such as the Salvation Army and the Brethren. The total membership for these independent churches in 1994 was only 3,840 compared with a combined total of 39,170 for the Church of Scotland, the Scottish Episcopal and Roman Catholic Churches.[40] Even so, many small Christian churches retained or expanded their number of adherents. The explanation for their relative success may lie partly in their smallness, which engendered a greater sense of loyalty and commitment, while some denominations, such as the Baptists, benefited from migration into the city and suburbs resulting from North Sea oil production. The torch of protestant fervour appears to have passed to ever smaller but more devout congregations.

A further exception to the downward trend was the Muslim community. In 1978 the Aberdeen Savings Bank building was purchased by the Muslims and converted into a mosque. It was estimated that there were 200 Muslims in the city representing 14 different nationalities, many of whom were students at Aberdeen University.[41] By 1984 membership had grown to 350 and permission was sought to extend the mosque. Expansion continued into the 1990s with an estimated Muslim population of 800 in 1996 and rising demands for a purpose-built mosque. In 1995 a site was identified near the junction of King Street and the Beach Esplanade, although it did not receive building permission.[42] The Jewish, Muslim and Roman Catholic communities all shared one obvious common feature in that their existence and growth were largely the result of migration into the city.

REASONS FOR DECLINE

It was during the twentieth century that the greatest decline in church membership and attendance was recorded. Indeed, at the end of the century Aberdeen had the lowest rate of church attendance in Scotland. There were two main historical trends which brought this about. Firstly there was a slowdown in the rate of expansion. Then there followed a loss of existing members, together with a haemorrhage of young people from the Christian churches. The movement of people away from many churches led to considerable debate amongst those who have remained within them. The decline was often attributed to changes in society, and the response to these changes, together with the methods used to present religion. In Aberdeen, the First World War led to a small increase in membership of the Church of Scotland which countered a small fall in membership in the decade before the Great War. This mirrored the national picture influenced by the tide of patriotism which accompanied the early years of war. In contrast, the Second World War led to a decline in membership and it was not until the 1950s that membership regained the 1938 level. The Second

World War seriously retarded the slow growth rate which had persisted throughout the first half of the century, partly because many conservative churchmen were out of step with the times. The Church of Scotland criticised the BBC for radio programmes such as ITMA (It's That Man Again), designed to raise civilian morale, which it regarded as vulgar. It also criticised the Government for allowing beer consumption to rise. However, the two world wars occurred in the midst of considerable social and economic change with the decline of the traditional forms of employment and work relationships. It has been argued that the Church of Scotland's response to poverty and unemployment 'seems if anything to have aggravated proletarian disaffection, and specifically by perpetuating notions of us and them'.[43] The traditional response of many presbyterian churches was to blame poverty and unemployment on moral and spiritual weakness thus alienating many people from those churches. While war and socio-economic problems partly explain the slowing in the rate of church growth in the early decades of the twentieth century it is more difficult to assign the sharp decline since the 1960s to these factors.

The development of North Sea oil protected Aberdeen from some of the worst effects of economic recession. Although the prosperity brought by North Sea oil coincided with the decline in church attendance and membership, this was a national trend experienced in areas unaffected by the oil industry. Despite this economic advantage, Aberdeen had areas of social and economic deprivation concentrated near the centre of the city. These areas were redeveloped and new housing schemes built on the periphery of the city. Many people moved to these new housing schemes, or to the suburbs. The major Christian churches were faced with the cost of maintaining expensive church buildings in central Aberdeen while at the same time attempting to relocate their activities to the newer housing areas. With the exception of some smaller denominations, church development into the suburbs and new housing schemes did not offset the effects of the declining membership of many older churches. Many members did not wish to transfer their loyalties, sometimes built up over many generations, to a different church building but found it increasingly inconvenient to travel into central Aberdeen for church services. Their connection with the churches was gradually lost.

For many people the 1960s and 1970s, in contrast to the 1920s and 1930s, were decades of improvement in the standard of living. Home entertainment replaced many traditional social activities provided by the churches, which also faced increasing competition from alternative Sunday activities. There were changes in social attitudes which were often viewed as being at variance with traditional Christian teaching. A Church of Scotland report in 1970 stated the dilemma.

For better or for worse we have entered upon an era when men and women will claim the right to decide, free from all dictation and direction by any authority, how they conduct themselves and live their lives. Need the church always deplore this new 'permissiveness' as an unalloyed disaster?[44]

A 1993 survey conducted among former churchgoers discovered that 62 per cent had left the Church because of its perceived lack of relevance to modern society.[45] In Aberdeen this crisis of relevance was most dramatically illustrated by the sharp decline in the membership of Sunday school and Bible class. In a damning report on its youth policy, the committee on parish education in the Church of Scotland argued that changes in youth culture were only partly to blame for the drop in Sunday school and Bible class attendance because many of the attitudes and policies of the Church had alienated young people. This report challenged many of the assumptions upon which the Church had based its work amongst teenagers. It criticised the view that the main aim of youth work was to ensure future members for the Church or that such work could be done on an 'austerity budget'. 'Could it be,' the report asked, 'that the prevalent culture which many people in the Church don't question leads to teenagers rejecting traditional Church practices and so losing all contact with the Faith?' A radical re-thinking was required into the ways in which religion was presented, taking into account changes in society, if the downward trend was to be reversed.[46]

Many of the above explanations could be applied to other Scottish cities and do not by themselves explain why Aberdeen had the lowest rate of church attendance in Scotland. Even in 1901 it was suggested that the church service which involved preaching 'at people' had 'been a complete failure' in Aberdeen. A more recent analysis, and one more specific to the city, argued that the reason lay in the small size of the Roman Catholic population. According to the 1984 Census of Religious Worship the two districts in Scotland with the highest proportion of Roman Catholics, Dunbartonshire, and Motherwell and Monklands, also had the highest church attendances apart from the Hebrides and Lochalsh. Lothian region had a smaller Roman Catholic population and average rates of church attendance but 'at the other extreme from west central Scotland is Aberdeen city with a very small number of Catholics and the lowest church going rate ... in the country'.[47] Many people within the Christian churches partly blamed their policies for the decline. But even in the nineteenth century the increase in church membership failed to keep pace with population growth in Aberdeen. In order to explain this divergence, and more fully explain the twentieth-century decline in churchgoing rates, it is necessary to analyse in greater detail patterns of religious adherence from different sections of society.

The Social Composition of Church Members

Church membership, as noted above, implied varying degrees of adherence to different denominations but only a small number of churches have retained the relevant church records to permit an analysis of their membership. The communicant roll books provide the most useful information, but relatively few of them are extant and many lack the requisite detailed information. This has been a particular difficulty with regard to the major presbyterian churches, for which baptismal registers provide a substitute for roll books to analyse church membership. Analysis is easier for the nineteenth century since few baptismal registers recorded parental names, address and occupations in the twentieth century. In the non-established presbyterian churches parents bringing their child for baptism were required to have firm links with the Church. The practice in Bon-Accord Free Church was typical since 'the children of those names on the Sessional Roll of Communicants shall receive baptism when required, without any further enquiry'. However, people 'not on the Sessional Roll of Communicants shall be required, before baptism is administered to their children, to produce the minister a line, signed by two of the Elders, testifying their belief of their being qualified by knowledge and character to have their children admitted into the Visible Church by baptism'.[48]

Baptismal procedures in the Church of Scotland permitted a looser connection with the Church. In 1875 the kirk session minutes of Woodside Parish Church recorded that 'the Session agreed to insert the names of all persons baptised in Communion with the Church, in a book to be kept for the purpose'.[49] This policy permitted both members and non-members to have their child baptised according to the procedures laid down by the Church. 'If either parent is a member of the Church the child has a right to baptism. If either parent is qualified, no other person is to be sponsor. But parents not entitled to church privileges must provide some fit person, if possible a relative.'[50] Therefore, some parents who brought their child for baptism were allowed to have more tenuous links with the Church of Scotland than those seeking baptism at one of the secession churches. Baptismal registers, nonetheless, provide an insight into the social milieu of church members. Both the Roman Catholic and Scottish Episcopal Churches were prepared to baptise non-church members as exemplified by practice at St. Mary of the Assumption in 1863 when 110 parents having their children baptised were protestant.[51]

Analysis of the characteristics of elders and deacons in Glasgow and Aberdeen presbyterian churches has shown that both offices were dominated by the middle class, although office bearers in the Church of Scotland were largely drawn from the upper middle class with the dissenting kirk session initially controlled by the aspirant middle class. This contrast was also noted by contemporary observers in Aberdeen in the 1840s.

We have heard ignorant … persons state it as a charge against Mr Foote [East Church], that in the selection of his elders, he chooses the monied men in his congregation … For the office of the eldership, the rich man … ought in every case to be preferred to the poor man … It would also be well if the Assembly would enact a law against appointing servants, managers and impudent boys to offices in the Church – a practice which prevails in the quod sacra parishes.[52]

Other denominations were just as explicit in the criteria for holding office. In George Street Congregational Chapel the office of deacon was regarded as 'a responsible one and those elected must be men of substance and position'.[53]

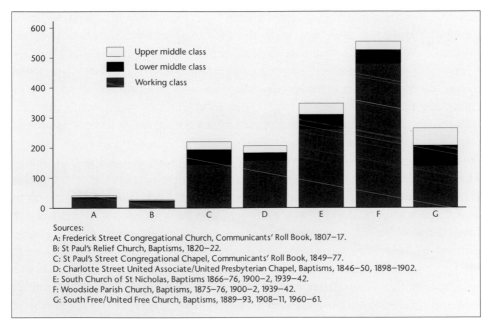

Sources:
A: Frederick Street Congregational Church, Communicants' Roll Book, 1807–17.
B: St Paul's Relief Church, Baptisms, 1820–22.
C: St Paul's Street Congregational Chapel, Communicants' Roll Book, 1849–77.
D: Charlotte Street United Associate/United Presbyterian Chapel, Baptisms, 1846–50, 1898–1902.
E: South Church of St Nicholas, Baptisms 1866–76, 1900–2, 1939–42.
F: Woodside Parish Church, Baptisms, 1875–76, 1900–2, 1939–42.
G: South Free/United Free Church, Baptisms, 1889–93, 1908–11, 1960–61.

Figure 13.2
Social composition of church membership.

The analysis of church members indicates that all denominations attracted a cross-section of Aberdeen's population and that the social make-up of office bearers was not an accurate reflection of the respective congregation. The Church of Scotland was more successful than the dissenting churches in attracting unskilled workers. Woodside Parish Church was composed of 37.6 per cent skilled workers and 62.4 per cent unskilled, while at the St Paul Street Congregational Chapel the equivalent ratios were 67.6 per cent skilled and 32.3 per cent unskilled. The Scottish Episcopal Church and the Roman Catholic Church were also successful in attracting significant numbers of the urban poor. Situated in the Gallowgate, St Margaret's Scottish Episcopal Church served the local working-class area. St Margaret's confirmation roll listed new members most of whom lived in the immediate vicinity of the Church.[54] In 1871, 113 children were baptised with all but five identified parents being working class, 47.8 per cent of whom were unskilled workers.[55] A sample analysis of parents bringing a child for baptism to St John's Episcopal Church in 1800 revealed that 69.4 per cent of parents were working class of whom 44.0 per cent were in unskilled occupations.[56] However, some of these parents would not have been members of the Scottish Episcopal Church. Throughout most of the nineteenth century, the Roman Catholic Church attracted rich and poor but, reflecting the social and economic structure of the Roman Catholic population, it had fewer middle-class adherents. Many of its wealthy members had deep roots in the community and included John Menzies of Pitfodels who, in 1802, gave £61 towards the building of a new Roman Catholic Chapel. Entries in the marriage register of St Mary's Cathedral, however, recorded a predominantly working-class congregation with significant numbers of unskilled workers.

This suggests that although the location of a church could influence its social composition all denominations contained a cross-section of social classes. Nonetheless, the Church of Scotland, the Scottish Episcopal Church and the Roman Catholic Church attracted a higher proportion of the urban poor than the dissenting Presbyterian churches. The socio-economic composition of the Presbyterian churches in Aberdeen was replicated in many other areas of Scotland. The pattern of membership in Aberdeen may also help to explain why the growth in church membership failed to keep pace with the city's expanding population in the nineteenth and early twentieth centuries. Many theories have been put forward to explain the relative failure of some denominations to attract a larger number of the urban poor. These theories range from the insistence on a strict dress code to the imposition of pew rents. However, there is no reason to believe that members of the Church of Scotland were less well-dressed than their dissenting contemporaries, while pew rents were charged by many denominations. There may have been certain unique features characteristic of the non-established Presbyterian churches which discouraged a greater presence on the part of the unskilled worker and the urban poor, namely the exacting financial obligations of church membership and, to a lesser extent, church discipline.

Kirk session discipline has been cited as an important factor in deterring people from joining the church. It has been argued that discipline was used by the middle class to impose its cultural and moral values on the working class, a process which alienated the latter from the church. However, 'there was a marked reluctance on the part of kirk sessions to proceed against individuals on socio-economic status.'[57]

Evidence from the Roman Catholic and Scottish Episcopal Church might seem to support this theory since neither exercised a Presbyterian form of discipline and had a high proportion of unskilled working-class members. Furthermore, the Church of Scotland was less authoritarian in the exercise of discipline, concentrating on cases involving antenuptial fornication. The dissenting denominations, which exercised the tightest form of discipline, had the lowest proportion of unskilled working class. In 1844 William Barry, a porter, appeared before South Free Church kirk session since he had 'been reported by several members of the session as habitually given over to intemperance.'[58] At Blackfriars Congregational Chapel, David Davidson was excluded from chapel membership 'for the sin of intemperance and for refusing to submit to discipline'.[59] Popular mythology detected more than a hint of double standards in such cases, particularly those involving extra-marital sex.

Middle-class church members were not entirely immune from prosecution. In 1807 David Gray, a merchant, was excluded from Frederick Street Congregational Chapel for 'telling lies'.[60] In 1848 Mr Urquhart, an elder of the South Free Church, appeared before his colleagues since at a dinner with members of the board of taxes he 'had partaken of some wines to the use of which he was unaccustomed'. Urquhart claimed that he had 'endeavoured to keep within the bounds of Moderation' but that on 'his way home along King Street had lost all consciousness, and had not the least recollection of anything which happened until he returned to his own house'.[61] But the majority of cases involved working-class members, who were in a majority within congregations. Church discipline long antedated industrialisation and urbanisation and its motives were partly theological since it allowed for public repentance of sin. While it may have deterred some people from joining the church there was a more potent disincentive. This was the financial burden of church membership.

THE COST OF CHURCH MEMBERSHIP

The non-established churches emphasised the financial imperative of church membership. This was most evident within the free churches which had to bear the cost of building new churches and supporting missionary work. Free church urban congregations were constantly reminded of their obligation to contribute towards the central sustentation fund which was used to subsidise less wealthy congregations. In March 1847 the Bon-Accord Free Church deacons' court heard from the presbytery clerk that 'the various Sessions and Deacons' Courts should immediately and without any delay visit and very solemnly converse with those Communicants in their congregations not yet contributing to the General Church Fund.'[62] The 1847 accounts recorded that contributions to the sustentation fund made up the largest single source of that church's income. Nonetheless, the deacons' court expressed concern that continual demands for increased contributions could prove to be counterproductive and that 'there might be considerable risk of irritating some who now contribute, if they were pressed too hard, and of thereby diminishing in place of increasing the amounts collected'.[63] Such contributions were additional to the normal church collection, or collections for missionary work, collections for the poor, and the payment of pew rents. Perhaps it was not surprising that some members fell into financial arrears as a result of church membership.

Congregational chapels were also dependent on the financial contributions of chapel members although at a reduced rate compared with the free churches. In 1895 the managers of St Paul's Congregational Chapel heard that there had been a decline of £11 in chapel collections between August and November and 'it was resolved that an intimation to that effect be made from the pulpit next Sunday with a request for increased liberality on the part of the congregation'.[64] Skilled workers enjoyed a higher income from which to support church membership, an option which could not be afforded by many unskilled workers and the urban poor. However, there is evidence to suggest that, soon after their formation, the free churches in Aberdeen lost members to the Congregational chapels where the financial demands were less onerous. The communicants' roll book for St Andrew's Street Congregational Chapel recorded the place or denomination of origin for each new member. Between 1847 and 1854, 35.7 per cent of new members came from the free churches and many of those who transferred their allegiance were skilled workers, 26 per cent were members by first profession, and 9 per cent had transferred from the Church of Scotland. Those denominations which set less stringent financial and disciplinary demands had the highest proportion of church members drawn from lower working-class groups. Furthermore, some members of the protestant working class chose to marry, or have their children baptised, in either the Roman Catholic or the Scottish Episcopal Church. Given that the major Christian presence in Aberdeen was represented by the Presbyterian denominations, within which the non-established churches were dominant, their combined relative failure to recruit higher numbers of lower working-class members helps to explain why church expansion did not keep pace with the rising population. This failure also sowed the seeds which germinated to reduce rates of church attendance in the twentieth century.

While social composition influenced church membership, it is clear that gender also influenced patterns of attendance and membership. In 1871 a total of 36 people were confirmed as members of the Scottish Episcopal Church in St Margaret's Chapel, of whom 14 new members were men and 22 were women. Equivalent figures for 1913 showed 32 women and 16 men. A similar distribution was found in St. Paul's Congregational Chapel. These figures replicate and confirm Field's analysis of the influence of gender on Baptist and Congregational nonconformity in England. Between 1826 and 1854 women represented 65.2 per cent of the total nonconformist membership within these denominations.[65] Field hypothesised that 'the less which was required of active involvement or personal sacrifice, the greater number of men'. For example, those professing allegiance to the free churches in England were almost in equal proportion men and women, but free church membership was disproportionately composed of women. Unless the dominance of men within the eldership, deacons and managers is regarded as an exceptional example of commitment, it is more difficult to apply this hypothesis to Aberdeen and other Scottish cities. The origin of this gender imbalance may lie in a combination of factors including the opportunities afforded by the church and chapel for a social life outwith the home as an alternative to the public house which was dominated by men. A less secular theory has suggested that many women traditionally had a stronger emotional susceptibility to religious forces.

THE SECULAR SOCIETY

Aberdeen's image as a churchgoing city has not always reflected reality. At no time since 1850 did more than 40 per cent of Aberdeen's population attend church, and by 1984 the city had the lowest churchgoing rate in Scotland. Only some smaller denominations and non-christian groups were able to counter the downward trend, partly as a result of migration into the city. The failure of the dissenting Presbyterian churches, in particular, to attract larger numbers of the urban poor helps to explain why the nineteenth-century expansion in church membership was outstripped by the growth of the city's population. Some people chose to attend church but many others retained only the most tenuous of links, looking to the churches only for baptism, marriage and burial. The increasing secularisation of society in the twentieth century, together with the erosion of many traditional social bonds, had a very marked effect on the visible strength of the Church as reflected in attendance at services.

14

Elite Society

I. G. C. HUTCHISON

Before 1830, much of the public life of Aberdeen was controlled by a tightly connected elite. The town council was a classic example of a self-perpetuating oligarchy before 1833. Between the beginning of the century and the reform of 1833 there were eighteen terms of the provostship. The office was held by nine individuals, two of whom, the brothers Gavin and James Hadden, each occupied the post four times. Two others, Thomas Leys and James Young, who enjoyed three terms between them, were business partners of the Haddens. Alexander Brebner, twice provost, was a business partner of Leys. Thus, only four of the nine men were not part of the Hadden–Leys business alliance, and these 'outsiders' shared the provostship only five times out of the eighteen terms.

Furthermore, most lord provosts had inherited, or acquired by marriage, their entrée into the municipal elite, rather than having risen on merit. Only one of the nine, Alexander Brown, who held office twice, was neither the son of a baillie nor married into the family of a baillie. There were five sons, plus one nephew of town councillors, totalling 11 provostships. In due course, three of James Hadden's four sons served on the town council. The marital ties were sometimes even more remarkable. Gavin and James Hadden married sisters, as did James Young and Alexander Fraser. Alexander Brebner was not merely in business with Thomas Leys, he was also his brother-in-law.

This intertwined network of blood and business was so restricted that it shocked a select committee of MPs, hardly a body of sea-green incorruptibles in the pre-reform age. In its report of 1819 into the town's municipal affairs, the select committee described the prevailing state of affairs in graphic terms.

> The old council elect their successors; by which means it is not only possible, but almost invariably happens, that by alternate election of each other, the same party maintain possession of the council, to the entire exclusion of the rest of the burgesses. And although, by the sett of the burgh, 15 out of 19 members composing the council must retire annually, it appears by the

return of members of council for the last 20 years, and by the evidence of the town clerk, that, during the said period, Provost [James] Hadden has been 15 times on council, his partner Provost Brebner 10 times, his partner Provost Leys, 10 times, his brother, Gavin Hadden, 10 times, &c, &c, and that the majority of the council have been the same individuals during that time and chiefly either relations or connexions in business of Provost Hadden, who has been considered the leader of the town council for the last 20 years, and this whether he was in or out of the council at that time.[1]

The committee unearthed evidence of rampant abuse of power by this self-appointing clique. The public coffers were raided for private gain. Land and rights were sold off to friends of the councillors. Council minutes were altered after being approved. No accounts were produced, and any public statements grossly misrepresented the true financial position. In 1812 civic debts were officially estimated at £6,874, when in reality they were £120,000-£140,000. At one key council meeting in December 1811, James Hadden, although not at that time a councillor, attended and played a decisive part in the deliberations.[2]

The MP for the Aberdeen Burghs seat between 1801 and 1818 was associated with the extended Hadden family network. James Farquhar was a first cousin of James and Gavin Hadden (their mothers were sisters) and nephew to James Young. Farquhar's wife was a sister of the two sisters who married the Hadden brothers. Even more incestuously, Farquhar's brother William married the sister of Gavin and James Hadden.[3] Farquhar's father was a director of Farquhar & Hadden, stocking manufacturers, and his mother was part of the other main textile manufacturing family in the city. Farquhar was a brother-in-law by marriage to his predecessor as MP, Alexander Allardyce, since they too had married sisters. Even the opposition to the Tory Allardyce-Farquhar-Hadden complex had family connections. In 1801, when a vacancy was created by Allardyce's death, the Whigs considered running Keith Jopp against Farquhar. Jopp was the uncle by marriage to Farquhar and had been a first cousin to Allardyce.[4] This domination of public life extended widely. In 1800, six of the fourteen police commissioners were town councillors, past or present.[5] James Hadden had been the driving force behind the establishment of the Aberdeen Banking Company. The Aberdeen Savings Bank, aimed at the less privileged, was set up in 1815 at a meeting heavily saturated with local eminences such as James Hadden. In 1830, six of the 20 directors of the Savings Bank also sat on the Banking Company board. But only one director of the Aberdeen Town & County Bank, a recently formed rival to the Banking Company, was also a member of the Savings Bank directorate. Wider community life was heavily permeated by these men.

The definition and measurement of an elite is notoriously difficult. The data assembled here to provide a general indication of the composition of the Aberdeen elite has been taken from Post Office directories and issues of the *Aberdeen Almanac*. Membership of the elite has been defined to include all those listed as JPs, sitting on elected bodies such as the town council or the school board, and those listed as directors of businesses. The eldership of the city's churches, then one of the significant indicators of status, was dominated by members of the elite.[6] Voluntary associations counted on the support of city notables as managers and directors. In 1830, exactly one-third of office bearers in ten selected societies were drawn from the elite. The occupational composition of the elite in 1830 was dominated by three groups, lawyers, manufacturers and large-scale merchants. They were key components of the ruling group, with the lawyers forming a professional and social bridge between the urban middle class and the gentry of the county. Smaller retailers, tradesmen and other non-legal professions were not well represented, and were excluded from politics under the unreformed system. During these early years of the century, there was little residential differentiation. Half of those identified as social leaders in 1830 had addresses within the central area, east of the Denburn, and a further quarter lived in the western part of Union Street. Some of the wealthier Aberdonians had two houses, both within the town. Gavin Hadden stayed at his property on the Green in winter, retreating in summer to his second home at Union Grove, just outside the city boundary.[7]

In the early nineteenth century many of the county gentry owned houses in Aberdeen, and spent part of the year engaged in the town's social round, preferring to stay in their country properties during the summer months. The lesser laird and Aberdeen merchant, James Forbes, lived at Springhill, three miles outside the town, in summer and moved to his property on Trinity Quay at the onset of winter. The widow of the fifth Burnett, laird of Kemnay, moved to Castle Street lodgings for the duration of the winter.[8] Dinners were attended by the upper echelons of the social pyramid, and frequently catered for large numbers of guests. Lord Kintore organised a dinner for 70 in the town to celebrate the victory at Trafalgar. Sir Alexander Bannerman recorded holding a dinner and dance for 60, but James Hadden easily surpassed that a week later, accommodating 120 for dinner. The meal at these dinners was taken at 5.30 in the evening, and would be followed by dancing, and a light supper would be available at the end of the night.[9] At the start of the calendar year it was the custom to have four assemblies, held at fortnightly intervals. Three or four balls were also held in winter, attended by the cream of local society. In addition, private dances were organised by individuals, the most prestigious being that of Lady Innes of Edingight, held in her Silver Street house.[10] Grand parties were also regular features of the time, and Sir Alexander Bannerman's brother, Thomas, held these frequently. One of his more spectacular events was a grand ball held on his 4,000 ton ship, *Arkwright*, otherwise used for the South

American cotton trade.[11] The most distinguished of these gatherings was the annual party hosted by Miss Betty Gordon of Leichesen, while other unmissable soirées were held by General Hay, in the Upperkirkgate, by Mrs Henry Lumsden and by Mrs James Farquhar, both in Union Terrace.[12]

A high-point in the social calendar came with the annual Aberdeen races. These attracted neighbouring aristocracy for the three days of sport, with the Duke of Gordon himself in attendance. During the time of the races, an 'ordinary' took place in the County Rooms. Events 'taking place there were considered to be of a higher class than elsewhere in town'; dinner was served at 5 o'clock, and cost the very high price of one guinea (£1 1s.), while the ball after the meal cost extra.[13] The Assembly Rooms were built to provide a town club for wealthy landowners, providing dancing, dining, gaming and billiards. The other major feature of elite entertainment in the first third of the century was theatre-going. The main, indeed the only respectable, theatre was the Theatre Royal, in Marischal Street, extensively patronised by fashionable society. Recalling the 1830s, one journalist observed: 'I have seen Marischal Street half lined with the waiting carriages of the best families of the town and county.'[14] Such a form of entertainment would shortly become unthinkable. The surge of evangelical zeal which grew in the 1830s and 1840s was blamed by some theatre devotees for the sad decline of the Theatre Royal, which retained but a shadow of its former glory by mid-century.

This small-scale and compact group controlled the economic, social, municipal and political levers of the city. The intimacy was emphasised by W. G. Blaikie, who grew up in the 1820s and 1830s. 'The town was compact and small enough to make it possible, not indeed for everybody to know everybody, but to have a tolerably general acquaintance with the community and especially to know

In the 1830s the theatre was still a 'respectable' pastime for the well-to-do. Later in the century it struggled against evangelical hostility.

THEATRE-ROYAL.
GRAND NIGHT'S PERFORMANCES.

Revival of Sir WALTER SCOTT's powerful Dramatic Romance of "THE LADY OF THE LAKE," with NEW DRESSES, and the following NEW SCENES. The Drawings taken on the spot by T. ALLOM, and Painted by Mr. OGILVIE.
A View of Loch Katrine.—Also, View of the Corra Lynn.

Positively the LAST NIGHT of the Grand Spectacle of "BLUE BEARD," and LAST but ONE of Mr. G. V. BROOKE's Appearance this Season.

On SATURDAY Evening, January 21, 1837,
Will be presented, a Dramatic Romance, taken from Sir Walter Scott's celebrated Poem, entitled THE

LADY OF THE LAKE.

With New and Appropriate Dresses, Scenery, and Decorations.
Fitz-james (Knight of Snowdon), Mr G. V. BROOKE
Roderick Dhu, ⎱ Outlawed Chiefs ⎰ Mr LAAGLEY,
Douglas, ⎰ ⎱ Mr MACKAY.
Malcolm Græme, Mr RYDER, Jun.   Murdoch, Mr SMITH.   Malise, Mr R. RYDER.
Brian, (a Monkish Hermit), Mr MACDONALD.   Allan Bane, (a Minstrel), Mr CRONE.
Ellen, (Lady of the Lake), Mrs RYDER.   Lady Margaret, Mrs TYRER.   Blanch, (a Manaic), Mrs NEWCOMBE.
Clansmen, Soldiers, &c. by Supernumeraries.

A Popular Dance - - - - - by Miss TYRER.

The whole to conclude with, for the last time, the Grand Eastern Spectacle of

BLUE BEARD;
Or, FEMALE CURIOSITY.

With New Scenery, Dresses, and Decorations.
Abomelique, (Blue Beard), Mr LANGLEY.   Selim, Mr MACDONALD.   Ibrahim, Mr CRONE.   Shaabac, Mr RYDER, Jun.
Hassan, Mr R. RYDER.   Spahis, Messrs. BONNAR, MACKAY, and SMITH.
Fatima, Mrs NEWCOMBE.   Irene, Mrs JACKSON.   Beda, Miss RYDER.

Incidental to the Piece, the following Songs, Duets, &c.
DUET—" Twilight glimmers," Mrs. NEWCOMBE and Mr MACDONALD.
QUARTETTO—" Ruthless Robber," Mr. MACDONALD, Mrs. JACKMAN, Mrs. NEWCOMBE, and Mr CRONE.
CHORUS—" Mark his approach with Thunder."
DUET—" Tinka ting," Mr RYDER, Jun. and Miss RYDER.
SONG—" While pensive I thought on my love," Mrs NEWCOMBE.
DUET—" All is hushed," Mrs NEWCOMBE and Mrs JACKMAN.
TRIO—" Look from the Turret," Mrs JACKMAN, Mrs NEWCOMBE, and Mr RYDER, Jun.
A Turkish Dance, by Miss TYRER and Miss RYDER.

The following NEW SCENERY, by Mr OGILVIE,—
Turkish Village—Procession of Blue Beard over the Mountains.
New Chamber and Garden.
Blue Chamber.
Horrid Spectacle of Blue Beard's Murdered Wives.
Turrets of Abomelique's Castle.
Terrific Denouement.

On MONDAY, Sheridan Knowles's New Play of " THE WIFE."—St. Pierre, Mr G. V. BROOKE.   The Wife, Mrs RYDER.
With " BLACK-EYED SUSAN."—William, Mr G. V. BROOKE ; and Susan, Mrs RYDER.—Being for the BENEFIT of Mr G. V. BROOKE, and his Last Appearance this Season.
Splendid Performances on Tuesday.

Boxes, 3s.   Pit, 2s.   Gallery, 1s.
Younger Branches of Families, under 12 years of age, admitted at half-price.—General Half-price, at Nine o'Clock.
DOORS OPEN AT SEVEN—THE PERFORMANCES TO COMMENCE AT HALF-PAST SEVEN EXACTLY.

J. Davidson and Co, Printers, Aberdeen.

"everybody that was anybody".'[15] Economic fluctuations, the rise of new industries and political reform soon swept away this world, and replaced it with a new social framework which persisted for much of the following century.

CHARACTERISTICS OF THE VICTORIAN ELITE

The impact of reform acts on parliamentary and municipal elections instigated a major change in the nature and composition of the elite. The collapse of the textile industry at the end of the 1840s destroyed much of the older urban ruling class. It was emblematic of the changes in power in the city that one of the old elite's establishments, the Aberdeen Banking Company, collapsed in 1849, coinciding with a remarkable burst of energetic creation which produced new financial companies, mainly involving Alexander Anderson. The expanding building industry was represented by provosts like Fleming, Leslie and Matthews, while the fishing and shipping trades produced provosts such as Thompson, Henderson, Meff and Mearns. Manufacturing contributed Blaikie and Stewart, mercantile interests included Jamieson, Mitchell and Esslemont. The legal profession was represented by Anderson, Webster and Wilson. This new elite represented a far greater diversity of interests than its predecessors.

Highly symbolic of the aspiration to a more open style of municipal administration was the decision of the councillors, prompted by the first post-reform lord provost, James Blaikie, to admit the public and the press to the deliberations of the town council.[16] But the change was not quite complete. Several of the old regime still found a place in municipal and community life. Members of the Hadden clan were still to be found in the council chamber nearly twenty years after the reform legislation. Links between old and new existed. Sir Thomas Blaikie, lord provost 1839–46 and 1853–55, married the niece of Provost Dingwall, 1799–1800. Nor did new men mean the abandonment of old practices. Among the provosts, intermarriage and blood ties were still in evidence. The two Blaikie brothers are one obvious instance, as is the tie between George Thompson and William Henderson, his son-in-law. Thompson was also related by marriage to the Blaikies, and to the McKinnon dynasty of ironfounders and lawyers. James Blaikie was connected through his wife to the Pirie dynasty of papermakers.[17] Two provosts, Alexander Nicol and John Webster, married sisters.

Efforts to guide and manipulate the composition of the town council persisted after reform. In 1883, John Morgan received an unsolicited letter from the current lord provost, James Matthews stating that 'I have been asked by an influential body of citizens to write to you to ascertain if you will allow yourself to be nominated for the Town Council.' Morgan agreed, and soon after joined the town council.[18] References in obituaries suggest that prominent individuals were frequently invited by unidentified social leaders to join the town council. Most such offers were declined, but the clear implication was that a seat was theirs for the taking. In a further echo of traditional practices, business links among councillors persisted. Matthews, an architect, was a business partner of John Morgan, a builder. They both sat on the board of a granite manufacturing concern, along with two other provosts, William Leslie and George Jamieson. A fourth, Alexander Nicol, was proprietor of the Seaton Brick & Tile Works which merged with the Northern Patent Brick Co., one of whose directors was John Morgan.[19]

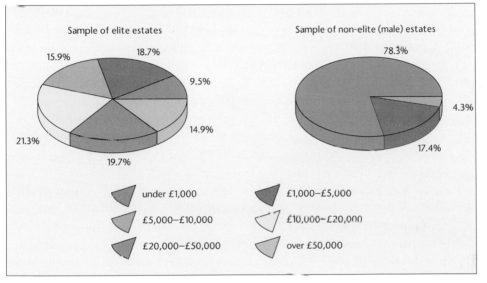

Figure 14.1
Value of estates left by elite and non-elite citizens of Aberdeen. (Source: NAS, Calendar of Confirmations, 1890-1930)

The economic base of the influential persons in this long century remained stable, but the balance did change noticeably from the earlier period. It is perhaps the clearest sign of the rise to prominence of the legal profession that nine of the ten provosts between 1707 and 1914 who were members of the Society of Advocates, as the local solicitors' body was called, held office after 1833. Of the groups that were dominant before 1830, manufacturers fell away, reflecting the altered economic structure of the city after the crises of the 1840s. The new elite included more small businessmen, such as retailers and tradesmen. The elite was reinforced in its close-knit identity by the development of interlocking business connections. The number of multiple directorships held by directors of bank and insurance companies rose markedly in the later nineteenth century. In 1830 a sample of 62 individuals held 112 directorships between them. By 1913 a larger sample of 79 individuals held 198 directorships between them. Thereafter the number of directorships fell to 150 by 1950 although the number of individuals remained virtually unchanged at 77.[20] Thus, an inner core tended to emerge,

George Jamieson 1809–93

Born in Perth, George Jamieson moved to Aberdeen at an early age and was apprenticed to Robert Troup, a grocer. For fifty years he ran a wholesale business, mainly as the senior partner of Jamieson & Mitchell. His extensive public service included membership of the police board 1839–41, dean of guild 1860–62 and 1866–68. He was a staunch defender of the Guildry and strongly supported its representation on the town council. In municipal affairs he was closely associated with Sir Alexander Anderson and Alexander Nicol. He returned to the town council in 1872, representing the fourth ward, and served as lord provost 1874–80. Union Terrace Gardens were set out during his term of office. He is credited with suggesting to Miss Duthie that a park might be an appropriate gift to the city. His role in the Harbour Act 1879 is commemorated in Provost Jamieson's Quay. He served as chairman of the St Nicholas parochial board 1865–69, was a director of the North of Scotland Bank, the Aberdeen Savings Bank, Fidelity Insurance Co., the Plate Glass Co., the Orkney, Shetland and North of Scotland Steam Navigation Co., the Hull & Newcastle Co., and the Heritable Securities Co. He was chairman of the Aberdeen District Tramways Company, and of the AAICP. He was a Liberal, but seceded to the Liberal Unionists in protest at Gladstone's policy on Irish home rule. He was a United Presbyterian, serving as an elder of Belmont Street Church.

identifiable as having a stake as director or proprietor in a number of ventures, where linkages with other leading players were established.

With Jamieson around the table at Fidelity Insurance were John Crombie Jr, a textile manufacturer who was also a director the North of Scotland Bank, J. W. Cruickshank, a farmer also on the North Bank's board and a director of three other companies, R. W. Mackay, a warehouseman and again a North Bank director, and John Sangster, a pharmaceutical chemist who was an Aberdeen Savings Bank board member. Shipping interests brought Jamieson into contact with another group of influential citizens, A. M. Ogston, chemical manufacturer (Town & County Bank, Scottish Provincial Assurance), David MacDonald, hide and leather merchant (Caledonian Insurance), Thomas Adam, shipowner (Great North of Scotland Railway), A. G. Pirie, paper manufacturer (Northern Assurance), Alexander Davidson, lawyer (Union Bank, Northern Assurance) and George Donald, glass merchant (North of Scotland Bank and Aberdeen Savings Bank).

The residential homogeneity of the pre-1830 era subsequently broke down. By the end of the century, only about 10 per cent of the elite were found in the old core of the city. The movement westward meant that by mid-century the area between the Denburn and Holburn Junction housed most of the elite. But increasingly thereafter the elite was found in the district to the west of Union Street, bounded by Union Grove and Albyn Place. By 1890 over 38 per cent of the

Some of Aberdeen's elite photographed by Washington Wilson, 1852–56.

elite lived in the West End. The most important addresses were initially on Albyn Place and Carden Place, but by the 1900s the locus of the elite was sited in Rubislaw Den and Queen's Road. In 1913 these two streets housed a cluster of the top Aberdonians, while King's Gate, Gladstone Place and Hamilton Place had become prestigious addresses. One who lived in the area described Queen's Road and its environs as consisting of 'solid houses of the more prosperous Aberdonians, of grey or pink granite, set well back in their gardens'.[21] The concentration is remarkable.

RUBISLAW TERRACE, ABERDEEN. 10,072. G.W.W.

Rubislaw Terrace on the north side of Albyn Place c. 1900 reflected both increased prosperity and the increasing segregation of social classes as the better-off moved steadily westward. Photograph by George Washington Wilson.

In 1913, there were over 500 streets in the city, but only 121 had a member of the elite in them, and 51 of these streets, less than 10 per cent of the total, contained 254, or about 80 per cent of these individuals. But about 20 per cent lived outside the city, primarily in Deeside villages such as Cults, Murtle and Peterculter.

The educational background of the entire spectrum of the elite is impossible to assess, as this is rarely given in obituaries. But a study of one important component group, the prominent lawyers, between 1800 and 1938 indicates the central importance of Aberdeen Grammar School, which produced 63 per cent of those whose schooling is recorded. Robert Gordon's College, converted to a school for the elite in the 1880s, made little impact before the Second World War, as only 3 per cent of lawyers attended the school. The only serious local challenge came from the Gymnasium, a private school in Old Aberdeen which operated in the second half of the nineteenth century.[22] Ten per cent of the top lawyers were old boys. It took boarders, but day pupils from the city also attended, including two members of the Crombie family. Herbert Grierson, later an Aberdeen professor, was a boarder. Very few of the members of the Society of Advocates were educated in private schools, only 4 per cent of them before 1939.[23] In addition, virtually all lawyers went to university in Aberdeen. Before 1860 Marischal College took 90 per cent and King's took the remainder. After the fusion in that year, 86 per cent of practising lawyers were graduates of Aberdeen University. Only five of the 154 lawyers included in the survey were educated elsewhere in Scotland, primarily in Edinburgh, while only three studied at Oxford or Cambridge. This common educational experience encouraged a very close community feeling among the elite, especially within the legal profession.

A survey of the ten largest Scottish gross estates left annually between 1876 and 1913 suggests that Aberdonians did not accumulate great wealth. Only three men from Aberdeen appeared in the sample, compared with 16 from Dundee and 13 from Paisley.[24] If these figures are expressed relative to the share of population, Aberdeen had a wealth:population ratio of 0:25 compared with the ratio for Dundee, which was 1:20, and the ratio for Paisley, which was 1:89. Moreover, not only did Aberdeen have fewer wealthy individuals, the average estate was significantly lower than in these other towns. Aberdeen recorded £219,469, compared with Dundee £283,494 and Paisley £832,258. The gross value of the majority of estates left by prominent citizens between 1890 and 1930 was below £20,000 (74 per cent) and almost half (44 per cent) was below £10,000.[25]

Aberdeen's business elite made few extravagant public donations. Duthie Park, opened in 1883, was perhaps the nearest equivalent. This was the gift of a family which belonged to the pre-reform generation, and whose line had effectively died out.[26] Generosity was more often shown by gifts to institutions. The wealthy merchant A. P. Fletcher gave money for the foundation of a chair of history at the University, and also made a substantial donation to the Royal Infirmary. Scott Sutherland's gift in 1952 of his extensive Garthdee mansion, which had 29 rooms, to provide spacious accommodation for the architecture department of Robert Gordon's Technical College, is a later example of this philanthropy. This more discreet form of endowment is consistent with the general modesty and reticence of the city's wealthy.

While the Aberdeen elite was perhaps less prone to indulge in building the grandiose houses which characterised many of their peers in other Scottish towns, a certain amount of style was adopted. Sir Thomas Blaikie created a stir in 1839 by installing two or three lavatories on each floor of the imposing new home he built in Union Terrace. The uniqueness of this was highlighted by the facilities in the house of his niece and her husband, a prominent lawyer, Lachlan McKinnon, Jr. In the new home on Union Street which they entered in the 1850s, there was no bathroom, no cold water above the first floor, and no hot water in the kitchen. There was no mains sewer, so household waste was collected in two cesspools positioned under back windows and covered by flagstones. Standards improved greatly in the next half century and, by the Edwardian age, private

David Stewart was educated at Dr Tulloch's Academy, the Gymnasium and King's College. After graduation he joined his father in the family firm, Messrs S. R. Stewart & Co., the largest combmaking business in the world, becoming owner in 1887. He was president of the chamber of commerce 1883–84, dean of guild 1885–89, a member of the school board 1885–88, and of the University Court 1889–1900. Elected for the Ferryhill ward in 1889, he served as lord provost 1889–95. His term of office witnessed the extension of the city to include Old Aberdeen, Woodside and Torry, and the new park in Woodside was named in his honour. In 1889 he became a member of the University Court and played an important part in the large expansion programme at Marischal College. He later became rector's assessor at the University. He stood unsuccessfully for the Unionists in Aberdeen South in the 1895 general election. He was knighted in 1896. He was deputy-lieutenant of Aberdeenshire and Kincardineshire, a livery-man of the City of London, and a director of the Northern Assurance Company. He became a director of the Great North of Scotland Railway in 1891 and served as chairman from 1904 until his death.

Sir David Stewart, combmaker, lord provost 1889–95. Portrait by William Orchardson, c. 1894.

bathrooms for the parents were provided in the Grierson family home in King's Gate.[27]

The interiors of some houses were substantial. Lord Cockburn noted in 1841 that the house of Baillie Crombie contained 'a more spacious lobby, staircase, dining-room and drawing-room than any house in the New Town of Edinburgh'.[28] Decoration tended in the later part of the century to the sombre. Mid-Victorian green and gold wallpapers, with drop crystal chandeliers, were discarded in the 1870s for the 'severe Cottier style' of subdued dull reds and blacks. Professor Sir Alexander Ogston's residence was described by his grand-daughter as having 'an atmosphere of solid ugliness', and the mood created by its dark, heavy furnishings and decoration seems to have made Ogston's daughter depressed.[29]

VALUES AND LIFESTYLES OF THE ELITE

New interests began to emerge among the elite in the later Victorian period, reflecting changing values. The badges of status consequently adjusted as time passed. Eldership in the Kirk, a very potent measure of status in the first half of the century, rapidly fell in significance in the last quarter of the century. It is no doubt significant that the *Aberdeen Almanac* ceased to list the elders of the various presbyterian churches after 1882. The experience of the most prestigious Free Church in Aberdeen, the West Free Church, is instructive. In 1889, the congregation elected ten men to serve as elders. But when the minister called on them, all of the ten initially declined to take up office, and it was only after a personal call from the

Mrs J. W. Crombie, wife of the leading textile manufacturer, J. E. Crombie. Portrait by J. S. Sargeant, 1898.

minister that five of them assented and were ordained.[30] This was not an isolated episode; if anything, the position deteriorated thereafter. In 1912–13, after approaching the twelve who topped the poll, the minister 'was sorry to report that with one exception, they all declined to accept office'. The situation was exacerbated by the feeling that the next eight on the list should not be invited to become elders. In the end, four of the top 20 agreed to serve. The consequence was that the church was perpetually understaffed from the 1890s onward, as normally only between one-half and two-thirds of the required posts could be filled. This situation persisted throughout the twentieth century.

The leisure time of the elite was more and more directed to less earnest activities. On the one hand, there was a resurgence of interest in aesthetic matters. The theatre, under a cloud from the mid-1830s, regained public acceptability in the 1880s. The

Aberdeen Theatre Company was formed by a key group of the inner core of the elite, and the resultant building of Her Majesty's Theatre replaced, in 1872, the virtually moribund Theatre Royal, which had staggered on for thirty years. By the turn of the century the pantomime at the 'HM' had become a regular institution for the middle class. Collecting works of art became a major preoccupation of the wealthy in the last quarter of the nineteenth century. Alexander Macdonald, a leading granite manufacturer, amassed around 150 paintings, mostly by contemporary artists. His collection was bequeathed on his early death to form the core of the city's Art Gallery, to which he left one-third of his estate, with instructions that only work created within 25 years of the date of purchase were to be acquired.[31] A contemporary, John Forbes White, also built up an impressive range of paintings. White specialised in the works of Corot, and was instrumental in setting up the Art Gallery in the 1880s.[32] Sir James Murray became chairman of the Art Gallery in 1901 and, by the time he left office in 1928, had transformed it into one of the finest municipal galleries in Britain. He created the sculpture court,

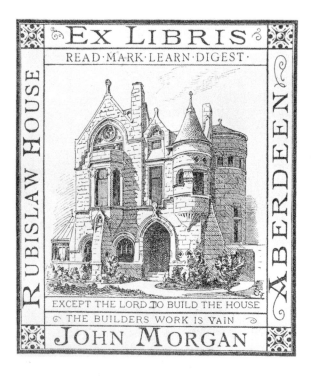

John Morgan was so proud of his new house that he had it on his book labels.

designed to inspire the granite trade, funded extensions, presented works from his own superb private collection, and secured endowments. His achievement was recognised when he was awarded the freedom of the city in 1931. Other keen collectors included Sir John Fleming who stressed, in an address to the Northern Arts Club in 1910, the importance of businessmen developing a lighter side to their lives, in his case by buying the works of contemporary Scottish painters.[33] Major patrons of art included J. E. Crombie, who commissioned Sargent to paint his wife. Book-collecting also flourished. Perhaps the most enthusiastic bibliophile was John Morgan. He possessed over 4,500 volumes, mostly rare or special items. The prime claim to fame of his library was that he held the finest collection of the works of Ruskin in Scotland. Perhaps the most revealing comment about Morgan's enthusiasm for books came in his obituary notice, which noted approvingly that 'not only did Mr Morgan possess books, but he also read them'.[34]

The landed class had been accustomed to foreign travel as a natural part of their lifestyle. Thus, in 1833, Alexander Bannerman toured Holland, Germany and Austria, as one of several such trips. The newer wealthy tended to go later in life.

John Morgan first went abroad when aged 35. Five years later he embarked on what he termed a grand tour to Naples, Rome, Florence, Venice and Basle. He was accompanied by a fellow successful builder, J. G. Bissett. For the most part these tours were educational, but frequently business was mixed with instruction. Morgan's visits to North America were partly in pursuit of contracts there. Even in the Eternal City, Morgan's Aberdonian business instincts were not abandoned. 'As Builders from the City of Granite, both Mr Bissett and myself were curious to know what the modern Romans could do in the way of building with granite.'[35] They were very impressed, finding Italian granite working far superior to methods at home. Sir John Fleming, likewise, embarked in middle age on a succession of travels which took him to most European countries, as well as to North America and the Holy Land. While for this earlier generation, the educational and instructional elements bulked large in the urge to visit abroad, this impulse seems to have diminished among those born later. Scott Sutherland went on numerous trips, mostly on luxury liners, and invariably in pursuit of pleasure. On the eve of the Second World War he embarked on a world cruise with 200 Americans who had especially chartered a liner for the trip.[36]

In summer, many of the more prosperous families retreated from the intolerable heat of the city, which occasionally rose above 60°F, to seek refuge in the countryside. Usually Deeside villages served as the bolt-holes for wealthy Aberdonians. The parents of the prominent lawyer, Harvey Hall, spent summers at Murtle, while his uncle went to Banchory Devenick. At the turn of the century, this practice was still evolving. John Morgan built a wooden bungalow, modelled on the style of American holiday homes, at Torphins for summer visits. It was surrounded by two acres of woodland, moor and garden. So attractive was his house that he was asked to construct others along Deeside for city businessmen.[37] The father would either travel daily to Aberdeen to work, or he would stay in the town during the week, going to the holiday home only at the weekend. Lachlan MacKinnon adopted the latter course from the 1890s when his family holidayed at Cullen. In the Deeside hamlets, too, bonds with other elite families were forged, as socialising was otherwise severely restricted.

Sport was another area where the elite found new outlets. Hitherto the only recreational association for the elite had been the (Royal) Aberdeen Golf Club. Re-formed in 1815, from 1827 onward the game was played in a uniform of a scarlet coat having gilt metal buttons embossed with the club's initials and a Scotch this-tle, and a black velvet cap. For club dinners, the colour of the coat was blue, but the trimmings were identical. The captains of the club were a roll-call of the city elite, and included five lord provosts.[38] Many of the new initiatives in sport after about 1860 were also launched by members of the top echelon of local society. Cricket was begun in 1857 under the auspices of A. G. Pirie (paper manufacturer), and James F. Lumsden, Alexander Edmond, and W. K. Burnett all lawyers. The Gymnastic Society was started in 1867 by five men who in later life became a stock-broker, a university professor (Sir Alexander Ogston), the Procurator-Fiscal (G. Cadenhead), a lawyer and a company director. The explanation offered for the prominence in gymnastics by a rising lawyer, George Cruden, sums up much of this new impetus.

> He has by the exercise of his innate energy, contrived to perfect himself in gymnastics, boating etc. – the muscular physique and enviable good health which he finds in such exercises enabling him to perform, with verve and success, the many important professional duties devolving upon him.[39]

For the less energetic, sporting initiatives of this era attracted an elite enrolment. Two lawn tennis clubs were established, both presided over by pillars of the community such as Jopp, Holland, and Henderson of Devanha House, and both located in the prime residential area of the West End. The Curling Club, begun in 1871, was sited in Fountainhall Road and included James Matthews, General Rutherford, Colonel Jopp and the ubiquitous W. K. Burnett on the committee. This club had a social side, with 152 members, but the 'playing club' contained a mere 60.[40]

The intimate nature of elite relations identified in the opening decades of the century became increasingly difficult to sustain as the city grew physically and numerically. Yet informal meeting-places still prevailed well into the second half of the century. A popular rendezvous was the Lemon Tree Inn, where Baillie William Fraser and his cronies gathered in an evening for debate and discussion.[41] Clubs began to appear offering venues in which the elite might do business without scrutiny from the rest of society. The Northern Club, established in 1854, was geared to accommodate the country gentlemen, but the real surge in membership came in the 1890s. In 1889 the University Club was launched. Its membership was largely drawn from the professional and business people residing in the city. Soon after, the Union Club was set up to cater for those of a Conservative or Liberal Unionist outlook. With fairly high fees and a controlled entry, often using a ballot to blackball applicants, the elite was set ever more socially apart. Yet even in the 1930s there still existed more informal meeting places for business and professional people. Scott Sutherland recorded that many of his age and type gathered each evening in Ma Cameron's bar which he described as 'Aberdeen's most discreet pub ... it was the Mecca of business and professional men who passed through its portals without being observed. No draught beer was served, hence the working man avoided it. Ma Cameron was the snob licensee of her day.'[42] For some of a later generation who remember Ma Cameron's, the concept of it as an elite howff might be somewhat difficult to grasp.

The role of voluntary organisations burgeoned in the mid-nineteenth century. The elite found these fulfilled a number of vital needs. Firstly, status and prestige were accorded to those who served on such associations. More importantly, perhaps, they permitted close direction of social policy by those with economic power and social standing, while by-passing official intervention by the state. A panoply of societies was founded to tackle the city's perceived needs and problems. The *Post Office Directory* and the *Aberdeen Almanac* for 1860 listed a comprehensive battery of agencies. These included 16 primarily religious societies, such as the Aberdeen Bible Society, founded in 1827, three temperance societies, 28 societies for the benefit of the poor or disadvantaged, such as the Industrial Asylum for the Rescue and Reformation of Females of Dissolute Habits, and the General Institution for the Education of the Deaf and Dumb, and five hospitals including the dispensary and the Hospital for Incurables. The ethos by which these institutions functioned was summed up in the note appended to the Clothing Society, founded in 1817, warning that 'imposture (would be) prevented by previous investigation'.[43] By 1890, membership of these committees was sought after by the elite. Some 31 individuals held multiple posts, 97 in all, or three per person, while others were content to be active in just one society. Some indeed appeared to collect committee posts. John Crombie Junior, William Henderson and William Yeats, an advocate, all held six, while George Jamieson, James Kinghorn and

---

Sir William Henderson 1826–1904

Born at Aberdour, William Henderson served an apprenticeship with the North of Scotland Bank at Fraserburgh. In 1850 he became a partner in George Thompson & Co., and between 1854 and 1857 acted as the London agent, subsequently returning to Aberdeen having married Thompson's daughter. He later became senior partner of the firm, and a partner in Walter Hood & Co. He was a director of the North of Scotland Bank, the Scottish Employers' Liability and General Accidental Insurance Company, the Bannermill Cotton Co., and was chairman of the Aberdeen Savings Bank 1897–1904. He served as a harbour commissioner 1869–81, and was a member of the school board 1873–78. He served as president of the Chamber of Commerce 1874–75, and was elected to represent his local ward, Ferryhill, on the town council in 1885. He served as lord provost between 1886–89 and was knighted in 1893. He served as deputy-lieutenant for Aberdeenshire. He played a major part in raising £30,000 for the rebuilding of the Aberdeen Royal Infirmary in 1887, including a donation of £1,000 from Andrew Carnegie. He contributed to this fund and to the University extension scheme, and supported the RAHSC. He was president of the Aberdeen Sailors' Institute. He was a Liberal and a Free Churchman. He played a major role in establishing the Ferryhill Free Church. On the death of his wife he established a medical missionary station in India in memory of her interest in such work.

Alexander Walker each had five. This of course reinforced the interlocking business relationships noted earlier.

Increasingly, however, as the religious-cum-moral drive of the evangelical generation was eclipsed, so the involvement of the elite in such organisations diminished. By 1938, only about 20 per cent of the elite were active in voluntary circles compared with one-third 50 years earlier, holding in total only 76 positions. A small group of 16 individuals held a significant number of multiple obligations. Furthermore, the number of voluntary associations began to decline. Another influence upon the dwindling male commitment to charitable efforts might have been the emergence of business-related associations. The Chamber of Commerce was, of course, the most important of these. From 148 members in 1872, its membership increased to reach 363 by 1933.[44] Prominent businessmen frequently became office-bearers, a sure sign of the significance of the Chamber. Single trade lobbies also emerged. The building trade seems to have been prone to forming groups. John Morgan, an active member of the Chamber of Commerce, explained the need for the Aberdeen Master Masons' Association, in which he was a central figure. 'Such associations have still a great deal to overtake for the benefit and betterment of their members, in the way of improving prices and reducing excessive and unhealthy competition.'[45] It is noticeable also that business-related social organisations flourished after 1918 (the Rotary Club, the Round Table, the Junior Businessmen's Club), simultaneously with the decline of involvement in socially concerned voluntary associations. The stress of intensified economic competition may have necessitated this redirection of attention and energy.

The desire to establish a more defensive posture in business matters might also be connected with the changes in freemasonry. Until the very late nineteenth century, masons were not very significant among the elite. Of the committee which organised a masonic bazaar in October 1896, and which was drawn from office-bearers, not one appeared on the list of nearly 200 individuals identified as the elite in 1890.[46] But recruitment to the most important lodge, No. 1, altered markedly at that time. While, between 1800 and 1890, the majority of entrants were manual workers, and lawyers comprised just 7 per cent, between 1890 and 1929, the figures for the two groups were 1 per cent and 34 per cent respectively. The lodge masters, for most of nineteenth century drawn from a mix of merchants and retailers, after 1900 were drawn primarily from the ranks of lawyers, engineers and manufacturers.[47] Even so, the number of freemasons among the elite remained very modest.

THE COUNTY ELITE

Increasingly after 1832, the gentry in the surrounding rural counties distanced themselves from the new urban dominant groups. Fewer of them kept town houses. Those individuals from the county who were active in the early-nineteenth-century social elite had virtually all disappeared by the 1860s. A handful only, including Innes of Learney, Nicholson of Glenbervie, and Irvine of Drum, kept a presence in the city. For others, the advent of the railway and the improved road network in the county made residence in Aberdeen less essential. The establishment of the Northern Club in 1854, with three-quarters of the membership drawn from the county landowning class, testifies to the changed relations with the city. Very few lairds mixed regularly with townspeople. Of the 36 Aberdeenshire and Kincardineshire families listed in Burke's 1953 edition of *Landed Gentry*, only four could be said to have intermarried since the early nineteenth century with Aberdonians. The Patons of Grandholm were fairly minor but long-established lairds who had leased the textile mill on their estate to the Crombies in the middle of the nineteenth century. Yet it was 70 years later before a marriage between the two families occurred, when John Paton wed Fenella Crombie.[48] Perhaps the landed family with closest links to Aberdeen were the Bannermans, one of whom became the first MP in the reformed parliament. Yet almost all the baronets in the Bannerman line wed landowning rather than urban brides, and after the death of Alexander, the seventh baronet, in 1840, the family retained only vestigial contacts with the city. The wealthier Aberdonians did sometimes acquire rural property. Frequently this comprised little more than summer holiday homes. Others bought small estates, often not much more than a large farm. James Blaikie, for example, bought Craigiebuckler in 1815, and showed his interest in agricultural improvement by developing it. Others who followed this trend included George Thompson, who bought Pitmedden near Dyce, David MacHardy, who bought Cranford near Ruthrieston, and Alexander Davidson who acquired Desswood. Few of these estates passed from one generation to another, but were usually sold on the death of the purchaser. The only urban elite families to secure an entry in the 1953 edition of Burke's *Landed Gentry* were Adam of Denmore and Pirie-Gordon of Buthlaw.

Social events reveal an interesting distinction. For certain public or ceremonial occasions, flocks of county landowners would descend upon the city. This was especially the case for any event at which royalty might be present. The commemoration of the Prince of Wales' marriage in 1863 attracted a vast array of nobility and gentry to Aberdeen, including Lords Aberdeen and Huntly.[49] Otherwise, involvement was patchy and not very exalted socially. The annual Royal Hotel salmon dinner, held at the opening of the fishing season, illustrates this point. In a random year (1863), the landowners present included Lord Saltoun, Gordon of Fyvie, Gordon the younger of Ellon, Colonel Kyle of Binghill, Lt Elphinstone the younger of Logie, and Major Gordon of Ellon. These individuals did not represent the highest echelons of Aberdeenshire society, but seem to have

County, university
and town elites
combine in 1931 to
confer the freedom
of the city on Sir
George Adam Smith.
From left to right:
Lady Adam Smith,
the Marchioness of
Aberdeen, Viscount
Arbuthnot (lord
lieutenant of
Kincardineshire),
Adam Smith's
grand-daughter, Sir
George Adam Smith,
Sir Robert Williams,
A. D. Buchanan-
Smith, Lord Provost
Rust, Mrs Rust, the
Marquis of
Aberdeen and
Tremor (lord
lieutenant of
Aberdeenshire).

been the best the citizens could expect to attract.[50] The sharpness of the break was reflected in the fact that Aberdonians did not attend county events even when they were held in the city. The annual hunt ball, held in Aberdeen's Beach Ballroom in the inter-war years, seems to have been patronised exclusively by county society.[51]

THE UNIVERSITY ELITE

Few university professors belonged to the civic elite before 1914. In part this reflected the fact that many of them lived in manses in Old Aberdeen, which was physically quite isolated from the city until after the First World War. When the Rev. George Adam Smith and his wife took a walk from the West End to Old Aberdeen in the 1880s, they felt quite removed from the modern city. 'We thought it all lovely, a bit of a quaint old world, of ancient days and homes of studious peace.'[52] The introversion of the professoriate was reinforced by their close inter-relationships. A remarkable number were connected to other professors. Fathers and sons holding chairs at Aberdeen included the Piries, the Ogstons and the Trails. Others were linked by marriage. Alexander Bain was succeeded as holder of the chair in logic and rhetoric by his son-in-law. Professor Milligan's daughter married the son of Professor Trail, who subsequently also became a professor. Professor Milligan's son, David, became a lawyer and partner in Davidson & Garden. He served as convener of the University business committee, factored University property as well as many county estates, and was extensively engaged in charitable work. The daughter of Professor Francis Ogston married Professor Henry Cowan, who then became son-in-law and brother-in-law to university professors. University people mixed almost exclusively with fellow-academics, and their children also played with each other.[53]

After 1918, the University became less isolated, as Old Aberdeen was integrated into the city. Access roads were built, a bus service was introduced, the quainter parts were altered to encourage the flow of traffic, and housebuilding spread down towards the sea.[54] The creation of new chairs meant more professors found houses outwith Old Aberdeen. As a result, more academics began to participate in civic affairs. John Clarke, a lecturer in education, sat on the town council between the wars. In the 1950s the University provided its first, and to date only, lord provost in John M. Graham. He was professor of systematic theology 1937-71, and represented St Nicholas ward 1947-52 and St Machar ward 1952-64 on the town council, serving as lord provost 1952-55 and 1961-64. In the 1970s and 1980s several lecturers also served on the town council, usually representing the Labour Party.

The Parliamentary Elite

While the county elite became separated from that of the city, and the academic elite moved slowly towards it, the parliamentary elite remained distant. The city has sometimes seemed highly reluctant to choose its MPs from its own citizens. From 1832 to 1847 the burgh MP, Alexander Bannerman, was a merchant shipowner in the city, as was George Thompson, who held the seat from 1852 to 1857. Thereafter it was nearly a quarter of a century before another townsman, John Webster, represented the city from 1880 to 1885. For the remaining thirty years until the First World War, there was normally a local man sitting for one of the two city seats, D. V. Pirie, G. B. Esslemont and Sir John Fleming forming this chain. For a half century after 1918, however, the absence of Aberdeen-based Members became endemic. Only J. G. Burnett, owner of the Powis estate on the edge of the city, was a local man, sitting from 1931 to 1935, the last MP to represent the Conservatives in Aberdeen North in the twentieth century. Labour had five MPs elected for city seats between 1918 and 1970, none of them hailing from the city. Robert Hughes, who won in 1970, worked in the city but was born elsewhere. Only in 1997 when Anne Begg won Aberdeen South was a native of the city returned to represent it at Westminster.

All the Aberdonians who represented the city before 1918 were undoubtedly drawn from the elite, as evidenced by their occupations as shipowners, lawyers, manufacturers and merchants. Four had held the office of lord provost, and all were active in a range of business and voluntary concerns. To some extent the choice of outsiders may reflect a desire to have a nationally renowned name represent the city, James Bryce being an obvious example. Labour's choice of William Wedgwood Benn, who went into the cabinet shortly after winning Aberdeen North, may have reflected similar aspirations. His successors, G. M. Garro-Jones and Hector Hughes, may also have been thought of as potential cabinet ministers, although both proved to be a grave disappointment. However, several Aberdonians did find seats elsewhere. J. W. Barclay, a prominent merchant and a leading councillor in the 1860s, represented Forfarshire, while J. W. Crombie represented Kincardineshire, and Peter Esslemont represented East Aberdeenshire. In the twentieth century too, politically ambitious Aberdonians had to look elsewhere. T. F. Kennedy, a socialist stalwart from the 1900s, represented Kirkcaldy between the wars, and James Lamond entered Westminster by courtesy of the voters of Oldham East.

CHANGING ELITES

The coherent social elite which dominated business, local politics and much welfare provision throughout the Victorian period became diffused in the twentieth century under the impact of a diversity of forces. For much of the twentieth century the local economy struggled with change and the commercial supremacy of textiles, shipbuilding, fishing, granite and papermaking all declined. Those industries which survived often saw ownership and control pass away from the city. In some cases control fell into the hands of managers who did not often settle long. Crombie & Co. suffered this fate in 1958, as did Davidson of Mugiemoss

---

Robert M. Williamson 1867–1955

Fourth son of George Williamson, farmer and land valuator, Robert Williamson was born at Duffus near Elgin and educated at local schools in Duffus, King Edward and then at Aberdeen Grammar School. He graduated in law from the University of Edinburgh before joining the partnership in 1891 which his elder brother George had started in 1881 with James Paull. He also lectured in constitutional law and history at the University of Aberdeen 1908–33, He served as a JP and Honorary Sheriff Substitute. He was a member of the University Senate 1925–33, president of the Chamber of Commerce 1932–33, chairman of the board of Aberdeen Royal Mental Hospital for eight years. He was appointed a member of the board of the Aberdeen Savings Bank in 1918, a trustee in 1922 and served as chairman 1928–53. He was treasurer of the Society of Advocates 1924–26, and president 1926–28. He served as vice chairman of Aberdeen Journals Ltd and was awarded a CBE in 1950. He was succeeded as senior partner of Paull & Williamsons and as chairman of the Aberdeen Savings Bank by his son, Sir George Williamson.

---

in 1953, and Donside mills in 1969.[55] The legal profession remained at the core of the commercial elite, providing necessary services to all business activity, so that it was the lawyers who provided the essential continuity within the commercial elite.

There were other manifestations of continuity, primarily through family dynasties. Three generations of the Irvin dynasty, major figures in the fishing industry, each sat on the board of the Aberdeen Savings Bank, and each had been captain of the Royal Aberdeen Golf Club.[56] George Robb sat on the boards of two banks, one insurance company and four other companies, while Sir Andrew Lewis served as director of a bank, an insurance company and three other businesses. The directors of the Aberdeen Savings Bank in 1965 included six men whose fathers had also been directors and, in two cases, their grandfathers as well.[57]

The growth and diversity of twentieth-century society produced a proliferation of elites. Many of these were professional. Characteristically, the major employers in the city in the last quarter of the century – higher education, the medical services, local government, and the oil industry – all contained professional elites. Those working within these sectors, and hoping to advance careers within them, would aspire to impress and, in due course, join their specific professional elite which would have a national and probably an international focus rather than one based on Aberdeen itself. This process itself generated the further dissipation of identifiable elites and their values. Other forces curtailed some of the activities which, hitherto, held the urban elite together. One of these was the decline of charitable societies. The rise of the welfare state eroded the importance of the voluntary associations. Gala dances for the elite had been a very popular means of raising cash for charity. The 1945 Royal Infirmary 'Springtime Ball' marked the end of this tradition. £1,700 was raised for the hospital, thanks to a committee drawn from the elite, including the wife of the University principal, a major trawler-owner and public-spirited citizen, James Mackie, and two eminent lawyers who were hospital directors, J. C. Duffus and J. Downie Campbell.[58]

Indications of the fragmentation of the elite are revealed by the fates of two important societies. The Royal Aberdeen Golf Club, an institution of high exclusiveness, which applied a ballot before new members were admitted, had in 1913 a waiting list of 73 and a membership of 300. By 1972, however, with the membership roll down to 283, drastic measures were introduced. Fees were cut from £25 to £15, and perhaps more importantly, the practice of balloting for membership was abandoned. Within one year the membership had risen to 350, and the club's future was secure. Yet sociability seemed in decline. The annual dinner, revived in 1936, was attended by 94 members, but when again resuscitated in 1975, a mere 51 came, despite the membership now being 20 per cent greater.[59] The Royal Northern and the University Clubs continued as separate entities until declining attendance forced them to merge in 1979. In 1975 the University Club reported that the decrease in numbers using the club's facilities was giving rise to concern, and the number of members was little altered from the inter-war period. In 1938 there had been 181 members, in 1975 there were 191. Similarly, the Royal Northern in 1975 had 210 members compared with 184 in 1936. Both had a membership which was overwhelmingly based on the city and its immediate surroundings, 249 members out of a combined total of 401 in 1975.[60]

Another social change which, slowly, eroded the traditional elite structure was the changing role of women. Women in the elite, until the 1880s, were confined to being wives or daughters following male interests. Primarily this involved church-related charitable work. In 1860, six bodies were administered by a female committee, three religious and three dealing with industrial schools, including an orphanage. Despite improvements in education for girls in the later nineteenth century, entry to the higher status occupations was not rapid. The first female lawyer was Miss H. Cassie, who practised in the 1930s. But the first woman member of the Society of Advocates was not admitted until 1962. Twenty years later, the number was still only seven, out of a total membership of 193.[61] Only a handful of women reached prominent positions in business. One of the first, Mrs John Hall, was a director in her husband's business, rather than holding an independent position. The first woman elected to the town council was Isabella Burgess, a teacher, who represented Gilcomston 1930-33. Lucy Ward, a headmistress, represented St Machar in 1932; Jeannie Black, a housewife (Woodside 1937-43) and Isabella Sharp (Ruthrieston 1938-45) were the other pioneers. A survey of 20 leading women in Aberdeen carried out in 1938 showed that at least eleven were included because of their family connections, as wives or daughters of prominent men, including Mrs Allan, the wife of a prominent member of the Chamber of Commerce, and the wife of Lord Provost Watt. Others were included because they held a professional position, as a headmistress, the head of nursing at the ARI or as director of the Red Cross in Aberdeenshire. One businesswoman as such was listed, Miss Cassie, the pioneering lawyer. The public life of these women suggests that much of the Victorian legacy was still present. Most seem to have been mainly or solely engaged in church-related affairs, and as noted elsewhere the main activity for women was confined to running charitable bodies. By 1938 there were 131 female office-bearers, compared with 181 males in the voluntary sector. In 1860, the respective figures had been 82 and 388.[62] For many, however, life in the inter-war years remained restrictive. Alison Cairns, the Cambridge-educated daughter of Professor Cairns, returned to Aberdeen after graduating, where she ran a drama club for working-class girls. Eventually she left for London, as local employment opportunities were too severely restricted. During the second half of the century women made modest progress in elite activities. More women served on the town council, two with long service, Ellen M. Williamson representing Torry 1956–75 and Margaret E. Farquhar representing Northfield and then Granitehill from 1972 onward and serving as the first woman lord provost 1996–99. At the close of the century a small number of women held professorial appointments at Aberdeen University.

FRAGMENTATION OF THE ELITE

For much of the last two centuries the elite in Aberdeen was a fairly stable group. Most were born in the area. Of the top lawyers between 1800 and 1937, 90 per cent were born in the city or county of Aberdeen, and 75 per cent of the brides of those who married had the same provenance. A narrow channel of educational experience and highly concentrated residential areas accentuated the group identity. In the accumulation and conspicuous consumption of wealth, they were more modest than the urban bourgeoisie elsewhere in Scotland, but their strong sense of belonging to the city gave them a drive to contribute to its development, social and moral as well as economic. After the Second World War, the power and prestige of the traditional ruling sector waned as a diversity of elites emerged and flourished, several of which aspired to function on a national or international stage. There emerged, in consequence, an array of elites. Within the city two elites still dominated. Within the commercial world, the legal profession remained the essential intermediary and thereby retained a status which it held throughout the past two centuries. Civic leadership necessarily falls to the city council, and this constituted the other principal elite. In the twentieth century, however, political change and especially the formation of highly organised political parties formed an elite quite different from the city fathers of the Victorian era.

Aberdeen's first woman lord provost, Margaret Farquhar, 1996–99.

15

Leisure and Culture:
The Nineteenth Century

IRENE MAVER

STREET LIFE

This chapter and the next elaborate on how Aberdonians spent their leisure time between the 1800s and 1990s, focusing on both continuities and changes within the range of pastimes that were pursued.[1] There is a chronological as well as thematic dimension to the analysis, which broadly divides the chapters according to the centuries. While there was no significant legislative turning point in leisure, apart perhaps from drink licensing laws, cultural change arising from shifts in the political power-base did affect recreational habits. That the civic authority also played a vital role in directing leisure pursuits, especially from the late nineteenth century onward, reveals the intricate relationship between politics and culture.

The substantial programme of city improvements that spanned the early decades of the nineteenth century served as tangible evidence to Aberdonians of changes in their community, with a warren of thoroughfares gradually cleared to give way to prestigious developments like Union Street and King Street. According to the enthusiastic account of historian Walter Thom in 1811, this not only 'greatly contributed to the elegance of the city', but enhanced the quality of street life, especially for the wealthier classes.[2] He identified part of Union Street as the favoured resort of 'the gentlemen of the town', who gathered in proximity to Alexander Brown's impressively stocked bookshop to exchange news and gossip, and peruse the titles of new publications.[3] A particular facet of Aberdeen culture was here conspicuously on display, and also revealed the complex interaction between the physical fabric of the city and its social life. The appropriate environmental conditions directed opportunities for a variety of activities. The broad new thoroughfares were especially suitable for the pastime of promenading, and traders could provide refreshment and entertainment, as well as consumer goods. In response to long-standing public demand to place Aberdeen on a par with Edinburgh and Glasgow, architect Archibald Simpson designed the imposing Grecian-style Assembly Rooms on Union Street, which were opened in 1822 with facilities for dining, dancing and other fashionable pursuits.[4]

On the other hand, Aberdeen's monumental reconstruction was not uniform. In 1850 tourists were advised that to take full advantage of the splendid view from Union Bridge they should keep their eyes firmly fixed on the hills of Torry, 'all near objects being of the most repulsive description – hovels, smoke, and impurities of every kind'.[5] Like other contemporary urban communities, the old co-existed uncomfortably with the new, although the past continued to have a significant influence on perceptions of the city's culture. This was apparent in the plethora of nostalgic reminiscences about bygone Aberdeen which appeared from at least the 1830s, usually as newspaper serialisations, and which evoked a far more favourable image of street life in the unimproved areas than the early tour-guide would suggest.[6] Some writers delved into their childhood memories to recreate the atmosphere of former times. This was a device that proved attractive to the reading public, both at home and among the expatriate community, as was shown by the North American success of James Riddell's *Aberdeen and Its Folk* from the 1860s onward. An array of street-traders, hawkers and itinerant chap-book vendors usually featured prominently in the narrative, their colourful sales-patter and flamboyant style having lingered long in the consciousness of the authors. Street musicians, especially the 'fiddling fraternity', comprised another group that made an impact, their repertoire chiefly catering for the taste in strathspeys and reels so enduringly popular in North-East Scotland.[7] While the distance separating the events and recollections have tended to give such works a disconcertingly rosy glow of retrospection, the robust nature of Aberdeen's street culture remains strikingly apparent.

TAVERN CULTURE

Taverns and public houses were another feature of city life that for some Aberdonian writers could evoke comforting nostalgia. However, as one historian has pointed out with reference to early nineteenth-century Scotland, such establishments were more than just premises for indulging in the more gregarious pastimes of eating and drinking for they also served as business and political centres.[8] This function was not confined to the working classes, who were restricted in their choice of available meeting places, but was ingrained in the habits of the more wealthy. Even in the 1850s William Carnie remembered the regular gatherings of 'the better known burghers of Bon-Accord' in a Guestrow tavern, where the editor of the *Aberdeen Herald*, James Adam, would check the newspaper galley-proofs while fortifying himself with whisky-toddy.[9] It was an overwhelmingly male environment with females usually present in a serving

Jane Ronald's Lemon Tree Hotel off Castle Street, a favourite haunt of businessmen and journalists. The men from left to right in the foreground are James Cooper (police constable), Chesser and Watson (sheriff officers), two detectives, Superintendent Duthie, John Watson (the town drummer), and George Robb (the town clerk depute).

capacity, although Jane Ronald, who for years ran the famous Lemon Tree tavern, was an astute businesswoman who knew precisely the preferences of her loyal clientèle.[10] Dining-out was an especially ritualised institution for those who could afford it. Aberdeen Golf Club, for instance, was known initially as much for its convivial suppers as sporting prowess. The unreformed town council was notorious for its magisterial banquets, while assorted friendly societies, sporting clubs, professional and learned associations contributed regularly towards the dining culture.

By 1845, the *New Statistical Account* was reporting a total of 193 inn-keepers and vintners in Aberdeen, including six hotels of the first-rank.[11] Several of these were described by Joseph Robertson in *The Book of Bon-Accord*, a pioneering tour-guide and history of the city, which appeared in 1839. A social hierarchy applied as to preferences for each establishment, with the New Inn patronised by persons 'of noble and gentle rank', and the Lemon Tree 'the place where merchants most do congregate'. Affleck's tavern was reckoned to be best of all for the quality of its cuisine, a haven where 'the curious in gastronomy flock thither to explore the deeper mystery of the science'.[12] Judging from Robertson's elaborate discourse on the correct way to prepare Finnan haddocks, a uniquely Aberdonian peat-smoked fish dish, he was no stranger to these mysteries. Yet while *The Book of Bon-Accord* was eloquent and entertaining, it was also consciously exclusive. Robertson regretted that there was 'no respectable Coffee-Room' in the city, although, at the time he was writing, Macdonald's temperance hotel was advertising the availability of 'best Mocha' and other non-alcoholic beverages.[13] Incompatible ideological differences help to explain this omission, and Robertson's refusal even to mention the hotel in his list of recommended places to stay. Among his many other occupations, Robertson was a Conservative newspaper editor, while Macdonald's was a meeting place for political radicals, notably the Aberdeen Working Men's Association, which was a Chartist organisation.

The significant shift in cultural habits that Macdonald's represented also would have been distasteful to a *bon vivant* like Robertson. Increasingly, the cosy image of Scottish conviviality, cultivated from the eighteenth century and exuberantly celebrated in the works of such cultural icons as Robert Burns and Walter Scott, was being questioned. The Assembly Rooms on Union Street had been erected partly because the old taverns were considered 'very incommodious' and 'ill adapted' for prestigious social gatherings.[14] At a different level, public drunkenness was increasingly associated with the tendency for taverns, taprooms and dramshops to serve as the social centres of communities, thus creating a spiral of alcohol dependency. This was especially identified in the newer industrial districts beyond Aberdeen's burgh boundaries. For instance, although the population of the textile village of Woodside had grown rapidly after 1800, amenities had not kept pace with demographic developments, and there was consequently scant opportunity for leisure outside the home apart from drinking. A nineteenth-century historian of Woodside, and a temperance sympathiser, pointed out that there was not even a place of public worship in the village, of any denomination, until 1819.[15]

The problem was compounded in Aberdeen because, until the early 1820s, it was quite usual for illicit spirits to augment the stock of drinking establishments. The city's coastal location and proximity to the Highlands made it a convenient outlet for the thriving trade in whisky produced by unlicensed distillers, until government regulation and much more vigorous enforcement procedures eventually put paid to such enterprise. Contraband gin and brandy from the continent were also widely available, and in their hey-day the North-East smuggling syndicates ran their operations with precision.[16] There was no stigma attached to the consumption of illicit alcohol and its abundance helped to entrench drinking habits, not only in Aberdeen but in fishing communities along the coast, where seafarers gained a notorious reputation because of their prodigious appetite for spirits. On the other hand, the legitimate drink trade was an important component of the city's economy, providing beer, ale and porter from local breweries, of which Aulton and Devanha were among the most enduringly successful. There were large-scale distilleries, too, such as Union Glen and later Bon-Accord, which manufactured pure malt whisky. Crucially, a number of eminent citizens enhanced the image of the trade and helped to counter the sustained attacks of temperance campaigners. William Cadenhead was a wine merchant and doyen of the Aberdeen Licensed Victuallers' Association, but he was also a well-known poet and writer, who in 1856 followed on directly from Joseph Robertson by producing the hugely successful *New Book of Bon-Accord* as a guide to the city.[17]

TEMPERANCE AND 'RATIONAL' RECREATION

Despite the resilience of Aberdeen's drinking culture, the emergence of the temperance movement both influenced and reflected the shift in leisure habits towards more 'rational' pursuits. In Scotland the organisation developed momentum during the 1830s, at a time when electoral reform was perceived as having purged some of the grosser malpractices of the old ruling order. Rejection of alcohol thus compounded the sense of moral cleansing associated with political regeneration. However, the Aberdeen Total Abstinence Society, which originated in 1837, firmly repudiated involvement in 'party politics, state affairs or sectarian peculiarities in religion', seeking instead to reconcile disparate elements of the community through the moderating influence of teetotalism.[18] The reality was rather different, as the leadership of the Aberdeen movement was overwhelmingly of a Liberal and evangelical Presbyterian persuasion, and remained so throughout the century. Moreover, the conviction that alcohol was 'the most prolific parent of every evil, and most stubborn barrier to every good' gave a millenarian dimension to the early temperance crusade. By the early 1840s there was a group of Aberdeen-based missionaries, who lectured regularly throughout the North-East. Their performances were often consciously theatrical, imbuing drunkenness with a vivid Gothic-horror quality intended to arouse queasy feelings of discomfort among the audience. The aim, as an editorial in the *Northern Temperance Record* starkly put it, was 'to cast the devil out of every drunkard in the land'.[19]

Yet while the Aberdeen campaigners were determined to reform hardened drinkers, they were also anxious to affirm the positive aspects of abstinence by creating a sufficiently attractive alternative culture to the public house. A range of social activities was encouraged, which characteristically had a strong family dimension. Saturday soirées were inaugurated from 1839, with recitations and singing directed by coffee-room proprietor Alexander Macdonald, who also happened to be an elocution and music teacher. Children were made welcome at such gatherings, the rationale being that the morally-elevating environment would help mould them into sociable and responsible adults. Leading on from the popularity of the weekly entertainments, the movement's first New Year Festival was held on 1 January 1841, attracting 1,200 to the new, custom-built Temperance Hall in George Street. The subsequent report in the *Northern Temperance Record* made pointed reference to the timing of the event, in the context of the traditionally boisterous celebration of Hogmanay in Scotland.

> The bacchanalian scenes that have so long disgraced our Christmas and New-Year's festivals are rapidly giving place to more rational and pleasurable sociability. Soirées are now 'the order of the day'; and it is truly pleasing to contrast the enjoyment to be derived in this way, with the cup that cheers, but also inebriates and unfits man for the exercise of his best faculties and feelings.[20]

Thereafter, the festival was a feature of the city's New Year celebrations for the remainder of the century. From 1845 onward the Aberdeen Temperance Society took over organisational responsibility, the new body being a more ambitious version of the Total Abstinence Society but with largely the same personnel. By the 1860s the festival was being conducted on an even grander scale, as Alexander S. Cook, the society's long-standing president, fondly recalled. The recently-inaugurated Music Hall proved to be an ideal venue, with over 2,000 enthusiasts from throughout the North-East participating in 'the largest tea-party in Scotland'.[21] Music was central to the entertainments, with choral singing especially favoured, because it was a shared activity, embodying the spirit of harmony so fundamental to temperance principles. However, there were also limits to what soirée culture could allow. Among temperance activists, dancing was thought to be a questionable pastime, because it dissipated self-control and dangerously aroused the passions. The maxim was that, 'if our dancing grieves a brother, or spreads a snare for him, as Christians and as teetotallers, we are bound to *abstain* from it'.[22]

The temperance movement was one significant strand of the rich associational culture that had been developing throughout the United Kingdom since the 1780s, and which covered a range of voluntary organisations, with assorted social, philanthropic and political objectives. Overwhelmingly, the stress was on 'rational' activity, which had a purposeful and practical end in view. Until the 1870s the most prominent in Aberdeen tended to focus on charitable and education work, with a particular abundance of Bible, tract and missionary societies. However, some of the organisations had a much more ephemeral existence, expressing interests that were a passing fashion of the time. Phrenology was popular from the 1830s, reflecting a vogue throughout Scotland which had been given considerable impetus by the ardent advocacy of the subject by the *Scotsman* newspaper.[23] The basis of phrenology is that character can be determined from the contours of the cranium, thus explaining behavioural patterns, especially why certain people or

Church and library offer alternatives to tavern culture. Rosemount Viaduct with the Central Library opened in 1892 and St Mark's Free South Church was built in the 1890s. The statue of Sir William Wallace was one of a number in Scotland paid for by the estate of John Steill. It was originally intended to stand in the Duthie Park, but was unveiled in July 1888 on Rosemount.

groups seem to be more creative and enterprising than others. Ironically, given the latitude that phrenology allows for race, class and gender stereotyping, it was considered to be a progressive movement, which pre-dated psychology in its attempt to come to grips with the working of the mind. In his memoirs, written in 1870, William Buchanan recalled his own youthful enthusiasm, serving as secretary to the Aberdeen Working Men's Phrenological Society.[24] William Carnie also remembered the obsessive interest in the city during his early career as an engraver, when a neighbouring shopkeeper, James Stratton, would come armed with measuring callipers to study the heads of the workforce. William Lindsay, the radical bookseller and writer, had such faith in Stratton's ability that for decades he kept a detailed chart of his own phrenological profile, which flatteringly calculated his 'cerebral capacity' as well above average.[25]

Despite its lack of scientific credibility and transient appeal, the example of phrenology reveals much about the receptiveness of Aberdonians to new ideas and how keenly they were prepared to pursue them. Indeed, for autodidacts like Buchanan, it was part of a general ethos of self-improvement, which aimed to prove that privilege was not a prerequisite for knowledge. Buchanan paid tribute to working-class associates from the old days as men 'fit to discuss almost any subject' because of their thirst for inquiry, although his pro-temperance commitment qualified this when he claimed that thirst of a different variety prompted the downfall of several erstwhile companions. One attempt to constructively channel such creative energy, the Mechanics' Institute, provided the opportunity for artisans to expand their working knowledge through lectures and use of a well-stocked library.[26] The Mechanics' Institute was by no means the only non-university library to operate in and around Aberdeen before the 1880s, and there was considerable expansion in the number of establishments that catered for reading, both general and specialised. Booksellers often ran circulating libraries, which were patronised by those who could afford it. For instance, Alexander Brown charged an annual subscription rate of half a guinea in 1800.[27] On the other hand, Woodside produced a number of smaller and more accessible libraries for the working community, including one opened in 1840 by the local temperance society. The Phrenological Society was listed in 1842 as possessing a particularly valuable library, while a prime motivation for membership of Aberdeen's Society of Advocates was use of its extensive law library.[28] George Walker, who ultimately became the proprietor of Brown's, patriotically described Aberdeen as 'the most literary city in Scotland', and recent research has confirmed that by mid-century there was a voracious appetite for reading, with a greater number of bookshops per head of population than either Dundee or Glasgow could muster.[29] The need to service the legal, religious and academic communities contributed substantially to this success, although the unprecedented popularity of Walter Scott created a taste for fiction, and from the 1830s weekly periodicals like *Chambers' Journal* and the *Penny Magazine* supplied demand for 'improving' but entertaining literature. Aberdonians consequently had access to a wide selection of reading material, and in 1850 the coming of the railways increased choice even further.

MUSIC AND DANCING

While temperance activists worked hard to popularise choral music in Aberdeen from the 1830s onward, they were building on a base of deep-rooted local interest. In February 1800 the *Aberdeen Journal* reported on a grand selection of music held in the concert hall, Broad Street, where *The Messiah* was performed 'with a degree of accuracy, which astonished the best judges'. Success was attributed to Mr Grenville, the conductor, who had made the most of local talent after hearing that 'a considerable number of tradesmen in town, had, for some time past, been in the way of amusing themselves with glee singing, for an hour in the evening after their work'.[30] Significantly, the concert was a charitable benefit, in aid of the city's poor, such formal entertainment often serving as an enticement to better-off members of the community to support worthy causes. The Aberdeen Musical Society was behind many of these initiatives, using its position as one of the most socially prestigious institutions in the city. From its inception in 1748, the society was distinguished as one of Scotland's main platforms for the promotion of concert music, its access to a wide range of instruments and use of professional as well as amateur performers maintaining consistently high standards.[31] The society declined during the 1800s, partly because its 'conservative and exclusive basis' was alienating Aberdonians. However, recurring attempts were made to revive high quality performances, notably in the critically acclaimed music festivals held in 1828 and 1834.

A regular feature of Aberdeen's concert programmes was the inclusion of 'Scots Tunes', along with the work of English and continental composers. These found favour with audiences, regardless of social status, and throughout the nineteenth century the traditional element held its own against changing musical preferences. The popularity of indigenous fiddle-playing was manifested not just through Aberdeen's corps of street performers, but by the demand for sheet music of compositions by the Gow family, an influential reel and strathspey dynasty from Perthshire. Niel and Nathaniel Gow were fashionable figures among Aberdeen's genteel society, largely because their music supplied such lively accompaniment to country dancing. Of course, 'country' here is a misleading term, as the old, uninhibited Scottish dance forms had absorbed refining urban influences, and Francis Peacock, one of the founders of the Musical Society, was a pioneer in teaching this sophisticated style. Although aged over eighty when he died in 1806, Peacock had been actively engaged in dance instruction until 1800, and his legacy still lingered.[32] Until the 1830s, Aberdonians with social pretensions learned the Peacock blend of country and continental dancing, the intricate steps and set figures displayed to best advantage in spacious premises like the new Assembly Rooms.

Yet despite the continuities, tastes in music and dancing gradually altered in Aberdeen to reflect much deeper changes in the nature of nineteenth-century society. The disdain of the temperance movement for dancing of any description meant more than just concern to exercise self-discipline; it also represented a political repudiation of assembly room culture, which was inextricably associated with the pre-Reform elite. In 1833 Alexander Bannerman, whose personal diary reveals a preoccupation with balls, stylish clothes and the cuisine at Affleck's, made regretful reference to the changing social habits that had emerged as a result of the divisions in opinion created by the reform debate.[33] The impact of evangelicalism, which was especially evident in the high level of Free Church adherence after 1843, further reinforced the new cultural mood within the city.

The prolonged crusade against 'promiscuous dancing' by the Rev. Alexander M. Bannatyne of the Union Free Church was aimed at preventing moral lapses among the upper classes as well as working classes. The waltz and its derivatives were his prime target, which in 1884 he famously described to the Aberdeen Free Presbytery as 'the flings and springs and the artistic circles, and the close-bosomed wheeling and whirling carefully taught or picked up by rule of thumb or toe'.[34] Bannatyne made considerable public impact with his colourful rhetoric, although in the long-term he could do little to dent the popularity of partner dancing or the rise of commercial dance schools in the city. By the 1890s Messrs Polsons' Dancing Academy was cheerfully proclaiming 'waltzing a speciality', with a course of twenty lessons available at eight shillings for women and half a guinea for men.[35]

Music also provoked moral concern among some sections of the community, although in a qualitatively different way from dancing. From the 1840s there was intense debate about the deficiencies of church music, which in Scotland's Presbyterian denominations had remained hidebound by post-Reformation strictures against ostentation, especially the supposed crypto-Catholic influence of the organ. Congregations remained seated to sing and were led by a precentor, who was given a stipend by the individual church for taking on this responsibility. They were not accompanied by the organ or any other instrument. At a well-attended public lecture in the forum of the West Free Church, given in 1854, journalist William Carnie lamented that Scottish psalmody had been allowed to degenerate into a 'vile and vapid style', where the participants went through the motions of a 'soulless ceremony' in praise of God. He made the revealing comment that some even regarded church music as too 'unfashionable', preferring to 'warble with finish and effect' in the luxury of drawing-rooms.[36] Carnie, who was a dominating influence on Aberdeen's musical life for the remainder of the century, advocated a robust approach to psalmody, in the belief that music was spiritually elevating, and that there should be no boundaries on its use for enhancing the experience of divine worship.

The prohibition of the organ and other instruments was eventually rescinded

The Rev. A. M. Bannatyne, the Union Free Church's 'presbytery policeman', who warned against the spread of dancing at church socials, particularly the 'flings, springs and close-bosomed whirls'. Northern Figaro, *10 January 1885.*

by the Established Church (1864), the United Presbyterians (1872), and the Free Church (1883). In Aberdeen there was fierce debate about this divergence from tradition, and it should come as no surprise that the Rev. Bannatyne was prominent in denouncing the intrusion of the organ. However, the pro-organ movement was strong and able to spread its beliefs widely through the local press.[37] That the city had a comparatively large episcopalian community, whose more expansive musical tastes influenced the presbyterians, was also of significance. Indeed, for all the differences among the denominations, music seems to have had a socially cohesive influence in Aberdeen, as was demonstrated by Carnie's persistent quest to raise the public consciousness. He was the conductor of the aptly-named Harmonic Choir, a group of young men and women who combined their talents in 1849, and became popular for their rendition of 'glees, part-songs, madrigals, anthems of the best composers – past and present'. At a time when the female presence in choirs was still not wholly accepted, Carnie acknowledged that the women of the Harmonic had been a driving force in its success. Moreover, although Carnie was a member of the established church, not all choir members shared this adherence. Such collective initiatives helped vocal music to flourish during the 1850s, the campaign to improve psalmody having an impact that went beyond the church domain, as the sheer pleasure of singing was generally recognised.

Indeed, in 1856 active discussions began about the need to provide a venue for more elaborate musical performances in the city. The *Aberdeen Journal* explained how much this deficiency was inhibiting the quality of cultural life.

> It has resulted in such vocalists as Jenny Lind, for example, never having been heard in Aberdeen, and to mention no other, a spirited attempt to send an operatic company even for one night, in the spring of this year, was defeated from the same cause. Another point, of greater importance, is that the influence of music cannot be brought to bear on anything like the extent that is desirable on the community at large, and especially as occupying, with pleasure and profit, part of the leisure time of those employed throughout the day.[38]

The reference to 'pleasure and profit' subtly indicated that a more commercial approach to entertainment also lay behind the moves to inaugurate a music hall in Aberdeen, capable of holding audiences of 2,500. The arrival of the railways had created unprecedented opportunities for bringing star attractions to the city, while the popularity of choral music clearly demonstrated market demand. Moreover, the success of concerts in Glasgow's City Hall and Edinburgh's Music Hall, erected during the 1840s, helped to stimulate the urge for emulation in the north. In 1858 the Aberdeen Music Hall Company, a recently created joint-stock enterprise, acquired the Assembly Rooms with the objective of enlarging and wholly restructuring them. By 1859 the new Music Hall was ready for public performances, and Swedish diva, Jenny Lind, made her long-awaited appearance in 1861.[39] This was also the year that the Music Hall Choral Union was inaugurated, as 'a concentration and embodiment of the different Musical Associations in the City', and which thereafter promoted a varied programme of events.

POPULAR ENTERTAINMENT AND THE THEATRE

Significantly, the Music Hall did not just focus on vocal virtuosity and oratorial performance on the grand scale. Aberdonians also appreciated comedy and a much pacier musical style, as was shown by the vogue for 'black-faced entertainers' that swept the city from the 1850s. In his reminiscences, William Carnie recalled that four visiting companies appeared in the Music Hall during 1860, including the African Opera Troupe, 'one of the very best combinations of the order that ever amused the North'.[40] The enduring appeal of minstrel troupes throughout the second half of the nineteenth century is intriguing, given that the genre was the

John Henry Anderson, 'the Wizard of the North, an illusionist of international fame whose grave in St Nicholas' churchyard was visited by Harry Houdini in 1909.

first in Scotland to directly include influences from African-American culture, albeit interpreted as pastiche by white performers. From its transatlantic origins in the 1840s minstrelsy soon hit the London theatres, and percolated northwards. The mysterious Signor Fumarolo, who ran variety entertainments at the Mechanics' Hall in Aberdeen, featured a highly competent local ensemble during the 1850s. According to Carnie, the first tenor not only 'sang Scotch songs with appreciative taste', but applied for a church precentorship 'during his black-faced period', and was successful.[41] A new generation of Aberdonians continued the tradition. In 1894 the *Bon-Accord* magazine featured the exploits of the Woodside Minstrel Troupe, who mixed American vaudeville songs like 'Carry Me Back To Old Virginny' with satirical sketches about contemporary life in Aberdeen.[42]

Minstrelsy was a form of pantomime, an entertainment based on stark role reversal with the incursion of a highly stylised rural fantasy into the supposedly practical and sophisticated urban sphere. In Aberdeen it also reflected a distinct predilection for the exotic, which belied preconceptions of the city as the dour and stolid centre of North-East Scotland. This glamorous alter ego was

*The Bool Road
'Penny Rattler'
theatre offered
cheap comedy and
melodrama until
the 1840s before it
was converted to a
mission hall.*

spectacularly displayed in the world of shows, circuses and the theatre. Two of the most renowned illusionists on the international variety circuit served their formative years in Aberdeen, John Henry Anderson, 'The Wizard of the North', and Dr Walford Bodie.[43] Their consummate showmanship was apparent in their striking physical appearance and gift for self-publicity, indicating the extent of professional organisation within the entertainment industry, especially from mid-century. In 1868 the Scottish comedy actor, Peter Paterson, gave behind-the-scenes insight into the reality of performing, revealing that public expectations were being raised deliberately in the direction of the unusual and sensational. In circuses and animal shows, especially, deeds of daring were the prime focus of attention. The display of equestrian ability lay invariably at the heart of these entertainments, the ubiquity of horses in pre-automobile society relating audiences readily to equine attractions. This was particularly evident in Aberdeen, where so many inhabitants had close connections with surrounding rural districts. The city thus became an important venue on the circuit of specialised companies, like 'Professor Norton B. Smith, Emperor of All Horse Educators', and top-class circuses like Cooke's and Sanger's.

As for drama, historians have repeatedly stressed the longevity of the tradition in Aberdeen. The earliest-known production of any play in Scotland was the fifteenth-century *Haly Blude*, which was revived as a pageant triumphantly celebrating the passing of the Reform Bill in 1832.[44] However, there was no permanent theatre in Aberdeen until 1795, and its existence was financially insecure until the Marischal Street premises were purchased outright by local merchant John Fraser.[45] Although the most prestigious, the Theatre Royal was not the sole outlet for dramatic performance in the city. The Bool Road Theatre, alternatively known as the 'Penny Rattler', provided cheap and accessible entertainment, with a strong emphasis on comedy and melodrama. It represented a dimension of popular culture that was viewed with mounting concern by the guardians of morality and sobriety in communities throughout Scotland. Temperance campaigner A. S. Cook gave a revealing appraisal of the Bool Road establishment as he remembered it during the 1840s.

> The plays performed were of the blood-and-thunder description. The players, not being numerous, had to represent two or three characters, and their tawdry dresses and general appearance showed a limited wardrobe. The elocution was declamatory and noisy, but heartily appreciated by their not very critical auditors, who were often engaged in personal squabbling and free fights, but that did not interfere very much with the progress of the performance. When this booth was removed to make way for an experiment in Home Mission work, there was a feeling of satisfaction expressed by the judicial authorities of the city that a moral nuisance had been removed.[46]

Cook was more appreciative of another popular theatre of the time, run by showman 'Big Scott' Longhurst, self-styled 'Emperor of All the Conjurers'. Longhurst blended melodrama with magic, his most famous illusion the 'gun-trick', in which he appeared to catch a marked bullet from a pistol pointed directly at him. Longhurst became the father-in-law of John Henry Anderson and was one of his key influences, with the gun-trick later serving as the centrepiece of the Wizard of the North's spectacular stage-show.[47]

Unquestionably, the Theatre Royal's main attraction was *Rob Roy*, which had been dramatised from Walter Scott's best-selling novel in 1818. As Peter Paterson put it, 'all over the north of Scotland, it had quite a tremendous success – Mr Corbet Ryder being the original, and by far the best, delineator of the bold outlaw'.[48] *Rob Roy* became a staple of the Scottish theatre, and was still going strong in Aberdeen at the end of the century, and its popularity in rural areas lasted until the 1930s. The play's association with the city made local drama critics acutely discerning about the quality of these later performances. The 1887 Grand Jubilee production at Her Majesty's Theatre was deemed a disappointment because the main character had 'too much of the English sportsman out on the moors about him'.[49]

The Marischal Street theatre was certainly far from the splendour of playhouses in Drury Lane or Covent Garden.[50] It was small and structurally unprepossessing.

Mrs Jessie Pollock 1805–75

The daughter of John Fraser, owner of the Theatre Royal, Jessie Pollock went on stage at the age of fifteen and became a highly accomplished actress. She married Corbet Ryder, who in 1817 had taken over the lease of the Theatre Royal as actor-manager and gained a legendary reputation for his swashbuckling style, probably in the early 1830s. The Ryders were instrumental in establishing Scotland's northern theatre circuit, using Aberdeen as their base, but taking the company for short seasons to Arbroath, Dundee, Montrose and Perth. After Corbet Ryder's death in 1842, his widow remarried, and as Mrs Pollock assumed responsibility for the management of the Theatre Royal over the next thirty years. Following the death of her second husband in 1855, she became director of the company. One obvious admirer wrote after her death in 1875 that loyalty to Aberdeen had stifled a glittering acting career, presumably on the London stage. She gave up the management of the theatre in 1869 but remained on stage almost until her death. On her final retirement she was presented with a life-sized portrait of herself in the role of Lady Macbeth.

But this made it conducive for direct audience participation, and Aberdonians were wont to greet stage hitches 'with sarcastic remarks in the quaintest of doric'. For all her pioneering role as actor-manager, Mrs Pollock also had conservative tastes in production, her offerings revolving round the classics, melodrama and the festive season pantomime. In their day these proved popular, but her retirement coincided with a fundamental change in the nature of the theatre, as London gained a near monopoly of professional drama north of the Border. Above all, the improved railway system made it much more economic for large-scale metropolitan companies to go on tour. The need for a prestigious venue to attract the southerners was quickly identified in Aberdeen, and in 1872 Her Majesty's Theatre and Opera House was opened on the initiative of a syndicate of local businessmen.[51] Ironically, the old Marischal Street theatre was sold to the Church of Scotland three years later. *Rob Roy* excepted, its style of acting was by this time perceived as drastically outdated by fashionable Aberdonians.

LANDSCAPE AND LEISURE

From the 1870s there was developing confidence about Aberdeen's future, tied to improved economic prospects. The extension of the burgh boundaries helped to reinforce the image of a burgeoning but administratively cohesive community,

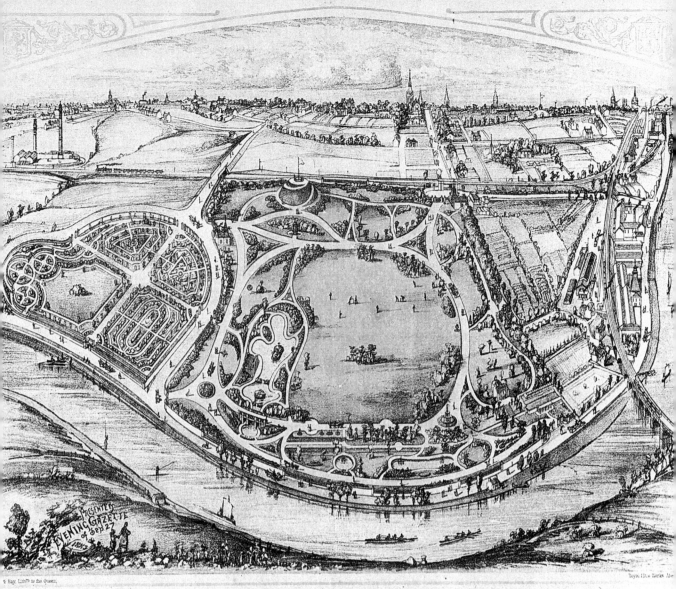

THE DUTHIE PARK,

PRESENTED BY MISS DUTHIE OF RUTHRIESTON TO THE CITY OF ABERDEEN

First Turf Out by Lord Aberdeen, Aug. 27, 1881; Opened by H.R.H. Princess Beatrice, Sept. 27, 1883.

with the town council playing a key role in shaping this identity. Throughout the United Kingdom municipalities were assuming a range of responsibilities intended to enhance the quality of urban life, and it is important to emphasise how much this new sense of commitment directed recreational preferences. In 1871 Aberdeen's councillors made a tangible declaration of their optimism for the future by sanctioning the landscaping of ground to the west of the city for use as a public park.[52] Compared with showpiece developments elsewhere, like Glasgow's Queen's Park, then extending to 90 acres, the 13-acre site that constituted Aberdeen's Victoria Park was small-scale. On the other hand, the venture was important for identifying Aberdeen with the long-established movement to promote recreational

A special supplement of the Evening Gazette *marked the formal opening of the Duthie Park in 1883.*

opportunities, in surroundings that would allow the population to benefit from the invigorating impact of fresh air and outdoor exercise. The acquisition of municipal parkland speeded up thereafter. Duthie Park was the 44-acre gift of wealthy heiress Elizabeth Duthie of Ruthrieston, its formal opening in 1883 providing the opportunity for one of the most elaborate ceremonials ever staged by the town council.[53]

In Scotland, public parks derived a good deal of their attraction from

---

Sir George Reid 1841–1913

Son of the manager of the Aberdeen Copper Co., George Reid was educated at the Trades School and Grammar School. At the age of twelve he was apprenticed to Keith & Gibb, lithographers. In 1860 he spent nine months in Edinburgh at art school seeking to become a portrait painter. He studied abroad in Utrecht, Paris and The Hague in 1863. He returned to Aberdeen to establish himself as a portrait painter whose subjects included important local figures such as Sir Alexander Anderson, George Thompson, Peter Esslemont and Sir William Henderson. He became a member of the Royal Scottish Academy in 1877 and president in 1891. He was knighted in that year. He was famous for his pen and ink sketches, especially the illustrations for *Johnny Gibb of Gushetneuk*. He was a strong supporter of the Aberdeen Art Gallery and opened the extension in 1905.

---

contemporary perceptions of the natural landscape, which embodied the qualities deemed so vital for restoring the well-being of enervated urban dwellers. From mid-century this was reflected in the work of Scottish painters like Horatio McCulloch and Sam Bough, who made a speciality of unspoiled scenic vistas, ranging from majestic Highland landscapes to rugged lowland seascapes. These proved popular, especially at a time when evangelicalism was ebulliently emphasising the wonder of God's creation and the need to recapture purer, pre-industrial values. In Aberdeen, even before 1871, the appeal of the landscape was potent. William Dyce was a gifted painter, who settled in London and absorbed influences from the luminous but intricately naturalistic style of the Pre-Raphaelites. His work had a strong religious underpinning, with the landscape used repeatedly as a device to expand the spiritual consciousness. At a less intensely cerebral level, James Giles was a fashionable landscape and animal artist, specialising in Highland scenes depicting dogs, deer and horses.[54] His illustrations of Balmoral Castle were impressive enough to convince Queen Victoria to lease the Deeside property in 1848. Significantly, Giles was also keen to demonstrate the practical application of the landscape aesthetic through garden design, and elaborately laid out the grounds of Haddo House, country home of the fourth Earl of Aberdeen, during the 1830s.

The interconnection between art and the landscape was reinforced in Aberdeen when the new process of photography became established during the 1850s. This was the decade when George Washington Wilson's company consolidated its reputation.[55] The growing tourist industry provided a natural complement in providing a demand for landscapes, helped by the fact that Aberdeen had become a focus for travellers to North-East Scotland. The commercialisation of the Scottish landscape was thus exemplified by the success of Wilson's company although, after 1900, technological changes sharply veered popular preferences in a wholly different direction, because of the rise of the cinematograph and the hand-held box camera.

George Washington Wilson, Scotland's best-known photographer between 1850s and 1880s. Many of our images of Scottish towns and landsapes in the nineteenth century are Wilson's.

George Washington Wilson 1823–93

Born at Carnousie, Banffshire, son of a farmer, G. W. Wilson was educated at the parish school and apprenticed to a carpenter and house builder at the age of twelve. At the age of 23 he moved to Edinburgh to learn the art of painting, and subsequently settled in Aberdeen about 1848 to work as a portrait painter. In 1853 he formed a partnership with John Hay, a photographer, and they were invited by Prince Albert to make a photographic record of the construction of Balmoral Castle. The partnership ended in 1855, financially insolvent. Wilson established himself as the leading society photographer in Aberdeen in the 1850s. His emphasis on quality reproduction meant that he was in great demand to provide pictorial embellishments for guidebooks and lantern slides for educational talks. Wilson's landscape work secured his reputation as a photographer of international quality and his work was further helped by the support and patronage of Prince Albert and Queen Victoria. Wilson was the only Scottish photographer to be awarded a medal in the photographic section of the London International Exhibition of 1862. By the 1860s he was producing half a million photographic prints per year. He built his house at Queen's Cross in 1875, and established a workshop in St Swithin Street. He retired in 1888, leaving the business to his three sons. It was undermined in the 1890s by a prosecution raised by the Inland Revenue claiming irregularities in the transfer of the business to Wilson's sons. The family lost the court case at great cost, and the business closed in 1902.

Aberdeen's coastal location provided another important dimension to the urban landscape. The traditional common lands of the burgh extended over the Links, a vast tract of undulating grassland and sand dunes between the city and the sea. These had long been used as a place of pleasurable resort, the terrain being especially suitable for physical exercise, whether strolling or more vigorous sporting pursuits. Golf was traditionally popular, one of the most socially-exclusive institutions being the Aberdeen Golf Club, which in the 1850s had taken a leading role in the campaign to stop a railway being pushed through the Links. The club was founded in 1815 on the initiative of local lawyers and businessmen, but the game had often languished behind the club's busy social calendar. Indeed, up to mid-century there were years when there were only two or three participants in the championship competition.[56] The keen debate over the colour of golfing coat to be worn by members also showed that style rather than substance could be a major motivation for joining.

Yet another attraction for Aberdeen's early golf *aficionados* was the thrill of betting on club performance, either in hard cash or magnums of claret. Betting was ingrained in upper-class sporting habits, taking the form of a direct 'gentlemen's agreement' between the parties making the wager. As well as adding piquancy to golf, it played a large part in sporadic efforts to turn the Links into a venue for horse racing. Successive meetings had been held between 1816 and 1829, when lavish prizes were offered.[57] These were closely tied to prestigious social events, like balls and assemblies, and there can be no doubt that racing's sharp decline in fortune after 1830 was due to the changing cultural and political climate in Aberdeen. Attempts to revive the horse-racing season met with particular hostility from evangelical agencies, and the Rev. Bannatyne's fulminations against 'dancing parties' in 1884 were related directly to the ongoing debate about racing and the associated iniquities of betting and drinking.

Quoiting and cricket were the two other main competitive pastimes popular on the Links. The first was a predominantly working-class activity, to some extent resembling bowls, but played with heavy metal rings and without the need for a carefully manicured green.[58] In 1879 William Cadenhead pointed out that bowls had also been played on the Links, but quoiting had much broader appeal until the town council began to lay out public bowling greens in the city's parks. The organisation of quoits is difficult to determine, although by the 1890s there was a league involving seven clubs from Aberdeen's outlying and suburban communities.[59] Cricket was much more of a middle-class pursuit, despite its popularity in Woodside, and from its competitive origins in the 1840s built up an enormous following. Aberdeenshire Cricket Club was formally constituted in 1857, under the energetic direction of lawyer James Forbes Lumsden, who helped to give the sport a much more professional status than had hitherto been recognised in the city.[60] The new club moved away from the Links in 1858, when it acquired its own grounds. It took the bold step two years later of appointing an English professional, Harry Lillywhite, to coach the players. Competition burgeoned as a plethora of clubs came into being, based on localities or institutions such as the University. English teams regularly visited Aberdeen, as well as the top-class Scottish clubs, like Edinburgh Grange and Perthshire.

Aberdeenshire Cricket Club led the way in radically reshaping perceptions of sport in the city from the 1860s onward. The Golf Club followed, with the old generation of worthies succeeded by competitive-minded enthusiasts, anxious to raise playing standards. In a flurry of organisational activity, a club house was erected on the Links in 1867, and a professional was engaged to look after the course and give lessons.[61] The club's monopoly of the Links ended in 1872, when Bon-Accord Golf Club was founded, with a much less exclusive membership base. Other clubs soon followed. This not only reflected a nationwide revival of interest in the game, but demonstrated popular demand for new leisure outlets. As a result of the buoyancy of the local economy, Aberdonians generally had more disposable income and could afford to indulge in a wide range of social activities. Opportunities were further expanded by a reduction in working hours and the introduction of the Saturday half-day holiday. Sport was only one facet of this changing cultural focus, but its rise in popularity by 1900 was spectacular. The level of participation in cycling, tennis, bowls, billiards, rugby and association football, as well as the three mainstays of the Links, was matched by rapidly increasing spectator interest. Inevitably, commercialisation also edged into the sporting world. While public use of the Links did not diminish, there were heightened expectations about quality of performance, which could be best achieved in congenial, custom-built surroundings. In 1888, the removal of Aberdeen Golf Club to its impressive new course of Balgownie, just outside the city, was a revealing example of this trend.

However, the most significant sporting shift of emphasis in Aberdeen during the 1890s was the consolidation of support for association football, another sport which had middle-class origins in the city. The game had taken longer than else-where to become established, and rugby football initially had a much higher profile, thanks to keen University patronage. 'Kick-Off', the football correspondent of *Bon-Accord* magazine, reported disconsolately in 1886 that 'a good Association game is rather a rarity in Aberdeen'.[62] This did not stop the Links being used by enthusiasts, and the number of association teams multiplied. Black Diamond, Bon-Accord Swifts, East End Swifts, Heatherbell and Woodside Hawthorn were among those playing competitively by the 1890s. In time, the clubs of Aberdeen, Victoria

United and Orion stamped their supremacy on the city, the last being the most consistently successful. The reversal of rugby fortunes was demonstrated in October 1894, when *Bon-Accord* reported that the North of Scotland Union had drawn 'a paltry £8 during the whole season', while at a recent Orion–Victoria United match the gate had been £70.[63] That the association game had firmly taken root in the city was also shown by the concern about the activities of English scouts, on the look-out for promising players to entice to professional clubs south of the Border. Professionalism had been sanctioned by the Scottish Football Association only in 1893, eight years after England, and in Aberdeen there was still a strong amateur commitment to the sport, elevating its 'manly' and character-forming qualities above its money-making potential. It was not until 1903 that the professional ethos came into its own, when the three premier teams were amalgamated, in a bid to integrate the city into the thriving Scottish football scene.

Apart from non-gender specific forms of recreational exercise, like walking and sea-bathing, opportunities for women to expend energy were severely limited in the early nineteenth century. Yet as the movement for political rights began slowly to assert itself from the 1860s, so too did female interest in sport. An important sign of changing times was the participation of women in cycling, as Katherine Trail recalled in the 1930s, when she looked back on her Victorian middle-class upbringing. She wrote with passion about the liberating impact of her first safety bicycle, and the unprecedented degree of mobility it allowed. The only obstacle to full enjoyment was the hopelessly impractical attire she was required to wear.

> Stiffly corsetted in stays whose bones very often cut into one's flesh, wearing skirts that reached to the ground, that measured about two and a half yards round the hem and were bound with braid to prevent the inevitable chafing, wearing sailor hats – the hardest and most unsympathetic headgear possible to imagine, which no amount of hatpins could persuade to remain firmly fixed on one's head – we yet managed to scour the country from end to end![64]

By the 1890s help was on hand for Aberdeen's flourishing corps of female cyclists in the person of Robert Coutts, who supplied tailor-made 'rational dress'.[65] That this was also considered suitable for golfing and tennis shows that horizons were beginning to broaden. When it came to football, however, withering scorn was poured on female aspirations by the sporting fraternity. The tour of Scotland by Lady Florence Dixie's British Ladies' Football Team was parodied by *Bon-Accord* in 1895, with the whole exercise depicted as grotesque and sinister.[66] At the same time, Sydney Grundy's successful London comedy about gender role reversal, *The New Woman*, was running at Her Majesty's Theatre, and further reinforced what was seen by beleaguered males as a destabilising trend towards female assertiveness.

NORTHERN BICYCLE MEET 1883
OFFICE BEARERS

THE VOLUNTEER MOVEMENT

The women were not helped by a heightened military outlook that prevailed in Aberdeen during the 1890s, and which was graphically displayed in the vogue for volunteering. The movement in Britain dated from 1859, the outcome of government anxiety about the preparedness of the nation to withstand hostile invasion. The volunteer force was effectively a citizens' army, intended to instil such morally-desirable qualities as loyalty, fellowship and motivation. William Carnie wrote of the enthusiasm originally engendered by the cause in Aberdeen, especially after the publication of poet laureate Alfred Tennyson's famous call to action, 'Riflemen Form'. By the end of 1859 well over 600 had joined assorted companies based on 'merchants', 'artisans' and other social groups.[67] There may have been social and professional pressures to aid recruitment. The directors of the North of Scotland Bank resolved unilaterally to supply their clerks with rifles, and sent them to drill on the Links along with the other volunteers.

Yet unquestionably there was keen interest, on the part of male and predominantly middle-class Aberdonians, not just in the allure of military spectacle, but in the promise of an active social life. By the 1890s the focus was on a distinctively masculine range of pursuits, including tactical war games, card-schools and 'smokers', this last taking the form of convivial evenings, centred

The office bearers of the Northern Bicycle meet, 1883, photographed by George Washington Wilson. Women had to await the arrival of the safety bicycle before they could participate.

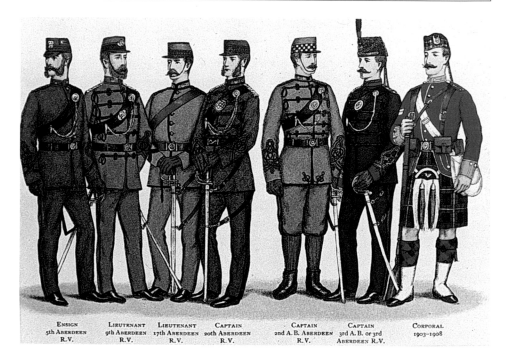

The Volunteer Movement from 1859 gave opportunities for parades and war games while maintaining clear social ranking.

| ENSIGN 5th ABERDEEN R.V. | LIEUTENANT 9th ABERDEEN R.V. | LIEUTENANT 17th ABERDEEN R.V. | CAPTAIN 20th ABERDEEN R.V. | CAPTAIN 2nd A.B. ABERDEEN R.V. | CAPTAIN 3rd A.B. or 3rd ABERDEEN R.V. | CORPORAL 1903–1908 |

around the consumption of alcohol and tobacco. There were strong echoes of the old tavern culture here, although in the context of a rigidly hierarchical organisation with a patriotic purpose. Volunteering retained its potent appeal until 1908, when the movement metamorphosed into the Territorial Army. That the Links featured so prominently on the volunteering agenda was testimony to the continuing importance of the landscape in directing social activities, even although the forms of these had altered over time.

The Evolution of Leisure

By 1900 Aberdeen aspired to the same cosmopolitan status as other United Kingdom cities and shared much in common in terms of its cultural profile. The commercialisation of leisure pursuits from mid-century contributed substantially to this process, especially after transport improvements had revolutionised communications to the north. On the other hand, there had been localised factors which helped to determine cultural preferences, especially arising from the particularly intense debate about the political power-base. The ruling elite during the pre-Reform era was associated with Toryism, the establishment and conspicuous consumption. The new elite after the 1830s reflected the rise of Liberalism, evangelical Presbyterianism and retrenchment. Evangelicalism aimed to impress the life-affirming qualities of godliness, and at the same time directed its adherents into patterns of behaviour that eschewed excess and self-indulgence, especially in the domain of drink. This does not mean that recreational activity was discouraged, rather that new forms were devised, with a strong moral underpinning, but which nevertheless afforded an outlet for much creative energy. 'Rational' recreation it may have been, but music especially benefited from the efforts of enthusiasts to provide entertainment that was both pleasurable and spiritually uplifting.

Moreover, the Aberdeen experience suggests that there was an interaction between the supposed polarities of 'sacred' and 'profane' culture that could be mutually reinforcing. Harry Gordon, Aberdeen's greatest star of the early twentieth-century Scottish variety theatre, made his debut appearance as a juvenile performer at a church soirée. Of course, the pronouncements of forceful personalities like the Rev. Bannatyne, who ironically had a strong theatrical streak in appearance and rhetorical style, indicate that moral strictures against recreational indulgence survived tenaciously in Aberdeen. Yet by the end of the century the city had come to represent an amalgam of assorted cultural components that went far beyond the sphere of influence of any one particular interest group.

16

Leisure and Social Change: The Twentieth Century

IRENE MAVER

NEW AND TRADITIONAL FORMS OF LEISURE

Leisure in twentieth-century Aberdeen was shaped significantly by technological developments, commencing with the cinema in the 1900s, the radio during the 1920s and television during the 1950s. The cultural impact of these phenomena show how swiftly and indelibly they altered social habits. Yet alongside innovative forms of entertainment, the traditional forms remained deeply entrenched. Local language and style influenced a range of performing disciplines, which penetrated the new broadcasting media and added a distinctively Aberdonian dimension. From a different perspective, the sustained attempts of the civic authority to create a popular and identifiable image for Aberdeen, notably through the cultivation of the beach as a pleasure resort, further boosted opportunities for leisure. Economic considerations underpinned municipal priorities, but the emphasis on Aberdeen's 'holiday' profile helped to encourage a more relaxed approach to social activities like drinking and dancing. Moral strictures did not disappear, but the increasingly commercial and secular climate muted their influence, especially after 1918. Sport and physical recreation were ardently pursued by Aberdonians, both as participants and spectators, and the expansion of opportunities proceeded at a brisk pace. Again, the municipal leadership played a pivotal role in directing activities, latterly using leisure as a key component in regeneration strategies in a bid to nurture and sustain the city's cultural identity.

THE BEACH AND THE SILVER CITY

Municipal interest in promoting Aberdeen as a holiday resort, based on the lyrical appellation of 'The Silver City By The Sea', was first activated during the 1890s. Throughout the nineteenth century the beach had been a popular attraction for visitors as well as locals, notwithstanding the vagaries of North-East weather. In 1818 William Kennedy gave the glowing testimony, 'No place in the Kingdom affords more excellent accommodation for sea bathing than Aberdeen', and went on to describe the facilities on offer, and the benefits to health for those taking advantage of the salt water.[1] However, there was no consistency of approach in the organisation of Aberdeen's bathing establishment, which was a major reason why councillors decided to direct matters themselves. There was also an emulative element, given that the turn of the century was the golden age of developing seaside culture in Europe and North America. The notion of the pleasure beach, with an eclectic array of entertainments and attractions, was spectacularly consolidated when Blackpool erected its famous tower in 1894, a development that was given much civic encouragement.[2] Aberdeen councillors took careful note of progress elsewhere, visiting sea bathing establishments in Scarborough and the south of England, as well as Boulogne and Trouville in France.[3] This laid the groundwork for their own plans for the development of the beach, which commenced in 1895. Compared with the efforts of successful southern resorts these were distinctly modest, although the inevitable outcry was raised against civic profligacy.[4] Yet within a short space of time the revitalised beach had endeared itself to the public, and was contributing a wholly new dimension to leisure in the city.

Central to the municipal programme was the construction of a bathing station, which took its lead from continental experience by providing luxurious private baths as well as one of the largest swimming pools in Scotland. A range of outdoor amenities was offered in close proximity, including sea-bathing facilities, a gymnasium, a bowling green and an 18-hole golf course. Despite the material improvements, there was still civic sensitivity about the unpredictability of the weather, which was perceived as a deterrent to prospective tourists. Aberdeen was consequently promoted as 'not inferior to the south of England' in terms of summer climate, and definitely superior to the notoriously rain-soaked west of Scotland.[5] Its bracing sea breezes were projected as a positive health advantage in an era when the menace of the 'smoke fiend' was recognised as a serious problem for urban dwellers. In this context, the image of the silver city was especially useful, because it consciously evoked the 'clean light appearance' of the local granite buildings, which contrasted starkly with the sooty and begrimed edifices of southern industrial centres like Glasgow. Moreover, *The Silver City* was the title of a famous poem, written by journalist William Forsyth, depicting Aberdeen as the kind of Arcadia that precisely met the objectives of the municipal public relations machine:

> My Silver City by the Sea,
> Thy white foot rests on golden sands;
> A radiant robe encircles thee
> Of woody hills and garden lands ...[6]

*Pierrots at the
Beach Pavilion
around 1900,
offering 'fun
without vulgarity'.*

Exploitation of these recreational opportunities was given practical assistance when Aberdeen's tramway system came wholly under civic control in 1898, thus allowing for greater ease of access to the beach and outlying beauty spots.[7] By then the railways had long served tourists, especially those anxious to follow the route to Royal Deeside and its romantic mountainous terrain.

Although councillors declared the health factor to be the motivating influence behind expanding beach horizons, they were soon encouraging new diversions to attract the people seawards. In 1902 George Sinclair and Fred Parr were given municipal sanction to stage open-air entertainments on a platform next to the bathing station, on payment of £25 for the season. Between June and September the Aberdeen Pierrots gave three daily performances, weather permitting, and proved to be hugely popular. This represented no localised phenomenon, as throughout the United Kingdom pierrot ensembles had become an integral part of the thriving seaside leisure industry. Such was their family-based appeal that they were seriously denting the long-standing supremacy of black-faced minstrel troupes in public affection. However, apart from a dramatic shift of emphasis in style to a romanticised French theatrical tradition, the pierrots followed the minstrels in offering a lively blend of music, dancing, comedy and speciality acts. In Aberdeen Messrs Sinclair and Parr advertised their shows as 'fun without vulgarity', and often featured visiting guest artists along with their stock players.[8]

The pair were London-based professionals, who had shrewdly detected a budding market for pierrot entertainment north of the Border. Their success in Aberdeen helped to stimulate an unprecedented surge of popular interest in the beach, to the extent that the bathing station committee was forced to recognise the gross inadequacy of amenities, both for the public and the pierrots. Matters were taken in hand with improved catering facilities and the construction of the

Alexander Ross 'Harry' Gordon 1893–1957

Born in Powis Place and brought up in Urquhart Road, he was the son of a plumber. Educated at King Street School and the Central School, he became a clerk for George Mollison & Sons, grain importers. In 1908 he won a talent competition at the Beach Pavilion and in the summer of 1909 joined a pierrot troup at Banchory. His first appearance in variety was at the Empire, George Street, in 1910. Subsequently he toured the north of Scotland, including Orkney and Shetland. Following military service during the First World War, he became master of ceremonies at the Beach Pavilion, in partnership with Mrs Cissy Murray, and was the driving force behind its success between the wars when his annual summer season made a major contribution to entertainment for holiday makers. In the 1930s he became sole leaseholder of the Beach Pavilion until the end of the Second World War. Between the wars he also worked on BBC radio and appeared annually in pantomime between 1929–54 in Edinburgh or Glasgow with a long unbroken run at the Alhambra, Glasgow from 1937–52. In 1943 he joined the 'Half-Past Eight' variety show with which he remained associated for the rest of his life. He died, while still appearing in pantomime, in January 1957.

Beach Pavilion in 1905, which allowed the performers a wind and weather-proof environment to stage their shows. The structure was not imposing, merely a wooden building with a corrugated iron roof, but the capable management of comedian David Thomson quickly established its reputation as one of the city's major summer attractions. Pierrot culture was booming, with Aberdonians filling the performing ranks and adding a unique dose of ethnic humour to the proceedings.

Appreciating the drawing power of 'Harry Gordon's Entertainers', the town council authorised the construction of a custom-designed Pavilion as part of a

So well-known was Harry Gordon, 'the Laird of Inversnecky', that he needed no identification on the Beach Pavilion's programmes of the 1930s.

beach improvement scheme, costing in total £53,000.[9] In 1928 the theatre opened with an audience capacity of 750, relatively small in scale but appropriate for the homely atmosphere of Gordon's shows. The process of beach expansion moved one step further with a prestigious new dance hall, the product of a joint initiative between the town council and American entertainment entrepreneur, John Henry Iles. The waltz was firmly legitimised in Aberdeen social life when the Beach Ballroom was formally opened by Lord Provost Andrew Lewis in 1929.[10] The proviso that 'the dancing entertainment shall be free from vulgarity', with alcohol strictly prohibited, showed that there was still a strong moral dimension to the promotion of certain leisure pursuits.[11] On the other hand, councillors were determined to maintain the viability of their investment. Iles was encouraged to erect an amusement park, complete with scenic railway, and the Codona family was given authority to run a fairground and carnival, on the understanding that noise levels would be 'discreet'. With such entertainments in place by the 1930s, the beach became a major attraction not just for Aberdonians, but for substantial numbers of visitors, notably Glaswegians during their traditional July Fair holiday.

The Rise of the Cinema

During the 1900s the success of the pierrots and the Beach Pavilion had encouraged an assortment of seaside attractions. In 1906 John Sinclair recognised the perennial fascination with animals and opened a small zoo, boasting the 'Finest Collection of Lions, Bears, Wolves, Hyenas' in the north of Scotland. Such was the success of the venture that Sinclair was encouraged to move the menagerie to winter quarters at the Alhambra Music Hall, which was transformed into an indoor pleasure-resort, complete with side-shows and assorted novelties. Along with the animals, the public was drawn to the Alhambra by the allure of the electro-graphic cinematograph, one of several motion picture entertainments operating in the city.[12] The new process was still in its pioneering days, and invariably featured as part of a package of live varieties. Indeed, Aberdeen's first public display of 'animated photographs' in September 1896 accompanied a one-man show at the Music Hall, where the star performer was a conjurer. Robert Calder, one of the city's early cinematographers, showed short films as part of an impressive concert programme, which included such luminaries as fiddling virtuoso James Scott Skinner and Violet Davidson, a soprano who soulfully interpreted Scots songs.

Keen Aberdonian interest in the early cinematograph is understandable, given the city's reputation for quality photographic reproduction, initiated in the mid-nineteenth century by George Washington Wilson. However, the potential of moving pictures had been recognised during the 1890s by William Walker, who ran a successful business specialising in magic lantern slides. Walker became a film-maker as well as an exhibitor, capturing vivid local events, such as the Gordon Highlanders on parade. Royal patronage was bestowed by Queen Victoria, who was fascinated by the camera, and summoned Walker regularly to Balmoral for command performances.[13] Following this success, a number of cinematographers became established in the city. One of the most flamboyant was Dove Paterson, who strikingly exemplified the mix of old and new culture. He exuded showmanship, having made his name as an elocutionist and concert promoter. Yet he was also an ardent temperance campaigner, who continued to organise the movement's traditional New Year Festival, complete with moving pictures.[14] Paterson ran the popular picture shows during the Alhambra Music Hall winter season, and went on to open the city's first permanent cinema, the Gaiety, in 1908. By 1914 a plethora of such cinemas had appeared, and that year the business entered a much more commercial and elaborate phase, with the construction of the custom-designed La Scala, which had a capacity of almost 1,000 seats.

It was profoundly ironic that, for all Paterson's emphasis on the moral integrity of his enterprise, particularly the educative value of films to the young, the cinema should have become a focus of debate about its supposed corrupting influence. This was not unique to Aberdeen, or even to Scotland, as in the United States moral reformers had led the way in putting pressure on the motion picture industry to temper the content of films. In 1913 an Aberdeen Citizens' Vigilance Committee was formed, encouraged by the evangelical Presbyterian Alliance. *Bon-Accord* identified a strong 'American element' among its influences, showing the starkly different ways that transatlantic culture could shape the public consciousness. The magazine's editorial was cautionary in its advice to the new body.

> There are many among our social reformers who, in their condemnation of street parading, picture palaces, and ice-cream shops, never for a moment pause to give a thought to the home-life of the poor. They do not seem to realise what the "call" of the street is to thousands, and the fascination it possesses.[15]

Street-promenading certainly had longevity as a pastime in the city, and 'walkin the mat', as it was known colloquially, continued well into the century, featuring especially on socially-restricted Sunday evenings before the liberalisation of Scotland's drink licensing laws in 1976.[16] In 1913, the concern of the reformers to clear the streets and direct young people into more respectable activities was inspired by profound unease about the disturbing trend towards the secularisation of urban life, and the dislocating impact of new and seemingly alien forms of culture. The cinema ranked with immigrant Italian ice-cream vendors and American ragtime as subversive. Such fears were also an indication of the fragile state of social equilibrium immediately before the trauma of the First World War.[17]

However, in Aberdeen the popular forms of entertainment held their own against the strictures of the morally-concerned. That the civic authority had a vested interest in encouraging the leisure industry also helped considerably in maintaining this resilience.

The war helped to legitimise cinema-going, not least because of the useful propaganda value of film. Technical progress also meant that the feature-film became a much more complex and creative entity, with D. W. Griffith's 1915 epic, *The Birth of A Nation*, running for twelve reels. By 1918 the United States dominated film output, having secured 80 per cent of the global market. In Aberdeen, control of the city's picture houses was virtually monopolised from the 1920s by two enterprises, headed respectively by James F. Donald and Bert Gates. Both men had started out in the pioneering cinematograph days, but their shrewd ability to anticipate changing film preferences allowed them gradually to overwhelm their rivals. The coming of talking-pictures to the city in 1929 forced a brisk pace of expansion, as the two equipped their establishments to cater for the innovative process. The impact this had on young Aberdonians was described retrospectively by one film devotee, 'we couldn't understand what the actors were saying, never having heard Americans speak, but soon we were saying "OK baby" in a poor imitation of the stars we so adored'.[18] Sumptuous picture-palaces were constructed to meet growing demand. Gates opened the Capitol in 1932, Donald the Astoria in 1934, reflecting the fashionable trend to provide auditoria that could seat 2,000 and more. According to figures quoted by *Bon-Accord* in 1936,

---

James F. Donald 1869–1934

Born in Newhills, James Donald was apprenticed to a coachbuilder in Rose Street, John F. Clark, and subsequently worked for the Great North of Scotland Railway Company at Kittybrewster. He opened an electro-plating and bicycle business in Rosemount. He was a cycle racing champion and temperance supporter, but was most enthusiastic about dancing. He opened his first dancing class, the Gondolier Quadrille Party in 1891 in the Lesser Albert Hall, Huntly Street, and in 1905 acquired a hall in North Silver Street for the Gondolier School of Dancing and Deportment. In 1921 he was elected president of the British Association of Teachers of Dancing. In 1915 he opened the West End cinema in a former billiard hall on Union Street. The lease expired in 1920 and, after presenting some shows at the Music Hall, he opened the Grand Central on George Street in 1922. In 1924 he opened the Cinema House in Skene Terrace. In the late 1920s he bought the properties on either side of the Grand Central and eventually reopened a refurbished theatre in 1929 with a capacity increased from 730 to 1,640. In 1933 he bought His Majesty's Theatre. He represented St Nicholas ward and then St Andrew's ward on the town council 1927–33. He was an active fund raiser for charities, especially for hospitals.

FRONT ELEVATION.

Aberdeen provided one cinema seat per seven inhabitants, more than double the ratio for London.[19]

During the 1930s John R. Allan identified the social life of the city as revolving around the polar institutions of church and cinema.

> The Church offers a great variety of entertainments, from Women's Guilds to Afternoon Whist, and gives almost continuous employment to those who are interested in good works. That being so, it is difficult to account for the even greater popularity of the Cinema, considering its tedious preoccupation with dramas of desire. But it may be that the frivolous passions shadowed on the screen offer the patrons a much-needed escape from their own intense and very practical affections.[20]

For Allan, authentic North-East passion was much more elemental and profound than the fare on offer at the Capitol or Astoria. It emanated from the landscape, 'a power of human nature that when roused is brother to the stormy seas'. His use of masculine and tempestuous imagery is revealing, because during the inter-war period the cult of the North Sea trawler-men preoccupied many film-makers and

Plans for Donald's 2,000-seater Astoria cinema in Clifton Road, built in 1934: one of the city's many cinemas between the 1920s and 1950s when cinema-going was at its peak.

writers. John Grierson led the way with his 1929 film about the herring fleets, *Drifters*, a documentary which emulated the gritty realism of the early Soviet film-makers. Harry Watt followed in 1938 with *North Sea*, where leading characters were played by actual fishermen, recruited from the Aberdeen labour exchange.[21] Among the writers, H. V. Morton accompanied the crew of the Aberdeen trawler *Majestic*, and marvelled at the precision of the enterprise. He commented, 'no man can work so hard and continuously unless they are united by a quality of mind which perhaps they would not recognise as pride or loyalty'.[22] Of course, trawler-life was often far from heroic, but its appeal must be understood in the context of the depression that was traumatising the heavily-industrialised regions of Scotland. In a climate of economic insecurity, the trawler-men were depicted as a stirring symbol of resilience, and did much to project a more positive national identity, influencing initiatives like the government-backed *Films of Scotland*, founded in 1938.

THE THEATRE AND PERFORMING ARTS

Dr Walford Bodie continued and developed Anderson's tradition of illusion as 'The Electric Wizard of the North'.

The 1900s was a decade of unprecedented theatre-building in Scotland, with the number of play-houses in the four major cities increasing from 32 to 53.[23] Glasgow claimed the lion's share, but Aberdeen's quota rose to three, comprising Her Majesty's Theatre (1872), the Palace Theatre (1898) and His Majesty's Theatre (1906). The Palace was built to replace a less elaborate theatre which had opened in 1888, the new structure seating 1,800 and with standing-room for 1,400.[24] The fare on

offer was strictly variety and some illustrious artists performed there, including Charlie Chaplin and Harry Houdini. In 1909 the American escapologist generated worldwide publicity for the Palace when he made one of his celebrated leaps, manacled, from the deck of a tug-boat into the North Sea. Houdini freed himself in 18 seconds. He also took time in Aberdeen to visit St Nicholas' churchyard and the grave of John Henry Anderson, who had died in 1874. A revered figure in the world of stage-magic, Anderson's charisma influenced more than just Houdini. Among his multiple stage personas, Aberdonian illusionist Dr Walford Bodie was 'The Electric Wizard of the North', and made the most of public awe about the new power source by appearing to have death-defying doses of electric current passed through his body.[25] Bodie attracted capacity audiences at the Palace, and was internationally so successful that he became second only to Harry Lauder as the highest paid Scottish music hall entertainer of the early twentieth century.

The size of the Palace Theatre indicated the expanding scale of theatrical operations in Aberdeen, which had come a long way since the days of Jessie Pollock's Theatre Royal. His Majesty's Theatre provided seating for 2,550 and was geared for profit, a development that did not meet with universal approbation among lovers of 'legitimate' drama in the city. With the theatre still in the process of construction, correspondence in the columns of *Bon-Accord* criticised the artistic control that London-based proprietor Robert Arthur was wielding in Aberdeen.[26] Having taken over Her Majesty's Theatre in 1891, he had become the driving-force behind the ambitious new venture. It was suggested that Arthur's offerings were over-dependent on the staples of melodrama, musical comedy and pantomime, limiting choice and rendering the season all too predictable. However, given Arthur's determination to build His Majesty's, he had a shrewd understanding of preferences among fashionable theatre-goers, and the likely return from his investment. At a cost of £35,000, and designed by specialist theatre architect Frank Matcham, Aberdeen's newest showpiece conformed to exacting safety standards.[27] Much was made of the skill of city craftsmen in the elaborate construction of the theatre, partly to deflect criticism of Arthur and his London sense of style. Yet His Majesty's was soon successful as a performing venue, the care taken in providing for space and comfort proving popular with actors and the predominantly middle-class audiences.

As for Her Majesty's Theatre, the interior underwent major reconstruction by Frank Matcham to bring it up to the necessary standards expected by audiences in the 1900s. It re-opened in 1910 as another variety venue, shedding the royal title to become the more down-to-earth Tivoli. Variety was booming during the immediate pre-war period, and the array of international vaudevillians who performed at the Tivoli and the Palace was of stellar quality. However, popular taste was already in the process of altering, owing to the rise of the cinematograph. While the Beach Pavilion triumphantly held its own, thanks to Harry Gordon and the holiday season, the larger theatres which were open throughout the year began to face stiff competition by the 1920s. After talking-pictures became firmly established, the Palace was restructured as a prestigious cinema, leaving the Tivoli as the city's sole home of variety. Times were especially lean for His Majesty's, which by 1931 was under threat of closure.[28] In that year a writer in the *Press and Journal* blamed the advent of cinema for the decline, but also referred to the impact of more relaxed leisure habits since the war. He claimed that theatre-going was no longer a 'dress-and-social matter', and that the well-groomed Edwardian culture associated with His Majesty's was now seen to be unfashionable.[29]

Ironically, it was cinema cash that came to the rescue of His Majesty's, as provided by James F. Donald. There had been prolonged unease about the barren prospects for professional drama in Aberdeen, until Donald purchased the theatre from the Robert Arthur enterprise in 1933. Blending civic pride with philanthropy, he acquired the building for £35,000 and invested a further £15,000 in refurbishment. Donald died in 1934, not long after His Majesty's celebrated its phoenix-like re-opening, but his four sons continued the family tradition, to the extent that the 'Donald dynasty' became long and inextricably associated with the promotion of entertainment in the North-East.[30] Even when His Majesty's was sold to the District Council in 1975, with substantial financial input from the Scottish Arts Council, James Donald and Peter Donald continued the family involvement with the theatre by acting successively as its manager.

From its early days His Majesty's featured a range of entertainment. Drama formed a segment of the seasonal programme, with plays performed invariably by prestigious professional touring companies. Unlike other Scottish cities, Aberdeen had no full-time repertory company, although 'Harry Gordon's Repertory Company' appeared at the Beach Pavilion during the 1950s. Locally-produced drama was overwhelmingly amateur, reflecting a phenomenon that flourished in Scotland during the inter-war period. The Scottish Community Drama Association was established in 1926 to co-ordinate activities, and strongly encouraged the use of local themes and language. Indeed, in much of Aberdeen's amateur output doric speech was consciously employed, representing a significant counter-side to the high-gloss metropolitan drama at His Majesty's. Established plays were even translated into the vernacular, such as the 1951 production of Ibsen's *The Lady from the Sea*.[31] The Aberdeen volume of the *Third Statistical Account*, published in 1953, devoted considerable space to community drama, pointing to successful doric plays such as Leonard Irwin's *The Land of the Living*, performed to critical acclaim by the city's Unity Players. However, by the early 1960s enthusiasm had waned, a columnist in the *Press and Journal* blaming the transfer of audience allegiance to the prolific output of television drama.[32] Scottish theatre generally suffered because of such shifting social preferences, which in turn drastically affected the viability of established performing venues, not least in Aberdeen.

Music remained deeply ingrained in local culture, and its forms became increasingly diverse. During the early twentieth century the theatres afforded a range of opportunities for performance, from light opera at His Majesty's to the syncopated rhythm of visiting dance bands at the Tivoli. Scottish traditional music consolidated its broad appeal, partly as a result of the surge in popularity for country dancing after the Scottish Country Dance Society was founded in 1923. Even the cinemas offered music, with the Symphonic Orchestra at the Palace a substantial ensemble, which accompanied films as well as performing in its own right. Yet ironically, during the 1920s the Music Hall was suffering from a similar crisis of confidence as His Majesty's. Changing tastes contributed to its declining fortunes, precipitated not just by the allure of cinemas and dance-halls, but competition from radio and its eclectic musical output. In 1928 the town council agreed to purchase the bankrupt concern for £34,000. Thereafter the building continued to serve as an important platform for concert and choral music, although there were those who felt that its function was being over-stretched in accommodating such pugnacious pursuits as boxing and wrestling. Moreover, the fabric of the building was deteriorating, so that by 1960 its down-at-heel discomfort was condemned witheringly by the *Press and Journal*.[33] Opinion became sharply divided as to the future of the Music Hall, with an influential lobby arguing for demolition. It was only after protracted public debate that the town council resolved in 1968 to retain its historic property.

BROADCASTING

Radio was one of the prime technological developments during the inter-war period, and had a profound impact on Aberdonian culture. Yet for all its subsequent reputation, entertainment was not the original rationale behind the establishment of the British Broadcasting Company in 1922. The BBC was a monopoly of assorted wireless manufacturers, who wanted to carve out a market for their receivers and restrict competition. The Government licensed the new enterprise, intent on ensuring that transmission would be regulated. The founding general manager of the BBC was John Reith, who became director-general in 1927, when the company was transformed into a public utility corporation. Described as 'a visionary whose cultural legacy endured deep into this century', Reith was born in the North-East, in Stonehaven, although he spent his formative years in Glasgow.[34] He directed BBC priorities into quality production, in adherence to his deeply-held evangelical commitment to provide a moral underpinning to broadcasting. Initially, he also allowed considerable regional latitude as far as programming was concerned. In Scotland there were two main stations, Glasgow and Aberdeen, both opened in 1923.[35] The new medium soon proved itself by providing distinctive and imaginative output, directly serving the local community.

The Aberdeen station moved ahead of its Glasgow counterpart in establishing the 2BD Repertory Players (2BD was the call sign of the station), who performed adaptations of the classics as well as numerous vernacular offerings. Not surprisingly, youngsters were readily attracted to radio's paradoxical blend of the familiar and the fantastic. During the 1930s, they avidly followed the activities of the 'Aberdeen Animals', brought to life on Children's Hour by producer Moultrie Kelsall, who consciously recreated the kind of cartoon characters made popular in contemporary comics like *Puck* and *Rainbow*.[36] Harry Gordon proved to have unique broadcasting talent. His humour did not depend on visual appeal but was crafted around the vernacular, with careful timing and a meticulous style of delivery.[37] In addition to his prolific radio output, he made countless gramophone recordings about Inversnecky, a mythical North-East village community, peopled by assorted functionaries, 'wifies' and 'bairns', thus continuing the long tradition of language as entertainment, identifiably stretching back to nineteenth-century popular theatre and soirée culture. Even the silent cinema was embellished by the Aberdonian flair for vocal improvisation. Dove Paterson, the elocutionist, pioneered 'real' talking pictures in the 1900s by providing lively dialogue accompaniment. Bert and Nellie Gates came from an acting background, and gave similar theatrical piquancy to the shows at their Star cinema.

The Second World War disrupted the BBC's golden age of regional broadcasting, although before this time there was a decisive shift in favour of London-centred production. For much of the 1930s radio 2BD was under threat, surviving only because of public pressure to defend its unique status in serving northern Scotland.[38] However, in 1938 it was downgraded from a main to a relay station. It has been suggested that the values and attitudes generated by the plethora of local BBC stations between the wars were deliberately eradicated, as the policy of broadcasting centralisation was consolidated in the 1950s. The Pilkington Report in 1962 eventually identified the need for a more devolved framework within the BBC monolith, but there was reluctance to invest resources in new stations until the Conservative Government sanctioned commercial radio in 1972.

Ironically, in their quest to attract advertisers, the independent radio stations targeted the population of central Scotland, especially Glasgow. Aberdonian interests were more immediately served by BBC Radio Scotland, created in 1974 in an attempt to compete with the commercial stations and break away from London domination. Local identity was further reinforced by the opening of BBC Radio Aberdeen but, despite a loyal following, the station was axed in 1993. Priorities became focused on Radio Scotland, and the BBC's Aberdeen base at Beechgrove Terrace steadily increased production for the national station. By the end of the century, Aberdonians could choose from the various permutations of BBC radio, London-based commercial stations, and local commercial offerings like NorthSound, which went on the air in 1981.[39]

Television first came to Aberdeen in 1954, when the BBC began transmission to the North-East.[40] Unlike the long-standing monopoly of radio, plans were already formulated to allow for competition, and in that year legislation was approved to establish the Independent Television Association. Commercial television was launched during 1955, although it was not until 1960 that the ITA invited applications to provide a station servicing Aberdeen and northern Scotland.[41] The

aptly-titled North of Scotland TV, led by cinema magnate, Sir Alexander King, and wealthy landowner, Captain Iain Tennant, was eventually given the seal of ITA approval. With a change of name to the more evocative Grampian Television, the new company started broadcasting in September 1961. Initially there was an element of local cynicism about its impressive mission statement, 'To bring the area to itself, to bring the area to the outside world, and to bring the outside world to the area'.[42] The *Evening Express* had to be given firm assurances about the quality of programmes likely to emanate from Grampian's studios, based in the old tramway depot at Queen's Cross. Accordingly, there would be no 'alien and mid-Atlantic mediocrity', with Grampian assiduously (if unhistorically) promoted as embodying the dual 'gaelic and nordic' cultures of northern Scotland.[43] Publicity material in the *Press and Journal* enthused that, 'the ground is richly fertile for the production of a variety of programmes concerning culture, history, customs, folk lore, myth and legend, religion, singing, dancing, mime, music and sport'.[44]

As it happened, Grampian's home-grown output attracted substantial audiences with such folksy offerings as *Bothy Nichts* and *Calum's Ceilidh*, the latter featuring Gaelic singer Calum Kennedy, whose tartan spectaculars were already hugely popular at the Tivoli Theatre. Looking back over the first decade in 1971, producer Jim Buchanan reaffirmed Grampian's broadcasting commitment, at a time when viewing audiences had risen from 98,000 to one million.

It is no part of Grampian's job to make the kind of shows which are produced in America, London or Birmingham. These shows can be, and are, bought and shown by the company, but you cannot buy from outside a programme in the language of Buchan or featuring music of the Highlands and North-East.[45]

However, from the 1980s Grampian's commercial underpinning made its management acutely sensitive to the technological changes that were broadening choices and boosting the potential for television to reach more specialised audiences. In consequence, Grampian expanded its range of production, notably into news coverage and documentaries. It successfully retained its licence under the 1990 Broadcasting Act, because of its commitment to maintain quality output.[46]

HEALTH AND SPORT

James Bryce MP campaigned for access to the mountains against the restrictions imposed by landowners.

Notwithstanding civic aspirations to develop Aberdeen as a tourist resort, much emphasis was placed on the health benefits of the beach, especially for the working classes. At the bathing station's formal opening in 1898, a leading councillor made pointed reference to the merits of 'the bath that cleanses the inward as well as the outward man'.[47] Moreover, exercise was thought to have a spiritually purifying influence. In 1907 the twin priorities of the 1st Aberdeen Company of the Boys' Brigade were itemised as 'development of the body' and 'religious training' in pursuit of 'Christian manliness'.[48] The identification of health with fresh air and the outdoors was consolidated after the First World War. More consistently than their Victorian and Edwardian counterparts, holiday makers sought the sun. While this was an unpredictable commodity in Aberdeen, the socially liberating impact of sun-culture proved to be a useful device for promoting the city. Gleaming youth and beauty reflected the more relaxed spirit of the times, as revealed in 1934 by the robust commentary to a *Bon-Accord* photograph of women sea-bathers.

Ten years ago such a picture would have surprised our citizenry. Today it is accepted as a perfectly natural expression of the healthy gaiety of free, untrammelled

RECTORIAL.

femininity that adds beauty to our glorious golden sands. This sort of thing is the complete answer to the lugubrious critics, such as the Wee Free Ministers, who rail against the pleasure-loving age. All the folks who come into our province in the summer months many not be fashioned on the lines of these strappin' lasses. Most of them have to take their fun with less abandon. But the point we make is that the Beach has justified the enthusiasm of civic leaders of a third of a century ago.[49]

If there was a disconcerting hint of 'strength-through-joy' in these observations, the waspish reference to outmoded moral attitudes revealed generational differences over restraints on leisure. There was a similar muscularity of approach in Aberdeen to the inter-war vogue for hiking. On the other hand, the call of nature and the countryside had deep roots in Scotland, tangibly demonstrated in Aberdeen when the Cairngorm Club was founded in 1889, with James Bryce MP as president, to encourage mountain-climbing and the accessibility of open spaces.

The municipal promotion of health broadened to include an assortment of sporting activities. Civic patronage undoubtedly helped to popularise bowls, with specially-constructed bowling greens forming an integral feature of the urban land-scape. In 1879 enthusiast William Cadenhead regretted that 'the game is nearly extinct about the town'. Just over a century later, in 1984, the venue for the World Bowls Championship was the city's Westburn Park. The surge of bowling interest was attributed to its 'cheap and sociable' nature, plus a keen following among both men and women. Tennis was another sport that benefited from substantial munic-ipal encouragement, although not until the inter-war period, when the panache of players like Suzanne Lenglen inspired emulation. Like bowls, tennis provided an opportunity for women to participate, although competition was dominated by the middle classes, whose domain lay in the exclusive private clubs of the suburbs. Swimming was yet another pursuit that was not gender-specific, and remained a consistent municipal priority. The town council opened its 'up-town baths' during the inter-war period, to provide centrally located facilities. The down-town bathing station became gradually run down, and was dismissed as 'unsightly' and out-dated in the ambitious *Plan for Aberdeen*, commissioned for the town council in the 1940s.[50] There was a scheme to replace it with a state-of-the-art lido, but it was not until 1973 that the familiar red-brick landmark was demolished.

Golf had a long pedigree in Aberdeen, and the municipality continued to provide facilities for clubs like Bon-Accord and Victoria to play on the Links. In 1920 councillors took the bold step of purchasing Hazlehead, an 800-acre estate to the west of the city, which they planned to transform into a municipal golfing centre. This included a nine-hole course promoted especially for the 'ladies', a recognition that women had established a niche in the sport.[51] However, the

Lord Provost Lewis drives off the first ball at the municipal golf course at Hazlehead, 2 July 1927: not quite the 'people's golf course' that it was claimed.

opening of the new municipal initiative in 1927 provoked controversy. The *Press and Journal* suggested that charges were too high for the use of facilities at the much-vaunted 'people's golf course', especially given the park's distance from the city.[52] For all its claims to serve popular needs, Hazlehead was perceived as a resort for better-off visitors, offering an environment that was more serene and edifying than the beach, with its amusements, entertainers and boisterous youngsters. Moreover, councillors were responding to the kind of style that was associated with prestigious out-of-town courses like Balgownie, at the Bridge of Don. This was the home of the Royal Aberdeen Golf Club, which had progressed far since it left the Links in 1888, with the 'royal' title bestowed by King Edward VII in 1903. In addition, the new and innovative course at Murcar was setting the pace for those who could afford it.

Outside the sphere of direct municipal influence, Aberdonians participated in an increasingly diverse range of sports, whether as players or spectators. However, there was a sharp decline in the popularity of cricket after 1900, despite the buoyant survival of the Aberdeenshire club. As a team sport, association football was claiming the single-minded loyalty of supporters. This was ironic, as cricket clubs like Orion had originally encouraged football as part of their activities during the winter season, only to become engulfed by the new sporting phenomenon. Rugby football experienced similar problems of declining support. For years the elite institutions of the University, Robert Gordon's College and the Grammar School constituted the heartland of Aberdonian rugby, although from the 1960s nationwide television gave it considerable exposure and helped to revive interest. Indeed, twentieth-century technology played a large part in nurturing new sporting activities. The invention of the electric hare was emblematic, as it created the cult of greyhound racing, which was eagerly followed by Scotland's working classes. Betting rather than canine prowess was the prime rationale for the sport's dramatic rise in fortune. By the 1950s, Aberdeen dog stadium featured two race meetings a week, catering for 3,000 spectators, and frequently attracting near-capacity attendance.[53]

ABERDEEN FOOTBALL CLUB

From 1900 sport in Aberdeen was dominated by the relentless rise of association football. Participation in the game multiplied at all levels, junior, amateur and professional, this last making the greatest impact on the public consciousness. Since the 1890s, the teams of Aberdeen, Orion and Victoria United had competed in Scotland's Northern League, but developed aspirations for more prestigious status. The Scottish Football League allowed competition with famous clubs like Celtic and Rangers, and was also a more commercial option for maintaining the game's momentum. However, a necessary first step towards the process of admission was the amalgamation of the three premier Aberdeen clubs. As *Bon-Accord* pointed out in 1902, there was still much spadework to be done before professional football in the city could be taken seriously.

> Even though the teams were brought together, it would be impossible to pick out from them an eleven likely to be worthy of the town. New players would require to be imported, while those left over could be held as substitutes playing in the 'A' team. Then, with hard training, there is no knowing what the 'Aberdeen' (which seems the only possible name for the combination) might do.[54]

In March 1903 the merger was agreed, and citizens were invited to take shares in the Aberdeen Football Club Limited, with a capital of £1,500.[55] The much-coveted entry to the Scottish League was delayed until 1904, but by the following year the new club was playing in the First Division. Despite initial anxieties it proved to be financially successful, making a comfortable profit of almost £320 by the end of the first season.[56]

In terms of playing performance the club proceeded solidly, if not spectacularly, during the first half of the century. John R. Allan commented in 1935 that the

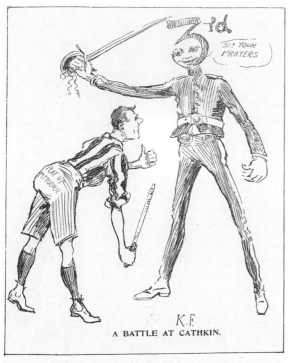

A BATTLE AT CATHKIN.

Aberdeen tackles the Third Lanark, at Glasgow, on Saturday, in the Third Round for the Scottish Cup.

Aberdeen FC v. Third Lanark FC, 1905. Aberdeen lost 4–1 to the eventual cup winners.

team's repeated failure to enter the glittering ranks of the champions provoked intense local passion, including 'newspaper correspondences of great bitterness besides some rare vituperation from the shilling side'. On the other hand, the club was a reliable investment and 'one of the few in Scotland to pay a regular dividend on its shares'.[57] The outbreak of war seriously disturbed the activities of Scottish football, because of the division of the country into 'safe' and 'unsafe' areas, where crowd sizes were restricted. Travel was also a major problem, and so Scotland was partitioned into local leagues, with Aberdeen a pivotal component of the North-East group of clubs. In the struggle to maintain the game's viability during profoundly unsettling times, the region demonstrated a capacity to attract much-needed revenue and spectators.[58] Football entered a particularly competitive phase in the aftermath of war, but Aberdonian angst about the elusiveness of honours dissolved in 1947 when the team defeated Hibernian to win the Scottish Cup Final. Fifty years of loyal following in the city was rewarded when Aberdeen became Scottish League champions in 1955. In describing Pittodrie Park, Aberdeen's home ground, about about this time, the contributor to the *Third Statistical Account* commented that the overwhelmingly male crowd averaged 15,000 out of a capacity of 44,000, with a charge of 1s. 6d. (7.5p) for admission to the stand.[59] The spectators, it added, 'are at all times responsive to the nicer points of play'.

Aberdeen's heroic years in football corresponded with fundamental changes in the game's organisation, as from the 1960s it became a very lucrative international business. Indeed, from the economic perspective, Aberdeen Football Club's success from the 1970s was based on the astute financial management that had characterised it from the fledgling days of the 1900s. The radical restructuring of the Scottish League in 1975 was the major catalyst for change, with the creation of an elite and highly competitive Premier Division. Chris Anderson, vice-chairman of Aberdeen FC and a key figure in its regeneration, explained what this new development had meant for the club.

We were very nearly relegated for the first time in our history which was the

Richard M. Donald 1912–94

Appointed manager of the Grand Central Cinema at age of 15 by his father, Richard Donald also acted as a dancing instructor at the Gondolier School. He played football for Aberdeen FC for ten years in the 1930s, interspersed by a short spell at Dunfermline. He became manager of the Astoria Cinema in 1936 when the family bought control and was primarily involved in managing the growing family cinema empire which also included the Ice Rink. In 1949 he became a director of Aberdeen FC and then chairman in 1970. He played a major role during the club's most successful period during which the Scottish League Championship was won three times. The Scottish Cup and League Cup and, most impressively, the European Cup-Winners' Cup were also won. It was a period in which the ground was renovated and developed. By 1978 it had become the first all-seated football stadium in Britain. A cantilever stand was built on the south side of the ground in 1980, followed by executive boxes in the main stand in 1985 and undersoil heating in 1987. The ground improvements were financed by success on the pitch especially in European competitions. A massive new stand was built at the beach end and opened in 1993. Fittingly it was named the Richard Donald Stand in recognition of the chairman's long and distinguished service to the club. Unfortunately his health had deteriorated so that he was unable to attend the opening ceremony.

Richard 'Dick' Donald, 1912-94, continued the tradition of the Donald family in shaping Aberdeen's leisure activities.

trigger for us to clear the decks and start afresh. We looked at everything, the players, the manager, the stadium, and the fact that Aberdeen was the offshore oil capital of Europe.[60]

The process had already started with the modernisation of Pittodrie, which eventually included all-seating facilities and a reduction of capacity to 22,600. It was more cost-effective to limit numbers, and the directors recognised that expectations were changing as far as comfort and amenities were concerned, especially during the affluent oil boom era. In the quest for ideas, Anderson visited the United States and made a careful study of the marketing and promotional activities of the financially successful North American Soccer League. From 1975 the club employed a series of inspired team managers, with Glaswegian Alex Ferguson ultimately securing immortal status. His personal rapport with

Aberdeen FC's greatest night. Willie Miller and his team celebrate their defeat of Real Madrid in the European Cup-Winners' Cup at Gothenburg, 1983. Leighton, Simpson and Miller are the three in front.

Aberdeen's owner, Dick Donald, and Chris Anderson was a vital factor in building up the club's confidence and ambition.

In 1980 the League Championship returned to Aberdeen for the first time since 1955. In May 1983 Aberdeen celebrated a major international achievement, defeating the illustrious Real Madrid 2-1 in the final of the European Cup-Winners' Cup. Ferguson paid tribute to the ever-loyal supporters, who crossed the North Sea to Gothenburg to cheer on the team.

> Our support that night was magnificent, absolutely great. 12,000 Aberdeen supporters, many of whom had begged and borrowed to be there. And the special thing about these people, for Aberdeen and the whole of Scotland, was that they were good-natured and good-humoured.[61]

LEISURE, OIL AND URBAN REGENERATION

As the experience of football demonstrated, the Second World War had a drastic impact on the organisation of leisure in Aberdeen. The beach became particularly dangerous territory, because of the persistent threat of German air raids. Harry Gordon finally closed the Beach Pavilion in 1940 and went on to boost wartime morale with touring shows. After the return of peace, the town council's priorities came to be focused on beach development as part of the long-term plan for the city. One of the first products of the new municipal publicity department was the slogan 'The Silver City with the Golden Sands' (see page 12), complete with Scottie dog mascot. By 1950 the campaign was bearing fruit, with Aberdeen named as Scotland's most popular holiday resort in a survey conducted by the Scottish Tourist Board.[62] However, respondents also criticised the standard of amenities and the blighting effect of the Scottish Sabbath on restricting the availability of entertainment and refreshments. Efforts were made to improve the image, including the pioneering promotional film *The Silver City* (1957), with commentary written and narrated by John R. Allan.[63] Not all Aberdonians were impressed; *Bon-Accord* described the city's resort pretensions as 'a big flop ... unless something happens to change our cold, wet, dull, blustery, topsy-turvy climate'.[64] To this were added dreadful smells from the gasworks and some of the less salubrious tenements. There were new initiatives, such as the children's adventure playground opened in 1962, but by this time the beach's hey-day had clearly passed. 'Now – It's the Glasgow Fair "Trickle"', observed the *Press and Journal* in July 1962, referring to Aberdeen's fading appeal as more glamorous destinations were targeted by holiday-makers, especially overseas.[65]

By 1970 there was considerable public cynicism about the beach's declining fortunes. Development proposals had come and gone, while the amenities languished. In the wake of Harry Gordon's death the Beach Pavilion closed in 1961. The Beach Ballroom survived, but there were conflicting ideas about using the loss-making property, which was regarded as a white elephant. Indeed, throughout the 1960s Aberdeen acquired several white elephants as a plethora of public buildings seemed to have outlived their usefulness. The Music Hall was a notorious example, although its architectural and cultural significance ultimately saved it from demolition. As a further sign of uncertain times, the ailing Tivoli Theatre became the Tivoli Bingo and Social Club. Bingo filled a social vacuum, created by the repudiation of older forms of entertainment and the rise of television. It first swept the city during the early 1960s, provoking immediate condemnation from the Church of Scotland about its supposed addictive qualities. Aberdeen Presbytery warned that it was 'a tragic irresponsibility in the use of leisure and money', while sanction for Sunday bingo was refused on the grounds that it would insidiously fuel the gambling habit. Nevertheless, the popularity of the new pursuit was tangibly demonstrated by the number of city cinemas switching to bingo, although this was not enough to rescue the Astoria from demolition in 1967.

Scotland the What? captured the ambiguous Aberdonian attitudes towards the

Overleaf:
The beach in the 1960s - past its glory days - looking north to the Bridge of Don before the housing developments there in the 1970s and 1980s. The Beach Ballroom is middle left.

ABERDEEN 1800–2000

city at this time. The song 'Cinemas' was an ironic lament for the changing urban landscape, with the demise of the 'picter hooses' symbolising the passing of an era.[66] Significantly, *Scotland the What?* expressed humour through language, in continuation of local tradition, but with trenchant satire in the lyrics and dialogue. On the other hand, Scottish-wide success also reflected the preoccupation with cultural identity during the 1970s, fuelled partly by the rise of political nationalism. This had the effect of attracting audiences back to the theatres, a development encouraged by local authorities, which increasingly provided maintenance and support for performing venues. Aberdeen's most

spectacular examples were the refurbishment of His Majesty's Theatre in 1982, and the Music Hall in 1986, at a cost to the community of £3.5 million for each building. There were mixed feelings about this civic commitment, which canny Aberdonians criticised as too extravagant. *Scotland the What?* mirrored the mood in the song '*That's Far A' the Money Went*', which wryly itemised the elaborate improvements to His Majesty's, including state-of-the-art computer technology.

By the 1980s Aberdeen's new-found status as offshore oil capital of Europe was boosting confidence in the city and redirecting priorities for development. Oil at first had been an unpredictable factor, with dire predictions of social fragmentation

Stephen Robertson, Buff Hardie and George Donald. Scotland the What? from the 1950s until 1997 built on the well-established North-East tradition of confident self-mockery.

Scotland the What?

This group had its origins in student review at Aberdeen University in the 1950s where Buff Hardie and Stephen Robertson met. After graduation they joined the Aberdeen Review Group where they met George Donald and James Logan. Logan acted as director/manager to the trio who appeared on stage. All retained and enjoyed successful careers: Robertson as a lawyer, Hardie rising to become secretary of Grampian Health Board, Donald as assistant rector of Perth Academy, and Logan as a research chemist. In 1969 the group made a farewell appearance at the Edinburgh Festival Fringe but this was so successful that appearances continued and increased. The group became a major attraction at theatres throughout Scotland and reached an even wider audience through television. Eventually the principals were obliged to abandon their other professions for the stage and continued to perform until the final tour in 1997.

as the new industry intruded brusquely into city life.[67] The Americanisation of Aberdeen was another anxiety fuelled by the media, as if transatlantic culture was a wholly new phenomenon. Conversely, the international spotlight concentrated civic energies on the need to promote a more cosmopolitan image. The city had become a major business centre, with expectations of high amenity standards. Yet in the early 1970s Aberdeen suffered from disadvantages, with Scotland's notoriously restricted drink licensing laws a persistent sore point in relation to tourism. Fortunately for the city's expanding economy, the issue was addressed in 1976 when hours were extended and Sunday opening permitted. Nevertheless, five years after this seminal social development, an investigation into Aberdeen's entertainment industry by the trade journal *Stage and Television Today* was scathing about continuing licensing constraints.[68] Over-caution and insularity on the part of councillors were blamed for not making the most of oil affluence. Discotheques had become the global emblem of fashionable night-life, but late licences in the city remained strictly limited, which scarcely enhanced perceptions of Aberdeen style. However, this snapshot view of the city in 1981 also identified positive trends, notably the 'astonishing amount' of free live music in pubs and hotels, especially traditional music.

By the 1990s the position had altered fundamentally. Aberdeen was being marketed as the 'Entertainment Capital of the North', and boasted the largest number of pubs and clubs per capita of all Scotland's cities.[69] It had also acquired, rather belatedly, a highly fashionable night club in Amadeus which proved to have a powerful attraction on the younger generation. Indeed, the apparent eagerness with which licensing applications were being granted by the city council provoked complaints from community organisations, concerned about noise levels and the unpredictable behaviour of revellers.[70] The conversion of churches and cinemas into nightclubs became a feature of this particular aspect of social transformation. The difficulty of satisfying consumer demand while preserving the integrity of the city was of course a perennial dilemma. However, the bolder approach to the promotion of leisure reflected a new emphasis on urban policy, which linked regeneration with recreational activities. Moreover, from the 1970s Aberdeen's civic leaders acquired a reputation for understanding the politics of environmental improvement, which formed a core component of regeneration strategies. With reference to the city's recurring success in the 'Britain in Bloom' competition, Lord Provost Alexander Collie had pointed out in 1982 that this was no frivolity. 'We ourselves and our families have to live and work in the circumstances we create in the city. It's all too easy to thrust care for amenity into the background when cuts are being made'.[71]

As for Aberdeen's 1990s status as a leisure and entertainment centre, this went beyond enthusiasm for night-clubbing and social drinking. Reflecting preoccupations of the previous century, the landscape was still a vital feature of community identity, although the 'Silver City' slogan had given way to the more nationalistic 'Flower of Scotland', as the efflorescent, blooming image was consolidated. With three times more public parkland per head of population than either Edinburgh or Glasgow, much was made of Aberdonian horticultural expertise in a bid to boost the use of open spaces. The beach remained a key priority, despite its prolonged fallow phase. In 1989 the £8 million Beach Leisure Centre opened as an all-year, all-weather family facility, offering fitness, health and sports. As if to emphasise that the sun no longer mattered for beach enjoyment, the Links Ice Arena opened two years later, to encourage skating and ice-sports. Yet some of the traditional attractions remained as an integral part of the development, notably the revived Beach Ballroom and Codona's amusement park. By the end of the century, Aberdeen was an active, modern city, that still retained a strong element of its old identity.

The Evolution of Leisure

Perceptions of Aberdeen in the 1900s were generally positive, due in part to the commitment of the civic leadership to promote the luminous image of the 'Silver City' and to establish a readily recognisable focus of identity. The extension of beach facilities was one of several municipally-inspired initiatives intended to nurture the kind of environment deemed so vital for ensuring the physical and moral welfare of the community. To a large extent, this was a continuation of nineteenth-century concern to provide for 'rational' recreation. Notwithstanding the doubts of middle-class moral reformers before 1914, the forms of entertainment that emerged during this controlled yet creative period were overwhelmingly associated with family values, and absorbed much from indigenous culture to strengthen their appeal. Even the icons of the twentieth-century communications' revolution – the cinema, radio and television – represented more than the intrusion of mass global entertainment, with its culturally levelling qualities. In their pioneering days, they reflected uniquely localised output, which gave a comforting dimension of homely familiarity to the new media. Moreover, as outlets for the deep-rooted Aberdonian preoccupation with language and performance, they served to consolidate cultural traditions, and helped to project them beyond the confines of the city. In this context, the progress of Aberdeen Football Club was significant. Its roots were localised and long-standing, but its success was achieved ultimately in the media-dominated, highly commercialised sporting arena. The past consistently reinforced the present throughout the century, due to the ability of Aberdonians to reconcile different and seemingly contradictory influences on their culture.

17

The Press

W. HAMISH FRASER

THE LITERARY TRADITION

The founding of the *Aberdeen Journal*, first issued as a weekly paper on 5 January 1748, launched a strong publishing tradition in Aberdeen.[1] The *Journal*'s founder and printer, James Chalmers, died in 1764 but was succeeded by his son, also named James, who continued to publish it until his death in 1810, when his son, David, took over. At the start of the nineteenth century the *Journal*'s politics, where apparent at all, were moderately Tory and no criticism of the dominating local elite appeared, although Chalmers' son-in-law, Alexander Brown, a bookseller and later lord provost, was prepared to sell Painite tracts and radical newspapers.[2] Its style and layout remained rigidly old-fashioned well into the nineteenth century, but it proved highly successful at attracting advertising.[3] There was some attempted rivalry with the appearance of the *Intelligencer* between 1752 and 1757 and the *Aberdeen Chronicle* in 1787. Chalmers took over the *Intelligencer* in 1757 thus removing the competition, and a serious alternative voice did not emerge until 1806 when John Bailie Booth launched a new version of the *Aberdeen Chronicle* offering a slightly less deferential tone towards the ruling order than did the *Aberdeen Journal*. Edited first by Andrew Sharpe, then by Dr Kerr, it was Foxite Whig in its politics and critical of the continuing war with France. This resulted in copies of the paper being burned in public. It took a moderately radical and vaguely republican line and seems to have found its main readership among the less well-off, although at sixpence (2.5p) an issue this must have been limited. However, as was the case until newspapers became much cheaper in the 1850s, there were reading groups who clubbed together to buy the paper and to pass it around. The city's bankruptcy in 1817 further fuelled the *Chronicle*'s vigorous demands for municipal reform, but after the legislation of the notorious Six Acts in 1817, its anti-government tone was somewhat modified. It continued, however, to push for parliamentary and burgh reform and backed Joseph Hume as MP for the Montrose Burghs. By the 1820s the *Chronicle*, or 'Johnny Booth's paper' as it was known locally, was beginning to struggle. It always had some difficulty in attracting advertisements and, in 1822, Booth sold it to a group of local Whigs.

There were also the beginnings of what was to become a strong tradition of satirical publication. An early one, the *Intruder*, survived for 16 fortnightly issues in 1802 and referred to a predecessor, the *Rambler*. It made fun of henpecked husbands, fashion-conscious young women and modern manners, but eventually concluded that 'this city is yet too small to give much scope to satire'.[4] A similar small publication, the *Inquirer*, published by the bookseller, William Gordon, had a brief existence in 1804-05. It was, however, in the late 1820s and 1830s that such papers came into their own, since it was only after 1825 that critics of authority could publish without fear of transportation. No fewer than 31 different periodicals appeared in the 1830s. Lewis Smith, a Broad Street bookseller, tried various short-lived literary enterprises in the 1820s including the *Aberdeen Censor* in 1825-27, a literary magazine that was published first fortnightly and then monthly, and the *Northern Iris* in 1826. The *Aberdeen Censor*, written largely by William Ferguson, the son of a local druggist, the Rev. John Jaffrey and Alexander Milne, a lawyer, was critical of Hume for campaigning for political reform and the repeal of the combination laws against trade unions. The *Northern Iris*, however, supported his campaigns as rector of Marischal College for student rights. Another printer and bookseller, Robert Cobban, offered the *Aberdeen Star: A Literary and Political Miscellany* for eighteen months in 1827-29, before it was closed by the government stamp office, and Thomas Spark produced its rival, the *Water Kelpie*.[5] There was also a radical *North Briton* in 1825 which was stillborn. Most of these newspapers were critical of the actions of the town council over the Harbour and the Police Bills, but not supportive of demands for an extended franchise. The arrival of a Whig government in 1830 and the mounting expectation of parliamentary reform produced the monthly *Aberdeen Independent*. It claimed to be a literary, political and commercial repository, 'of a decidedly liberal and independent character', although a supporter of the established church. It denounced the extravagance of the town council and tried, with little success, to rally support from the Trades House and the Guildry for burgh reform. The radical schoolmaster, John Warden, became editor and he gave coverage to the emerging working-class demands for political reform, which he actively supported, and for shorter factory hours and poor law reform. An attempt to relaunch the paper in October 1831 as the *Aberdeen New Independent* did nothing to help its fortunes and it folded at the end of the year. A *Scots Champion and Aberdeen Free Press*, published by John Watt, a printer of many political broadsides, proposed to be 'Liberal, patriotic and free' and started in October 1832 but never managed more than the first issue.

On the Tory side, the *Aberdeen Observer* appeared in 1829 published by Thomas Spark and John Davidson. It defended the town council, and Joseph Robertson, popularly known as 'Provost Hadden's Prime Minister', was a contributor under the pseudonym of 'Beppo'. It survived until 1837 when it was succeeded by the

Aberdeen Constitutional. It started as mildly Tory but hardened its attitudes in the aftermath of 1832. The coming of steam printing presses and the excitement of the parliamentary reform debates encouraged a flourishing of papers and periodicals. Young Tories subscribed to the *Aberdeen Magazine* in 1831–32, published by Lewis Smith and very much in the style of Blackwood's *Edinburgh Magazine*, and there was talk of producing a working-class paper. A hefty stamp duty deliberately kept the price of newspapers and periodicals high and, in the 1830s, there were a variety of short-lived unstamped, satirical publications, which changed their names regularly to avoid the attentions of the stamp office. The *Squib* in 1832, essentially a comic, was published by Cobban & Co. of Guestrow. The *Aberdeen Pirate*, published every Saturday by John Anderson & Co., lasted from the summer of 1832 until the end of 1833 when it was replaced by the *Aberdeen Mirror*, which too was stopped by the stamp office. This, in turn, gave way to the *Aberdeen Shaver*, a monthly satirical magazine also produced by John Anderson, which attacked the insistence by the Guildry that businesses should pay for their 'freedom' to trade, exposed brothels in the city and uncovered a cartel of book-pricing among local booksellers. It lasted through 64 issues from 1834 to July 1838 when it was driven out of business by the last of many libel actions. An *Aberdeen New Shaver* was published for 25 issues between July 1837 and 1840 but was 'badly printed and miserably edited' according to Bulloch. In politics it claimed to be neither Whig, Tory nor Radical, but it was firmly opposed to the new enthusiasm for teetotalism.[6] John Watt also produced other short-lived papers such as the *Letter of Marque*, the *Artizan*, the *Budget*, the *Quizzing Glass* and the *Aberdeen Monitor*. The first urged all classes 'to be contented with their condition, and trust to Providence for improvement' but the others tended to take a more radical stance. It appears that the same group of young men, with different political views but a common ambition to become writers, probably started and contributed to most of these short-lived magazines. The group included John Ramsay, Joseph Robertson, James Bruce, William Duncan, Thomas Spark and Robert Brown, close companions and regulars at Susie Affleck's public house.[7]

The Emergence of the *Herald*

By far the most significant development was the merger of the *Chronicle* with the *Aberdeen Gleaner* in August 1832 to form the *Aberdeen Herald*.[8] It was committed firmly to support of the Whig reforms and when its first editor, John Powers, was succeeded by the portly and prickly James Adam it became effectively the creator of Liberal politics in Aberdeen. Adam attracted around him a circle of Liberal radicals, regularly ensconced in the Lemon Tree Tavern, who pushed the reform causes of the day.

The paper became increasingly critical of Bannerman, the local MP, for his luke-warm attachment to the more radical politics of people like Hume, and Bannerman's brother, Thomas, tried to launch a rival *Aberdeen Advertiser and Town and Country Journal* in 1835. It took up the cause of university reform which was being pressed by Alexander Bannerman, who wanted the merger of King's College and Marischal College, but when that cause failed in the autumn so did the newspaper. Like all good Liberals, Adam was committed to the expansion of education, 'as absolutely necessary to ensure civil and religious liberty'. Adam favoured an educational electoral qualification rather than the manhood suffrage of the Chartists and he frequently clashed with the more militant Chartists. But after 1842 he became sympathetic to the Complete Suffrage Union committed to uniting working-class and middle-class reformers, and the paper, to the disquiet of some of the proprietors, gave extensive reports on working-class meetings, and began to campaign for household suffrage and triennial parliaments 'to prevent the popular agitation from being turned to bad purpose by wicked and designing demagogues'.[9] Adam was unrelenting in his attacks on the local clergy for their failure to support the 1834 General Assembly's declaration of the right of congregations to veto the choice of minister. When the minister of the Union Chapel-of-ease, John Allan, responded to persistent assaults on clerical hypocrisy by accusing Adam of being 'an infidel villain, a blasphemous villain ... and a satanic agent' he found himself having to hand over £1,000 in damages.[10] In March 1839 Adam challenged Baillie Chalmers to a duel. With remarkable courage, Adam regularly confronted powerful members of the Aberdeen elite and clearly the excitement of his style was effective since by the 1840s the circulation of the *Herald* at 2,300 was coming close to challenging the *Journal* which sold about 2,800 copies at that time.[11]

The Chartists tried to launch their own papers, the *Aberdeen Patriot*, which the Workingmen's Association published for two months in the winter of 1838–39, and John Legge's *Northern Vindicator* in 1839, but with little success.[12] However, the Complete Suffrage Union from April 1843 until the end of 1844 had the *Aberdeen Review and North of Scotland Advertiser*, which supported both teetotalism and free trade. It was edited by the moderate Chartist bookseller, John Mitchell, and was backed financially by the future MP for the city, Dingwall Fordyce. Against them was a short-lived Tory paper, the *Aberdeen Monthly Circular* in 1840 edited by James Bruce, who abused the Chartists 'without mercy' and the *Aberdeen Monthly Chronicle*, which claimed to be Liberal but was hostile to the Chartists and to the evangelicals.[13] A small satirical magazine, *Random Recollections*, published by Daniel of the Columbian Press, lampooned the clergy for a few months in 1841, while a twopenny monthly, the *Aberdeen Spectator and Monthly Advertiser*, was highly critical of Bannerman, and sympathetic to radical political reform. It ran from July 1841 until February of the following year.

Church politics and free trade overshadowed everything in the early 1840s and the press reflected this. Despite the fact that the *Herald* was aimed at a middle-class readership from among the class who were to form the backbone of the Free Churches, Adam had no sympathy with the evangelical clergy and taunted them ruthlessly in the months before the Disruption as being more concerned with their livings than their principles. The non-intrusionist cause and temperance were taken up by the *Aberdeen Banner*, edited from 1839 to 1842 by the former editor of the innovative and radical *Montrose Review*, the Stonehaven-born George Troup, vigorously supporting the dissident cause in the Marnoch resistance to an imposed minister in 1841. Although Troup described himself as an 'independent Liberal', he remained a firm opponent of free trade and his main ties were increasingly with the Conservatives. He had a wide experience of journalism, and was one of the most eloquent and fearless promoters of the temperance movement as well as a 'no compromise' sabbatarian. His paper proved a wonderful foil for James Adam's barbs in the *Herald*. After Troup's departure for Ulster, frustrated by too much clerical interference in editorial matters, the *Banner* was edited first by David Masson and then by Dr Longmuir and it survived as the main Free Church newspaper until 1851.

The *Aberdeen Constitutional*, the successor to the *Observer* as the defender of the Conservative and Established Church causes, was run first by Robert Cruickshank, followed Dr R. Shelton Mackenzie in 1839 and then by Joseph Robertson, an historian, future Keeper of Register House in Edinburgh and the founder of the Spalding Club.[14] The *Constitutional* did not long survive the Disruption of 1843 and the *Herald* celebrated its demise with a mock black border. A monthly rival, the *Bon-Accord Reporter* appeared in 1842 published by Robert Edward. It was Liberal-Radical in its politics and a supporter of 'the sensible, liberal right-hearted people of the Free Kirk', but it folded in 1844. The *Aberdeen Journal*, with John Ramsay as editor, gradually responded to competition with a more attractive lay-out and, bearing in mind its rural readership in the country areas, a firm commitment to defence of the Corn Laws against the increasingly loud demands for repeal. It could celebrate its centenary in January 1848 with reasonable confidence.

Yet another challenge to the *Herald* came in April 1847 with the appearance of the *North of Scotland Gazette*. While in some ways its politics were little different from those of the *Herald*, Adam by his anti-evangelical stance had forfeited the support of many of the radical middle-class. The *Herald* had no sympathy for the burgeoning temperance movement and was scathing about the limitations on alcohol consumption imposed by the 1853 Forbes Mackenzie Act, while the *Gazette* was edited by Dr J. H. Wilson, founder of the Aberdeen ragged kirk and a vice president of the Total Abstinence Society. Wilson had previously been a reporter and sub-editor on the *Herald* before departing for Birmingham. His assistant was William Carnie, who was to become one of the city's best-known journalists. The *Gazette*, 'a newspaper established for the promotion of Liberal and Nonconformist principles', paved the way for the *Aberdeen Free Press* which first appeared on 6 May 1853.[15]

THE ADVENT OF THE *FREE PRESS*

The men behind the *Free Press* regarded themselves as radical Liberals and were religious dissenters with different concerns from those which had shaped the *Herald.* David Macallan, a cabinetmaker and upholsterer, the main promoter of the venture, was a Baptist member of the town council who had resigned from his business partnership in 1848 rather than swear an oath of allegiance when the firm received a royal warrant. George King, a Congregationalist like many booksellers, was radical in his politics. William McCombie, also a Baptist, the editor until his death in 1870, was an author and farmer from Cairnballoch near Alford and had latterly edited the *Gazette*. The new paper supported the disestablishment of the Church, something which Macallan had long favoured, and 'the principles of Joseph Sturge' for moderate parliamentary reform which would maintain the unity of middle class and working class. McCombie also pushed for an expansion of education and for a number of social reforms and, in 1865, he was at the forefront of the campaign for the the rights of tenant farmers along with his cousin, also William McCombie, the famous cattle breeder, and J. W. Barclay, landowner and leading businessman.

Several factors emerged to encourage McCombie to try a twice weekly issue. These included the end of the stamp duty and the tax on advertising, and the advent of the electric telegraph, plus the appearance of the first penny daily, the *Northern Telegraphic News and Northern Advertiser*, edited and owned by Alexander Mowat, in 1855. It was published on Tuesday as well as the usual Friday as the *Penny Free Press* but, largely because of lack of advertising, this experiment was abandoned after eight months and not until 1865 did a regular Tuesday issue again appear. The new opportunities also encouraged rivals. The *Aberdeen Citizen*, edited by Dr John Christie in 1858–59 'to rebuke the jobber and expose cant', attacked the property qualifications which restricted membership of the police board and the town council, called for a public park, supported half-day holidays on a Saturday for workers and complained about the increasing pollution in the city. Other similar publications included the *Northern Examiner*, edited by the temperance campaigner, A. S. Cook, for a few months in 1860, and the *Aberdeen Saturday Post and Northern Counties Chronicle* edited by John Spark which, although surviving only briefly in 1861, attracted contributions from well-known local writers like William Alexander, James Valentine and W. S. Lindsay. Nor did the satirical

William Carnie 1825–1908

Born in the Poynernook district of the city, William Carnie received little education and was apprenticed at the age of 13 to an engraver, John H. Stephen, in the Netherkirkgate. He was very musical and became a member of the West Parish Church choir. After the Disruption he went to Banchory Devenick as leader of the Psalmody, becoming precentor in 1845. In 1847 he became inspector of the poor for Banchory Devenick and collector of the poor assessment for the parochial board. He attended classes at the Mechanics' Institute and, in 1849, became a part-time reporter for the *North of Scotland Gazette*. He abandoned engraving for journalism and, in 1852, became reporter and sub-editor of the *Aberdeen Herald*. In 1861 he changed career again, becoming clerk and treasurer of the ARI and the Royal Lunatic Asylum, posts he held until 1898. He continued his journalistic work, serving for many years as the drama critic of the *Free Press* and the Aberdeen representative of *The Times*. He also continued his musical activities, becoming precentor of the West Church in 1855, and musical director of the Aberdeen General Association for the Improvement of Psalmody, and compiling the *Northern Psalmody*. He was a poet and, in retirement, compiled three volumes of *Reporting Reminiscences* covering the local history of the period 1850–76. His portrait was painted by Sir George Reid in 1897.

William Carnie, journalist, who perhaps did more than anyone to encourage the development of music and drama in the city. Portrait by Sir George Reid.

tradition disappear entirely. The *Chameleon* lambasted local worthies in the early 1850s and again in the lively local politics of the 1860s and early 1870s and there was an attempt to revive the *Aberdeen Magazine*.

Both the *Herald* and the *Journal* could unite in their hostility to the fusion of King's College and Marischal College in 1859, and the professors who supported it came in for the same rough treatment from Adam as had the clergy of 1843.[16] William Forsyth's style in the *Journal*, despite the fact that he had learned his trade under Adam, was altogether more gentle. Under his editorship the *Journal* was brought back to the middle-ground of politics, although remaining decidedly old-fashioned in appearance and tone. Not surprisingly it supported Lord Aberdeen, the Prime Minister, in 1853 against Palmerston's bellicose demands for war with Russia. In the early 1860s it was sympathetic to the northern states in the American Civil War and resisted calls for British intervention. But both papers were beginning to struggle against the *Free Press*. Adam remained at the *Herald* until 1862 but his successor, Archibald Gillies, never managed to capture a consistent voice to suit the 1860s. The launching of an Aberdeen, Banff and Kincardine edition of the Dundee-based *People's Journal* in 1861 must also have taken its toll. It was aimed at the same sort of plebeian radical readership to which the *Herald* had once appealed. James Whyte Duncan, radical Liberal and United Presbyterian, edited the Aberdeen edition from 1865 until 1902. The first evening paper, the *North Star*, also Liberal in politics, selling at one halfpenny appeared in 1870. It was bedevilled with disputes

William Alexander 1826–94

Born at Rescivet, Chapel of Garioch, William Alexander was the son of a blacksmith who took over the tenancy of Damhead Farm, Pitcaple. He attended the parish school at Daviot, and intended to follow his father into farming. The loss of a leg in an accident necessitated a change of career and, in 1852, as the result of writing a prize-winning essay on farm servants and attracting the attention of McCombie, owner of the *North of Scotland Gazette,* he joined the paper as reporter and sub-editor, moving to the *Free Press* one year later. In 1870, on the death of McCombie, he became editor of the paper, but stood down two years later, on health grounds, when it began daily publication. He continued to edit the weekly edition and to propagate strong radical views particularly on behalf of the rights of tenant farmers. He was an elder of the Free Church, a director of the Royal Infirmary, and a member of the public library committee. He was a member of the council of the Aberdeen Philosophical Society, and a founder member of the council of the New Spalding Club. He was the first president of the local branch of the Institute of Journalists and a vice president of the Institute. His most famous book was *Johnny Gibb of Gushetneuk*, first published in serial form in the *Free Press* in 1869–70, and as a single volume in 1871, subsequently passing through many editions. The illustrations were drawn by Sir George Reid. His other publications included *Sketches of Life Among My Ain Folk* (1875), a volume of rural life in the north in the eighteenth century (1877), and a study of the rinderpest outbreak in Aberdeenshire in the 1860s (1882). His name is commemorated in 'Mount Alexander' in New Guinea, a tribute from a friend and explorer.

among the printers and survived for only seven months. The *Free Press* was gaining ground both in Aberdeen itself and in the farming areas, thanks to the rural interests of McCombie and the man who increasingly ran the paper, William Alexander. The author of that remarkable evocation of rural life in Aberdeenshire of the 1840s, *Johnny Gibb of Gushetneuk*, Alexander steadily began to professionalise the paper. On McCombie's death, in 1870, he became editor and shook his rather lackadaisical rivals by publishing daily in 1872 and dropping 'Aberdeen' from the title in 1874. The *Daily Free Press* under Alexander's editorship was the main voice of Gladstonian Liberalism in the North, and defended Professor Robertson Smith against conservative forces within the Free Churches. In 1876 the proprietor of the *Free Press*, now Alexander Marr, bought out the fading *Herald*.

The *Free Press* led a vigorous protest against the foreign policies being pursued by Disraeli's government in the late 1870s. It rallied to Gladstone's denunciations of Turkish atrocities against their Christian subjects in the Balkans in 1878, rejected the imperial expansionism of Disraeli, and condemned army excesses in Afghanistan and Southern Africa. The increasingly imperialist policies being pursued were blamed on London Jingoes and even the fall of Khartoum in 1885 and the death of General Gordon stirred no imperialist calls for revenge, but a view that 'it will be a happy day of deliverance when the last British soldier plants his last footsteps on that portion of the African continent'.[17] Meanwhile, the *Aberdeen Journal*, which had remained in the hands of the Chalmers family, was purchased by a group of county Conservatives, led by Thomas Innes of Learney, who had been trying since 1866 to get a newspaper to revive the Conservative cause in the North-East and to counter the anti-landowner stance of the *Free Press*. The directors included William Yeats of Anquharney, Innes of Learney, Ferguson of Kinmundy, Alexander Walker, James Badenoch Nicolson of Arthur House, Henry Wolrige Gordon of Hallhead and Esslemont, James Chalmers and his brother, John.[18] The new company, the Aberdeen and North of Scotland Newspaper and Printing Company, took over in May 1876 and, in August, turned the *Journal* into a daily paper, while continuing with a weekly digest in the form of the *Aberdeen Weekly Journal*. Shares were taken up by the leading Conservative worthies including the Duke of Richmond and Gordon, the Earl of Aberdeen, the Earl of Crawford and Balcarres and the Earl of Seafield, Gordon of Cluny, James Baird (the Ayrshire ironmaster), and William Cosmo Gordon of Fyvie Castle among others, but they struggled to sell the 2,000 shares and operated precariously on loans for some years. Archibald Gillies from the defunct *Herald* was appointed editor in 1879, replacing the gentle poet and angler, William Forsyth, who found adjustment to the world of daily newspapers rather difficult.[19] The *Journal* struggled to survive against the aggressive marketing and style of the *Free Press*, which had eight pages to the *Journal's* four in 1878, and decades of rivalry were to follow. In 1879 Gillies launched the *Aberdeen Evening Express* at one halfpenny and for many years it was the profits of the *Express* which kept the *Journal* going.[20]

The political excitement of the 1880 election, when there were some thirteen Liberals competing for the candidacy, stimulated a new penny weekly, *Bon-Accord*, published by Henry J. Clark of Rettie's Court. It was to offer 'Satire, Music, Art, Drama and Gossip' as well as comic banter. It proposed a New Year's resolution that the citizens might 'think it possible that, after all, the town council is not the most extravagant and reckless set of men in existence'.[21] In politics it was against the *Free Press* and the group who ran the new Liberal Association. It attacked the *People's Journal* as communist because it had opposed the scheme for reorganising the Grammar School on the grounds that it would disadvantage the working class. Clark tried to hedge his bets by also launching, in January 1881, the *Mirror of the North* as a radical and progressive paper. But it collapsed at the end of March and the *Bon-Accord* was brought down with it. However, the early 1880s saw a fresh spate of satirical and literary papers, some 28 of them during the decade according to Bulloch. The *Comet* was a series of letters addressed to named individuals, such as the superintendent of police, Thomas Wyness, who was famous for his vigorous anti-drink campaign during his term of office 1880-1902, notably by clamping down on the 'treacle-cask', illegal drinking in grocery shops. Other recipients included the Rev. A. M. Bannatyne, the 'presbytery policeman', with his denunciations of promiscuous dancing, and the Rev. James Stark, who was denouncing evolutionary theory. The *Northern Figaro*, edited by Frank Clements, first appeared in November 1884 as a halfpenny weekly. It concentrated mainly on sport, the theatre and music, with just the occasional political comment and cartoons pointed at local worthies. It survived until 1895. The following year brought a short-lived *Aberdeen Reformer*, the *Meteor*, and the reappearance of a little magazine which had been issued at various times since 1852, the *Chameleon*. It usually appeared at times when there was an outcry against municipal extravagance, and the 1880s was one such period. Some of the new ideas of evolution and socialism were briefly propagated in the Rev. Alexander Webster's monthly, the *Ploughshare*, which sought to offer a journal of 'radical religion and morality'. In the great political debate of 1886 over Gladstone's Irish Home Rule Bill both the daily papers adopted a unionist stance. Henry Alexander and William Watt took the *Daily Free Press* into the Liberal Unionist camp. However, the *Evening Gazette*, which the *Free Press* brought out in 1882 with Alexander McGilligan as editor, and which was reputed to be the most popular paper among the working class, remained Gladstonian in its sympathies. The *Weekly Free Press*, edited by the kenspeckle William Alexander, the brother of Henry, followed the same line. A number of leading Liberals, including Peter Esslemont, James Crombie, William Henderson, Professor Minto and the Earl of Aberdeen tried to fill the lack of a Liberal morning daily paper in 1891 with the *Northern Daily News*. When that failed to attract readers, they tried a *Northern Evening News* but it lasted only six months before being absorbed by the *Evening Express*.

The Revival of the *Journal*

Both the *Free Press* and the *Journal* had offices in Fleet Street, and there were well-used networks which stood many young budding writers and journalists from the North-East in good stead. There were regular Monday evening gatherings of what was nicknamed the 'tobacco parliament' in Fleet Street in the offices of the *Journal* in the 1870s. Aberdeenshire-born, J.Morrison Davidson, was a link with a range of radical left-wing bodies. George Washington Wilson's son, Alexander, was a sub-editor on the *Economist* under Bagehot, and later was editor of the *Standard* and the *Pall Mall Gazette*, and founder of the *Investor's Chronicle*. Another key link was the Dufftown-born William Robertson Nicol who edited the immensely influential nonconformist weekly, the *British Review*, and knew everyone.[22]

The *Journal* still struggled to survive. In 1886 it had a circulation of less than 10,000 and there was talk of closure. Three years later the *Free Press* offered to purchase the title for £4,000. It was saved by a legacy worth £10,000 from John Gray Chalmers, which allowed the company to pay off its debts and to buy premises in Broad Street. By 1895 it was at last in profit. The transformation in the fortunes of the *Journal* came as a result of the vigorous and provocative editorship of David Leith Pressly, previously chief editor at the strongly 'Orange' *Belfast Evening Telegraph*. He had succeeded James McKay in 1894, soon after the *Journal* offices moved from the Adelphi to Broad Street, and he adopted a more aggressively conservative tone and made the *Journal* a force in local politics. His successor Robert Anderson continued to build up its readership.

The key event of 1886 in local journalism was the appearance of a relaunched *Bon-Accord, The Illustrated News of the North*. The man behind it was the editor of the *Evening Express*, William Dallas Reid, who was much influenced by American approaches to journalism. The *Bon-Accord* was a lively weekly with satire, gossip and comic strips, full of in-jokes about the town council, and offering an extensive coverage of theatre, music and entertainment in the city. Its masthead of the city's skyline and many of its line drawings were first produced by a French artist, Pierre Delavault, and then by Edward Rodgers. It had a difficult time in its early years suffering from a considerable turnover of editors and owners. Ross sold the paper to Andrew Robb of the firm of Charles Playfair & Co., who in 1896 sold to William Smith, who in 1905 sold to Henry Munro. Gradually, however, it began to attract extensive advertising. Verse and popular columns attracted a growing following, most famously the observations of 'Peter Birse', first from the pen of Dr Maitland

The tower of recently-built Town House dominates the skyline in the Bon-Accord's *elaborate masthead designed by Pierre Delavault.*

Moir and then for years from other hands. It concentrated on entertainment and cultural activities and its political coverage was limited, but when it did comment it was firmly Liberal, with regular references to Aberdeen's radical tradition, and offered support to a broadly-based progressive politics in the early twentieth century. It presented itself as the 'week-end family journal', with lots of local news covering much of the North-East and with increasing numbers of good-quality photographs. By the 1930s and 1940s a glossy outer wrapping of photographs had replaced the former cover which had been devoted to advertisements. It showed a particular penchant for bathing belles and health and beauty groups, and also an increasing number of wedding photographs. A rival *Holloa*, run by Robert Houston, a poet, and J. G. Murray, an artist, failed to take off in 1887 and the *Northern Life* had a 'brief but merry' existence in 1896–97, but soon folded for lack of capital. The *Bon-Accord* ceased publication at the outbreak of war in August 1914, but was revived in 1926 as the *Bon-Accord and Northern Pictorial*, adding 'Aberdeen' to its title in 1927. The inter-war years saw the *Bon-Accord* at the peak of its success. Munro owned several papers as well as his travel agency in Crown Street. He published the *Perthshire Advertizer*, and the *Mearns Leader* and the trade paper of the licensed trade, the *National Guardian*. All the publications appear to have been treated as part of a single venture, and included the provision of pictures for the *Glasgow Herald* and the *Evening Times*.

The emergence of the independent labour movement brought a number of attempts to establish a socialist press. In 1891 James Leatham launched the *Workers' Herald*, the first socialist paper in Scotland, which lasted for a few weeks. H. H. Champion issued first the *Fiery Cross* and then the *Aberdeen Labour Elector* during his election campaign of 1892, and this was transformed into the *Aberdeen Standard* in 1893–94, edited by George Gerrie, a clerk in the Aberdeen Savings Bank, and later by Alexander Catto. It supported the cause of Independent Labour and gave space to the future editor of the *Bon-Accord*, J. F. George, who although a Tory, under the *nom de plume* of Nestor, 'weekly belaboured "nasty bodies" of the bourgeois order in its leading columns'.[23] It also provided a temporary haven for the extraordinary Frederick Rolfe, Baron Corvo, author of *Hadrian the Seventh*. He had come to Aberdeen as tutor to the sons of James Gordon Hay of Seaton, but quickly lost his position. He then inveigled his way into the photographic firm of Washington Wilson only to be quickly dismissed. However, Champion took him on as his secretary in 1893 and he wrote a few pieces for the *Aberdeen Standard*, including one in which Aberdeen houses were described as 'granite rabbit hutches'.[24] The *Standard* also had a lively sports page with extensive coverage of football and cycling in particular. The Social Democratic Federation had its own occasional journal, the *Comet*, which survived for a decade after 1908. Socialism had less appeal than sport at the turn of the century, however, and in 1911 both the *Evening Express* and the *Evening Gazette* issued Saturday special football editions.

Only the Bon-Accord *supported the local MPs Bryce (right) and Pirie (left) in their criticism of the South African War.*

The Boer War saw all four Aberdeen daily and evening papers take a strong pro-war stance. With William Alexander gone and replaced as editor by his brother Henry, the *Evening Gazette* had lost its remaining radical tinge and became a mere satellite of the *Free Press*. However, both the *Bon-Accord* and the *People's Journal*, still edited by the radical Duncan, condemned 'Rhodes the Raider', backed Bryce and Pirie and supported the Liberal radical cause.

TRUE TO THE OLD FLAG.

BON ACCORD, October 1, 1900.

Our Buyers have returned from London and Paris with all the latest novelties of the season. PRATT & KEITH

MERGER

It was perhaps a sign of the fading fortunes of Liberalism that John Bruce of the *Free Press* approached the *Aberdeen Journal* in 1920 about a possible amalgamation. Since 1904 the *Free Press* had been edited by William McCombie Alexander and was owned by a partnership including himself, his brother, Henry, Robert Bruce and Edward William Watt. The editor of the *Aberdeen Journal* from 1910 until 1927 was Sir William Maxwell, a passionate Unionist in politics committed to breaking the Liberal hold on Aberdeen. According to his obituary, he 'early became convinced that if a Socialist government came into power it would break up the Empire, and all his energies were directed to prevent that happening'.[25] A native of Castle-Douglas in Galloway, Maxwell worked as a journalist for the *London Gazette,* the *London Evening Standard,* the *Pall Mall Gazette,* and *The Scotsman* before coming to Aberdeen. Under his editorship the *Aberdeen Journal* had picked up readership from 6,000 in 1912 to 16,000 by 1921. The circulation of the *Evening Express,* in the same period, had risen from 42,000 to 52,000. A merger was accomplished in 1922 when a new company, Aberdeen Newspapers Ltd, with a share capital of £200,000, issued the new *Aberdeen Press and Journal.* The *Evening Gazette* disappeared. William Maxwell remained as editor and the new paper pushed a Conservative and imperialist line despite attempts by the *Free Press* partners to commit it to 'a moderate but at the same time progressive policy'.[26] He was obliged to retire from the editorship on health grounds in 1927, but remained a member of the board of directors to which he had been appointed two years earlier, and was knighted in 1928.

Harmony among the directors did not last long and, early in 1926, the Alexander brothers seem to have been pushed out and were replaced by members of the Conservative county gentry. By

Cartoon of Sir Henry Alexander, nephew of William, editor of Aberdeen Free Press 1914-22, lord provost 1932-35.

Sir Henry Alexander 1875–1940

Born into a journalistic family, Henry Alexander was educated at the Grammar School and Aberdeen University. In 1914 he succeeded his father as editor of the *Aberdeen Free Press* retiring in 1922 when the paper merged with its erstwhile rival. He represented Rubislaw on the town council 1925–35 and served as lord provost 1932–35. He was convener of the editorial committee of the *Aberdeen University Review* 1914–28, and was a member of the University Court 1932–40. He served as deputy lieutenant for the County of the City and as a JP. He served as president of the Aberdeen branch of the Territorial Army Association, the British Red Cross Society, the National Lifeboat Institution, the Playing Fields Association and the Royal Northern Agricultural Society. He was chairman of the Aberdeen and district joint town planning committee which prepared a scheme for an area covering 96 square miles in the city and its adjacent counties. The scheme, which was approved in 1933 after five years of preparation, was regarded as a major pioneering study in town planning. He was a staunch supporter of the Scottish Mountaineering Club and of the Cairngorm Club. He wrote for the journals of both societies and edited the *Cairngorm Club Journal* 1924–26.

this time the new paper had a circulation of 25,000, while the *Evening Express* had 62,000. During the General Strike of May 1926 roneo sheet strike bulletins were produced for five days and, like many of the provincial newspapers, the company took the opportunity offered by the collapse of the strike to exclude trade unionism from its staff. This led to the foundation of a rival paper, the *Aberdeen Citizen*, in the summer of 1926 but it failed even after a relaunch in 1927. In 1928 the *Press and Journal* and the *Evening Express* titles were bought by the Berry Brothers' Allied Newspapers, battling with Lord Rothermere for control of whole areas of the British provincial press. It was a move which was unsuccessfully resisted in the courts by Robert Bruce and other old *Free Press* shareholders. When the Berry brothers' enterprise split apart in 1937, the titles came under the control of Gomer Berry's Kemsley Press.

The *Aberdeen Bon-Accord* continued to survive. It was taken over by Outram & Co. after the Second World War but, by the 1950s, like other illustrated magazines, it was struggling to find a niche. Increasingly it appeared to be aimed at women, with recipes and fashion advice while, at the same time, producing rather ponderous editorials on the need for everyone to work harder. This may have reflected internal tensions within the company as the paper ceased publication abruptly in 1959 following a dispute. There were still opportunities for literary amateurs to try their hand in the *Aberdeen University Review* and in the *North-East*

Broad Street was the home of Aberdeen Journals from the 1890s until 1970. This photograph is from the 1960s.

Review. The latter ran for six years during the Second World War, backed by a local businessman, Garnet R. Fraser. It contained an eclectic range of articles by authors who included R. F. Mackenzie, Jessie Kesson, Professor Rex Knight, and many budding poets.

SURVIVAL

As part of the Kemsley Empire and with no local competition, the *Press and Journal,* ('Aberdeen' having been dropped from the title in May 1939), pursued a bland conservatism, and by the 1950s despite the lack of competition it was again struggling to survive. Circulation had fallen from a wartime peak of 99,000 to 89,000. In 1956 it lost £40,000 and there was talk of closure unless its fortunes could be turned around within two years. The slide downwards continued and the *Weekly Journal* was abandoned in 1957. In 1959 the Canadian Roy Thomson, for whom, according to Stephen Koss, 'newspaper ownership was not so much a vocation as an addiction', bought over the Kemsley Newspapers. But there was still a real danger that the *Press and Journal* would close.[27] The strategy for salvation was initiated by the new editor 'Jimmy' Grant. He opted for a much greater focus upon local news with seven regional editions. Circulation steadily picked up until by the 1970s it was approaching 118,000.[28] In 1970 the presses were moved from the increasingly confined space of Broad Street to a custom-built site at Mastrick on the edge of the city. There were occasional attempts to challenge the monopoly of the *Press and Journal* with an *Aberdeen Clarion* between 1958 and 1966 and the *Aberdeen People's Press* between 1973 and 1976. The latter, describing itself as 'a community newspaper' was published fortnightly for a couple of years and then monthly by a small co-operative group of left-wing enthusiasts for community politics. It thus continued the tradition of the nineteenth-century alternative press, lambasting town councillors, investigating corruption and challenging the domination of the oil companies and their associates with articles on 'Who runs Aberdeen?'.

The 1980s and 1990s saw a proliferation of free newspapers financed by advertising and reviving some of the old names. Most were produced by Aberdeen Journals, presumably with the intention of seeing off any potential rivals. The third *Aberdeen Citizen* from 1982 gave way in 1988 to the *Aberdeen Herald* and the *Aberdeen Post* which soon merged into the *Aberdeen Herald and Post.* A more critical *Silver City,* appearing on a Sunday, managed seven monthly issues from October 1994 until May 1995 and took up matters like the dirtiness of parts of the city and the fact that Ayrshire-made 'butteries' were being sold in the city. Later the *Aberdeen and District Independent* emerged from the Aberdeen Journal's offices.

As with many other newspapers in the 1980s there was growing conflict

between the National Union of Journalists (NUJ) and management. This culminated in an effort by the Thomson organisation to break the hold of the NUJ by introducing personal contracts. In August 1989, 100 of the 180 journalists at Aberdeen Journals went on strike for three weeks. A settlement was reached, but six weeks later trouble flared again over victimisation, and 116 journalists were sacked. As a result, one of the most bitter strikes in the history of the city continued for nearly a year. In the second strike the journalists resorted to fund-raising efforts, including the production of their own *Free Press* Newspaper. Those reporters who remained with the *Press and Journal* and the *Evening Express* found themselves ostracised by many organisations, and local councils boycotted the papers. The circulation of the *Press and Journal* during 1990 fell by nearly 20,000 copies. Although a final settlement was achieved in September 1990 few of the dismissed journalists found their way back and the company would no longer recognise the NUJ.[29]

An attempt to capture some of the qualities of the *Bon-Accord* together with the bite of some of the nineteenth-century periodicals was made in 1974 with the launch of the monthly periodical, *The Leopard*, subtitled *The Grampian Magazine*. Under the editorship of Diane Morgan, for 14 years it combined a wide range of well-illustrated articles on aspects of the North-East with some pointed editorials on developments in city planning. Doric humour in the form of pieces by 'Jamie Fleeman' and cartoons of 'Councillor Swick' by Steve Robertson and Buff Hardie, with Sandy Cheyne as artist, continued the tradition of scathingly calling attention to examples of local pomposity. Acquired by John and Edna Coyne in 1988, it was taken over by George Outram & Co. in 1989 and lost its editorial bite. In the summer of 1992 it again faltered with the disappearance of Outrams. It was revived in October of the same year as a result of the enterprise of the farmer and writer, Charlie Allan, and his daughter Susan. The ever-popular Councillor Swick, back from a fact-finding trip to Maastricht, returned to its pages.

In 1995 the Thomson organisation sold Aberdeen Journals to Northcliffe Newspapers, the regional newspaper company of the Daily Mail Group. The matter was referred to the Monopolies and Mergers Commission which gave approval on the assurance that the, now ten, local editions of the paper would be maintained. By 1995 circulation of the *Press and Journal* had reached a daily average of 108,963 while the *Evening Express* averaged 70,346. Change of ownership did not bring much change in the style and presentation of the *Press and Journal* as it celebrated two and a half centuries of continuous operation. It remained, as someone described it to the Monopolies Commission, 'a local weekly paper that came out every day'. But this is not to deride the immense influence it has had on local affairs and the extent to which both the *Press and Journal* and the *Evening Express* played a vital role in giving identity to the local community and in enabling the voice of that community to be heard by decision makers. Nor can one exaggerate the extent to which Aberdeen's papers acted, over two centuries, as a training ground for generations of distinguished journalists.

18

Villages and Suburbs

JOHN S. SMITH

PATTERNS OF URBAN GROWTH

A variety of academic hypotheses have been developed to explain urban land use and patterns of growth. The classic urban models are mainly based on the discipline of distance, notably the way in which improved transport technology increasingly permitted people to live farther from their place of work. In the recent past this has been linked to the perception that the ideal life style was to combine residence in the countryside with work in the town or city. One hypothesis envisaged an ideal western world city consisting of a succession of concentric rings of land use around a hub comprising a central business district complete with public buildings and market square. This would be surrounded by an inner ring of low-grade housing and factories, with an outer ring of higher-grade housing located at the edges close to the countryside. A slightly more sophisticated thesis envisaged that the rings of similar land usage would be broken by fingers of higher-cost residential development which naturally gravitated towards the edges of higher ground, along which pre-existing roads and tracks headed outward into the countryside and beyond. These long sectoral fingers of development would tend to avoid valley bottoms because of cold air, drainage and the dangers of flooding. Once the restrictions on mobility were broken by trams, buses, trains and eventually the private car, fingers of urban-supported development would extend outwards and absorb pre-existing settlement nuclei which had previously been both geographically and administratively isolated.

Gilcomston, Ruthrieston and Footdee were examples of this process of progressive absorption. Similar patterns of growth were encouraged around the edges of Aberdeen's western outskirts by the landowners of suburban estates who planned and inaugurated residential developments on their property, specifying styles of building and employing local architects. The lands of Rubislaw were the property of the Skene family, whose members were closely involved in the development of Albyn Place. Archibald Simpson was commissioned to design a series of villas along this generously proportioned street, and these were occupied by surgeons, lawyers and bankers, paying their feu duties to James Skene. About

1852, Skene promoted a further piece of sectoral planning in the form of a development of 50 houses along Rubislaw Terrace, immediately behind Albyn Place. It was not only landowners who were involved in the nineteenth-century urban expansion which absorbed or expanded small nuclei, but a number of corporate groups, including the Incorporated Trades' Guild and, most influential of all, the City of Aberdeen Land Association (CALA). The main strategy employed by the latter was to purchase or to take out an option to purchase, land in large blocks on the edge of the city, and subsequently to feu or sell in small parcels to private individuals or builders. Usually the purchases were located outwith the burgh boundary but within reach, and at a location judged as likely to prove attractive to developers in the not-too-distant future. The potential value of the property developed on such land was sometimes enhanced by buying or by negotiating a link with the existing public municipal water and gas service. In the first year of its operation, CALA bought the properties of Fountainhall and Morningfield in the western suburbs of the town, and the lands of Torry and Craiginches in Kincardineshire on the south bank of the Dee, all for a remarkably small total expenditure of £134,000.

By the later years of the reign of Queen Victoria the town council, wherever possible, purchased land ringing the city which was often owned in the form of small estates or farms. It eventually gained complete control of the development of the intersectional areas required for residential developments. Despite this, land for development was in short supply after the Second World War especially in the private sector, as large areas had been earmarked for council housing, and for industrial estates, leaving only relatively small areas within the burgh boundaries for private developments such as Deeside Gardens and Countesswells. By now, the days of the Victorian mansion with resident domestic staff had virtually gone, and the areas where the prosperous Victorian and Edwardian citizens had lived were increasingly invaded and converted to professional offices. Private housing demand was increasingly accommodated by land freed for housing in the counties of Aberdeenshire and Kincardineshire. This was particularly significant in lower Deeside where more efficient transport, both public and private, generated much residential growth around the suburban villages of Cults, Bieldside and Culter. Similarly Dyce and Stoneywood were eventually to be absorbed into the city as Woodside and Old Aberdeen had been in 1891. In the 1920s when the town council purchased the lands at Hazlehead, the *Aberdeen Journal* commented that the city might be expected to continue to develop in that direction and speculated that some day in the future the tramway might extend for several miles into the countryside. However, the introduction of the motor bus during that same decade, with its advantages of novelty, cheapness and speed, began the inexorable process of increasing access far beyond the city boundaries. The enforcement of green belt

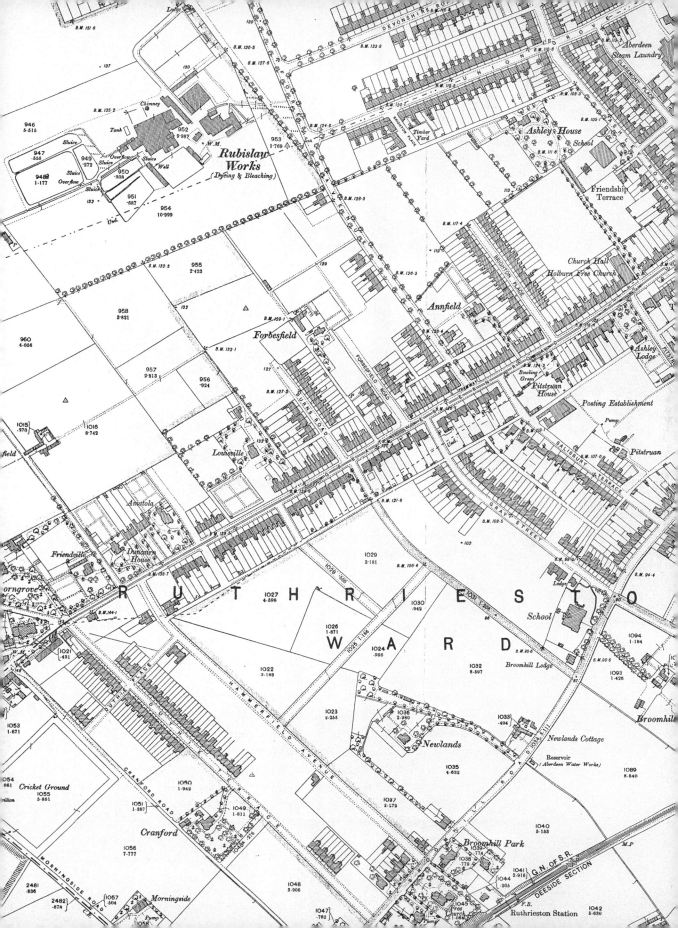

TO & FROM THE STEWART PLEASURE PARK WOODSIDE

KITTYBRE...R WOODSID...

WOOD... 5

protection policy in the twilight zone west of the city, between town and county planning authorities, ensured that further residential developments were added to existing communities, or at least located nearby as at Westhill and Kingswells. Here, as at Altens, Cove and Portlethen on the coast, and at Bridge of Don, Scotstown and Persley, existing nuclei became surrounded by an upsurge of residential and service-based facilities. Such was the acceleration in the city's built environment that there was little opportunity to generate a sense of community in architectural or social terms, although community schools and sports centres, and even shopping centres, served as partial substitutes.

In short, Aberdeen's pattern of growth over the last two centuries, while unique in its fine detail, in general has been completely typical of most western cities. The principal topographic features were characterised by an unusually diverse physical site in which twin valleys, a large estuary and surrounding heights were the prominent elements. Superimposed on this were established historical routes drawing visitors and travellers into the city, and leading towards the historical centre around the Castlegate and the Green. A surrounding pattern of land ownership and country estates planned with field boundaries, lanes, avenues,

Looking north in the 1970s to the expanding suburbs beyond the Bridge of Don. Pittodrie Stadium is beside the large gasometer.

farms, estate policies and mansions was developed upon the physical framework and exerted an increasingly active set of pressures to sell, develop and relocate for residential, industrial and recreational land uses. These were superimposed and accommodated by a succession of journey-to-work transport innovations, driven by economic advance. In time the built-up area of the city spread outward, absorbing historically isolated hamlets and villages, and closely followed by the expanding outer boundary of the town council's authority. In the most recent past, the patterns and directions of growth involved the use of zoning restrictions as a major tool in planning development and, within that, the provision of open space with future built environments regarded as having a highly beneficial visual and psychological role in enhancing the quality of life of city dwellers. Although predictions for new household formation continued to attract ambitious schemes for urban village growth in the countryside, as at Blairs College, by the 1990s the urban view of the peri-urban countryside had changed. The perception current after the Second World War, that the countryside was primarily a vital resource to be protected for food production, became modified to an apparently all-pervading belief that such environments represent a playground for the urban dweller, whether resident in the city or the countryside. This investigation of Aberdeen's villages and expanding suburbia explores their origins and their development in the last 200 years, during which, in some cases, their individuality as a recognisable community was greatly diminished or even disappeared and, in others, the most recent, it was scarcely discernible.

RUTHRIESTON, TORRY AND FOOTDEE

The township of Ruthrieston, originally Ruadri's settlement, was established in the twelfth century at a river crossing point over the Dee by a ford guarded by a timber motte castle. The township sat on the long established routeway of the Hardgate, but lay for centuries beyond the burgh boundaries of Aberdeen, holding its monthly cattle markets at a stance whose site was still indicated on the 1869 edition of the first Ordnance Survey map. Beyond Ruthrieston, the sixteenth-century Bridge of Dee pointed the traveller to the Causeymounth and the way south. This historical highway was traversed by many worthy folk such as Dr Johnson and Robert Burns, and led them to Aberdeen's Castlegate and their probable destination at the New Inn, reached via Windmill Brae and the Green. The road was only to be superseded as the southern entry to the town with the construction of Union Street and the gradual extension of Holburn Street towards the south-west during the nineteenth century. Holburn Street passes over the line of the Howburn, one of the several streams which provided water and power for domestic manufacturers within the burgh. The traditional name of How Burn was altered to Holborn when the street which spanned it was initiated, to hint at its namesake, the great London thoroughfare, but subsequently it was renamed Holburn. It was the Howburn which provided a water supply for the North of Scotland distillery, an enterprise which ended dramatically in a spectacular fire on 27 September 1904, and which resulted in the complete destruction of granary, malthouse, kilns, stills and bonded warehouses. It was estimated that 800,000 gallons of whisky were lost, most of which flowed down the burn. Further downstream, and having been joined by the Ferryhill Burn, water from the Howburn drove the machinery of the Ferryhill mills which processed waste wool and cloth, its lowest portion marking the eastern edge of Aberdeen's freedom lands, granted to the burgh by a charter authorised by Robert the Bruce in 1319. The Howburn depression remained a significant obstacle to the expansion of the city until the linking arteries of Crown Street and Bon-Accord Street were completed in the 1880s, forming direct links with Ferryhill. The joint How Burn/Ferryhill Burn entered the estuary of the Dee at Clayhills, where the estuarine clays provided employment for the inhabitants of the hamlet of Potters' Creek. This hamlet was replaced in 1805 by the planned square of Dee Village, laid out by Dingwall Fordyce of Arthurseat House. By the end of the nineteenth century, the site of the village lay vacant, awaiting the construction of the new electricity works, completed in 1903, together with an adjoining tram/repair works of the Ferryhill branch line, and the 130 metre high power station chimney which was eventually demolished in 1969.

The genesis of new Torry, as opposed to old Torry which had been located close by the riverside and east of the brickworks, was intimately tied to the progressive southern extension of Market Street. This was only made possible through the diversion of the channel of the River Dee to occupy a new totally-engineered and stable bed at the southern edge of the originally large but shallow and geomorphologically-dynamic estuary. Before the successful diversion, which was completed about 1880, the main channel ran seawards and almost parallel to the line of the Caledonian Railway, then turned to the east to enter the estuary outlet in the vicinity of Point Law, its old channel marked by the outline of the Albert Basin. The estuary reclamation work, which enabled Market Street to be extended, was derived partly from excavation of the new channel and partly from city landfill sites. The land reclamation from the original estuary during this project permitted the feuing of the Old Ford, Russell, Raik and Stell Roads, the last two being Old Scots names for the long-established salmon pools located in what had been the main channel of the Dee. The prolonged negotiations required to buy out the Raik and Stell salmon fishing interests delayed the completion of the Dee diversion project by several years. As the work on these reclamation projects proceeded, the urgency of providing a bridge downstream of the Wellington chain bridge was heightened by a ferryboat disaster during the April spring holiday of 1876 when 32 people returning from a day trip to the popular beach at the Bay of Nigg were drowned as the overcrowded ferry was swamped. The Victoria Bridge was projected. Several parties had an interest, and a liability for the costs, including the town council, the harbour commissioners and the CALA which owned the land. While a substantive proportion of the finance for the bridge came from the city's long-established bridge fund, a significant contribution came from the Land Association which had previously acquired a portion of prime development land on the southern edge of the estuary on which a part of the new suburb of Torry would be built. The Victoria Bridge was eventually opened in 1887. Very soon after the bridge was completed, carrying gas and water services over the river as well as traffic, the first houses in new Torry sprang up on Victoria Road. The rapid expansion of Aberdeen's trawler-dominated fishing industry created a demand for tenement accommodation near to the harbour, and for fish processing work near to the quay. A variety of types of residential accommodation developed to cater for crewmen, skippers and fish merchants. Many of them came to live in Torry from as far away as Grimsby, Hull and Tyneside as well as from the many small fish landing villages of North-East Scotland, the former inward migration spawning an infusion of English surnames to set among a predominance of local names. Torry was to become a very distinctive suburb of granite mansions, despite early administrative amalgamation with Aberdeen in 1891. Churches were built to meet the spiritual needs of Torry's growing population which increased from 1,117 in 1881 to 9,386 in 1901. The massive red granite structure of St Peter's Episcopal Church was built in 1897. New factories, storage and distribution yards, especially for fish processing and timber, were sited on prime locations along the Dee and in the Albert Basin. The nearness of Torry to the new fish market, opened in 1899 on Albert Quay, gave a definite focus to Aberdeen's then extremely prosperous and expanding fishing industry, from which Torry clearly benefited.

Sir Andrew Lewis 1875–1952

Educated at Old Aberdeen Grammar School, Andrew Lewis joined the family shipbuilding and trawling firm of John Lewis & Co., rising, in due course, to become senior partner. He served on the harbour commission, and represented Ferryhill on the town council 1919–29. He served as lord provost 1925–29, and during that period he played a major part in bringing the joint hospital scheme to a successful conclusion. He served as a director of the National Bank of Scotland, and as chairman of the Millom Askam Hematite Co., the Aberdeen, Edinburgh and London Trust, the North Eastern Ice Co., and John Lewis Ltd, coal factors. He also served as vice chairman of the Aberdeen Mutual Insurance Co.

The distinctive regular layout and generally low cottage-style buildings of Footdee on the northern flank of the Dee estuary are eloquent evidence of its planned fisher town origins. The original village was situated just seaward of the former Waterloo railway goods station, a position that it had occupied for at least 500 years previously. It is shown in early maps as six rows of cottages hard by the Fishers' Haven and physically isolated from the burgh of Aberdeen. The male occupations were white fishers, pilots and seafarers, a distinctive community of people who seldom intermarried with those of any other occupation. White fishing by long line was very much a team effort in that bait had to be collected, lines baited and coiled and catch marketed or preserved. This was customarily undertaken on a family or extended family basis, and a fisherman was understandably unlikely to find a partner willing to take responsibility for these essential and physically demanding duties, and cope with them successfully, other than from another fisher family. The existence of a remarkably close and supportive village community is revealed in the surviving minute book of the Footdee Society, covering the period of its existence between 1761 and 1822, indicating a high level of community care for orphans and widows. In 1809, the city magistrates deliberated upon the final stages of the 1810 Harbour Act. This included following the necessary procedures for the acquisition of the property and site of old Footdee as part of the plans to develop further the northern shore of the Dee estuary, an activity which had been in process for several years. A newly designed settlement for the displaced community, comprising initially 56 houses set in squares, was constructed to plans devised by the city architect on a site levelled out of the sandhills of Sandness, at the northern side of the estuary, just west of the proximal end of the north pier of the navigation channel. The original cottages included the traditional loft for storing nets and rope together with sail

Salmon fishers with their nets at the mouth of the River Don, c. 1900.

Salmon Fishers, Bridge of Don

cloth internal divisions. In the late 1850s, Footdee witnessed an intense religious revival inspired by the skipper of a becalmed Fraserburgh boat, named Summers, and thereafter religious activities tended to be concentrated in the Footdee mission hall in the village's North Square. Although there were 27 white fishing boats and 33 herring boats based in the village in the late 1870s, towards the end of the nineteenth century, the occupational structure of the community began to change, with shipbuilding, joinery and masonry assuming a larger role. These changes were partly a reflection of a major storm in 1881 which left a number of families fatherless, and partly a response to the introduction of steam trawling, which was much opposed by the Footdee fisher families because some trawlers operated during the Lord's Day. However, the same industry provided growing employment in the nearby shipyards and the women could augment the household income by following the trawler fleet southward to English ports on the east coast as fish gutters and packers.

Alexander Nicol 1810–80

Son of a shipowner and insurance broker, Alexander Nicol followed the same profession and owned the first Aberdeen clipper, the *Scottish Maid* built in 1839. He served as a harbour commissioner 1841–47 and again 1860–63. He also served as provost of Old Aberdeen and dean of guild 1853–55. He represented the first ward on the town council 1847–52, 1856–59 and 1863–69 and served as lord provost 1866–69, playing a major role in obtaining the Harbour Act of 1868 which authorised the diversion of the Dee, the creation of the south breakwater and the extension of the north pier. He supported the construction of a bridge to Torry but opposed the purchase of Torry Farm. He lost his seat in 1869. He served as chairman of the Association for Improving the Condition of the Poor, and was very active in the 1870s in the Church of Scotland Extension and Territorial Home Mission Association.

GILCOMSTON, MANNOFIELD AND OLD ABERDEEN

Writing in the 1830s with the flowing narrative one might expect of a minister, the contributor of the Oldmachar parish account noted that

> this parish rises in a gentle slope from the sea, and though there is no eminence in it that deserves the name of a mountain, its surface is beautifully diversified by rising grounds. The windings of the Dee and the Don, the

manufactories and the woods on the banks of the latter, some detached clumps of planting on the rising grounds, interspersed with a number of gentlemen's seats and villas ... together with the various prospects of the sea, the rivers, the Cities of Old and New Aberdeen, and the villages of Gilcomston and Woodside ... give a pleasant variety to the general appearance of the parish.[1]

The lands of Gilcomston lying astride the Denburn Valley were purchased from the Menzies family of the Pitfodels estate in the 1670s by the town council, probably in part to gain a measure of management control over the outflow from the Gilcomston dam whose waters drove the town's mills as well as many small basement workshops. Gilcomston grew as Aberdeen's first industrial village in the eighteenth century, as a plethora of narrow lanes and alleyways most of which survived until the area was redeveloped in the 1960s. It was initially populated by weavers, shoemakers and tradesmen working in the nearby Loanhead quarry which was situated at the top of Craigie Loanings, and which provided granite for a number of Aberdeen's buildings, including those on Marischal Street and the Gilcomston chapel of ease, later the Denburn Church, designed in 1771 by architect William Smith. Developed before the days of Rosemount Viaduct, the church was intended to accommodate a congregation drawn from a maze of streets and lanes, and served a mainly working-class population. The story of the village of Gilcomston is encapsulated in the composite story of the four separate congregations which eventually became amalgamated into the present Denburn parish church. The original 1771 part of the building was designed as a means of easing the burden of the journey to worship in St Machar's Cathedral in Old Aberdeen. A disagreement over the appointment of a minister led to a breakaway congregation, St Paul's, whose building was for some time located at the corner of Gilcomston Park and Rosemount Viaduct. A third Union Church was housed in a building on Shiprow, and a fourth, the Bon-Accord congregation which was founded in 1828, eventually settled in 1896 in a new building on Rosemount Viaduct with a prominent campanile tower, now the place of worship for the members of the Bon-Accord congregation. The four restored houses at Skene Place, dating from 1815, in classical style with stair flights to front door, exhibited a benign elegance, repeated below by the burnside buildings of Mackie Place, generously proportioned merchants' houses, two with Dutch-style gables, and a single pantiled weaving shed. Only these, together with the place names and churches, remain to recall the community whose size and religious vigour spawned a parish church seating 2,000 worshippers.

The strong sectoral development patterns, which characterised the expansion of the city in the late nineteenth and early twentieth centuries along the new roads and tramway network, were particularly evident in Mannofield as well as Ruthrieston. The historic Old Deeside Road, which remained as an address on the suburban list of the city street directory of 1893 was, by 1900, all but obliterated by its successor, Broomhill Road. While the old Skene turnpike, heading for Alford and beyond, retained its name west of Rubislaw quarry, it was named Queen's Road at its eastern end. The construction of Great Western Road linked up with the Deeside turnpike to provide an imposing entry to the small separate hamlets of Cults and Bieldside. These new roads encouraged residential villa development in a ribbon along their edges, and relieved the pressure on the old estate lanes such as Countesswells Road which, in 1900, was known as Mid-Pitfodels Road, and Craigton Road, the back road to Cults via Jacob's Ladder. Residential infill behind these ribbon developments became primarily private housing schemes of bungalows. Thus the growing city persistently engulfed small estates, country mansions and hamlets such as Ruthrieston and Mannofield. The speed of development at the end of the nineteenth century was such that private mansion houses such as Beech-hills on Countesswells Road which entered its address in the 1893 street directory as being 'two miles from Holburn Street' had by 1900 defined itself as being 'about half a mile from Mannofield'.[2] The suburb of Mannofield derived its name from an Aberdeen merchant, Robert Balmanno, who in 1772 purchased part of Aberdeen's former freedom lands from the Rubislaw estate. The 'inclosures' which Balmanno reclaimed from 'foul moors' became substantially improved. Balmanno's fields yielded, among other market garden products, an annual crop of high-quality strawberries, for some time rated as the cream of the Scottish crop, and sold as such at Covent Garden, London. His little estate extended eastwards and included the properties of Ashley, Louisville and Wellbrae. The proprietor built for himself the fine Georgian house of Friendville, and this name, together with Friendship Terrace and Friendship Farm on Stanley Street, commemorated the estate owner's Quaker ancestry. The Friendville estate later passed through the hands of several owners and the lands around were gradually sold off and feued for residential development. The adjoining mansion of Thorngrove was to become the home of the architect J. Russell Mackenzie, and may have been the first house in Aberdeen to install electric lighting in 1894. Community status for Mannofield was confirmed by the opening of Mannofield Church in 1882, and more recently but, perhaps less impressively, by the presence of the Mannofield shopping centre.

The outward spread of residential developments was, as indicated earlier, only made possible by the development of horse buses and horse trams. The essential link which permitted Balmanno's hamlet to grow was probably the opening of the Mannofield horse tramway in 1880, running from Market Street with a 30 minute frequency, which was increased to 15 minutes in 1889. The fare from Mannofield to Market Street, both inside and outside seating, was two pennies, and children under two years of age could travel free. Most of the other horse tramways in Aberdeen included a reduction in the fare for outside travel. The district tramways had a depot at Mannofield, but the cars were actually based at the Queen's Cross depot on the site later occupied by Grampian Television, so that the facility at Mannofield could be used for storing the horse buses which initially acted as feeders from the villages of Cults and Bieldside, operating at an hourly frequency. This relatively low frequency of feeder provision was probably a recognition of the competing suburban rail service via the Great North of Scotland Railway Company.

Henry J. Butchart 1882–1971

The son of an Aberdeen lawyer, Henry Butchart was educated at the Grammar School and the Universities of Aberdeen and Edinburgh. He formed a law partnership in 1908 with Ernest Rennet to whom he had previously been apprenticed. In 1920 he was appointed secretary and factor of Aberdeen University. He served as a JP and was county commissioner for the City of Aberdeen Boy Scouts. During the First World War he served with the Scottish Horse Regiment of Cavalry and with the Australian and New Zealand Light Horse, holding a variety of staff appointments and rising to the rank of major. He was awarded the Distinguished Service Order the TD (Territorial Division), and the Star of Roumania. In the Second World War he served as a sergeant in C Company of the City of Aberdeen Battalion. He was a founder member of the Scottish Ski Club and became president in 1950. He played a major role in planning and developing the University's sports facilities, and the physical recreation centre which now bears his name. In 1948 he was appointed deputy lieutenant of the County of the City of Aberdeen. He received an OBE in 1951. He retired from the post of secretary in 1952, but remained the University's law agent until 1967. He secured a considerable amount of property in Old Aberdeen for the University at modest prices.

Although Old Aberdeen lost its administrative independence in 1891, it retained its ecclesiastical and academic distinctiveness accumulated over 500 years as home to King's College. Its historical framework of the High Street, Don Street and the Chanonry, the tight layout, high walls and physical separateness from the residential communities which surrounded it, together with the Spital extending southwards as a tail towards new Aberdeen, included many architecturally distinguished historical buildings. The twin western towers of St Machar's Cathedral and the elegant crown tower of King's College Chapel remain the best known landmarks in Old Aberdeen, perhaps evocative of the role of the church in temporal as well as in spiritual matters. The tightly-packed houses, some crammed with gables facing onto the High Street hint at a shortage of space or money, or possibly both, constraining the plans of the founder, Bishop Elphinstone. They also represent a trading burgh juxtaposed with a well-established Cathedral quarter to the north and small academic quadrangle to the south hard by the boggy ground of the Powis Burn. To the east lay the inviolate open space of the King's Links, with its long established devotion to recreational use. Inland of the low ridge of drier ground, on which the bishops' burgh of barony was established, lay an area of wetter ground with streams and springs, whose landward slope fed the former loch of Old Aberdeen and provided a stance for the market and horse fair which was held every six months. The remarkable survival of the classic medieval burgh street plan and the physical land boundaries, violated only by the link road of St Machar Drive, was a result, in part, of the successful completion of King Street and eventually of the new Bridge of Don in 1836. This diverted most of the traffic away from Old Aberdeen and eventually permitted the closure of the old Brig of Balgownie crossing of the river to all but pedestrian traffic. A policy of land acquisition and land retention adopted by the University Court, driven by the vision of a single campus, innate canniness and conservatism, and generally cordial relations with Old Aberdeen's residents, all assisted in retaining the individuality of the settlement as a living campus. When a shortfall in university funding by the Government cast its shadow on the University of Aberdeen, plans to exploit infill or redevelopment sites within the burgh, notably in Don Street, soon aroused the ire and eventually the opposition of the Old Aberdeen Residents' Association. Although enfiladed in the inter-war and post-war period with council house estates in various architectural styles, the university presence of around 10,000 students, and several halls of residence still provides a sense of community in the Aulton. Equally, however, although many of the surrounding residential schemes suffer from deprivation, there exists a distinct sense of community support and hope for the future, enhanced by community centres and community schools as social neighbourhood foci.

THE SUBURBAN VILLAGES OF LOWER DEESIDE

The Rev. James L. Thomson, writing about the parish of Peterculter in the early 1950s, stated that it consisted of the villages of Cults, Bieldside, Milltimber and Culter, but he also noted later in the same account that 'now the houses are almost continuous along the stretch of the road from Mannofield to the bridge over the Culter Burn'.[3] Culter might be regarded as the senior member of the quartet, growing around the site chosen by Bartholomew Smith in the middle of the eighteenth century to establish a small paper mill, based on the waters of the Culter Burn. A lease of the Waulkmill of Craigtown and the privilege of using the water was met by a yearly rent of £60 Scots, and extended to 114 years. It was initially a very small family business, involving Bartholomew, his wife, and two sons, one of whom, Richard, succeeded him. When his son, in due course, took over the operation, the mill had expanded its production to employ 50 persons. In the early years of its existence the Smith family relied on rags of all kinds collected from Aberdeen each Friday by horse and cart. By the 1840s, the New Statistical Account described the large paper manufactory of Messrs Arbuthnott and McCombie as

> a large chaste pile of the necessary buildings in excellent repair; its internal machinery is of the most approved modern description. The necessary movements in the machinery are produced by two large powerful water wheels – the one placed a little bit above the other – and both turned by the same stream, brought from an artificial reservoir by a wooden aqueduct. The papers made at this work are browns, cartridge and all sorts of wrapping papers … giving employment to upwards of 60 people.[4]

Alexander Pirie's paper mill at Culter, which survived until the early 1980s.

The rural situation of the paper mill in the hollow immediately below the gorge of the Culter Burn inspired the minister's vision and verbal eloquence to quite a remarkable level, not encountered in the near contemporary companion accounts of industrial lower Donside. The Victorians clearly admired romantic scenery and the harnessing of nature by technology.

> The beauty of the situation and scenery of this establishment is much admired. The extent of artificial works, the large pile of buildings on the left, the spacious reservoir on the right, with an occasional cascade over the dike; the aqueduct supported in the air, with its large column of rolling water passing under the spacious bridge, with the surrounding rocks and woods – all at this point burst upon the eye of the traveller and present to his view a combination of the beauties of nature, and the works of art in a variety and to an extent seldom if ever to be met with in so narrow a compass.[5]

In 1865 the company was taken over by Alexander Pirie of Stoneywood, steam boilers were installed, the sylvan character violated by the construction of a 200 foot high brick chimney, and two blocks of workman's cottages built on the Deeside turnpike which, in 1843, was described as 'one of the best public roads in the North', the Braemar mail coach providing a daily service. The mill continued to expand its production and workforce, and in the 1950s employed about 600 personnel, providing the mainstay of Culter's local economy and spending power, as only 100 of the work force were daily commuters from the city. Its demise in the early 1980s was a blow to the community in terms of both loss of earnings and sense of community. Nonetheless the support of the residents for community ventures such as the Culter gala week, survived and most village-led social activities maintained their support.

At the eastern end of suburban lower Deeside, the village of Cults was rooted in more rural origins. Its early-nineteenth-century kernel lay in the environs of the Den of Cults whose waters, enhanced by small reservoirs, drove water mills for cutting timber and grinding grain near the line followed by the old Deeside Road in the years before the turnpike. It ran westwards from the old Bridge of Dee via Inchgarth, through what became Allan Park and the Deeside Golf Club (on the southern edge of the first fairway). The village focus emerged, and remained at Cults Square, centred on the hotel and post office, on the route of the North Deeside Road turnpike, a site originally occupied by blacksmith and shoemaker and, perhaps fittingly, later partly occupied by the Village Garage. The early-nineteenth-century feuing of the Pitfodels estate in geometric blocks permitted the construction of early Victorian mansion houses, sitting with ample grounds and enjoying open views over the River Dee towards rural Kincardineshire. The spiritual needs of the village and its surrounding farms were catered for by a Free

Church built in 1843 and located on Kirk Brae (Damhead), and by the Parish Church of Banchory Devenick, situated on the southern side of the River Dee and reached by ferry, until the completion of the Rev. George Morrison's irreverently termed shakkin' briggie in 1837. The operation of the Deeside Railway between Aberdeen and Banchory from September 1853, and the opening of Cults railway station, proved the stimulus to further residential growth within easy walking distance of the station, particularly when the 'subbie service' (the suburban transport system) was inaugurated in 1894. The prospectus for the Deeside Railway envisaged considerable potential revenue from the villas of the 'merchant princes' which they thought would spring up on the southerly facing slopes of the valley. It was an inspired prediction as the census records confirm. In Cults in the 1880s, an average of 15 per cent of all residents were domestic servants, and the villa-owners were lawyers, teachers, bankers and merchants, with a sprinkling of widows and spinsters of ample means. Coachmen and gardeners soon began to outnumber agricultural farm servants although these, together with quarrymen, remained a feature of the social profile of the Victorian village. Dairying, market gardens and plant nurseries were also characteristic activities. Growth was confirmed by the establishment of three churches on the north bank of the Dee, with Cults West effectively replacing Banchory Devenick as the parish church.

In 1891, Cults was transferred from the parish of Banchory Devenick to the parish of Peterculter. By that time, the village and its surroundings enjoyed a prosperous air of Victorian and Edwardian gentility which its elder counterpart of Culter with its mill-based origins did not aspire to, despite its sharing the 'subbie service' and equally attractive southerly outlook. There was a period of consolidation in the first half of the twentieth century, during which sites for residential building were gratefully exploited by city dwellers and ex-colonials, no doubt attracted by the lower feu duties associated with living in the county rather than the town. Thereafter, residential development boomed in the mid-1970s, mainly in the Abbotshall, Hillview and Hilltop areas, a surge of growth up the slope of the valley which was paralleled at Bieldside and at Milltimber in the following decades, leaving palpable gaps of relatively green belt at Pitfodels and between Bieldside and Milltimber at Murtle. Although well-used local names for quite specific geographical areas, neither Bieldside nor Milltimber could justifiably claim village status, either through distinctive settlement history or social coherence, although the Camphill (Rudolf Steiner) School created a coherent and exceptionally well integrated community in its own right at Bieldside. Development up the side of the valley continued as demand for further private residential developments increased in response to the influx of oil executives. The parish of Peterculter was absorbed into the city in 1975. The possibility of future growth had been hinted at as early as 1966 when the old Cults School on the North

Looking east towards Seaton along St Machar Drive. The buildings in the foreground are the University with the striking dome of the natural philosophy (physics) department.

Deeside Road closed and was replaced by Cults Academy, located, it seemed at the time, in an improbably peripheral location relative to the heart of the community. The shift in the residential centre of gravity reflected the growing multiple car ownership patterns of a prosperous suburb, the lack of alternative sites appropriate for development, and was further confirmed in 1974 with the opening of the Cults community centre and primary school complex.

The Villages of Suburban Donside

The River Don, Scotland's sixth river by length, ends in a sand-spit encumbered small tidal estuary, immediately downstream of Balgownie gorge and the great meander channel bend running through Seaton Park. The park was once envisaged as a potential site for Aberdeen's first aerodrome. The agricultural products of the Don river basin are claimed to be worth 'twa o' Dee – except for salmon, stone or tree'. In other words, cattle and cereals were, historically, its key products. However, over its last few kilometres the River Don cascades over a number of rock outcrops in its channel bed and these spawned the growth of a succession of village communities along its banks and tributaries, deriving their growth from industries requiring water and water power, principally paper and woollens. Most of these Donside industries originated before the days of granite quarrying in the Bucksburn, Auchmill and Hilton areas. Until the second half of the eighteenth century plaidings and woollen articles were produced domestically in both town and countryside. The stimulus to create larger units, in mills and small factories, was helped by the activities and promotions of the various boards set up in the aftermath of the battle of Culloden. The boards encouraged new branches of textile manufacture, and in 1779 a cotton factory was established in Woodside, with raw material imported from abroad. Power-driven machinery for spinning and, eventually, weaving came to the area at the very end of the eighteenth century. There was a search for appropriate water power sites both on the Don and its tributary streams, such as Bucks Burn, as well as within Aberdeen itself. The early stages in developing sites, and establishing companies were often promoted by estate owners. In the parish of Newhills, the villages of Bucksburn, Bankhead and Stoneywood all developed in this way. Still properly described as villages in 1951, Bucksburn then had the largest population of the three with 3,750. Paper making was the main industry, and the two mills located within Newhills parish provided employment at that time for approximately 2,000 people, about half of whom travelled daily from Aberdeen. In that same year, the last burst of granite quarrying was being conducted at Sclattie with a workforce of around two dozen men. There were still limited quarrying operations at Bankhead, Dancing Cairns and Bucksburn.

George Moir, a member of a staunchly Jacobite family, acquired the lands of Stoneywood in 1671. The family was exiled after Culloden, but Moir returned from Sweden in 1761 to develop the village. It had a sugar refinery and a woollen mill, and was almost a classic planned village. Subsequently a paper mill was started in 1770, with a lease granted to John Boyle and Richard Hyde, and subsequently to an Aberdeen wigmaker, Alexander Smith. These were small enterprises. The mill in 1787 consisted of two vats, with sixteen employees making paper by hand. The mill eventually passed to Alexander Pirie, a young man only 22 years old, who probably merits the title of founder of the Pirie paper dynasty. The family enhanced the sense of community by accepting extensive social responsibilities for their workers including the provision of a library, sports club and canteens. The company merged with Wiggins Teape & Co. in 1922. Almost equally famous was the woollen mill of Crombie & Co. at Grandholm, opposite Woodside on the north bank of the Don. This establishment was a descendant from the original works of Leys, Still & Co. started in 1749, and which subsequently became Leys, Masson & Co. The original company was bankrupted in the economic depression of the 1840s and subsequently rescued by the Crombie family in 1859. It built up a world-wide reputation for quality overcoats, as displayed in the greatcoats of the Russian Army, and in Crombie cloths, and the company still had over 800 employees as late as the 1950s although independent ownership ended in the 1990s. Woodside, which became a police burgh in 1868 with a population of just under 5,000, extended at that time from Powis Terrace to the city boundary at Scatterburn, and included Tanfield, Cotton and Middlefield.

James E. Crombie 1862–1932

After graduating from Aberdeen University, James Crombie joined the family business of woollen manufacturers, and remained a director for 30 years. He was a member of the University Court and played a major role in the extension scheme and the quatercentenary celebrations. He served as rector's assessor 1900–08 and chancellor's assessor 1913–32. He was both a manager and a substantial benefactor of the Sick Children's Hospital and an original trustee of the Newhills Convalescent Home. He gave generously to the Royal Infirmary. He was a strong supporter of the Liberal Party and served as vice president of the Scottish Liberal Federation. He also served as a JP.

The village of Dyce, last of the significant suburban Donside villages, grew up around the railway station, established in 1861 at the junction of the Inverness line with the Buchan and Formartine line to Peterhead. Those who pass through or around Dyce en route to Kirkhill industrial estate each day or who regularly travel out by air from Dyce will read the following account, written 1950, with some incredulity. With reference to the village of Dyce, since its foundation in 1861 as a station hamlet, 'it has grown steadily and is now a built-up area with over 1,000 of a population'.[6] The 1950 description of 'the aerodrome' is equally illuminating.

An aerodrome was established in the Farburn district to the west of Dyce and some six miles from Aberdeen. During the war, it was used as an RAF station

Aberdeen Airport at Dyce, transformed by the oil industry into the country's busiest heliport.

but in 1946 was taken over by the Ministry of Civil Aviation. British European Airways now operate daily services south to Edinburgh and Glasgow and north to Inverness and the islands. The three runways at Dyce … are short by modern requirements, and the topography of the area and the layout of the road and rail communications, prevent any great extension being made to them. This seriously handicaps the creation of continental services, which would require larger landing facilities than Dyce can provide.[7]

The message and the verbal forms of expression delivered by the 1950s commentary quoted above are redolent of an almost Arcadian state where a travel-to-work journey of even a few miles was still regarded with mild surprise, even distaste, and air passengers from Aberdeen had to be content with limited travel horizons. The airport grew substantially in response to the demands of the oil industry. The first oil-support helicopter flights took place in 1967, and increased rapidly thereafter. In 1972 the airport was taken over by the Civil Aviation Authority, and this presaged considerable development of runways and a wide range of facilities for passengers and commercial operators.[8] By the close of the century, it had become one of the busiest airports in the United Kingdom.

New Villages on Greenfield Sites

Villages on greenfield sites represent a new breed of planned settlement which share some common origins with the landowner's planned villages established in the Scottish Lowlands. They also incorporate and represent some of the design aims and objectives of Ebenezer Howard's late-nineteenth-century 'garden settlements'.

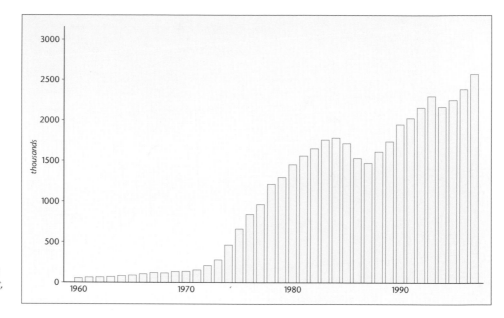

Figure 18.1
Numbers of
passengers arriving
at Aberdeen Airport,
1960-97.

They were envisaged by planners as offering an alternative to piecemeal residential developments which constantly gnaw away at green belts and buffer zones. They also enable careful attention to be given to the quality of life for a whole new community, and permit, through the use of a greenfield site, maximum freedom to be paid to variety in layout and design. Such planning proposals for the area around the city generally originated from predictions of housing need, that is the number of households, which were then increased further by *ad hoc* development consortia who identified what they deemed to be appropriate sites after consultation. In all cases, it should be stressed, these new designer 'villages', however large in comparison with their eighteenth-century ancestors, such as the frequently-proposed development at Maryculter which planned to cater for 2,750 houses and 10,000 people in the later 1970s when it was first suggested, are specifically residential and involve a journey to the work place. They are not envisaged as new towns. Kingswells in Newhills parish serves as one example which was developed in the 1980s around a small hamlet situated in the city's green belt. At Kingswells, the initial scheme involved 49 new houses grouped around the existing church, inn, shop, garage and primary school, but subsequently increased to 1,000 in the early 1990s, and later to a total of 3,000. Significantly the small shopping centre was not successful, presumably because of the proximity of Aberdeen. The term 'village' applied to a designer settlement like Kingswells is appropriate in terms of scale. But the provision of a new home in a pleasant setting, within easy travelling distance to city and countryside, does not necessarily have any community 'feel' other than street 'neighbourhood' watch.

Its near-neighbour of Westhill, just beyond the city boundary, was also designed as a sort of garden suburban village, not associated or intended to be integrated with any existing settlement or town. It was first actively promoted as such in the early 1960s on a proposed 450-acre site which included 150 acres identified for a golf course, hotel, schools, open space and shopping centre. The number of houses built and proposals for more was greatly augmented by the growth of the oil industry, so much so that by the late 1990s the target ceiling population seemed to be nearer 10,000 than the 5,000 initially envisaged as an upper limit. Such rapid development provides a dilemma for planners who must constantly revise their housing requirements to allocate space for demand as the economy fluctuates and household requirements change. It also provides a different type of dilemma for the individual householder who perhaps paid a high price for a rural retreat only to find that subsequent planning proposals for further residential developments, or western peripheral roads, with even more residential possibilities, emerge to threaten this rural idyll.

The ever-expanding city: the fashionable garden suburb of Westhill in the 1980s.

Epilogue
The City and its People

George Gordon, Lord Byron, the most famous product of Aberdeen Grammar School declared that

> I live not in myself, but I become
> Portion of that around me.

So a city shapes its citizens by its topography, its architecture and, most of all, by how its past is read. Set between a grey North Sea and the hard-won farmlands of Buchan, built of the hardest granite, Aberdeen proudly presides as capital of Scotland's north-east lowlands. It is quite separate from the Highlands in language, culture and experience but, at the same time, so different from the industrial heartland of central Scotland. Its past is read as one of struggle with the elements, but also of faith in an ability to master them and civilise them. Like the land from which it grew, it is a city that reflected an environment which required hard work and fortitude to wrest a living. Its granite buildings seem to project these qualities: stolid, firmly-based, grey in the rain, but sparkling in its aftermath; comfortable and bourgeois like the bungalows of Anderson Drive but, equally, bold and soaring in aspiration, like the spires of Marischal College. Few who know it fail to recognise its independence, its self-sufficiency, its deep sense of its own worth and values, and its confidence that it can find its own solutions. Such, with some justification, is its reading of its own history.

In writing the history of a city, it is natural to attribute to it characteristics reflecting economics, politics, culture and a variety of other activities. In this volume Aberdeen has been described as politically radical, as generating a powerful literary tradition, as having a strong commitment to dealing with the problems of poverty and health, and as being the oil capital of Europe. But, of course, the city does none of those things. It is the people of the city who are the active agents who undertake such activities and it is they who create the character and personality of the city. Throughout this study a sustained effort has been made by the authors to identify some of the individuals who contributed to the historical evolution of Aberdeen. Some were major political and business figures, like the Hadden family, Sir Alexander Anderson, James Barclay and Peter Esslemont each of whom played a major part in the development of the city. Others, like Archibald

Simpson, John Smith and Scott Sutherland, shaped the physical environment. Yet others shaped the culture of the city and the North-East, as in the literary contributions of the Chalmers and the Alexander families, and, in entertainment, with a tradition running from Jessie Pollock to Harry Gordon and *Scotland the What*. Some few like Boyd Orr, Sir Dugald Baird and Sir Ian Wood, have achieved eminence in their sphere of activity to acquire recognition on an international scale. One group has, however, been largely overlooked and it is appropriate that it too should be recognised.

In concentrating on the history of the city itself, those sons and daughters who moved away to pursue their lives elsewhere tend to be ignored. But they too are part of the history of the city, carrying its traditions and formative influences with them. Scotland has a long tradition of outward migration to all parts of the globe, and the North-East has been no exception. In the nineteenth century, while the city drew migrants from its rural hinterland, others moved away to seek their fortunes elsewhere. There was always a strong military/medical tradition from Sir James McGrigor at the start of the period to Sir Alexander Ogston later in the nineteenth century. On a less exalted level, many others joined the colours, and saw service in far flung corners of the Empire, before returning home. Enlistment for military service provided one obvious solution to a lack of work during trade depressions.

Others moved to take advantage of career and business opportunities. The celebrated Stephen shipyard on the Clyde had its origins in Aberdeen. So too did the business career of Charles Mitchell, who established one of the shipyards of the Tyne, when it too was one of the great shipbuilding centres of the world. Mitchell, like many of his successful peers, freely disbursed his abundant wealth both in his adopted home of Newcastle and in his native city. His debt of gratitude to Marischal College is fittingly commemorated in its Mitchell Hall and Mitchell Tower.

Some Aberdonians have had to migrate in order to realise their talents on a larger scale. Few who saw Denis Law play at his peak doubt that he deserves inclusion in the highest echelon of professional football. But he never played professionally in Scotland other than in international matches. The son of a North Sea trawlerman, he left his native city at the age of 15 to join Huddersfield Town, later playing for the two Manchester clubs, as well as having a spell in Italy. Rather more recently, and in a different branch of the entertainment industry, Annie Lennox achieved fame and fortune as a singer. Another performer of truly international status, she enjoyed two decades as a major star, performing initially with the Eurythmics and later as a solo performer.

Scholars have also customarily travelled, and are sometimes never known outside their esoteric discipline. One such was John Rae, born in 1796, who studied at Marischal College and, subsequently, at Edinburgh as a medical student. In 1822 he migrated to Canada where he took a number of positions as a village schoolmaster. He later worked in the timber trade and as a doctor, went to California in the gold rush and, in his later years, became a teacher, a medical officer, and a local judge in Hawaii. He finally returned to the United States and died at Staten Island in 1872. The enduring product of this varied life was a volume entitled *Statement of some New Principles on the Subject of Political Economy*, published in 1834, and which has become recognised as an important contribution to the literature of economic theory. Indeed, Rae has been recognised and feted in his adopted land as Canada's greatest economist.

Some have found fame and returned. John Macleod, graduate of Aberdeen University and Nobel Laureate, returned at the end of his academic career to the city where it began. James Lamond served on Aberdeen town council between 1959 and 1971, and as lord provost in 1970-71. He was then elected as labour MP for Oldham East and later for Oldham Central and Royton. When he retired from Parliament in 1992 he resumed his service in local government on Grampian regional council and then on the new city council, where he joined his wife June, who had also achieved a long record of service to local government. Another son of the city who chose to leave and return has been C. Duncan Rice. In 1996, after a quarter of a century in the United States, where he had been a Professor of History and Dean of Arts and Science and then Vice-Chancellor of New York University, he returned to become Principal of Aberdeen University.

To write the history of a city is a challenge for historians. The task of integrating what is unique to the particular city with what is common to all cities, and to find the correct balance between them, is difficult. Inevitably limitations of space mean that only a fraction of the past can be encompassed, and many of those who made a distinguished contribution to the life of the city in their day have gone unrecorded. In the end, the history of a city lies not just in the written records, from which historians conjure their explanations, but in the hearts and minds of its people.

> City of granite tower and granite spire
> Of grim, indomitable granite will,
> Deep in your granite heart the cosmic fire
> Is burning still ...

So wrote Ronald Campbell MacFie. These chapters may not have entirely captured that elusive spirit of place which gives Aberdeen its uniqueness, but perhaps they have evoked some 'portion of that around me' and stirred thoughts about that past. It is to be hoped that they have generated understanding of both the turning points and the continuities of its long and particular history. At the same time, the fact that individuals like Lamond and Rice returned to the city in which their careers began is, in part, a reflection of the increasing internationalisation of life at the start of the new millennium. This was clearly and most strongly manifest in Aberdeen in the last three decades of the twentieth century by virtue of the emergence of the oil industry. There is no doubt that the new century will advance and confirm that process, and that Aberdeen will have to review and formulate its role for the future within that new and international context.

Notes

Notes to Chapter 1:
The Growth of the City, by John S. Smith

1. Alexander A. Cormack, *Poor Relief in Scotland* (Aberdeen 1923), p. 51.
2. BPP, *Laws Relating to the City of Aberdeen, viz the Police Act* (Aberdeen 1795), pp. 3-4.
3. *Aberdeen Town Council Minutes*, 2 July 1894.
4. *Ibid.*, 5 February 1894, 19 March 1894.
5. John R. Turner, *Scotland's North Sea Gateway: Aberdeen Harbour AD 1136-1986* (Aberdeen 1986), pp. 203-8.
6. William Robbie, *Aberdeen: Its Traditions and History* (Aberdeen 1893), p. 369.
7. *Town Council Minutes*, 18 October 1920.
8. *Ibid.*, 3 August 1853.
9. *Ibid.*, 21 June 1926.
10. *Ibid.*, 16 April 1923.
11. *Ibid.*, 7 February 1938, 7 March 1938.
12. *Aberdeen Journal*, 28 April 1869.
13. *Ibid.*
14. *Ibid.*
15. *Town Council Minutes*, 7 March 1953.
16. *Ibid.*, 15 June 1925.
17. W. D. Chapman and C. F. Riley, *Granite City - A Plan for Aberdeen* (1952)
18. *Town Council Minutes*, 7 October 1957.
19. *Ibid.*
20. *Ibid.*, 6 September 1976.
21. Michael J. R. Mitchell, 'Municipal Transport in Aberdeen, 1898-1975' (University of Aberdeen PhD thesis, 1993), p. 21.
22. John Smith, 'Tramways, Subbies and Suburbia - Aberdeen, 1860-1958', *Aberdeen University Review*, LII, 1987-88, pp. 221.
23. *Town Council Minutes*, 5 October 1959.
24. *Ibid.*, 6 June 1960, 6 March 1961.
25. *Ibid.*, 6 March 1850.
26. Aberdeen Herald (publisher), *Report of the Evidence Taken before the Committee of the House of Commons on the Subject of the Proposed Interference with the Public Links belonging to the Community of Aberdeen* (Aberdeen 1856), pp. 5, 38.
27. City of Aberdeen District Council, Department of Planning and Building Control, *Aberdeen District Local Plan - Final Written Statement* (Aberdeen 1989).
28. *Town Council Minutes*, 3 July 1967.
29. *Ibid.*, 19 May 1980.
30. *Ibid.*, 4 September 1950.
31. Grampian Regional Council, *Grampian Structure Plan Written Statement* (Aberdeen 1995).

Notes to Chapter 2:
People in the City, by Andrew Blaikie

1. The author wishes to thank: the staffs of the General Register Office and New Register House, Edinburgh; Aberdeen and North East Scotland Family History Society; Aberdeen University Library (Queen Mother Library and Special Collections); Fiona Watson, Northern Health Services Archives; Norman Bonney, Napier University; Eilidh Garrett, University of Cambridge; and Tony Glendinning, University of Aberdeen for providing useful advice.
2. Sir John Sinclair (ed.), *The Statistical Account of Scotland*, XIV, Kincardineshire and South and West Aberdeenshire (Edinburgh, 1796-97), the 'Old' Statistical Account (OSA) [Wakefield, 1982 edition], pp. 285, 294-6.
3. Aberdeen City Council, Planning and Strategic Development Department.
4. H. C. Mackenzie, *The City of Aberdeen Third Statistical Account of Scotland* (TSA), p. 107.
5. William Watson, *Pauperism, Vagrancy, Crime and Industrial Education in Aberdeenshire 1840-1875* (Aberdeen 1877), pp. 11-12.
6. James Valentine, 'Illegitimacy in Aberdeen and Other Large Towns of Scotland', *Report of the British Association for the Advancement of Science* (1859), pp. 224-6.
7. These data are taken from the Detailed Annual Reports of the Registrar General for Scotland.
8. Rachel Filinson, 'Illegitimacy in Aberdeen', *Journal of Biosocial Science*, 14 (1982), pp. 149-50.
9. Andrew Blaikie, 'A Kind of Loving: Illegitimacy, Grandparents and the Rural Economy of North-East Scotland 1750-1900', *Scottish Economic and Social History*, 14 (1994), pp. 41-57.
10. Aberdeen Town Council, *Public Health Committee*, 19 September 1934. Note the eugenicist element in the resolution.
11. Janet Askham, *Fertility and Deprivation: A Study of Differential Fertility amongst Working-Class Families in Aberdeen* (Cambridge 1975), pp. 10, 65.

12. Colin Pritchard and Barbara Thompson, 'Starting a Family in Aberdeen, 1961-79: The Significance of Illegitimacy and Abortion', *Journal of Biosocial Science*, 14 (1982), p. 128.
13. *Ibid.*, pp. 133-4.
14. C. H. Lee, 'Regional Inequalities in Infant Mortality in Britain 1861-1971: Patterns and Hypotheses', *Population Studies*, 45 (1991), p. 57.
15. Debbie Kemmer, 'Investigating Infant Mortality in Early Twentieth Century Scotland using the Civil Registers', *Scottish Economic and Social History*, 17 (1997), p. 9.
16. Registrar General, *Census of Population* 1891, Old Machar, 168b.
17. Aberdeen Town Council, *Report of the Medical Officer of Health, 1907* (Aberdeen 1908), p. 59, Appendix (Table C).
18. Robert A. Cage, 'Infant Mortality Rates and Housing. Twentieth Century Glasgow', *Scottish Economic and Social History*, 14 (1994), pp. 77-92.
19. *Report of the Medical Officer of Health (1908)*, p. 60.
20. Edwin van Teijlingen and Rose Barbour, 'The MRC Medical Sociology Unit in Aberdeen: Its Development and Legacy', in A. Adam, D. Smith and F. Watson (eds), *To the Greit Support and Advancement of Helth* (Aberdeen 1996), pp. 54-63.
21. Lesley Diack, '"A Woman's Greatest Adventure": The Development of Maternity Care in Aberdeen since the Eighteenth Century', in T. Brotherstone and D. J. Withrington (eds), *The City and Its Worlds: Aspects of Aberdeen's History since 1794* (Glasgow, 1996), p. 126.
22. Scottish Health Department, *Infant Mortality in Scotland: The Report of a Sub-Committee of the Scientific Advisory Committee* (Edinburgh 1943), pp. 15, 56-8.
23. I. D. G. Richards, *Infant Mortality in Scotland* (1971), pp. 32-4.
24. Mackenzie, *The City of Aberdeen*, pp. 101-2.
25. Ian Carter, *Farm Life in North-East Scotland 1840-1914: The Poor Man's Country* (Edinburgh 1979), pp. 76-97; Andrew Blaikie, *Illegitimacy, Sex and Society: North-East Scotland 1750-1900* (Oxford 1993), pp. 52-8.
26. Katherine Pacitti, 'Boom Blamed for Out-Patient Delays', *Press and Journal*, 4 November 1994.
27. *Planning and Strategic Development Department*.
28. The sample areas are as follows: Footdee Squares - North Square, South Square, Middle Row, Pilot's Square; City Centre - Netherkirkgate, Flourmill Lane, Barnett's Close, Guestrow, Thornton Place, Thornton Court; Elite Quarter - Bon Accord Terrace, Bon Accord Square, Bon Accord Street, Springbank Terrace, East Craibstone Street, West Craibstone Street, Union Place, Union Street.
29. *The New Statistical Account of Scotland*, XII, Aberdeen (NSA), (Edinburgh, 1845), p. 74.
30. Diane Morgan, *Footdee and Her Shipyards* (Aberdeen 1993), p. 48.
31. For the Scottish influence overseas, including Aberdonians such as Robert Laws, Patrick Manson, Mary Slessor, and Thomas Sutherland, see Olive and Sydney Checkland, *Industry and Ethos: Scotland 1832-1914* (Edinburgh 1989), pp. 155-64.
32. *OSA*, XIII, p. 424; Paul Thompson, Tony Wailey and Trevor Lummis, *Living the Fishing* (1983), pp. 227-63.
33. Morgan, *Footdee*, p. 45.

34. Blaikie, *Illegitimacy, Sex and Society*, pp. 129, 139.
35. Cf. Theodore Koditschek, *Class Formation and Urban-Industrial Society: Bradford 1750-1850* (Cambridge 1990), pp. 218-21; Hugh Mcleod, 'White Collar values and the Role of Religion', in G. Crossick (ed.), *The Lower Middle Class in Britain 1870-1914* (1976), pp. 63, 79.
36. Catherine Marsh and Andy Teague, 'Samples of Anonymised Records from the 1991 Census', *Population Trends*, 69 (1992), pp. 17-26. On-line access to SAR from 1991 Census was provided by the Census Microdata Unit, University of Manchester. All data are Crown Copyright.
37. The category 'married with dependent children' included a total of 1,315 individuals of which 650 were the dependent children themselves.
38. G. A. Mackay and Anne C. Moir, *North Sea Oil and the Aberdeen Economy* (Glasgow, 1980).
39. Michael J. Flinn (ed.), *Scottish Population History from the Seventeenth Century to the 1930s* (Cambridge 1977), pp. 387-420.
40. Michael Anderson, 'The Emergence of the Modern Life-Cycle in Britain', *Social History*, 10 (1985), p. 70.
41. Scottish Office, *Scottish Abstract of Statistics* (1995), p. 7.

Notes to Chapter 3:
The Nineteenth-century Economy by Richard Perren

1. James R. Coull, 'The Historical Geography of Aberdeen', *Scottish Geographical Magazine*, 72, 1963, pp. 86-8.
2. William Robbie, *Aberdeen: Its Traditions and History* (Aberdeen 1893), p. 366, 1841 Census.
3. John S. Smith, 'Modern Times', in Donald Omand (ed.), *The Grampian Book* (Golspie 1987), p. 190.
4. Robbie, *Aberdeen: Its Traditions and History*, pp. 361-4; William Watt, 'Fifty Years' Progress in Aberdeen', *Transactions of the Aberdeen Philosophical Society*, IV (1910), pp. 100-1; John R. Allan (ed.), *Crombies of Grandholm and Cothal 1805-1960* (Aberdeen 1960), pp. 22, 67-71, 118; Hugh C. Mackenzie, The City of Aberdeen, *Third Statistical Account of Scotland* (Edinburgh 1953), pp. 282-6; British Association, *Report of the British Association for the Advancement of Science*. Appendix (London 1934), pp. 103-5; British Association, *The North-East of Scotland: A Survey prepared for the Aberdeen Meeting of the British Association for the Advancement of Science* (Aberdeen 1963), pp. 173-6.
5. Thomas Donnelly, 'Shipbuilding in Aberdeen, 1750-1914', *Northern Scotland*, 4 (1981), pp. 24-7, 33; Victoria E. Clark, *The Port of Aberdeen* (Aberdeen 1921), pp. 140-2; *Aberdeen Chamber of Commerce Journal*, 50 (1969), p. 277.
6. Anthony Slaven, 'Shipbuilding in Nineteenth-Century Scotland', in S. Ville (ed.), *Shipbuilding in the United Kingdom in the Nineteenth Century: A Regional Approach* (Newfoundland 1993), pp. 153-5.
7. Clark, *The Port of Aberdeen*, pp. 141-2; Boyd Cable, 'The World's First Clipper', *Mariner's Mirror*, 29 (1943), p. 73.
8. *Aberdeen Chamber of Commerce Journal*, 11, 1930, p. 55; *British Association 1934*, Appendix, pp. 92-3, 95; J. Neville Bartlett, *Davidsons of Mugiemoss: A History of C. Davidson & Sons Makers of Wrapping Papers, Paper Bags, Paperboard and Plasterboard Liner* (1997), pp. 1-3.

9. Robert Wilson, *An Historical Account and Delineation of Aberdeen* (Aberdeen 1822), p. 218.

10. Thomas Donnelly, *The Aberdeen Granite Industry* (Aberdeen 1994), pp. 14-17.

11. William Diack, *Rise and Progress of the Granite Industry in Aberdeen* (London 1950), pp. 29-30; W. Knight, 'The Granite Quarries of Aberdeenshire', *Transactions of the Highland and Agricultural Society*, 2nd ser., 11, 1862, p. 64; Jean Lindsay, 'The Aberdeenshire Canal, 1805-1854', *Journal of Transport History*, 6 (1963-64), pp. 158, 164; *The New Statistical Account of Scotland*, XII Aberdeen (Edinburgh, 1845), pp. 68-9; Joseph Priestley, *Historical Account of the Navigable Rivers, Canals and Railways of Great Britain* (1831), pp. 2-4.

12. W. Gordon, *et al., A Directory for the City of Aberdeen, 1824-25* (Aberdeen 1824), pp. 113-16; *NSA*, p. 96; Richard Perren, 'Changes in Aberdeenshire Farm Livestock', *The Ark*, 2 (1975), p. 289.

13. James Anderson, *General View of the Agriculture and Rural Economy of the County of Aberdeen* (Edinburgh, 1794), pp. 81-2, 164-6.

14. Ranald C. Michie, 'Trade and Transport in the Economic Development of North-East Scotland in the Nineteenth Century', *Scottish Economic and Social History*, 3 (1983), pp. 67, 69-70; J. H. Smith, 'The Cattle Trade in Aberdeenshire in the Nineteenth Century', *Agricultural History Review*, 3 (1955), p. 114. C. H. Lee, 'Some Aspects of the Coastal Shipping Trade: The Aberdeen Steam Navigation Company, 1835-80', *Journal of Transport History*, New Series, 3 (1975), pp. 94-5.

15. Wilson, *Historical Account of Aberdeen*, p. 207; *The Bon-Accord Directory 1840-41* (Aberdeen, not dated), pp. 183-4.

16. William Kennedy, *Annals of Aberdeen from the Reign of King William the Lion, to the end of the year 1818*, Vol. II (1818), pp 195-8.

17. Charles W. Munn, *The Scottish Provincial Banking Companies 1747-1864* (Edinburgh 1981), pp. 85-8.

18. Sydney G. Checkland, *Scottish Banking: A History 1695-1973* (Glasgow, 1975), pp. 346-7.

19. Ranald C. Michie, *Money, Mania and Markets* (Edinburgh 1981), pp. 93-4.

20. *Aberdeen Herald*, 22 March 1845; Watt, 'Fifty Years' Progress', p 104.

21. BPP 1845 XL, *List of Names, Descriptions, and Places of Abode of all Persons Subscribing to the Amount of £2000 and upwards, to any Railway Subscription . . . during the Present Session of Parliament . . .*, pp. 1-149.

22. Michie, *Money, Mania and Markets*, pp. 60-1; Alexander Keith, *Eminent Aberdonians* (Aberdeen 1984), pp. 1-2, 22-4; J. J. Waterman, *The Coming of the Railway to Aberdeen in the 1840s* (Aberdeen 1976), pp. 17-21.

23. Watt, 'Fifty Years' Progress', pp 105-7; Keith, *Eminent Aberdonians*, p. 10.

24. *TSA*, p. 47; Coull, 'Historical Geography', p. 90.

25. Robbie, *Aberdeen: Its Traditions and History*, pp. 340-2.

26. Lee, 'Coastal Shipping Trade', pp. 94-107; Robert Duncan, *Textiles and Toil: The Factory System and the Industrial Working Class in Early 19th Century Aberdeen* (Aberdeen 1984), pp. 52-3.

27. Alexander Newlands, *The Scottish Railways: A Sketch of their Growth and Recent Developments* (1921), pp. 6, 7; *TSA*, p. 61; H. A. Vallance, *The Great North of Scotland Railway* (1965), *passim*; John Thomas and David Turnock, *The North of Scotland: A Regional History of the Railways of Great Britain* (Newton Abbot 1989), pp. 143-214.

28. *Aberdeen Chamber of Commerce Journal*, 58 (1977), pp. 359-61.

29. *Aberdeen Journal*, 3 April 1850; Waterman, *The Coming of the Railway*, p. 26.

30. William McCombie, *Cattle and Cattle Breeders* (Edinburgh, 1886, 4th edn), p. 82.

31. James Allan and Alexander A. Cormack, *Agriculture in Aberdeenshire in the Nineteenth Century* (Arbroath 1927), p. 15.

32. George M. Fraser, *The Old Deeside Road* (Aberdeen 1921), pp. 33-6; Richard Perren, 'John Moir Clark', in A. Slaven and S. G. Checkland (eds), *Dictionary of Scottish Business Biography*, 2, 1860-1960 (Aberdeen 1990), pp. 122-3.

33. James Valentine, *Statistics of Aberdeen for 1868* (Aberdeen 1869), p. 14; McCombie, *Cattle and Cattle Breeders*, p. 83, fn. 3.

34. Lindsay, 'The Aberdeenshire Canal', pp. 158, 164; David Pearson, 'The Aberdeenshire Canal', *Aberdeen University Review*, LI (1986), pp. 285-306.

35. Diane Morgan, *Footdee and her Shipyards* (Aberdeen 1993), pp. 125, 143; Clark, *The Port of Aberdeen*, pp. 141-2.

36. Hazel M. Carnegie, 'Aberdeen Ships and Shipbuilders 1839-1880', *Aberdeen University Review*, XLVII (1977), pp. 161-3.

37. *Aberdeen Chamber of Commerce Journal*, 14 (1932), p. 6; 50 (1969), p. 277.

38. Clark, *The Port of Aberdeen*, p. 160; James R. Coull, 'The Trawling Controversy in Scotland in the Late Nineteenth and Early Twentieth Centuries', *International Journal of Maritime History*, VI (1994), pp. 108-9.

39. Malcolm Gray, *The Fishing Industries of Scotland 1790-1914: A Study in Regional Adaptation* (Aberdeen 1978), pp. 166-80.

40. John S. Smith, 'Aberdeen Harbour – The Taming of the Dee', in J. Smith and D. Stevenson, *Aberdeen in the Nineteenth Century*, p. 100; *Proceedings of the Institute of Mechanical Engineers*, July 1907, pp. 799-800.

41. British Association 1963, *The North-East of Scotland*, pp. 142-3.

42. *Aberdeen Free Press*, 9 January 1904.

43. *Aberdeen Journal*, 13 January 1905; *Aberdeen Free Press*, 14 January 1905.

44. *Aberdeen Chamber of Commerce Journal*, 49, 1968, pp. 171-2.

45. Post Office, *Aberdeen Directory 1846-47*, p. 163; 1875-76, p. 305.

46. Post Office, *Aberdeen Directory 1879-80*, pp. 312-3; 1913-14, pp. 561-3.

47. Donnelly, *The Aberdeen Granite Industry*, pp. 53-4.

48. *Ibid.*, p. 57.

49. *British Association* 1934, Appendix, pp. 93-5; *Aberdeen Chamber of Commerce Journal*, 49 (1967), p18; J. Neville Bartlett, 'Alexander George Pirie', in A. Slaven and S. G. Checkland (eds), *Dictionary of Scottish Business Biography* Vol. 2, 1860-1960 (Aberdeen 1990), pp. 202-3.

50. J. Neville Bartlett, 'Alexander Pirie and Sons of Aberdeen and the Expansion of the British Paper Industry, *c.* 1860-

1914', *Business History*, XXII (1980), p. 26; idem, 'Investment for Survival: Culter Mills Paper Company, 1865-1914', *Northern Scotland*, 5 (1982), pp. 32-3.

51. Richard G. Burnett, *Though the Mill: The Life of Joseph Rank* (1945), p. 22; Joseph Rank Limited, *The Master Millers: the Story of the House of Rank* (1955), pp. 19, 21; John S. Reid, *Mechanical Aberdeen* (Aberdeen 1990), pp. 46-7.

52. Ian Carter, *Farm Life in North-East Scotland 1840-1914, The Poor Man's Country* (Edinburgh 1979), pp. 76-97.

53. John McRobb, *Then and Now, 1854-1912: A Short History of the Aberdeen Lime Company* (Aberdeen 1912), pp. 7, 18-28, 31-2.

54. Allan, *Crombies of Grandholm*, pp. 103-7, 115; Richard Perren, 'Management Style and Business Crises in the Aberdeen Textile Industry', in D. H. Aldcroft and A. Slaven (eds), *Enterprise and Management: Essays in Honour of Peter L. Payne* (Aldershot 1995), pp. 260-3.

55. Alexander Keith, *The North of Scotland Bank Limited 1836-1936* (Aberdeen 1988), pp. 90-148; *TSA*, pp 313-16.

Notes to Chapter 4: Survival and Decline: The Economy 1918-1970 by Richard Perren

1. Aberdeen Chamber of Commerce, *Report by the Council for the Year 1916*, 1917, pp. 23-4; *Report by the Council for the Year 1917*, 1918, p. 21; Alexander Keith, *The North of Scotland Bank 1836-1936* (Aberdeen 1936), pp. 149-50.

2. Richard Perren, 'Management Style and Business Crises in the Aberdeen Textile Industry', in D. H. Aldcroft and A. Slaven (eds), *Enterprise and Management: Essays in Honour of Peter L. Payne* (Aldershot 1995), p. 264.

3. *Report by the Council 1916*, pp. 26-7; *Report by the Council 1917*, pp. 24-5.

4. Ethel Kilgour, *A March of Time* (Aberdeen 1996), pp. 56-7.

5. *Ibid.*, p. 245; Henry Hamilton, 'The Granite Industry', in Michael P. Fogarty (ed.), *Further Studies in Industrial Organization* (London 1948), pp. 207-8.

6. *Aberdeen Chamber of Commerce Journal*, 49 (1967), p. 19.

7. Peter Myers, *The Aberdeen Colliers* (Aberdeen 1987), p. 44.

8. Hugh C. Mackenzie, *The City of Aberdeen, Third Statistical Account of Scotland* (*TSA*) (Edinburgh 1953), p. 329.

9. Diane Morgan, *Round About Mounthooly* (Aberdeen 1995), pp. 169-70.

10. *Aberdeen Chamber of Commerce Journal*, 48 (1966), pp. 709-11.

11. John R. Allan (ed.), *Crombies of Grandholm and Cothal 1805-1960* (Aberdeen 1960), pp. 129-31.

12. *TSA*, pp. 190-1; Paul Thompson, *et al.*, *Living the Fishing* (1983), pp. 111-14.

13. *Aberdeen Chamber of Commerce Journal*, 1 (1919), pp 16-17; James R. Coull, 'The North Sea Herring Fishery in the Twentieth Century', in *International Ocean Institute, Ocean Yearbook 7* (Chicago 1988), pp. 121-2.

14. BPP 1935-36 X, *Second Report of the Sea Fish Commission for the United Kingdom. The White Fish Industry*, pp. 329, 417; *Aberdeen Chamber of Commerce Journal*, 17 (1936), p. 25.

15. The Scottish Council (Development and Industry), *Report of the Committee on the Aberdeen Fishing Industry* (Edinburgh 1951), pp. 9-10, 18.

16. Gavin Cargill, *Blockade '75: The Story of the Fishermen's Blockade of the Ports* (Glasgow, 1976), pp. 3, 9, 34-5, 39.

17. James R. Coull, 'Fishing', in Donald Omand (ed.), *The Grampian Book* (Golspie 1987), p. 235; Fishery Economics Research Unit, *The Fisheries in the Grampian Region: A Study in Conservation & Development* (Edinburgh 1982), pp. 10-12, 33, 37.

18. Michael P. Fogarty, *Prospects of the Industrial Areas of Great Britain* (London 1945), pp. 133-4.

19. *Aberdeen Chamber of Commerce Journal*, 10, 1929, pp. 30; 17 (1936), p. 25.

20. William Russell, *Aberdeen: Industries and Attractions* (Aberdeen 1938), p. 46; British Association, *Report of the British Association for the Advancement of Science. Appendix* (1934), p. 105; *Aberdeen Chamber of Commerce Journal*, 18 (1937), p. 25; Morgan, *Round About Mounthooly*, pp. 149-52.

21. *Aberdeen Chamber of Commerce Journal*, 46 (1965), pp. 361-2.

22. *Ibid.*, 39 (1957-58), pp. 77-9.

23. Diane Morgan, *Footdee and her Shipyards* (Aberdeen 1993), pp. 131, 181-6.

24. *Aberdeen Chamber of Commerce Journal*, 18 (1937), pp. 23-4; William Diack, *Rise and Progress of the Granite Industry in Aberdeen* (London 1949), pp. 103-4.

25. William S. Grant, *Reminiscences* (Aberdeen 1949), pp. 20-1; T. Donnelly, *The Aberdeen Granite Industry* (Aberdeen 1994), pp. 102-4.

26. Post Office, *Aberdeen Directory* 1918-19, pp. 562-4; 1929-30, pp. 618-20; 1938-39, pp. 667-8.

27. *Aberdeen Chamber of Commerce Journal*, 18 (1937), p. 23; 39, 1958, pp. 127-8; *TSA*, pp. 245-50.

28. *Aberdeen Chamber of Commerce Journal*, 39 (1958), p. 127; 44 (1962), pp. 55-7.

29. John S. Smith, 'The Rise and Fall of Aberdeen's Granite Industry', *Aberdeen University Review*, XLIX (1982), p. 167; Post Office, *Aberdeen Directory* 1977-78, pp. 80, 251.

30. John McLaren, *Sixty Years in an Aberdeen Granite Yard: The Craft and the Men* (Aberdeen 1987), pp. 105-6.

31. British Association 1934, Appendix, p. 96; *Aberdeen : Industries and Attractions*, p. 41; *TSA*, p. 276.

32. *Aberdeen Chamber of Commerce Journal*, 48 (1967), p. 77.

33. *Ibid.*, 49 (1967), pp. 18-19.

34. *Aberdeen Chamber of Commerce Journal*, 59, 1978, pp. 519-22; J. Neville Bartlett, *Davidsons of Mugiemoss: A History of C. Davidson & Sons Makers of Wrapping Papers, Paper Bags, Paperboard and Plasterboard Liner* (1997).

35. Great North Review, 32, 1995, p. 167.

36. *Aberdeen Chamber of Commerce Journal*, 1 (1919), p. xxix; 9 (1928), p. 24; 10 (1929), p, 27; Charles A. Oakley, *Scottish Industry To-day* (Edinburgh 1937), pp. 18-19.

37. Perren, 'Management Style', pp. 269-70; Oakley, *Scottish Industry To-day*, p. 3.

38. Allan, *Crombies of Grandholm*, pp. 124-7; *Aberdeen Chamber of Commerce Journal*, 42 (1961), pp. 335-6.

39. *Aberdeen Chamber of Commerce Journal*, 38 (1956), pp. 17-19; British Association, *The North-East of Scotland: A Survey prepared for the Aberdeen Meeting of the British Association for the Advancement of Science* (Aberdeen 1963), pp. 179-80.

40. *British Association* 1934, Appendix, p. 102; *Aberdeen Chamber of Commerce Journal*, 15 (1934), pp. 25–6; 18 (1937), p. 22; Michael Thomson, *Silver Screen in the Silver City. A History of Cinemas in Aberdeen, 1896-1987* (Aberdeen 1988), pp. 83, 186, 213.

41. *Aberdeen Chamber of Commerce Journal*, 38 (1957), pp. 115–17; 45 (1964), pp. 133–7; 45 (1964), pp. 191–4; W. Mackie, *A Century of Craftsmanship* (Aberdeen 1980), pp. 74–6.

42. Richard Perren, *John Fleming & Company Ltd, 1877-1977* (Aberdeen 1977), pp. 65–7.

43. *Aberdeen Chamber of Commerce Journal*, 56 (1975), pp. 741–4.

44. Keith, *North of Scotland Bank*, pp. 154–7; *TSA*, p. 314.

45. British Association, *The North-East of Scotland*, p. 180; Morgan, *Round About Mounthooly*, p. 137.

46. Dick Jackson and John Emslie, *Great North Memories: The LNER Era* (Aberdeen 1993), pp. 1, 27, 39.

47. *TSA*, pp. 146–7.

48. *Aberdeen Chamber of Commerce Journal*, 42 (1960), pp. 233–5; 54 (1975), pp. 871–2; Perren, *John Fleming*, pp. 76–7.

49. *Aberdeen Chamber of Commerce Journal*, 41 (1960), pp. 179–80.

50. C. H. Lee, *British Regional Employment Statistics 1841-1971* (Cambridge 1979).

51. Donald I. Mackay, 'Regional Planning for the North of Scotland', *Aberdeen University Review*, XLI (1965), pp. 76–7; *Aberdeen Chamber of Commerce Journal*, 50 (1969), p. 319.

52. Scottish Office Regional Development Division, *North East Scotland: A Survey of its Development Potential* (Edinburgh 1969), pp. 6, 12, 132.

53. *TSA*, pp. 299, 303–5.

54. *The Leopard*, 91, July/August 1983.

55. *The Railway Magazine*, XLVIII (1921), pp. 4–5; *Great North Review*, 29 (1992), pp. 344, 346.

56. Fogarty, *Prospects of the Industrial Areas*, p. 133.

57. AULSC, OD. T2, *London and North Eastern Railway* (Northern Scottish Area) (1938*), Excursion and Special Train Arrangements, passim*; City of Aberdeen, *Official Guide* (Aberdeen 1939), p. 104.

58. Aberdeen Corporation, *Royal Burgh and City of Aberdeen Official Guide* (Cheltenham 1930s), pp. 56, 66, facing 91, 106.

59. *Aberdeen Chamber of Commerce Journal*, 8 (1927), p. 19.

60. AULSC, OD. U2. 7, *Railway and Sporting Guide to the Highlands* (Glasgow, 1926), pp. 186–7.

61. AULSC, OD. U2. 6, *Aberdeenshire and the Moray Firth* (no date), p. 7.

62. Edward W. Watt, 'Aberdeen in the Twentieth Century', *Transactions of the Aberdeen Philosophical Society*, V (1938), pp. 198–200.

63. Ethel Kilgour, *A Time of Our Lives* (Aberdeen 1992), pp. 42–7; Aberdeen Corporation, *City of Aberdeen Official Guide*, pp. 40–5, 88–9.

64. AULSC, OD. U2. BR. SC, British Railways, *Holiday Guide, Area No. 1 Scotland* (Perth 1952), pp. 185–7.

65. Harry Webber, *City of Aberdeen Official Handbook* (Cheltenham 1954), p. 65.

66. All the sources used for this paragraph come from the local pamphlet collection (Lo P. 914. 125) held by the Aberdeen Central Reference Library (ACRL): Lo P. 914. 125.

Ab3, *Aberdeen Holidays* (Aberdeen 1951), Lo P. 914. 125. M46, Corporation of the City of Aberdeen, *General Information* (Aberdeen 1953), p. 1; *Aberdeen Illustrated Guide* (Aberdeen 1960), pp. 1, 65.

67. ACRL, Lo P. 914. 125. Ab3, *Aberdeen: Garden City by the Sea* (Aberdeen c. 1968), pp. 11–14; *Around and About Aberdeen by Car* (Aberdeen 1970), p. 36.

Notes to Chapter 5:
The Oil Economy by David Newlands

1. A. Hogg, 'The North-East and Tayside' in A. Hutcheson and A. Hogg (eds), *Scotland and Oil* (Aberdeen 1975).

2. M. Gaskin *et al., North East Scotland: A Survey of its Development Potential* (Edinburgh 1969).

3. Hogg, *North-East and Tayside*, p. 84.

4. *Ibid.*, p. 87.

5. G. A. Mackay and A. Moir, *North Sea Oil and the Aberdeen Economy* (1980), p. 14.

6. A. Harris, M. G. Lloyd, A. McGuire and D. Newlands, 'Incoming Industry and Structural Change: Oil and the Aberdeen Economy', *Scottish Journal of Political Economy*, 34 (1987).

7. A. Harris, M. G. Lloyd, A. McGuire and D. Newlands, 'Who Gains from Structural Change? The Distribution of the Benefits of Oil in Aberdeen', *Urban Studies*, 23 (1986).

8. The editors are grateful to Ms Joanna Robertson for this information.

9. Mackay and Moir, *North Sea Oil*, p. 85.

10. M. G. Lloyd and D. Newlands, 'The Interaction of Housing and Labour Markets: An Aberdeen Case Study', *Land Development Studies*, 7 (1990).

11. Harris *et al.*, 'Who Gains from Structural Change?'

12. S. McDowall and H. Begg, *Industrial Performance and Prospects in Areas Affected by Oil Development* (Edinburgh 1981).

13. Grampian Regional Council, 'House Prices', *Grampian Quarterly Economic Review*, Summer (Aberdeen 1984).

14. Grampian Regional Council, 'The Fish Processing Industry', *Grampian Quarterly Economic Review*, Autumn (Aberdeen 1982).

15. P. Scrimgeour and M. Wight, 'Manufacturing Employment Change in the Scottish Regions', *Scottish Economic Bulletin* (1983).

16. Mackay and Moir, *North Sea Oil*.

17. P. Hallwood, 'The Offshore Oil Supply Industry in Aberdeen', *Aberdeen University, Department of Economics, North Sea Study Paper* 23 (Aberdeen 1986).

18. Mackay & Moir, *North Sea Oil*, p. 61.

19. *Sunday Times*, 11 April 1999.

20. N. Williams, 'Differential Perceptions of the Benefits of North Sea Oil by Aberdeen Residents', *Cambria*, 16 (1991).

21. A. Harris, M. G. Lloyd and D. Newlands, *The Impact of Oil on the Aberdeen Economy* (Aldershot 1988).

22. M. Deakin and D. Kerr, 'Flexibility in the Restructuring of a Service Economy: The Case of Aberdeen', paper presented to the *ESRC Urban and Regional Economics Seminar Group* (Lancaster 1987).

23. A. Salmond and J. Walker, 'The Oil Price Collapse: Some

Effects on the Scottish Economy', *Fraser of Allendar Institute, Quarterly Economic Commentary*, November 1986.

24. Lloyd and Newlands, 'Housing and Labour Markets'.
25. M. Beck and C. Woolfson, 'The Hidden Deregulation of Britain's Offshore Oil Industry', St Andrews University, Centre for Research into Industry, Enterprise, Finance and the Firm, *Discussion Paper 95. 11* (St Andrews 1995).
26. Grampian Regional Council, *Oil and Gas Prospects - 1992 Update* (Aberdeen 1992).
27. *Ibid.*, p. 26.
28. Aberdeen City Council, *Oil and Gas Prospects - 1997 Update* (Aberdeen 1997).
29. D. Newlands, H. Battu, J. Finch and M. Parker, *The Economic Impact of Aberdeen University on the North East of Scotland*, Report for Aberdeen University Principal C. Duncan Rice, Economics Department, Aberdeen University (Aberdeen 1997).
30. *Times Higher Education Supplement*, 18 December 1998.

Notes to Chapter 6:
Working Life in the City by William W. Knox

1. R. Duncan, *Textiles and Toil: The Factory System and the Industrial Working Class in the Early Nineteenth Century* (Aberdeen 1985), p. 9.
2. W. Thom, *Rhymes and Recollections of a Handloom Weaver* (Paisley 1880), p. ix.
3. Duncan, *Textiles and Toil*, p. 15.
4. *Ibid.*, p. 50.
5. J. H. Dawson, *An Abridged Statistical History of Scotland* (1853), p. 8.
6. *Daily Free Press*, 15 August 1887.
7. P. Thompson, *Living the Fishing* (1983), pp. 120-8.
8. T. Donnelly, 'Shipbuilding in Aberdeen, 1750-1914', *Northern Scotland*, 4 (1981), p. 41.
9. L. G. Gibbon, *Scottish Scene or the Intelligent Man's Guide to Albyn* (1934), pp. 130,151.
10. T. Donnelly, *The Aberdeen Granite Industry* (Aberdeen 1994), pp. 130,151.
11. H. Hamilton, 'The Granite Industry', in M. P. Fogarty (ed.), *Further Studies in Industrial Organisation* (1947), pp. 193-5.
12. J. MacLaren, *Sixty Years in an Aberdeen Granite Yard* (Aberdeen 1987), p. 105.
13. W. Skene, *East Neuk Chronicles* (Aberdeen 1905), pp. 16, 27.
14. R. E. Tyson, 'The Economy of Aberdeen', in J. S. Smith and D. Stevenson (eds), *Aberdeen in the Nineteenth Century* (Aberdeen 1988), p. 33.
15. A. Gaffron, *A Patchwork of Memories* (Aberdeen 1986), pp. 20, 29.
16. *Glasgow Herald*, 11 January 1907.
17. AULSC, Aberdeen Trades Council Minutes, 29 August 1917. The 'buttery' is a bread roll made to a particular North-East recipe.
18. M. Watt, 'Aberdeen', in Nigel Gray (ed.), *The Worst of Times: An Oral History of the Great Depression in Britain* (1985), p. 158.
19. T. Harris *et al.*, 'Oil and the Aberdeen Economy', in P. Cooke (ed.), *Global Restructuring: Local Responses* (1986), p. 49.
20. City of Aberdeen Medical Officer of Health, *Annual Report 1958*, pp. 2-4.
21. N. Bonney, 'Aberdeen and Dundee: A Tale of Two Cities in the Oil Era', in *Global Restructuring*, p. 188.
22. P. Theroux, *Kingdom by the Sea* (1983), p. 295.
23. G. A. Mackay and A. C. Moir, *North Sea Oil and the Aberdeen Economy* (1980), p. 38.
24. C. H. Lee, *Scotland and the United Kingdom: The Economy and the Union in the Twentieth Century* (Manchester 1995), p. 55.
25. Bonney, 'Aberdeen and Dundee', p. 190.
26. E. Bain, *Aberdeen Incorporated Trades* (Aberdeen 1887), p. 246.
27. National Archives of Scotland (NAS), CS 96/1943. *Minute Book of the Woolcombers' Society in Aberdeen* (1755).
28. Bain, *Incorporated Trades*, p. 261.
29. National Library of Scotland (NLS), NE 3C 27, *Aberdeen Female Operatives Union*.
30. W. Diack, *History of the Trades Council and Trade Union Movement in Aberdeen* (Aberdeen 1990), pp. 49-50.
31. Thompson, *Living the Fishing*, p. 135.
32. *United Operative Masons' and Granite Cutters' Journal*, February 1902.
33. Maclaren, *Sixty Years ... Granite Yard*, p. 21.
34. *Operative Masons' and Granite Cutters' Journal*, February 1905.
35. Aberdeen Ladies' Union, *Annual Reports 1884-91*.
36. AULSC, *Trades Council Minutes*, 10 June 1901, 8 July 1905, 8 May 1906.
37. *Daily Journal*, 16, 17 April 1913.
38. AULSC, *Trades Council Minutes*, 11 June 1913.
39. Thompson, *Living the Fishing*, p. 137.
40. E. Kibblewhile and A. Rigby, *Aberdeen in the General Strike* (Aberdeen 1989), p. 6.
41. Angus Macdonald, *Organising Trade Unions in Aberdeen, 1927-1939* (Aberdeen 1986).
42. T. Geiger, 'Opposition in the Shadows of an Emerging Conflict: The Aberdeen Trades Council, Government Policy and Voicing Dissent in the Cold War', *Northern Scotland*, 13 (1993), p. 107.
43. D. Hunt, 'The Sociology of Development: Its Relevance to Aberdeen', in R. Parsler and D. Shapiro (eds), *The Social Impact of Oil in Scotland* (1980), pp. 113,117.
44. *The Guardian*, 20 September 1973. I am grateful to Diane Morgan for this reference.
45. C. Woolfson *et al*, *Paying for the Piper: Capital and Labour in Britain's Offshore Oil Industry* (1997), pp. 47, 112, 489.
46. AULSC, Aberdeen Trades Council, *Annual Reports 1989-91*.
47. A. Bowie, 'A History of Aberdeen Union of Masons', *United Operative Masons' and Granite Workers' Journal*, 15 (1916).
48. *Aberdeen Free Press*, 16 October 1868; *Aberdeen Herald*, 21 November 1868.
49. AUL, Trades Council Minutes, 4 July 1883, 15 August 1883, 17 June 1884, 30 October 1884.
50. *Daily Free Press*, 1 March 1889.
51. *Ibid.*, 24 November 1887, 2 February 1888.
52. AULSC, *Trades Council Minutes*, 11 September 1895.
53. Kibblewhile and Rigby, *Aberdeen in the General Strike*, p. 29.

54. AULSC, *Trades Council Minutes*, 13 October 1886.
55. *Ibid.*, 8 May, 2 July 1890.
56. Aberdeen Liberal Association, *Annual Report 1891*.
57. *Aberdeen Labour Elector*, 1,7 January 1893.
58. *Workmen's Times*, 21 January 1893.

Notes to Chapter 7:
Politics Before 1918 by W. Hamish Fraser

1. W. Kennedy, *Annals of Aberdeen from the Reign of William the Lion to the end of the Year 1818* (1818), pp. 337-9.
2. *Aberdeen Journal*, 4, 11 May 1814.
3. *Ibid.*, 30 September 1818.
4. *Aurora Borealis Academica, Aberdeen University Appreciations* (Aberdeen 1899), pp. 1-3.
5. *Aberdeen Journal*, 18, 25 August 1830.
6. Alexander Keith, *Eminent Aberdonians* (1984), p. 158; *The Northern Iris*, March-May 1826.
7. *Aberdeen Journal*, 1 December 1830.
8. *Ibid.*, 15 December 1830.
9. *Aberdeen Independent*, Vol. 1 No. 10, May 1831.
10. *Aberdeen Herald*, 12 October 1831.
11. *Ibid.*, 26 October 1831.
12. *Aberdeen Journal*, 27 June, 30 August, 5, 12 September, 19 December 1832.
13. *Aberdeen Herald*, 21 January 1835, 15 July 1837.
14. *Ibid.*, 22 May, 7 June 1841.
15. R. Duncan, 'Chartism in Aberdeen: Radical Politics and Culture 1838-48', in T. Brotherstone (ed.), *Covenant, Charter and Party* (Aberdeen 1989), pp. 78-82.
16. *Aberdeen Herald*, 15 February, 5 September, 17 October 1840.
17. *Ibid.*, 13, 20 March 1841.
18. Duncan, *Chartism in Aberdeen*, p. 79.
19. A. A. MacLaren, 'The Disruption of the Establishment', in John S. Smith and David Stevenson (eds), *Aberdeen in the Nineteenth Century* (Aberdeen 1988), pp. 114-18.
20. A. S. Cook, *Pen Sketches and Reminiscences of Sixty Years* (Aberdeen 1901), p. 17.
21. *Northern Star*, 30 October 1841.
22. *Ibid.*, 20 November 1841; *Aberdeen Herald*, 12 February 1842.
23. *Aberdeen Herald*, 29 January, 19 March, 24 September, 1, 8, 22 October 1842.
24. ACA, *Squibs, Cartoons and Broadsheets and other Fugitive Writings Relating to Aberdeen, 1785-1890*, No 36, 37.
25. R. E. Tyson, 'The Economy of Aberdeen', in Smith and Stevenson, *Aberdeen in the Nineteenth Century*, p. 22.
26. Michael Dyer, *Men of Property and Intelligence: The Scottish Electoral System prior to 1884* (Aberdeen 1996), p. 74.
27. *Ibid.*, pp. 76-81.
28. *Aberdeen Free Press*, 4, 11 September, 2 October 1868. I am grateful to Dr Jane Rendall for drawing my attention to J. D. Milne.
29. *Aberdeen Journal*, 18 November 1868.
30. *Ibid.*, 3 July 1872, 4 February 1874.
31. *Daily Free Press*, 22 May, 10 October 1882; *Aberdeen Working Men's Conservative Association*, Address 21 March 1883.
32. A. S. Cook, *The Aberdeen Liberal Association: The Story of its Formation* (Aberdeen 1907).
33. AULSC, *Aberdeen Trades Council Minutes*, 7 February, 2 March 1877; C. C. MacDonald, *Sermon Preached by the Rev. C. C. MacDonald on Sabbath 7th September to the Delegates Attending the Congress at Aberdeen, 1884* (Aberdeen 1884).
34. *Ibid.*, 23 December 1884.
35. *Inverness Courier*, 24 January 1885.
36. Tom Stephenson, *Forbidden Land: The Struggle for Access to Mountain and Moorland* (Manchester 1989).
37. H. A. L. Fisher, *James Bryce* (Viscount Bryce of Dechmont O. M.), 1 (1927), p. 215.
38. Alexander Webster, *Memories of Ministry* (1913), p. 31.
39. AULSC, *Trades Council Minutes*, 7 July, 13 November 1886.
40. *Ibid.*, 8 May, 2 July 1890.
41. Aberdeen Liberal Association, *Annual Report 1891*.
42. *Workman's Times*, 23 July 1892.
43. A. E. Fletcher to Tom Mann, 21, 22 April 1896.
44. R. Price, *An Imperial War and the British Working Class: Working-Class Attitudes and Reactions to the Boer War 1899-1902* (1972), pp. 82-3.
45. *Minutes of Scottish Workers' Parliamentary Committee*, 5 January 1901.
46. *Social Democrat IV*, 11 November 1900.
47. C. W. M. Phipps, 'The Aberdeen Trades Council in Politics 1900-1939: The Development of a Local Labour Party in Aberdeen', University of Aberdeen MLitt thesis (1980), p. 49.
48. John Paton, *Proletarian Pilgrimage: An Autobiography* (1935), pp. 114-16.
49. *Forward*, 23 February 1907.
50. L. Leneman, 'The Women's Suffrage Movement in the North of Scotland', *Northern Scotland*, 11 (1981), pp. 31-2.
51. *Glasgow Herald*, 20, 24 March 1917.
52. Thanks are due to Dr Martin Mitchell for his help with research on the 1880s.

Notes to Chapter 8:
Twentieth-century Politics by Michael C. Dyer

1. C. W. M. Phipps, 'The Aberdeen Trades Council and Politics 1900-1939: The Development of the Local Labour Party in Aberdeen' (University of Aberdeen MLitt thesis, 1980), p. 195.
2. D. Hatvany, 'The General Strike in Aberdeen', *Scottish Labour History Society Journal*, X (1976).
3. Phipps, 'Trades Council and Politics', p. 205. At least 18 Aberdonians fought for the Republicans in the Spanish Civil War, five of whom were killed.
4. Hatvany, 'General Strike in Aberdeen'.
5. *Aberdeen Journal*, 30 December 1918.
6. Phipps, 'Trades Council and Politics', pp. 141-52.
7. *Aberdeen Journal*, 1 November 1922.
8. *Ibid.*, 17 November 1922.
9. *Press and Journal*, 20 November 1923.
10. Phipps, 'Trades Council and Politics', p. 143.
11. *Press and Journal*, 30 November 1923.
12. *Ibid.*, 6 December 1923.
13. *Ibid.*, 24 October 1924.
14. *Ibid.*, 15 October 1924.

15. Phipps, 'Trades Council and Politics', pp. 148-52.
16. *Press and Journal*, 8 August 1924.
17. *Ibid.*, 13 August 1928.
18. *Ibid.*, 10 August 1928.
19. *Ibid.*, 30 May 1929.
20. *Ibid.*, 25 May 1929.
21. *Ibid.*, 27 May 1929.
22. *Ibid.*
23. *Ibid.*, 30 October 1931.
24. *Ibid.*, 14 October 1931.
25. *Ibid.*, 15 October 1931.
26. *Ibid.*, 16 October 1931.
27. *Ibid.*, 12 October 1931.
28. *Ibid.*, 16 October 1931.
29. *Ibid.*, 22 April 1935.
30. J. H. Smith, *Joe Duncan: The Scottish Farm Servants and British Agriculture* (Edinburgh 1973).
31. *Press and Journal*, 16 May 1935.
32. Phipps, 'Trades Council and Politics', pp. 167-70.
33. *Press and Journal*, 7 November 1935.
34. *Ibid.*, 29 October 1935.
35. *Ibid.*, 18 November 1946.
36. S. Rose and J. H. Burns, 'A Scottish Constituency', in D. E. Butler (ed.), *The British General Election of 1951* (1952), p. 185.
37. Some copies of this address are lodged in the local collection of Aberdeen Central Library.
38. This was despite the fact that another Hughes had represented the constituency since 1945.
39. M. C. Dyer and J. G. Jordan, 'Who Votes in Aberdeen? Marked Electoral Registers as a Data Source', *Strathclyde Papers on Government and Politics*, 42 (1985), pp. 26-9.
40. At the time of the 1971 Census of Population, 64. 9 per cent of households in Aberdeen North were council house tenants.
41. AULSC, MS 3037/1/4/15/a, Letter from the Chairman of Aberdeen North Liberal Party to Mary Esslemont.
42. M. C. Dyer, 'The 1979 Referendum Campaign in Aberdeen and Grampian', in J. Bochel (ed.), *The Referendum Experience: Scotland 1979* (Aberdeen 1981).
43. One of those meetings, on the Tillydrone housing estate, was attended by Miss Watt, her constituency chairman and an observer (myself).
44. M. C. Dyer, 'The 1992 General Election in Grampian', *Scottish Affairs*, 1 (1992), pp. 27-35.
45. Election Pamphlet 'Fighting for Scotland'.
46. Nicol Stephen, 'It's Time for a Change' stated: 'Nicol Stephen is closing in fast on the Conservative - with Labour and SNP out of the race . . . Backing either Labour or the SNP this time could simply let the Conservative back in. '
47. Labour Pamphlet, 'Dishonest Politics'.

Notes to Chapter 9:
Local Government by Clive H. Lee

1. Alexander Clark, The Town Council and the Merchant Guild: A Study in Local Government (Aberdeen 1938), pp. 40-1.

2. Stanley Horsfall Turner, *The History of Local Taxation in Scotland* (Edinburgh 1908), pp. 145, 188.
3. BPP, *Report from the Select Committee to Whom the Several Petitions from the Royal Burghs of Scotland were Referred.* (Edinburgh, 1819), pp. 42-3.
4. William Kennedy, *Sketch of the Affairs of the Treasury of Aberdeen under the Administration of the Trustees* (Aberdeen 1821), p. 15.
5. Alexander M. Munro, *Memorials of the Aldermen, Provosts and Lord Provosts of Aberdeen, 1272-1895* (Aberdeen 1897), pp. 260-7.
6. *Report . . . Royal Burghs of Scotland*, p. 40.
7. *Ibid.*, pp. 51-2.
8. Clark, *Town Council and Merchant Guild*, pp. 56-7.
9. Oliver MacDonagh, *Early Victorian Government 1830- 1870* (1977), p. 122.
10. Rosemary Tyzack, 'The Growth of Civic Consciousness in Aberdeen with Particular Reference to the Work of the Police Commissioners', in Terry Brotherstone and Donald J. Withrington (eds), *The City and its Worlds: Aspects of Aberdeen's History since 1794* (Glasgow, 1996), p. 151.
11. I am grateful to Mr Brian T. Jones of the North of Scotland Water Authority for this information and for the data upon which Figure 9. 1 is based.
12. Anon, *The Diced Cap: The Story of Aberdeen City Police* (Aberdeen 1972), pp. 10, 47-9.
13. BPP, *Aberdeen Municipality Extension Bill 1871*, Minutes of Proceedings, 25 April 1871, p. 78.
14. James A. Ross, *Record of Municipal Affairs in Aberdeen* (Aberdeen 1889), p. 98.
15. *Ibid.*, p. 121.
16. *Ibid.*, pp. 125-6.
17. Munro, *Memorials*, pp. 278-9.
18. See above, pp. 33-5.
19. BPP, *Aberdeen Municipality Extension Bill*, p. 80.
20. Ross, *Record of Municipal Affairs*, pp. 60, 63.
21. John S. Reid, *Mechanical Aberdeen: Industries and Services 1888-1913* (Aberdeen 1990), pp. 17-28.
22. Michael J. R. Mitchell, 'Municipal Transport in Aberdeen, 1898-1975' (University of Aberdeen, PhD thesis, 1993), p. 21, 24-9; M. J. Mitchell and I. A. Souter, *The Aberdeen Suburban Tramways* (Dundee 1980), p. 10.
23. Mitchell, *Municipal Transport*, pp. 86, 89.
24. AULSC, *Annual Accounts of the City of Aberdeen* (1901), p. 227.
25. *Ibid.*, p. 186.
26. Douglas E. Ashford, 'A Victorian Drama: The Fiscal Subordination of British Local Government', in Douglas E. Ashford (ed.), *Financing Urban Government in the Welfare State* (1980), p. 74.
27. Arthur Midwinter, 'A Return to Ratepayer Democracy? The Reform of Local Government Finance in Historical Perspective', *Scottish Economic and Social History*, 10 (1990), p. 64.
28. Aberdeen City Council, *Council Tax Information Leaflet 1999-2000*; AULSC, *Annual Accounts of the City of Aberdeen*.
29. AULSC, *Aberdeen Town Council Minutes*, 5 September 1877, 30 October 1877, 4 September 1878.

30. *Ibid.,* 14 October 1885.
31. Kenneth D. Buckley, *Trade Unionism in Aberdeen, 1878 to 1900* (Edinburgh 1955), p. 123.
32. *Ibid.,* p. 141.
33. C. W. M. Phipps, 'The Aberdeen Trades Council and Politics 1900-1939: The Development of a Local Labour Party in Aberdeen'. (University of Aberdeen, MLitt thesis, 1980), pp. 86-7.
34. Mabel Atkinson, *Local Government in Scotland* (Edinburgh 1904), p. 34.
35. *Ibid.,* pp. 177, 183.
36. Mitchell, 'Municipal Transport', Appendix 8A and Maps 2. 1 to 2. 4; Ross, *Record of Municipal Affairs*, pp. 5-60.
37. William Miller, 'Politics in the Scottish City 1832-1982', in George Gordon,(ed.), *Perspectives of the Scottish City* (Aberdeen 1985), p. 203.
38. Mitchell, 'Municipal Transport', Appendix 8A.
39. Miller, *Politics in the Scottish City*, p. 207.
40. Arthur Midwinter, *The Politics of Local Spending* (Edinburgh 1984), p. 46.

Notes to Chapter 10:
Social Welfare: Poverty and Health by Clive H. Lee

1. BPP, *Report of the Royal Commission on the Poor Laws and Relief of Distress (Scotland)*, Cd 4922, 1909, p. 493.
2. Jean Lindsay, *The Scottish Poor Law: Its Operation in the North-East from 1745 to 1845* (Ilfracombe 1975), p. 50.
3. *Aberdeen Journal*, 25 November 1812.
4. Paul Johnson, *Saving and Spending: The Working-Class Economy in Britain 1870-1939* (Oxford 1985), p. 81; Mary Mackinnon, 'Living Standards 1870-1914', in Roderick Floud and Donald McCloskey (eds), *The Economic History of Britain since 1700: Volume 2: 1860-1939* (Cambridge 1994), pp. 277-8.
5. Lindsay, *The Scottish Poor Law*, pp. 142, 238-9.
6. Alexander A. Cormack, *Poor Relief in Scotland* (Aberdeen 1923), p. 84.
7. T. Ferguson, *Scottish Social Welfare 1864-1914* (Edinburgh 1959), p. 246.
8. BPP, *Royal Commission on the Poor Laws*, pp. 76-7.
9. Cormack, *Poor Relief in Scotland*, pp. 81-2.
10. Lindsay, *The Scottish Poor Law*, pp. 70-1, 76-7.
11. Cormack, *Poor Relief in Scotland*, pp. 89-90.
12. Lindsay, *The Scottish Poor Law*, pp. 232-7.
13. Cormack, *Poor Relief in Scotland*, p. 84.
14. T. Ferguson, *The Dawn of Scottish Social Welfare* (Edinburgh 1948), p. 195.
15. Lindsay, *The Scottish Poor Law*, pp. 167-8.
16. *Aberdeen Journal*, 6 January 1830.
17. Hugh C. Mackenzie, The City of Aberdeen, *Third Statistical Account of Scotland* (Edinburgh 1953), p. 74.
18. Anon, *Aberdeen Savings Bank: Its History from 1815 to 1965* (Aberdeen 1967), p. 6.
19. BPP, *Royal Commission on the Poor Laws*, pp. 492-3.
20. *Ibid.,* pp. 499-500.
21. Anon, *Aberdeen Old People's Welfare Council: The First Twenty Five Years* (Aberdeen 1971), p. 2.
22. *Evening Express*, 26 January 1999.
23. I am very grateful to Mr Dennis Nicol for taking the time to explain the development of the Instant Neighbour charity.
24. I am grateful to Dr David Smith for this information. A research project to undertake a comprehensive study of the epidemic commenced, in 1999, in the Department of History at Aberdeen University under the co-ordination of Dr Smith. The investigation was funded by the Wellcome Trust.
25. Iain Levack and Hugh Dudley, *Aberdeen Royal Informary: The People's Hospital of the North-East* (1992), pp. 12, 25; Cormack, *Poor Relief in Scotland*, p. 177.
26. *Aberdeen Magazine*, March 1831.
27. BPP, *Royal Commission on the Poor Laws*, p. 695.
28. N. J. Logie, 'History of the Aberdeen Joint Hospital Scheme', in George P. Milne (ed.), *Aberdeen Medico-Chirurgical Society: A Bicentennial History 1789-1989* (Aberdeen 1989), pp. 166.
29. *Ibid.,* p. 174.
30. Roy Weir, 'The Medical School and Health Care in the Region', in John D. Hargreaves and Angela Forbes (eds), *Aberdeen University 1945-1981: Regional Roles and National Needs* (Aberdeen 1989), p. 51.
31. Grampian Health Care, *Application for N. H. S. Trust Status* (Aberdeen, 1993).
32. G. A. G. Mitchell, 'The Founder of the Aberdeen School of Anatomy', in George P. Milne (ed.), *Aberdeen Medico-Chirurgical Society: A Bicentennial History 1789-1989* (Aberdeen, 1989), pp. 78-81.
33. Donald J. Withrington, 'The "Mysterious" Road to Union: The Making of the New University of Aberdeen, 1858-60', *Aberdeen University Review*, 190 (1993), pp. 147-8.
34. Weir, 'Medical School and Health Care', p. 55.
35. E. H. B. Rodger, *Aberdeen Doctors at Home and Abroad* (Edinburgh, 1893), pp. 282-5.
36. Fiona Watson, *Westburn Medical Group 1896-1996: A Centenary History* (Aberdeen 1996).

Notes to Chapter 11:
Housing by Nicholas J. Williams

1. The author wishes to acknowledge the assistance of Fred Twine with respect to material on municipal housing in the inter-war period and helpful comments on drafts of this chapter by Judith Cripps
2. W. Robbie, *Aberdeen: its Traditions and History* (Aberdeen 1893), p. 500.
3. H. J. Dyos and D. A. Reeder, 'Slums and Suburbs', in H. J. Dyos and M. Wolff (eds), *The Victorian City* (1973), pp. 359-86.
4. AULSC, MS 2626/2, *Prospectus of the City of Aberdeen Land Association 1874.*
5. AULSC, MS 2626/2, *Memorandum and Articles of Association of the City of Aberdeen Land Association 1874.*
6. AULSC, MS 2626/2, Financial details are derived from the Association's Annual Reports.
7. AULSC, MS 2626/2, *Prospectus.*
8. A. A. MacLaren, 'The Disruption of the Establishment: James Adam and the Aberdeen Clergy', in J. S. Smith and

D. Stevenson (eds), *Aberdeen in the Nineteenth Century* (Aberdeen 1988), pp. 106-20.

9. AULSC, Robert Anderson, Water Works Engineer, *Report on the Sewerage of the City of Aberdeen* (Aberdeen 1865).

10. ACA, L1B/6, *The Aberdeen Police and Waterworks Bill 1862*, Minutes of Evidence to the House of Commons Select Committee on Private Bills.

11. AULSC, *First Annual Report of the Aberdeen Lodging-House Association 1850*.

12. AULSC, *Third Annual Report of the Aberdeen Lodging-House Association 1852*.

13. Details are taken from the Annual Reports of the Aberdeen Association for the Improvement of the Dwellings of the Labouring Classes (AULSC), and the Annual Accounts of the Association (ACA, Accession 13).

14. AULSC, *The Plague is Begun: God's Warning Voice to all Classes on the Cholera* Sermon given by the Reverend David Simpson (Aberdeen 1832).

15. *Monthly Report of the Medical Officer of Health, to the Public Health Committee of the Town Council*, May 1882.

16. *Medical Officer of Health Report*, July 1883.

17. ACA, ML/62 and PA/13, Legal and Parliamentary Papers.

18. *Medical Officer of Health Report*, December 1889 and February 1890.

19. *Medical Officer of Health Report*, July 1894.

20. AULSC, *Aberdeen Town Council Minutes*, 20 August 1894.

21. ACA, PA/15, Legal and Parliamentary Papers.

22. *Annual Report of the Medical Officer of Health*, 1905.

23. AULSC, MS2853, Paper presented by Matthew Hay on the Glasgow Corporation Water and City Improvements Bill 1902.

24. AULSC, *Town Council Minutes*, 3 February 1896.

25. The Corporation Lodging-House was subsequently demolished and the site redeveloped by Langstane Housing Association as permanent housing for 34 single homeless persons, opened in 1994.

26. AULSC, *Town Council Minutes*, 19 June 1893.

27. *Ibid.*, 15 February 1897.

28. *Ibid.*, 15 March 1897.

29. *Medical Officer of Health Report*, 1908.

30. A. Gaffron, *A Patchwork of Memories* (Aberdeen 1985).

31. *Memorandum by the Medical Officer of Health*, 8 October 1917.

32. AULSC, *Town Council Minutes*, 15 October 1917.

33. A capital subsidy to private enterprise was also available under the 1919 Act, but only 63 dwellings were built under this scheme.

34. T. Scott Sutherland, *Life on One Leg* (1957).

35. Forty wooden semi-detached bungalows were built in Smithfield Road under the 1924 Act.

36. AULSC, *Town Council Minutes*, 4 March 1935. Ironically, the only four-storey tenements built by the Council during this period, the Rosemount Square development constructed during the Second World War, was awarded the Diploma for the best designed local authority housing project 1939 to 1947 by the Saltire Society in 1949. Rosemount Square differs from the rest of the 1930s stock, consisting of a continuous façade of tenements on four sides pierced by three archways. It was influenced by social housing developments in Vienna.

37. F. E. Twine and N. J. Williams, 'Social Segregation in Public Sector Housing: A Case Study', *Transactions of the Institute of British Geographers*, 8 (1983), pp. 253-66.

38. Gaffron, *A Patchwork of Memories*.

39. AULSC, *Town Council Minutes*, 16 March 1936.

40. The Jute Works were evacuated in 1940, but the Torry Point Battery was used for housing until 1953 and the Castlehill Barracks until 1961.

41. *Memorandum of Information for Councillors* 1945.

42. *Press and Journal*, 21 August 1946.

43. *Ibid.*, 9 September 1946.

44. Scottish Office Building Directorate, *A Guide to Non-traditional Housing in Scotland* (Edinburgh 1987). The Orlit houses required less skilled labour than a traditionally built dwelling and it was estimated that it required 1,000 man-hours to build the former compared to 2,000 man hours for the latter.

45. J. Sewel, F. E. Twine and N. J. Williams, 'The Sale of Council Houses – Some Empirical Evidence', *Urban Studies* 21 (1984), pp. 439-50.

46. C. Jones and D. Maclennan, 'The Impact of North Sea Oil Development on the Aberdeen Housing Market', *Land Development Studies* 3 (1986), pp 113-26.

Notes to Chapter 12:
Education by Sydney Wood

1. David Masson, *Memories of Two Cities: Edinburgh and Aberdeen* (Edinburgh 1911), p. 234.

2. BPP, XIX, 1841, *Answers made by Schoolmasters in Scotland to queries circulated in 1838 by order of the Select Committee on Education in Scotland*, p. 11.

3. Committee of the Council of the City of Aberdeen on the Town's Public Schools, *Interim Report* (Aberdeen 1834), p. 26.

4. BPP VI, 1867-1868, Schools Inquiry Commission, *General Reports of the Commissioners on Burgh Schools in Scotland*, p. 66.

5. BPP, *Third Report of the Commissioners on Schools in Scotland 1867-68*, p. 113.

6. BPP, *Burgh Schools in Scotland*, p. 65.

7. Committee of the Council, *Interim Report*, pp. 3-6.

8. *Report on the Grammar School and other educational institutions under the patronage of the Town Council of Aberdeen* (Aberdeen 1854), pp. 41-53.

9. *Ibid.*, p. 12.

10. Deed of Mortification, 1729, quoted in Robert Anderson, *The History of Robert Gordon's Hospital Aberdeen, 1769-1881* (1896).

11. BPP, *Commissioners on Schools in Scotland 1867-68*, Appendix, p. 59.

12. Robert Anderson, *The History of Robert Gordon's Hospital 1769-1881* (Aberdeen 1896), p. 61.

13. *Foundations, Statutes and Rules of Robert Gordon's Hospital* (Aberdeen 1823).

14. ACA, *Aberdeen School Returns*, 1833

15. BPP XLII, 1839, *Reports from Inspectors of Factories relating to the Educational Provisions of the Factory Act*, p. 65.

16. *Answers made by schoolmasters*, p. 6.

17. BPP, *First Report from the Commissioners on the Employ-ment of Children and Young Persons in Trade and Manufactures*, Appendix, *Reports and Evidence, Lucifer Match Manufacture*, 13 (1863), p. 100.

18. *Report of the Committee for the Erection of Schools in Bon Accord Parish* (Aberdeen 1839), p. 10.

19. BPP III, 1816, *Report on the minutes of evidence on the state of children employed in the manufactories of the United Kingdom*, pp. 240-3.

20. R. D. Anderson, *Education and the Scottish People 1750-1918* (Oxford 1995), pp. 129-30.

21. BPP Part 2, XX, 1834, *Factory Inquiry Supplementary Report, Employment of Children in Factories*, p. 41.

22. D. Mackinnon, *School Board Directory and Educational Year Book* (Edinburgh 1874).

23. Alexander Thomson, *Industrial Schools, their Origins, Rise and Progress in Aberdeen* (Aberdeen 1847), p. 7.

24. William Watson, *Pauperism, Vagrancy, Crime and Industrial Education in Aberdeenshire* (Aberdeen 1877), p. 43.

25. *Ibid.*, p. 49.

26. R. A. Bayliss, *The Aberdeen School of Domestic Science* (Aberdeen 1979), p. 10; J. Smith, *Mrs Elmslie and her Female Orphan Asylum* (Aberdeen 1882).

27. A. Gordon, *An Address to the Inhabitants of Aberdeen on the Necessity of Establishing Schools especially for the Poorer Classes* (Aberdeen 1831), p. 8.

28. H. M. G. Duncan and G. I. Duthie (eds), *Albyn School Centenary* (Aberdeen 1967), p. 20.

29. *St Margaret's School Chronicle*, Centenary Edition (Aberdeen 1946), p. 4.

30. ACA, GR6S/A65/1/1, *Skene Square School Logbook*, 1864-99, 4 April 1864.

31. A. L. McCombie, *Aberdeen and its First School Board* (Aberdeen, undated).

32. ACA, ASB1/1, *Aberdeen School Board Minutes*, 5 November 1873.

33. *Report of the Committee of Council on Education*, 1891 p. 287.

34. *Deeside Field*, 17 (1935), p. 47.

35. ACA, ASB1/6, *Aberdeen School Board Minutes*, 11 April 1888.

36. ACA, ASB1/14, *Aberdeen School Board Minutes*, 17 March 1898.

37. ACA, ASB1/15, *Aberdeen School Board Minutes*, 19 January 1899.

38. Alexander Walker, *The Aberdeen Educational Trust* (Aberdeen 1898).

39. J. T. C. Scotland, *A History of Aberdeen College of Education*, supplement to *Education in the North*, VI (Aberdeen undated).

40. ACA, ASB1/1, *Aberdeen School Board Minutes*, 10 September 1874.

41. BPP (LXIII 1895), *Minutes of Evidence taken before the Royal Commission on Secondary Education*, p. 297.

42. Anderson, *History of Gordon's Hospital*, pp. 89-95.

43. *The First Report of the Committee of the Aberdeen Mechanics' Institute* (Aberdeen 1824), p. 2.

44. *The Second Report of the Committee of the Aberdeen Mechanics' Institute* (Aberdeen 1825), p. 4.

45. R. B. Strathdee, *Scientia et Opera* (Aberdeen 1971), p. 27.

46. R. D. Anderson, *The Student Community at Aberdeen 1860-1939* (Aberdeen 1988), p. 56.

47. C. Pennington, *The Modernisation of Medical Teaching at Aberdeen in the Nineteenth Century* (Aberdeen 1994).

48. *Ibid.*, p. 56.

49. ACA, ASB1/15, *Aberdeen School Board Minutes*, 16 February 1899.

50. David Newlands, Harmindar Battu, John Finch and Margaret Parker, *The Economic Impact of Aberdeen University on the North East of Scotland* (Mimeo, Aberdeen 1997), p. ii.

Notes to Chapter 13:
Religion by Peter Hillis

1. I would like to thank Dr Sheila Oliver for her assistance in analysing the social status of church members.

2. Sir John Sinclair (ed.), *The Statistical Account of Scotland*, XIV Kincardineshire and South and West Aberdeenshire (Edinburgh, 1796-97), p. 185.

3. BPP, *Census of Great Britain 1851*, Report and Tables on Religious Worship and Education.

4. *Aberdeen Journal*, 18 April 1901.

5. *Report to the General Assembly of the Church of Scotland 1990*.

6. *The Catholic Directory for Scotland*, 1992, p. 479.

7. ACA, CC/1/6, *George Street Congregational Chapel, Deacons' Court Meeting*, 28 September, 1 November 1865.

8. *Aberdeen Journal*, 18 April 1901.

9. A. A. MacLaren, *Religion and Social Class: The Disruption Years in Aberdeen* (1974), p. 215.

10. Peter Brierley and Fergus MacDonald, *Prospects for Scotland* (Edinburgh 1985), p. 70.

11. James Martin, *Eminent Divines of Aberdeen and the North: Their Work and Influence* (Aberdeen 1888), p. 211.

12. MacLaren, *Religion and Social Class*.

13. A. Gammie, *The Churches of Aberdeen* (Aberdeen 1905).

14. *Letter to the Rev. Charles Fraser, officiating priest at the Roman Catholic Chapel, Aberdeen, from the Rev. Joseph Thorburn, Minister of Union Chapel* (Aberdeen 1831).

15. MacLaren, *Religion and Social Class*, pp. 47-8.

16. W. Lindsay, *Some Notes: Personal and Public* (Aberdeen 1898), pp. 105-10.

17. James Cooper, *Disestablishment and Disendowment: Contrary to Holy Scripture* (Aberdeen 1885).

18. The adherents were known as Morrisonians after the Rev. James Morrison who was ejected from the Secession Church in 1844 for believing that all could achieve salvation.

19. *Popery in the Scotch Episcopal Church. An Examination of a Sermon Preached by the Rev. P. Cheyne before the Bishops and Clergy of the Diocese of Aberdeen in Synod Assembled* (Aberdeen, 1844).

20. Canon Gibb N. Pennie, 'The Trial of Patrick Cheyne for erroneous Teaching of the Eucharist in Aberdeen in 1858', *Records of the Scottish Church History Society*, 23 (1987), pp. 77-93.

21. J. H. S. Burleigh, *A Church History of Scotland* (Oxford 1960), p. 387.

22. R. H. Story, *Life and Remains of Robert Lee DD* (1870), pp. 152-70.
23. Douglas M. Murray, 'James Cooper and the East Church Case at Aberdeen, 1882-83: The High Church Movement Vindicated', *Records of the Scottish Church History Society*, 19 (1977), pp. 217-32.
24. He went on to become Professor of Arabic at the University of Cambridge. His successor at the Free Church College was George Adam Smith.
25. Margaret Knight, *Morals without Religion and Other Essays* (1955), pp. 22-3.
26. Callum Brown, *The Social History of Religion in Scotland since 1730* (1987), p. 83.
27. *Aberdeen Journal*, 15 April 1901.
28. *Report of the Schemes of the Church of Scotland*, 1889, 1904.
29. *The Roman Catholic Directory for Scotland*, 1866, 1893, 1894, 1895, 1896.
30. Brierley and MacDonald, *Prospects for Scotland*, p. 132.
31. *Ibid.*, p. 70.
32. *Church of Scotland Year Book*, 1934, 1989.
33. Brown, *Social History of Religion*, p. 85.
34. *Aberdeen Journal*, 15 April 1901
35. *Catholic Directory for Scotland*, 1950. The 1994 figure was provided by Bishop Mario Conti.
36. Brierley and MacDonald, *Prospects for Scotland*, p. 9.
37. Figures provided by Bishop Mario Conti.
38. Brierley and MacDonald, *Prospects for Scotland*, p. 132.
39. Figures provided by the Baptist Union of Scotland.
40. Brierley and MacDonald, *Prospects for Scotland*, p 132.
41. *Press and Journal*, 6 November 1978.
42. *Evening Express*, 7 November 1995.
43. Brown, *Social History of Religion*, pp. 210-12, 218.
44. *Report of the Committee on Moral Welfare to the General Assembly of the Church of Scotland*, 1970, p. 397.
45. Brierley and MacDonald, *Prospects for Scotland*, p. 22.
46. *Report of the Committee on Parish Education to the General Assembly of the Church of Scotland*, 1980, pp. 389-96.
47. Brown, *Social History of Religion*, p. 80.
48. NAS, CH3/874/6, Bon-Accord Free Church, Kirk Session Meeting, 19 January 1844.
49. NAS, CH2/777/46, Woodside Parish Church, Kirk Session Meeting, 5 April 1875.
50. William Mair, *A Digest of Church Laws and Decisions* (4th edn, Edinburgh 1923), p. 89.
51. *Cathedral of St Mary of the Assumption, Souvenir Brochure* (1863), p. 7.
52. MacLaren, *Religion and Social Class*, pp. 69-144; *Aberdeen Monthly Circular*, July 1840.
53. ACA, CC/1/6, Deacon's Court Minutes, George Street Congregational Chapel, 9 April 1866.
54. St Margaret's Church Confirmation Roll, 1871-1913. (Records held by Church).
55. St Margaret's Church Baptismal Register, 1867-1884.
56. St John's Scottish Episcopal Church Baptismal Register, 1778-1855.
57. Brown, *Religion and Social Class*, p. 130.
58. NAS, CH3/488/8, South Free Church, Kirk Session Meeting, 30 June 1844.
59. ACA, CC/5/1, Blackfriars Congregational Chapel, Minute Book, 2 October 1844.
60. Ronald Leith, 'The Membership Role of Frederick Street Congregational Chapel 1807-1859', *Aberdeen and North-East Scotland Family History Society* (1986), p. 1.
61. NAS, South Free Church, Kirk Session Meeting, 21 April 1844.
62. NAS, CH3/874/6, Bon-Accord Free Church, Deacons' Court Minutes, 5 March 1847.
63. *Ibid*, 5 July 1848.
64. ACA, CC/2/7, St Paul's Congregational Chapel, Managers' Minute Book, 25 November 1895.
65. Clive Field, 'Adam and Eve: Gender in the English Free Church Constituency', *Journal of Ecclesiastical History*, 44 (1993).

Notes to Chapter 14:
Elite Society by I. G. C. Hutchison

1. BPP. VI. 1819, *Report of Select Committee on Petitions . . . from Royal Burghs of Scotland*, p. 21.
2. *Ibid.*, pp. 21-7.
3. A. W. Johnstone, *A Short Memoir of James Young, Merchant Burgess of Aberdeen, and Rachel Cruickshank, his Spouse, and of their Descendants* (Aberdeen, not dated but c. 1860).
4. R. G. Thorne (ed.), *The History of Parliament. The House of Commons, 1790-1820*, II (1986), pp. 590-2; III (1986), pp. 61-2, 727-9.
5. R. Tyzack, '"No Mean City"? The Growth of Civic Consciousness in Aberdeen with particular reference to the Work of the Police Commissioners', in T. Brotherstone and D. J. Withrington (eds), *The City and its Worlds. Aspects of Aberdeen's History since 1794* (Glasgow, 1996), pp. 150-67.
6. A. A. MacLaren, *Religion and Social Class. The Disruption Years in Aberdeen* (1974), pp. 69-99, 218-20.
7. L. I. Lumsden, *Memories of Aberdeen a Hundred Years Ago* (Aberdeen 1927), pp. 16-17.
8. *Ibid.*, pp. 3-4; S. Burnett, *Without Fanfare* (Kemnay, 1994), pp. 174-5.
9. Aberdeen Central Reference Library, Sir A. Bannerman Diaries [typescript extracts], 3 February and 10 February 1836; Lumsden, *Memories of Aberdeen*, pp. 19-20.
10. Burnett, *Without Fanfare*, pp. 174-5; Lumsden, *Memories of Aberdeen*, pp. 19-20.
11. Bannerman Diaries, 22 March 1835, 24 October 1834.
12. Lumsden, *Memories of Aberdeen*, pp. 19-20.
13. A. S. Cook, *Aberdeen Amusements Seventy Years Ago* (Aberdeen 1911), p. 18.
14. W. Carnie, *Additional Aberdeen Reminiscences* (Aberdeen 1906), p. 71.
15. W. G. Blaikie, *An Autobiography. Recollections of a Busy Life* (1901), p. 49.
16. *Ibid.*, pp. 20-1.
17. *Ibid.*
18. Aberdeen Central Reference Library, Memoirs by John Morgan, Builder (typescript, c. 1902), pp. 165-6.
19. *Ibid.*, pp. 171-2.
20. *Aberdeen Almanac* (annual); Post Office, *Aberdeen directories* (annual).
21. G. S. Fraser, *A Stranger and Afraid. The Autobiography of an Intellectual* (Manchester 1983), pp. 37-8.

22. A. Shewan, *Spirat Adhuc Amor. Records of the Gym (Chanonry House School), Old Aberdeen* (Aberdeen 1923) lists all the pupils. Shewan was himself an Aberdeen lawyer.
23. The material for this and the succeeding paragraph is derived from: J. A. Henderson, *History of the Society of Advocates in Aberdeen* (New Spalding Club, Aberdeen 1912), and *A Supplemental History of the Society of Advocates in Aberdeen, 1912-1938* (Third Spalding Club, Aberdeen 1939). Only those advocates who participated in the public life of the city are included in this survey.
24. All the data in this paragraph is derived from: R. Brittan, 'Wealthy Scots, 1876-1913', *Bulletin of the Institute of Historical Research*, 58 (1985), pp. 78-94. The Aberdonians were: Alex. Pirie, papermaker (1876), £169,393; J. Crombie, textile manufacturer (1894), £253,262; John Fyfe, granite manufacturer (1906), £253,272.
25. NAS, *Calendar of Confirmations 1890-1930*.
26. Anon, *The Duthie Park. A Descriptive and Historical Sketch* (Aberdeen 1883), pp. 3-5, 103ff.
27. L. McKinnon, *Recollections of an Old Lawyer* (Aberdeen 1935), pp. 66-70; J. Teissier du Cros, *Cross Currents. A Childhood in Scotland* (East Linton, 1997), pp. 21-5.
28. Lord Cockburn, *Circuit Journeys* (2nd edn, Edinburgh 1889), p. 140. McKinnon, *Recollections*, p. 66.
29. du Cros, *Cross Currents*, pp. 26, 65.
30. NAS, CH3/821/4, Aberdeen Free West Church, Kirk Session Minute Book, 5 December 1889, 12 December 1889, 5 January 1890.
31. C. Carter, *Alexander Mcdonald, 1837-84. Aberdeen Art Collector* (undated), pp. 5-8.
32. I. M. Harrower, *John Forbes White* (Edinburgh 1918), pp. 55-71. White was forbidden, as a child in the 1840s, to venture anywhere near the local theatres.
33. Sir J. Fleming, *Looking Backwards for Seventy Years, 1921-1851* (Aberdeen 1922), pp. 364-9. He made eighteen tours abroad between 1875 and 1920.
34. Memoirs by John Morgan, pp. 98, 151, 246-56.
35. *Ibid.*, p. 202.
36. T. Scott Sutherland, *Life on One Leg* (1957), pp. 158-60.
37. Memoirs by John Morgan, p. 231.
38. J. A. G. Mearns, *Two Hundred Years of Golf, 1780-1980. The Royal Aberdeen Golf Club* (Aberdeen 1980), pp. 12-15.
39. *Northern Cricket Annual* (1889), p. 8.
40. *Ibid.*
41. W. Carnie, *Further Reporting Reminiscences* (Aberdeen 1904), pp. 311-12.
42. Scott Sutherland, *Life on One Leg*, p. 136.
43. *Aberdeen Almanac*, 186, p. 249.
44. *Aberdeen Chamber of Commerce*, Annual Reports. I am grateful to Dr R. Perren for making these available to me.
45. Memoirs by John Morgan, pp. 77-8.
46. *The Book of the Masonic Craft. The Masonic Bazaar, Aberdeen, 8 & 9 October, 1896* (Aberdeen 1896) gives a full list of the committee.
47. J. A. Parker, *Roll of Lodge of Aberdeen No. 1* (Aberdeen 1929).
48. *The Leopard*, October-November 1985.
49. *Aberdeen Journal*, 25 February 1863, 11 March 1863.
50. *Ibid.*, 4 February 1863; Carnie, *Further Reporting Reminiscences*, p. 364.

51. *Bon-Accord*, 8 September 1938.
52. L. A. Smith, *George Adam Smith. A Personal Memoir and Chronicle* (1904), p. 41.
53. *Ibid.*, pp. 42-4; A. M. Stoddart, *John Stuart Blackie* (Edinburgh 1895), p. 222; du Cros, *Cross Currents*, pp. 34-5.
54. Smith, *George Adam Smith*, p. 228.
55. J. R. Allan, *Crombies of Grandholm and Crothal, 1805-1960. Records of an Aberdeenshire Enterprise* (Aberdeen 1960), pp. 5-6; J. Fedo, *Mill on the Don. The Story of the Donside Paper Company* (Aberdeen 1993), pp. 19-21, 46-9.
56. *The Leopard*, February 1985.
57. *Aberdeen Savings Bank*, pp. 63-71.
58. *Aberdeen Bon Accord & Northern Pictorial*, 26 April 1945
59. Mearns, *Two Hundred Years of Golf*, pp. 19 ff
60. Aberdeen, Royal Northern and University Club, Aberdeen University Club MSS, Annual Report (1975); Royal Northern Club MSS, Membership List (1975).
61. G. F. Collie, *Society of Advocates in Aberdeen. Some Notes on the Recent History of the Society* (Aberdeen 1983), pp. 5-6, 11.
62. *Aberdeen Almanac* and Post Office, *Aberdeen Directory*, 1860 and 1937-38); Aberdeen Central Agency. Appeal on Behalf of Charitable Organisations (1937).

Notes to Chapter 15: Leisure and Culture: The Nineteenth Century by Irene Maver

1. I am most grateful to Mairianna Birkeland and Mhairi Dewar for invaluable help in researching this and the following chapter. I must also express thanks to Hamish Fraser for his constructive comments and for pointing me in the direction of that formidable Victorian anti-dancing divine, the Rev. Alexander M. Bannatyne.
2. Walter Thom, *The History of Aberdeen: Containing an Account of the Rise, Progress and Extension of the City*, II (Aberdeen 1811), p. 28.
3. *Ibid.*, p. 48; Iain Beavan, 'All New Works of Interest Received on Publication: Aberdeen and its Access to the Printed Word 1800-1850', in Terry Brotherstone and Donald J. Withrington (eds), *The City and its Worlds: Aspects of Aberdeen's History since 1794* (Glasgow, 1996), pp. 95-6.
4. Miles Glendinning, Ranald Macinnes and Aonghus MacKechnie, *A History of Scottish Architecture from the Renaissance to the Present Day* (Edinburgh 1996), p. 215.
5. Lewis Smith (publisher), *A Guide to Aberdeen with Illustrations and a Plan of the City* (Aberdeen 1850), pp. 5-6.
6. An early example is W. Bannerman, *The Aberdeen Worthies: or Sketches of Characters Resident in Aberdeen during the End of the Last and the Beginning of the Present Century* (Aberdeen 1840). See also Donald J. Withrington, 'Aberdeen as Place and Community', in Brotherstone and Withrington, *The City and its Worlds*, p. 5.
7. James Riddell, *Aberdeen and its Folk from the Twentieth to the Fiftieth Year of the Present Century by a Son of Bon-Accord in North America* (Aberdeen 1868), pp. iii, 129-32.
8. W. Hamish Fraser, 'Developments in Leisure', in W. H. Fraser and R. J. Morris (eds), *People and Society in Scotland*, II (Edinburgh 1990), p. 240.

9. William Carnie, *Reporting Reminiscences* (Aberdeen 1902), pp. 169-70.
10. Robert Murdoch Lawrence, *The 'Lemon Tree' Hostess and Aberdeen Tavern Lore* (Aberdeen 1927); George Walker, *Aberdeen Awa': Sketches of its Men, Manners and Customs as Delineated in Brown's Bookstall 1892-94* (Aberdeen 1897), pp. 285-6.
11. *The New Statistical Account of Scotland*, XII Aberdeen (Edinburgh 1845), p. 102.
12. Joseph Robertson, *The Book of Bon-Accord: or A Guide to the City of Aberdeen* (Aberdeen 1839), pp. 6-7.
13. *Ibid.* ; advert in the *Aberdeen Teetotaller and North of Scotland Abstinence Advocate,* May 1839.
14. William Kennedy, *Annals of Aberdeen from the Reign of King William the Lion to the End of the Year 1818*, II (1818), p. 283.
15. Patrick Morgan, *Annals of Woodside and Newhills: Historical and Genealogical* (Aberdeen 1886), pp. 11, 34-5.
16. Victoria E. Clark, *The Port of Aberdeen: A History of its Trade and Shipping from the Twelfth Century to the Present* (Aberdeen 1921), pp. 136-40.
17. *Bon-Accord*, 26 January 1896; William Cay and Sons (publisher), *In Memoriam: An Obituary of Aberdeen and Vicinity for the Year 1904* (Aberdeen 1904), pp. 12-17.
18. *Aberdeen Teetotaller*, May 1839.
19. Rev. R. G. Mason, *Northern Temperance Record and Aberdeen Abstinence Advocate*, March 1841, November 1842.
20. *Ibid.,* February 1841.
21. A. S. Cook, *Pen Sketches and Reminiscences of Sixty Years* (Aberdeen 1901), p. 170.
22. *Northern Temperance Record*, September 1842.
23. R. M. W. Cowan, *The Newspaper in Scotland: A Study of its First Expansion 1815-1860* (Glasgow, 1946), pp. 126-7.
24. William Buchanan, *Glimpses of Olden Days in Aberdeen: Being Sketches from Memory and Incidents and Characters in and about Aberdeen during the Last Fifty Years* (Aberdeen 1870), pp. 23-4.
25. William Lindsay, *Some Notes, Personal and Public* (Aberdeen 1898), pp. 227-8.
26. James H. Wilson, *Bon-Accord Repository of Local Institutions* (Aberdeen 1842), pp. 188-91; G. M. Fraser, *Aberdeen Mechanics' Institute: A Record of Civic and Educational Progress* (Aberdeen 1912), p. 15.
27. *Aberdeen Journal*, 7 July 1800.
28. *Bon-Accord Repository*, p. 191; Kennedy, *Annals of Aberdeen*, II, p. 168.
29. *Aberdeen Awa'*, pp. 9-10; Beavan, 'All New Works . . . ', pp. 95-6.
30. *Aberdeen Journal*, 24 February 1800.
31. Henry George Farmer, *A History of Music in Scotland* (1947), pp. 312-16; Thom, *History of Aberdeen*, pp. 199-203.
32. *Aberdeen Journal*, 20 October 1800; George S. Emmerson, *A Social History of Scottish Dance: Ane Celestial Recreation* (Montreal, 1972), pp. 117-18, 160.
33. Aberdeen City Reference Library, Summary of a Diary of Sir Alexander Bannerman (not dated), p. 11.
34. Alexander M. Bannatyne, *Dancing: A Sermon* (Aberdeen 1885), p. 21; Alexander Gammie, *Churches of Aberdeen, Historical and Descriptive* (Aberdeen 1909), p. 224.
35. *Bon-Accord*, 25 March 1894.

36. William Carnie, *Psalmody in Scotland: A Lecture Delivered to the Aberdeen Young Men's Literary Union and Early Closing Association* (Aberdeen 1854), pp. 3,16.
37. Alexander M. Bannatyne, *Hearts and Voices, the Only Organs for Christian Praises* (Edinburgh 1865), pp. 9-14; Walker, *Aberdeen Awa'*, p. 221.
38. *Aberdeen Journal*, 15 October 1856.
39. Jim Pratt, *The Music Hall: A Short History* (Aberdeen 1993), pp. 6-7.
40. Carnie, *Reporting Reminiscences*, p. 363.
41. *Ibid.,* p. 239.
42. *Bon-Accord*, 8 December 1894.
43. Carnie, *Reporting Reminiscences*, pp. 299-301; James H. Littlejohn, *Aberdeen Tivoli* (Dyce, 1986), pp. 30-2.
44. Kennedy, *Annals of Aberdeen*, I, pp. 89-94; Robb Lawson, *The Story of the Scots Stage* (Paisley, 1917), pp. 39-62; Donald Campbell, *Playing for Scotland: a History of the Scottish Stage 1715-1965* (Edinburgh 1996), p. 58.
45. J. Keith Angus, *A Scotch Play-House being the Historical Records of the Old Theatre Royal, Marischal Street, Aberdeen* (Aberdeen 1878), pp. 21-6.
46. A. S. Cook, *Aberdeen Amusements Seventy Years Ago* (Aberdeen 1911), p. 7.
47. Constance Pole Bayer, *The Great Wizard of the North: John Henry Anderson* (Watertown, 1990), pp. 11-12.
48. Peter Paterson, *Glimpses of Real Life as seen in the Theatrical World and in Bohemia: being the Confessions of Peter Paterson, a Strolling Comedian* (Edinburgh 1868), p. 80.
49. *Bon-Accord*, 14 May 1887.
50. Angus, *A Scotch Play-House*, p. 26.
51. Littlejohn, *Aberdeen Tivoli*, pp. 7-11.
52. William Robbie, *Aberdeen, its Traditions and History, with Notices of Some Eminent Aberdonians* (Aberdeen 1893), pp. 451-2.
53. Aberdeen Free Press (publisher), *The Duthie Park: A Descriptive and Historical Sketch* (Aberdeen 1883), pp. 41-82.
54. Andrew Gibbons Williams and Andrew Brown, *The Bigger Picture: A History of Scottish Art* (1993), pp. 102-6; Robbie, *Aberdeen, Traditions and History*, pp. 482-3.
55. Roger Taylor, *George Washington Wilson: Artist and Photographer 1823-93* (Aberdeen 1981), p. 11.
56. Charles Smith, *The Aberdeen Golfers: Records and Reminiscences* (1909), p. 43.
57. J. Fairfax-Blakeborough, *Northern Turf History, IV: History of Horse-Racing in Scotland* (Whitby 1973), pp. 302-7.
58. N. L. Tranter, 'Organised Sport and the Working Classes of Central Scotland 1820-1900: The Neglected Sport of Quoiting', in Richard Holt (ed.), *Sport and the Working Classes in Modern Britain* (Manchester 1990), pp. 45-66.
59. *Bon-Accord*, 21 April 1896.
60. Aberdeenshire Cricket Club (publisher), *Aberdeenshire Cricket Club: A Historical Survey* (Aberdeen 1983), pp. 2-3.
61. *Aberdeen Golfers*, pp. 43-4.
62. *Bon-Accord*, 6 November 1886.
63. *Ibid.,* 6 October 1894.
64. Katherine E. Trail, *Reminiscences of Old Aberdeen* (Aberdeen 1932), p. 78.
65. See adverts in *Bon-Accord*, 13 April 1895 and 18 June 1896.
66. *Ibid.,* 13 March 1895 and 1 June 1895.
67. Donald Sinclair, *The History of the Aberdeen Volunteers,*

embracing also some Account of the Volunteers of the Counties of Aberdeen, Banff and Kincardine (Aberdeen 1907), pp. 160-3.

Notes to Chapter 16: Leisure and Culture: The Twentieth Century by Irene Maver

1. William Kennedy, *Annals of Aberdeen from the Reign of William the Lion to the End of the Year 1818*, II (1818), pp. 285-6.
2. John K. Walton, 'Municipal Government and the Holiday Industry in Blackpool 1876-1914', in John K. Walton and James Walvin (eds), *Leisure in Britain 1780-1939* (Manchester 1983), pp. 159-86.
3. *Aberdeen Town Council Minutes*, 2 January 1894.
4. *Bon-Accord*, 9 April 1896.
5. Aberdeen Corporation, *The Silver City by the Sea* (Aberdeen 1899), p. 6.
6. William Carnie, *Reporting Reminiscences* (Aberdeen 1902), p. 53.
7. Henry Munro (publisher), *Aberdeen Today: A Record of the Life, Thought and Industry of the City Forming the Majority Number of Bon-Accord 1886-1907* (Aberdeen 1907), pp. 28-31.
8. *Bon-Accord*, 3 July 1902.
9. *Press and Journal*, 3 May 1928.
10. *Ibid.*, 4 May 1929.
11. *Town Council Minutes*, 9 January 1929.
12. Michael Thomson, *Silver Screen in the Silver City: A History of Cinemas in Aberdeen 1896-1987* (Aberdeen 1988), p. 34.
13. Janet McBain, *Pictures Past: Recollections of Scottish Cinemas and Cinema-Going* (Edinburgh 1985), pp. 1-2.
14. Thomson, *Silver Screen*, pp. 34-7.
15. *Bon-Accord*, 25 June 1913.
16. Griselda Sarah McGregor, *Grit, Growth and Sometimes Groovy: Aberdeen in the '60s* (Aberdeen 1990), p. 3.
17. Callum G. Brown, 'Popular Culture and the Continuing Struggle for Rational Recreation', in T. M. Devine and R. J. Finlay (eds), *Scotland in the Twentieth Century* (Edinburgh 1996), p. 219.
18. Ethel Kilgour quoted in T. C. Smout and Sydney Wood, *Scottish Voices 1745-1960* (1991), p. 193.
19. Thomson, *Silver Screen*, p. 233.
20. J. R. Allan, 'The North-East: The Cold Shoulder of Scotland', in George Scott-Moncreiff (ed.), *Scottish Country: Fifteen Essays by Scottish Authors* (Edinburgh 1935), p. 12.
21. Forsyth Hardy, *Scotland in Film* (Edinburgh 1990), pp. 31-2.
22. H. V. Morton, *In Scotland Again* (1933), p. 330.
23. David Hutchison, '1900 to 1950', in Bill Findlay (ed.), *A History of Scottish Theatre* (Edinburgh 1998), p. 207.
24. J. H. Littlejohn, *The Scottish Music Hall 1880-1990* (Wigtown 1990), p. 87.
25. Edward Holmes, 'The Electric Wizard of the North' in *The Book of the Braemar Gathering* (1971), pp. 149-57; Jim Pratt, 'Dr Who? The Amazing Stage Career of Walford Bodie MD (Merry Devil)' in *The Leopard*, March 1990; J. H. Littlejohn, *Aberdeen Tivoli* (Dyce 1986), pp. 30-2.
26. *Bon-Accord*, 18 and 25 February, 3 and 17 March 1904.
27. John Malcolm Bullock, *The Playhouse of Bon-Accord Being a Short Survey of the Actors' Art in the City of Aberdeen from Forgotten Times to the Erection of His Majesty's Theatre* (Aberdeen 1906), pp. 27-8.
28. Elizabeth Adair, 'The Story of His Majesty's Theatre', *The Leopard*, July/August 1977, pp. 7-8.
29. *Press and Journal*, 9 October 1931.
30. Campbell Anderson, 'The Story of His Majesty's Theatre: The Donald Dynasty', *The Leopard*, October 1977, pp. 7-8.
31. *Bon-Accord*, 19 July 1951.
32. *Press and Journal*, 12 September 1962.
33. Jim Pratt, *The Music Hall: A Short History* (Aberdeen 1993), p. 8.
34. D. L. LeMahieu, 'John Reith 1889-1971: An Entrepreneur of Collectivism', in Susan Pedersen and Peter Mandler (eds), *After the Victorians: Private Conscience and Public Duty in Modern Britain* (1994), p. 189.
35. W. H. McDowell, *The History of BBC Broadcasting in Scotland 1923-1983* (Edinburgh 1992), pp. 15-16.
36. Howard Lockhart, *On My Wavelength* (Aberdeen 1973), p. 29.
37. Iain Watson, *Harry Gordon: The Laird of Inversnecky* (Aberdeen 1993), pp. 58-9.
38. McDowell, *BBC Broadcasting*, p. 17.
39. Bill Aitkenhead, 'NorthSound, the North-East's New Independent Radio Station', *Aberdeen Chamber of Commerce Journal*, 62 (1981), pp. 310-11.
40. Jane Ancona, 'Golden Anniversary: 50 Years of the BBC at Beechgrove', *The Leopard*, July 1989, p. 23.
41. Bernard Sendall, *Independent Television in Britain II Expansion and Change 1958-1968* (1983), p. 60.
42. Magnus Linklater, 'The Media', in Magnus Linklater and Robin Dennison (eds), *Anatomy of Scotland: How Scotland Works* (Edinburgh 1992), p. 137.
43. *Evening Express*, 29 September 1961.
44. *Press and Journal*, 31 October 1961.
45. *Evening Express*, 30 September 1971.
46. Andrew Davidson, *Under the Hammer: The Inside Story of the 1991 ITV Franchise Battle* (1992), p. 174.
47. *Aberdeen Journal*, 14 July 1898.
48. J. F. Anderson, *21 Years of the 1st Aberdeen Company of the Boys' Brigade* (Aberdeen 1907), p. 146.
49. *Bon-Accord*, 2 June 1933.
50. W. Dobson Chapman and Charles F. Riley, *Granite City: A Plan for Aberdeen* (1952), p. 91.
51. Aberdeen Corporation, *The Royal Burgh and City of Aberdeen* (Aberdeen 1934), pp. 7-8.
52. *Press and Journal*, 4 July 1927.
53. Hugh C. Mackenzie, The City of Aberdeen, *Third Statistical Account of Scotland* (Edinburgh 1953), pp. 569-70.
54. *Bon-Accord*, 18 December 1902.
55. *Ibid.*, 26 March and 23 April 1903.
56. Jack Webster, *The Dons: A History of Aberdeen Football Club* (1990), p. 13.
57. Allan, *Cold Shoulder of Scotland*, p. 11.
58. Bob Crampsey, *The Scottish Football League: The First Hundred Years* (Glasgow, 1990), p. 128.
59. *TSA*, p. 558.
60. Roddy Forsyth, *The Only Game: The Scots and World Football* (Edinburgh 1990), p. 128.

61. Alex Ferguson, *A Light in the North: Seven Years with Aberdeen* (Edinburgh 1985), p. 91.
62. *Bon-Accord*, 6 March 1950.
63. Hardy, *Scotland in Film*, p. 109.
64. *Bon-Accord*, 25 July 1957.
65. *Press and Journal*, 14 July 1962.
66. Buff Hardie, Stephen Robertson and George Donald, *Scotland the What? Collected Sketches and Songs* (Edinburgh 1987), p. 35.
67. *Evening Express*, 7 July 1975.
68. *Stage and Television Today*, 18 November 1981.
69. *Glasgow Evening Times*, 1 October 1998.
70. *Evening Express*, 15 March 1997.
71. *Aberdeen Chamber of Commerce Journal*, 63 (1982), p. 438.

Notes to Chapter 17:
The Press by W. Hamish Fraser

1. Anyone working on the press in Aberdeen has the advantage of the pioneering work undertaken by the journalist and antiquarian John Malcolm Bulloch, published in *Scottish Notes and Queries*, a journal edited by his father. He also collected newspaper cuttings which are available in the Aberdeen University Special Collections. In addition there is the invaluable *Waterloo Directory of Scottish Newspapers and Periodicals 1800-1900* (Waterloo 1989).
2. Iain Beavan, 'All New Works of Interest Received on Publication', in T. Brotherstone and D. J. Withrington (eds), *The City and its Worlds: Aspects of Aberdeen's History since 1794* (Glasgow, 1996), pp. 95-6.
3. R. M. W. Cowan, *The Newspaper in Scotland: A Study of its First Expansion* (Glasgow, 1946), pp. 19, 47.
4. *The Intruder*, 22 October 1802.
5. *Scottish Notes and Queries*, 1 (1888), p. 21.
6. The first meeting of theTotal Abstinence Society was 20 November 1838. *Aberdeen New Shaver*, VI, December 1838.
7. Alexander Walker, *The Selected Writings of John Ramsay M.A.* (Aberdeen 1871).
8. John Booth was the main shareholder. Others included James Nicol, Alexander Jopp, John Angus, William Allardyce and several members of the Blaikie family.
9. AULSC, Herald - King Collection, 1842.
10. Cowan, *The Newpaper in Scotland*, p. 149.
11. The *Journal* was edited from 1834 to 1848 by John Ramsay who had been the private secretary to Joseph Hume M.P.
12. It may have been absorbed into the Glasgow paper, the *Scottish Patriot*.
13. *Scottish Notes and Queries*, IV (1890).
14. The Spalding Club was founded in 1839 to publish historical records of North-East Scotland.
15. A. S. Cook, *Pen Sketches and Reminiscences of Sixty Years* (Aberdeen 1901), p. 15.
16. I am grateful to Dr Allan MacLaren for information on Adam's attitudes.
17. *Daily Free Press*, 7 February 1885.
18. Garden A. Duff of Hatton Castle served as chairman of the Board of Directors between 1884-1933.
19. William Donaldson, *Popular Literature in Victorian Scotland: Language, Fiction and the Press* (Aberdeen 1986), pp. 9-10.
20. 'Aberdeen' was dropped from the title in 1899.
21. Harry Dunn, 'The Bon-Accord and Northern Pictorial', *The Leopard*, 39 (1978), pp. 6-8.
22. A. F. Murison, *Memories of 88 Years* (Aberdeen 1935).
23. *Bon-Accord*, 'Aberdeen Today', 1907.
24. Miriam J. Benkowitz, *Frederick Rolfe: Baron Corvo* (1977), pp. 60-70.
25. *Press and Journal*, 22 May 1947.
26. AULSC, MS2770.
27. S. Koss, *The Rise and Fall of the Political Press in Britain* (1990), p. 1099.
28. Norman Harper, *First Daily: A 250-Year Celebration of the Press and Journal* (Aberdeen 1997).
29. *Ibid.*, pp. 144-8; Jack Page (ed.), *Strike!* (Aberdeen 1990).

Notes to Chapter 18:
Villages and Suburbs by John S. Smith

1. *The New Statistical Account of Scotland*, XII Aberdeen (Edinburgh 1845), p. 1075.
2. Post Office, *Aberdeen Street Directory*.
3. Henry Hamilton, *Aberdeenshire, Third Statistical Account of Scotland* (Glasgow, 1960), pp. 111-12.
4. *NSA*, p. 112
5. *Ibid.*
6. *TSAC*, p. 171.
7. *Ibid.*, p. 167.
8. James D. Ferguson, *The Story of Aberdeen Airport 1934-1984* (Glasgow 1984).

Index of Names

(*biog*): principal biographical details

Abercrombie, Charles (architect), 22
Aberdeen, Lady, 58, 392
Aberdeen, Lord (landowner) 302, 391-2, 415, 454, 456-7
Adam of Denmore (landowner), 391
Adam, Brian (town councillor), 227, 230
Adam, James (newspaper editor), 81, 180, 182-4, 399, 450-2, 454-5
Adam, Thomas (shipowner), 380
Adam, William (lawyer), 81
Adams, Gordon C. (town councillor), 224
Affleck, Mrs Susie (innkeeper), 400, 406, 450
Albert, Prince Consort, 415
Alexander, Henry (journalist), 457, 460
Alexander, Prov. Sir Henry (newspaper editor/town councillor), (*biog*) 461
Alexander, William (author/journalist), 186, 453, (*biog*) 455, 456-7, 461
Alexander, William McCombie (newspaper editor), 460
Allan, Charlie (farmer/journalist), 465
Allan, Rev. John, 451
Allan, John R. (writer), 10, 429, 439, 443
Allan, Susan, 465
Allardyce, Alexander (MP), 176, 201, 375
Anderson, Chris (football club director), 440-2
Anderson, John (publisher), 450
Anderson, John Henry (illusionist), 409-11, 430
Anderson, Robert (water engineer), 299
Anderson, Prov. Sir Alexander (businessman/town councillor), 10, (*biog*) 32, 33, 81, 183, 187, 244-5, 280, 298, 378, 414
Annand, J. W. (trade unionist), 173
Archibald, G. (Labour candidate), 210
Arthur, Robert (theatrical impressario), 270, 431-2
Asquith, H. H. (MP), 198, 208

Bagehot, Walter (writer), 458
Bain, Prof Alexander (professor of logic), 341, 392
Bain, William (bus company owner), 40

Baird, Prof. Sir Dugald (professor of medicine), 54, (*biog*) 55, 56, 72
Baird, James (industrialist), 456
Baird, Lady Matilda (doctor/town councillor), (*biog*) 55, 291
Balmanno, Robert (businessman), 478
Bannatyne, Rev. Alexander M., 407-8, 416, 421, 457
Bannerman, Alexander (landowner), 391
Bannerman, Sir Alexander (MP), 177-8, (*biog*) 179, 182-3, 201, 289, 376, 386, 393, 406, 451
Bannerman, Patrick (lawyer), 357
Bannerman, Thomas (shipowner), 376, 451
Barclay, James William (MP), 34, 185, 201, 245, (*biog*) 246, 394, 453
Barrie, Maltman (politican), 194, 197, 202
Barry, William (porter), 371
Begg, Miss Anne (MP), 227, 393
Bell, Dr Andrew (educationalist), 328-9, 332
Berkeley, R. C. (Liberal candidate), 212
Berry, Gomer (newspaper proprietor), 462
Betjeman, Sir John (poet), 16, 26
Beveridge, Dr A. T. G. (town councillor), 195
Bisset, George (trade unionist), 174, 192
Bisset, J. G. (builder), 387
Blaikie, James (lawyer/landowner), 378, 391
Blaikie, John (lawyer), 33
Blaikie, Prov. Sir Thomas (industrialist/town councillor), 43, 183, 244, 378, 383
Blaikie, W. G. (writer), 377
Black, Mrs Jeannie (town councillor), 396
Black, Professor (academic), 332
Bodie, Dr Walford (illusionist), 410, 430
Bond, Stephen (businessman), 143
Booth, John Bailie (newspaper proprietor), 448
Boothby, Robert (MP), 212
Bough, Sam (artist), 414
Boyd Orr, Lord John (scientist), 54, 72, (*biog*) 347

Boyle, John (paper manufacturer), 485
Bramley, Frederick (MP), 197-8, 203
Brebner, Prov. Alexander (cotton manufacturer/town councillor), 374-5
Bremner, Alexander (head of Demonstration School), 339
Brewster, Rev Patrick, 182
Brown, Prov. Alexander (bookseller/town councillor), 374, 398, 405, 448
Brown, Robert (writer), 450
Bruce, James (writer), 450-1
Bruce, John (newspaper owner), 460
Bruce, Robert (newspaper owner), 460, 462
Bruce, Robert the, 473
Bryce, James (MP), 190, 193, 195, 197, 200, 202-3, 394, 436-7, 460
Buchanan, James (television producer), 435
Buchanan, William (member, phrenological society), 404-5
Bulloch, J. M. (writer), 331, 450, 457
Burgess, Miss Isabella (teacher/town councillor), 396
Burnett, John George (estate owner), 33, 213, 393
Burnett, W. K. (lawyer), 388
Burnett, Lady, of Kemnay, 376
Burns, Robert (poet), 401, 472
Butchart, Henry J. (lawyer/university adminstrator), (*biog*) 479
Butchart, James (lawyer), 186

Cadenhead, G. (lawyer), 388
Cadenhead, William (wine merchant), 402, 416, 437
Cairns, Miss Alison, 396
Calder, Robert (cinematographer), 426
Cameron, 'Ma' (publican), 388
Cant, John (tanner), 179
Carnegie, Andrew (industrialist/philanthropist), 389
Carnegie, Sir James (MP), 177-8, 201
Carnie, William (journalist/musician), 399, 404, 407-9, 419, 453, (*biog*) 454

Carry, William (jeweller), 118
Cassie, Miss H. (lawyer), 396
Catto, Alexander (trade unionist), 460
Catto, George (trade unionist), 213
Chalmers, David (newspaper proprietor), 187, 448, 451
Chalmers, James (newspaper proprietor), 448
Chalmers, John (newspaper proprietor), 456
Chalmers, John Gray (newspaper proprietor), 458
Chalmers, Patrick (newspaper proprietor), 187
Chalmers, William (town councillor), 260
Chamberlain, Joseph (MP), 186, 193, 196-7
Champion, Henry Hyde (socialist), 192-4, 197, 202, 459-60
Chaplin, Charlie (entertainer), 430
Cheyne, Sandy (artist), 465
Cheyne, Rev. Patrick, 359
Christie, Dr John (newspaper editor), 453
Clark, Henry J. (publisher), 457
Clarke, John (lecturer/town councillor), 393
Clements, Frank (editor), 457
Cobban, Robert (printer/bookseller), 449-50
Cockburn, Lord, 384
Codona, Mark (fairground owner), 123, 426
Collie, Alexander C. (trade unionist/town councillor), 262, 446
Collie, Mrs George, 213
Collins, Sir Godfrey (Secretary of State for Scotland), 215
Comper, Rev. John, 356
Cook, Alexander S. (temperance reformer), 164, 166, 186, 403, 411, 453
Cooney, Robert H. (Communist candidate), 218
Cooper, Alexander (mill manager), 155
Cooper, Rev. Prof. James, 359, (biog) 360
Cooper, William (town councillor), 195
Coutts, Robert (tailor), 418
Cowan, Prof. Rev. Henry, 354, 392
Coyne, Edna (magazine owner), 465
Coyne, John (magazine owner), 465
Craig, David (trawler owner), (biog) 104
Crawford and Balcarres, Earl of (landowner), 456
Crawfurd, Mrs Helen (Communist candidate), 213-14
Crichton Smith, Iain (poet), 2-3, 12
Crombie, Mrs J. W., 385
Crombie, J. W. (MP), 394
Crombie, James E. (textile manufacturer/philanthopist), 281, 385-6, 457, (biog) 486
Crombie, John (textile manufacturer/philanthropist), 190, 380, 389

Cruden, George (lawyer), 388
Cruickshank, Miss Christine (philanthropist), 280
Cruickshank, J. W. (farmer), 380
Cruickshank, Robert (journalist), 452
Cunninghame-Graham, R. B. (MP), 195, 197

Davidson, Alexander (lawyer), 380, 391
Davidson, John, (philanthropist) 328
Davidson, John (printer), 179, 449
Davidson, J. Morrison (politician), 458
Davidson, Violet (singer), 426
Davison, Emily (suffragette), 198
Delavault, Pierre (artist), 458-9
Dewar, Rev. Dr Daniel (university principal), 351, 358
Dewar, Donald C. (MP), 221
Diack, Peter (secretary and superintendent, AAICP), 274-5
Dingwall, Prov. (town councillor), 378
Dingwall Fordyce, Capt. Alexander (MP), 183-4, 201, 451, 473
Disraeli, Benjamin (MP), 185, 187, 456
Dixie, Lady Florence (manager of ladies' football team), 418
Don, Lawrence (handloom weaver), 265
Donald, George, (glass merchant) 380
Donald, George,(comedian/musician) 21, 445
Donald, James F. (dancing teacher/cinema proprietor), (biog) 428, 429, 432
Donald, James (theatre manager), 432
Donald, Peter (theatre manager), 432
Donald, Richard M. (cinema manager/football club chairman) , (biog) 441, 442
Doran, Frank (MP), 226-7
Downie Campbell, J. (lawyer), 395
Duffus, Alexander (town councillor), 190, 242, 246, (biog) 274
Duffus, J. C. (lawyer), 395
Dunbar, Rev. Sir William, 359
Duncan, Miss Isabella (school teacher), 331
Duncan, James Whyte (newspaper editor/radical), 455, 460
Duncan, Miss Jean (school teacher), 331
Duncan, John (cattle dealer), 83, 359
Duncan, Joseph F. (trade unionist), 174, 196-9, 214-15
Duncan, William (writer), 450
Duthie, John (shipbuilder), 64, 76, 91
Duthie, Miss Elizabeth (philanthropist), 302, 380, 414
Dyce, William (artist), 414

Edmond, Alexander (lawyer), 388
Ellis, Alexander (architect), 356
Elphinstone, Bishop, 3
Elphinstone, Lieutenant (landowner), 391
Elrick, J. H. (trade unionist), 196

Emslie, Mrs Mary (school teacher/philanthropist), (biog) 331, 334
Esslemont, George Birnie (MP), 57, 197-9, 203, 393
Esslemont, Dr Mary (doctor), (biog) 57, 221, 292
Esslemont, Peter (MP), 57, 186, 188, 191-2, 197, 245, (biog) 248, 249, 274, 378, 394, 414, 457
Ewan, Dr Elizabeth (doctor), 292

Farquhar, Sir Arthur (Tory candidate), 180, 201
Farquhar, James (MP), 176-7, 201, 375
Farquhar, Mrs James (society hostess), 377
Farquhar, Mrs Margaret E. (town councillor), 397
Farquhar, William (industrialist), 375
Ferguson, Aitken (Communist candidate), 211-12
Ferguson, Sir Alex (football club manager), 441-2
Ferguson, William (writer), 449
Ferguson of Kinmundy (landowner), 456
Finlay, Alec (comedian), 14
Fleming, Sir John (MP), 197, 199-200, 203, 208-9, 386-7, 393
Fletcher, A. P. (journalist), 194, 383
Foote, Rev., 369
Forbes, James (town councillor), 259
Forbes, James (merchant), 377
Forsyth, William (newspaper editor), 423, 454, 456
Fraser, Alexander, 374
Fraser, Garnet R. (businessman), 463
Fraser, John (merchant), 411-12
Fraser, Peter L. (Conservative candidate), 224
Fraser, William (town councillor), 388
French, Prof. George (professor of chemistry), 288
Fumarolo, Signor (theatrical impressario), 409
Fyfe, John (granite merchant), (biog) 92

Galen, Dr, 292
Gardiner, Rev. Thomas, 40
Garro-Jones, G. M. (MP), 215-16, 394
Gates, Bert (actor/cinema owner), 428, 434
Gates, Nellie (actor/cinema owner), 434
Gerrie, George (journalist), 460
George, J. F. (journalist), 460
George, Henry (writer), 189
Gibb, James (architect), 349
Giles, James (artist), 414
Gill, Thomas (trade unionist), 186
Gillies, Archibald (newspaper editor), 455-6
Gladstone, W. E. (MP), 186-8, 190, 248, 456

Glass, A. P. (town councillor), 195
Gordon of Cluny (landowner), 456
Gordon of Fyvie (landowner), 391
Gordon of Khartoum, General Charles, 336, 456
Gordon, Major (landowner), 391
Gordon, Rev. Abercromby, 327, 330
Gordon, Miss Betty (society hostess), 377
Gordon, Father Charles, 357-8
Gordon, Duke of (landowner), 179, 377
Gordon, Alexander Ross 'Harry' (comedian), 12, 421, *(biog)* 425, 431-2, 434, 443
Gordon, George (Lord Byron) (poet), 490
Gordon, Henry Wolrige (newspaper shareholder), 456
Gordon, John, of Murtle (landowner), 280
Gordon, William (bookseller), 449
Gordon, William Cosmo (newspaper shareholder), 456
Gow, Nathaniel (fiddler), 406
Gow, Niel (fiddler), 406
Graham, Prov. Prof. John M. (theologian/town councillor), 393
Grant, James C. (newspaper editor), 463, *(biog)* 464
Grant, John Lyall, 31
Grassic Gibbon, Lewis (writer), 159
Gray, John (philanthopist), 341, 353
Grenville, Mr. (orchestral conductor), 405
Grierson, Prof. Herbert, 382
Grierson, John (film maker), 430
Griffiths, D. W. (film maker), 428
Grundy, Sydney (playwright), 418
Guthrie, Rev. Thomas, 330

Hadden, Prov. Gavin,(textile manufacturer/town councillor) 176, 238, 374-6
Hadden, Prov. James (textile manufacturer/town councillor), *(biog)* 23, 154, 176, 178-80, 183, 238-9, 244, 374-6
Hall, Harvey (lawyer), 387
Hall, James (shipbuilder), 85, 87, 158-9, 183
Hall, Mrs John (businesswoman), 396
Hall, William (shipbuilder), 84-5
Hamilton, Prof. Robert (professor of mathematics), 268-9
Hardie, Buff (comedian/writer), 21, 445, 465
Hardie, Keir (MP), 192
Harney, George Julian (chartist), 181
Harper, J. E. (engineer/lawyer), 216
Hay, General (society host), 377
Hay, James (lawyer/golfer), *(biog)* 121
Hay, James Gordon, of Seaton (landowner), 460
Hay, Maj. Malcolm (landowner), 31
Hay, Prof. Matthew (doctor/moh), 53-4,

(biog) 55, 72, 282-3, 304-6, 308
Henderson, Prov. Sir William (industrialist/town councillor), 280, 378, 388, *(biog)* 389, 414, 457
Henderson, Rev. William, 63
Hetherington, Henry (trade unionist), 215
Houdini, Harry (escapologist), 409, 430
Houston, Robert (poet), 459
Howard, Ebenezer (architect), 487
Hughes, Hector S. J. (MP), 216, *(biog)* 218, 219-20, 394
Hughes, Ian (lecturer/nationalist), 222
Hughes, Lord Robert (MP), 221-2, *(biog)* 213, 226-7, 393
Hume, Joseph (MP), 177-8, 201, 448, 451
Humphrey, J. M. Marcus (Conservative candidate), 218
Huntly, Lord (landowner), 391
Hunter, Thomas 'Cocky' (general dealer), *(biog)* 116
Hunter, William Alexander (MP), 190, *(biog)* 191, 194, 200, 202, 334
Hutcheon, Henry (granite master), 212
Hyde, Richard (paper manufacturer), 485
Hyndman, H. M. (socialist), 195

Ibsen, Henrick (playwrite), 432
Iles, John Henry (entertainment organiser), 426
Inglis, John (Lord Advocate), 289
Innes, Lady (society hostess), 376
Innes of Learney (landowner), 391, 456
Innes, William, of Raemoir (landowner), 182, 456
Irvine of Drum (landowner), 391
Irvine, Arthur J. (Labour candidate), 217
Irvin, Sir John (president, Aberdeen Liberal Association), 209, 212
Irwin, Leonard (playwright), 432

Jackson, Dr Henry (police commissioner), 299
Jaffrey, Rev. John, 449
Jaffrey, Sir Thomas (banker/philanthropist), *(biog)* 113, 281
Jamieson, Prov. George (businessman/ town councillor), 31, 259, 378-9, *(biog)* 380, 389
Jessiman, John (trade unionist), 172
Joad, Dr C. E. M. (broadcaster), 216
Johnston, W. (trade unionist), 195-6
Johnstone, James (Liberal candidate), 208
Jones, Ernest (Chartist), 183
Jopp, Andrew (town councillor), 177
Jopp, Keith, 375
Jopp, Col. William (wine merchant/volunteer), 388, *(biog)* 420

Kellas, Rev. James, 212
Kelsall, Moultrie (broadcaster), 433
Kennedy, Calum (singer), 435

Kennedy, Rev. John, 359
Kennedy, Thomas F. (MP), 195-6, 198-9, 202, 394
Kennedy, Mrs Thomas, 197
Kennedy, William (writer), 422-3
Kerr, Dr (newspaper editor), 448
Kesson, Jessie (novelist), 463
Kidd, Rev. Dr James, 351, *(biog)* 352
Kilgour, Dr Alexander (doctor), 292
Kilgour, James (textile manufacturer), 97
King, Sir Alexander (cinema magnate), 435
King Edward VII, 438
King Edward VIII, 286
King, George (bookseller), 453
Kinghorn, James (lawyer), 389
Kinloch, Dr J. Parlane (doctor/moh), 283
Kintore, Lord (landowner), 376
Knight, Mrs Margaret (humanist), 361
Knight, Prof. Rex (professor of psychology), 361, 463
Kyle, Colonel (landowner), 391

Laing, Sir John (businessman), 96
Lamond, James (MP/town councillor)), 221, 394, 492-3
Lamond, Mrs June (town councillor), 493
Lancaster, Joseph (educationalist), 329
Lang, Rev. Marshall (university principal), 360
Lauder, Harry (comedian), 431
Law, Denis (footballer), 491
Leatham, James (socialist), 192, 459
Lee, Rev. F. G., 359
Legge, John (Chartist), 181, 451
Leith, John Farley (MP), 184-6, 201
Leith Hay, Sir Andrew (soldier), 184
Lenglen, Suzanne (tennis player), 437
Lennox, Annie (singer), 491
Lennox, Prov. Robert S. (trade unionist/town councillor), *(biog)* 170
Leslie, Prov. William (builder/town councillor), 245, 378-9
Lewis, Prov. Sir Andrew (shipbuilder/town councillor), 283-5,, 395, 426, 438, *(biog)* 474
Leys, Prov. Thomas (textile manufacturer/town councillor), 239, 374-5
Lillywhite, Harry (cricket professional), 417
Lind, Miss Jenny (singer), 408-9
Lindsay, William S. (newsagent and radical), 164, *(biog)* 165, 183, 186, 273, 404, 453
Lloyd George, David (MP), 198, 208
Locke, Alasdair (oil industy executive), 142-3
Logan, James (theatrical manager), 445
Longhurst, 'Big Scott' (conjuror), 411
Longmuir, Dr (newspaper editor), 452
Lowery, Robert (Chartist), 182, 201, 352

Lumsden, James Forbes (lawyer), 210, 388, 417
Lumsden, Mrs Henry (society hostess), 377

Maberly, John (textile manufacturer), 79–80, 329
Macallan, David (cabinet maker/town councillor), 359, 453
McCombie, Baillie (landowner), 237–8
McCombie, William (cattle breeder), 83, 453
McCombie, William (newspaper editor), 453, 455–6
Maconnachie, George (town councillor), 259
McCulloch, Horatio (artist), 414
McCullugh, James Gordon (Conservative candidate), 193, 202
Macdonald, Alexander (granite merchant), 386
Macdonald, Alexander (coffee house proprietor), 401–2
Macdonald, Rev. C. C., 189–90
MacDonald, David (hide and leather merchant), 380
MacDonald, D. C. (lawyer), 189
MacDonald, Ramsay (MP), 196, 200, 213
MacFie, Ronald Campbell (poet), 492
McGilligan, Alexander (newspaper editor), 457
MacGillvray, Rev. Walter, 358
McGrigor, Sir James (doctor in military service), 491
MacHardy, David (landowner), 391
Macintosh, A. Fraser (trade unionist), 215–16
Macintosh, William (draper), 248
MacIntosh, George R.'GR' (joiner/trade unionist), 215–16
McKay, James (newspaper editor), 458
Mackay, R. W. (warehouseman), 380
Mackenzie, J. Russell (architect), 478
Mackenzie, A. Marshall (architect), 298, (biog) 316
Mackenzie, Robert, F. (schoolmaster), 338–9, 463
Mackenzie, Dr R. Shelton (newspaper editor), 452
Mackenzie, Thomas (architect), 298
Mackie, James (trawler owner), 395
Mackie, Sir Maitland (farmer), (biog) 132
McKinnon, Lachlan (lawyer), 383, 387
MacLaren, Rev. J. Ross, 348
Macleod, Calum Alexander (lawyer/businessman), 151, (biog) 152
Macleod, Professor John J. R. (doctor/Nobel laureate), (biog) 284, 347, 492
McNeill, Ronald J. (journalist/Unionist candidate), 197, 203
MacPherson, John (combmaker), 182–3
MacQueen, Dr Ian (doctor/moh), 278

Magee, Frank (town/regional councillor), 218
Mahon, John Lincoln (socialist), 192, 194, 202
Mair, Rev. Michael, 276
Maitland, George (philanthropist), 359
Mallet, Sir Charles E. (Liberal candidate), 208–9
Malone, P. Gerald (MP), 225–6
Mann, Tom (MP), 194, 197, 202
Marr, Alexander (newspaper proprietor), 456
Marshall, John (factory owner), 327
Masson, David (newspaper editor), 452
Matcham, Frank (theatre architect), 431
Matthews, Prov. James (architect/town councillor), 43–4, (biog) 298, 316, 378–9, 388
Maxwell, James Clerk (scientist), 344
Maxwell, Sir William (newspaper editor), 460
Mearns, Prov. (ship merchant/town councillor), 378
Meff, Prov. (ship merchant/town councillor), 378
Melvin, George (schoolmaster), 325
Melvin, James (schoolmaster), 271, (biog) 323, 324–5
Menzies, John, of Pitfodels, (landowner), 33, 370, 477
Middleton, Robert (town councillor), 224–6
Mill, John Stuart (economist/writer), 185
Miller, Willie (footballer), 442
Milligan, David (lawyer), 392
Milligan, Prof., 392
Milne, Alexander (lawyer), 449
Milne of Kinaldie (landowner), 33
Milne, James (marine engineer), 143
Milne, James (trade unionist), 175, 220
Milne, John Duguid (lawyer), (biog) 185
Milne, Stewart (builder), 138
Minto, Prof. (Liberal supporter), 457
Mitchell, Adam (builder), 297
Mitchell, Charles (shipbuilder/philanthropist), 491
Mitchell, John (bookseller/Chartist), 181, 183
Mitchell, Sir Thomas (town councillor), 261
Moir, Dr Andrew (anatomist), 288–9
Moir, George (landowner), 485
Moir, Dr. Maitland (surgeon), 189, 458–9
Morgan, Mrs Diane (editor/writer), 464–5
Morgan, John, 28–9 (builder/town councillor), (biog) 297, 316, 378–9, 386–7, 390
Morrison, Rev. George, 483
Morton, H. V. (film scriptwriter), 430
Mount-Stephen, Lord George (railway magnate), 200–1, 280
Mowat, Alexander (newspaper proprietor), 453

Munro, Alexander Macdonald (city chamberlain), (biog) 249
Munro, Henry (travel agent/newspaper proprietor), 458–9
Murray, Mrs Cissy (theatrical impressario), 425
Murray, Sir James (art collector/philanthropist), 199, 386
Murray, J. G. (artist), 459
Mutch, Alexander 'Sandy' (businessman/town councillor), 221, 262

Nicol, Prov. Alexander (shipowner/town concillor), 354, 378–9, (biog) 476
Nicol, Dennis (charity organiser), 276
Nicol, John (republican), 172
Nicol, John (councillor), 34, 245
Nicol, William Robertson (newspaper editor), 458
Nicholson of Glenbervie (landowner), 391
Nicolson, James Badenoch (newspaper shareholder), 456

O'Connor, Feargus (Chartist leader), 182
Ogilvie, James (president, Liberal Party), 209
Ogilvie, James (principal, Normal School), 339
Ogston, A. M. (chemical manufacturer), 380
Ogston, Prof. Sir Alexander (surgeon), (biog) 290, 384–5, 388
Ogston, Prof. Francis (surgeon), 290, 392
Orchardson, William (artist), 384
Owen, Robert (reformer), 165–7

Palmerston, Lord, 184–5, 455
Pankhurst, Mrs Emmeline (suffragette), 197–8
Parker, Rev. Gavin, 351
Parnell, Charles Stewart (politician), 193
Parr, Fred (theatrical entertainer), 424
Paterson, Dove (elocutionist/concert promoter), 427, 434
Paterson, Peter (actor), 410
Paton, Mrs Fenella, 50–1, 391
Paton of Grandholm (landowner), John, 51, 391
Paton, John (socialist), 196, 209, 211
Paull, James (lawyer), 394
Peacock, Francis (dance teacher), 406
Pethick-Lawrence, F. W. (pacifist), 200, 203
Phillips, Caroline (journalist), 198
Pirie-Gordon of Buthlay (landowner), 391
Pirie, Alexander George (paper manufacturer), (biog) 95, 380, 387, 482, 486
Pirie, Duncan Vernon (MP), 194–5, 197, 199, 202–3, 208, 393, 460

Pirie, F. Logie (paper manufacturer), 186
Pirie, Patrick (paper manufacturer), 76-7
Pirie, Rev. Dr (university principal), 332, 360
Pollitt, Harry (Communist), 212
Pollock, Mrs Jessie (actress/theatre manager), *(biog)* 412, 431
Powers, John (newspaper editor), 450
Pressly, David Leith (newspaper editor), 458
Pyper, William (shipowner/town councillor), *(biog)* 89

Queen Elizabeth II, 279
Queen Victoria, 119, 180, 414-15, 427

Rae, John (schoolmaster/writer), 491-2
Ramsay, John (MP), 177, 201, 450
Ramsay, Lady (suffragette), 198
Reid, Sir George (artist), 271, *(biog)* 414, 454-5
Reid, William Dallas (newspaper editor), 458
Reid, William R. (lawyer), 190
Reith, John (general manager, BBC), 433
Rhodes, Cecil (politician), 195
Rice, Prof. C. Duncan (university principal), 492-3
Richmond and Gordon, Duke of (landowner), 456
Riddell, James (writer), 399
Ritchie, Alexander (socialist), 195
Robb, Andrew (newspaper proprietor), 458
Robb, George (company director), 395
Robertson, Joseph (writer), 400-2, 449-50, 452
Robertson, Raymond (MP), 226-8
Robertson, Stephen (comedian/writer), 21, 445, 465
Rodgers, Edward (artist), 458
Rolfe, Frederick (writer), 460
Ronald, Mrs Jane (hotel proprietor), 400
Rose, Donaldson (landowner), 31
Rose, Frank H. (MP), 200, 203, 208-11, 213
Rose, Margaret (guest house proprietor), 218
Ross, Horatio, of Rossie (army captain/sportsman), 178, 201
Ross, James (upholsterer/philanthropist), 328
Rothermere, Lord (newspaper magnate), 462
Rowett, John Quiller (philanthropist), 347
Ruskin, John (writer), 386
Rust, Prov. (town councillor), 392
Rutherford, General (curling club committee member), 388
Ryder, Corbet (actor), 411-12

Saltoun, Lord (landowner), 391
Sandeman, Dr Laura (doctor), 211-12, 292

Sangster, John (pharmaceutical chemist), 380
Sargeant, J. S. (artist), 385-6
Savidge, Malcolm (MP), 227
Scott, Sir G. Gilbert (architect), 298
Scott Skinner, James (fiddler), 426
Scott Sutherland, Thomas (architect/town councillor), 312, *(biog)* 318, 343, 383, 387-8
Scott, Sir Walter (writer), 401, 405, 411
Seafield, Earl of (landowner), 456
Shanks, Rev., 357
Sharar, John (political reformer), 185
Sharp, Miss Isabella (town councillor), 396
Sharpe, Andrew (newspaper editor), 448
Shaw, James (ironmaster), 185, 187, 201
Shirras, William (wholesale draper), 248
Simon, Sir John (MP), 215
Simpson, Archibald (architect), 5, 9, 25, *(biog)* 26, 279-80, 298, 343, 349, 398, 466
Simpson, Dr W. J. (doctor/moh), 303-4
Simpson, Mrs Wallis, 286
Sinclair, George (theatrical entertainer), 424
Sinclair, John (zookeeper), 426
Skene, James (landowner), 466-7
Skinner, Bishop, 359
Smith, Alexander (wigmaker), 485
Smith, Bartholomew (paper manufacturer), 480-1
Smith, Sir George Adam,(clergyman/university principal), 354, *(biog)* 355, 392
Smith, George 'Chicago'(financial speculator), 81
Smith, John (architect/superintendent of public works), 5, 24-5, *(biog)* 36
Smith, Lewis (bookseller/publisher), 449-50
Smith, Lewis (paper manufacturer), 76
Smith, Prof. Norton B. (theatrical entertainer), 410
Smith, Sir Robert (Liberal candidate), 226
Smith, Prof. William Robertson (theologian), 355, 361, 456
Smith, William (architect), 35, 477
Smith, William (newspaper proprietor), 458
Soddy, Prof Frederick (chemist/Nobel laureate), 346
Spankie, James (television presenter), 435
Spark, John (newspaper editor), 453
Spark, Thomas (publisher), 449-50
Sproat, Iain M. (MP), 221, 224, 226
Stark, Rev. James, 457
Steill, John (nationalist), 404
Stephen, Miss (school teacher), 331
Stephen, Nicol (MP), 228, 230
Stewart, Prov. Sir David (industrialist/town councillor), 194, 202, 252, 378, *(biog)* 384

Still, George (town councillor), 177
Stirling, Rev. James, 352
Stopani, Rt. Rev. Monsignor William, 272, 356, *(biog)* 357
Stopes, Dr Marie (birth-control pioneer), 51
Stratton, James (shopkeeper), 404
Stronach, 'Sandy' (SNP candidate), 222
Sturge, Joseph (Chartist), 453
Summers, Capt. (seafarer/evangelist), 476
Suther, Rev. Thomas George, 359
Suttie, Ian (businessman), 143
Sykes, Col. William H. (MP), 183-5, 201

Taggart, Prov. Sir James (granite merchant/town councillor), *(biog)* 160, 209-10, 280
Taylor, Alexander (manager, Co-operative Coal Society), 186
Tennant, Capt. Iain (landowner), 435
Tennyson, Lord Alfred (poet), 419
Thain, James (merchant/philanthropist), 328
Thom, Walter (historian), 398
Thom, William (handloom weaver/poet), 155
Thompson, Prov. George Jr. (MP), *(biog)* 86, 183-4, 201, 378, 389, 391, 393, 414
Thompson, James C. (trade unionist), *(biog)* 173
Thompson, William (shipbuilder), 64
Thomson, Dr Agnes (doctor), *(biog)* 51
Thomson, David (comedian), 425
Thomson, Prof David (professor of natural philosophy), 344
Thomson, Sir Frederick C. (MP), 200, 203, 208-9, 212-13, *(biog)* 214
Thomson, Sir George Paget (professor of physics/Nobel laureate), 346
Thomson, Sir J. Douglas W. (MP), 214-15
Thomson, Rev. James L., 480
Thomson, Roy (newspaper magnate), 463
Trail, Miss Katherine, 418
Trail, Prof. (academic), 392
Troup, George (newspaper editor), 452
Tweedsmuir, Lady (previously Lady Grant) (MP), 216, *(biog)* 217, 218, 220, 222

Valentine, James (writer), 453

Walker, Alexander (merchant/ philanthropist), 186, *(biog)* 271, 389, 456
Walker, Austin W. (chartered accountant), 216
Walker, George (bookseller), 405
Walker, Thomas (textile manufacturer), 97
Walker, William (film maker), 426-7
Ward, Miss Lucy (headmistress), 396
Warden, John (schoolmaster), 178-9, 449

Warrack, Miss Harriet (school teacher), 331

Washington Wilson, Alexander (journalist), 458

Washington Wilson, George (photographer), 10-11, 20, 354, 381-2, *(biog)* 415, 419, 426

Watson, Prof. J. Robertson (professor of chemistry), 199-200, 203

Watson, Sheriff William (educationalist), 49, 329, *(biog)* 330

Watt, Miss E. Maureen (SNP candidate), 224-5

Watt, Edward William (newspaper proprietor), 460

Watt, Dr George (doctor), 280

Watt, Harry (film maker), 430

Watt, John (printer), 449-50

Watt, William (newspaper proprietor), 457

Watts, Dr Annie (doctor), 292

Webster, Rev. Alexander, 191-2, 195, 198, 457

Webster, Prov. John (MP), 186, *(biog)* 187, 190, 201, 245, 378, 393, 420

Webster, Ron (trade unionist), 175

Wedgwood Benn, W. (MP), 211-13, 215, 394

West, Dr Alexander (college principal), 343

White, John Forbes (art collector) 190, 386

Wilkie, Alexander (town councillor), 254

Williams, C. B. (inspector of poor), 274

Williams, Robert (Liberal Unionist candidate), 195, 202

Williamson, Mrs Ellen M. (town councillor), 397

Williamson, Robert M. (lawyer), *(biog)* 394

Wilson, Harold (MP), 223

Wilson, Dr J. H. (newspaper editor/home missions activist), 359, 452

Wisely, Mrs Jill (town councillor), 227

Wood, Sir Ian (businessman), 142, *(biog)* 143

Wood, John (businessman), 112

Wyness, Prov. James (town councillor), 263

Wyness, Thomas (superintendent of police), 457

Yeats, William (landowner), 389, 456

York, Duke of, 286

Young, Prov. James (town councillor), 374-5

Zwart, Klass (businessman), 143

Index of Subjects

Aberdeen
  Adelphi, 458
  Albyn Place, 26, 50, 253, 466
  Anderson Drive, 29-30, 38, 264
  Broad Street, 353, 405, 449, 458, 462-3
  Castlegate, 8, 15, 20, 25, 192, 237, 256, 301, 470, 472
  Castle Street, 22, 28, 252274, 290, 295, 301, 376, 400
  Causeymounth, 472
  Crown Street, 299, 353, 459, 473
  Gallowgate, 41, 79, 115-16, 165, 273, 276-7, 295, 303, 305, 330-2, 356, 370
  George Street, 79, 89, 116, 134, 296, 299, 301, 353-5, 358, 403, 425, 428
  Great Western Road, 29, 41, 160, 478
  Guestrow, 26, 28, 31-2, 61, 68, 199, 273, 282, 288, 295, 302, 399, 450
  Hardgate, 272, 472
  Holburn Street, 328, 472
  King Street, 22-3, 26, 50, 237, 297, 301, 305, 311, 314, 330, 332, 335, 350, 371, 398
  Marischal Street, 295, 377, 411-12, 477
  Market Street, 30-1, 34, 40, 118, 256, 274, 296, 473, 478-9
  Schoolhill, 11, 23, 155, 249, 297, 323
  Shiprow, 31, 256, 301, 328, 351, 477
  Shorelands, 295, 299, 304
  The Green, 18-19, 23, 79, 81, 155, 295, 470, 472
  Union Street, 2, 3, 8-9, 11-12, 20, 22-3, 25, 28, 30, 41, 44-5, 50, 53, 61, 79, 116, 119, 132, 134, 205, 252-3, 296, 376, 383, 398-9, 401, 428
  Union Terrace, 15-16, 113, 249, 377, 383
  Upperkirkgate, 11, 16, 28, 31, 295, 328, 330, 332, 377
  West End, 380-2, 388, 467
  Woolmanhill, 279-80, 283-4
Aberdeen Citizen's Vigilance Committee, 427
Aberdeen Philosophical Society, 297, 455
Aberdeenshire, 45-6, 59, 63, 78-9, 93, 129, 132, 154, 240, 279, 330, 391, 467

Aberdeenshire Canal, 38, 78, 95
Aberdour, 389
Aboyne, 82, 246
agriculture (see also food research), 78, 96-7, 114, 121, 188, 191
Airport, 129, 136-7, 205, 486-8
Alford, 453, 478
Altens, 30, 45, 129, 320, 322, 470
American Civil War, 455
Americanisation, 427-8, 446
Anti-Corn Law Association, 181, 183-4
Arbroath, 176, 412
Ardersier, 63, 127
Ardoe House, 298
arts, 349, 414, 432
Art Gallery, 113, 270, 298, 316, 386, 414
Ashgrove, 320
Assembly Rooms, 377, 398-9, 401, 409
association football (see also Pittodrie Stadium), 20, 417-18, 439-42, 491
association football clubs
  Aberdeen, 138, 417-18, 439-42, 447
  Celtic, 439
  Dunfermline Athletic, 441
  Hibernian, 440
  Orion, 418, 438-9
  Rangers, 439
  Real Madrid, 442
  Third Lanark, 440
  Victoria United, 417-18, 439
Australia, 107, 197

Balfour Commission, 335
Balmoral Castle, 36, 121, 414-15, 427
Balnagask, 316, 318
Banchory, 48, 82, 138, 322, 425, 483
Banchory Devenick, 387, 454, 483
Banff, 118
Banffshire, 154, 224, 279, 357, 415, 455
banks, 79-80, 97-8, 112, 298, 375, 378, 380, 474
  Aberdeen Banking Co., 79-80, 82, 98, 298
  Aberdeen Savings Bank, 113, 271, 273, 297, 365, 378, 380, 389, 394-5, 460
  North of Scotland Bank, 26-7, 86, 98-9, 112-13, 298, 380, 389, 419

Bankhead, 485
Battle of Trafalgar, 376
Beach, 2, 11, 117, 119-20, 122, 422-3, 442-4, 447
  Bathing Station, 42, 118-22, 436
  Beach Ballroom, 392, 426, 443-4, 447
  Beach Boulevard, 12, 15
  Beach Leisure Centre, 447
  Beach Pavilion (see theatres)
  Links, 42-3, 122, 155, 179, 416-17, 419, 437-8, 480
Belfast, 352
Bieldside, 29-30, 39, 322, 467, 479-80, 483
bingo, 443
Birmingham, 452
Blackpool, 423
Blairs, 357, 472
Boer War, 195-6, 290, 460
booksellers, 399, 405, 448ff
Boulogne, 423
bowls, 416, 437
  World Bowls Championship, 437
Boys' Brigade, 436
Braemar, 121, 287
Brechin, 51, 176-7, 227, 355
breweries, 401
Bridge of Don, 30, 38, 40-1, 59, 73, 138, 261, 322, 339, 365, 470
Bridge of Don Fund, 34
'Britain in Bloom', 446
British Association for the Advancement of Science, 187
Broomhill, 28, 312, 318
Bucksburn, 43, 97, 347, 485
Burke's Landed Gentry, 391
bus companies, 39-41, 256
bus wars, 256
butteries, 163

cabinet making, 111
Cairngorm Club, 437, 461
Cairnton, 241
CALA, 296-9, 311, 467, 473
Canada, 107, 151, 281, 492
canning industry, 91
Canterbury, 277
cattle trade, 83-4

Census of Church Attendance 1901,
    1984, 1994; 349, 362-4, 367
Census of Population, 53, 67, 70-3, 75,
    204
Census of Religous Worship 1851; 348-9,
    353, 362
Chamber of Commerce, 41, 114-15, 384,
    389-90, 394, 396
Chapel of Garioch, 455
charitable institutions & organisations
    Association for Teaching the Blind
        in their Homes, 271
    BBC 'Children in Need' Fund, 277
    Clothing Society, 271, 389
    Female Society for the Relief of Aged
        & Indigent Women, 271
    House of Bethany, 272
    House of Refuge for the Elderly
        (Oakbank), 271, 280
    Industrial Asylum for the Rescue &
        Reformation of Females of
        Dissolute Habits, 389
    Instant Neighbour, 276-7
    MacRobert Trust, 281
    Nazareth House, 272, 357
    Poverty Action Liaison, 276-7
    Public Soup Kitchen, 268, 271, 329
    Repository for Female Industry, 271
    Safe and Sound Project, 276
    Sick Man's Friend, 271
    Society for the Suppression of
        Begging, 268
    United Coal Fund, 271
charity concerts, 405
Charity Organisation Society, 274
chartism, 9, 86, 181-2, 273, 451-2
    Aberdeen Charter Union, 181-3
    Aberdeen Working Men's
        Association, 181, 184, 401, 451
    Chartist Association, 165
    Chartist Convention, 181
    Complete Suffrage Union, 183, 451
China, 151, 184
Chinese restaurants, 73
church
    attendance, 348, 353, 362
    discipline, 370-2
    finance, 371-3
    government
        Free Presbytery of Aberdeen, 40,
            407, 443
        General Assembly of the Church
            of Scotland, 269, 360, 451
        Kirk Session, 268-9
        Moderator of the General
            Assembly, 355, 360
    and elites, 385
    and the media, 366
    ssions, 357, 389, 402
    ible Society, 389
    urch of Scotland Extension &
        erritorial Home Mission
        ociation, 354, 476

    Society for Promoting the
        Religious Principles of the
        Reformation, 357
    and social problems, 366
        Church of Scotland Poverty
            Committee, 276
    and social structure, 368-73
    and youth, 363, 365, 367
    membership, 362ff
    officers, 368ff
churches (Christian)
    Baptist, 351, 364-5, 373
    Brethren, 365
    Chartist, 182, 352
    Church of Scotland, 180, 182, 184
        Bon Accord, 351, 371, 477
        East Parish Church of St Nicholas,
            349, 353, 359-60
        Gaelic, 350, 354
        Gilcomston Chapel of Ease, 351-2,
            477
        Greyfriars Kirk, 257, 349, 352-3
        North Parish Church of St
            Nicholas, 25, 349-51, 357
        St Clement's, 351
        St Machar, 350, 477, 479
        South Parish Church of St
            Nicholas, 351, 369
        Trinity, 350-2, 354
        Union, 350-1, 451
        West Parish Church of St
            Nicholas, 16, 177, 271, 349,
            352-4, 454
    Congregational, 351, 373
        Albion Street (ragged kirk), 359,
            452
        Blackfriars, 371
        Frederick Street, 25, 369, 371
        George Street, 348, 369
        John Street, 173
        St Andrew's Street, 372
        St Nicholas, Belmont Street, 39,
            298, 348
        St Paul Street, 369
        St Paul's, 372-3
        Trinity, 359
    Episcopalian
        Ferryhill, 354
        Rosemount, 354
        Rubislaw, 92, 354
        St Andrew's, 25-6, 351, 359, 364
        St James', 364
        St John the Evangelist, 351, 356-7,
            359, 364, 370
        St Margaret's, 357-8, 363-4, 370,
            372
        St Mary's, 271, 359, 364
        St Paul's, 268, 351, 359, 420, 477
        St Peter's, Torry, 474
    Evangelical Union, 359
    Free Church, 183-4, 406
        Bon Accord, 368
        Beechgrove, 363

    Causewayend, 354
    Charlotte Street, 369
    Craigiebuckler, 89
    Cults West, 483
    Denburn, 477
    East, 353
    Ferryhill, 354, 389
    Gilcomston, 249, 358, 360
    Holburn West, 276
    John Knox Gerrard Street
        Church, 284, 351
    Mannofield, 212, 478
    Queen's Cross, 297, 354-5
    Ruthrieston, 354
    St Clement's, 36
    St Columba's, 354
    St Paul's Relief, 369
    South, 36, 329, 353, 369, 371, 404
    Torry, 354
    Trinity, 86
    Triple Kirks, 9, 16, 25-6, 38, 349,
        353
    Union, 407, 477
    United, 358, 363, 369
    West, 298, 353, 385, 407
    Woodside, 369
    Presbyterian Alliance, 427
    Roman Catholic, 272, 348, 357, 367
        St Joseph's, 363
        St Mary of the Assumption
            (Cathedral), 297, 355-7, 363-4,
            368, 370
        St Mary's College, Blairs
        St Peter's, 351, 355, 357, 363
    Salvation Army, 11, 365
    Secession, 351-2
    Unitarian, 351-2, 358
    United Presbyterians, 248, 355-6, 358,
        380
    other denominations, 351
churches and education, 325-32, 336-40
churches and music, 360-1, 407-8
churches (non-Christian), 348, 365
cinemas (see films), 422, 426-30, 445
    Astoria, 318, 428-9, 441
    Capitol, 111, 428-9
    Cinema House, 428
    City, 318
    Gaiety, 427
    Grand Central, 428, 441
    La Scala, 111, 427
    Majestic, 318
    Palace, 170, 431
    Regent, 318
    Star, 434
    West End, 428
circus, 410
clipper ships, 76, 84-5
    Scottish Maid, 84, 476
    Thermopylae, 86
civil disorder, 167, 176, 181-2, 288, 336
Codona's Pleasure Park, 426, 447
Columbian Press, 451

combworks, 110-11
Stewart & Co., 156, 169, 384
Communist Party, 170, 207, 211, 213-14, 216, 219-20, 260
Conservative politics, 180, 183-7, 195, 197, 200, 220-2, 229, 384, 434, 456, 460-1
Conservative Association, 126, 194, 226, 271
Conservative & Unionist Party, 208, 211-12, 262, 393
Liberal Conservative Association, 186
Official Conservatives, 262
Progressive Party, 217, 261-2
Scottish Unionist Party, 221
Working Men's Conservative Association, 186
construction industry, 109, 112
Corn Laws, 86, 176, 180-1
Countesswells estate, 467
Cove, 29, 138, 292, 322, 470
Covent Garden, 478
Cowdray College of Nursing Club, 113
Cowdray Hall, 316
Craigiebuckler, 37, 347, 391
Cranford estate, 391
cricket clubs, 42, 416
Aberdeenshire, 416-17
Edinburgh Grange, 417
Orion, 138
Perthshire, 417
Cruden Bay, 114
Cullen, 387
Cullen Report, 150
Cults, 29, 36, 138, 191, 322, 365, 382, 467, 479-80, 482-4
Cummings Park, 319
Curling Club, 388
cycling, 418-19

dance bands, 432
dancing, 407, 426
British Association of Teachers of Dancing, 428
Gondolier Quadrille Party, 428
Gondolier School of Dancing & Deportment, 428, 441
Polsons' Dancing Academy, 407
Scottish Country Dance Society, 432
dean of guild, 242, 246, 260, 263, 271, 280, 380, 384, 476
Dee Village, 332, 473
Denmore, 320
Deputy Lieutenant of the County of the City of Aberdeen, 461, 479
Deputy Lieutenant of Aberdeenshire & Kincardineshire, 384, 389
Desswood estate, 391
Devanha House, 388
disestablishment, 86, 185, 187, 248
Disruption, 9, 269, 299, 323, 328, 351-7
distilleries, 401-2, 472
distributive trades, 117-18
dog racing, 439

domestic servants, 273
domestic service, 58, 61-4, 66-7, 70, 156, 330
Dufftown, 280, 458
Dunbartonshire, 367
Dundee, 1, 32, 45, 49, 53, 56, 70-1, 128, 153, 156, 162-3, 166, 173, 208, 340, 383, 405, 412, 455
Dunkeld, 284
drink licensing laws, 249, 427, 446, 457
drink trade, 401-2
Dyce, 29-30, 38, 40, 45, 59, 111, 129, 255, 264, 467, 486-7

earnings, 133-6, 144-5, 154, 157, 162-4, 170
Edinburgh, 1, 8, 11, 22, 55-6, 70, 79-80, 98, 114, 163, 176, 208, 270, 301, 339, 384, 398, 408, 414-15, 425, 445, 447, 452
education
Aberdeen Educational Society, 329
Aberdeen Educational Trust, 335
Aberdeen Endowment Trust, 341
eight-hour day, 173, 192-4
elections
local, 178, 183, 222, 259, 261
parliamentary, 178, 180, 182-3
pre-reform, 176-9, 201
(1832), 179-80, 201
(1835), 189, 201
(1837), 180-1, 201
(1841), 182, 201
(1847), 183-4, 201
(1852), 184, 201
(1857), 184, 201
(1859), 185, 201
(1865), 185, 201
(1868), 185, 201
(1872 by election), 185-6, 201
(1874), 185-6, 201-2
(1880), 186-7, 202
(1885), 190, 202
(1886), 190-1, 202
(1892), 193, 202
(1895), 193-4, 202
(1896 by election), 194-5, 202
(1900), 195, 202
(1906), 196-7, 202-3
(1907 by election), 197, 203
(1910), 199, 203-4
(1917 by election), 199-200, 203
(1918), 200, 203, 207-8
(1922), 208-9, 230
(1923), 209-10, 230
(1924), 210-11, 230
(1928 by election), 211-12, 231
(1929), 212-13, 231
(1931), 213-14, 231
(1935 by election), 214-15, 231
(1935), 215-16, 231
(1945), 216-17, 231
(1946 by election), 217, 231
(1950), 204, 217-18, 232
(1951), 218, 232

(1955), 218, 232
(1959), 218, 232
(1964), 218, 221, 232
(1966), 219-22, 232-3
(1970), 221-2, 233
(1974), 222-4, 233
(1979), 224-5, 233-4
(1983), 225-6, 234
(1987), 226, 234
(1992), 226-7, 234
(1997), 227-9, 234-5
Scottish Parliament, 230, 235
electoral constituencies (parliamentary)
Aberdeen, 190-1, 195, 197-200, 204-5, 208, 210, 215-17, 227, 384, 393-4
East Aberdeenshire, 191-2, 212, 248, 394
Forfarshire, 246, 394
Glasgow Bridgeton, 199
Glasgow Govan, 222
Kincardineshire, 394
Kircaldy, 394
Montrose district of burghs, 176, 448
Oldham Central & Royton, 492
Oldham East, 394, 492
West Aberdeenshire, 217, 222
electoral wards (local govt)
post-1883
Cairncry, 261
Castlehill, 262
Ferryhill, 248, 384, 389, 474
Gilcomston, 261, 396
Granitehill, 397
Greyfriars, 196, 248, 261, 297
Holburn, 262
Mastrick, 261
Northfield, 261, 397
St Andrew's, 196, 248, 259-61, 428
St Clement's, 205, 248, 260, 262
St Machar, 248, 259, 260-1, 393, 396
St Nicholas, 248, 261, 393, 428
Rosemount, 248
Rubislaw, 248, 298, 461
Ruthrieston, 318, 396
Torry, 261, 397
Woodside, 261, 396
electricity production, 252
electronics industry, 142
Elgin, 287, 316, 360, 464
elites, 421
business, 379-80, 383, 397
county, 388, 390-2
municipal, 374-5, 378, 387
parliamentary, 393-4
social, 376-78, 380-84, 387
university, 392-3
and education, 382-3
and leisure, 385-90
and wealth, 379, 383
and women, 396-7
Ellon, 48, 59, 73, 322

employment, 61–4, 97, 105, 114, 124, 133–6, 144, 148–50, 154–62
Encyclopaedia Britannica, 361
engineering industry, 100–2, 341, 378
epidemics, 269, 277–8
   cholera, 277, 292, 303
   measles, 277, 303
   scarlet fever, 303
   smallpox, 278, 281
   tuberculosis, 277, 303
   typhoid, 124, 278, 303
   typhus, 277–8, 303

families, 64–70
family planning, 292
Faroes, 107, 141
fascism, 207
Ferrier/Sandilands, 276
ferry disaster, 473
Ferryhill, 28, 39–40, 157, 252, 299, 312, 342, 472–3
fiddle-playing, 399, 406, 426
Fife, 142
films, 428
   Birth of a Nation, 428
   Drifters, 430
   North Sea, 430
   The Silver City, 443
Films of Scotland, 430
financial services, 80, 114, 297, 318, 380, 389, 474
   North of Scotland Fire & Life Assurance Co., 80
   Northern Assurance Co., 297–8, 316, 380, 384
Findhorn, 87
Findochty, 65
First World War, 29, 36, 40, 58, 91, 97, 99–100, 157, 162, 169, 199–200, 207, 290, 365, 425, 428, 459, 479
fishing, 83–4, 87–91, 98, 100, 102–5, 114, 141, 143, 156–9, 429–30, 474
   finnan haddock, 400
   fish market, 31, 103
   herring, 90, 103
   salmon, 34, 473, 475
   Torry Fishery Research Station, 284
   trawlers, 11, 87–91, 103, 159, 474
   white fish, 87–8, 90, 103, 159
Fleet Street, 458
flour milling, 96
food processing, 96, 100, 111, 113, 141–2
Footdee, 36, 61–2, 64–6, 69, 72, 159, 308, 327–8, 351, 466, 474–6
Fountainhall estate, 28, 298, 467
Foresterhill, 53, 151, 282–5, 345
franchise, 177–80, 185
Fraserburgh, 87, 118, 187, 318. 389, 476
freedom lands, 472–3, 478
free trade, 183, 193
freedom of the city, 355, 386, 392
freemasons, 390
French Revolution, 176

Friendville estate, 478
friendly societies, 272
Froghall, 314
further education
   Aberdeen College, 342
   Aberdeen Technical College, 342
   Gray's School of Art, 298, 343, 353
   School of Art and Science, 341
   School of Domestic Economy, 341
   School of Librarianship, 343
   Scott Sutherland School of Architecture, 318, 341, 343
   Robert Gordon Institute of Technology, 142, 343
   Robert Gordon's Technical College (see also universities), 341–3, 383

Garthdee, 42, 44, 205, 314, 316, 319, 343
Garthdee House, 318, 343, 383
gas production, 244–5, 252
Gaskin Report, 45, 115
General Strike 1926; 169–70, 175, 207–8, 462 (see strikes)
Gilcomston, 280, 302, 350–2, 466, 477
Girdleness, 109, 316
Glasgow, 1–2, 12, 32, 38, 53–6, 63, 70–1, 79, 83, 96, 98, 112, 156, 163, 167, 173, 277, 355, 368, 398, 405, 408, 413, 423, 425, 430, 433, 447
Glasgow Fair, 120, 170, 426, 443
golf, 121–2
golf clubs, 437
   Bon-Accord, 417, 437
   Hazlehead, 121, 124, 437–8
   Royal Aberdeen, 121, 387, 395, 400, 416–17, 438
   Royal Deeside, 482
   Victoria, 437
golf courses
   Balgownie, 417, 438
   Links, 416–17, 423, 437
   Murcar, 438
   Westhill, 489
Gordon district, 59, 71, 205
Gordon Highlanders, 427
Gothenburg, 442
government agencies, 138, 143
government departments
   Inland Revenue, 415
   HM Treasury, 289, 310–12
   Scottish (Scotch) Education Department, 331, 334, 338–41
   Scottish Office, 46, 285, 287
Grampian Industrialist of the Year, 138
Grampian Region, 135, 140, 144, 147, 149, 163, 205
Grangemouth, 112, 128
granite industry, 77–8, 92–4, 99, 101, 108–10, 156, 159–62
granite processors, 109–10, 112
granite quarries, 92–4, 109, 125, 478, 485
Grandholm, 51, 74, 76, 82, 101, 155, 486
green belt, 37, 44

Greenock, 55, 63, 208
Gymnastic Society, 388

Haddo House, 415
Harbour, 25–8, 31, 33, 38, 77, 90, 101–2, 128–31, 141, 178, 316, 473
   Board, 33–4, 128, 191, 241–3, 246, 298, 389, 474, 476
Haudagain, 314
Hayton, 36, 276, 316
Hazlehead, 29, 31, 37, 121, 125, 240, 320, 339, 467
Hilton, 36, 41, 312, 318, 336, 340, 343
Hogmanay, 403
Holburn, 351, 472–3
holiday industry, 422–6
home rule
   Ireland, 190–1, 248, 274, 380, 457
   Scotland, 191, 193
Honourable County Club, 280
horse racing, 42, 377, 416
hospital and health administration (see also medicine), 55–6, 284, 286, 291
hospitals and clinics
   Aberdeen Royal Mental Hospital, 394
   Asylum for the Blind, 280
   City Hospital, 276, 282–4
   Denburn Centre, 292
   General Dispensary, Vaccine and Lying-In Institution, 32, 281–2, 389
   Hospital for Incurables, 389
   Infirmary, 279
   Institution for the Deaf and Dumb, 389
   Kingseat, 274
   Lunatic Asylum for the Mentally Ill, 280
   Maternity Hospital, 55
   Morningfield Hospital, 280
   Newhills Convalescent Home, 281, 486
   Oldmill Hospital, 280, 283, 286
   Ophthalmic Institution, 280, 290
   Royal Aberdeen Hospital for Sick Children, 51, 160, 280–2, 285, 389, 486
   Royal Infirmary, 86, 111, 121, 259, 279–92, 383, 389, 454–5, 486
   Royal Lunatic Asylum, 454
   Woodend Hospital, 284, 286
hospital trusts, 287
hotels, 114, 119, 123, 134–5, 400
   Balmoral, 316
   Caledonian, 297, 316
   Douglas, 297
   Imperial, 297
   Macdonald's Temperance, 401
   Palace, 119, 298
   Royal, 391
   Station, 120
   Willowbank, 316

house builders
  Bisset & Son, 312
  City of Aberdeen Land Association
    (see CALA)
  Hall & Co., 320
  Modern Homes (Aberdeen), 312, 318
  Morgan & Co., 28-9
  North of Scotland Housing Co., 312
  Northern Garden Suburbs, 312
  Shirras & Son, 312
  Stewart Milne Group, 138, 143, 277,
    338
  Tesswell Construction, 312
House of Commons, 299
House of Lords, 181, 188
  People's League for the Abolition of
    the House of Lords, 191
housing agencies
  Association for the Improvement of
    the Dwellings of the Labouring
    Classes, 302
  Lodging-House Association, 302
  Scottish Special Housing Association,
    35, 137, 319
housing costs
  prices, 139, 149-50
  rent, 137, 147, 163, 311-13
  rent rebates, 314
housing provision, 54, 137, 144-5, 163
  council housing, 30, 33, 36, 38, 147,
    306ff
  'elite' housing, 383-5
  'granite rabbit hutches', 460
  lodging-houses, 301, 305
    Corporation Lodging-House, 307
    Victoria Lodging-House, 61, 302,
      307
  owner-occupation, 65, 69, 138-9, 145,
    310, 314-15, 321-2
  policy, 38
  stock, 310
  temporary, 314, 316-18
Hull & Newcastle Co., 380
hunt ball, 392
Huntly, 29, 82

Ice Rink, 441
Iceland, 107, 141
Incorporated Trades, 178, 246, 268, 272,
  280, 355, 467
industrial estates, 129, 486-7
Inverbervie, 176
Inverness, 63, 277
Inverurie, 48, 53, 59, 83-4, 138
Ireland, 180, 188

Japanese navy, 87
Junior Business Men's Club, 390

Kaimhill, 318
Keith, 4, 82
Kemnay, 138
Kennethmont, 297

Kepplestone Farm, 343
Kincardineshire, 45, 63, 71, 182, 205, 228,
  279, 391, 455, 467
Kincorth, 30-1, 33, 36-7, 41, 205, 318-19
Kingswells, 488
Kintore, 78
Kittybrewster, 4, 39, 79, 297, 428

Labour politics, 200, 205, 207-8, 219, 229
  Aberdeen Labour Party, 198
  Aberdeen Socialist Club, 199
  Aberdeen Workers' Election
    Committee, 196, 260
  Clarion Club, 196
  Independent Labour Party, 174-5,
    193-7, 208, 219, 260-1
  Industrial League, 199
  Industrial Workers of the World, 199
  Labour Party, 170, 199, 210-12, 215,
    225, 227, 260, 312, 316, 393
  Labour Representation Committee,
    197
  Marxian Socialist Club, 199
  Scottish Labour Party, 193
  Scottish Socialist Federation, 193
  Scottish Trades Councils' Labour
    Party, 193
  Scottish Workers' Parliamentary
    Elections Committee, 195-6
  Social Democratic Federation, 193-5,
    197-8, 260, 460
  Socialist Labour Party, 199
land reform, 188, 191, 436
  Aberdeen Land Law Reform
    Association, 189-90
  Scottish Land Restoration League, 191
  Scottish Land and Labour League,
    192
Laurencekirk, 287
leather & footwear manufacture, 96
leisure, 118-25
Leith, 78, 128, 208
Lerwick, 128
Liberal politics, 180, 183, 185, 207-8,
  221-2, 229
  Aberdeen District Council of
    National Liberals, 209
  Junior Liberal Association, 188, 191
  Liberal Association, 165, 186-8, 190,
    197, 209, 218, 248-9, 457
  Liberal Democratic Party, 205, 227-8,
    230
  Liberal Party, 197, 199, 207
  Liberal Unionists, 187, 190, 194-5, 199,
    207, 246, 420
  National Liberal Federation, 186
  National Liberal Party, 208
  Radical Association, 188, 191, 274
  Social Democratic Party, 225
Liberation Society, 187
literary works (see also Statistical
  Account)
  Aberdeen and its Folk, 399

Book of Bon-Accord, 400
Hadrian the Seventh, 460
Johnny Gibb of Gushetneuk, 414,
  455-6
New Book of Bon-Accord, 402
New Principles on . . . Political
  Economy, 492
Reporting Reminiscences, 454
Sketches of Life Among My Ain Folk,
  455
The Silver City, 423
Liverpool, 96
local government, 133, 146, 236-64
  pre-reform Town Council, 177,
    236-40, 374-5, 400
  Aberdeen District Council, 38, 41-2,
    45-6, 137, 147, 205, 262-3. 432
  Aberdeen Police Commission, 237,
    240-3, 245-6, 299, 375
  Aberdeen Town Council, 25, 30-3,
    44, 51, 129, 160, 183, 186, 207, 433,
    492
    bankruptcy, 177, 238-9, 244, 448
    electorate, 247-8
    finance, 257-8
      bell and petty customs, 236,
        244
      common good fund, 30, 33,
        277
    municipal buildings, 45
    officers, 185, 249, 297
    planning, 38-9, 44-6, 437, 461
    public health department (see
      medical officer of health)
  Grampian Regional Council, 41-2,
    45-6, 146-9, 256, 258, 262-3, 492
Local Government Board, 310
London, 56, 78, 83, 96, 136, 151, 167, 182,
  298, 310, 412, 415, 424, 429, 431, 434,
  472
Lord Advocate, 176, 289
Lothian Region, 142, 367

Macaulay Institute, 347
Mannofield, 14, 29, 40, 205, 241, 255, 312,
  318, 478-9
Marine Research Institute, 347
Maritime Museum, 359
Maryculter, 488
Mastrick, 21, 30, 41, 48, 170, 222, 348, 463
May Day, 193
Mechanics' Institute, 271, 340-1, 405, 409,
  454
Medical Officer of Health, 25, 51, 53-4,
  278, 282, 290, 303ff
Medical School, 51, 55-6, 86, 282, 284-91,
  345
medical services, 292
Medico Chirurgical Society, 282, 285,
  287, 290, 292
Middlefield, 276, 313
Midstocket, 312
Milltimber, 30, 42

Mitchell Hall, 491
Monopolies and Mergers Commission, 465
Montrose, 87, 128, 177, 208, 216
Morningfield estate, 298, 467
Motherwell, 367
Mounthooly, 299
municipal trading, 40, 252-6
Murtle, 280, 382, 387, 483
music, 399, 401ff
    entertainment
        Aberdeen Musical Society, 406
        African Opera Troupe, 409
        Eurythmics, 491
        Harmonic Choir, 408
        Music Hall Choral Union, 409
        Symphonic Orchestra, 432
        Woodside Minstrel Troupe, 409
    religious, 405, 407, 454
Music Hall, 13, 20, 25-6, 34, 187, 198, 217, 298, 403, 409, 426, 428, 432-3, 443, 445

Napoleonic Wars, 269, 448
Narrow Wynd Society, 272
National Lifeboat Institution, 461
national lottery, 277
National Health Service, 286, 289
nationalisation, 191, 195, 197, 212
Newcastle, 491
New Year Festival, 402, 427
New York, 56, 209
Newhills, 45, 165, 428, 485, 488
newspaper companies
    Aberdeen Journals, 394, 462-3
    Aberdeen Newspapers, 461
    Aberdeen & North of Scotland
        Newspaper and Printing Co., 456
    Allied Newspapers, 462
    Barclay Brothers, 465
    Kemsley Press, 462-3
    Northcliffe Newspapers, 465
    Outram & Co., 462, 465
    Thomson Group, 465
newspapers and journals (see also periodicals)
    Aberdeen Advertiser & Town and Country Journal, 451
    Aberdeen Banner, 452
    Aberdeen Citizen, 453, 462-3
    Aberdeen Chronicle, 448, 450
    Aberdeen Clarion, 463
    Aberdeen Constitutional, 450, 452
    Aberdeen Evening Express, 198, 207, 435, 457-8, 460-4
    Aberdeen Gleaner, 450
    Aberdeen Herald, 80-1, 180, 182, 184, 399, 450-6
    Aberdeen Herald & Post, 463
    Aberdeen Journal, 91, 155, 178, 185-7, 197, 207, 209, 405, 408, 448, 451, 455-6, 458-61
    Aberdeen Labour Elector, 174, 459

Aberdeen Observer, 449, 452
Aberdeen Patriot, 452
Aberdeen People's Press, 463
Aberdeen Review & North of Scotland Advertiser, 451
Aberdeen Saturday Post & Northern Counties Chronicle, 453
Aberdeen Standard, 460
Aberdeen Weekly Journal, 456, 463
Aberdeen & District Independent, 463
Belfast Evening Telegraph, 458
Daily Despatch, 215
Evening Gazette, 413, 455, 457, 460
Evening Times, 459
Fiery Cross, 459
Free Press, 254, 361, 453-8, 460-1
Glasgow Herald, 162, 459
Intelligencer, 448
Investor's Chronicle, 458
London Evening Standard, 458, 461
London Gazette, 461
Mirror of the North, 457
Montrose Review, 452
Moray & Nairn Gazette, 464
North Briton, 449
North Star, 455
North of Scotland Gazette, 359, 452, 454-5
Northern Daily News, 458
Northern Evening News, 458
Northern Examiner, 453
Northern Scot, 464
Northern Telegraphic News & Northern Advertiser, 453
Northern Vindicator, 451
Penny Free Press, 453
People's Journal, 193, 455, 457
Press & Journal, 127, 217, 219-20, 260, 431-3, 438, 443, 461-3, 467
Scots Champion & Aberdeen Free Press, 449
Silver City, 463
Sunday Times, 142
The Gazette, 453
The Scotsman, 403, 461
Weekly Free Press, 457
Workers' Herald, 459
newspapers and politics, 448
Nigg, 33, 63, 77, 127
night clubs, 354, 446
Nobel Prize, 55, 284, 346-7, 492
North Eastern Ice Co., 474
Northern Arts Club, 386
Northern Co-operative Society, 115-16, 207, 221, 262, 273
Northern Club, 388, 391, 395-6
Northern Patent Brick Co., 379
Northern Shooting Club, 268
Northfield, 30, 37, 41, 46
Norway, 93, 103, 107, 141

office rents, 140
Ogston & Tennant, 113

oil companies
    Amerada Hess, 132
    British National Oil Corporation, 38
    Britoil, 148
    British Petroleum, 38, 126-7, 129, 151
    Chevron, 151
    Halliburton, 277
    Occidental, 38
    Shell UK, 27, 38, 127
    Texaco, 151
oil industry, 14, 38, 58, 112, 115, 125-52
oil tool manufacturers & supply services, 129, 143
    Abbott Group, 143
    Baker Oil Tools, 129
    Balmoral Group, 143
    Orwell Group, 143
    Petroline Wellsystems, 143
    Smith International, 129
    Vetco Offshore, 129
    Wood Group, 107, 112, 142-3
Old Aberdeen, 3, 28-9, 39, 170, 179, 205, 252, 392-3, 467, 476-7, 479-80, 484
Old Deer, 280
Old Deeside Road, 478
Oldmachar parish, 22, 45, 266, 269, 327, 350, 476
    parochial council, 243, 274-5
Oldmill Reformatory, 278, 280, 330
Orkney, 83, 106, 118, 146, 425
Orkney, Shetland & North of Scotland Steam Navigation Co., 106, 380
Oxford Movement, 359-60

Paisley, 208, 383
paper industry, 94-6, 109-10, 114, 141, 480-2
paper manufacturers, 76, 96, 101, 110, 142, 394, 482
Paris, 136
parks, 437, 447, 482
    Duthie, 44, 252, 380, 383, 404, 413-14
    Stewart, 252, 384
    Union Terrace Gardens, 41, 44, 380
    Victoria, 35, 43, 413
parliamentary legislation
    Aberdeen Act 1469, 1800; 236-7
    Abortion Act 1967; 52
    Artisans' and Labourers' Dwelling Improvement Act 1875; 304, 307
    Broadcasting Act 1990; 436
    Corporation Act 1881, 1891; 303-5
    District Tramways Act 1872; 253
    Education (Scotland) Act 1872, 1918, 1945; 247, 331, 334, 336, 341
    Electric Lighting Act 1882; 252
    Emergency Powers Act 1920; 208
    Equal Franchise Act 1928; 204
    Extension and Improvement Act 1883; 248
    Factory Act 1833; 326
    Harbour Act 1810, 1829, 1843, 1868, 1879, 1960; 33, 237, 243, 380, 475-6

Housing of the Working Classes Act 1890; 35, 304, 307
Housing Act 1919, 1923, 1935; 311-14
Improvement Confirmation Act 1884; 188, 304
Improvement Scheme Provisional Order Confirmation Act 1896; 305
Local Government (Scotland) Act 1894, 1929, 1981; 256, 264, 275
Municipality Extension Act 1871; 28, 245, 248
National Health Service and Community Care Act 1990; 287
Police Act 1795, 1818, 1829, 1833, 1857, 1892; 23, 241-2, 257, 329
Police and Waterworks Act 1862; 299
Poor Law Amendment Act 1845, 1894; 269, 274
Prisons Act 1839; 257
Public Health (Scotland) Act 1867; 282
Representation of the People Act 1918, 1968; 204, 207
Royal Burghs (Scotland) Act 1833; 239
Scottish Reform Act 1832; 179-80, 204, 221, 411
Scottish Universities Act 1858; 289
Six Acts 1817; 448
Town Councils (Scotland) Act 1900; 247
Town and Country Planning (Scotland) Act 1947; 46, 318
Party of Progress, 35, 187, 245, 248
Paull and Williamsons, 394
periodicals and pamphlets (see also newspapers)
  Aberdeen Almanac, 376, 385, 389
  Aberdeen Censor, 449
  Aberdeen Independent, 449
  Aberdeen Magazine, 282, 450, 454
  Aberdeen Mirror, 450
  Aberdeen Monitor, 450
  Aberdeen Monthly Chronicle, 451
  Aberdeen Monthly Circular, 451
  Aberdeen Pirate, 450
  Aberdeen Reformer, 457
  Aberdeen Shaver, 450
  Aberdeen Spectator & Monthly Advertiser, 451
  Aberdeen Star, 449
  Artizan, 450
  Blackwood's Edinburgh Magazine, 450
  Bon-Accord, 409, 417-18, 427-8, 431, 436-7, 439, 443, 457
  Bon-Accord: The Illustrated News of the North, 458-9
  Bon-Accord & Northern Pictorial, 459-60, 462-3
  British Review, 458
  Budget, 450
  Chambers' Journal, 405
  Chameleon, 454, 457

  Comet, 457, 460
  Holloa, 459
  Inquirer, 449
  Intruder, 449
  Leopard: The Grampian Magazine, 464-5
  Letter of Marque, 450
  Mearns Leader, 459
  Meteor, 457
  National Guardian, 459
  North-East Review, 462-3
  Northern Figaro, 407, 457
  Northern Iris, 409
  Northern Life, 459
  Northern Temperance Record, 402
  Pall Mall Gazette, 458, 461
  Penny Magazine, 405
  Perthshire Advertiser, 459
  Ploughshare, 457
  Quizzing Glass, 450
  Rambler, 449
  Random Recollections, 451
  Squib, 450
  Stage & Television Today, 446
  Water Kelpie, 449
Persley, 41, 154, 470
Perth, 1, 412
Perthshire, 406
Peterculter (Culter), 30, 40, 42, 45, 76, 95, 264, 322, 382, 467, 480-3
Peterhead, 14, 87, 118, 128, 133, 173, 486
philanthropy, 164
phrenology, 403-5
Pilkington Report, 434
Piper Alpha disaster, 150, 171
Pirie's Act, 360
Pitfodels, 42
Pitfodels estate, 477, 482
Pitmedden estate, 391
Pittodrie, 312, 319
Pittodrie Stadium, 342, 440-1, 470
Plate Glass Co., 380
Playing Fields Association, 461
poor law, 266, 268, 273
poor relief
  Board of Supervision, 274-5, 298
  Inspector of Poor, 265, 274
  Oldmill Poor House, 274
  Poor's House, 266, 274, 298
  Poor's Hospital, 266, 268-9, 273, 279
population, 22, 47, 59, 82, 138-9
  baby boom, 49, 57
  birth control, 50, 52, 56
  birth control clinic, 50-1
  birth rate, 48, 50, 59
  death rate, 48-9, 52-3, 57, 59, 71
  density and overcrowding, 299ff
  fertility, 71, 73
  illegitimacy rate, 49-50
  infant mortality, 53, 56, 71
  marriage rate, 49, 315
  migration, 48, 57-9, 70-1, 163, 362, 364, 474

Portlethen, 38, 59, 73, 322, 470
Portsoy, 287
Post Office directories, 376, 389
Powis, 33, 276, 313, 318, 393
Poynernook, 454
Primrose League, 89
Printfield, 276
prostitution, 49
Provost Ross' house, 295
Provost Skene's house, 295, 301
public health (see medical officer of health)
pubs & taverns, 399-402
  Affleck's, 400, 406, 450
  Archibald Simpson's, 32
  Lemon Tree, 43, 268, 388, 400, 450
  Ma Cameron's, 388
  New Inn, 400, 472
public library, 404
public transport, 424, 478-9

Quakers, 478
Queen's Jubilee, 280
quoits, 42, 416

radio, 366, 422, 433-4
  NorthSound, 434
  2BD Repertory Players, 433-4
railways, 78, 80-1, 80, 83-4, 88, 113, 120, 137, 281, 486
railway companies
  Aberdeen Railway, 38, 81
  Aberdeen, Peterhead & Fraserburgh Railway, 42, 416
  Caledonian Railway, 38, 473
  Deeside Railway, 32, 483
  Denburn Valley Railway, 25, 297, 353
  Great North of Scotland Railway, 32, 39, 80, 82, 86, 113, 119-20, 253, 380, 384, 428, 479
railway stations, 15, 39, 198, 483
ratepayers, 269, 271
Referendum (1979), 224
Register House, 452
relief work, 265
River Dee, 240-1, 472-3
River Don, 154, 241, 485
Rochdale Co-operative Society, 273
Rome, 387
Rosehill, 318
Rosemount, 28, 301, 305, 342, 404
Rosemount Square, 276
Rosemount Viaduct, 9, 31, 40, 188, 297, 404, 477
Rotary Club, 390
Round Table, 390
Rowett Research Institute, 284, 347
Royal Atheneum, 25-6
Royal Charter, 272, 279-80, 282
Royal Commission on Housing 1917; 214-15
Royal Infirmary Springtime Ball, 395
Royal Northern Agricultural Society, 461